Teaching Reading in the Elementary School

Eldon E. Ekwall
THE UNIVERSITY OF TEXAS AT EL PASO

James L. Shanker
CALIFORNIA STATE UNIVERSITY, HAYWARD

COLUMBUS TORONTO LONDON SYDNEY

Published by Charles E. Merrill Publishing Co.
A Bell & Howell Company
Columbus, Ohio 43216

This book was set in Univers and Century Schoolbook
Production Coordination: Ben Shriver
Cover Design Coordination: Cathy Watterson
Cover Photo: Tom McGuire
Title Page Photo: David Strickler
Text Design: Cynthia Brunk and Ben Shriver

Library of Congress Catalog Card Number: 84–43017
International Standard Book Number: 0–675–20121–7
Printed in the United States of America
1 2 3 4 5 6 7 8 9 10—89 88 87 86 85

to Dr. Cornelius K. Blesius
for his compassion, competence,
and sense of humor

to Susan, Michael, and
Kenneth Shanker

Preface

This is a book about teaching developmental reading in the elementary school. It is meant to be used primarily as a developmental reading methods book. We believe, however, that it is a rare classroom where all students learn everything taught by the teacher the first time it is presented. When a certain amount of reteaching becomes necessary, based on assessment that discovered which students did not learn the material during the original presentation, you become involved in corrective reading instruction. Therefore, we have sought to include throughout this book procedures for both developmental and corrective teaching. We would hope, then, that the order of events in your classroom reading program would take the following sequence: assess (as necessary); teach (including direct instruction, guided practice, and reinforcement); reassess (to see who has not yet learned); and reteach constantly so that all children progress successfully in every area of reading instruction.

We break with the traditional format of developmental reading books in chapters 1 through 12, by including a section entitled Review of the Research. These sections emphasize aspects of the research that are crucial to you as an elementary school teacher trying to develop a successful reading program. The reviews give you the background to understand why experts in the field of reading advocate certain instructional procedures and not others. You will find that substantially more research information is presented in Chapters 1 through 7. The importance of the topics covered in these chapters, as well as the controversial nature of some of the content, warrants additional emphasis on the research findings.

After the research section (generally), the main topic of each chapter is presented. In Chapters 4, 5, 6, and 7, we address the subjects of reading readiness, sight word learning, decoding skills, and comprehension by focusing first on the assessment, then on the teaching, of these skills. This repeated order of presentation of material should clarify the distinction between testing and teaching, and at the same time enhance your understanding of how these processes work together to promote student learning.

Following the summary at the end of every chapter you will find a group of review questions. We hope that these sections will reinforce your understanding of the information presented in each chapter.

This book contains thirteen chapters. Chapter 1 presents a framework for understanding and teaching reading that should help you put in place the important topics subsequently developed in the book. Chapter 2 describes the major approaches to the teaching of reading, while Chapter 3 presents specific procedures for organizing and managing your classroom reading program. Many reading methods texts present the information on approaches and management much later in the book. We have placed this information early for two reasons. First, many prospective teachers are anxious to get a picture of what reading instruction actually looks like in an elementary classroom. Second, obtaining a feeling for the rigorous demands made on you by conducting daily reading instruction will give you a sense of the urgency of all the teachings presented in the book. Many returning graduate students have told us that they felt inadequate, as beginning teachers, when it came to organizing and managing daily reading instruction. We also realize that reading methods texts are often criticized for providing too much theory and not enough practical content. We are confident that the material in Chapters 2 and 3 answers these concerns.

Chapter 4 addresses the complex, fascinating issues that surround reading readiness and offers specific procedures for assessing and teaching various readiness skills. Chapter 5 presents the assessment and teaching of sight words and basic sight words. Chapter 6 deals with assessing and teaching the various decoding skills, paying particular attention to phonics, structural analysis, and context clues. It is one of the longer chapters; however, we believe that a teacher who masters this information, as well as that presented in the surrounding chapers on sight words and comprehension, will be well-grounded in the teaching of basic reading skills.

As noted, Chapter 7 focuses on reading comprehension, including vocabulary. Clearly, this is a timely topic in reading, judging by interest among professionals and laypersons alike. Chapter 8 teaches content area reading and the study skills, which we refer to as *learning for a lifetime of learning*. This chapter was written by a specialist in the area, Ellsworth A. Berget, Professor of Teacher Education, California State University, Hayward.

Chapter 9 addresses a practical subject—analysis of oral reading errors. In this chapter you will discover how oral reading errors, once coded and understood, can become a blueprint for instruction.

Chapter 10 presents techniques for matching children and reading materials. We firmly believe that many of our students who fail to learn to read do so because in the beginning of their schooling they were not matched with reading material at a proper level to ensure them success.

Chapter 11 addresses a subject frequently neglected—how to begin and maintain a sustained silent reading program. We believe that many, many children learn how to read, but fail to become adept at reading simply because they take little or no time to practice the act of reading.

Chapter 12 helps you deal with the many challenges presented by trying to teach children with special needs, including problem readers, gifted students, and students who speak other languages or dialects.

Finally, Chapter 13 is on the history of reading instruction and what it has taught us. Whatever interest you may take in the history of reading instruction, we hope that you will note well some of the promising newer research, as well as certain lessons that seem to have been proven time and again through research and experience.

You will notice that throughout this book certain themes are repeated, beliefs about reading instruction that we hold strongly. These beliefs are supported not only by a substantial body of research, but by our own practical experience and the experience of many others. Among these themes are the following:

1. You the teacher are the most important factor in the reading instruction your students receive in school. In order to be most effective, you need to understand how children learn to read and understand fully the advantages and disadvantages of using various approaches, methods, and materials in the classroom.
2. Although the skills required to teach children to read in an elementary school classroom are formidable and complex, they are learnable. Good teaching is a craft that is developed over time. With patience, guidance, and some assistance, you can become a successful teacher of reading.
3. The teaching of reading is not a mystical process. Although much remains to be learned about how children learn to read and how we can best help those who are failing, we do know which practices succeed most often. These include the following:
   a. Most students require a certain amount of systematic, sequential skill instruction to learn how to decode or pronounce unknown words.
   b. Most students require direct instruction in which the teacher presents information to the students and monitors the pace of their learning of new material.
   c. All students should be taught at an appropriate level of difficulty so that they can experience frequent success.
   d. All students need a substantial amount of practice in the act of reading, to ensure that important skills are learned and utilized, and to promote an appreciation for the value and joy of reading.
4. Children vary in their reading abilities, just as they do in other areas. Your task as a teacher is to help each child reach his or her potential as a reader.
5. Learning to read should be a fun, exciting, and satisfying activity for your students. Similarly, the teaching of reading should be a stimulating, challenging, and rewarding activity for you.

We hope you find reading this book to be an enjoyable experience and the information it conveys to be beneficial to you in the future as a reading teacher.

We would like to thank a number of people who have in some way contributed to the completion of this book. First, thanks to Richard Wohl, who helped us in the initial stages of the project, and Vicki Knight, Bev Kolz, John Nee, and Beth Dougherty of the Merrill staff, who provided a great deal of assistance throughout the preparation of the manuscript. It has been a joy to work with our editors at Merrill.

Our appreciation also extends to research assistant Wedge Johnson, who gave so freely of his time in assisting us, and to Mable Chew and Judy Filler, expert typists.

We also wish to thank Richard L. Allington, State University of New York at Albany, Susan J. Daniels, The University of Akron, Janet L. Prange, Texas A&I University, John Savage, Boston College, Leo Schell, Kansas State University, and James D. Walden, Indiana University, who reviewed the manuscript and contributed many scholarly suggestions. We offer our appreciation to the many fine students who have taken our classes in the past, who—along with our own teachers—have helped us learn what we have attempted to convey to you in this text.

James Shanker would especially like to thank his friends Cheryl Milner, Barbara Polito, and Jay Rowley for their advice and interest, and his family for their unfailing support.

Eldon Ekwall would like to thank his wife, Carol Ann, for her patience and understanding during the writing of his part of the text.

Contents

1

A Framework for Understanding and Teaching Reading

Considerable controversy about how to teach reading exists in the field of reading education. Some authors believe teachers should approach reading holistically, teaching it without any concern for subskills. Others claim children must learn a definite sequence of subskills to become fluent readers who understand what they read. The position taken on this issue ultimately influences the shape reading materials for young children take, the content of reading methods courses, and the content of courses in the diagnosis and remediation of reading disabilities.

This chapter presents a logical framework for understanding and teaching reading. It also includes a comprehensive chart (Figure 1–7) that shows when many reading skills are usually mastered. This chart should help teachers determine which students need corrective help. Note that some skills are mastered once and for all, such as being able to instantly recognize a certain group of often-used words. On the other hand, some skills, such as reading graphs and maps, may continue to be extended and refined throughout our lifetime as we read more complicated graphs and maps. Finally, a review and assessment of the research on reading as a whole versus reading as a combination of skills concludes the chapter.

Once you understand the reading process, you will have a framework in which to work: you will know what to listen for as children read out loud and what to ask children about when they finish reading.

The various reading skills outlined in this chapter *do* exist. However, some children seem to learn some or even most of these skills with very little instruction. For example, they learn new words with ease even though they do not know vowel rules or syllable principles. On the other hand, many children need to learn various phonic word attack skills systematically before they can decode new words. As a teacher, then, you will need to distinguish between those children who have automatically learned how to "crack the code" and those who need to learn individual skills.

A FRAMEWORK FOR UNDERSTANDING AND TEACHING READING

Most definitions of reading are similar to the following one: Reading is a process whereby the reader attempts to construct in his mind what the writer had in her mind when the material was written. This definition is logical, but it cannot help us understand the wide scope of reading skills.

Reading can be divided into two basic categories, *recognizing and analyzing words* and *understanding words and ideas.* Then the scope of reading skills looks like Figure 1–1.

Teachers often say, "I have a student who reads well, but he can't seem to understand anything he reads." Yet others say, "I have a student who just doesn't know the words, but if I read it to her, she seems to understand perfectly well." Such statements clearly show that reading is neither just calling words nor just understanding what is heard. It is a combination of being able to almost instantly recognize or analyze every word and understand what they mean when they are strung together in a sentence, paragraph, or longer passage. Thus, the teacher who says, "I have a student who reads well, but he can't seem to understand anything he reads," is technically wrong in stating that the student *reads.* It would be more correct to say, "I have a student who calls words well, but he can't seem to understand the meaning of those words."

Recognizing and Analyzing Words

The category of recognizing and analyzing words can be further subdivided. Words a student already knows by sight and does not have to

Figure 1–1   Two basic categories of reading

Note. Adapted from *Diagnosis and Remediation of the Disabled Reader*, 2nd ed., by E. E. Ekwall and J. L. Shanker (Boston: Allyn and Bacon, 1983), 69. Copyright 1983 by Allyn and Bacon. Figures 1–1 through 1–6 all adapted by permission.

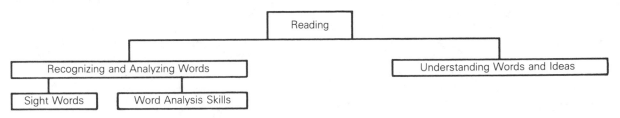

Figure 1–2   The two main subcategories of recognizing and analyzing words

analyze each time they are encountered are *sight words.* On the other hand, if a student encounters an unfamiliar word, then he has to use *word attack* or *word analysis skills.* (These two terms mean the same thing—methods of determining the pronunciation of a word unknown to the reader—and will be used interchangeably in this text.) The scope of reading skills increases, as shown in Figure 1–2.

Sight Words.   There are two types of sight words, *basic sight words* and *other sight words.* Basic sight words are those words of very high utility. For example, if you count all the words on this page, you will find that *a, and*, and *the* account for about 10 percent of the total, and approximately ten words of the highest utility account for about 25 percent of the total. Obviously, writers use some words over and over again, and if a student is to learn to read fluently, then she must learn to instantly recognize these very high utility words.

When does a researcher end a list of high utility words? As one moves down a list, the words, of course, decrease in utility. Therefore, most researchers in reading have agreed that words on these lists can only be considered basic sight words if they are among the first 200 or 300 words, and at most 500 words, of highest utility. Several writers and researchers have developed basic sight word lists which will be discussed in Chapter 5. These words are sometimes referred to as a student's *basic sight vocabulary.* (The word *vocabulary* itself is confusing, since most teachers mean the study of word meaning when they use it. Most researchers, however, including us, reserve the term vocabulary for those words students have in

their meaning vocabulary.) Basic sight vocabulary or basic sight words mean that a student recognizes those words and can say them instantly but may or may not know their meanings. The words on most basic sight word lists are of such high utility that they are usually in the listening and speaking vocabularies of beginning readers and therefore also in the students' meaning vocabularies. However, remember that the term does *not* refer to word meaning. Actually, a basic sight word is a word of high utility that appears on someone's list as a word of high utility. *Other sight words* are all words instantly recognized by a reader that do not happen to appear on a basic sight word list. These words might be a child's name, easily recognized product or store names, or other words that are significant to the child.

Some basic sight word lists have been divided so the words are listed according to the grade level at which the words are usually learned. The first-grade words are usually divided into three levels: pre-primer, which refers to words learned in the first third of the year; primer, which refers to words learned in the second third of the year; and first grade, which refers to words learned in the last third of the year. Second grade lists are often broken down into two halves, the first being 2–1 and the second being 2–2. Some basic sight words may appear on third-grade lists, but when they do, they are simply called third-grade words. Very few words are called basic sight words at the third-grade level.

Why are these words related to certain levels? Words used most by very young children will most likely be listed at the pre-primer level. Lower utility words are placed at progressively higher levels. After the third grade, most words of high utility would have already appeared on one of the lower level lists.

Words are also listed as pre-primer, primer, first grade, etc. because *readability formulas* help writers write at a certain level and help teachers decide the grade level at which certain materials are written. A readability formula is a method of determining how difficult reading materials are. Readability is usually shown by grade level, such as 3.8, which means the material is appropriate for a third grader in the eighth month of school (provided the student is reading at grade level). Such formulas are often based on the percentage of difficult words in a passage and the length of sentences. Creators of readability formulas usually look at past lists or at what words are already used in pre-primer books, primer books, etc. So a never ending circle develops: words traditionally appearing as pre-primer words tend to reappear as pre-primer words.

A sight word is *any* word known instantly by the reader. The word has been encountered so many times that the reader no longer has to use word analysis skills to say it. Beginning readers, of course, have very few words in their sight vocabulary. They might have some words such as *stop*, from reading stop signs on the highway or various other words that they have seen many times. Some readers also learn sight words after fewer repetitions than other readers do. These readers do not necessarily have higher IQs than

others, but they may have a higher "potential for learning words." For this reason the term "potential for reading" is probably more accurate than "intelligence" when discussing why one student is able to learn a word more easily than another.

As we grow older and read more we develop a much larger sight vocabulary. The size of our sight vocabulary depends on such factors as our occupation, the amount we read, and our potential for learning words.

See Figure 1–3 for this enlarged scope of reading skills.

Word Attack Skills.   If a student does not instantly know a word, he must then use one or more of the word analysis skills. These skills contain five main categories—configuration clues, context clues, phonetic analysis, structural analysis, and dictionary skills—and one minor category, study skills, that is used infrequently as a word attack skill.

Configuration Clues

Configuration clues are the overall characteristics of how a word looks. Configuration clues include the length of a word (*Mississippi* vs. *it*), **ascenders** and **descenders** (lowercase letters that rise above and fall below the x-height, letters such as *l* and *y*), double letters (g*oo*se, l*oo*k), and overall word form.

More experienced readers rely less on configuration clues; however, for a beginning reader

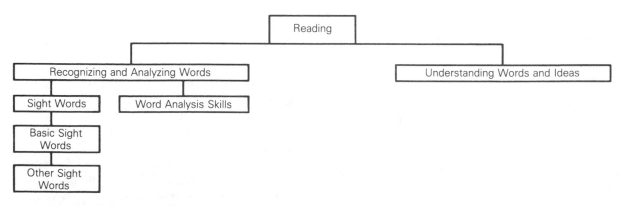

Figure 1–3   The two subcategories of sight words

learning the difference between two words, they can be very important. For example, it is much easier to teach the word *yellow* to a beginning reader than it is to teach the word *then*, partly because *yellow* has more immediate meaning for the student than the word *then*, but also because *yellow* has ascenders, decenders, and double letters that help it stand out as a new word.

Configuration clues play a more important part in helping both adults and children recognize words than one might realize. For example, note it is not difficult to read all uppercase letters when the bottom half of a sentence is covered:

ARE THESE WORDS DIFFICULT TO READ?

On the other hand it is quite difficult to read all capital letters when the top half is covered.

ARE THESE WORDS DIFFICULT TO READ?

When the bottom part of *lowercase* letters is covered, they are not nearly so difficult to read because of the top coastline configuration. Note the following sentence:

these words are much less difficult to read

Thus we see that the ascenders in words make them much easier to read. Note the following sentence written with all descenders and ascenders missing and replaced with *x*:

ix is mucx more xixxicuxx xo reax wxen xxe xescenxers anx ascenxers are xexx oux.

Although substituting *x* for letters also changes the overall appearance of the word, the absent descenders and ascenders make the words even more difficult to read. Now look at the following sentence written with all of the *x* height letters missing:

thxx xx xxt xx hxxd tx xxxd.

(This is not so hard to read.)

Context Clues

Context clues come from the meaning of a word as it is used in a sentence (*semantic* clue) or from guessing what word is coming next according to the way a reader usually uses oral language (*syntactic* clue). In reality semantic clues and syntactic clues often overlap. However, observe the following semantic clue, provided by the context of a sentence:

The barking _____ chased the cat over the fence.

In this case, a student would know that *dogs* sometimes chase cats and that dogs bark. Syntactic clues are based on **syntax**, or the way we are used to stringing words together in our oral language patterns. For example, look at the syntactic clue in the following sentence:

Even though it was only four o'clock in the afternoon, the sandstorm caused it to be _____ dark as if it were midnight.

In this case, a student would know the missing word was probably *as* since she often uses the phrase *as* _____ *as*.

Beginning readers use context clues to analyze a new word or to learn what a new word may mean. Context clues are probably the most used word analysis skills. Adults probably learn a much higher percentage of the total words they know, both pronunciation and meaning, from context than from any other method. Context clues include two subcategories: *word or sentence context clues* and *picture context clues.* Anyone who has taught beginning readers has observed them constantly checking to see if there is a picture because it can give them clues to the meaning of new or unknown words. Sentence or word context clues may be either semantic or syntactic in nature, or they may be a combination.

Phonetic Analysis

Phonetic analysis usually refers to the sound–symbol or **phoneme-grapheme** relationships (the grapheme is the written representation of a phoneme, which is the smallest unit of speech sound in the language) between the smaller nonmeaning-bearing parts of words. Phonics includes learning the sounds represented by consonants, vowels, consonant blends, consonant digraphs, vowel digraphs, diphthongs, vowel teams, and special letter combinations. Phonetic analysis often includes the rules for syllable principles; however, syllabication can also be considered part of structural analysis or even a separate category.

Structural Analysis

Structural analysis usually refers to the analysis of larger meaning-bearing parts of words such as root words, suffixes, prefixes, word endings, apostrophe *s* for possession, compound words, and contractions. It may include syllabication, since dividing words into syllables often means dealing with prefixes and suffixes that carry meaning. Structural analysis can also refer to a student's ability to derive meaning from words; however, when used this way, it describes a student's meaning vocabulary, not a word attack skill. Structural analysis is also referred to as **morphology**, the study of **morphemes** or the meaning bearing units of the language.

Dictionary Skills

Dictionary skills are such skills as alphabetizing letters, locating words, using preferred spellings, using guide words, etc. However, using the dictionary to check on pronunciation is using a dictionary skill as a word analysis skill.

Study Skills

In addition to these five main categories, some **study skills** can be considered word attack skills. For example, one study skill is learning how to look up certain topics or words in an encyclopedia. When a student uses an encyclopedia to look up the pronunciation of a word, then the study skill has become a word analysis skill. Note that a broken line connects the study skills with the other word analysis skills in Figure 1–4, indicating that they may be used as word attack skills but are not directly defined that way. The addition of word analysis skills makes the scope of reading skills look as it does in Figure 1–4.

Understanding Words and Ideas

Vocabulary (word meaning) is a subskill of understanding words and ideas (comprehension).

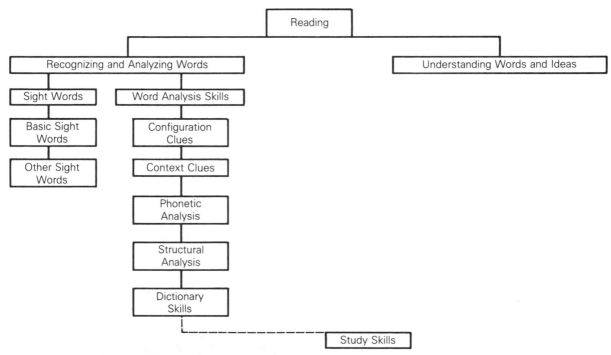

Figure 1–4   Scope of reading skills with specific word attack skills

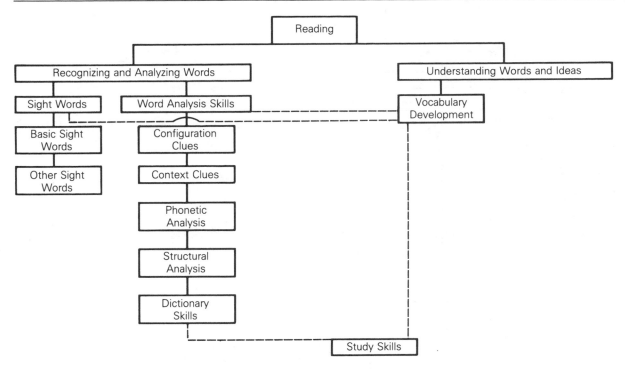

Figure 1–5　　Scope of reading skills, including vocabulary

Before a word can be read with meaning, the reader must either instantly recognize it or use word attack skills on it. For this reason vocabulary has been connected to both sight words and word attack skills with a broken line in Figure 1–5 to show that both processes are involved. Sometimes we use an encyclopedia to derive the meaning of a word. Thus, vocabulary is connected to the study skills with another broken line. With vocabulary as a subskill of comprehension, the scope of reading skills now looks like Figure 1–5.

Subskills of reading comprehension are more difficult to isolate than word analysis subskills. The literature on comprehension shows that researchers cannot agree on what subskills it contains. For teaching purposes, perhaps the categories suggested by Thomas Barrett (1967) are most useful. These categories include:

1. Getting literal meaning
2. Making inferences
3. Evaluating
4. Appreciating

Using certain study skills can also promote comprehension, as discussed in Chapter 8, so comprehension is connected to the study skills with a broken line. Adding the comprehension categories completes the scope of reading skills, as shown in Figure 1–6.

As a teacher, you will want to know when authors of some *basal readers* expect students to have mastered various reading skills. (A basal reader is a textbook used for teaching reading.) Figure 1–7 indicates, not the time when these various skills *should* be taught, but the time that most basal readers actually cover these skills. It is not possible to indicate when each of these skills should have been taught since the authors of basal readers do not completely agree. In *developmental reading*, the program for normally achieving students, most skills would be taught during the semester immediately preceding the point listed. In *corrective reading*, the program for students with minor reading problems, the points show when each skill should be mastered. If a skill is not mastered by then

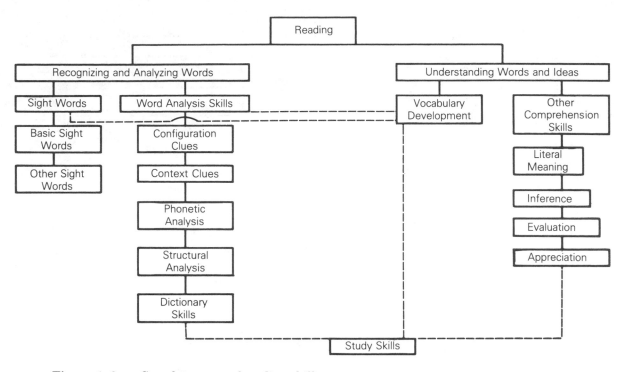

Figure 1–6   Complete scope of reading skills

(and you believe the student needs that skill), then teach the skill immediately so that the child will not develop a more serious reading problem.

Although comprehension is as important as the other skills listed on the chart, no accurate list of comprehension skills has been developed. Also, because the skills that make up comprehension (such as vocabulary or word knowledge) change and grow constantly, no accurate point of mastery can be determined. Therefore, comprehension is not included on the chart.

REVIEW OF THE RESEARCH

The *skills oriented approach* to reading (based on the belief that there are certain skills most students must learn in order to learn to read) was outlined by Susan Gross, Martha Luke Carr, Allan Dornseif, and Sally Mitts Rouse (1974). The authors assert,

A critical part of any reading or language arts program is the teaching of the skills underlying the

reading process. Without the basic skills of word discrimination, vocabulary development, and comprehension, it is virtually impossible for a student to read new material with success. (p. 782)

However, the authors also point out,

Skills development is only a part of the total reading program and should occupy no more than one-fifth to one-fourth of class reading time. A natural division would be one or two class periods a week spent on skills development. (pp. 782–83)

The authors then provide several pages of *behavioral objectives* related to such skills development. (A behavioral objective states the nature and degree of measurable performance expected for a specified instructional outcome under certain conditions.)

In contrast, Richard Allington (1977) expresses concern about using the skills approach. In the *Journal of Reading*, Allington states,

The recent trend throughout the educational system to depict learning as a hierarchical series of small steps has run amuck. Learning, but particularly learn-

SKILL	Grade 1	Grade 2	Grade 3	Grade 4	Grade 5	Grade 6	Grade 7+
Knowledge of Dolch Basic Sight Words (or similar)							
First Half		▨	▨	▨	▨	▨	▨
Second Half			▨	▨	▨	▨	▨
Other Sight Words							
Configuration Clues[a]	▩	▩	▩	▩	▩	▩	▩
(Word length, capital letters, double letters and letter height)							
Context Clues	▩	▩	▩	▩	▩	▩	▩
(Pictures and words)							
Phonic Analysis							
Single initial consonants (all but soft c and g)		▨	▨	▨	▨	▨	▨
soft c			▨	▨	▨	▨	▨
soft g			▨	▨	▨	▨	▨
Initial consonant blends							
bl, br, fl, fr, gr, st, tr, cl, cr,			▨	▨	▨	▨	▨
dr, pr, sl, sp			▨	▨	▨	▨	▨
pl, gl, sk, sm			▨	▨	▨	▨	▨
sn, thr, sw, wr				▨	▨	▨	▨
tw, sch, sc, squ, str, spl, spr, scr				▨	▨	▨	▨
shr, dw				▨	▨	▨	▨
Ending consonant blends							
st			▨	▨	▨	▨	▨
ld, nd, ng			▨	▨	▨	▨	▨
nk, nt				▨	▨	▨	▨
ft, mp				▨	▨	▨	▨
lt				▨	▨	▨	▨
Consonant Digraphs							
sh, th (three, this), wh (which, who),			▨	▨	▨	▨	▨
ch (church)			▨	▨	▨	▨	▨
ck, ng				▨	▨	▨	▨
gh, ph				▨	▨	▨	▨
Silent Consonants							
kn, gh(t), wr				▨	▨	▨	▨
mb				▨	▨	▨	▨
gn					▨	▨	▨

 Skill firmly established ▩ Skill extended and refined, but has been introduced

[a] The use of configuration clues is taught in grade one, but older students continue to use and improve in this skill as their knowledge of structural analysis increases.

(cont.)

Figure 1–7 The scope and sequence of various reading skills

SKILL

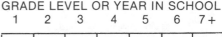

Short Vowel Sounds
  a, e, i, o, u
Long Vowel Sounds
  a, e, i, o, u
Vowel Teams and Special Letter combinations
  ay, ee
  oo (book), oo (moon), ea (each),
  ea (bread), oe, ai, oa, ow (cow),
  ow (snow), ir, ur, or, ar, aw, ou, er
  oi, oy, al, au, ew
Rules for Y sound
  at end of multi-syllable word
  at end of single syllable word
Vowel Rules For Open and Closed Syllables
Contractions
  didn't, won't, can't, isn't, don't
  let's, it's, that's, wasn't, hadn't, I'll,
  I'm, he's
  we'll, I've, he'll, hasn't, haven't,
  we're, you're, what's, there's, she's,
  they'd, she'll, here's, ain't, couldn't,
  they're, you'll, she'd, weren't, I'd,
  you've, you'd, we'd, anybody'd, there'll,
  we've, who'll, he'd, who'd, doesn't,
  where's, they've, they'll
  aren't, wouldn't
Possessives
Accent Rules[b]
1. In two syllable words the first is
   usually accented.
2. In inflected or derived forms the
   primary accent usually falls on
   or within the root word.
3. If two vowels are together in the
   last syllable of a word it may be a
   clue to an accented final syllable.
4. If there are two unlike consonants
   within a word, the syllable before
   the double consonants is usually
   accented.

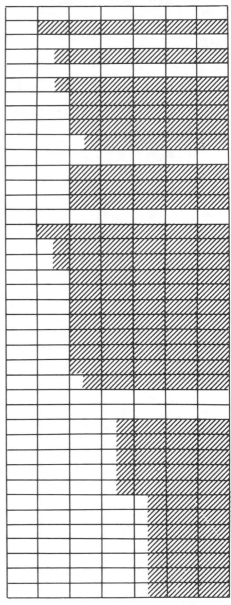

[b] At present no definitive research is available as to which accent generalizations are of high enough utility to make them worthwhile to teach. The four listed here are believed to be quite consistent and also of high utility.

(cont.)

Figure 1–7   (continued)

SKILL

Prefixes (recognition only)[c]
  a
  un, re
  dis
  in, per, pre, al, be, de, con
  im, under, mid
  for, ex, over, ad, sub, photo, en,
  com, pro, non, fore, anti, out
  auto, mis, trans
  inter, self, tele, counter, ab
Prefixes (meaning only)
  re (back or again), *un* (not)
  pre (before, prior to)
  ex (out, forth, from)
  de (from, away, from off)
  dis (apart, away from), in (into), in (not)
  en (in, to make, put into), sub (under)
  com (with, together)
Suffixes (recognition only)
  ly
  est, er
  y, less
  fully, self, en, full, ness,,ily, ty
  an, ier, some, ish
  ern, ite, ion, able, ment, ology, ous,
  or, ward, al, th, ious, ese, hood, ship,
  ist, ure, ive, ible, age
  ity, ation, ant, ian, ent
  ance, ence, ic, ical, ling, eer, ery,
  ey, most, wise
  ary
Syllable Principles
  1. When two like consonants stand between
    two vowels the word is usually divided
    between the consonants.

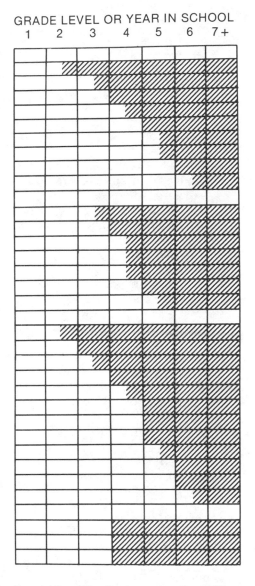

GRADE LEVEL OR YEAR IN SCHOOL
1 2 3 4 5 6 7+

[c]The prefixes *un* and *re* should be known by the middle of the third year in school. From that point on, the student should continue to extend and refine his or her knowledge of prefixes. This extension and refinement would continue throughout his or her elementary and high school years. The same is true of the suffixes such as *est* and *er* which should be known by the end of the second year of school but would be extended and refined throughout the student's elementary and high school years. (The authors suggest that "known" in this case only means that the student recognizes the prefix and/or suffix, but that he or she not be required to know its meaning.)

(cont.)

Figure 1–7 (continued)

GRADE-LEVEL OR YEAR IN SCHOOL

1   2   3   4   5   6   7+

2. When two unlike consonants stand between two vowels the word is usually divided between the consonants.
3. When a word ends in a consonant and *le,* the consonant usually begins the last syllable.
4. Divide between compound words.
5. Prefixes and suffixes are usually separate syllables.
6. Do not divide letters in consonant blends and consonant digraphs.

Dictionary Skills
   Alphabet in order
   Alphabetizing letters
   Alphabetizing words to first letter
   Alphabetizing words to second letter
   Estimating location of a word
   Alphabetizing words to third letter
   Using guide words
   Interpreting symbols
   Interpreting accent and stress
   Selecting word meaning from context
   Interpreting pronunciation key
   Using cross reference
   First and second spellings
   Word origin
   Parts of speech

Study Skills
   Table of Contents
   Index
   Glossary
   Encyclopedia (Find topic)
   Encyclopedia (Use index volume)
   Encyclopedia (Use cross-reference)
   Almanac
   Telephone Directory
   Interpret tables
   Library card index
   Read maps
   Read graphs, charts, and diagrams
   Skimming

Figure 1–7   (continued)

Note. From *Diagnosis and Remediation of the Disabled Reader,* 2nd ed., by E. E. Ekwall and J. L. Shanker (Boston: Allyn and Bacon, 1983), 72–75. Copyright 1983 by Allyn and Bacon. Reprinted by permission.

ing to read, has been presented in a variety of skills-based formats, but it seems that the poorest readers receive the heaviest doses of skills instruction. Skills instruction is not inherently bad but it is argued that skills are not enough. . . . In fact, when reading takes a back seat to skills instruction, one has to ask the age old question about the cart and the horse.

It should seem clear to anyone who examines the issue that reading is not responding to flashcards, nor is it filling in blanks, marking vowel values, or responding to graphemes presented in isolation. Reading ability is not necessarily facilitated by, nor does it necessarily require the ability to perform, the above acts. To develop the ability to read fluently requires the opportunity to read—a simple rule of thumb. (p. 58)

Roger Shuy (1981) warns teachers against rigidly adhering to any "set" of reading skills. He writes,

As one who helps to develop teacher's manuals for reading, I live in mortal fear that what we say in these manuals will prevent good teachers from applying our materials individually to the specific learning styles of their pupils. Most of the sequentially developed materials on the market gear to some anonymous norm which, as we all know, does not match one-to-one with many of our students. If pushed, most of us who develop teacher's manuals will admit this and clearly state that we produce a sort of menu of approaches to reading which each teacher, in wisdom, must use to select from in relationship to each individual child in a given classroom. The simple and unvarnished truth is that we who develop manuals do not know your children at all. Even clearer is the fact that you *do*. We can do no better than to provide a menu and it is up to you to determine what to order for your students. If we have put our menus together well, you will have some useful things to choose from to create an effective reading program for each child in your class. If we present only part of a program, your children will not be adequately nourished. (p. 920)

Shuy also points out that *letter-sound correspondence* (the relationship between a letter and the sound it stands for) is crucial to some children as a starting skill but that it grows less important as the reader becomes more proficient. In addition, not only do some children learn to read only through letter-sound correspondence while others learn with only the look-say or whole

word method, but also some children who learn using the look-say method develop letter-sound correspondence abilities on their own. Shuy thinks a good reading program is obliged to provide "multi-language accesses" to its students although not all children will need the same techniques in the same proportions. The teacher must then decide what types of instruction and how much of each type the individual child needs.

John D. McNeil (1974) attempted to determine if certain abilities must precede being able to pronounce a word or read a passage. First, he identified 15 skills assumed to be prerequisites for reading, such as being able to match rhyming words or to recognize compound words. McNeil then selected 150 children, ages 7–9, to demonstrate competence in reading aloud and to complete 15 objective-based measures of "highly valued skills in word attack" (p. 422). Of those children, 24 were competent readers, and 24 were unable to perform the transfer task showing reading proficiency.

McNeil theorized that skills unsuccessfully mastered by the competent readers are *false prerequisites*: "One cannot claim a skill as a prerequisite to reading if competent readers have not acquired it" (p. 422).

McNeil discovered that prerequisite skills actually fell into the following three categories:

1. *False Prerequisites.* Those skills which were unattained by most (75% or more) competent readers.
2. *Skills that may be necessary but not sufficient.* Those skills displayed by nearly all competent readers (90%) and by 50% or more of the incompetent readers.
3. *Skills associated with competency.* Those skills achieved by most competent readers (75% or more) and few incompetent readers (less than 25%). (p. 425)

Three skills, such as selecting words with prefixes and/or suffixes, were false prerequisites, and another was suspected false. McNeil found four skills possibly necessary but not sufficient for learning to read, such as matching the beginning sound to a written single letter. Seven skills were achieved by nearly all competent readers and only a very few of the incompetent readers. McNeil concludes that

Some skills regarded by many in the field of reading as prerequisites to word attack lack validity. . . .

When one considers that only a few of the skills which a consensus regards as essential were treated in this study and that from this small sample three were found to be false prerequisites, then it is likely that many more nonessentials are being taught in skill development programs. (p. 426)

McNeil believes some readers acquire some of these skills *after* or *as* they learn to read but not necessarily *before.* However, teachers should teach those skills found necessary but not sufficient because some of these skills might be helpful to particular learners.

In her article, "Whose Skills System? Mine or Penny's?" Louise A. Jackson (1981)* tells about a third grade girl who did not do well in school. Jackson writes,

Until mid-October, Penny was a blurred image, always hovering on the edges of our third grade class. In the mornings, she eased through the door sideways, her back against the door-jamb. Her clothes were faded and worn. Her voice was soft and hesitant. The other children had to be reminded to choose her for a game.

Penny's academic work was equally tentative. She read considerably below grade level. Her written work had little to commend it. Even her pencil seemed reluctant to make a decisive remark.

Imagine my surprise, then, when Penny first tugged at my skirt. She had a new third grade basal reader hugged to her chest, and her upturned face seemed more sharply focused. Punctuating her words with another tug, she asked, "If I can learn to read this book, will you let me read in Jody's group?"

Quickly, patronizingly—because I hadn't learned to have hope for children that I have now—I promised rashly, "Sure, Penny, when you can read that book and tell me about it, you can read in Jody's group." (p. 260)

Jackson then explains how Penny kept reading the book in all her spare time and constantly asked the teacher about words she couldn't pronounce. However, in the skills pages she was rarely successful.

Jackson says one day Penny came to her and said, "I can read this book now, Teacher. I'm ready to read in Jody's group" (p. 261). Jackson explains,

There was no way that she could function adequately in Jody's group.

But I was wrong. Penny *could* read that book! Furthermore, she understood what she was reading. "She's memorized it," I told myself. Aloud I said, "Very good, Penny! Now let's see if you can read *this* book. You've never seen this one!" She read that one, too, sailing smoothly through all sorts of new words with minimal hesitation. We sampled several other books and talked about them. The same thing happened. Penny, who couldn't do the simplest word attack skills lessons and had trouble with easier books, could read and understand third grade books she had never seen before.

What should I do? I knew she couldn't do the skills in the new workbook. I knew you were supposed to be sure pupils mastered skills at one level before moving to another level. I knew lots of things because I had been taught them, everybody else said so, and they seemed logical.

I put her in Jody's group anyway. And it worked out just fine. (p. 261)

Jackson concludes,

After all, why do we teach skills, why should we try to superimpose a formal system after the fact?

I have long since concluded that I'll offer formal word attack help where there is a clear need, and I'll put my trust in the children themselves if they already read successfully. (p. 262)

In "Reading: Skills or Competencies?" A. Sterl Artley (1980) discusses the danger of teaching the same reading skills to all students regardless of whether or not they have already developed a word system of their own. He concludes his article by saying,

Without realizing what would ultimately take place we have been walking the road of performance objectives, mastery teaching, and back-to-basics under the false assumption that if readers demonstrate the mastery of skills, ipso facto they will be effective readers. We have measured children's progress by tests rather than by the extent to which they read and enjoy reading. We have made reading less interesting and more of a task to be learned, with the result that for many children, "reading just isn't any fun." What

---

*"Whose Skills System? Mine or Penny's?" by L.A. Jackson, *Reading Teacher*, 1981, *35*, 260–62. Copyright 1981. Reprinted with permission of L.A. Jackson and the International Reading Association.

is needed is a change in the teacher's perception of the nature of the reading process, followed then by changes in teaching strategies. (p. 549)

John Downing (1982) quotes several experts in the field of reading to make his point about reading as a skill. For example, S. Jay Samuels indicates that learning to read is so complex, a validated hierarchy (proof that a certain set of skills must be taught in a certain order) does not exist. Frederick J. McDonald believes that when reading is broken up into a series of discrete responses that are practiced separately, then those skills are practiced in ways they will never be used.

Downing summarizes,

In other words, reading is a skill, and, therefore, no matter what framework of teaching methods and materials we set reading in, its essential psychological features assert themselves. The brain processes that determine the course of skill development operate constantly in learners despite the variety of methods and materials used in reading instruction. . . .

These remarks should not be misunderstood as cynicism about teaching methods and materials. On the contrary, teachers, their methods and their materials do make a difference in children's success and failure in learning to read. They make their difference to the extent that they approximate the natural course of skill development. For example, the need to practice integration from the very beginning is catered to much better by a language experience approach than by the "skills" approach. Imagine learning to fish by a "skills" approach! (p. 537)

Although these researchers believe too much emphasis on reading skills can be counterproductive, S. Jay Samuels, in John T. Guthrie, ed. (1981), also notes that four successful schools shared a decoding emphasis. Samuels states,

An early emphasis was given to what may be called a code-breaking subskill approach to reading rather than a holistic meaning emphasis. This should not be taken to mean that comprehension was unimportant, but that an early focus was given to those skills which facilitate word recognition. (p. 258)

Note also that in a table compiled by S. Jay Samuels (see Chapter 13), three of the fifteen variables common to very successful schools

Skills charts accompanying basal readers help teachers assess those learnings which should be mastered at each grade level.

were specific reading objectives, skills centered curriculum, and instruction and materials relevant to goals (p. 265).

Comprehension

The subskills of reading comprehension seem to be even more elusive than those of word analysis. Researchers have tried to pinpoint these subskills, but in most cases, have been less than successful. Frederick B. Davis (1972) summarizes one of the earlier "armchair analyses" (nonstatistical) of reading done by William S. Gray, an early pioneer in the field of reading. Gray's subskills, in the *Eighteenth Yearbook* of the National Society for the Study of Education in 1919, were as follows:

1. To read for the purpose of giving a coherent reproduction;
2. to determine the central thought or the most important idea of a selection;
3. To select a series of closely related points and their supporting details;
4. To secure information which will aid in the solution of a problem;
5. To gain a clear comprehension of the essential conditions of a problem;
6. To discover new problems in regard to a topic;
7. To determine the lines of argument which support the point of view of the author;
8. To determine the validity of statements. (p. 631)

Davis also discussed E. L. Thorndike's study of elementary school students whom he had asked to write answers to some questions on paper. From this study Thorndike derived the following information, according to Davis:

Understanding a . . . printed paragraph is then a matter of habits, connections, mental bonds, but these have to be selected from so many others, and given weights so delicately, and used together in so elaborate an organization that "to read" means "to think" as truly as does "to evaluate" or "to invent" or "to demonstrate" or "to verify." (1917c, p. 114) (p. 663)

Dolores Durkin (1978) lists several factors affecting comprehension: the way a piece of material is written; the information the reader brings to the printed page, such as her sight vocabulary and ability to decode; past experiences; intelli-

gence; and ability to remember (p. 418). Frederick B. Davis (1972) comments on many of these studies,

During the present century, innumerable writers have presented analyses of the processes or skills thought to be involved in comprehension in reading. The characteristics that all of the analyses mentioned in this section have in common is a lack of association with any specific experimental data that provide empirical support for them. Nonetheless, all of them are based on wide-ranging experience in the teaching of reading and familiarity with experimental studies in the field. (p. 631)

Researchers usually use a statistical technique called factor analysis in trying to determine whether there are, in fact, subskills of reading comprehension that exist as separate entities. Even when researchers claim to have isolated various subskills of comprehension, other researchers and writers doubt, or are unable to duplicate, those findings.

In perhaps the best known study of possible comprehension subskills, Davis (1944) examined the literature and isolated nine such factors. Davis lists these possible subskills as follows:

1. Knowledge of word meanings
2. Ability to select the appropriate meaning for a word or phrase in light of its particular contexual setting
3. Ability to follow the organization of a passage and to identify antecedents and references in it
4. Ability to select the main thought of a passage
5. Ability to answer questions that are specifically answered in a passage
6. Ability to answer questions that are answered in a passage but not in the words in which the question is asked
7. Ability to draw inferences from a passage about its contents
8. Ability to recognize the literary devices used in a passage and determine its tone and mood
9. Ability to determine a writer's purpose, intent, and point of view, i.e., to draw inferences about a writer (p. 236).

After a thorough statistical analysis of these subskills, Davis states that all except numbers 2, 3, and 4 can be measured. He also thinks that factors 5 through 9, although important, account for only a small part of the overall skill of comprehension.

In spite of Davis' work and other studies, most attempts to measure the subskills of comprehension have failed or have been discounted by other researchers. Also, George D. Spache and Evelyn B. Spache (1977) in their introduction to the study of comprehension state,

Recent studies by tests and interviews are beginning to raise questions about this multiplicity of comprehension subskills. It appears that what the reader retains while reading reflects such influences as (1) his purpose in reading or what he intends to retain; and (2) the instructions he is given before reading, which may lead him to find only the precise answers to specific questions or to secure a broader comprehension if the questions are more general. (3) Comprehension is affected even more, however, by the pattern of questions the child learns to anticipate. He learns to read with only those types of thinking that the teacher's questions demand. Since teacher's questions appear to be limited in type and depth, children's thinking (or comprehension) tends to be superficial and stereotyped, and lack critical thinking. (p. 439)

Most of the writers and researchers do, however, agree that the subskill *vocabulary* or word knowledge exists as a separate entity. Most lump together the rest of the skills in a category named "other comprehension skills." In a critique of the Davis study, Dale D. Johnson, Susan Toms-Bronowski, and Ray R. Buss (1983) state,

Further investigation of the critical skills of comprehension is sorely needed, especially at the elementary-school level. Nonetheless, the works reviewed here indicate that vocabulary knowledge *is* critical to comprehension. If you don't know the words, you're not going to understand the passage. (p. 254)

Thomas Barrett (1967) suggests four cognitive categories for comprehension skills: literal meaning, inference, evaluation, and appreciation. Literal meaning conveys the explicit ideas and information in the reading selection. To get the literal meaning of a passage, students need two skills, recognition and recall. Inference, Barrett states, occurs when the student "uses the ideas and information explicitly stated in the selection, his intuition, and his personal experience as a basis for conjectures and hypotheses" (p. 22). Barrett explains evaluation as follows:

Purposes for reading and teachers' questions, in this instance, require responses by the student which indicate that he has arrived at a judgment by comparing ideas presented in the selection with external criteria provided by the teacher, other authorities or written sources, or with internal criteria provided by the reader's experiences, knowledge, or values. In essence, evaluation deals with judgments and focuses on qualities of correctness, worthwhileness or appropriateness, feasibility, and validity." (p. 22)

The last category, appreciation, involves all the other levels of thought, but goes beyond them. About this category Barrett states,

Appreciation, as used here, calls for the student to be emotionally and aesthetically sensitive to the written work and to have a reaction to its psychological and artistic elements. For example, when a student verbalizes his feelings about part or all of a reading selection in terms of excitement, fear, dislike, or boredom, he is functioning at the appreciational level. (p. 23)

Barrett's classification of comprehension skills probably cannot be defended in terms of statistical analysis, but it gives us a logical framework for teaching comprehension.

Assessment of Research

Reading much of the literature on teaching various word analysis skills can easily lead one to believe it is innately bad to focus on skills. During the past decade some linguists have influenced the teaching of reading by claiming that there is no hierarchy (or certain sequences built on one another) of reading skills and that a child should be allowed to guess at words or take chances in reading. But we have seen the results of too much of this type of instruction in our respective clinics: many disabled readers. These readers have often not learned a method of attacking new or strange words and so make wild or unmeaningful guesses at words. As a result, they have an inadequate sight vocabulary for reading.

Reading fluently with good comprehension is the ultimate goal in teaching reading. However, to reach that goal, children must learn some word attack skills. There is nothing wrong with a skills oriented program *provided* time is also given to practice the act of reading. Skill building at the expense of actual reading time can be harmful because then many readers never relate the skills they learn to future reading enjoyment. However, successful schools usually have a set of objectives for reading skills, and the teachers teach directly to those objectives. Teachers monitor children's achievement of these objectives closely, and if students have not achieved certain skills, they are given corrective work until they learn them.

On the other hand, some children, like Penny, develop their own method of attacking words. A teacher must not insist that children master all the skills lessons if they can already accomplish what the skill is supposed to help them accomplish. For example, children are taught to divide words into syllables so they will know what sounds to give the vowels. Thus, a teacher has to teach syllable principles and then certain vowel rules. These syllable principles and vowel rules are a *means* to an *end.* However, if a child can look at almost any word and pronounce it, then that child is already *at* the end and need not be taught these particular skills.

Reading teachers, then, need a skill building program that allows them to help any child who has difficulty with certain skills, to monitor children to see if they have already accomplished what a skill is supposed to accomplish, and to relate the word attack skills being taught to the children's overall skill and pleasure as readers. In addition, children must have a lot of time to actually practice reading. This precept is so important that an entire chapter (Chapter 11) is devoted to ways of getting children to read, read, read.

SUMMARY

This chapter presents the reading skills that can be identified. Most of the skills in the area of sight words and word attack skills are easy to identify. However, it is much more difficult to identify comprehension subskills. A scope and sequence of reading skills is included to help you determine what students should have been taught when they reach the grade level you teach, to help you realize what reading skills you are responsible for teaching, and to help you determine which students need corrective reading instruction. Finally, the research about the controversy in teaching reading is reviewed and a possible compromise is suggested.

REVIEW QUESTIONS

1. Reading has two main categories. What are they?
2. Explain the danger in viewing reading as only a series of skills.
3. Explain the danger in taking a completely holistic view of reading.
4. After reading the various comments and research presented in this chapter, how do you view reading?
5. What are the five main subcategories of word analysis?
6. Why have studies attempting to identify some subcategories of comprehension met with little success?
7. What is the difference between a sight word and a basic sight word?
8. Explain the relationship between vocabulary and comprehension.
9. Why is one study skill included in the word attack skills?
10. Why does the subcategory syllabication fit equally well under the word analysis skills of phonetic analysis and structural analysis?

REFERENCES

Allington, R. If they don't read much, how they ever gonna get good? *Journal of Reading*, October 1977, *21*, 57–61.

Barrett, T. C. (Ed.). The evaluation of children's reading achievement. *Perspectives in reading No. 8*. Newark, Del.: International Reading Association, 1967.

Artley, A. S. Reading: Skills or competencies. *Language Arts*, May 1980, *57*, 546–49.

Davis, F. B. Fundamental factors of comprehension in reading. *Psychometrika*, 1944, *9*(3), 185–97.

Davis, F. B. Psychometric research on comprehension in reading. *Reading Research Quarterly*, 1972, *7*(4), 628–78.

Downing, J. Reading—Skill or skills? *Reading Teacher*, February 1982, *35*, 534–37.

Durkin, D. *Teaching them to read* (3rd ed.). Boston: Allyn and Bacon, 1978.

Gross, S., Carr, M. L., Dornseif, A., & Rouse, S. M. Behavioral objectives in a reading program, grades 4–8. *Reading Teacher*, May 1974, *27*, 782–89.

Jackson, L. A. Whose skills system? Mine or Penny's? *Reading Teacher*, December 1981, *35*, 260–62.

Johnson, D. D., Toms-Bronowski, S., & Buss, R. R. A critique of Frederick B. Davis' study: Fundamental factors of comprehension in reading. In L. M. Gentile, M. L. Kamil, & J. S. Blanchard (Eds.), *Reading Research Revisited*. Columbus, Ohio: Charles E. Merrill, 1983.

McNeil, J. D. False prerequisites in the teaching of reading. *Journal of Reading Behavior*, December 1974, *6*, 421–27.

Samuels, S. J. Characteristics of exemplary reading programs. In J. T. Guthrie (Ed.), *Comprehension and teaching: Research reviews*. Newark, Del.: International Reading Association, 1981.

Shuy, R. W. What the teacher knows is more important than text or test. *Language Arts*, November/December 1981, *58*, 919–28.

Spache, G. D., & Spache, E. B. *Reading in the elementary school* (4th ed.). Boston: Allyn and Bacon, 1977.

2

Major Approaches to the Teaching of Reading

Today's elementary teachers use three major approaches to teach children to read: the basal reader approach, the language experience approach, and the individualized reading approach. An overwhelming majority of these teachers use basal readers as the primary component of their reading instruction. With the *basal reader approach* the teacher relies on a series of graded books, with accompanying teacher's manuals, workbooks, and testing materials, to teach the students to read. Different types of basal readers have different underlying assumptions or philosophies about teaching children to read. Produced by fifteen different American publishing houses, modern basal readers are much more attractive, motivating, and comprehensive than their earlier counterparts.

Because much of the planning is already done for the teacher in the basal reader approach, the major challenges are to manage the materials properly, group the students appropriately, and teach the lessons effectively.

Teachers primarily use the *language experience approach* for beginning or remedial reading instruction because it recognizes that children's oral language background can be used to develop their reading skills. The teacher transcribes the child's own words to create stories that are then used as the child's first reading material. Several variations on the dictation, story writing, and reading procedures exist, but all language experience approaches believe in individualizing and personalizing instruction. Reading skills are generally taught as they become necessary rather than in the basal reader's systematic and sequential fashion.

The *individualized reading approach* contrasts sharply with the basal reader approach. For example, the teacher encourages students to choose their own reading materials from the large selection provided. The students' personal interests lead them to books that motivate them to read. In addition to self-selection, the individualized reading approach usually includes ample time for individual silent reading of library books, individual conferences between teacher and pupil, small groups that form and disband as necessary to learn specific reading skills, and individual record keeping.

Although each of these approaches has its distinctive features, many teachers use a combination to teach reading in the elementary grades.

REVIEW OF THE RESEARCH

Researchers have difficulty deciding which approach is best for teachers to use. First, most investigations show that differences between teachers are greater than differences between methods. Second, the approaches themselves are not always sufficiently different from each other to yield results that clearly point to the superiority of one method over another. Third, approaches have changed over time. For example, modern basal readers bear little resemblance to the basals used in the 1950s. Fourth, comparisons of approaches require very large groups of students and teachers and rigorous experimental controls to yield legitimate and meaningful results. Fifth, from what we know of child development and learning, no one method or approach is best for all children. Indeed, our present knowledge of how individual children learn to read makes it almost impossible to determine—from a research perspective—which approach is most effective for most children. Finally, teachers' preferences affect how children respond to any approach. Keep these limitations in mind as you read the results of investigations into reading instruction approaches.

The research summary falls into three categories: (1) beginning reading approaches—code emphasis vs. meaning emphasis; (2) the language experience approach compared to other approaches; and (3) the effectiveness of the individualized reading approach.

Code–Emphasis vs. Meaning–Emphasis Programs

For decades educators, laymen, and self-styled reading authorities have debated the merits of code-emphasis and meaning–emphasis approaches to beginning reading instruction. *Code–emphasis programs* initially emphasize decoding skills, specifically phonics; students learn sound-symbol correspondences and the application of phonic generalizations. *Meaning–emphasis (eclectic) programs* emphasize reading for meaning or comprehension. During the 1950s and early 1960s most American school children were taught in basal reading programs that emphasized reading for meaning and a whole word approach to decoding.

Rudolf Flesch, in his popular book, *Why Johnny Can't Read* (1955), suggested that a strong emphasis on phonics was essential to the nation's literacy. Flesch's book evoked considerable response from the public and was generally well received by the nation's press, if not by professional educators. By 1959 the debate was at its peak and led directly to a critical analysis of the research on the various methods of teaching beginning reading. Jeanne Chall, a member of the National Conference on Research in English, conducted a study and published her results in *Learning to Read: The Great Debate* (1967). Chall found that

a code–emphasis method—i.e., one that views beginning reading as essentially different from mature reading and emphasizes learning of the printed code for the spoken language—produces better results, at least up to the point where sufficient evidence seems to be available, the end of third grade.

The results are better, not only in terms of the mechanical aspects of literacy alone, as was once supposed, but also in terms of the ultimate goals of reading instruction—comprehension and possibly even speed of reading. The long-existing fear that an initial code emphasis produces readers who do not read for meaning or with enjoyment is unfounded. On the contrary, the evidence indicates that better results in terms of reading for meaning are achieved with the programs that emphasize code at the start than with the programs that stress meaning at the beginning. (p. 307)

Chall strongly emphasized that no one code–emphasis approach was superior to any other, and she recommended the code-emphasis approach only for beginners. Chall also noted that a poor method used by a good teacher probably yielded better results than the favored approach taught by a poor teacher. Finally, Chall pointed out that a code-emphasis approach was not a panacea for reading problems and that some pupils would indeed learn better through other approaches.

Chall's findings did not end the debate. The results of the Cooperative Research Program in First-Grade Reading Instruction, as reported by Guy Bond and Robert Dykstra (1967), supported many of Chall's findings, but also suggested that factors *other* than method might account for differences in reading achievement among early readers. These studies indicated that

1. Word study skills must be emphasized and taught systematically regardless of what approach to initial reading instruction is used.
2. Combinations of programs, such as a basal program with supplementary phonics materials, often are superior to single approaches.
3. Reading programs are not equally effective in all situations. Evidently, factors other than method, within a particular learning situation, influence pupil success in reading.
4. Future research might well center on teacher and learning situation characteristics rather than method and materials. . . . To improve reading instruction, it is necessary to train better teachers of reading rather than to expect a panacea in the form of materials.
5. Children learn to read by a variety of materials and methods. . . . No one approach is so distinctly better in all situations and respects than the others that it should be considered the one best method and the one to be used exclusively.
6. Initial reading vocabulary should be selected with a greater balance between phonetically regular words and high utility words. It is likely that introducing words solely on the basis of frequency of use presents an unusually complex decoding task for the beginning reader. On the other hand, it appears that presenting only phonetically regular words makes it very difficult to write meaningful material. (pp. 122–24)

The findings of the First-Grade Reading Studies point to the importance of a balanced approach.

Dykstra (1968a) summarized the findings of the second-grade phase of the Cooperative Research Program Studies and reported similar results. In a follow-up article, Dykstra (1968b) suggested it was not possible to attribute students' reading success to the superiority of a particular approach.

In spite of the careful, large-scale studies reviewed above, no clear resolution to the code-emphasis versus meaning-emphasis debate has emerged. The best evidence suggests that educators ask the wrong question when they ask whether the code-emphasis or meaning-emphasis program is superior. Too many other factors determine whether a child learns to read successfully. Some of these factors, particularly the teacher's effectiveness and the child's disposition, may be more important than method. For example, in their report on a study seeking to determine whether teachers made a difference in the reading achievement of their first-grade pupils when the *same, given* reading method was used, Jeanne Chall and Shirley Feldman (1966) found that several teacher characteristics were what correlated with pupils' reading achievement at the end of first grade. Chall and Feldman concluded "that teachers using one given method vary in their implementation of that method, that these differences in implementation can be observed reliably, and that the observed practices are not related to those the teachers themselves report" (p. 574).

Remember, however, that both Chall's research and the First-Grade Reading Studies were based on reading materials that are now obsolete. Contemporary basal readers are unlike those used in earlier studies. Even the eclectic basal readers published today place stronger emphasis on a phonic approach then did the basals of the 1950s and early 1960s.

Probably the best conclusions one can draw from these historic studies are: (1) all methods will be successful with some students and unsuccessful with others; (2) the teacher is probably a more important factor than the approach used; and (3) given the range of children's abilities and needs, an eclectic, balanced program, adapted as necessary for pupils who exhibit reading failure, seems most sensible for general classroom use.

Research on the Language Experience Approach

Considerable research has been conducted over the last fifty years to determine the value of the language experience approach to reading. Mary-Anne Hall (1978), in her synthesis of this research, points out that much of it supports the language experience approach as an effective method for teaching reading and language skills. Studies com-

paring the language experience approach to other approaches have generally found the language experience method equally satisfactory in terms of pupil achievement, and in some instances, superior. For example, Bond and Dykstra (1967) and Dykstra (1968a) found no significant differences in the achievement of pupils taught by language experience or basal reader approaches at the end of either first or second grade. But Elaine C. Vilscek (1968) found that much research on the language experience approach has yielded conflicting results because of several weaknesses in the research methodology used.

Hall reports that language experience has also been researched in relationship to pupil learning in specific skill areas, such as reading readiness, oral language, vocabulary, word analysis, creative writing, spelling, and reading comprehension. For example, Mary Ann Dzama (1975) found that the words used by first graders in the language experience program provided adequate models for learning phonic generalizations. Ronald L. Cramer (1970) found that students taught by the language experience approach were significantly better spellers, both in writing tasks and on word lists, than students taught with a basal reader approach. A more recent investigation by Christopher J. Ramig and Hall (1980) revealed that first-grade children taught by language experience and basal reader methods used the same reading strategies when reading a story out loud.

Much research recommends that teachers use language experience activities with second-language speakers, children with nonstandard dialects, economically disadvantaged students, adult illiterates, and other remedial students. Blanche L. Serwer (1969) and Cramer (1971), among many others, recommend the language experience approach for teaching beginning reading to black children, and Ricardo L. Garcia (1974) offers a similar recommendation for Mexican American children. While acknowledging that language experience has been shown to be an effective method for teaching disadvantaged pupils to read, Hall (1972) believes that further research is needed to justify its exclusive use with special populations.

Research on the Individualized Reading Approach

Most research on the individualized reading approach was conducted during the 1950s and 1960s, and much of it has been criticized for its poor quality. Sam Duker (1968), in a comprehensive review of research in individualized reading, acknowledges the shortcomings, stating:

Much of the reported research suffers from poor research design, inadequate sampling, careless measurement, and a biased attitude on the part of the investigator. (p. 25)

Duker's review also reveals that some studies support the use of the individualized reading approach while others do not.

Harry W. Sartain (1969) also reviewed the research on this topic. His tentative conclusions were:

1. Individualized reading can be somewhat successful under certain conditions.
2. It requires highly competent teachers, and those who are not particularly capable should not be asked to adopt it.
3. Children usually enjoy the personal attention of the individual conference and, as a result, develop favorable attitudes toward reading.
4. They often, but not always, read more books.
5. The less capable pupils and those having special problems are likely to be less successful in individualized reading than in more structured programs.
6. The lack of a sequential skills program and opportunities for readiness instruction cause teachers to be doubtful about the adequacy of skills learning.
7. Teachers are constantly pressed for time to provide conferences that pupils should have. (pp. 526–27)

Mary C. Austin and Coleman Morrison (1963) conducted their landmark study of reading in the elementary schools by examining more than 1000 school systems through questionnaires and direct observations. With respect to the individualized reading approach, they reported:

1. Of 407 school administrators questioned, only 24 clearly preferred this approach, 350 did not approve of it, 26 would prefer to use it in combination with a basal reader, and 7 were insufficiently knowledgeable to offer an opinion.

2. The reasons offered for not favoring the approach were: "(1) too few teachers possessed the ability and/or knowledge necessary to conduct this approach with success, and (2) even if all teachers were endowed with the attributes of a 'master' teacher, an adequate supply of books and materials was not to be found in the classroom at the present time. . ." (p. 88). Administrators were also concerned that reading skills would not be developed adequately with this approach, children would select improper materials, teachers would not be able to handle the variety of materials and record keeping, and children would not receive a sufficient amount of teacher time.

3. Those who favored the approach believed that children would be more motivated to read widely and would attain higher reading achievement.

Jeannette Veatch, an advocate of the individualized reading approach, and others (1979) claim that "the preponderance of support for the individualized approach using self-chosen, noncommercial books is unmistakable, regardless of textbook authors' and publishers' opinions" (p. 213). Veatch and others state that research clearly shows the following advantages with the individualized reading approach:

1. Marked and immediate improvement in attitude towards reading.
2. Dramatic increase in the amount of reading within a relatively short span of time.
3. Unusual approval by teachers and children of the individual conference.
4. Achievement rarely less, usually markedly higher in any of the skill areas studied.
5. Improved self-concept. (p. 213)

Even this cursory review of the research shows that no one method is clearly superior to any other. However, each method has its distinct advantages and disadvantages. These disadvantages can be somewhat mitigated by combining the three major approaches.

The major approaches to reading instruction usually require the teacher to meet with small groups of students.

THE BASAL READER APPROACH

Austin and Morrison (1963) reported that more than 95% of primary grade teachers and 90% of intermediate grade teachers relied on basal reading materials as their primary tool for instruction. Although more recent large-scale research is not available, it can be assumed that nearly all elementary teachers continue to use the basal reader in some way. Thus, teachers need to be thoroughly familiar with the modern basal reader program. Although many teachers develop the organizational and instructional skills to go "beyond the basal" and use other materials in their reading programs, they succeed with a multiple approach because they have experience with the basal reader approach.

What is a Basal Reader?

A *basal reader program* includes a series of books ranging from small paperbacked pre-primers to increasingly long and difficult books for students up to the sixth- or eighth-grade level.

Basal readers are designed to be comprehensive, developmental, continuous progress programs, providing for the sequential and systematic learning of all reading skills. In addition, such programs include teachers' manuals with detailed lesson plans, workbooks for student practice of specific skills, testing materials, ditto masters, instructional aids, and other materials.

Pupil Text Materials.   A group of 15–16 basal texts would typically follow this progression.

Pre-kindergarten, kindergarten, and some first-grade pupils use *one or more readiness level books* with accompanying materials. These materials are designed to help children develop a range of readiness skills, including language development skills, auditory and visual skills, letter knowledge, some beginning phonics skills, and recognition of a few sight words. Extra materials may include charts, manipulative devices, audio-visual materials, games, and story books. The pupils' books are usually in workbook form. (For a thorough discussion of reading readiness, see Chapter 4.)

The first graders' package includes two or three pre-primers, a primer, and a first-grade reader. Pre-primers have stories that may begin with one word per page and usually increase to about eight lines per page. Basal readers provide the tightest control of vocabulary at this stage. *Controlled vocabulary* means that new words are carefully introduced and limited and frequently repeated so the child can learn them easily. Writers of pre-primers must control vocabulary and create exciting and interesting stories at the same time. Writers also try to include language that is more natural and consistent with that spoken by six-year-olds. Frequently, the pre-primers introduce a set of characters that the children can get to know and follow in succeeding levels of the series.

The primer is usually the first hardbound book of the series, and it and the first reader continue to expand vocabulary. Vocabulary control becomes less rigid, and texts may distinguish between words the children can decode and those that require the teacher's assistance. The primer emphasizes the development of decoding skills, especially phonics, and focuses on other reading skills. The workbook accompanies the basal textbook, reinforces skills taught in the lesson, and is part of all subsequent levels.

Two second-grade and two third-grade readers present a greater variety of literature while reinforcing previously taught skills and emphasizing new ones. The comprehensive chart in Figure 1–7 (chapter 1) provides specific information on the skills taught at these levels.

On the fourth-grade, fifth-grade, and sixth-grade levels, one reader per grade is assigned. Word analysis skills continue to be taught, but in the intermediate grades, increased emphasis is placed on higher-level comprehension skills, content area reading skills, and study skills. Students read more nonfiction selections on a range of subjects as well as longer selections. See the figures in Chapter 1 for more specific information about the skills emphasized at the intermediate level.

Most publishers of basal readers also provide texts for pupils in *seventh and eighth grades.*

Grade Level Designations. Indicating that students' texts are assigned to certain grade levels is not entirely accurate. At one time these books were so labeled. For example, average students were expected to complete two books each in second grade; these were labeled 2^1 and 2^2, with the 2^1 book for the first half of the year and the 2^2 book for the second half. Third grade books had similar designations, the fourth grade book was labeled level 4, the fifth grade book level 5, and so forth.

Such labeling created problems. By arbitrarily labeling a book a 2^1 reader, for instance, a publisher created the illusion that all the book's selections were written at a 2^1 level. However, even though each successive book in a series was more difficult to read than the previous book, the readability levels of the selections within any one book varied significantly. Therefore, a student might be placed properly in a book yet find that some selections were too difficult and others too easy. In addition, many teachers frequently misused basal readers by steadfastly assigning their students to ''grade level'' books regardless of their actual reading ability; unfortunately, administrators often encouraged such assignments. Publishers intended for students to be grouped and placed in basal readers according to their reading levels, but instead, teachers often automatically assigned the upper half, for example, of a second grade class to the 2^2 text and the lower half to the 2^1 reader.

Modern basal readers usually designate levels with letters or numbers that do not correspond to specific grade levels. In fact, some publishers do not match their level designations to grade levels at all, preferring teachers to group and place students properly, then move them sequentially through the books. But old notions fade slowly and parents (as well as teachers) still want to know the grade level of the book their children are placed in. Sometimes, publishers make grade level assignments reluctantly; other times, they are made without the publisher's endorsement. Examples of present level designations from two of the most popular series are shown in Table 2–1.

Table 2–1   Basal series designations and equivalent grade levels

Series	Book level	Approximate grade level
Series A	A	Readiness
	B	Pre-primer[1]
	C	Pre-primer[2]
	D	Pre-primer[3]
	E	Primer
	F	First Reader
	G	2^1
	H	2^2
	I	3^1
	J	3^2
	K	4
	L	5
	M	6
	N	7
	O	8
Series B	1	Readiness
	2	Pre-primer[1]
	3	Pre-primer[2]
	4	Primer
	5	First Reader
	6	2^1
	7	2^2
	8	2, 3
	9	3, 4
	10	4
	11	4, 5
	12	5, 6
	13	6, 7
	14	7–8
	15	7–8

Referring to a level 10 book as a fourth-grade reader does no harm as long as teachers recognize the book is suitable *only* for those students reading on a fourth-grade level. Since in many fourth grades reading abilities range from first-grade to seventh-grade levels, teachers must form many groups or use some other administrative devices to meet pupils' needs when they assign students to any basal reader.

Other Components.   The basal reader program also contains other components that make the system effective.

Teacher's Manual

Essential to the proper use of the program, the teacher's manual includes a statement of the program's philosophy, a description of the program's components, detailed lesson plans for each selection with suggestions for teaching the recommended skills, supplementary activities for review and enrichment, scope and sequence charts of the skills presented, and other information. Teacher's manuals may contain reduced copies of each pupil page.

Student Workbooks

Workbooks, which may be called practice books, study books, or skill books, give students practice using the skills taught in the basal reader lesson. Workbook activities reinforce vocabulary, decoding, comprehension, and study skills.

Teacher's Edition of Workbooks

Some series include separate teacher's editions of workbooks. Designed to assist the teacher in checking pupils' work, the teacher's edition has the answers.

Testing Materials

The basal program may include a variety of testing materials. Typically, a group placement test is included to help the teacher properly place students. Publishers sometimes include individual reading inventories that help a teacher examine students' oral and silent reading to gain more diagnostic information. Basal programs also include mastery tests covering each unit or book; these measure whether or not students have learned the specific skills presented to that point. Charts and other record keeping devices are provided to help the teacher manage the testing component.

Duplicating Masters

Reproducible ditto masters provide independent skill practice for students in a variety of areas. In some cases, teachers can use duplicating masters instead of workbooks.

Instructional Aids

Publishers may include aids such as picture or word cards that drill students on new vocabu-

Unit 3. *Skylights* (22–33)   Word Recognition (R)
Directions **After children have read the directions, say:** When you have filled in all the blanks in the story,
read the story again to make sure that it makes sense with the words you have chosen.

⑧

This story is about Jane and her mouse Sam.
Some of the words are missing. The missing words
are at the right of the story. Find the word
that makes sense in each sentence. Then print
the word in the blank where it belongs.

Sam is missing. Jane can't find him anywhere.

She is sad enough to ___cry___.

___Everybody___ will help look for Sam.

Even Jane's ___aunt___ will help.

But finding Sam will be ___hard___ to do.

Sam is a very small ___animal___. He is

as white as ___snow___. Maybe Jane

could see him better if he were ___black___.

"I ___believe___ I see him over there,"

says Jane with a big smile on her face.

hard

black

cry

animal

aunt

everybody

believe

snow

● Can you find Sam? Put a line around him.

Figure 2–1   A sample page from the teacher's edition of a workbook

Note. From *Skylights: Practice Book* by W. K. Durr, J. M. LePere, and J. J. Pikulski (Boston: Houghton Mifflin, 1981), 8.
Copyright 1981 by Houghton Mifflin. Reprinted by permission.

E TEST TWO
Sound Associations for **ow**

Read each sentence below. Use what you know
about the sounds for **ow** and the sense of the other words
to read the new word in heavy black letters. Then put
a line around the picture at the right that goes
with the sentence. The first one shows you how.

★ I started to **mow** the grass.

1. We laughed at the funny **clown.**

2. Lynn has a **bow** on her dress.

3. The man has a **crown.**

4. The wind is **blowing.**

5. The dog began to **howl.**

UNIT 13   SKILL D1·7m   Number Correct _____

Figure 2–2   A sample page from a test manual accompanying a basal text

Note. From *Skylights: Test Manual* by J. Brzeinski and H. Schoephoerster (Boston: Houghton Mifflin, 1981), 18. Copyright
1981 by Houghton Mifflin. Reprinted by permission.

lary, pocket charts that hold word cards, games or other materials that reinforce new skills, or charts that present essential information from the lesson.

Supplementary Readers

Most series make sets of supplementary books available. These books may be paper or hardbound, coincide with different reader levels, and provide students with an opportunity to practice reading. They are usually attractive and motivating for students.

Miscellaneous Components

In addition, basal programs may include: dictionaries, cassette recordings with filmstrips, other audiovisual equipment, independent supplemental reading kits, magic slates, and reading machines.

Features Common to Basal Readers

Several features are common to most basals. Robert C. Aukerman's excellent resource, *The Basal Reader Approach to Reading* (1981), reviews the 15 American basal readers and describes the physical components, the materials and methods used, the literary and graphic arts components, the materials for directed learning and individualized reading, and the resources for assessment, evaluation, and management. Remember, however, that basal series are revised frequently. To obtain accurate information about the *latest* edition of a particular series, you will probably need to examine the publisher's catalogue or the actual series materials.

The following features are among those that Aukerman lists as common to *most* basal readers:

1. A readiness component.
2. Pre-primers, beginning with picture books that have very few words and gradually increasing to real stories.
3. Instruction in word analysis skills running concurrently with the basal stories.
4. A complete set of comprehension questions for each story.
5. A comprehensive teacher's manual with detailed lesson plans.
6. Suggestions for teaching the other language arts skills (listening, speaking, and writing) along with reading skills.
7. A wide range of literary selections, both fiction and nonfiction.
8. Study skills instruction.
9. Outstanding art work.
10. Student workbooks for follow-up practice.
11. Provision for students who fail to master new skills the first time they are taught.
12. Various testing devices for assessment and evaluation.

In addition, Aukerman notes that basal readers are very expensive to produce—ranging from $10 million to more than $20 million—that they are usually developed by leading authorities in the field, and that they constantly undergo revision, with new editions appearing at least every five years.

Listed below are the names and addresses of the publishers of American basal readers. You may wish to request catalogues describing their latest programs from some of these companies.

- American Book Company, 136 West 50th Street, New York, N.Y. 10020
- The Economy Company, 1901 North Walnut Street, Oklahoma City, OK 73125
- Ginn and Company, 191 Spring Street, Lexington, MA 02173
- Harcourt Brace Jovanovich, Inc., 757 Third Avenue, New York, N.Y. 10017
- Harper & Row, Publishers, 10 East 53rd Street, New York, N.Y. 10022
- Holt, Rinehart and Winston, 383 Madison Avenue, New York, N.Y. 10017
- The Houghton Mifflin Company, One Beacon Street, Boston, MA 02107
- Laidlaw Brothers, Thatcher and Madison, River Forest, IL 60305
- J. B. Lippincott Company, East Washington Square, Philadelphia, PA 19105
- The Macmillan Publishing Company, 866 Third Avenue, New York, N.Y. 10022

- Charles E. Merrill Publishing Co., 1300 Alum Creek Drive, Columbus, OH 43216
- Open Court Publishing Company, P. O. Box 599, La Salle, IL 61301
- The Riverside Publishing Company, 1919 South Highland Avenue, Lombard, IL 60148
- Scott, Foresman and Company, 1900 East Lake Avenue, Glenview, IL 60025

Different Types of Basal Reading Programs

Basal reader programs fit into two broad categories: (1) the more common "eclectic" or "balanced" basal programs that rely on a core vocabulary and analytic phonics; and (2) the phonics-based programs. Remember, however, that even within these categories, not all basals are the same. Each program is distinctive in number of skills introduced, vocabulary load, instructional procedures to be followed, etc. In a series of studies at California State University, Hayward, Diane Rogers (1977), Martha Wall (1975), and Nancy Roetzer (1979), respectively, compared components of readiness levels, vocabulary load and word analysis skills at the primary levels, and vocabulary load and word analysis skills at the intermediate levels in several of the most popular basal series. Each researcher found a wide discrepancy among the contents of the series.

Table 2–2   Publishers of different types of basal reader programs

Eclectic, balanced, or meaning-based (usually core vocabulary with analytic phonics)	Phonics-based
• Allyn and Bacon	*Analytic Phonics*
• American	• Economy
• Ginn	
• Harcourt Brace	*Synthetic Phonics*
• Harper & Row	• Open Court
• Holt	
• Houghton-Mifflin	*Linguistic*
• Laidlaw	• Lippincott
• Macmillan	• Merrill
• Riverside (Rand-McNally)	
• Scott-Foresman	

Meaning-based Basal Programs.   An *eclectic or meaning-based basal program* usually emphasizes language development and other readiness skills and then introduces a core vocabulary of words to be learned as sight words. Vocabulary is controlled, with words repeated frequently so that students master them. The core vocabulary words are also used to develop phonics skills through an *analytic* approach.

In an analytic approach, students are taught that letters *stand for* sounds rather than *make* sounds. For example, using familiar words such as *ball, bat, base,* and *banana,* the approach leads students to recognize that all these words begin with the same sound and the letter *b* stands for that sound. Students learn that whenever they see a word beginning with the letter *b,* they can *think* of the sound the letter stands for and begin to decode the unknown word. Usually, the teacher carefully avoids teaching the children that *b* says *buh.*

Basal reading programs that rely on a core vocabulary and analytic phonics are frequently called "meaning-based" programs because they emphasize context clues for decoding and focus on reading as a language-based activity. Phonics is *not* taught in isolation, but as a tool to be used in combination with context clues. Teachers usually introduce new words in context and encourage children to use other words in the sentence *and* phonics clues to decode them.

Sometimes basals of this type are called "sight-word basals," presumably because some words are taught as whole words rather than "sounded out," but this label is inappropriate and misleading. The popular basal readers of the 1950s and early 1960s did indeed de-emphasize phonics instruction and promote sight word learning, but the newer meaning-based basals place strong emphasis on phonics instruction—even in the earliest parts of the programs—and so the "eclectic" label is more accurate.

Phonics-based Basal Programs   The other broad category of basal readers contains the *phonics-based programs.* A phonics-based program places a much stronger emphasis on phon-

READING THE SELECTION

Introducing New Words

Today you will read about a family that moves to the city. Here are some words that may be new to you.

See pages 5–6 for model.

▲ apartment

Print: We live in the **apartment** next door to you.

Checking words: appointment *(no sense)*

building *(wrong sounds)*

▲ sneakers

Print: I have new **sneakers** on my feet.

Checking words: boots *(wrong sounds)*

snacks *(no sense)*

Instruction Charts: Unit 3

Assessment: Forms A, B

Noting Correct Sequence

Reading Bonus: Unit 3

Language Bonus: Unit 3

Figure 2–3   Sample page from a meaning-based basal reader teacher's manual, level 9, 2[1]

Note. From *Skylights: Teacher's Guide* by W.K. Durr, J.M. LePere, and J.J. Pikulski (Boston: Houghton Mifflin, 1981), 30. Copyright 1981 by Houghton Mifflin. Reprinted by permission.

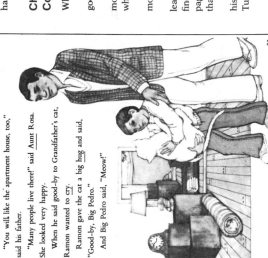

Setting the Scene

Have you ever moved from one place to another? . . . How did you feel about moving? . . . Today you will read about a family that has to move.

Print *Ramon.* This is the name of the boy in the family — Ramon (rah mohn).

Print *Aunt Rosa.* Here is the name of someone else who lives with Ramon and his parents. Her name is Aunt Rosa (ro sah).

Print *Big Pedro.* This name is Big Pedro (pay dro). When Ramon moves, he will have to leave Big Pedro. You'll find out who Big Pedro is when you read.

Open your books to page 22. Who will read the title of the story for us? . . . The author's name is right next to the title. The name of the woman who wrote this story is Lilian Moore.

Grownups
Are
Funny   by LILLAN MOORE

"Grownups are funny," thought Ramon.
"It is so nice here. Why would they want to move to an apartment house?"
"Do not be sad, Ramon," said his mother.

"But I like it here in Grandfather's house," said Ramon.
"You will like the apartment house, too," said his father.
"Many people live there!" said Aunt Rosa.
She looked very happy.
When he said good-by to Grandfather's cat, Ramon wanted to cry.
Ramon gave the cat a big hug and said,
"Good-by, Big Pedro."
And Big Pedro said, "Meow!"

22

23

Pages 22–23

Motivation and Silent Reading

Read pages 22 and 23 and find out who Big Pedro is and why Ramon has to leave him.

Checking and Developing Comprehension

Who was Big Pedro?
   Why did Ramon have to say good-by to Big Pedro?
   What kind of house is Ramon moving to? . . . Who can tell us what an apartment house is?
   How did Aunt Rosa feel about moving? . . . Why?
   How did Ramon feel about leaving Big Pedro? . . . Who can find and read aloud the sentence on page 23 that helps you to know that?
   Do you think Ramon will like his new home? . . . Let's find out. Turn to page 24.

SKYLIGHTS Unit 3 (22–33)   31

Figure 2–4   Sample page from a meaning-based basal reader teacher's manual, level 9, 2[1]

Note. From *Skylights: Teacher's Guide* by W.K. Durr, J.M. LePere, and J.J. Pikulski (Boston: Houghton Mifflin, 1981), 31. Copyright 1981 by Houghton Mifflin. Reprinted by permission.

Fun in the Sun
pages 1–4

OBJECTIVES

DECODING

COMPREHENSION

ORAL LANGUAGE

The student should be able to:

- decode the vocabulary in the selection.
- recognize that a word may have multiple meanings. (vocabulary development)
- recall the sequence of events. (literal)
- draw conclusions. (inferential)
- discuss similar incidents from personal experiences.

MATERIALS

Textbook pages 1–4
Duplicating Master no. 1
word cards: cross, Don, from

SYNOPSIS

Fran and Don are at a lakeside beach. Fran drops sand on Don as he snoozes in sun. Cross at first, Don chases Fran with sand. She flops on the sand and Dan drops sand on her. Both laugh. The story reviews sound/symbols that have been previously introduced; no new sound/symbols are taught in this lesson.

Warm-up

Have students pretend they are playing a horn in a band when they hear a word that rhymes with **band.**

grand	march	sand	jog
milk	hand	thank	stand
stamp	land	trim	drive

I. PREPARING FOR READING

Introducing the Selection

Ask students if they have ever been to the beach, and if so, whether it was at the ocean or on a river or lake. Discuss how a mountain lake would differ from the ocean. Tell them that the story they are going to read is about two children having fun at a lakeside beach.

Vocabulary Study

Write the following on the chalkboard:
Don is <u>cross</u>.
Did the cat <u>cross</u> the grass?

<u>Hand</u> the drum to Ann.
It is in his <u>hand</u>.

Pat can <u>dump</u> sand on Dad.
Dad can get sand from the <u>dump</u>.

Figure 2–5   Sample page from a phonics-based basal reader teacher's manual, level B, primer

Note. From *Exploring: Teacher's Edition* by C.C. Walcutt and G. McCracken (New York: Harper & Row [Lippincott], 1981), 39. Copyright 1981 by Harper & Row. Reprinted by permission.

Have each pair of sentences read silently then aloud. Have students explain the different meanings of the underlined words in each pair. Give assistance as needed. Then, explain that many words have more than one meaning.

Skill Review

Write the following on the chalkboard:
  Fran runs from Don.
  Is Fran on the sand?
  Cross the grass fast!

Have students read each sentence to themselves and then aloud. Draw your hand under each sentence from left to right as students read aloud. Ask why **Don** is capitalized. (person's name) Point to the period at the end of the first sentence. Have students identify it. Then point to the question mark at the end of the next sentence. Ask students to name it and tell its purpose. (shows person is asking a question) Point to the exclamation point at the end of the third sentence. Have students name it and tell its purpose. (shows person is speaking with excitement, surprise, anger) Have sentences read aloud with the proper intonation.

II. GUIDING THE READING

Silent Reading/Comprehension

1. Ask students to turn to the CONTENTS page. Review how it is used. *Read the title and page number of the first story.* (Fun in the Sun, page 1) *Turn to page 1.*

2. *Read the first sentence to find out what kind of day it is.* (hot, sunny)
   Read the next sentence to find out what Don does. (naps)
   Read the next three sentences to find out about Fran. What does she have? (cup)
   What does she do with it? (digs in the sand)
   Is she having a good time? (Yes, it is fun.)
   Now, let's look at the picture. Where are Don and Fran? (at the beach)

3. *What is going to happen at the beach? Read the first four sentences on page 2.*
   What does Fran have? (sand in cup)
   What does Fran do with the sand? (dumps sand on Don)
   Does Fran think it is fun? (yes)
   What does Don do? Read the next three sentences. (sits up)
   Is Don enjoying Fran's sand? (no, cross)
   What does Don want to do? (get Fran)
   What do you think that means? (get back at her in some way)

Fun in the Sun

It is hot in the sun.
Don naps on a rug.
Fran has a cup.
Fran digs in the sand.
It is fun.

1

Fran stands up.
Fran has sand in the cup.
Fran dumps the sand on Don.
Fran grins.

Don sits up.
Don is cross.
Don must get Fran.

2

Figure 2–6 Sample page from a phonics-based basal reader teacher's manual, level B, primer

Note. From *Exploring: Teacher's Edition* by C.C. Walcutt and B. McCracken (New York: Harper & Row [Lippincott], 1981), 40. Copyright 1981 by Harper & Row. Reprinted by permission.

ics as a decoding skill. Phonics-based programs may use an analytic approach, a synthetic method, or a linguistic approach.

Unlike the analytic approach, the **synthetic phonics method** teaches children the sounds of letters and then teaches them how to decode words by blending the letter sounds. Often the vowels are taught before the consonants. Letters are sounded in isolation. For example, a student might learn that *b* says *buh*, short *a* says *ă*, and *t* says *tuh*; when these letters are synthesized, they form the word *bat*. In the early reading stages, most synthetic phonics programs present stories with only a few words, and those have regular spelling patterns. These stories may be less interesting for pupils to read, but they are easier to decode.

Many teachers favor the synthetic approach, although no research evidence clearly proves it is any more or less effective for decoding than an analytic approach. Usually the method chosen reflects personal preference, but each method has its advantages and disadvantages. Proponents of the synthetic method claim it produces independent decoders more quickly, while proponents of the analytic approach argue that synthetic phonics results in blending problems, later difficulties with reading comprehension, or readers who "sound out" every word. Evidence shows, however, that either method succeeds with some pupils and fails with others. Teachers should supplement instruction when necessary to compensate for the weaknesses in both approaches and to help the maximum number of pupils achieve success.

The linguistic approach is not easy to define, first because the term is a misnomer and second because not all linguistic programs are alike. Linguistics is the study of human speech in its many facets including the nature, structure, and development of language. But so-called *linguistic reading programs* focus on only a narrow aspect of linguistic science, instruction that emphasizes the regularity of letter-sound associations through consistent spelling patterns. These spelling patterns usually appear in the form of

graphemic bases,[1] such as *-an* or *-at*. These consistent ending sound patterns are then used to form sentences and "stories," such as *Can Dan fan Nan?* or *Pat a fat cat, Matt.*

Linguistic programs present a few irregular sight words when necessary to form sentences. Phonics generalizations are usually not taught; rather, the students learn to generalize through repeated exposure to word patterns. Some programs use nonsense words, others do not. Some include illustrations while others omit them, thinking they will distract students from focusing on the words.

The obvious advantages of this approach are that it makes the process of beginning reading regular and structured, it may facilitate rapid decoding skill because of minimal contrast between words and frequent repetition, and it lessens the child's confusion.

The disadvantages are that stories contain unnatural language, are drawn less often from good children's literature, and may, therefore, be much less interesting and motivating for the child.

In addition to the linguistic basal programs noted in Table 2–2, some *nonbasal* reading programs use a linguistic approach. These include the *Miami Linguistic Readers* (Heath), the *Palo Alto Program* (Harcourt), and the *SRA Basic Reading Series* (SRA).

The *Distar* program (SRA) is another well-known nonbasal phonics-based program. It is a highly structured program that requires the teacher to follow the manual without deviation. The teacher uses a set of signals to prompt pupil responses. Instruction is programmed and includes much drill and repetition.

Criticisms of Basal Readers

Although basal readers are almost universally used in our public schools, they are also frequently criticized. Some of the criticism reflects disenchantment with aspects of the basal reader

---

[1]The following terms are often used synonymously with the term *graphemic base*: *phonogram, word element, word family, vowel family,* and *graphoneme.*

A Cap in a Bag

Dan's cap is on a mat.

Nat looks at the cap.

He bit it and hit it.

He hit it into a bag.

Dan had to look for his cap.

Tam is with Dan.

"Look in the bag, Dan," she said.

Dan said, "It's in the bag.

It's a rag!"

Figure 2–7   Sample page from a pupil text of a linguistic basal reader program, level B, 2nd pre-primer

Note. From *Dig In* by R.G. Wilson and M.K. Rudolph (Columbus, Ohio: Charles E. Merrill, 1980), 20. Copyright 1980 by Charles E. Merrill. Reprinted by permission.

approach, some is aimed at the quality or content of the materials themselves, and some is actually a comment on the misuse of these programs.

The Approach Itself.   Some critics simply oppose the use of graded materials with systematic progressions for skill instruction. They say such an approach is depersonalizing, if not dehumanizing. Advocates of basal readers can say very little in response to criticism of this type except to note that: (1) the basal reader approach should not be used as a *total* program for any child, and (2) for some children, it should not be used as even the *core* or basic program.

Although basal readers are marketed as "complete programs" designed to "meet the needs of every reader," the programs cannot be complete because the number of reading selections must be limited. Also, students at the extreme ends of reading ability will tend to be either bored or frustrated by the materials and instruction. Some pupils read before they enter kindergarten. To require these very able readers to go step-by-step through the skills and practice activities provided in the basal reader may be unwise. These students may need more enrichment, variety, and challenge than a basal reader can offer. At the other extreme are students who fail in their initial attempts to learn to read. They may be unable to keep up with other children in basal groups or, if older, may feel demeaned by being placed in a "baby" book. These students may require smaller increments of learning, a different approach, or greater individualization.

The strength of the basal program, however, lies in its usefulness for the large majority of elementary school pupils. Probably 80 to 90 percent of all pupils can learn to read successfully using the basal reader for the basic day-to-day developmental program—especially if certain aspects of other approaches are also employed.

Controlled Vocabulary and Uninteresting Content.

Using controlled vocabulary in the beginning levels of basal readers has been criticized. Because of the limited vocabulary, basals are accused of not reflecting children's actual language and of being too dull and repetitive. However, basals have changed a great deal since the early 1960s. Most basals still maintain some control over vocabulary, but much less so than in the past. The language in today's pre-primers and primers tends to be more natural, less stilted. A study conducted by R. Timothy Rush, Alden J. Moe, and John C. Manning (1979) found that the language used in basal readers by the beginning second grade text approximated that spoken by first grade children. The results of this study contradict the notion that children's oral language is more complex than that used in the basal materials they are given to read.

Today's basal reader stories are also more interesting and varied than those in earlier series. Many more selections from outstanding children's literature are included. At the lower levels, a lot of intentional repetition occurs to help young children develop the sufficient vocabulary recognition required for successful reading. But with the proper use of language experience activities and pattern books to supplement basal lessons, even very young children should have ample opportunity to read interesting stories.

Basal readers are often criticized for not providing stories that reflect the interests of intermediate-grade pupils. However, after comparing the expressed interests of intermediate students with the content of eight basal series, Florence T. Pieronek (1980) concluded that "current basal readers, with minor exceptions, do reflect reasonably well the reading interests of intermediate children" (p. 411).

Readability Problems and Other Criticisms.

The increased use of selections from children's literature and the accompanying decontrol of vocabulary, particularly at upper grade levels, have resulted in less reliable readability levels among basal readers. All selections in a book called a fourth-grade reader should be written at or near a fourth-grade level of difficulty. Furthermore, the fourth-grade level book of series A should be comparable in difficulty to the fourth-grade book of series B. However, John M. Bradley and Wilbur S. Ames (1977) examined selections from six basal readers and found "extreme basal reader variation" and "substantial intra-book story differences" (p. 182). The level of difficulty varying among books at the same level produced by different publishers *and* varying within each book may create difficulties for some students. Although it is unrealistic to expect publishers to produce books with precise readability control, it would be helpful if they provided teachers with more information about the actual difficulty of the various selections in the books.

Some basals have been criticized for not emphasizing decoding skills enough. This criticism may have been justified in the past; today, however, basal programs are more likely to be guilty of overkill in this area. Some programs do a better job than others of providing selections that allow students to practice specific decoding skills while reading the complementary lesson. All basals today, however, present comprehensive coverage of phonic and other decoding skills.

Basal readers have been criticized in the past for unrealistically portraying only the happy events of life and avoiding conflict. This criticism is also no longer valid. Earl H. Cheek, Jr. and Martha C. Cheek (1979) reviewed three basal series published since 1976 and examined the stories and illustrations from 629 selections. They found that the story content depicted real-life problems 33 percent of the time. They classified 73 percent of the stories as realistic and 27 percent as unrealistic. The illustrations were nearly equally divided between those that portrayed happiness and those that portrayed conflict.

In recent years basal readers have been criticized for negative or inaccurate portrayals of minority groups, women, and family structures. Gwyneth E. Britton (1975) has decried the negative portrayal of women and minorities, but Laurel A. Marten and Margaret W. Matlin (1976) and Diane W. Kyle (1978) have acknowledged the improvements made while calling for more progress. The McGraw-Hill Book Company (1975) has prepared a set of guidelines for equal treatment of the sexes in written publications, and publishers of basal readers have made a concerted effort to respond.

Carol J. Hopkins (1982) found that handicapped individuals are rarely portrayed in basal selections. Hopkins analyzed twelve major basal reading series and observed that less than 1 percent of the stories included handicapped characters. None of these portrayals appeared before the third-grade level readers. Hopkins pointed out, however, that several publishers were planning to depict more handicapped individuals in future editions.

Finally, textbook adoption committees, usually at the state level, have attacked publishers of basal programs. Writing in *The Reading Teacher,* Smith (1982) cites a political effort in Texas that had the following results:

Nearly every basal, with the exception of straight decoding approach [phonics-based] basals, was attacked with 30-80 pages of remonstrances dealing with objections to represented role models, values, teaching techniques, story resolutions, and story topics. (p. 575)

Although such attacks have not yet resulted in direct censorship of basal materials, several educational organizations oppose efforts by such pressure groups to impose their preferences on others.

Misuses of Basal Readers

The potential misuses of basal readers create more problems than the construction of these programs does. The most common misuses of basal readers are: (1) improper pupil placement and inappropriate grouping; (2) improper use of the teacher's manual; (3) lack of direct instruction; (4) improper and excessive use of workbooks; and (5) lack of program stability. Although authors of basal readers do not necessarily cause these misuses, if they modified certain areas and included more guidance about using their materials, they might reduce the incidence of these misuses.

Improper Pupil Placement and Inappropriate Grouping. Since the basal program is predicated on the students' systematic and sequential progression through a series of skills, students *must* be placed appropriately. The child placed in a too difficult book may become frustrated and discouraged, and the student placed in too easy material may become bored and unmotivated. In either case, the students fail to learn at the proper rate.

Albert J. Harris (1979) reported on research that shows students placed in easier materials make greater progress than students placed in more difficult materials. Students placed in easier materials also tend to exhibit better behavior in the classroom. Thus, the teacher who is in doubt should place pupils in easier books; certainly students are often placed in basal readers that are too difficult.

There are several reasons for improper placement, most of them preventable. First, teachers may simply fail to use appropriate procedures to determine pupil placement. Such procedures include the testing instruments provided by the basal publisher, individual pupil assessment when any doubt arises, and careful, continuous observation. But teachers often place students in reading groups based only on the previous teacher's recommendation or on a rudimentary observation of the students' oral reading. Or teachers may conscientiously rely on the publisher's assessment test only to later discover that it is inadequate. For example, some publishers encourage teachers to use a group administered, multiple-choice test to arrive at pupil placement. But many times, only a teacher's careful, individual observation of pupils *in the act of reading* can determine proper placement. Also, some publishers may provide informal reading inventories (IRIs) for individual assessment, but fail to match the content of the IRI selections with the basal selections. When aware of the shortcomings of the assessment instruments provided with some basal readers, teachers can develop their own inventories to aid in pupil placement.

Improper pupil placement may also occur because teachers are unable or unwilling to form enough groups to meet all their pupils' needs. For example, some teachers—even in the primary grades—have only one or two reading groups for the entire class, and so many students are misplaced. Even when teachers prepare daily and attempt to manage six or more groups at different reading levels, they cannot always place all students properly because of the wide range of abilities found in their classrooms. Classroom teachers face great difficulties in organizing and managing multiple reading groups, and of course, they can only do so much—not every student can be properly placed all the time. Nonetheless, with appropriate support from administrators, teachers can do more to ensure adequate group placements for students. (See Chapter 3 for procedures to follow to achieve this goal.)

Furthermore, not understanding what proper placement is or what criteria should be used to match students with reading materials both cause incorrect placement. Teachers generally assume that students should be assigned to basal reading groups according to their *instructional reading level*, when the student can recognize at least 95 percent of the words and comprehend at least 75 percent of what is read. Anything below these levels is the student's *frustration*

reading level. (See chapter 10 for a discussion of how reading levels are determined.) But Harris reported that students made the best gains when their word recognition was at least 97 percent; anything below 95 percent was considered frustration level for primary children. Even if you use the 90 percent criterion, your students should miscall no more than one word out of every ten to be properly placed in their basal readers. Many teachers disregard the guidelines for proper placement because they mistakenly think basal texts should constantly challenge their students.

Finally, old notions about grade level designations still persist, to the detriment of young readers. Some teachers still believe that if they teach second grade, then half of their students must be placed in the 2^1 book and half assigned to the 2^2 book. Others feel pressured by administrators, colleagues, and parents to ignore placement guidelines and push students into more difficult books so they will achieve better. However, their students are likely to learn less rather than more.

Several grouping problems may arise when basal programs are used. Some teachers fail to form enough groups. In most classrooms, teachers should form three or more reading groups for at least three different basal levels, which requires substantial time management and organizational skills. Also, the best instruction occurs when the teacher meets with each group every day. Adequate provision for individual differences can be achieved through carefully managed small group instruction.

Improper Use of the Teacher's Manual. Problems also occur as a result of improper use of the teacher's manual. The teacher's manual outlines lesson steps to follow in presenting the basal selections and accompanying skills learnings. Every publisher of basal readers seems to follow the edict, "Let no teacher ever run out of things to do"! As a result, teacher's manuals present far more activities and directions than any mortal teacher can accomplish in a reasonable amount of time. Procedures that should take twenty minutes will, in fact, take up to three times that long if the teacher tries to follow all the lesson steps outlined. To conduct small group instruction, the teacher has to modify prescribed procedures and skip over some recommended activities or instructions. Teachers can do these things, but surely authors of teachers' manuals could be more selective and indicate which procedures are essential and which are optional or supplementary. Many of the procedures presented are excellent, but some teachers may ignore the strengths of the lesson plan because they do not have time to select the crucial teaching procedures.

Lack of Direct Instruction.   If the quality of direct instruction is poor, one of the major strengths of the basal reader approach is negated. For example, in spite of almost universal condemnation, many teachers still use a round robin oral reading format for daily lessons; children take turns reading orally while the other group members follow along silently. Boring for the more able oral readers and agonizing for children who read slowly or haltingly, round robin oral reading also usually hinders development of reading comprehension skills.

No basal program recommends the frequent use of round robin oral reading; instead, basal manuals usually recommend that students spend a substantial amount of time reading selections silently and in small increments. After silent reading, the teacher may ask questions or have students read orally to answer specific questions. When used in appropriate ways for specific purposes, oral reading can be an effective activity.

The importance of practice *in the act of reading* cannot be overstressed whether it takes the form of silent reading or appropriate oral reading in context, such as choral reading or an oral reading approach where *each* child reads at length.[2] Richard L. Allington (1977) reported on

informal observations showing that low achieving students read only between 24 and 110 words in context during their reading instruction sessions. Instead of practicing reading, students received isolated skills instruction. But if students do not read in context, Allington wonders, "How they ever gonna get good?"

Improper and Excessive Use of Workbooks. Proper use of the basal reader program requires the teacher to select activities from the teacher's manual that balance direct instruction of reading skills and ample opportunity to apply these skills while reading. Teachers who provide little or no direct instruction and minimal reading practice, who ignore the teacher's manual and concentrate on workbook exercises, misuse the basal program. Unfortunately, it is easy to find teachers who view the basal reader program as a series of stories with accompanying workbook pages to be assigned and corrected in order.

Again, publishers of basal readers provide many more workbook pages and activities than are necessary. Workbooks can properly serve either of two purposes: (1) to provide practice that reinforces previously taught reading skills; or (2) to keep a group of children independently busy *for a short time* so the teacher can concentrate on another group of students. Ideally, all workbook pages would fit into the first category. Realistically, of course, assignments sometimes fit into the latter category. In either case, however, teachers cannot assume that workbook pages "teach" new skills or replace the directed reading lesson.

Because they may occupy a third or more of the students' reading instruction time, workbook pages must be used properly. Therefore, teachers should consider these guidelines when assigning workbook pages to elementary school pupils.

1. The total amount of time allocated for workbook tasks should not exceed 20 minutes per day.

2. The teacher should selectively assign pages. Workbook pages may be inappropriate: un-

---

[2]In addition to choral reading, effective oral reading approaches include the Neurological Impress Method, echo reading, repeated readings, paired reading, tape recorder activities and others. For descriptions of various oral reading methods, see the section on Efficiency Skills in Chapter 5 of Ekwall, E.E. & Shanker, J.L. *Diagnosis and Remediation of the Disabled Reader* (2nd ed.). Boston: Allyn and Bacon, 1983.

related to skills previously introduced, too lengthy, too difficult, or too confusing. (Sometimes, even the teacher has to look up the answers in the teacher's edition and work backwards to understand how to arrive at the correct answers. Then you *know* the pages are inappropriate!)

3. Teachers should remember that practice work should not be too difficult even if directions are clear. Workbook pages should not constantly test students. If students are properly placed and have received appropriate instruction on the skill, they should be able to complete the workbook pages with about 90 percent accuracy. Workbook pages should not be graded on the bell-shaped curve; rather, teachers should strive for and be pleased when all students complete their pages correctly. If a student fails to achieve 90 percent accuracy—and the failure is not caused by lack of effort—then the teacher should assume that: (a) the student is not placed at the proper level; (b) the teacher did not adequately teach the material; or (c) the workbook page in question is inappropriate for that student. The teacher should *not* automatically have the student do the page over or assign similar pages.

4. When teachers assign workbook pages, they should always give clear directions on how to complete them. The best time to assign pages is at the end of the reading group just before the students actually begin their seatwork. Then the teacher can go over one or two items on each page before dismissing the students. In addition, students should always be given *written* directions that clarify which pages to do and when to have them completed.

5. Workbook pages should be corrected promptly. When the reading group meets, students and teacher can discuss and resolve any problems that arise. By taking these few minutes daily, teachers can effectively reduce the time spent correcting individual workbooks. This approach also motivates students to complete their work on schedule. If workbook pages are to reinforce skills just taught, students must not be allowed to fall behind.

Administrative Problems. Teachers use a

basal program more effectively if they have the opportunity to use it over a period of time and become familiar with its strengths and weaknesses. In addition, basal reading programs are very costly. However, administrators frequently do not understand the value of stability in a reading program, and change basal programs constantly, presumably so that the district can have the latest program. Sometimes changes are made from one type of program to another, which may create additional confusion for children. In many schools teachers choose from among a variety of series, and some teachers use more than one series in their classrooms. This undoubtedly makes daily lesson planning more difficult.

Many students have severe reading difficulties because they are confused about what the reading process is. These students have often been exposed to several conflicting approaches to beginning reading instruction. For example, it is not unusual to see students who were taught with Distar in kindergarten, a phonics-based basal in first grade, a language experience approach in second grade, a linguistic basal in third grade, and a meaning-based basal in fourth grade. These students are understandably perplexed about how to attack words. They cannot succeed in reading because they have not received consistent instruction.

School districts should adopt a single series for grades K–6. Some advantages of using one basal throughout a school district over this period of time are:

1. Teachers become thoroughly familiar with a series. They know the strengths and weaknesses of the series and can supplement the weak areas as needed.

2. This approach is cost effective. Supplementary materials (word cards, etc.) can be printed by the district if all teachers are using the same materials. Consumable materials (workbooks, ditto masters) are more likely to be available because they can be ordered in larger quantities. If materials temporarily run out, they can be borrowed easily from other schools.

3. Teachers adjust more easily to changes in assignment to new schools or grade levels since they are already familiar with the basal approach used district-wide.

4. Children do not become confused by a variety of approaches. Similarly, children can be placed more quickly and can progress satisfactorily if they transfer to a different school within the school district.

5. School or district reading staff development efforts succeed more often if all teachers are using the same core approach.

Some teachers and administrators will disagree because they think using only one series stifles a teacher's individuality and that various offerings must be provided for children who fail to learn with the mandated program. However, the single series adoption is *not* a total reading program, only the foundation for skills development in the developmental program. Teachers can go beyond the basal program with supplemental approaches when appropriate and enrich instruction according to individual styles and talents. Also, it may be shortsighted to assume certain children fail to learn because of a particular basal program. Shifting children to different core programs does not result in success either. Other factors are more likely to have led to some pupils' reading failure. Also, school reading specialists who give extra help to those pupils who need it will be more effective if they can tailor their assistance to a program being offered in all the school's classrooms.

Summary of the Strengths and Weaknesses of the Basal Reader Approach

Obviously, the basal reader program can be an important and valuable part of the classroom reading program. It is not, however, a panacea, a total program, or an essential component that has no faults. Table 2–3 summarizes the basal approach's strengths and weaknesses. As a professional teacher, you will decide how and to what extent the basal reader can assist you in teaching children to read.

THE LANGUAGE EXPERIENCE APPROACH

MaryAnne Hall (1978) defines the *language experience approach* (LEA) as follows:

The language experience approach for teaching reading is a method in which instruction is built upon the use of reading materials created by writing down children's spoken language. The student-created reading materials represent both the experiences and the language patterns of the learner. The communication processes of listening, speaking, reading and writing are integrated in language arts and reading instruction. (pp. 1–2)

LEA has won the support of many devoted teachers, some of whom use it exclusively, others of whom use it with another approach.

Roach Van Allen (1968) captures the conceptual framework for the language experience approach in these statements:

What I can think about, I can talk about.
What I can say, I can write (or someone can write for me).
What I can write, I can read.
I can read what others write for me to read. (p. 1)

Allen believes that each child's oral language background is vital to the program. The teacher writes down a child's thoughts, as expressed in spoken words, and then the child reads those words. This basic dictation approach has a number of variations and ultimately enables the child to read other writers' words as they appear in books or other written forms. Supporters claim the language experience approach will also lead to improved spelling and writing.

Unlike the basal reader approach, the language experience approach does not require the teacher to depend on textbooks or other commercially prepared materials. LEA may, however, supplement a basal or individualized approach.

No built-in scope and sequence of skills or vocabulary control exists in the language experience approach. Skills and vocabulary are learned as they arise during dictation, or small groups may be formed as needed. Ability grouping, common with basal approaches, is definitely not recommended when LEA is used as an exclusive

Table 2–3   Strengths and weaknesses of the basal reader approach

<table>
<tr><th colspan="2">Strengths</th></tr>
<tr><td>1.</td><td>Basal readers provide a comprehensive program with numerous materials.</td></tr>
<tr><td>2.</td><td>Basal readers provide a sequential, systematic presentation of vocabulary, decoding, comprehension, and study skills.</td></tr>
<tr><td>3.</td><td>Basal readers provide for a systematic review of skills as students progress through the program.</td></tr>
<tr><td>4.</td><td>Controlled vocabulary in the early stages helps students achieve initial success with decoding.</td></tr>
<tr><td>5.</td><td>A system for placing students and evaluating their progress is included.</td></tr>
<tr><td>6.</td><td>Workbooks and other reinforcement materials are included to aid the teacher in planning and carrying out instruction.</td></tr>
<tr><td>7.</td><td>The teacher's manuals provide daily lesson plans and a wealth of other instructional resources.</td></tr>
<tr><td>8.</td><td>Basal readers are designed for small-group instruction.</td></tr>
<tr><td>9.</td><td>The programs are written by reading experts.</td></tr>
<tr><td>10.</td><td>Basal readers are attractive and carefully packaged.</td></tr>
<tr><td>11.</td><td>Basal readers provide a variety of literary forms carefully selected from outstanding children's literature.</td></tr>
</table>

<table>
<tr><th colspan="2">Weaknesses</th></tr>
<tr><td>1.</td><td>Vocabulary may be either too restricted or not restricted enough. Ranges in readability increase as levels become more difficult.</td></tr>
<tr><td>2.</td><td>Language patterns of basal stories at the earliest levels may not match children's oral language.</td></tr>
<tr><td>3.</td><td>The variety and number of selections cannot be as great as that found in actual trade books. Some selections lack literary merit.</td></tr>
<tr><td>4.</td><td>The systematic, sequential approach to skill development is considered inappropriate by some.</td></tr>
<tr><td>5.</td><td>The structured nature of basal programs may decrease individualized instruction and limit a teacher's choices.</td></tr>
<tr><td>6.</td><td>Basal programs tend to be less effective for both the very able and the slowest readers.</td></tr>
<tr><td>7.</td><td>Teacher's manuals may contain too much information, requiring the teacher to determine which parts of the lesson are essential and which are supplementary.</td></tr>
<tr><td>8.</td><td>Workbook materials can be misused because there are so many inappropriate pages.</td></tr>
<tr><td>9.</td><td>Basal selections have been criticized for inadequate or inappropriate portrayal of ethnic and racial minorities, women, and the handicapped.</td></tr>
</table>

method. Rather, LEA requires a flexibility of approach.

In addition, the language experience approach is characterized by:

1. A warm and stimulating classroom environment.

2. The encouragement of oral expression among the children.

3. A reliance on each child's spoken language, rather than strict adherence to standard English as the only form of acceptable language.

4. An emphasis on familiar words, such as those that appear on labels, signs, and television.

5. Opportunities for children to share their individually authored stories.

6. An emphasis on expressive activities, such as dramatics, art, music, and cooking.

7. The early development of students' writing skills.

8. The use of materials that are already available, such as basal readers, trade books, magazines, recordings, filmstrips, art work, and science materials.

9. An ungraded, individualized method in which students progress at their own rates.

10. The early fostering of students' independence and self-directed learning.

11. The involvement of several adults in the classroom, such as team teachers, instructional aides, and volunteers.

The language experience approach is generally used with beginning or remedial readers but may be used as an adjunct to reading programs at nearly all levels. Research often shows that LEA is an effective method with some special advantages.

However, this method also has potential disadvantages, such as the lack of structure. The approach's major weakness is that it places unusual demands on the teacher who uses it as an exclusive method for beginning reading instruction. Thus, many experts suggest that language experience not be used as a *total* program but as a complement to other approaches.

Many basal programs now incorporate language experience activities. Roach Van Allen and Claryce Allen's (1974) multimedia kit, *Language Experience in Reading*, provides a comprehensive and creative collection of resources for the classroom teacher. There are also a number of excellent guidebooks and texts on language experience procedures, such as those written by Roach Van Allen and Claryce Allen (1982), Hall (1981), Dorris M. Lee and Roach Van Allen (1966), Russell G. Stauffer (1980), and Jeannette Veatch,

With the language experience approach, dictation can be taken from the whole class.

Florence Sawicki, Geraldine Elliott, Eleanor Flake, and Janis Blakey (1979).

Language Experience Procedures

There are five main language experience techniques: the key vocabulary approach, the group experience chart, individual descriptions of illustrations done in a group setting, the individual experience story, and individual experience stories using the tape recorder.

The Key Vocabulary Approach.   The description of the key vocabulary or key words to reading approach is drawn from Veatch and others (1979). These authors credit Sylvia Ashton-Warner for their inspiration in developing the key vocabulary procedures. Ashton-Warner's book, *Teacher* (1971), described the approach that she used to teach Maori children in New Zealand.

In the *key vocabulary approach* the teacher

elicits words from the child that have special meaning. Drawn from the student one at a time, the words are then manipulated and gradually expand to whole sentences that the student soon learns to write down. This leads to the first child-authored stories, which may be shared with other students.

The specific steps presented by Veatch and others are as follows:

1. *Elicit a key word from each child.* These are words of high emotional value, such as *love, Mommy, blood, ghost* or *teacher.* To elicit the key word the child is asked questions such as, "What is your favorite word?" or "What is your scariest word?" The greater the emotional value of the word the better.

2. *Print the word on a piece of tagboard.* The child whispers the word to the teacher, who prints it on a large piece of tagboard (8½" × 11") while the child observes closely.

3. *Let the child trace the word.* The child presses a finger to the tagboard and traces the word. At this stage the child may pronounce the whole word while tracing it or simply name the letters.

4. *Let the child do something with the word.* The child gets actively involved with the word by drawing a picture of it, copying it on the chalkboard or a slate, showing it to others, etc.

5. *Review words with the child.* The child regularly brings the words to the teacher, who then asks the child to pronounce them as they are rapidly flashed. No effort should be made to have the child "sound out" the words. Words not instantly recognized should be discarded on the assumption that they are not sufficiently important to the child yet.

6. *Store the words.* To store the accumulating words, the teacher may give individual folders to the children, make ring files by punching holes in the cards and arranging them on a ring, or give them word banks. Word banks may be created from cigar boxes, file boxes, shoe boxes or other types of containers that the students may decorate. Although the key vocabulary steps

are obviously designed for beginning readers, word banks appeal to all elementary children.

Veatch and others also suggest a variety of group and individual activities to extend the learning of key vocabulary words after the six steps outlined above have been followed. Some of the extended group activities are: telling stories spontaneously, classifying words, exchanging words, coauthorship, and acting out words. The recommended individual activities include: making booklets, illustrating words, typing words, and tracing words on felt, sand or salt.

The Group Experience Chart. The *group experience chart* or whole class dictation approach, used for many years in first-grade classrooms, has a group or the entire class develop a story that the teacher prints on the chalkboard or a large chart. Students may reread the story individually, with the teacher, and again as a large group. A variety of follow-up activities provide additional vocabulary or skill instruction, or give students additional practice in reading words in context. Typically, the teacher goes through the following steps when using this method:

1. *Motivation.* Before actual dictation begins, the teacher must create the proper climate for the experience story. Once the children are comfortable and can see teacher and chart, the teacher may stimulate interest by reading to the students, showing them an unusual object or picture, or recalling a strange or exciting event. The teacher's goals are to focus the children's attention, build their enthusiasm for the activity, and promote active discussion. Teachers learn through experience how to motivate the children without losing control of the ensuing discussion. Commercial materials, guidebooks, and texts assist teachers with motivational ideas and often include lists of motivating topics. Generally, however, experienced teachers have little difficulty motivating students. After some success with this approach, students are usually eager to participate and will often suggest their own topics.

2. *Discussion of the topic.* Once a topic is chosen, the teacher gives the children time to

discuss the story before the dictating and story writing begin. Frequently, this step and the first step are indistinguishable. Be sure students' oral contributions are encouraged. The teacher may focus the discussion by printing the story title at the top of the chart and having the students repeat it. Next the teacher should encourage as many students as possible to tell what they want to contribute to the story.

3. *Dictation and story writing.* When the teacher feels the children are ready, she begins the actual process. Individual students contribute words, usually one sentence at a time, to compose the story. The teacher involves as many volunteers as possible in this process. The teacher carefully prints the words on the chalkboard or chart, clearly pronouncing the words as they are written. Usually the teacher will have the students repeat the words after each sentence is written. The teacher may run her hand or a pointer under each word as it is pronounced to help students match the written words to their spoken sounds. Using a hand or a pointer also familiarizes the students with left-to-right progression and the return sweep that occurs at the end of a line of print. Experts usually recommend that teachers not edit the students' words in any way, including inappropriate grammar or usage. According to this view, the experience story should correspond as closely as possible to the students' spoken language. At some point, the teacher must conclude the story, which can be difficult with an enthusiastic group of children. The teacher may be forced to ask: "Who can give us the words we need to end our story?"

4. *Reading the completed story.* After the story is completed the teacher may wish to have the students reread it. The teacher may first reread the entire story using a hand or pointer while the students observe silently. Then the entire group or individuals may do another reading. Many variations can be used. Surprisingly, students usually enjoy the repeated readings. The teacher usually observes more students participating with each reading. (Of course, many participating students are not actually *reading* the story. They are, in fact, repeating words that

they memorized with the assistance of visual cues. This is fine. It is a beginning step to actual decoding. Perhaps what is most important is that the students think that they are reading.) When teachers find it easier to use the chalkboard for the dictation, they should copy the story onto chart paper later. The stories should be permanent so that students can reread them on subsequent days.

5. *Follow-up activities.* Follow-up activities tend to be of two types, skill work and application. Teachers may use the completed story to teach or reinforce nearly any reading skill, including the readiness skills of auditory discrimination, visual discrimination, and sequencing, plus basic sight vocabulary, other vocabulary, phonics, context clues, and comprehension. The teacher may put words from the story on flashcards or have the story reprinted on a ditto for instructional purposes. Or, the teacher may prefer to have the pupils do follow-up activities that do not involve specific skill instruction, but rather focus on the enjoyment of reading. In this case, the teacher might prepare copies of the story for the children to illustrate and read with a friend or take home to read to parents. The teacher might have the children decorate the original chart for display in the room, on a hallway bulletin board, or in the principal's office. Other possibilities would be for the teacher to have the children act out the story or for the teacher to send one or more children with the chart to an upper grade classroom to read the story to older students.

The following story illustrates one way to use the group experience chart. A sixth-grade teacher in a Midwestern inner-city school teamed with a first-grade teacher to pursue several reading related activities.

Each day, after the first-grade children had composed their experience story, two of them practiced it until they could read it without error. Later that day, these two went to the sixth-grade room on the third floor to read their story to the older students.

The sixth-grade students were carefully trained for this activity (meaning that the teacher threatened them with bodily harm if they failed to perform their role properly!). Actually, the older students enjoyed the reading because it provided a brief diversion from the normal instructional routine and an opportunity to let off steam.

The two first graders were ushered into the room, dragging their experience chart rack with them. After appropriate introductions and a symbolic drum roll from an older student, the two small children, with nervous, squeaky voices, read their story out loud to the attentive older children. A typical story might go like this:

> *The Duck Pond*
> We went to the duck pond.
> It was fun.
> Rolando fell in.
> He got wet.
> The teacher was mad.
> Ha–ha–ha.
> The End

At the end of the reading, the attentive audience erupted in loud cheering and applause. Some of the students beat on their desks. Four students charged to the front of the room and hoisted the first graders in the air. This led to more applause and, on cue, a chant of "Read it again! Read it again!"

By now the first graders were in their glory and the second reading was performed with loud and enthusiastic voices. More cheering. More beating on the desks. On one occasion, one of the little ones shouted: "Do you want us to read it again?" Laughter, more applause, and a third, even more enthusiastic, reading.

After the two beaming children departed, the teacher—relishing the moment—praised his troops for their contribution to literacy before returning to the rigors of rational numbers. Although the teacher could never follow one of the little ones home, he always imagined a six-year-old bursting through the door and shouting: "Mommy! Mommy! I learned to read in school today!"

One special advantage of language experience activities is that they offer unusually satisfying teaching experiences.

Individual Descriptions of Illustrations Done in a Group Setting. A third type of langauge experience activity is individual descriptions of illustrations done in a group setting. Again the teacher motivates the children and leads a brief discussion on the topic. The children then draw pictures of the topic. Some sample topics for this type of activity might be:

1. Happiness is
2. Sadness is
3. A friend is
4. I feel afraid when
5. If I were the teacher I would
6. If I had a million dollars I would

The children decide how they will finish the sentence and begin their illustrations. The teacher (and other adults, if available) circulates quickly about the room and writes down the children's words, such as "A friend is my Daddy," or "A friend is someone who rides bikes with you," or "A friend is a big yellow zebra." The teacher writes down the exact words the student says. With practice, the teacher can catch all the students' responses while they illustrate. Then, the teacher collects the pictures and binds them and the sentences into a book that the children can later read.

A collection of these student books often becomes the single most popular item in the classroom. The students eagerly read them many times and learn to recognize not only their own words but also the words dictated by their peers.

The Individual Experience Story. The *individual experience story* is the most common language experience activity. The teacher uses the same basic procedures as with the group experience chart, but in this case, the stories are individually dictated. This method demands the most time from the teacher. It is nearly impossible to take regular individual dictation from all students without the help of others. However, this is clearly the most powerful of all language experience methods. The effect of the direct personal contact between teacher and student is often pronounced. Also, the teacher can focus instruction to meet the child's specific needs. In using this approach, you may wish to try the following steps:

1. *The teacher motivates the student to talk about a subject or describe a certain event.* This step may be difficult at first, but with patience and a careful choice of topics, teachers usually succeed in motivating even reluctant children.
2. *The teacher writes down the student's dictated words.* Place the student next to you so that she can see the words as they are printed.
3. *The child and the teacher read the story together after it is completed.* The teacher points to each word as it is read. If the student hesitates, the teacher simply tells the words to the student.
4. *The child rereads the story while the teacher observes.*
5. *The child recopies the story if possible.* Copying is beneficial here because it reinforces words for the student.
6. *The child illustrates or decorates the recopied story.*
7. *The teacher does something special with the story.* The teacher may display the story prominently or bind the story into a book. Children are then encouraged to read each other's books. Sometimes teachers select individual children's stories to be read out loud to the class.

Individual Experience Stories Using the Tape Recorder. A variation of the individual experience story is when *the student dictates into a tape recorder.* The teacher listens to the stories later and transcribes them into a printed or typed form. This procedure requires less direct contact by the teacher during class time, but it lacks the intimacy and immediacy of a person-to-person dictation. For this reason, it is not often used with beginning readers.

Teachers are likely to find that combinations of language experience procedures are effective. As the process develops, many children begin writing their own stories and no longer depend on an adult to take dictation. Early language experience efforts become later creative writing activities. As Mark W. Aulls (1982) has pointed out, regular use of language experience techniques has many advantages:

Each of these standard methods of story dictation open the way to learning to read. It is very important to recognize that there is no need to expect children to learn all the words in every story. By doing stories every day (or every other day), each child will begin to: (1) learn some words, (2) understand how text is read, (3) learn something about organizing words as they read, and (5) enjoy the pride of doing reading. (p. 148)

Criticisms of the Language Experience Approach

Some of the obvious problems with the language experience approach include the unusual demands placed upon the teacher, the lack of a preplanned program of skills instruction, and the absence of vocabulary control. Several other criticisms can be made about this method: the issue of teacher editing, the transition to real books, and the problem of students copying each other.

Experts recommend that teachers write down students' words exactly as they are said so that they do not criticize children's natural language and to provide a close match between the students' spoken words and the written stories. Many teachers, however, find it difficult to avoid editing the stories when inappropriate grammar or nonstandard language is used. This need not be an either/or issue. If teachers use good judgment and do not embarrass or humiliate children, editing is justified at times. For instance, it might make good sense to edit stories that are to be displayed or sent home. Six-year-olds are capable of understanding the rules of propriety. Similarly, teachers may find that modifying children's words can broaden their language facility.

Some critics of the language experience approach suggest that children who learn to read child-authored selections may have difficulty making the transition to adult-authored materials.

Table 2–4   Strengths and weaknesses of the language experience approach

Strengths

1. The approach motivates students highly. Language experience matches the students' interests with learning activities.
2. The approach is enjoyable and satisfying for most teachers.
3. Children are "reading" early. Substantial success is built-in.
4. The approach is individualized. Because children can progress at their own rates, there is less stigma for slower readers.
5. The approach is especially appropriate for children who speak a second language or dialect.
6. Children are more likely to become self-directed learners.
7. There is an integration of all the language arts—listening, speaking, reading, and writing.
8. The approach does not require expensive materials.

Weaknesses

1. The approach demands a great deal from the teacher. The teacher must organize instruction, take dictation, plan individual students' programs, and monitor their progress.
2. No daily lesson plans are provided.
3. There is no preplanned scope and sequence of skills to be mastered.
4. There is no control of the initial vocabulary presented.
5. Only a limited number of commercial programs are available to assist the teacher.

However, such difficulty need not occur. Whether language experience is used as an exclusive approach to beginning reading instruction, or with a basal approach, children should receive ample exposure to trade (or library) books. The experience of many teachers has shown that the language experience method need not limit children's ability to read real books.

Every teacher who uses language experience activities or teaches creative writing faces the problem of children copying each other's ideas. This problem is normal and temporary. Many children have so little faith in their own ideas that they repeat the thoughts of others. With patience and praise for each individual's unique efforts, teachers find that the copycat problem soon disappears. If you are impatient, you may limit the oral discussion activities to minimize copying, which would be unfortunate, since the discussion step is a critical part of the language experience process.

Table 2–4 summarizes the strengths and weaknesses of the language experience approach.

THE INDIVIDUALIZED READING APPROACH

The *individualized reading approach* (IR) was quite popular in the 1950s and 1960s. This approach was partly a response to the somewhat dull and inflexible basal reader methods common in those decades. Today the individualized reading approach is frequently misunderstood, so it may be helpful to clarify what individualized reading is *not*. IR is *not* a system of instruction in which each student works independently at his own level without benefit of teacher instruction. So-called individualized reading programs exist in which students have almost no contact with their teachers. These programs may be very loosely structured—students have the option to wander aimlessly about the room—or quite rigid—students must go step-by-step through a "contract" or other prescribed set of activities—but in either case, the lack of direct instruction and the depersonalization are contrary to the principles of the individualized reading approach.

IR is also *not* merely unsupervised recreational reading. Although students do read widely from books that they enjoy in the individualized reading approach, the teacher is aware of the students' reading habits and concerned about their reading skills development.

Finally, individualized reading should not be confused with *individualized instruction*. IR does not mean that the teacher provides only one-to-one instruction. Flexible grouping is, in fact, a part of the individualized reading method.

Individualized reading is, on the other hand, a way to organize reading instruction according to certain major tenets, such as the ones Richard C. Wilson and Helen J. James (1972) note.

1. Children are encouraged to select reading materials that interest them.
2. Children may read at their own pace rather than at a pace set by the teacher or group leader.
3. There is no set *amount* of required reading. The children themselves determine the quantity of reading they do.
4. There is no static grouping of children by ability for the purpose of reading instruction.
5. Evaluation of reading ability is not determined solely by prepared tests. The teacher evaluates students' reading performance using materials chosen during individual conferences or group sessions.
6. Both teacher and pupils share responsibility for record keeping.
7. Skills are taught as needed. Skill instruction may occur in individual, small group, or whole class settings.
8. Oral reading is used for diagnosing a student's reading difficulties.
9. Silent reading is emphasized to encourage wide reading and to promote students' reading comprehension.
10. The teacher uses records for each pupil in planning specific instruction and activities.
11. Since students seldom hear each other read orally or discuss specific selections, their curiosity about available books remains high.
12. Teachers are encouraged to draw upon commercially prepared materials and aids for use in the total reading program.

The successful implementation of the individualized reading approach as an exclusive method requires an unusually skilled teacher. Duker (1968) recommends a number of ways in which a teacher might prepare to use this approach. These include: (1) wide reading on the subject, (2) visiting classes or at least observing films of classes where the approach is used successfully, and (3) attending staff development sessions or college courses in which the approach is presented by knowledgeable and experienced individuals.

A key element of the approach is *self-selection*; students choose their own instructional materials. Many trade books and other reading materials must be available in each classroom, at least 3 to 10 times as many books as students. Students are then encouraged to choose books that appeal to them. If a book is no longer interesting, it should be replaced by another. Students are often encouraged to apply the "rule of thumb" in selecting books: the child opens a book to a full page of print and begins reading. When she comes to a word she does not recognize, she places one finger on the page and continues reading. As other unknown words are encountered, additional fingers are placed down. If the child gets to her thumb before completing the page, the book is considered too difficult and should be replaced. This obviously translates into a maximum of five errors per page. Unfortunately, because the number of words on any particular page varies greatly, it is not possible to compute a consistent percentage of accuracy required for selection when using the "rule of thumb." For this reason, this technique is often criticized. However, the technique is a guide not a rule. Children find it useful because it is simple and they can judge, on their own, their ability to read a particular book.

Self-selection is essential because it provides motivation and satisfaction for young readers. Critics of IR, however, note several disadvantages to self-selection. For example, can pupils select material at the proper level? Theodore A. Mork (1973) found that nearly 40 percent of the third through fifth grade students studied could not choose books at the appropriate reading level. Also, the poorer readers were least likely to make proper selections. Critics are also concerned about children reading only one type of book instead of reading widely, or choosing very easy books to read. And what of the child who chooses not to read at all? Advocates of IR argue that in practice these are not serious problems and that the benefits of self-selection outweigh the potential disadvantages.

Another key element of the individualized reading approach is the individual conference. These conferences may be organized and scheduled in a variety of ways. Some teachers adhere to a strict schedule, while others meet with children as the need arises. Students must learn to come prepared and teachers must learn to use conference time efficiently. The purposes of the conference include on-going diagnosis, instruction as needed, discussion of the child's reading progress and interests, and record keeping. Record keeping is usually viewed as a joint responsibility of teacher and student.

Other features of the individualized reading approach include provision for skill grouping, using learning centers, and time for students to informally discuss books they've read with each other.

Extraordinary teachers can successfully implement an individualized reading approach. Teachers with the talent and inclination should not be discouraged from pursuing it. But many fine teachers have become overwhelmed and frustrated in their attempts to meet children's reading needs through IR. Some of their students could operate in an individualized fashion while others could not, or all could, but for only part of the time. Many of these same teachers developed successful and satisfying reading programs that drew on some of the elements of individualized reading. There is no reason, for instance, why teachers who use a basal reader approach cannot give students time to self-select

and silently read trade books. The classroom reading program need not be an either/or proposition. The truly successful teacher may well be the one who selects the best aspects from various approaches and presents them in a carefully managed program.

The strengths and weaknesses of the third major approach—individualized reading—are summarized in Table 2–5.

OTHER APPROACHES TO THE TEACHING OF READING

In addition to the three major approaches to developmental reading instruction, other approaches have been used in American schools: (1) modified alphabet approaches; (2) programmed materials approaches; and (3) management systems approaches.

Modified Alphabet Approaches

Some experts believe that a major cause of reading difficulty for English-speaking children is the lack of a perfect correspondence between the sounds and the symbols of the English language. The 26 letters in our alphabet actually represent between 40 and 50 different speech sounds, depending on the linguist doing the estimating. This causes little difficulty for the fluent reader. But our spelling system poses many difficulties to the beginning reader. So certain reformers—including George Bernard Shaw and Benjamin Franklin—have sought to modify our existing alphabet.

Though no one has as yet succeeded in adding a 27th letter to the standard English alphabet, a number of modified alphabets have been developed to aid the beginning reader. The most well known of these is the Initial Teaching Alphabet or i.t.a.

The i.t.a. consists of 44 symbols, one each to match the 44 sounds or phonemes of English. These symbols are shown in Figure 2–8.

The i.t.a. is *not* a method for teaching reading, but merely an alternative alphabet system. It

Table 2–5   Strengths and weaknesses of the individualized reading approach

Strengths

1. The approach is highly motivating for students.
2. The approach may be satisfying for the teacher.
3. The approach is individualized. Students are able to progress at their own rates. There is less stigma for slower readers.
4. Children are more likely to become self-directed learners.
5. The approach is flexible.
6. The elements of self-selection and self-pacing are consistent with the goal of developing reading as a lifelong habit.

Weaknesses

1. The approach presents substantial organizational and management challenges for the teacher. It requires a lot of preparation time, and individual conference time may be difficult to arrange.
2. The approach becomes increasingly difficult to implement as class size increases and as the range of reading abilities or the number of problem readers increases.
3. The teacher must be unusually knowledgeable about the reading process, as neither a preplanned scope and sequence of skills nor daily lesson plans are provided.
4. There is no control of the initial vocabulary presented.
5. There are a limited number of commercial programs available to assist the teacher.
6. Many trade books are needed. Some publishers provide excellent sets or kits, if money is available.
7. Some students may be unable to self-select materials at the proper level.
8. Some students may lack the self-discipline needed to profit from this approach.

has been used rather widely in Great Britain, but its use has all but disappeared in American schools.

The obvious advantage of a modified alphabet approach is that children can decode more rapidly and effectively. Proponents argue that the transition to the traditional alphabet can be made easily, and texts gradually diminish the unconventional letters. Also, i.t.a. fosters increased writing skill sooner since children do not struggle with English spelling.

Critics of i.t.a. do not think children make the transition to traditional materials easily. Very few written materials exist in i.t.a., which prevents beginning readers from reading widely. Perhaps the biggest problem occurs for students who move frequently and so do not spend enough time in a classroom where i.t.a. is presented. One can only imagine the difficulties faced by children, teachers, and parents in schools with significant turnover in population.

Programmed Materials Approaches

Programmed materials, designed to teach students with procedures drawn from behavioral psychology, usually take the form of small paperback workbooks, through which students progress independently and at their own paces. Students receive continual feedback on their performances, learning occurs in small increments, and skills are presented in a sequential and systematic way. Usually, a linguistic approach to decoding is employed. In addition to the programmed workbooks, publishers usually provide storybooks and testing materials.

Teachers often use programmed materials with remedial reading students or sometimes with beginning readers. The two best known programmed approaches are the *Sullivan Remedial Reading Program* (Behavioral Research Laboratories) and *Programmed Reading* (McGraw-Hill).

This approach gives the teacher more time

a	æ	ɑ	au	b	c	ɔh
at	ate	arm	all	bed	cat	chap
d	e	ɛɛ	f	g	h	i
dog	elm	even	fox	go	hat	it
ie	j	k	l	m	n	ŋ
ice	jug	kite	like	mad	note	ring
o	œ	ω	ῶ	ɔi	ou	p
on	over	took	soon	oil	out	put
r	ɾ	s	ʒ	ʃh	ʒ	t
run	her	sit	is	shoe	measure	top
ʇh	ɾh	u	ue	v	w	wh
thin	then	up	use	vase	web	what
y	z					
yet	zip					

Figure 2–8   The Initial Teaching Alphabet

since the materials are largely self-instructional. Teachers know that students are receiving systematic and carefully presented instruction in small segments. Students can progress at their own individual rates and should succeed.

But the approach has many disadvantages. First, students lose personalized, direct teacher instruction, which is essential for many pupils' reading success. Additionally, many students are bored by the approach and the materials. They often learn how to get the answers right without actually proceeding through the lesson steps. No real advantage to succeeding exists, since they just have to do more of the same. Students read fewer trade books because of time spent in programmed workbooks. Last, this approach does not work well on higher level comprehension skills.

A place for programmed materials exists in the reading program if a knowledgeable teacher carefully selects which pupils will participate and for how long. Also, the teacher should use programmed approaches as an adjunct to, rather than a substitute for, a teacher-directed reading approach.

Programmed instruction particularly lends itself to technological applications. For example, the *System 80* program (Borg-Warner) has students view slides on a screen and listen to instructions on record. The student pushes appropriate buttons to respond to the directions, and the program continues if the correct answer is given. Placement and mastery tests are available, and various reading and language arts kits may be purchased for use on the machine.

Computers and Reading Instruction.   Computers are certainly in the reading teacher's future. Many educational publishers are already developing highly sophisticated programs for computers that will diagnose, teach, practice, and evaluate reading in every school, if not classroom, in the country. Although some heralded curricular and technological changes failed in the past, the potential assistance computers can give the teacher is exciting. The key word is assistance. No machine can replace the classroom teacher as an absolutely essential element in learning to read.

Using computers in reading instruction depends, of course, on the software. Software may come in the form of discs, cartridges, or cassette tapes. Presently, software programs serve three different functions:

1. Diagnostic-prescriptive programs focus on specific skill development, including pre-testing, mastery-testing, and record keeping. Students who lack skills in certain areas can be directed to practice activities in only those areas.
2. Programmed instruction is self-paced and self-checking.
3. Drill and practice programs focus on specific vocabulary or decoding skills. A computer program might, for example, assist students with basic sight words, basal reader vocabulary words, or phonics skills.

Management Systems Approaches

The management systems approaches have already been influenced by computers. **Management systems**, often called "skills management systems," "objective-based systems," or "diagnostic-prescriptive programs," are designed to provide an individualized, carefully monitored, skill-specific approach to reading instruction. In some schools or districts, the management system *is* the reading program. In others the system is used alongside of or in addition to the basal reader program.

There are different types of management systems. Program dependent types are designed to be used with basal readers. Program independent types are usually used independently of the basal. Management systems may be published by basal reader companies, other educational publishers, or prepared by local school districts.

The program independent systems usually include the following components:

1. A list of behaviorally stated reading objectives that range from prereading to upper-grade skills. Some systems contain hundreds of specific skill objectives.
2. A set of criterion-referenced tests that determine if students have mastered specific objectives. These tests are individually administered.
3. Record keeping devices such as pupil profile cards that detail progress and may inform parents.
4. Guides for matching various instructional and practice materials to the specific objectives. The guides may direct teachers to basal materials, other published materials, or teacher-developed activities.

Under this system, each child is pre-tested and placed on the skills continuum. Students are instructed either individually (usually with programmed materials) or in small groups formed according to skill levels. When the small group format is used, students move around to various classrooms as necessary. After receiving instruction, the children are post-tested. Students passing the test move to the next skill while students failing receive more instruction on that skill. Periodically, students take mastery tests covering a broad range of skills to insure that retention of learning has occurred.

Table 2–6   Strengths and weaknesses of the management systems approach

Strengths

1. Students uniformly progress through the reading skills.
2. The approach allows for individualized instruction. Students can proceed at their own paces.
3. A wide range of materials and methods may be used.
4. The approach is efficient. Students work only on those skills identified as necessary for them.
5. The teacher has a written profile of specific reading strengths and weaknesses for each child.
6. A thorough report of students' progress can be given to parents.
7. If used properly, students achieve continual success as they progress through the skills.
8. The approach allows for flexible and cross-age grouping.
9. The criterion-referenced testing accurately measures students' abilities on specific skill tasks.

Weaknesses

1. The approach views reading as a collection of specific skills and focuses on skill instruction at the expense of other essential activities, such as practice in the act of reading and reading for pleasure.
2. No one has yet established an absolute, verifiable hierarchy of reading skills.
3. The tests focus on the more easily measured skills, such as decoding. Higher level skills, such as comprehension, are much more difficult to measure.
4. The approach may become mechanical and depersonalized.
5. Too much testing may be required.
6. Too much paperwork may be required.
7. Although the approach is designed to *facilitate* management, daily management may be more difficult to achieve.
8. Teacher-directed instruction may be deemphasized.
9. Important instructional time may be lost due to group rearrangement and the necessary movement of pupils.
10. The approach usually requires a wide variety of materials for instruction and reinforcement of skills.

The teacher must assume responsibility for administering, scoring, and recording test information, assigning students to proper skill instruction, teaching skills as needed, retesting and reassigning when necessary, and communicating with parents and other teachers. Many teachers feel overwhelmed by the amount of testing and paperwork involved. However, this problem should decrease as the use of computers increases.

Examples of program independent systems are: *Wisconsin Design for Reading Skill Development* (Interpretive Scoring Systems), *Fountain Valley Teacher Support System* (Richard L. Zweig Associates), *Prescriptive Reading Inventory* (CTB/McGraw-Hill), SCORE (Westinghouse Learning), and *High Intensity Learning System 2* (Random House).

Program dependent systems, available through several basal publishers, are similar to program independent systems but are integrated into the existing basal program, thus making them easier for teachers to adjust to.

The use of management systems for reading instruction remains controversial. Some teachers view these systems as rigid, depersonalized, too skills oriented, and ineffective. Management systems are often the subject of acrimonious debate among teachers, administrators, school board members, and the general public. The use of these systems is, in some school districts, a specifically negotiated item in the teachers' contract. Because of public demands for accountability and the expanded use of computers, however, this approach will continue to be used. The strengths and weaknesses of management systems for reading are listed in Table 2–6.

SUMMARY

This chapter covers the major approaches to the teaching of reading in American schools. A review of the pertinent research shows that no one approach is clearly superior to the others. Each approach has its distinctive strengths and weaknesses. Yet educators continue to debate about and search for *the* best method. Richard J. Smith and Dale D. Johnson (1980) have summarized the state of affairs about approaches to teaching reading:

The search for better ways to help children learn to read has resulted in such diverse innovations as: tachistoscopic devices and mechanized speed regulators; talking typewriters and audio cassettes; new orthographies and old ones with color; books with no pictures and books with no words; ability grouping, achievement grouping, interest grouping, randomized grouping, and no grouping at all; dialect stories, experience stories, relevant stories, teaching sounds and teaching words; early instruction and delayed instruction; training teachers this way or that way or no way. There have been countless innovations, changes, panaceas, fads. Some have worked and linger on, while others have failed. Nothing has worked for everyone; everything has worked for someone. (p. 222)

The basal reader approach, the language experience approach, and the individualized reading approach are the three major approaches used by today's elementary teachers. These approaches may be used exclusively or in combination. Other methods, such as modified alphabet approaches, programmed materials, and management systems are used to a lesser extent. The best evidence suggests that all methods succeed with some students and do not succeed with others, the teacher is the most important factor in any method's success, and an eclectic or balanced approach seems most sensible.

REVIEW QUESTIONS

1. Compare and contrast the three major approaches to teaching reading in the elementary school.
2. What conclusions can be drawn from the research on code-emphasis versus meaning-emphasis approaches to beginning reading instruction?
3. Discuss the research findings on the language experience and individualized reading approaches.
4. List the elements common to most basal readers.
5. What is the distinction between eclectic or meaning-based basal programs and phonics-based basal programs? List the four phonics-based basals.
6. Basal readers may use either of three approaches to phonics instruction: (a) analytic; (b) synthetic; or (c) linguistic. Describe each.
7. Discuss the strengths and weaknesses of the basal reader approach.
8. Discuss the common misuses of basal reader programs.
9. Describe the language experience approach including at least four different procedures a teacher may use.
10. Discuss the advantages and limitations of the language experience approach.
11. What are some common misconceptions about individualized reading?

12. List the major characteristics of individualized reading as a way of organizing reading instruction.
13. What are the strengths and weaknesses of the individualized reading approach?
14. Briefly describe the following approaches to reading instruction: (a) modified alphabet approaches; (b) programmed materials approaches; and (c) management systems approaches.
15. In what ways might computer-assisted instruction improve the teaching of reading? How might computers prove harmful to quality reading instruction?
16. What is controlled vocabulary? How does it affect materials developed for early reading instruction?
17. What is i.t.a.?
18. Which major approach is most likely to include the teaching of key vocabulary?
19. What are the typical grade level designations used in basal readers? What are some of the dangers of these designations?
20. Why should school districts use a single series adoption of a basal reader as the core program for grades K–6?

REFERENCES

Allen, R. V. How a language experience program works. In E. C. Vilscek (Ed.), *A decade of innovations: Approaches to beginning reading*. Newark, Del.: International Reading Association, 1968.

Allen, R. V., & Allen, C. *Language experience in reading: Teacher's resource book, levels 1, 2, 3 and 4*. Chicago: Encyclopedia Britannica, 1974.

Allen, R. V., & Allen, C. *Language experience activities* (2nd ed.). Boston: Houghton-Mifflin, 1982.

Allington, R. L. If they don't read much, how they ever gonna get good? *Journal of Reading*, October, 1977, *21*, 57–62.

Ashton-Warner, S. *Teacher*. New York: Bantam Books, 1971.

Aukerman, R. C. *The basal reader approach to reading*. New York: John Wiley, 1981.

Aukerman, R. C., & Aukerman, L. R. *How do I teach reading?* New York: John Wiley, 1981.

Aulls, M. W. *Developing readers in today's elementary school*. Boston: Allyn and Bacon, 1982.

Austin, M. C., & Morrison, C. *The first R: The Harvard report on reading in elementary schools*. New York: Macmillan, 1963.

Bond, G. L., & Dykstra, R. The cooperative research program in first-grade reading instruction. *Reading Research Quarterly*, Summer, 1967, *2*, 5–142.

Bradley, J. M., & Ames, W. S. Readability parameters of basal readers. *Journal of Reading Behavior*, Summer, 1977, *9*, 175–83.

Britton, G. E. Danger: State adopted texts may be hazardous to our future. *Reading Teacher*, October, 1975, *29*, 52–58.

Chall, J. S. *Learning to read: The great debate. An inquiry into the science, art, and ideology of old and new methods of teaching children to read, 1910–1965*. New York: McGraw-Hill, 1967.

Chall, J., & Feldman, S. First grade reading: An analysis of the interaction of professed methods, teacher implementation, and child background. *Reading Teacher*, May, 1966, *19*, 569–75.

Cheek, E. H., Jr., & Cheek, M. C. A realistic evaluation of current basal readers. *Phi Delta Kappan*, May, 1979, *60*, 682.

Cramer, R. L. An investigation of first-grade spelling achievement. *Elementary English*, February, 1970, *47*, 230–37.

Cramer, R. L. Dialectology—A case for language experience. *Reading Teacher*, October, 1971, *25*, 33–39.

Duker, S. *Individualized reading: An annotated bibliography*. Metuchen, N.J.: Scarecrow Press, 1968.

Dykstra, R. Summary of the second-grade phase of the cooperative research program in primary reading instruction. *Reading Research Quarterly*, Fall, 1968a, *4*, 49–70.

Dykstra, R. The effectiveness of code- and meaning-emphasis beginning reading programs. *Reading Teacher*, October, 1968b, *22*, 17–23.

Dzama, M. A. Comparing use of generalizations of phonics in LEA, basal vocabulary. *Reading Teacher*, February, 1975, *28*, 466–72.

Flesch, R. *Why Johnny can't read and what you can do about it*. New York: Harper and Row, 1955.

Garcia, R. L. Mexican Americans learn through language experience. *Reading Teacher*, December, 1974, *28*, 301–305.

Hall, M. A. *The language experience approach for the culturally disadvantaged*. Newark, Del.: International Reading Association, 1972.

Hall, M. A. *The language experience approach for teaching reading: A research perspective*. Newark, Del.: International Reading Association, 1978.

Hall, M. A. *Teaching reading as a language experience* (3rd ed.). Columbus, Ohio: Charles E. Merrill, 1981.

Harris, A. J. The effective teacher of reading, revisited. *Reading Teacher*, November, 1979, *33*, 135–40.

Hopkins, C. J. Representation of the handicapped in basal readers. *Reading Teacher*, October, 1982, *36*, 30–32.

Intellectual and academic freedom: Issues and strategies for reading educators. *Reading Teacher*, February, 1982, *35*, 574–77.

Kyle, D. W. Changes in basal reader content: Has anyone been listening? *Elementary School Journal*, May, 1978, *78*, 305–311.

Lee, D. M., & Allen, R. V. *Learning to read through experience* (2nd ed.). Englewood Cliffs, N.J.: Prentice-Hall, 1966.

Marten, L. A., & Matlin, M. W. Does sexism in elementary readers still exist? *Reading Teacher*, May, 1976, *29*, 764–67.

McGraw-Hill Book Company. Guidelines for equal treatment of the sexes. *Elementary English*, May, 1975, *52*, 725–33.

Mork, T. The ability of children to select reading material at their own instructional level. In W. H. MacGinitie (Ed.), *Assessment problems in reading*. Newark, Del.: International Reading Association, 1973.

Pieronek, F. T. Do basal readers reflect the interests of intermediate students? *Reading Teacher*, January, 1980, *33*, 408–412.

Ramig, C. J., & Hall, M. A. Reading strategies of first-grade children taught by a language experience approach and a basal approach. *Reading World*, March, 1980, *19*, 280–389.

Roetzer, N. *A comparative study of the reading skills presented in the fourth, fifth, and sixth grade levels of selected basal reading series.* Unpublished master's thesis, California State University, Hayward, 1979.

Rogers, D. *A comparative study of the readiness components of selected basal reading series.* Unpublished master's thesis, California State University, Hayward, 1976.

Rush, R. T., Moe, A. J., & Manning, J. C. A comparison of basal reader language and the oral language of beginning first-grade children. *Journal of Educational Research*, September/October, 1979, *73*, 12–15.

Sartain, H. W. The research base for individualizing reading instruction. In J. A. Figurel (Ed.), *Reading and realism.* Newark, Del.: International Reading Association, 1969.

Serwer, B. L. Linguistic support for a method of teaching reading to black children. *Reading Research Quarterly*, Summer, 1969, *4*, 449–67.

Smith, R. J., & Johnson, D. D. *Teaching children to read* (2nd ed.). Reading, Mass.: Addison-Wesley, 1980.

Stauffer, R. G. *The language experience approach to the teaching of reading* (2nd ed.). New York: Harper & Row, 1980.

Veatch, J. *Reading in the elementary school* (2nd ed.). New York: John Wiley, 1978.

Veatch, J., Sawicki, F., Elliott, G., Flake, E., & Blakey, J. *Key words to reading: The language experience approach begins* (2nd ed.). Columbus, Ohio: Charles E. Merrill, 1979.

Vilscek, E. C. What research has shown about the language-experience program. In E. C. Vilscek (Ed.), *A decade of innovation: Approaches to beginning reading.* Newark, Del.: International Reading Association, 1968.

Wall, M. *Comparison of word-analysis skills and vocabulary load in three basal reading series.* Unpublished master's thesis, California State University, Hayward, 1975.

Wilson, R. C., & James, H. J. *Individualized reading: A practical approach* (2nd ed.). Dubuque, Iowa: Kendall/Hunt, 1972.

3

Organizing and Managing Classroom Reading Instruction

One of the greatest challenges the elementary school teacher faces is organizing and managing the classroom reading program. Defined as the skills required to conduct efficient, effective reading instruction, management includes organizing and planning, arranging the room, disciplining students, establishing routines, correcting and following up work, and using paraprofessionals or other aides.

With some study and effort most teachers can acquire the knowledge and skill needed to teach a child to read. Teaching reading to thirty or more students in a classroom, however, is a formidable task, involving many difficulties and challenges. Without the skills required to organize and manage daily instruction for an entire class of pupils, a teacher's knowledge of the reading process, fine materials, and effective instructional techniques have little value. Furthermore, this skill does not necessarily develop over time. Veteran teachers, without appropriate direction and assistance, may struggle with the same problems that beginning teachers face.

In this chapter, the necessary information you need to conduct a successful classroom reading program will be presented. The principles and procedures described work; many classroom teachers have developed successful reading programs based on the recommendations presented here.

THE CHALLENGE OF MANAGING A READING PROGRAM

To illustrate the challenge of managing the reading program, an experienced primary grade teacher lists his concerns about his own program. This teacher held a reading specialist credential, was unquestionably dedicated, and was regarded by administrators, peers, parents, and students as an excellent reading teacher. But as part of a graduate assignment, he wrote:

I am concerned about the following aspects of my present reading program:

1. The use of my aide in an instructional capacity.
2. My pace through the basal reader. I think I'm going too fast.
3. The quality of activities provided for follow-up, reinforcement, and/or enrichment.
4. The lack of diversity in materials.
5. My lack of ready knowledge about the scope, sequence, and philosophy of the newly adopted basal series.
6. My inability to differentiate between valuable basal activities and inappropriate ones.
7. Keeping up with all the correcting and busy work. I simply don't have time to plan effective lessons and spend hours of each day correcting.
8. Dealing with the students who choose to sit with their heads down instead of reading during the regular silent reading time.
9. Students below grade level who do not receive adequate instruction. They get no help outside of the regular program.
10. Finding a way to solve these problems so I can feel satisfied with my reading program.

With some guidance and assistance, this dedicated and open teacher was able to resolve most of the problems in a few weeks, and by the end of the school year, did feel satisfied about his program.

Certain prerequisites must be met to have a successful reading program. These include the following *beliefs*:

1. The teacher is the critical factor.
2. The teacher controls the important variables. (There are always three kids who create havoc, unforeseen interruptions, and inadequate materials and space).
3. The skills required to effectively organize and manage classroom reading instruction can be learned. They are neither magic nor limited to a few teachers.

In addition to these beliefs, four conditions must exist:

1. The teacher must have reasonable working conditions. The teacher must be comfortable with the number of students to teach and the number and range of groups. (Reasonable is difficult to define; today, it probably means up to at least thirty pupils per class. Forty or more students is clearly unreasonable, but between

thirty and forty may be reasonable for some and not for others.)

2. The teacher must maintain the program's quality and be knowledgeable about it. The program should be sensible, balanced, and stable.

3. The teacher must maintain effective student discipline and be able to handle discipline problems. (Discipline is the major management problem for most teachers.)

4. The teacher should have assistance and some direct supervision to develop effective management skills. For most teachers, reading about good management or even observing it first hand are not sufficient. Assistance should come from people who are excellent classroom managers and who work effectively with teachers. These individuals need not be administrators or supervisors. In some cases, other teachers or reading specialists can be valuable resources.

If these beliefs and conditions are present, you can use the information presented here to successfully structure your reading program.

Effective classroom reading programs can be easily identified. Although excellent programs may vary in structure, they all have the same key characteristics. Excellent classroom reading programs are characterized by:

1. An orderly, structured learning environment in which students maintain maximum *on-task time* (the amount of time a student is actually involved in a task).
2. Direct instruction of essential reading skills to pupils in small groups that are at the proper instructional level.
3. Sufficient opportunities for students to practice the act of reading.
4. A classroom environment that encourages productive learning, high expectations, success, enthusiasm, and joy for teacher and pupils.

This chapter contains a review of the research pertinent to this topic, a description of various organizational plans and grouping strategies, and a detailed description of reading program management. It also includes the components of the directed reading lesson, offers some guidance on lesson planning, and briefly explores the issue of discipline.

Managing reading instruction for an entire class is a formidable task.

REVIEW OF THE RESEARCH

This section covers some of the research conducted to identify specific instructional characteristics associated with high pupil achievement in reading. These research findings will be applied to a specific model for classroom reading instruction.

William H. Rupley and Timothy R. Blair (1980) reported on two of the pioneers in teacher effectiveness research, William S. Gray and Arthur I. Gates. Gray completed a landmark five-year investigation in 1930. Although Gray did not explore the specific instructional procedures associated with student achievement, he identified the teacher as the most important variable, listed "principles that underlie good procedure," and enumerated "conditions essential to success." Gray's work set the stage for future research efforts designed to translate reading theory into classroom practice.

Gates conducted research in 1937 to determine the relationship between mental age and the reading achievement of first graders, but he found that quality of instruction was more important than mental age. Rupley and Blair note that "a major influence of Gates' research was that it turned attention away from the individual child to the importance of the teacher in effective reading instruction" (p. 53).

In the late 1960s and 1970s *process-product research* identified many teacher behaviors that influence student learning. These studies evaluated relationships between *processes* of teaching (actual behaviors in the classroom, such as the clarity of instructions or the use of praise) and *products* of this instruction (usually the students' achievement gain as measured by standardized reading tests). Much of the process-product research focused on reading instruction in the elementary grades. More recent research not only explores the process-product dimension but also examines student variables, such as student attention, content learned, and learning conditions.

A few cautions about teacher effectiveness research are in order. First, not all the research conducted on teacher effectiveness is reviewed here. We shall try to present some of the most significant and representative findings and draw on the conclusions of investigators who have published reviews of a number of studies. Second, not all the findings agree. For example, they may vary according to the population studied. What works with students from a low socioeconomic background may not work with students from a high socio-economic background, and techniques effective with first graders may not be effective with intermediate pupils. Third, some studies suffer from methodological flaws. Most process-product research has been correlational; that is, researchers find significant correlations between certain teaching processes and subsequent pupil achievement. However, correlations do not prove cause. Thus, this research does not *prove* that a certain factor leads to higher student achievement. Finally, research results are limited by measures used and areas explored. Most of the research has used standardized test data to evaluate pupils' growth in reading or math. These data may not be the only, or even the most accurate measures of this growth, and the findings may not apply to other curriculum areas.

Nonetheless, these research findings offer teachers the best information currently available for planning a reading program. The results are consistent with common sense and answer some important questions about teaching.

In a frequently cited review, Donald Medley (1977) analyzed 14 teacher effectiveness studies out of the 289 he examined. Medley found that effective teachers:

1. Devote more class time to task-related activities. Students spend more time in structured learning.
2. Run more orderly classrooms.
3. Provide more direct instruction to pupils in small groups.
4. Produce improved self-concepts among pupils as well as higher achievement.

Reports of the six-year Beginning Teacher Evaluation Study, presented by Frederick Mc-

Donald (1976) and Marjorie Powell (1979), noted that

1. The more time teachers spend in direct instruction, the more students learn.
2. The more time students are engaged in their work (on-task), the more they learn.
3. Some teachers are more effective than others in keeping their students on-task.
4. Some teachers are more effective than others in assigning instructional tasks that lead to a high success rate.
5. The more time spent in reading instruction, the more students learn in that area.
6. The teachers who place greater emphasis on "academics" and have higher expectations for students produce students with higher achievement.
7. In higher achieving classrooms, teachers and students demonstrate greater respect for each other and work in a more cooperative atmosphere.

Wilbur Brookover and Lawrence Lezotte (1979) found that emphasizing "basics" makes a major difference between improving and declining schools. Staffs of improving schools emphasize basic reading objectives, devote more time to achieving these objectives, and believe *all* their students can master basic skills. Brookover and Lezotte also found that improving schools have assertive principals who take responsibility for evaluating student performance.

Jane Stallings and others (1978) compared secondary classes with high gains in reading to those with low gains. They concluded that a structured program, clear expectations, and minimal time wasted during instruction were associated with high gain classrooms. In high gain classrooms, teachers also gave students written assignments rather than oral ones, varied the activities, closely monitored seatwork, and provided supportive feedback to students.

Albert J. Harris (1979), in a review of research that identified characteristics of effective reading instruction, found the following:

1. Formal educational programs are superior to informal programs with respect to student achievement.
(Formal programs tend to be teacher-directed, sequential, and systematic while informal programs tend to be student-centered, involve more choices, and place the teacher in the role of facilitator.)
2. The amount of instructional time allocated to the subject is positively related to student reading gains, particularly at primary levels.
3. The amount of on-task time is positively related to student achievement.
4. Effective teachers use praise and encouragement more than ineffective teachers do.
5. Effective teachers are good classroom managers who teach in an orderly environment.
6. Effective teachers are perceptive of individual and group needs, keep a close watch over the progress of their pupils, and provide help promptly when a difficulty becomes evident. (p. 138–39)

Clearly, certain characteristics are consistently and positively associated with students' achievement gains. One of these factors is *direct instruction.* According to Barak V. Rosenshine (1979):

Direct instruction refers to academically focused, teacher-directed classrooms using sequenced and structured materials. It refers to teaching activities where goals are clear to students, time allocated for instruction is sufficient and continuous, coverage of content is extensive, the performance of students is monitored, questions are at a low cognitive level so that students can produce many correct responses, and feedback to students is immediate and academically oriented. In direct instruction the teacher controls instructional goals, chooses materials appropriate for the students' ability, and paces the instructional episode. Interaction is characterized as structured, but not authoritarian. Learning takes place in a convivial academic atmosphere. The goal is to move the students through a sequenced set of materials or tasks. (p. 38)

In his review of the research, Rosenshine reported that effective teachers allocated substantial time to academic pursuits, acted as strong leaders, gave students fewer choices, and taught in a direct and businesslike way.

Rosenshine also reported on research that found that highly individualized instruction was negatively related to achievement. The most successful teachers worked with students in small and large groups. Rosenshine assumed that students received better supervision when placed in groups, whereas individualized instruction resulted in more off-task time and more time lost on transitions.

Rosenshine's review also explored the types of activities that typically occur in formal classrooms during the reading period. He reports that students spend from 50 to 70 percent of their time in seatwork or self-paced activities and from 11 to 30 percent of their time with the teacher. Rosenshine acknowledges that management of the reading program is a major problem for teachers. He states:

Although it is not difficult to manage a small group of students that a teacher is working with, the management of seatwork for the remaining students is a difficult and relatively unstudied task. (p. 46)

Instructional time relates closely to a formal, direct-instruction approach. John T. Guthrie, Victor Martuza, and Mary Seifert (1979) reanalyzed data collected by the Educational Testing Service from a study of compensatory reading programs. The sample studied included 264 schools and 57,694 children. Guthrie, Martuza and Seifert concluded that direct instruction, as measured by the amount of formal instructional time, was beneficial for primary-aged students and intermediate-aged students from lower socioeconomic backgrounds. They stated: "We are compelled to draw the conclusion that what children learn about reading in one year is determined primarily by the quantity of instruction they receive" (p. 177).

Albert J. Harris and Blanche L. Serwer (1966) compared type of approach used to amount of instructional time for effects on reading achievement and found that reading time was more critical; it positively correlated with reading achievement for all methods studied. Harris and Serwer also found that "when teachers of reading spend substantial amounts of time on activities that involve little or no practice in reading, the results in reading achievement tend to be unfavorable" (p. 56).

In another research study, Herbert Kiesling (1977–78) reported that when teachers provided both small and large group instruction, instruc-

tional time was positively related to reading achievement. The relationship was especially strong for students who read at or slightly below grade level.

In this process-product type of research, conclusions are drawn from correlational findings. The First-grade Reading Group Study conducted by Linda M. Anderson, Carolyn M. Evertson, and Jere E. Brophy (1979) went one step further. These researchers attempted to translate research findings into actual classroom practice. A manual describing 22 principles of effective reading instruction drawn from process-product research was given to 17 first-grade teachers (the experimental group). Ten other first-grade teachers were the control group and had no list of principles to follow. Care was taken to control other variables. At the end of the school year, the reading achievement data of the pupils in all 27 classes were examined along with observational records used to evaluate the degree of implementation of the principles.

The researchers found that the students taught by teachers who received the manuals scored significantly higher on reading tests than did the students of teachers in the control group. The investigators also determined that some, though not all, of the principles were indeed used more by the experimental group of teachers than by the control group. However, a number of effective techniques were used by both groups.

Anderson, Evertson, and Brophy reported that most of the principles had a strong positive relationship to the students' achievement. Among these variables were: efficient transitions, appropriate teacher seating, and moderate and specific use of praise. Other variables not among the list of principles were also related to achievement: amount of time spent on lessons and the success rate of the students. After examining more than 500 variables, the researchers concluded:

Good classroom management underlies all the other principles and makes it possible to implement them in instruction. In the well-managed classroom, students use efficient routines for carrying out daily tasks, and students work without distraction in a calm, pleasant environment. The teacher prevents behavior problems, and the students concentrate on the tasks at hand. (p. 222)

These research efforts add to our knowledge about the effects of teacher behaviors on students' achievement and also show that teachers can learn these behaviors and translate them into classroom practice.

To summarize the research that evaluates the effect of teaching behaviors on pupil achievement, Jere Brophy (1979) concluded:

1. Teachers make a difference. Some teachers encourage more learning in their students than others do.
2. Teacher expectations for student learning are important.
3. Effective teachers are good classroom managers.
4. Effective teachers provide a maximum amount of instruction on critical skills, with minimal time wasted.
5. Students who receive a great deal of direct instruction in a structured curriculum have the highest achievement.

ORGANIZATIONAL PLANS AND GROUPING STRATEGIES

To effectively organize and manage instruction and to meet the needs of individual learners, teachers rely on various organizational plans and grouping strategies. Their plans may be influenced by the architecture of the school or district programs over which the teacher has little or no control. These factors may in turn be influenced by current educational fashion, pupil attendance patterns (small schools versus large schools), transportation (assignments may be influenced by bus schedules), or economics (during times of limited financial resources schools may be closed, class sizes may increase, specialists and aides may be eliminated, physical space may be reduced, and materials and supplies may diminish).

Educators have used several different organizational and grouping plans to improve the qual-

ity of reading instruction: grouping by age or heterogeneous grouping, homogeneous grouping, nongraded schools, the Joplin plan, staggered reading, departmentalization, team teaching, and open schools. Most often, students are first grouped heterogeneously by age in self-contained classrooms, then divided into ability groups for specific reading instruction.

Class Size

Teachers use different grouping plans to minimize the difficulties created by large classes. Most teachers today instruct classes of 25 to 35 pupils. In addition, because of declining enrollment, many more teachers must teach combination classes, such as a group of first and second graders instead of only first graders. Such classes create an even broader range of reading abilities. In the past, teachers could expect a smaller total of pupils if the class was a combination one, but financial restraints have made lower teacher-pupil ratios less feasible.

Nearly every teacher believes that better instruction will occur in smaller classes, but research has not necessarily supported this view. Richard D. Arnold (1974) reviewed the research on the relationship between class size and student reading achievement and found contradictory and inconclusive data. Arnold did note, however, that:

1. Small classes seem most important in the early grades. . . . when children are beginning to learn to read, carefully monitored attention by the teacher is crucial.
2. There is an abundance of evidence that individual and small group reading instruction has proven beneficial to many disabled readers. . . .
3. Other factors being equal, teacher training and morale are important. . . . if the teacher is well trained and dedicated to providing the best instruction possible for each child in his class, it seems logical to expect that he will be able to accomplish more if he has fewer children with whom to work. (p. 419)

Homogeneous and Heterogeneous Grouping

American schools group nearly all children by age: 6-years-olds are assigned to first grade,

7-year-olds are assigned to second grade, etc. Sometimes schools group two age groups together for combination classes.

When students are assigned on the basis of age, they are in *heterogeneous groups.* If other factors are used in determining placements in a class, such as IQ or academic ability, then students are in *homogeneous groups.* Homogeneous grouping is rare at the primary level and tends to occur with greater frequency in the upper grades.

Both types of grouping have advantages. Proponents of homogeneous grouping argue that: (1) teachers can better meet students' individual differences when the range of abilities is narrower because they can provide more individual attention and more easily gear materials to the proper level; and (2) students feel less failure and more challenge if grouped with peers of similar ability. Advocates of heterogeneous grouping argue that: (1) it is democratic and reflects the conditions in which people live and work in the real world; (2) it need not stigmatize lower ability pupils; (3) students can learn best from each other and the teacher if placed in groups with a range of abilities; (4) it is impossible to form truly homogeneous groups; and (5) there is less likelihood that students will be divided according to race or class.

A review of the research presented by Dominick Esposito (1973) showed little evidence for grouping class units homogeneously. Such an organizational plan tends to have a negative effect on the self-esteem of average and below average students and does not demonstrate consistently positive academic benefits for any group.

However, most of this research criticizes the homogeneity of whole classes. But *tracking*, the inflexible assignment of students to the same ability groups for all academic subjects, does not typically occur in the elementary grades. Rather, what usually occurs is the assignment of a heterogeneous class of students into subgroups according to ability for reading instruction. These same students may be grouped in other subject areas as well, and not necessarily with the same students or at the same levels.

The *ability grouping* usually used for reading instruction—subgrouping by ability within a heterogeneously grouped class—is designed to enable the teacher to teach pupils of diverse ability efficiently.

Nongraded Schools

Nongraded elementary schools, popular in the early 1960s, grouped students in a nongraded unit replacing grades 1, 2, and 3. Nongraded programs do not usually exist at higher grade levels. The nongraded primary unit has no grade labels, students are usually allowed to complete the curriculum in three or four years, and flexible grouping occurs. Reading instruction is generally organized into sequential units of work through which all students proceed at their own rates.

In a review of early research on nongraded programs, Louis T. DiLorenzo and Ruth Salter (1965) reported mixed results. However, in a more recent review, Lyn S. Martin and Barbara N. Pavin (1976) claimed that:

Generally, students in nongraded programs have been doing as well as or better than their peers in the graded programs—usually better, according to several comparative studies. . . . It is probably safe to conclude from these studies that nongraded programs can enhance academic achievement and foster positive attitudes among children. (p. 312)

Nongraded programs are not as prevalent now as they were in the recent past.

The Joplin Plan

In a normal classroom the teacher must teach students at several different reading levels. To reduce the number of preparations, many schools group children across grade or class levels. Interclass or intergrade grouping has been used in some form since 1929, according to John F. Newport (1967). But it was not until 1957 that the *Joplin Plan* (popularized in Joplin, Missouri) gained national attention. Schools using this plan implement it as follows:

1. Near the end of a school year all students entering grades 4, 5, or 6 the next year

are evaluated and tentatively assigned to reading groups.

2. If, for instance, each grade level has three teachers, then nine teachers teach grades 4, 5 and 6. Because each teacher teaches only one reading level, as many as nine different reading-level groups could be formed.

3. For reading, each student has the teacher who teaches that student's level. Thus, the reading teacher may not be the student's homeroom teacher.

4. Reading instruction is scheduled at the same time for all students to accommodate the necessary shifting of students.

5. Teachers are expected to regroup as necessary within each level.

6. Placements remain flexible so that students are not "stuck" in one group indefinitely. Also, because initial placements are made the previous spring, teachers must carefully observe and reassess in the fall when instruction begins.

7. Other modifications and considerations may be made according to the needs of the school. In some schools fourth graders cannot be placed above a certain level and sixth graders cannot be placed below a certain level so that students will not be uncomfortable.

8. A 20-minute silent reading period is scheduled daily. Students remain in their homerooms and read interesting materials in a relaxed setting. No reading groups are formed during this period.

9. Thorough communication among homeroom teachers, reading teachers, and parents is required.

Although the Joplin Plan is typically used for intermediate grades, this or similar intergrade plans are occasionally employed at primary levels.

The advantages of the Joplin Plan approach are as follows:

1. Students are more likely to be placed in the proper levels.

2. The teacher can teach better because she can concentrate more energy on fewer preparations.

By contrast, the Joplin Plan has the following possible disadvantages:

1. Teachers often fail to regroup students. They may assume that regrouping and small group or individualized instruction are unnecessary because the students assigned to them are supposedly reading at the same level.

2. Because the reading teacher may not be the same person as the homeroom teacher, the homeroom teacher may be less aware of the child's needs and therefore unable to adapt other instruction during the school day to the student's reading needs. Reading may be thought of as something separate from the rest of the curriculum.

3. Certain social and emotional pressures may result from students of different ages being assigned to the same reading class.

4. The same time schedule for all may limit flexibility. Teachers may lose some "teachable moments" because of time pressure. Time will be lost daily for transitions and behavior problems may be exacerbated by this movement.

5. Communication difficulties may lead to teacher/teacher or parent/teacher disagreements, especially when different teachers use different criteria for evaluating student performance.

The first disadvantage listed above is not a criticism of the method but an abuse of the plan. Nonetheless, teachers' failure to regroup students is more the norm than the exception. Although the advantages of the Joplin Plan are significant, there are better ways to minimize the number of preparations and still place students in appropriate groups.

However, many teachers succeed with the Joplin Plan. When teachers work diligently to minimize the disadvantages, it is a workable and appropriate plan.

Research on the effects of the Joplin Plan is

inconclusive. Donald C. Cushenbery (1967), a proponent of the plan, reports that research on this approach shows generally promising results. However, Wilma H. Miller (1969) and John F. Newport (1967) claim that the research evidence is essentially unfavorable.

Staggered Reading

Staggered reading directly addresses the issue of class size. After an initial period of testing and adjustment (usually two to three weeks), students in each class are divided into two groups. These groups are typically called early birds and late birds or morning readers and afternoon readers. The school day is adjusted so that the early birds arrive one hour earlier in the day for reading instruction and the late birds stay one hour later for the same purpose. Thus, one half of the students might be scheduled from 8:00 a.m. to 2:00 p.m. and the other half of the students might attend school from 9:00 a.m. to 3:00 p.m.

The teacher can therefore group students and individualize instruction more easily, teaching half the normal number of students in the first hour (usually the lower-ability students) and half in the last hour (usually the more able students). Theoretically, teachers are on duty for additional time under this plan. However, in practice this is not necessarily the case, since the length of the school day may vary considerably from state to state and district to district irrespective of a staggered reading plan.

This approach only proves effective if teachers make morning or afternoon assignments according to student needs and not parent convenience. Staggered reading was not designed to place teachers in the role of babysitter, which can be a problem when school administrators fail to persuade parents that children must attend school at the prescribed time. Students who are in the classroom during nonassigned times may disrupt the instruction of others.

Staggered reading also does not benefit children if teachers fail to take advantage of the chance to provide individualized or small group instruction. When teachers merely divide their class into two reading groups and then plan and conduct the same instruction for one group in the morning and the other group in the afternoon, they work contrary to the purposes of staggered reading.

Departmentalization

In a *departmentalized* format teachers teach specific subject areas. For instance, one teacher might teach reading classes, another teacher might teach math classes, etc. The standard format above sixth grade, this approach allows each teacher to teach the subject or subjects that she is most proficient in, but the disadvantages are similar to those noted with the Joplin Plan.

Although a departmentalized format is occasionally used in elementary schools, a *semi-departmentalized plan* is more common. In such an approach, one or more teachers may be assigned to teach a language arts block (reading, writing, and spelling) while other teachers are assigned another subject block, such as math/science. In this arrangement, students go to the ''specialist'' teacher for the block subjects, but remain with the homeroom teacher for all other subjects. The Joplin Plan is not really the same as a semi-departmentalized approach since all teachers teach all subjects under the Joplin Plan.

Team Teaching

In some schools teachers work together to teach some or all subjects. If the architecture of the school permits, classes may be combined in a common area or students may shift from class to class according to grouping arrangements. *Team teaching* narrows the range of groups for which each teacher is responsible and allows teachers to use their particular strengths. But for the approach to be successful, teachers must work together well. Thus, the approach requires additional preparation and good communication.

Open Schools

The term *open schools* may refer to an architectural arrangement or a teaching philosophy, but not necessarily the two together. In the mid-70s many schools were constructed around a *pod* arrangement: classrooms with few or no interior walls surround an open-space area that can be used as a learning laboratory or for large-group activities. All classes in the pod share this space. Open space schools are often built for economic reasons, forcing teachers to adjust to a physical arrangement that may not match their teaching approach. Because many teachers are simply not comfortable with the noise and confusion generated by as many as 150 children, many open space buildings have been gradually transformed to traditional self-contained classrooms by the addition of interior walls or partitions. In other cases, however, teachers have embraced open space construction and have modified their instructional programs to take advantage of the flexible space.

The *open school* approach may or may not be used in open space areas. Open schools suggests a teaching philosophy somewhat different from the traditional approach used in elementary schools. Instruction is highly child-centered and individualized. Students are viewed as willing, self-directed learners who are usually given some freedom to choose what, when, and how they will learn. The teacher is often a facilitator rather than an authoritative or authoritarian leader. Flexible scheduling, self-discipline, and discovery teaching approaches are also often a part of this type of schooling. Open schools are often nongraded.

The many variations to the approach reflect the differences in teachers and administrators who work in these settings. Open schools may be set up as alternative schools in a particular school district or may exist within traditionally organized schools.

The reading instruction program usually employed in an open school is either an individualized reading approach, a language experience approach, or both. (See Chapter 2.) There is usually considerably less pressure on students to achieve by a certain time. Children may not be instructed in reading until they demonstrate a desire to learn to read.

No clear evidence exists to indicate whether children benefit from an open school approach in terms of their reading achievement. Usually the children are placed in such settings by parents, so these pupils' achievement may be influenced by some nonschool factors. The research reviewed in this chapter suggests that many of the important principles of effective reading instruction may not occur in open schools, such as substantial direct instruction of critical reading skills in a structured environment. However, research on the effect of open schooling on reading achievement is mixed. Martin and Pavin (1976) noted that, taken as a whole, the studies do not suggest that open schools lead to significant differences in student learning.

Frequently a single school uses a combination of these grouping strategies. For instance, students in one school may receive reading instruction in a staggered reading program using ability groups taught by team teachers. This same school has a nongraded, open school which provides individualized reading instruction in a nonstaggered format.

Ability Groups Within a Self-Contained Classroom

The most common grouping arrangement in American elementary classrooms is ability grouping within self-contained classrooms. A *self-contained classroom* is the traditional organizational arrangement in American schools: one teacher teaches all subjects to a group of approximately thirty students in one classroom.

Rationale. To better understand the necessity of teaching students in subgroups by ability you may examine Figure 3–1. The normal range of reading ability in elementary classrooms extends from 2.5 years at the second-grade level (from a low of 1.3 to a high of 3.8) to 7 years at the sixth-grade level (from a low of 2.5 to a high of 9.5). Thus, it is obviously not possible for teachers to meet students' needs without some sort of ability grouping.

Emerald V. Dechant (1982) lists the follow-

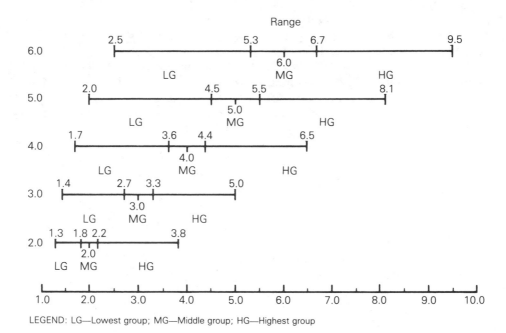

LEGEND: LG—Lowest group; MG—Middle group; HG—Highest group

Figure 3–1   Normal range of reading ability found in typical classrooms of grades two through six at the beginning of the school year

Note. From *Reading Difficulties: Their Diagnosis and Correction*, 4th ed., by G.L. Bond, M.A. Tinker, and B.B. Wasson (Englewood Cliffs, N.J.: Prentice-Hall, 1979), p. 30. Copyright 1979 by Prentice-Hall. Reprinted by permission.

ing advantages of ability grouping for reading instruction:

1. It makes it easier for the teacher to provide the experiences and materials of instruction which each level needs.
2. It does not waste the time of the superior readers nor bore them.
3. It does not undermine the self-esteem of the poor readers by throwing them into constant comparison with the superior readers.
4. It is more economical; there is obviously no economy in trying to teach students what they are not ready to learn or for that matter in making students who have already learned a skill mark time until all others in the class have learned the same skill. (p. 426)

Dechant points out that ability grouping can not resolve all differences, even between children reading at the same level. It is certainly not a panacea. But what are the alternatives for the teacher responsible for teaching reading to 25–35 pupils? Although most authorities agree that an

individualized format is desirable, it is simply not possible for teachers to provide 25–35 individual programs. Furthermore, reading is only one of the subject areas for which the elementary school teacher must plan. Experts also agree that whole class, undifferentiated instruction is unacceptable. Thus, most teachers accept ability grouping as a practical, though imperfect, approach to teaching reading. By grouping effectively, the teacher can teach consistently with the sound instructional procedures identified in the research.

Forming Reading Groups.   Most elementary schools randomly assign students to classes according to age. If this approach is used, a third-grade teacher might have thirty pupils ranging in ability from the 1.4 to the 5.0 grade level. (See Figure 3–1.) Fourth–, fifth–, and sixth-grade teachers must teach increasingly diverse groups of pupils. Bond, Tinker, and Wasson designate three groups for each grade level. The third-grade teacher, for instance, would instruct a low group of students whose abilities range from 1.4 to 2.7, a middle group from 2.7 to 3.3, and a high group from 3.3 to 5.0.

Normally, teachers conduct three groups during the reading period, but beginning teachers may find that they can handle only two groups comfortably. With more experience, some teachers organize children into five or six different reading groups. Usually each group represents an additional preparation for the teacher, although sometimes two groups at the same reading level reduces the teacher's preparation time somewhat.

If, however, the typical third-grade teacher forms three groups, then both the low group and the high group contain students whose reading ability varies by more than one grade level. By sixth grade, the range is nearly three grade levels for the low group, about a grade level and a half for the middle group, and nearly three grade levels for the high group.

Can the teacher really provide the same instruction to small groups of children when their reading abilities vary so greatly? If not, and if more than three groups is not practical from a preparation and management standpoint, then what can be done?

One possible solution, of course, is the Joplin Plan, but it has some serious drawbacks. Students must change classes, which is especially difficult for primary-aged children, time is lost for transitions, teachers are less aware of the reading needs of some of their "own" students, communication difficulties may arise, and so forth.

Another possibility, which requires a lot of administrative leadership and support, has been successfully instituted in many elementary schools. This plan embodies most of the advantages of the Joplin Plan without the disadvantages. The key is *not* to assign students to classes randomly. Students need not be tracked or assigned homogeneously to classes, however.

Unfortunately, this plan works only where there are two or more classes at each grade level—the more the better. If a school has only one third-grade class, for instance, then little can be done to reduce the range of reading abilities or the number of groups, short of shifting some of the students out of the classroom for reading instruction. Where more than one class exists per grade level, the range of reading abilities in each group and the number of groups can be reduced without shifting children.

Prerequisite Steps for Forming Reading Groups

1. Administrative leadership and support.
2. Understanding of the procedure by teachers and willingness to try the approach.
3. Use of the same basal reader or core approach by all teachers in the school or grade levels involved.
4. Ability of each teacher to manage three groups during the reading period.
5. Accurate assessment of all students' reading abilities with respect to the instructional materials in which the students are placed.

Steps 1 and 2 do not require explanation. However, administrative leadership and support does not mean only administrators can initiate the plan. Teachers or reading specialists may persuade administrators to direct and support the implementation of this approach. On the other hand, the plan simply will not work if, for whatever reason, classroom teachers are unwilling to cooperate.

Although it is not essential for teachers to use the same core program (Step 3), it makes good sense. One of the main purposes for grouping students is to guide them through a systematic and sequential set of reading sub-skills. If a variety of basal readers are used, this purpose is defeated because all basal programs do not follow the *same* sequence of skills. A student moving into a new book in a different series may be at the proper level but have difficulty because prerequisite skills were not introduced in the previous series. This problem may occur even within a single series because the basal readers lack appropriate continuity. However, this problem only worsens if more than one series is used for the core program.

Careful grouping does not insure effective teaching if the teacher lacks the skills to manage daily instruction (Step 4). If discipline or management are problems, later sections of this chapter should prove helpful.

Step 5 is very important. Teachers should be certain that placement is based on a student's ability to handle new material as well as to master previous material. Such placement should not necessarily be determined by the previous teachers' recommendations or by the last books "completed" by students (they may have been completed unsuccessfully). Certainly, placement in reading groups *cannot* be determined by standardized tests. (For a discussion of appropriate procedures for placement in basal readers see "Misuses of Basal Readers" in Chapter 2.)

Once the prerequisite steps are taken, use these procedures to form classroom reading groups:

Steps in Assigning Students to Classroom Reading Groups

1. Based on late spring estimates, determine number of students and teachers at each grade level.
2. Determine number of students assigned to each basal reader level in the fall.
3. Assign tentative reading groups to each teacher.
4. Reassess students in the fall and reassign to other classrooms if necessary.
5. Shift students to other classes for reading instruction as a last resort.

To illustrate, consider a hypothetical situation in which ninety students assigned to three teachers enter third grade. According to the estimates previously given, these students will range in reading ability from 1.4 to 5.0 grade level. What we need to know, however, are the students' estimated basal reader placements. Once these are determined and charted, the estimated number of reading groups can be determined. Figure 3–2 shows these figures for our hypothetical third graders.

Now tentative classroom assignments may be made to coincide with reading group placements. These assignments are also shown in Figure 3–2. Each teacher has three groups with students of low, average, and high ability. Teacher A, for example, has groups of students reading in the levels 1, 3^1, and 4 basal readers, quite a range of reading ability. However, Teacher A does *not* have students reading at other basal levels; thus he can accommodate that range of abilities with only three basal preparations.

Also note that the number of students in each teacher's 3^1 group can be adjusted to allow each teacher to have the same total number of students in the class.

The figures presented in Figure 3–2 represent a somewhat ideal picture because the distribution conveniently allows for appropriate group size. Figure 3–3 also presents hypothetical data, this time for ninety sixth graders. As can be seen, a bit more adjustment was required to provide each teacher with a range of abilities and comparable total numbers of students. Note, too, that three groups are called "special groups" because the reading ability of these students suggests that basal readers may be inappropriate. These students meet in reading groups, however, even if their instruction comes from a source other than a basal program. Having these special groups acknowledges the limitations of basal readers.

Unfortunately, in the fall students do not always read at the levels projected in the spring. Some children have either dramatically improved or regressed in reading ability so that the tentative placements are no longer appropriate. Or some children do not come to school at all, having transferred to another locale only to be replaced by students who read at different levels. These factors need not cause the plan to fail, however. To address this problem, teachers may need to reassess some students in the fall to determine appropriate placements. Although some students will be reassigned, the majority of spring projections will probably be accurate.

Next, permanently reassign students to other teachers' classrooms to reestablish balance in the reading groups. Usually the most difficult,

Range of Ability

Reading level	1.4	2.7 3.3 3.0	5.0
Number of students	30	30	30

Estimated Basal Reader Placements

Basal reader level	1	2^1	2^2	3^1	3^2	4	5
Number of students	8	10	12	30	12	10	8
Number of reading groups	1	1	1	3	1	1	1

Assignment of Reading Groups to Teachers

Teacher	Level	Number of Students
A	1	8
	3^1	12
	4	10
B	2^1	10
	3^1	8
	3^2	12
C	2^2	12
	3^1	10
	5	8

Figure 3–2   Grouping of ninety entering third graders

this step requires the greatest administrative support. The school principal should explain to parents that reassigning children will lead to more effective reading instruction. The necessary shifts can be completed within the first few weeks of the school year, and it is common for children to be reassigned anyway because of staff adjustments. Parents must accept this. Reassigning a few students to preserve reading group arrangements is feasible and justified.

When reassignment is not possible, shifting students to other classrooms only for reading may be considered. Effective teachers usually prefer to teach reading to their own students, but sometimes a teacher must choose between

regular instruction in another teacher's reading group or erratic instruction in the home classroom because no appropriate group exists. Then shifting a student for reading may make sense. Of course, teachers must be sure that students are not shifted in an emotionally upsetting way.

Frequently students enter a school during the year. When effective grouping is practiced these students are screened to determine their reading placement and then assigned to a class where they fit into an existing group. When this is not possible because of an enrollment imbalance, shifting may again be resorted to.

While implementing this grouping process, an on-site reading specialist can provide valuable

Range of Ability

	2.5		5.3	6.7		9.5
Reading level	⊢—————————————					⊣
				6.0		
Number of students		30		30		30

Estimated Basal Reader Placements

Basal reader level	LSP*	4	5	6	7	HSP**	HSP**
Number of students	8	10	18	20	16	10	8
Number of reading groups	1	1	2	2	2	1	1

Assignment of Reading Groups to Teachers

Teacher	Level	Number of Students
A	LSP*	8
	6	13
	HSP**	10
B	5	9
	6	7
	7	6
	HSP**	8
C	4	10
	5	9
	7	10

*LSP indicates low special placement.
**HSP indicates high special placement.

Figure 3–3   Grouping of ninety entering sixth graders

assistance. In schools that implement this plan most successfully, the principal, reading specialist, and classroom teachers all cooperate to make it work. Then the results are satisfying for all.

Issues and Concerns Related to Grouping

Several issues or concerns about this plan for forming reading groups may have occurred to you. Some of these concerns will be raised and then answered in this section.

1. *Why should students' reading levels be a major criterion for classroom assignments?* Why not? Teachers are likely to group reading students by ability anyway. It is sensible to reduce the number of groups and/or preparations the teacher must face, especially without tracking the students or distributing the instructional bur-

dens unequally. Sometimes teachers want to separate certain children or accommodate occasional parental requests, both of which can usually be done if there are three or more classes per grade level.

2. *What about flexible grouping? If this method is used to form reading groups, won't students get stuck in the same groups?* This plan, in fact, may limit group flexibility. However, teachers often prefer to keep groups together from a management standpoint and deal individually with students who cannot keep up with the group or who accelerate beyond the group. Flexible grouping may be oversold. Teachers, after all, must provide reading instruction to pupils in less than ideal circumstances. If class sizes were 10 to 1 or even 20 to 1, teachers might have more options. The teacher who wishes to group children in a highly flexible manner must consider the consequences: it will be more difficult to keep track of children as they progress through their developmental reading skills; group management and discipline will be more challenging, since teacher and students will have to adjust to new learning groups and time schedules frequently. And the teacher will need to prepare for and teach more reading groups. This sounds fine in theory and may work for teachers in certain situations. But teachers can only expend a given amount of time and energy for reading instruction. If this energy is concentrated on a reasonable number of groups and preparations, then the teacher likely does a commendable job with each group. If more groups are formed and more preparations are necessary, then each group will probably receive less effective instruction.

To be sure, once students are placed in a group they do not have to remain there until the end of the year. If students are monitored properly their performance will show if they are consistently failing to keep up with the group or if they are clearly able to move up to a higher group. In these cases teachers can modify instruction or teachers may move the student to a different group. If a new placement is required teachers usually send the misplaced child to another classroom for reading instruction. In practice, this change does not happen often, and when it does, the transfers usually even out. In any case, when children are clearly misplaced, their placement in an appropriate group should be accommodated.

3. *If a three-group format is used, how can the teacher provide for individual differences?* There is nothing magical about three reading groups. However, three groups is usually the minimum number required to provide adequate differentiation of instruction, and most teachers find it difficult to manage more than three groups. Also, the time budgeted for daily reading often makes more than three groups impractical. Of course, teachers with the ability and time to teach more groups should be encouraged to do so. Teachers who teach in staggered reading programs can usually handle five or six groups (though more than one may be at the same level), and teachers in schools that allow more than 70 minutes per day for reading may also direct more than three groups. Generally, schools allocate 60–70 minutes per day for developmental reading instruction.

To meet individual needs, a teacher must carefully observe students in the small group setting, modify instruction to foster individual growth, and adjust assignments of follow-up work. Teachers may also personalize instruction by scheduling alternative days when reading groups do not meet and other activities take place.

4. *Won't the lower-ability children be stigmatized by their placement in the bottom groups?* All teachers who group children for instruction, regardless of the plan employed, are concerned about this problem. But it is fruitless to try to disguise children's abilities. Most elementary school children can name the top and bottom students in their class in reading, math, and spelling. They can also name students who have the best abilities in various athletic pursuits, art, and other areas. No matter how we label books or name reading groups, children perceive each other's abilities.

However, children need not be stigmatized

by placement in low reading groups. One of the teacher's most important responsibilities is to help children understand and accept their individual differences. If assignments to reading groups are handled in a sensitive way, there should be no long-term ill effects. The purpose of grouping children for reading instruction is to help them achieve their potential as readers.

Some teachers refer to their reading groups by book level: "Ok, level 4 group, you'll be working with me while the level 6 group works quietly at their desks." These group designations are inappropriate. Without realizing it perhaps, this teacher calls attention to the students' differences in a negative way. It is like saying: "OK, all the good kickball players line up here and all the lousy kickball players line up over there."

A simple solution is to let students name their own groups. They enjoy doing this and it helps build camaraderie within the group. Then the teacher could say: "OK, lions, you'll be working with me while the giraffes work quietly at their desks."

5. If this plan is used for reading instruction five days a week, won't the teacher and children find it boring and limiting? Quite possibly. However, instructional reading groups need *not* meet five days a week. Teachers can certainly schedule *Plan B* days, or alternative days, for more individualized and varied instruction as well as a number of special reading activities or events.

6. What if I think this is a terrific plan but am employed in a school that uses a different approach to grouping students? Since the plan requires the cooperation of all teachers, you will probably have to follow the scheme employed in the school, even if it means you will have to teach students with a wider range of reading abilities. If, over time, other teachers at your grade level want to try this approach, you may be able to convince your principal to use this strategy at just the one grade level.

No perfect organizational strategy for classroom reading instruction exists. All plans have certain advantages and disadvantages. Teachers are individuals, and what works for one may not

work for another. Also, teachers and teacher-trainers may have preferences that conflict with some aspects of this plan. Nonetheless, the following specific system for managing reading instruction should be considered because:

1. The plan is based on sound principles of effective instruction.
2. The plan is based on common sense and the realistic limitations of elementary school teaching.
3. The plan includes enough specific information that teachers can implement it on their own.
4. This plan, though not perfect, has the maximum number of advantages and minimum number of disadvantages.
5. The plan is structured enough to be followed by most teachers yet flexible enough to accommodate a range of teaching styles.
6. This plan works. Teachers can dramatically improve the management of their reading programs, leading to demonstrably higher pupil achievement and improved teacher morale and job satisfaction.

MANAGING THE CLASSROOM READING PROGRAM

This plan is not radical or new, but an adaptation of a traditional, three-group reading program. To help you understand the critical elements of a classroom reading program, we have presented ten guidelines for a well-managed reading program in Figure 3–4. Under each guideline are observable teacher behaviors or classroom conditions associated with effective programs. The information presented in Figure 3–4 has been used by administrators and supervisors to evaluate classroom reading instruction, by teachers for self-evaluation, and may be used by you to recognize or better understand what an excellent classroom program looks like. Study each of the points carefully before reading further in this chapter, because some points will be discussed later.

Guideline 1: Instruction begins on time.

- The teacher is in the room, prepared, and waiting for the students.
- The students know what to do when entering the room.
- All materials are at hand (workbooks, readers, supplementary materials, etc.).

Guideline 2: The classroom is calm and quiet.

- There are no on-going discipline problems.
- The teacher has rules posted.
- The teacher uses a discipline system.
- The teacher is consistent.
- The teacher follows through.

Guideline 3: Clear routines have been established.

- The teacher's direct teaching time is not interrupted.
- Expectations have been explained and are reviewed periodically.
- Transitions to new activities take place quickly and quietly.
- Procedures for movement, pencil sharpening, etc. are followed.

Guideline 4: Children are on task; the teacher exhibits appropriate teaching intensity.

- The students are engaged in assigned activities.
- Only appropriate reading activities take place.
- The children are challenged and productive.
- The teacher holds each student accountable.
- An appropriate amount of time is spent on actually teaching the subject.
- An appropriate amount of time is spent on directions and supervision of seatwork.

Guideline 5: Instruction is planned to teach appropriate reading skills.

- The teacher knows the subject matter.
- Some lesson plan form is used.
- Lessons are planned in advance.
- Materials are at the direct teaching area and ready for use.
- The teaching area is free of clutter.
- The lessons are appropriate to the needs of the students.
- The teaching intensity and pacing are appropriate for each group.
- The teacher uses high-interest materials.

Figure 3–4   Critical elements of a well-managed classroom reading program

Note. From C. Milner, Principal, and L. Fulvio, Principal, Hayward Unified School District, Hayward, California. Reprinted by permission.

Obviously, effective reading instruction is not easy. The teaching skills involved are seldom developed quickly. Most teachers succeed only after substantial experience and frequent failure. Rarely does a teacher regularly exhibit all these behaviors. In addition, some behaviors may not be appropriate for every teacher. For instance, many teachers can maintain a calm and quiet learning environment (Guideline 2) without relying on a specific discipline system or posted rules. The guidelines themselves, however, are important and can serve as an

Guideline 6: Grouping techniques are implemented to help meet the needs of students.

- The teacher uses assessment information to appropriately group students and plan instruction.
- The physical arrangement of the room lends itself to effective group activities.
- Appropriate materials have been selected or developed to meet the needs of the groups and to motivate students to learn.
- Appropriate activities have been planned and implemented to meet the needs of each group.

Guideline 7: The teacher interacts with each reading group to motivate and stimulate learning.

- The teacher meets with each group each day.
- The teacher gives appropriate directions and speaks clearly.
- The teacher maintains the students' attention.
- The teacher is enthusiastic, energetic, and involved.
- The teacher is confident.
- The teacher communicates clear, positive, high expectations.
- The teacher gives appropriate, sincere praise.
- The classroom climate promotes dignity and respect.
- The teacher encourages appropriate student input and response.
- The students and the teacher have a cooperative relationship.

Guideline 8: Seatwork assignments are clear and at the proper level for independent practice.

- Assignments focus on follow-up practice of skills taught in the directed lesson.
- Directions for seatwork are given at the end of the directed lesson.
- Written directions are provided for the students to refer to and follow.
- Students are provided with a list of things to do when the assigned seatwork is completed.
- Necessary supplies are easily accessible.

Guideline 9: Independent activities are appropriate, clear and well-organized.

- Appropriate independent activities are selected by the teacher.
- Students know what to do to begin, conclude, and change activities.
- Activities must not disrupt other students in the class.
- Equipment and materials are ready and at the activity area.

Guideline 10: Teacher aides, if available, are used in an appropriate manner.

- Good communication exists between the teacher and the aide(s).
- The teacher and the aide(s) plan jointly.
- The aide(s) is not used to supplant instruction that should be provided by the teacher.
- The aide(s) has been trained in advance.
- The aide(s) is used effectively throughout the reading period.

Figure 3-4 (continued)

accurate barometer of a reading program's quality.

The Basic Instructional Plan

Teachers have used this basic instructional plan for many years. The grouping arrangement and daily schedule for this plan are presented in Figure 3–5. The basic plan assumes three reading groups with a 60-minute reading period. Variations are shown in Figure 3–6. The first variation is for two groups in a 60-minute period, perhaps appropriate for a beginning teacher or a teacher

	(Low) Group I	(Middle) Group II	(High) Group III
8:30 - 8:50	D.T.	I.A.	S.W.
8:50 - 9:10	S.W.	D.T.	I.A.
9:10 - 9:30	I.A.	S.W.	D.T.

Activities

D.T. - Directed Teaching

S.W. - Seatwork

I.A. - Independent Activities

Figure 3–5   The basic instructional plan

in a staggered reading format. The second variation is for four groups in a 90-minute period.

Some advantages of the basic instructional plan are:

1. The teacher meets with the low group first, when both teacher and students are fresh, for directed instruction.
2. Seatwork follows directed teaching immediately for the two lower groups.

3. The more capable students (who are also most often able to learn independently) begin with seatwork and independent tasks.
4. The teacher meets with each group daily, which helps students to maintain task attention and teachers to maintain continuity of instruction. Although 20 minutes may seem too short for directed teaching,

	(Low) Group I	(High) Group II
8:00 - 8:30	D.T.	S.W. and I.A.
8:30 - 9:00	S.W. and I.A.	D.T.

	(Low) Group I	(Low-average) Group II	(High-average) Group III	(High) Group IV
8:30 - 8:40	Large group activities with whole class			
8:40 - 9:00	D.T.	I.A.	I.A.	S.W.
9:00 - 9:20	S.W.	D.T.	I.A.	I.A.
9:20 - 9:40	I.A.	S.W.	D.T.	I.A.
9:40 - 10:00	I.A.	I.A.	S.W.	D.T.

Figure 3–6   Variations of the basic instructional plan

most teachers find that if they focus on the lesson's crucial aspects, students make satisfactory progress. Transitions, however, must be made swiftly and smoothly.

Generally, teachers should adhere to the same schedule whenever the basic instructional plan is used. Students usually benefit from a set routine. They adjust their work habits so they can move to the next activity automatically, *if* that activity occurs at the same time each day. Even first graders who may be unable to tell time will know by watching the hands on the clock when it is time to proceed to the next activity.

Some teachers prefer to meet the whole class for a short period before commencing reading instruction. The second variation in Figure 3–6 shows how this time might be scheduled. The teacher may use this time to review plans for the reading period with the children or to handle other administrative tasks. Other teachers prefer to begin reading instruction immediately. Since reading is usually taught at the beginning of the school day in the elementary school, teachers can eliminate one transition and save time if the first group begins instruction at the start of the period. This approach is particularly appropriate in staggered reading programs where only half of the students are present and attendance and other administrative activities must wait for the entire class to arrive.

Activities During the Three Periods

Directed Teaching

During this period, the teacher directly teaches pupils in a small group setting. During this time the effective teacher follows the principles outlined in the Guidelines. Most teachers rely on a basal reader approach to present the daily lesson and so must select the critical aspects of the lesson from the many suggestions usually offered in the teacher's manual. Typically, the lesson steps focus on four types of activities: (1) lesson motivation; (2) vocabulary development; (3) guided reading; and (4) extended reading activities. Some teachers also include language-experience activities in the directed teaching time.

For the directed lesson the teacher relies on a lesson plan prepared before the group meeting. If a basal reader approach is used, the teacher knows the story and the skills to be covered and has the teacher's manual handy. Other materials are out and ready to use so that no time is lost searching for flash cards, workbooks, etc. Many teachers keep a can of pencils on the table for students who forget to bring their pencils, again saving time. Marking the pencils keeps them from disappearing when the group disbands.

Most teachers prefer to teach children at a table placed near a chalkboard, and some are fortunate enough to have U-shaped tables for this purpose. These tables can usually accommodate up to eight students comfortably. When these tables are unavailable, teachers often use standard rectangular classroom tables that can seat eleven or twelve students.

Figure 3–7 shows both types of table and where students sit. Some positions allow for better eye contact between teacher and child and a better view of the chalkboard for the student. Such postions are therefore considered more favorable for the child. At the U-shaped table the most favorable positions are numbers 5 and 6, and the least favorable are numbers 1 and 2. For children who have an especially difficult time sitting still, positions 1 and 2 are more favorable because the teacher is in easy reach. In any case, if seat assignments are made, the teacher should consider where children actually sit at the teaching table. Some teachers feel that assigning seats eliminates arguments and allows them to place certain students in more favorable learning positions. Other teachers let students select their own seats, but make sure it is done without disruption.

In some cases, teachers simply do not have enough furniture or space to have a separate reading group area. Then the teacher may provide directed instruction to pupils at their desks. They usually have students move to desks in a certain area of the room or, if necessary, actually move some desks. Such an arrangement

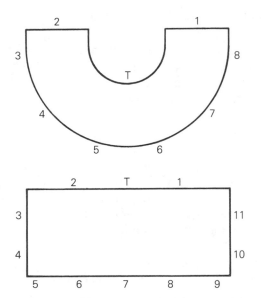

Figure 3–7   Placement of students around two types of tables for reading instruction

can be satisfactory, especially for intermediate pupils. Younger children usually need to be closer to the teacher to stay on-task.

Some teachers, particularly at the primary level, prefer to have their students sit on the floor or on a rug for reading group instruction, but this arrangement is usually not a good idea. When students are on the floor, they have trouble doing written work, lose their places more often when reading, and often wiggle or misbehave. Many teachers enjoy the cozy atmosphere that such an arrangement creates, and in certain situations, such as when the teacher reads to students, its use is warranted. But for directed reading instruction, students should sit at tables or desks.

The teacher should organize the direct instruction area so that it is free of unnecessary clutter. Pupils can put their books and materials on the floor during the lesson to keep the teaching table clear. Other distracting items, such as coats, hats, gloves, and toys, should be put in their appropriate places before the group convenes. The teacher may also place a small bookshelf or table near the teaching table to store

the various manuals, books, and teaching devices needed for the lesson.

Several important teaching behaviors should be exhibited during the directed teaching segment. Of course, the teacher wants to spend enough time actually teaching the subject, but this task may be more difficult than it seems. When in small groups, children enjoy talking with the teacher. Many normally shy students can be highly verbal in the small group setting. Some exchange of ideas among students is important for developing reading ability, so the challenge for the teacher is to balance student discussion and the task at hand. Sometimes students will make "off the wall" comments or humorous remarks that make it difficult for everyone to stay on-task. Experienced teachers know that it often takes a good deal of discipline and sensitivity on the teacher's part to redirect the students to the day's lesson.

Much of the process-product research reviewed earlier in this chapter shows that higher student achievement is associated with teachers who: (1) give appropriate directions and speak clearly; (2) maintain the students' attention; (3) are enthusiastic, energetic, involved, and confident; (4) communicate clear, positive, high expectations; (5) give appropriate, sincere praise; (6) see to it that children are challenged and productive; (7) hold each student accountable; (8) encourage student participation; (9) establish a classroom climate that promotes respect and dignity; and (10) maintain a cooperative relationship with children. To do all these things all the time would require a teacher who walks on water! To exhibit these effective teacher behaviors even most of the time requires a teacher who not only knows the subject but also has remarkable skill in working with children. For some teachers, who seem to be gifted in this regard, these skills come easily. Other teachers need a great deal of conscious effort to learn these behaviors. But these behaviors *can* be learned. With the proper attitude and appropriate assistance, teachers can learn to teach in a way that will promote high student achievement.

One specific teacher behavior has not been

explored in the research: allowing interruptions during the directed lesson. Many teachers allow students to interrupt them almost constantly. Reasons for the interruptions may vary, but include requests for assistance with seatwork, requests to sharpen pencils or go to the bathroom, tattling, and other complaints. The result, however, is always the same, a significant loss of teaching time. How significant? It is not unusual for students to lose 50 to 80 percent of their direct teaching time because of interruptions. Teachers are often not aware of the problem or its significance, or they justify it on the basis of "meeting students' needs." The teacher may either be a poor classroom manager, set low expectations for students, or both. Fortunately, most teachers make adjustments and eliminate interruptions once they are aware of the problem.

One of the best things teachers can do to eliminate interruptions is to be sure to meet each group each day. If students know they can meet with the teacher and not be disturbed every day, they are more likely to respect the rights of their peers. A teacher can also spend the first few minutes of the reading group reviewing the seatwork from the previous day and the last few minutes of group time carefully assigning the seatwork to follow.

Seatwork

In the basic instructional plan, seatwork activities follow immediately after directed teaching for two of the three groups. Seatwork activities should be completed by students individually, without teacher assistance. Seatwork activities usually consist of the workbook or spirit master pages accompanying a basal reader. For students to complete these pages without assistance, the teacher should be sure that:

1. *The student is properly placed in the basal reader.* If the material is too difficult, the student becomes frustrated and seeks assistance, fails to complete the work, completes the work improperly, or misbehaves.

2. *The pages are carefully selected.* Inappropriate or inscrutable pages should not be assigned.

The best pages are those that give the student practice on skills that were just taught. Then workbook pages should be easy. If the student understands the skill and tries, the pages should be completed accurately. The teacher can appropriately expect 90 percent accuracy on students' seatwork pages.

3. *Time is spent at the end of the reading group to familiarize students with the assignment.* In addition to reviewing the directions for each page, teachers should go over one or two items on each page or have students actually complete the items in the reading group to be sure that students understand *what* to do and *how* to do it.

4. *Directions are provided in writing as well as orally at the end of the reading group.* Some children have an amazing ability to forget what they are told immediately after they hear it.

5. *An appropriate amount of time is allocated to seatwork.* Some teachers assign an hour or more of reading seatwork daily, but students cannot be expected to maintain attention on such a relatively unstimulating task for this long. A maximum of 20 minutes per day of seatwork works well.

6. *An appropriate amount of seatwork is given for the allocated time.* Do not expect students to complete 30 minutes of seatwork in a 20-minute period. All students do not work at the same rate. Assign all students an amount that can be completed by the slower children. The faster (though not necessarily more capable) students can be given additional or special assignments.

7. *The reading group begins with an examination of the previous day's assignment.* It takes only a few minutes to review each student's seatwork, yet doing this daily can save hours of the teacher's time. The teacher can easily hold students accountable for the work assigned, and they will not fall behind in their seatwork.

As can be seen, assigning seatwork is not simple. Teachers must take time and effort to prepare and present seatwork tasks. However, the time is well spent. If these steps are followed,

Name: _____ Snow L.6

#1 Copy each new word twice:
    softly   flakes   pretty   soft

_____ _____ _____ _____

_____ _____ _____ _____

#2 Make compound words by drawing lines between words.

	Write each compound word.
police light	_____
day man	_____
snow day	_____
some balls	_____
	_____

#3 Do page 45 in your Studybook. Write the answers and trace the words here.

1. _____ and _____ made the snowman.

2. The boys weren't in school because It was _____ .

Figure 3–8   One week's seatwork for a group of second graders

Note. From P. Rothling, Teacher, Hayward Unified School District, Hayward, California. Reprinted by permission.

2.

Snow L.6
U.3

3. Mr. Migs had the

_____.

4. I think Mr. Migs will

_____.

#4 Do Skilpak page 61.

#5 Write all the words that you
underlined on Skilpak page 61.

_____ _____

_____ _____

_____ _____

_____ _____

#6 Do Skilpak pages 62 and 63.

#7 Draw a picture of a
snowman here.

Figure 3–8 (continued)

students learn more and so teaching time becomes more enjoyable.

Item 4 suggests you give written directions for seatwork assignments. Figure 3–8 shows an example of one week's seatwork for a group of second graders.

In the form's upper right hand corner, the teacher indicates the name of the story and the book and unit levels. There is also a space for the student's name at the top of the page. The numbers down the left hand column correspond to the seatwork activities. Each day the teacher circles the numbers of activities to be completed, and after the student finishes the work, marks an "X" through the numbers that were circled. The assignment sheet reminds the student about assigned seatwork after that seatwork is introduced.

The teacher prepares this sheet for each group and then duplicates it. Such sheets can be revised or used again for other groups when they are reading at this level.

Most teachers initially assign the same seatwork to every child in the group, making it easier to plan and correct seatwork. Later, as individual needs and abilities become more apparent and the groups are functioning smoothly, seatwork activities can be more individualized. The teacher can use the same form by circling only those numbers appropriate for a particular child.

The type, variety, and length of seatwork activities vary according to the students' ages and abilities and the teacher's instructional goals. Teachers usually find it helpful to provide some variety for students; however, if too many different activities are assigned, students may not learn to attend to a task well.

Listed below are some other possible seatwork activities:

1. Recopy and illustrate a language experience story.
2. Complete a book report activity.
3. Do free reading.
4. Do flash card drill or practice with self-checking materials designed for individual reinforcement of specific skills.

5. Work with cross-age tutors or parent volunteers.
6. Do creative writing activities.
7. Write thank you notes, birthday cards, cards to a sick child, etc.
8. Read books authored by classmates from the language experience center.
9. Write an article for the class newspaper or magazine.
10. Do paired oral or silent reading with a partner if this can be done in a secluded area without disturbing others.

Seatwork should reinforce the reading skills presented in the directed reading lesson. Therefore, the above activities should be used only for those students who have mastered the skills or for those who have completed the specific practice. Teachers often vary the presentation of work-sheets to motivate students to complete them. You might place pages in plastic sheets and provide students with grease pencils or markers, or occasionally give students individual chalkboards or magic slates for their work. Even cutting around the edges of seatwork pages with pinking shears can improve students' motivation.

To manage seatwork assignments, give students individual but inexpensive folders. For example, use two sheets of 12" by 18" construction paper and a stapler to make folders, as shown in Figure 3–9.

Label the two inside pockets *Do* and *Done* to correspond to the student's work. The student pulls the papers out of the *Do* side, completes them, then places them in the *Done* side. Each student's folder might include a weekly and/or daily schedule or contract, the daily seatwork, progress charts, extra activity pages, and *bonus cards*. The teacher may periodically place bonus cards in individual folders for a change of pace and some excitement. The cards may or may not be used as rewards. The bonus may be a special activity, a small prize, or the "reward" of erasing the chalkboards.

Students often take pride in their personal folders and should be encouraged to illustrate or decorate them. The folders may also be color-

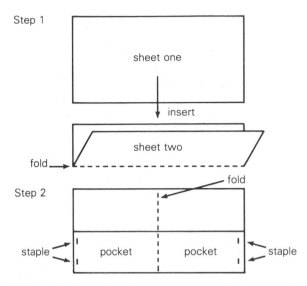

Figure 3–9   Simple construction of an individual student folder

coded by groups. As part of the management plan teachers should instruct students to put their folders in a specific location when they are not being used. Many teachers provide "mailboxes" in a central place for students to store their folders and other reading materials.

Independent Activities

Independent activity time allows students to practice reading in another setting and in a motivating way. The amount of freedom provided varies according to the needs and talents of teacher and students, amount and kinds of materials available, number of aides or volunteers present, and other factors. For students to work independently in a successful way it is *essential* that they learn to clean up after themselves, settle (or avoid) their own disputes, help each other, share, and cooperate quietly. Noise from independent activities must never disturb or disrupt students working at their desks or in a group.

Independent activities may be structured loosely or scheduled specifically. Students may have the option of choosing from a variety of activities or be assigned to an activity or sequence of activities. Usually teachers begin by limiting the choices.

The best independent activity is silent reading. Easy to plan, it gives students crucial practice in the act of reading and helps them appreciate the value and joy of reading. If students can read quietly on their own, by all means allow them to do so for the entire independent activity period, if possible. Even first-grade children can spend 20 minutes reading or looking at picture books without direct supervision or calamity. Some teachers prefer to introduce independent activities by providing a controlled activity or learning center, such as a listening center where students can listen to tapes or read along with stories.

Teachers use a variety of devices to manage independent activities: student contracts, time schedules, sign up sheets, or room arrangement devices (for example, with four chairs at the listening center, no more than four students may go to that area at one time).

Teachers also manage independent activities by using student helpers, teacher aides, or parent volunteers. These assistants, if reliable and properly trained, can monitor independent activities by setting up and operating equipment, keeping students on task, assisting students when necessary, or directing specific activities. If paid aides are unavailable, you can sometimes recruit volunteers or student assistants. If these are also unavailable then students within the class can assume some monitoring tasks and the nature of the activities provided can be modified.

If you wish to set up a number of learning or interest centers, or provide a variety of reading kits, games or other reinforcement activities, careful planning is essential. The materials used must be well organized, durable, and introduced to the students one at a time. The materials or activities may be grouped according to reading group or skill level and color-coded. You should try to match the activities to the students' specific needs and this may require continual assessment and monitoring.

Teachers need to resist the temptation to assign fun activities or custodial tasks that do little more than keep children entertained or

Computer-assisted instruction can help teachers manage students' independent work.

occupied. Independent activity time succeeds when children actually use the time to improve their ability and desire to *read*.

Independent activities can include many of the activities listed under seatwork, as well as the following:

1. Visiting the room library for browsing, checking out books, and free reading.
2. Going to the "buddy center" for tutoring, paired reading (with another student), or reading with a parent or aide.
3. Going to a secret hideaway or loft for silent reading *only*. The teacher may also provide a reading chair or sofa, a rug, or a bathtub!
4. Working at the "recording studio"; students read into a tape recorder, rewind the tape, and listen to or read along with the playback.
5. Working at the "conference center" and meeting with the teacher or another adult. Such conferences may be used to

discuss reading progress or share interests in materials being read.
6. Visiting the "drama center" where students use puppets, masks, costumes, and simple props to dramatize stories or act out plays.
7. Practicing reading skills through the use of kits and reinforcement games and materials.
8. Working at the language experience/creative writing center or preparing book reports.
9. Working at the "listening center" where commercial or teacher-made tapes are played on an audio recorder while students listen to or read along with the story.
10. Using audio-visual equipment to practice reading skills.

Of course it will not be possible to provide a physical place for all of the centers or activities to occur at the same time. However, many of

Name _____

Directions: On the lines to the left of each statement below, please rate the following elements of a well-managed reading program as they are implemented in your classroom. An *A* placed on the line indicates that you *always* implement that element. An *S* indicates that you *sometimes* implement that element and an *N* indicates that you *never* implement that element.

A = Always   S = Sometimes   N = Never

Directed Teaching Lesson

_____ 1. The teacher uses a lesson plan form.
_____ 2. Each day's lesson is planned in advance.
_____ 3. All materials are at the directed teaching area and ready for use.
_____ 4. The students have assigned seats.
_____ 5. The students' ability and distractibility were considered when assigning seats.
_____ 6. The teaching area and chalkboard are free of unnecessary clutter.
_____ 7. Instruction is planned to teach appropriate reading skills at the proper level.
_____ 8. Instruction starts on time; no time is wasted.
_____ 9. The teacher interacts with each group each day to motivate and stimulate learning.
_____10. The previous day's seatwork is reviewed at the beginning of the lesson and directions for subsequent seatwork are given before the group is dismissed.

Seatwork

_____11. Written directions are provided for seatwork assignments.
_____12. Students know where and how they will get workbooks or worksheets and where to put them when finished.
_____13. Students know how to use individual student folders and where to put them when finished.
_____14. There is a list of things to do when the assigned seatwork is finished. This list is visible.
_____15. Necessary supplies are at each student's desk.
_____16. An appropriate amount of time is allocated for seatwork and an appropriate amount of seatwork is given for the allocated time.
_____17. Seatwork assignments are clear and at the right level for independent practice.
_____18. All skills have been taught and students have been checked for their understanding of these skills prior to the assignment of seatwork activities.

Independent Practice

_____19. An activity is usually chosen by the teacher. Beginning activities are simple and without choice by students.
_____20. Equipment and materials are ready and at the activity area(s).
_____21. Where necessary, monitors have been selected and trained to handle equipment and other materials.

Figure 3–10   Classroom management evaluation form
Note. From P. Landsberg, Reading Specialist, C. Milner, Principal, and L. Fulvio, Principal, Hayward Unified School District, Hayward, California. Reprinted by permission.

_____22. If available, student helpers, teacher aides and parent volunteers are trained in advance and used effectively throughout the reading period.

_____23. All students and helpers know what to do to start an activity.

_____24. All students and helpers know what to do when they finish early.

_____25. All students and helpers know what to do when it is time to change activities.

Establishment of Routines

_____26. Pencil sharpening plans have been established (regular and emergency).

_____27. A regular and an emergency plan has been established for getting drinks and using the restroom.

_____28. A routine has been established for using student folders.

_____29. A time indicator is used (bell, timer, voice, or other signal).

_____30. A routine has been established for moving from one activity to the next.

_____31. A routine has been established for greeting guests or messengers.

_____32. A procedure has been established for taking roll, noting tardies, collecting notes from home, etc.

_____33. Students know the procedures to follow when they are finished or stuck.

_____34. Students know what to do when they need additional paper or supplies.

_____35. Transitions to new activities are quick and quiet.

_____36. The teacher and students feel comfortable with the procedures that have been established.

_____37. Procedures are explained and reviewed periodically.

_____38. The teacher rehearses the procedures for transitions with students before implementing them.

Expectations

The teacher has established the following expectations with the class:

_____39. Reading starts on time.

_____40. Everyone stays at her reading task.

_____41. Reading time is for reading activities.

_____42. The teacher cannot be interrupted during the directed reading lesson.

The teacher has made an effort to communicate:

_____43. Clear, positive, high expectations.

_____44. Appropriate praise.

_____45. Knowledge of students' progress by checking and returning students' work promptly.

Grouping for Instruction

_____46. The teacher has appropriately grouped students.

_____47. The teacher has effectively used assessment information for grouping and instruction.

_____48. Appropriate materials have been selected or developed to meet the needs of the groups and to motivate the students to learn.

_____49. Appropriate activities have been planned and implemented to meet the needs of each group.

_____50. The physical arrangement of the room lends itself to effective group activities.

Figure 3–10   Classroom management evaluation form

the activities can be combined in one area or they can be rotated periodically. Also, some of these suggestions may be impractical because of noise unless space exists away from the regular classroom.

Students should not run out of things to do in the reading classroom. Since students always have the option of free reading, this should not be a problem. But just in case, many teachers post a large chart titled *What To Do When You're Through*, listing suggestions like:

1. Have you read any of the new books on display at the reading center?
2. Have you done your room job yet?
3. Is your desk cleaned out?
4. Do you have a suggestion for the suggestion box?
5. See what's new at the science center.

Evaluating the Basic Instructional Plan   The basic instructional plan just discussed is the type of plan that occurs most often in elementary reading programs. Figure 3–10 presents a classroom management evaluation form for evaluating this plan in your own classroom. Teachers whose reading programs reflect the specific elements listed in Figure 3–10 have well-managed programs in which students learn successfully.

Plan B Days

The basic instructional plan need not be used every day; alternative or Plan B days may also be scheduled. Teachers will vary how often they use Plan B days. Some teachers may think their students need a structured program four or five days per week, while others may find that three days of the basic program are enough and two days can be scheduled for different kinds of reading activities. Teachers may have to consider the age or ability of the pupils and the school schedule when planning alternative days. Some schools adjust the entire school schedule and dismiss students early on one or more days a month for teacher inservice. These "minimum days" may cause the regular program to be modified.

Plan B days may be scheduled for any of the following reasons:

1. A change of pace.
2. A time for individual conferences with students to check progress or to listen to them read.
3. A time for grouping according to interests or friendships.
4. A time for special activities such as speeches, plays, or book selling.
5. A time to *observe* students as they read and work together.
6. A time for intensive individual or small group tutoring.

The activities taking place during Plan B days will, of course, vary according to the teacher's purpose. Many language experience and individualized reading techniques can be applied on days when the basic instructional plan is not followed.

Plan B days should be scheduled rather than be chosen on the spur of the moment. Students need the routine of consistency, structure, and an opportunity for a calm, productive learning environment.

Establishing Routines

Establishing routines is critical to the smooth operation of the reading program. Students function best when clear limits are set for their classroom behavior. You should clarify appropriate procedures for all the little necessities, such as sharpening pencils, getting drinks, using the restroom, getting materials, and beginning and ending activities. It is helpful to appoint aides, volunteers, student helpers, or classmates to answer questions or provide assistance. The effective reading teacher establishes an appropriate climate for learning, one in which students are taught to get settled quickly, stay on task, and listen carefully to directions. A teacher can not afford to waste time repeating directions, disciplining students, passing out materials, picking up after students, giving instructions to aides, or collecting lunch money during reading time.

Time can also be easily lost during transitions between the three major group activities (directed teaching, seat work, and independent activities). However, you can take several specific steps to help students make these transitions quickly and quietly. First, be sure the room is appropriately arranged for small group reading instruction. Second, take time to clearly explain to students where they are to go for each major group activity. Then, walk the students through the transitions as many times as necessary to establish this routine, perhaps for several days. Students can then learn specific times to move and the traffic patterns to follow. Adhere to the daily time schedule while teaching these transitions so that the children begin to pace themselves and anticipate transition times by looking at the clock.

In a well-managed reading program, transitions should require only 30 to 60 seconds. For example, one minute after you dismiss students in the low group from directed teaching, they should begin their seat work.

Most teachers challenge students to make transitions quickly by timing them with a stopwatch, making this approach into a game or fun activity. Frequently teachers use a timer or ring a bell when it is time for groups to move. In any case, it is usually better to use a simple signal rather than verbal directions.

Certainly a mechanized or inflexible atmosphere should not exist, but efficient classroom procedures can be employed within a warm and humane environment. Indeed, students welcome a well-managed and productive reading period.

Sometimes the teacher should reinforce classroom procedures. Certainly halt a lesson if the noise level or off-task behavior requires admonishment or additional practice. But once routines are clearly established you may find that the reading period is one of the most satisfying and productive periods of the day.

Time may also be lost or used unwisely in the directed reading lesson. Efficient use of this time requires thorough and careful planning. Even with careful planning, however, difficulties may arise when certain instructional techniques are used. The round robin oral reading technique is ineffective, and the teacher must judiciously select from the many recommended basal reader activities in teachers' manuals.

Also inefficient is sending one student to the chalkboard to write a word, for example, while asking the other students to merely watch. It is better to have the other students at least do the same activity at their seats on paper, individual chalkboards, magic slates or other media. Having as many pupils as possible respond not only improves behavior and on-task time, but also facilitates learning.

It is usually helpful to eliminate hand raising during the reading group. Two things often occur when students raise their hands to answer questions. First, some students—unable to restrain themselves—wave their hands frantically in hopes of being called on. Some students even grunt, which can be annoying. Second, perhaps as a result of the first, some students are called on more often than others. In fact, most teachers tend to call on students who can provide the answer correctly. This is probably just human nature; however, there are alternatives that you can employ that will yield highly satisfactory results.

Teachers can teach students that, whereas hand raising is an appropriate procedure for large group activities, in the reading group students should not raise their hands to answer questions. Initially, the teacher states the student's name first, then asks the question. For example, "Rita, what do you think this story will be about?"

Students take a while to adjust to this approach and to unlearn their almost automatic tendency to fling their hands in the air as soon as they sense a question coming. Once the proper pattern is established, however, the teacher can maintain everyone's attention by asking the question and then selecting an individual to answer. This approach has several advantages: (1) it eliminates irritating hand waving and squirming; (2) students attend better, for they cannot avoid being called on by not raising their hands; (3) less aggressive students also participate; indeed, more equal participation by all students is likely; and (4) the teacher can more easily check individuals' understanding of the concepts presented.

If you wish to pose a question for *any* child to answer, direct the children to raise their thumbs rather than their hands. For example, you might say: "I'm going to let one of you tell us what your favorite part of the story is. If you want to tell us, pop up your thumb." Children enjoy this approach and it does eliminate hand raising. "Thumbs up" also serves as a good signal for students to use if they wish to ask a question or indicate that they have completed a particular task.

Other techniques, known as ***every-pupil-response techniques*** (EPRT), can be used in directed reading groups. EPRT requires all students to simultaneously answer a question so that they cannot copy each other's answers. Used properly, EPRT also enables the teacher to assess individual students' mastery of concepts. These techniques are appropriate for "yes/no" or "right/wrong" type questions or for having students give an oral group repetition response, such as repeating a list of vocabulary words. Several every-pupil-response techniques follow (Ekwall and Shanker, 1983):

1. *Yes/no cards*—to provide group response to "yes–no" or "right-wrong" questions. For example, the teacher might say, "I am going to read some words that start with the 'b' sound and some that start with other sounds. If the word I read starts with the 'b' sound, hold up your 'yes' card. If it starts with another sound, hold up your 'no' card. Does everybody understand? Good. Ready? *ball, tree, house, bat, Bill, dig,*" etc.
2. *Thumbs up, thumbs down*—the same as yes-no cards; thumbs up indicates "yes," thumbs down indicates "no."
3. *Open eyes, close eyes*—the same as above; this method has the added advantage of eliminating the possibility that students will mimic the responses of others.
4. *1, 2, 3 . . .*—to provide a group repetition response. For example, the teacher might say, "Printed on this chart are a number of words that begin and end with sounds you know, so I know you will be able to read them. Say each word on the signal as

I point to it. Ready? . . ." As the teacher points to each word, he or she says: "1, 2, 3 . . ." the students then read the word quickly. After the list is read in order, the teacher may use the pointer to point to words quickly in random order. Students enjoy the speed and challenge of this technique and it provides excellent practice. (pp. 156–57)

A final consideration for the efficient use of time in the directed reading group is the pace at which instruction occurs. It is difficult to guide teachers in this regard; they must rely on their judgment, experience, and careful observation of the students' progress. You want to move briskly, yet take the necessary time to reteach a crucial skill if students have difficulty with it.

Room Arrangement

Room arrangement directly affects the management of the reading program. Teachers often have difficulty with their reading instruction because they have overlooked relatively simple but important physical considerations. Sometimes minor changes in this area can make a big difference.

Figures 3–11, 3–12, and 3–13 illustrate three actual classrooms. Figures 3–11 and 3–12 show primary classrooms, with 30 and 28 students respectively, and Figure 3–13 shows an intermediate grade classroom with 25 students. In the first two examples the teacher directs the reading group at a reading table, while in the third the students sit at desks at one side of the room facing the teacher. Otherwise all three classrooms have common features.

The teachers separated the directed teaching, seatwork, and independent activities areas. Arrows in the figures indicate patterns the children follow during transitions. Often teachers place the directed teaching area and the independent activities area at opposite ends of the room with the seatwork area in the middle, thus minimizing distractions between groups.

At the directed teaching area, face the room and have students face the wall. Then you can observe what other children are doing and the students in the reading group will be less dis-

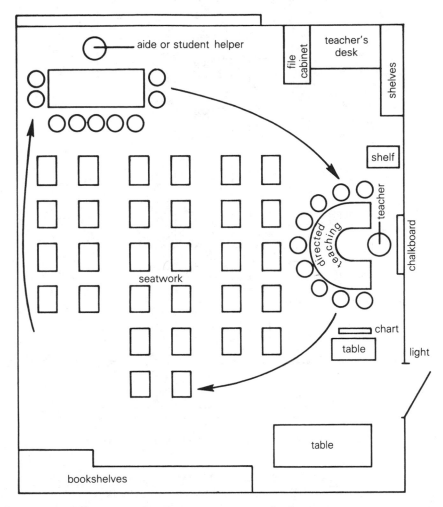

Figure 3–11   Room arrangement for a primary grade classroom

tracted by other activities in the classroom. Of course, place the reading group students where they can easily see the chalkboard and chartrack, if one is used.

No best room arrangement for reading exists. The classroom itself often limits the teacher's options. But teachers' classrooms can reflect their personalities in much the same way their homes do. Beyond the illustrations provided and the suggestions made about some basic structural considerations, you can do a lot to create a comfortable, warm, and stimulating environment.

Using Teacher Aides, Parent Volunteers, and Student Helpers

Paid teacher aides can greatly contribute to the elementary school reading program. But recently, the number of these paraprofessionals has begun to decrease as a result of financial constraints in the public schools. In some cases, parent volunteers or student helpers can fulfill some of the same roles as those assumed by teacher aides.

Karl Koenke (1979) in a review of research on the effective use of teacher aides found that, in programs where teachers work closely with

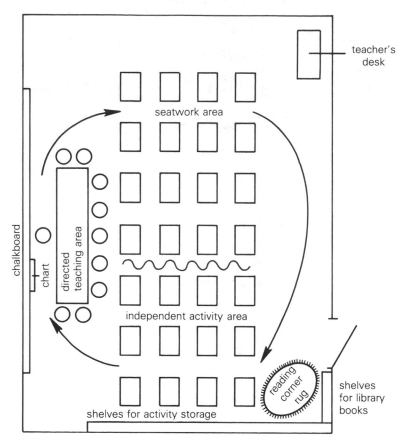

Figure 3–12   Another room arrangement for a primary grade classroom

trained aides, the results are often very satisfying. A caring, effective, dependable, and dedicated individual usually does well, whether aide or volunteer. Other characteristics that help teacher aides or volunteers succeed include: facility with the English language, understanding of children with special needs, familiarity with instructional media, knowledge of the curriculum, emotional stability, and a willingness to make a long-term commitment to the program.

Most teachers find that aides or volunteers who possess the important personal qualities can develop the necessary instructional knowledge and skills. Teachers and aides must work closely together, plan cooperatively, be attuned to each other's personal and professional needs, and maintain open communication. Teachers should schedule regular times to meet with their

aides or volunteers to share concerns and plan for future instruction.

Aides or volunteers should be given clear guidelines or role descriptions both in writing and through thorough discussion. Teacher and aide or volunteer should agree on the definition of roles and responsibilities.

Using teacher aides, volunteers, or student helpers usually requires some extra time and effort. However, the contributions made by a well-trained aide or volunteer more than make up for it.

Aides and volunteers can assume several roles, but they should *not* provide direct instruction of skills not previously taught to students. Too often aides have complete responsibility for a group of students, often the lowest group, which is unfortunate and inappropriate, regard-

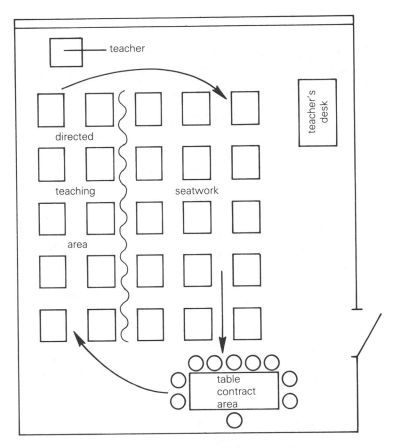

Figure 3–13   Room arrangement for an intermediate grade classroom

less of the aides' competence. Only the teacher should be directly responsible for all children's reading instruction. Certainly the aide or volunteer may assist the teacher or groups of children or supplement instruction, but they should *not* supplant the teacher. Aides, volunteers, or helpers can be effective by

1. Answering students' questions or helping students complete seatwork assignments.
2. Monitoring seatwork or independent activities to keep students on-task.
3. Taking language experience dictation and completing follow-up language experience activities.
4. Drilling students on high-frequency sight words or practicing other decoding skills.

5. Supplementing the teacher's direct teaching.
6. Listening to students read orally.
7. Reading to students.
8. Discussing books students have read.
9. Directing learning centers; for example, playing assigned reading games with students to reinforce skills.
10. Handling record keeping tasks.
11. Running off and organizing weekly seatwork materials.
12. Correcting workbooks or ditto pages.
13. Constructing game or reinforcement materials under the teacher's direction.

Teacher aides or volunteers need not be assigned only to specific classrooms. In some schools they work with a reading specialist or other school personnel. For example, in one school parent volunteers staff an area of the reading specialist's classroom, working individually with low readers in carrels. They see certain children according to a set schedule, spending time on such activities as numbers 3 through 8 above, all under the direction of the classroom teacher and reading specialist.

This program succeeds: children enjoy the personal attention; parent volunteers gain satisfaction for their important contribution; and students make excellent progress because of the cooperative planning of teachers and volunteers.

Although the tasks listed above are appropriate for well-trained aides or adult volunteers, some of them could be assumed by older student helpers or, in some cases, students in the regular classroom. When paid aides or dependable parent volunteers are unavailable, some teachers train students to help each other with monitoring tasks, language experience activities, reading practice activities, seatwork, and so forth. Such cooperative learning among students can be effective and rewarding.

Reading Activities for the First Few Weeks of School

It usually takes about two weeks for teachers to form reading groups under the basic instructional plan. During this time, teachers and reading specialists test new students, reassess returning students, and check records. Under a staggered reading program, the split sessions usually do not begin for two or three weeks.

However, reading instruction can occur during this period. Many valuable instructional activities can take place, such as those described for Plan B days. In addition, consider the following:

1. Do a variety of language experience or creative writing activities. Autobiographies dictated or written by the students are particularly appropriate—they are enjoyable for the children and informative for the teacher.
2. Read to the class and then discuss what was read.

3. Allow children to form their own reading groups; they can select favorite stories, plays, or poems from basal readers previously read.
4. Use out of date and discontinued basal readers.
5. Have students select, practice, and read short passages or favorite poems to the class.
6. Begin a sustained silent reading program so that students get into the habit of taking time for recreational reading.
7. Take a trip to the public or school library. Help students select books and acquire their own library cards.
8. Use old Weekly Readers or subject matter textbooks.
9. Have children create their own stories and books. Their words can be typed or written on dittos, duplicated, assembled, and distributed to the whole class.
10. Prepare packets of interesting, varied, and relatively easy seatwork for children to complete. These can occupy students while you test or work with other children.

THE DIRECTED READING LESSON

The teacher teaches the directed reading lesson during the directed teaching segment of the basic instructional plan. The basal-reader teacher's manual provides specific, daily directions. Although basal readers vary somewhat, most present similar basic steps or components for the directed reading lesson.

Components of the Directed Reading Lesson

The directed reading lesson or directed reading activity can be divided into a number of steps or components. Mark W. Aulls (1982) lists eight different steps as follows:

1. Introduction, background, or motivation.
2. Presentation of new vocabulary or review of previous vocabulary.
3. Guided silent/oral reading.

4. Discussion of the story.
5. Rereading of the story.
6. Evaluation of vocabulary or skills.
7. Specific word identification or comprehension skills instruction.
8. Enrichment activities. (p. 135)

Frank B. May (1982) lists thirteen different steps, but many authors combine the steps into three or four components. Such an approach makes the components applicable to more basal series. Four critical components of the directed reading lesson are:

1. Lesson motivation
2. Vocabulary development
3. Guided reading activities
4. Extended reading activities

Lesson Motivation. The teacher stimulates the children's interest in the reading selection by providing some background for it, discussing its purpose with students, looking at some of the illustrations, relating the topic to the students' experiences, and so on. Presented on the first day to introduce the selection, this step typically takes only a few minutes. Often teachers also supplement the story with library books, illustrations, or personal materials to increase students' interest.

Vocabulary Development. Next, the teacher presents new vocabulary words. These words may be written on the chalkboard or presented on large flashcards. Manuals encourage teachers to present new words in context so that students not only learn to recognize them but also develop meaning for them. Also, new words often prepare students for the selection's new concepts. The number of new words introduced and the amount of time spent on vocabulary instruction varies according to difficulty and pupils' needs.

Again, vocabulary is generally presented on the first day of the lesson, right after the lesson motivation. Many teachers, however, take a few minutes on subsequent days to review, reinforce, or extend vocabulary.

Guided Reading Activities. This part of the lesson begins on the first day and may continue on the second or even the third day of covering the story. The teacher asks the children to read part of the story silently, which may be preceded by specific questions. The silent reading done without interruption varies from one or two lines to many pages, depending on the students' reading level and the teacher's purposes. After the silent reading, the teacher discusses the material with students. The basal-reader manual usually provides many questions at a variety of levels to stimulate thinking and to evaluate students' comprehension. Teachers can ask students to paraphrase answers or to reread parts of the selection orally for specific purposes, but should not ask students to take turns reading out loud. Rather, use the basal manual's suggestion for purposeful oral reading: oral reading to answer specific questions, oral reading for expression, oral reading to demonstrate or identify dialogue, and choral or paired reading for fluency.

Extended Reading Activities. In this part of the directed lesson, specific skills are taught and practiced. These skills may include vocabulary development, decoding skills (phonics, structural analysis, or context clues), comprehension skills, or study skills. In addition, various enrichment activities may be presented as time allows. These include such areas as language development, poetry, music, art activities, and creative dramatics. Once again the teacher's manual serves as an invaluable source of suggestions for teaching important skills. The teacher can correlate such skills with specific workbook pages introduced and explained in the directed lesson. Some basal programs indicate whether the skill on a particular workbook page is being introduced or repeated. This information helps a teacher decide which pages to skip.

Basal programs also provide tests for evaluating students' progress at the end of units or books. The teacher usually administers these tests during directed teaching time.

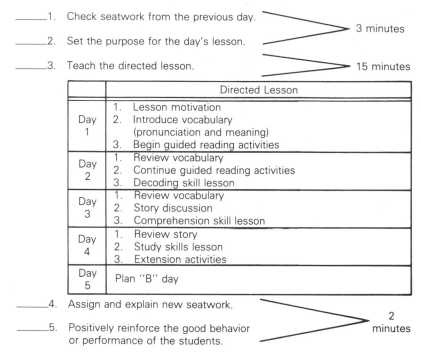

_____1. Check seatwork from the previous day.

_____2. Set the purpose for the day's lesson.

> 3 minutes

_____3. Teach the directed lesson.

> 15 minutes

	Directed Lesson
Day 1	1. Lesson motivation 2. Introduce vocabulary (pronunciation and meaning) 3. Begin guided reading activities
Day 2	1. Review vocabulary 2. Continue guided reading activities 3. Decoding skill lesson
Day 3	1. Review vocabulary 2. Story discussion 3. Comprehension skill lesson
Day 4	1. Review story 2. Study skills lesson 3. Extension activities
Day 5	Plan "B" day

_____4. Assign and explain new seatwork.

_____5. Positively reinforce the good behavior
or performance of the students.

> 2 minutes

Figure 3–14   Daily reading lesson checklist

Note. From C. Milner, Principal, Hayward Unified School District, Hayward, California. Reprinted by permission.

Planning the Directed Reading Lesson

To cover these four basic steps in the 20-minute directed teaching period usually requires three to five days, depending on the group's level, the story's length, the teacher's skill, and other factors. Figure 3–14 shows a daily reading lesson checklist of the types of activities that might occur in a typical directed reading group over a four-day period. Each day the teacher (1) checks the previous day's seatwork; (2) sets the purpose for the day's lesson; (3) teaches the directed lesson; (4) assigns and explains the new seatwork; and (5) positively reinforces group members. Components of the directed reading lesson are under item 3. Also, the approximate time for each activity is noted.

Figure 3–15 illustrates an actual lesson plan for one day's directed teaching period, day 3 on the chart in Figure 3–14. The lesson was planned for a group of fourth graders and should be completed in about twenty minutes.

Alternatives to the Directed Reading Lesson

Although basal reader programs recommend the directed reading lesson most often, other approaches are sometimes used. Russell G. Stauffer (1981) describes two such alternatives, the Directed Decoding Activity (DDA) and the Directed Reading-Thinking Activity (DRTA).

The **_Directed Decoding Activity_** is often used for first and second graders in phonics-based basal programs using a synthetic method. According to Stauffer, the DDA uses the following steps:

1. Teacher models
2. Pupils imitate
3. Teacher reinforces or remodels. (p. 66)

The manual urges the teacher to follow directions precisely. Specific and detailed, the directions may include a series of hand or voice signals. The method emphasizes training pupils to associate letters with sounds and to use that information in decoding. Ample repetition is provided and students receive verbal praise when

Date: ___11-16___   Room: ___20___   Teacher: ___Cheryl Milner___

Objective:
1) Review vocabulary.
2) Finish story discussion.
3) Students will find the topic sentence of a given paragraph.

Number of students: ___8___   Ginn Level: ___9 - "Discovering Dinosaurs"___
pp. 184–97

Materials:
1) Dinosaur-shaped Vocabulary Chart T.M. 152.
2) Class Checksheet of names.
3) Chalkboard & partial list of facts about "Dinosaurs."
4) Charts - Main Idea Steps & Paragraph pp. 190, 194.
5) Story paper for class books. Six Skilpaks.

Procedures:
1) *Check Seatwork from Previous Day*

2) *Purpose/Motivation* - "Today we will:
   a. Check to see how many of the new vocabulary words each of you remember."
   b. Complete our list of facts about dinosaurs."
   c. Each be able to find the topic sentence of a paragraph I give you."

3) *Vocabulary* - "Use your fingers to show me the number of the word I give the definition for. Wait until I say show me." "Read the word—." (Record words missed on checksheet)

4) *Discussion* of Story Facts T.M. 153
   a. Complete the list of facts started yesterday. Students may use lists from their seatwork assignment.
   b. "Which facts suggest that dinosaurs were unusual animals?"

Figure 3–15   Lesson plan for one day's directed teaching period

Note. From C. Milner, Principal, Hayward Unified School District, Hayward, California. Reprinted by permission. Plan organized around a story from *Inside Out* by T. Clymer, D. J. Bissett, and G. Wulfing (Lexington, Mass.: Ginn, 1976), 184–97.

they successfully imitate the teacher's modeling of decoding tasks. Stauffer describes the DDA approach as:

. . . a sound-letter naming technique that is basically a mechanical way of blending sounds into spoken word units. The tactical phase of D-D-A instruction is one of pupil imitation and repetition totally teacher oriented. (p. 67)

The *Directed Reading-Thinking Activity*, which Stauffer advocates, uses the following steps:

1. Identifying purposes for reading.

   a. Individual pupil purposes
   b. Group purposes
2. Adjusting the rate of reading to the purpose(s) declared and to the nature and difficulty of the material.
3. Achieving reading purposes.
4. Developing comprehension. (p. 70).

The DRTA differs from the traditional directed reading lesson. For example, pupils largely determine the purposes for reading. They must generate questions about the selection, read the selection, and then validate the answers to their

5) *Topic Sentences* T.M. 159 (comprehension)
   a. Review definitions of topic sentence.
   b. Review steps to find topic sentence/main idea.
      Chart:
      1. *Read* the paragraph.
      2. *Study* each sentence.
      3. *Ask yourself:* What one thing were all the sentences about?
      4. *Find* the topic sentence or main idea.
      5. *Check* each sentence in the paragraph with your answer.
   c. Use chart p. 190 to do each step aloud with the group.
   d. Use chart p. 194 (numbered sentences). Ask students to follow the steps, and at signal (show me) have students hold up fingers to indicate the number of the topic sentence.
   e. If students need more guided practice use the first paragraph on Skilpak p. 64.

6) *Closure*
   "Today we learned some ways that dinosaurs were unusual. At your seat, you are going to illustrate one fact about dinosaurs for our book.

   You also found topic sentences of paragraphs using the steps on the chart. You are going to practice this by yourself at your seat."

7) *Follow-up*
   Give directions for seatwork and independent activity. Praise students appropriately.

Evaluation:
   1) Every pupil response to vocabulary activity.
   2) Illustration for class book.
   3) Skilpak p. 64.

Follow-up Activities:
   1) Skilpak p. 64. (Seat)
   2) Illustrate and write one fact about dinosaurs. (Seat)
   3) Independent activity - Read books about dinosaurs. (Table)

Figure 3–15   (Continued)

questions through group judgment. The teacher serves as a catalyst or agitator by providing thoughtful questions. Stauffer outlines the teacher's responsibilities as follows:

1. Activate pupil thoughts (What do you think?)
2. Agitate reflective thought (Why do you think so?)
3. Require evidence (Prove conclusions) (p. 70)

The DRTA approach is often considered a more thought-provoking and creative strategy and probably requires more skill on the part of the teacher than the traditional directed reading lesson.

Florence T. Pieronek (1979) suggests an "ideal integrated reading lesson plan." This approach combines the crucial aspects of the DRTA and the traditional directed reading lesson and consists of the following steps:

1. Concept development
2. Vocabulary recognition
3. Setting overall goals for comprehension
4. Directed reading and thinking activity
5. Purposeful oral reading
6. Follow-up activities
7. Enrichment

DISCIPLINE

Although discipline is rarely covered in reading methods texts, it is imperative to alert the beginning teacher to this problem. Almost every survey of teachers, school administrators, and parents in recent years has named discipline as the number one problem in American schools. It is impossible to be an effective teacher of reading, regardless of instructional knowledge and skill, unless one can also work effectively with problem children. Schools or classrooms without any discipline problems are rare.

Teachers in inner-city schools often remark that capable suburban teachers would not last a week in overcrowded settings where discipline presents a constant challenge. Today, however, many of the problems that were once limited to schools in economically poor communities now appear in schools that serve middle class and affluent students. Causes of discipline problems are complex, but are finally unimportant to the teacher who wants to help children learn. What matters is solutions.

It is sad to see many otherwise capable and potentially successful teachers leave the profession because of their inability to handle discipline problems. Such an exodus is unnecessary, because the skills required to effectively handle discipline problems *can be learned* if teachers are given proper guidance and assistance. Beginning teachers should not have to learn how to handle discipline problems "off the seat of their pants."

One teacher's experiences can show how discipline problems ruin a reading program and nearly destroy self-confidence. Susan had been teaching for eight years when she was assigned a first-grade class in an urban school. A full-time aide was assigned to the class and teachers could draw on an impressive collection of the latest teaching materials and instructional aids. When the reading consultant first observed Susan's class, he saw a teacher attempting to instruct a group of students on a rug around her, most of whom were off-task. Some students occasionally punched each other, and elsewhere in the room, children were rude and abusive to the aide and each other. One child, for example, continually left his seat, went to the drinking fountain, took a mouthful of water, and spit it at another child on his way back to his seat. Another child was so boisterous that the teacher finally interrupted the group and attempted to discipline him. This 6-year-old child responded by raising his middle finger in the familiar salute of contempt. A few well-behaved children sat with their heads on the table and their arms over their heads as if for self-protection. The teacher had lost control, and the class was in chaos, not only during the reading period but also the rest of the day.

Such a situation is not really unusual. At an inservice session for about forty school principals, the consultant remarked that in nearly every elementary school, at least one classroom exists in which the teacher has lost control. No one disagreed. One principal said, "I was a principal at _____ school for ten years and we *never* had a class like that. But the school I am assigned to this year must have at least four."

Susan, however, had several advantages: she freely admitted that she had a problem, that she was part of the problem, and that she was open to help. She was getting discouraged and planned to resign from teaching if the same thing happened again.

As is frequently the case, Susan's difficulties were exacerbated by discipline problems elsewhere in the school, especially on the playgrounds, while students were lining up, during lunch period, and so forth. The consultant first persuaded the principal and other staff members to address the problem schoolwide. Susan then received a pep talk from the consultant, support from other teachers, and, most important, a specific plan for solving her problems.

The consultant worked with Susan, but had no magical cures. Rather, Susan worked hard, planned carefully, practiced new teaching behaviors, in particular learning how to assert herself, and closely observed the consultant when he demonstrated effective discipline practices. The room was reorganized, expectations for the children's behavior were made clear, positive rewards and negative consequences for children's behavior were established, and parents were involved. Susan learned a series of effective management techniques, such as providing enough work to keep students busy, that helped keep her students on-task, let her students know that she liked them, and emphasized the positive. When children misbehaved, Susan learned to discipline them quickly, consistently, and dispassionately. She learned to always follow through.

For Susan, the most difficult aspect of her retraining was learning to assert herself with her students, to let them know that she meant what she said. This is important for any teacher, but it is essential with a group of children—even first graders—who are out of control. The consultant's demonstrations were particularly helpful in this regard. One day, during a large group lesson, a number of children became boisterous and unruly. When Susan began to lose control, the consultant, with Susan's permission, took over the lesson. He reestablished good behavior by asserting his authority; he used his voice and body language to let students know their misbehavior would not be tolerated. Susan then resumed the lesson without further problems and taught the rest of the day without incident. Later the consultant asked her what made the difference. Susan replied:

I observed you do it and saw that the kids were behaving. I just decided that from then on I would pretend I was you. When a kid did something that he wasn't supposed to do, I tried to react as I thought you would. It worked. I really think I can handle these kids now. I feel wonderful.

The teacher realized she had to change her *behavior*, and, to her credit, she kept trying until she did.

Susan's class did not become a group of angels overnight. Indeed, Susan had to maintain firm control for the remainder of the year. Although not the most desirable way to teach, such control is certainly preferable to chaos.

The following fall Susan once again taught first grade. She decided it was her "make it or break it" year. She specifically requested a disproportionate number of low readers for her room because she wanted to use her skills as a reading teacher.

Both Susan and her children performed admirably. Discipline problems became a thing of the past. Her new techniques were a part of her; she had stage presence. As the year progressed, Susan saw she could give these students much more freedom than she thought possible, for her classroom was now a model of cooperative, calm, productive, stimulating, and joyful learning.

Some time later, the consultant conducted an unscientific investigation of the achievement of Susan's pupils. The consultant examined the mean or average pre– and post–test reading scores of Susan's former students. (In this school, all students were tested on a standardized achievement test in the fall and spring of each year.) Over a three-year period, the students' average reading growth was charted:

Year One (before Susan received any assistance): Mean growth per child = 0.4 years

Year Two (while Susan was receiving assistance): Mean growth per child = 0.7 years

Year Three (after Susan received assistance): Mean growth per child = 1.7 years

Again, no *one* approach works for all teachers. Teachers' individual teaching styles and the situations they are in determine which approach is best. Some experts advocate a democratic approach in which students decide what is appropriate school behavior. Other experts recommend an authoritarian approach in which the teacher assumes a benevolent dictator role. (For those who would like to read more about approaches to effective discipline, see the Additional Reading list at the end of the chapter.)

The following list includes some suggestions for establishing and maintaining classroom discipline. Neither all-encompassing nor novel, these ideas *are* effective for most teachers in most situations. Keep these suggestions in mind when you find it difficult to maintain appropriate student behavior.

1. Be fair, be firm, be consistent. Do *not* be mean. Teachers need to establish their authority, but this can be done in a positive and caring way.

2. Do not be afraid to let children know

that you are a person. (They do think teachers sleep in their desk drawers, you know.) Share your personal experiences and feelings with students.

3. Make school fun, interesting, nonthreatening, and less frustrating. Although school and learning cannot be these things all the time, they can certainly be like this some of the time.

4. Keep students busy. Idle minds may lead to disruptive behavior.

5. Set clear limits for student behavior on the first day of school. Most teachers find it helpful to post *a few* rules and to discuss expectations for behavior with students.

6. Provide clear, specific consequences for infractions and some reward or recognition for good behavior. These consequences usually do *not* work:
   a. group punishment of any kind for the misdeeds of a few—this is not only ineffective, it is also immoral;
   b. humiliation, embarrassment, or sarcasm;
   c. idle threats;
   d. write 100 times;
   e. extra homework;
   f. denial of recess (except for students who misbehave *during* recess) or some other enjoyable part of the day;
   g. a bawling out;
   h. stand in the corner, head down on the desk, etc.

   Here are some consequences that sometimes work:
   a. removal from the class for a period of time;
   b. parent notification;
   c. involvement of the principal or other school authority figure;
   d. detention;
   e. suspension or expulsion.

   These steps can be followed if negative consequences are necessary:
   a. *one* (and only one) warning;
   b. letter sent (via U.S. mail) to parents notifying them of infraction;
   c. exclusion (to another classroom or principal's office where student will be supervised) for a minimum of one-half day, with another note to parents;
   d. four-way conference (teacher, parent, principal, child) to issue final warning, clarify concerns;
   e. suspension (length will vary according to school district code, seriousness of problem, etc.)
   f. expulsion (may now be a legal matter, may not even be a possibility in some schools regardless of offense);
   g. for serious offenses, such as violence, threats, severe defiance, go immediately to steps d or e; otherwise always go through steps in order;
   h. if it is necessary to go beyond step b for more than a few students, something is wrong. Have a supervisor, principal, or colleague intercede and give you direct assistance. Most teachers get to step d sooner or later but many never find it necessary to suspend a child.

   Here are some suggestions for rewards or recognition:
   a. parent notification;
   b. certificates;
   c. publication of achievement in parent newsletter, school newspaper, bulletin boards, etc.;
   d. special privileges or activities;
   e. special treats, such as special time with teacher, small prize, or trip.

7. Be sure that all students and parents have received a written copy of the school and classroom rules and the series of positive and negative consequences. Parents should sign a form indicating that they have read the discipline policy and the parents' signatures should be kept on file.

8. Teachers *must* follow-through with disci-

plinary actions quickly, consistently, and, if possible, dispassionately.

9. Teachers should keep records of specific incidents committed by problem students.

10. Always inform the principal if you are having difficulties but do not expect her to solve your discipline problems for you.

11. Consider visiting with parents in their homes. Some teachers try to visit the parents of all their students. This takes time but can have enormous benefits and actually save time in the long run.

12. Promote camaraderie, spirit, and good morale within your class. Let students know you think they are special.

13. Do not *try* to get kids to like you or to be their pal.

14. Expect to have one or more students who "don't belong in a regular classroom" each year.

15. Do not attempt to deal with a student if he is angry. Always let the student cool off first.

16. Do not get into arguments with students. Even when you win, you lose.

17. Do not ever chase students (unless you are absolutely sure you can catch them!).

18. Never make a threat that you are not prepared to carry out. Better yet, think carefully before you make any threats.

19. Try not to reveal your favorites, although it is impossible not to have them.

20. Do not lose your temper (too often).

21. Eliminate the words "the next time" from your vocabulary.

22. Beware of the self-fulfilling prophecy. Do not lie in wait for a student to misbehave. Try to challenge yourself to be the most successful with students who have a history of discipline problems.

23. Do not be afraid to laugh at yourself or admit mistakes. Try not to take students' misbehavior personally.

24. Reach back for your reserve supply of self-confidence. If it is hiding, then pretend. Your goal is to master stage presence. Be patient. It takes time to learn how to handle such a difficult task.

SUMMARY

This chapter covers various aspects of organizing and managing classroom reading instruction. The recent research on teacher effectiveness has helped educators identify the crucial classroom conditions and teacher behaviors that promote student achievement in reading. Also, a variety of organizational plans and grouping strategies have been devised to improve the quality of classroom reading instruction. The chapter covers the advantages of ability grouping, explores some of the issues surrounding this practice, and provides a step-by-step procedure for effectively grouping children for instruction.

A basic instructional plan for the daily reading program enables the teacher to meet with each group each day by allocating time for directed teaching, seatwork, and independent activities. Several types of activities can take place during each of these periods. Management concerns, such as room arrangement, establishing routines, and using aides and volunteers, are also discussed.

The last part of the chapter describes the directed reading lesson, offers suggestions for planning lessons, and discusses the maintenance of good student discipline.

Several checklists can help you understand the concepts presented.

The tasks of organizing and managing effective reading instruction are not mastered quickly or easily. For most teachers success only comes after substantial experience and frequent failure. Though difficult and complex for the beginning teacher, these organizational and management tasks can be achieved. Many teachers run excellent, well-managed reading programs that follow the guidelines presented. These teachers enjoy the process of teaching children to read, and their students do indeed learn to read successfully.

REVIEW QUESTIONS

1. What are the three critical beliefs and four critical conditions necessary for successful classroom reading programs?
2. List some of the observable characteristics of effective classroom reading programs.
3. What are some of the critical classroom factors and teacher behaviors identified with high reading achievement?
4. What are some of the limitations of process-product research?
5. What is direct instruction? How might it be distinguished from other activities that occur in elementary classrooms?
6. What is the relationship between class size and student achievement?
7. Briefly describe or define each of the following organizational plans or grouping strategies: (a) homogeneous grouping; (b) heterogeneous grouping; (c) nongraded schools; (d) Joplin plan; (e) staggered reading; (f) departmentalization; (g) team teaching; (h) open schools.
8. What are the advantages and disadvantages of grouping students by ability for reading instruction?
9. What procedures should be followed in assigning students to classroom reading groups?
10. Describe the basic instructional plan for reading instruction. What are some of the advantages of this plan?
11. What steps can you take to organize yourself for efficient direct instruction?
12. What considerations should you keep in mind when assigning workbook pages?
13. What activities can be assigned as alternatives to workbook pages?
14. Suggest some activities that would be appropriate for the independent activities segment of the basic instructional plan. What activity is *most* appropriate?
15. How might you help students effectively establish a routine for quick, quiet transitions between reading group activities?
16. Give some examples of every-pupil-response techniques. Why use these activities?
17. What ways can teacher aides, parent volunteers or student helpers assist you in the reading program?
18. Describe each of the four basic components of the directed reading lesson.
19. How does the directed reading-thinking activity differ from the directed reading lesson?
20. Provide lists of appropriate classroom rules and steps to follow in dealing with students' good behavior and misbehavior. How should these lists be communicated to students and parents?

REFERENCES

Anderson, L. M., Evertson, C. M., & Brophy, J. E. An experimental study of effective teaching in first-grade reading groups. *Elementary School Journal*, March, 1979, *79*, 193–223.

Arnold, R. D. Class size and reading development. In J. E. Merritt (Ed.), *New horizons in reading*. Newark, Del.: International Reading Association, 1974.

Aulls, M. W. *Developing readers in today's elementary school*. Boston: Allyn and Bacon, 1982.

Brookover, W. B., & Lezotte, L. W. *Changes in school characteristics coincident with changes in student achievement.* East Lansing, Mich.: Institute for Research on Teaching, 1979.

Brophy, J. E. *Advances in teacher effectiveness research.* East Lansing, Mich.: Institute for Research on Teaching, 1979.

Clymer, T., Bissett, D. J., & Wulfing, G. *Inside out—Reading 720, Level 9.* Lexington, Mass.: Ginn, 1976.

Cushenberry, D. C. The Joplin Plan and cross grade grouping. In W. Z. Ramsey (Ed.), *Organizing for individual differences.* Newark, Del.: International Reading Association, 1967.

Dechant, E. V. *Improving the teaching of reading* (3rd ed.). Englewood Cliffs, N. J.: Prentice-Hall, 1982.

DiLorenzo, L. T., & Salter, R. Co-operative research on the nongraded primary. *Elementary School Journal,* February, 1965, *65,* 269–77.

Ekwall, E. E., & Shanker, J. L. *Diagnosis and remediation of the disabled reader* (2nd ed.). Boston: Allyn and Bacon, 1983.

Esposito, D. Homogenous and heterogenous ability grouping: Principal findings and implications for evaluating and designing more effective educational environments. *Review of Educational Research,* Spring, 1973, *43,* 163–79.

Guthrie, J. T., Martuza, V., & Seifert, M. Impacts of instructional time in reading. In L. B. Resnick & P. A. Weaver (Eds.), *Theory and practice of early reading* (Vol. 3). Hillsdale, N.J.: Lawrence Erlbaum Associates, 1979.

Harris, A. J. The effective teacher of reading, revisited. *Reading Teacher,* November, 1979, *33,* 135–40.

Harris, A. J., & Serwer, B. L. The CRAFT project: Instructional time in reading research. *Reading Research Quarterly,* Fall, 1966, *2,* 27–56.

Kiesling, H. Productivity of instructional time by mode of instruction for students at varying levels of reading skill. *Reading Research Quarterly,* 1977–78, *13,* 554–82.

Koenke, K. Toward effective use of teacher aides. *Reading Teacher,* May, 1979, *32,* 996–99.

Martin, L. S., & Pavin, B. N. Current research on open space, nongrading, vertical grouping and team teaching. *Phi Delta Kappan,* January 1976, *57,* 310–15.

May, F. B. *Reading as communication.* Columbus, Ohio: Charles E. Merrill, 1982.

McDonald, F. *Beginning teacher evaluation study: Phase II, 1973–74.* Princeton, N. J.: Educational Testing Service, 1976.

Medley, D. *Teacher competence and teacher effectiveness: A review of process-product research.* Washington, D.C.: American Association of Colleges of Teacher Education, 1977.

Miller, W. H. The Joplin Plan—Is it effective for intermediate-grade reading instruction? *Elementary English,* November, 1969, 951–54.

Newport, J. F. The Joplin plan: The score. *Reading Teacher,* November, 1967, *21,* 158–62.

Pieronek, F. T. Using basal guidebooks—The ideal integrated reading lesson plan. *Reading Teacher,* November, 1979, *33,* 167–72.

Powell, M. New evidence for old truths. *Educational Leadership,* October, 1979, *37,* 49–51.

Rosenshine, B. V. Content, time, and direct instruction. In P. L. Peterson & H. J. Walburg (Eds.), *Research on teaching: Concepts, findings and implications.* Berkeley, Calif.: McCutchan Publishing, 1979.

Rupley, W. H., & Blair, T. R. Research revisited: Teacher effectiveness research in reading instruction: Early efforts to present focus. *Reading Psychology*, Fall, 1980, *2*, 49–56.

Samuels, S. J. Characteristics of exemplary reading programs. In J. T. Guthrie (Ed.), *Comprehension and teaching: Research reviews.* Newark, Del.: International Reading Association, 1981.

Stallings, J., Cory, R., Fairweather, J., & Needles, M. *A Study of basic reading skills taught in secondary schools.* Palo Alto, Calif.: Stanford Research Institute, 1978.

Stauffer, R. G. Strategies for reading instruction. In M. P. Douglass (Ed.), *Reading: What is basic? 45th Yearbook, Claremont reading conference.* Claremont, Calif.: Center for Developmental Studies, 1981.

ADDITIONAL READING

Canter, L., & Canter, M. *Assertive discipline: A take charge approach for today's educator.* Los Angeles: Lee Canter and Associates, 1976.

de Zafra, C., Jr. *62 suggestions to improve classroom discipline.* Fairfield, N.J.: The Economics Press, 1968.

Epstein, C. *Classroom management and teaching: Persistent problems and rational solutions.* Reston, Va.: Reston Publishing Company, 1979.

Howell, R. G., Jr., & Howell, P. L. *Discipline in the classroom: Solving the teaching puzzle.* Reston, Va.: Reston Publishing Company, 1979.

Koerner, T. F. (Ed.). *NASSP Bulletin*, 1981, *65*, 1–78.

Martin, R., & Lauridsen, D. *Developing student discipline and motivation.* Champaign, Ill.: Research Press, n.d.

Wallen, C. J., & Wallen, L. L. *Effective classroom management* (abridged ed.). Boston: Allyn and Bacon, 1978.

4

Readiness for Reading

Reading readiness fascinates scholars from several different disciplines, so a lot of research has been done in the field. But many questions about children's early reading development remain unanswered. The literature is replete with claims, counterclaims, and opinions. Experts do not agree on how or when children should learn to read. Nor do they concur on the timing or practices that teachers and parents ought to use to ready youngsters for learning to read.

The term *reading readiness* can mean two different concepts. On the one hand, reading readiness refers to the child's *state of prepared-*

ness for the reading task. A child is ready when he has mastered the various skills thought to be prerequisites to reading. Unfortunately, experts do not agree on what skills or abilities are essential prereading tasks. Furthermore, some skills seem to be prerequisites for some children but not for others. The term reading readiness also refers to the *type of instruction* that children receive before actually learning to read. Once again experts disagree about what constitutes appropriate reading readiness activities.

Albert J. Harris and Edward R. Sipay (1979) define reading readiness so that it incorporates both of these notions. They state:

> Reading readiness is the state of general development of children that allows them to learn to read without undue difficulty. A reading readiness program comprises the methods and materials used to help children who have not yet attained the needed level of maturity. (p. 34)

A persistent question about beginning reading instruction is: When is a child ready to read? Seemingly an innocent question, it generates considerable debate and disagreement. The problem is that the question does not define the terms *ready* and *read*. As Walter H. MacGinitie (1976) points out: "We cannot answer 'Is the child ready?' unless we specify 'Ready for what?' " (p. 879). Although many children are not ready to receive formal decoding instruction until at least age six, nearly all four- and five-year-olds can benefit from exposure to language and books. MacGinitie suggests that when, how, and what readiness activities should begin depends on the type of instructional program planned for children.

READING READINESS AND BEGINNING READING PROGRAMS

At present, a dichotomy exists between reading readiness programs and beginning reading programs. The former often begin in preschool, kindergarten, or first grade, while the latter begin for some children in kindergarten and for most in first grade. However, a child does not suddenly graduate from readiness prepared for beginning reading instruction. Rather, the process is a continuum over which children move at individual rates.

Usually, predecoding skills, such as auditory and visual discrimination and letter knowledge, are taught in reading readiness, while word recognition and word analysis skills, such as recognizing sight words and learning phonics skills, are taught in beginning reading programs. However, many readiness programs also include components for teaching sight words and sound-symbol correspondence.

Teachers often present reading readiness activities in a relaxed, flexible atmosphere. They may feel little pressure to insure that all students get to a certain point by a certain time. By contrast, the first-grade teacher, usually seen as most responsible for the development of beginning reading skills, often feels considerable pressure about children's reading progress. That pressure may partly cause the less flexible, more structured, more intensive teaching usually associated with beginning reading instruction. Although the reading readiness/beginning reading dichotomy may be an artificial distinction, actual teaching practices in kindergartens and first grades may differ a lot. For example, many kindergarten teachers do not want to form assigned reading groups, while most first-grade teachers take for granted the necessity for small group instruction.

Presently more children are taught to read at an earlier age, which may explain why some of the differences between typical kindergarten and first-grade reading programs are decreasing. Lloyd O. Ollila (1980) has pointed out that reading instruction rarely occurred before first grade in American schools until the early 60s. In the kindergarten "there was no deliberate, systematic, sequential program for developing prereading skills" (p. 5). Even children who could read when they entered kindergarten usually received no help and little encouragement. According to Ollila, several factors have altered that situation: (1) the launching of Sputnik; (2) numerous reports in the literature and popular press about early readers; and (3) increased early childhood education experiences, such as nursery schools, day care centers, Head Start programs, and TV programs such as *Sesame Street*.

As a result, Ollila reports that most kindergarten teachers now teach reading readiness, and approximately 25 percent of these also teach beginning reading skills. However, kindergarten programs still range from some teachers steadfastly refusing to expand the kindergarten program beyond play and socialization activities, to others devoting an inordinate amount of time to paper and pencil tasks.

REVIEW OF THE RESEARCH

Much of the research on reading readiness focuses on the relationship between these factors and future reading success: age; intelligence; visual skills; auditory skills; metalinguistic skills; letter knowledge; language development; other readiness factors.

Age

For many years teachers and parents have wondered when to begin reading instruction. Several different but related questions about age and beginning reading include: To what extent does the student's age, when beginning reading instruction, affect future reading success? Is there an optimal age for reading instruction to begin? Should children learn to read before entering school? Will early reading instruction prove beneficial or harmful to children in later years, with respect to both attitudes and reading abilities?

These questions are not easy to answer. Generally, little relationship exists between students' chronological age when they begin to read and their later reading achievement. In the United States, children usually begin reading instruction at age six. Children in British schools begin at age five, and in Sweden reading instruction begins at age seven. No evidence suggests that *any* of these ages is optimal.

It used to be assumed that children should

not learn to read until they reached a mental age of six years and six months on an intelligence test. An early study by Mabel Morphett and Carlton Washburne (1931) concluded that the high correlation between mental age and reading achievement justified such an arbitrary criterion. Although based on some false assumptions and containing methodological flaws, Morphett and Washburne's study contributed to the persistent notion that reading instruction should be delayed. Not until the mid 60s did the majority of educators seriously consider possible advantages of an earlier start in reading.

Dolores Durkin, a well-known investigator of early readers, began her first study of such children in 1958. Durkin (1977) states:

At that time, reading for children younger than six was hardly being encouraged. Instead, both professional educators and society as a whole openly frowned upon this type of precociousness and predicted nothing but problems for early readers once school instruction began. (p. 1)

She identified a first-grade population in Oakland, California of 5,103 children, of whom 49 (or approximately 1 percent) could read when they entered first grade. None of these children had received reading instruction in kindergarten. Durkin followed these children through sixth grade and found they maintained their advantage as readers. Durkin (1966) reported:

the average achievement of early readers who had had either five or six years of school instruction in reading [some of the children were double-promoted], was significantly higher than the average achievement of equally bright classmates who had six years of school instruction but were not early readers. (p. 41)

Durkin's second longitudinal study, begun in 1961 and covering three years, was conducted in New York City and, unlike the first study, examined the preschool experiences of nonearly readers as well as early readers. In this study, 156 (or approximately 3½ percent) of 4,465 first-grade children were early readers. Durkin again found that early readers maintained their reading achievement advantage over their counterparts.

In a third longitudinal study, Durkin (1974–75)

examined the reading performance of children who had received reading instruction as part of a language arts program for two years prior to first grade. These children were followed through grade four. Durkin found that the reading achievement of the early readers again exceeded that of the control group in each of the grades one through four. However, the differences were not significant in grades three and four. Thus, it appeared there may be no lasting advantage to an early start in reading. Durkin's observations of the classrooms persuaded her, however, that the early readers might have had higher achievement if teachers had taken advantage of the children's head start in their instruction.

Other studies of early readers have been reported by Michael Sampson and L. D. Briggs (1981), Durkin (1977), and William H. Teale (1980). Teale's excellent annotated bibliography includes summaries of more than one hundred studies of early readers. In addition to the Durkin studies, the investigation conducted by Joseph E. Brezeinski (1964) is cited most often. Brezeinski's work in Denver involved 4,000 entering first graders, 2,000 of whom composed the experimental group and received formal reading instruction in kindergarten. In grade one, one-half of the experimental group received adjusted instruction that capitalized on the early reading instruction, while the other half was placed in a regular program. Brezeinski found that the students receiving adjusted instruction maintained a reading achievement advantage through fifth grade over children who began reading in grade one. Those students not receiving adjusted instruction did no better than their counterparts who began to read in grade one. Although the Denver study has been criticized for a number of methodological flaws, the results and implications are similar to Durkin's.

In summarizing the research on early reading, Ollila (1972) concluded:

1. Most studies lend support to the claim that children who have an early start in reading will exhibit higher reading achievement than their later-starting counterparts and will maintain this advantage, especially if adjusted instruction is provided.

2. There is an indication that attitudes of kindergarteners toward reading may be partly related to the teacher's selection of children to participate in the early reading program.
3. So little is known about the effects of early reading on eyesight that even the most enthusiastic advocates should take cautious note.
4. Early reading seems neither to create nor prevent reading disabilities, problems of boredom, school adjustment, or psychological problems. (pp. 59–60)

Teale (1978) examined numerous studies of early readers to determine which environmental factors were repeatedly associated with early success. Four factors seemed to be closely related to an early start in reading:

1. A large number and great variety of reading materials were present in the home.
2. A great deal of reading took place in the home.
3. A variety of paper and pencil activities occurred in the home.
4. Parents and other important people in the child's life responded to the child's early reading efforts.

Research on early readers has helped to answer many questions about the effects of early reading and the characteristics of early readers. However, Judi Lesiak (1978) suggests that the following questions remain unanswered:

1. Which methods and materials are most effective for teaching kindergarten reading?
2. For how long should instruction take place?
3. How should early reading achievement be measured?
4. Is an early start really beneficial in the later grades?
5. What effect does early reading instruction have on the child's social and emotional development?
6. How do educators determine which children will benefit most from early reading instruction?

Based on the best information currently available, (1) there is no optimal age for beginning reading instruction; (2) many children can learn to read before entering first grade; and (3) an early start in reading does not harm children in later school years. As Albert J. Harris and Edward R. Sipay (1979) succinctly state:

Attempting to teach all nursery school or kindergarten children to read has little to recommend it. On the other hand, those who are ready to read and want to learn to read should not be denied the opportunity. (p. 73)

Intelligence

The role intelligence plays in learning to read is complex and not fully understood. Although IQ relates to both reading readiness and later reading achievement, no specific minimum IQ is necessary for reading ability and no maximum IQ guarantees reading success. Some children with relatively low IQs learn to read quite well while some extremely intelligent children have serious reading difficulties. Thus, though intelligence correlates with early reading success, intelligence tests simply cannot predict reading achievement with great accuracy.

As noted in Ekwall and Shanker (1983), IQ scores seem most predictive of reading scores for pupils with either very low or very high IQs. For the majority of students, with IQs between 85 and 115, the correlation with reading achievement is less significant, and many other readiness factors are probably more important.

Jane W. Torrey (1979) examined eleven studies of early readers and found early readers usually had high intelligence test scores. However, in most of the studies at least some students had average or below average scores. Torrey concluded that "intelligence is therefore not a crucial factor in reading" (p. 118).

Visual Skills

Since eyes play an obvious and important role in reading, children should receive regular and thorough vision screenings. Almost all experts agree that the vision screening customarily provided in schools does not detect many of the potentially serious vision difficulties children may possess. Teachers need to be alert to students' symptoms of possible vision problems: headaches, squinting, closing or covering one eye, tilting the head while working at a desk, or a variety of possible eye movement difficulties, such as omitting words, losing place, head movements, or finger pointing. A checklist of observable clues to classroom vision problems can be found in Ekwall and Shanker (1983, pp. 290–291).

It is difficult to determine the extent to which vision problems contribute to reading failure, partly because of the range of possible difficulties. For instance, the student may lack *visual acuity*, or the ability of the eyes to accurately resolve detail. Such problems can usually be identified through a proper visual examination by a professional vision specialist and may be corrected by prescription lenses. The teacher should refer the child for a complete evaluation if such difficulties are suspected.

However, a student may possess good visual acuity but still lack other necessary visual skills required for translating written symbols into meaning. According to the American Optometric Association (*A Closer Look at Reading and Vision*, 1979), seven other visual skills must be successfully integrated for a child to read efficiently: visual fixation, accommodation, binocular fusion, convergence, stereopsis, field of vision, and form perception. But *visual discrimination* has been studied most thoroughly as a factor in reading readiness. Visual discrimination refers to the child's ability to discriminate or see the likenesses and differences among visual stimuli, particularly letters and words.

In a comprehensive review of the research on the relationship between measures of visual discrimination and first-grade reading achievement, Thomas C. Barrett (1965) concluded that visual discrimination of letters and words was a better predictor of first-grade reading performance than visual discrimination of geometric designs and pictures. Barrett could not determine whether discrimination of letters or discrimination of words was the best predictor.

Other research studies and reviews (Paradis, 1974; Santa, 1975; Paradis and Peterson, 1975; and Downing and Lundsteen, 1980) have shown that most entering first graders can successfully discriminate letter and word forms. For the few students who cannot, providing visual discrimination exercises with pictures or shapes does not help. Rather, it is more appropriate to provide visual discrimination training with either letters or words. Carol M. Santa (1975) found that pretraining with words provided the greatest transfer to word learning.

Auditory Skills

Auditory acuity, like visual acuity, is considered a prerequisite for reading. It refers to the ability to hear sounds at various pitches (or frequencies) and at different volume levels; it can be evaluated quite easily by a trained professional. Auditory acuity problems are also often reflected in observable symptoms: cupping the hand behind the ear, tilting the head while listening, inappropriate responses to oral questions, and so forth. Other auditory abilities often assumed to be related to learning to read include *auditory attention, auditory closure, auditory blending*, and *auditory memory.* These abilities are not always defined by experts precisely or consistently, which makes their evaluation and relationship to reading somewhat difficult to establish.

Good auditory acuity is required for *auditory discrimination*, most often considered a crucial readiness factor. Auditory discrimination refers to the child's ability to hear the likenesses and differences among spoken sounds, which usually means the smallest units of sound or the *phonemes.* Much research has been conducted to determine the predictive value and the necessity of auditory discrimination as a prereading skill. Teachers assume that to use phonic skills to decode words, a child must first be able to distinguish the various sounds for which the letters stand. However, research has not shown that auditory discrimination ability is required for learning to read.

Some research reveals a positive relationship between auditory discrimination ability and reading achievement (Guy Bond and Robert Dykstra, 1967; Jerome Rosner, 1973; Gerald Strag and Bert Richmond, 1973). Edward Paradis and Joseph Peterson (1975) have noted that children from lower socio-economic backgrounds often have difficulty with auditory discrimination skills.

However, Dykstra (1966) concluded that, although auditory discrimination ability was highly correlated with reading achievement, no direct cause and effect relationship has been proved. He stated:

In view of the relatively low relationships found between the auditory discrimination abilities . . . and success in learning to read, the first-grade teacher should not expect that developing auditory discrimination of her pupils will be sufficient to insure their success in mastering the reading task. (p. 32)

Patrick Groff (1975) reviewed research on this topic and found ample justification for a cautious, skeptical attitude about the importance of auditory discrimination in learning to read. Susan Neuman's study (1981) found that auditory training could improve auditory skills but transferred little to actual reading ability.

Karl Koenke (1978) reported that three commonly used tests of auditory discrimination failed to agree on which students lacked the skill. Mary Ann Geissal and June Knafle (1977) noted that auditory discrimination tests were complicated by a number of factors, such as dialect differences, vocabulary range, and examiner bias. Thus, researchers cannot provide definitive measures of auditory discrimination ability, and its relationship to reading achievement is unclear.

After a thorough review of the literature, Reid Lyon (1977) concluded:

Although many of the investigations cited indicate that poor readers do manifest difficulties in auditory perception, an equal number of studies found good readers who demonstrated deficits in auditory skills and poor readers who demonstrated adequate auditory-perceptual abilities. (p. 570)

Metalinguistic Skills

Several researchers have tried to solve the puzzle of beginning reading development by examining children's acquisition of metalinguistic abilities. Linnea C. Ehri (1975) defines *metalinguistic skills*

Kindergarteners can learn to read many words.

as the child's "conscious awareness of and ability to manipulate language as an object" (p. 204). Karen K. Allan explains further:

Prior to schooling or reading, children use language for functional, communicative purposes. They are conscious of the content of their messages but not the language they are using to communicate their ideas. In this experimental use of language, children do not need consciously to analyze language. However, when they enter school and reading lessons begin, the metalinguistic viewpoint, or the conscious, analytic view of language is emphasized. Thus, the children's use of language needs to evolve from an unconscious, experimental use to a conscious, metalinguistic use. (p. 89)

One type of metalinguistic ability is the child's awareness of specific terms and concepts related to reading. Another type is the child's ability to identify and isolate linguistic segments or units of language.

Awareness of Specific Reading Concepts.
John Downing's theory of *cognitive clarity* (1979) suggests that children are confused about what they are supposed to learn when they approach the task of reading. Most children figure out how the written system matches oral language and thus understand how the alphabetic code translates to speech sounds.

But children may not understand specific reading terms or concepts. For example, many children do not understand the terms *word*, *sound*, and *letter*. To this list, Albert Harris (1979) adds *page*, *sentence*, *line*, *first*, *last*, *middle*, *before*, *after*, *above*, and *below*. Harris also points out that beginning readers may not know to move their eyes across the page from left to right and down the page from top to bottom.

Martha Evans, Nancy Taylor, and Irene Blum (1979) examined the predictive value of a series of written language awareness tests. They found that a *metalinguistic interview* given to first graders in September was the best predictor of reading ability in June. The metalinguistic interview consists of questions designed to assess the children's knowledge of the specific concepts described above.

Metalinguistic Ability to Isolate Segments of Language.   The term *segmentation* refers to a child's ability to recognize that when oral language is translated into print, the language is divided into discrete units, such as sentences, words, and phonemes (or individual sounds). Research by Downing and Peter Oliver (1973–74) found that preschool, kindergarten and first-grade children all confused isolated phonemes and syllables with spoken words. Normally, young children have difficulty recognizing these segments, which can impede the learning-to-read process since teachers name these units when teaching reading. Recent research has explored both the predictive value of several segmentation tasks (particularly those related to words) and the importance of these abilities in the readiness program. Allan (1982) found that segmentation ability tends to increase with reading ability and facilitates, though not necessarily causes, improved reading ability. Allan noted that children move from aural to visual contexts in their ability to segment words into their constituent phonemes. Similar findings were reported by Ehri (1975).

Nancy K. Lewkowicz (1980) examined several segmentation abilities and found that blending and oral phonemic segmentation were most closely related to reading and therefore should be taught in reading readiness programs. Lewkowicz defined **blending** as "responding to a sequence of isolated speech sounds by recognizing and pronouncing the word that they constitute" (p. 688). For example, if the teacher says, "What word is this—/F/,/I/,/Š/?", the child responds by pronouncing the word *fish*. Lewkowicz defined **oral phonemic segmentation** as the opposite process of "separately articulating (isolating) all the sounds of a word, in correct order" (p. 688). In this case, for example, the teacher would ask the child to say the sounds in the word *fish*.

Lise Wallach, Michael Wallach, Mary Dozier, and Nancy Kaplan (1977) concluded that the difficulty many disadvantaged children had with sounds did not stem from inadequate auditory discrimination but rather from their inability with tasks of phonemic analysis.

Tessa Roberts (1975) analyzed the skills of analysis (oral phonemic segmentation) and synthesis (blending) in the beginning stages of reading and ordered four skills from easiest to hardest:

1. *Auditory Synthesis* (no written material required): The child hears the sounds /F/, /I/, /Š/, and then blends them to pronounce the word *fish*.
2. *Auditory Analysis* (no written material required): The child hears the word *fish*, and then pronounces the phonemes in order.
3. *Auditory-Visual Synthesis:* The child looks at the written word *fish* and then pronounces the word.
4. *Auditory-Visual Analysis:* The child hears the word *fish*, and then writes the word correctly.

Roberts says the analysis skill is more difficult than the synthesis skill and that auditory-visual analysis is required for writing, not reading. Roberts also found that boys had more difficulty with all of these skills than girls had. Roberts points out (and much of the research verifies) that the first two skills are a more appropriate focus for reading readiness instruction than the type of auditory discrimination training often provided.

Letter Knowledge

Research shows that a child's ability to recognize and name the letters of the alphabet is highly correlated with later reading achievement. In their analysis of the First-Grade Reading Studies, Bond and Dykstra (1967) found that a letter-names test was the single best predictor of first-grade reading success. Because they concluded that the predictive validity of this single subtest equaled the predictive validity of an entire reading readiness battery, they said teachers should administer only a letter-names test for predicting students' future reading performance.

Robert E. Lowell (1971) also found that knowing letter names appeared to be the only item in the reading readiness battery that had significant predictive value. However, at the time of this research, many factors now considered important—such as metalinguistic abilities—were not routinely tested.

Margaret Ann Richek (1977–78) examined seven reading readiness tasks and two word-learning tasks (tasks that parallel sight and phonics approaches respectively) and once again found that the children's ability to recognize letters was the best predictor for either task. Richek also found that other readiness skills were highly predictive depending on the word-learning approach used. For the sight approach, visual discrimination skills and digit span memory (an auditory memory task in which the child repeats a series of digits back to the examiner) were highly predictive. For the phonics method, the child's ability to produce letter sounds and the ability to blend words together were highly predictive. Richek also determined that visual memory and auditory discrimination were *not* highly predictive regardless of approach used.

Thomas C. Barrett (1965) also identified letter knowledge as the best predictor of first-grade reading achievement. However, Barrett and other researchers have emphasized the distinction between correlations and causes. Barrett stated:

Children who were able to visually discriminate and name letters and numbers upon entrance into first grade very likely came from environments that had developed and reinforced this behavior as well as other abilities that, if measured in the study, would have aided in predicting first grade reading achievement. In other words, such an ability may be a symptom of many kinds of experiences with letters, numbers, words, and stories; therefore, it should not be assumed from this study that success in first grade reading will be insured by simply teaching children to discriminate, recognize, and name letters and numbers. (p. 281)

Thus, the best evidence suggests it is worthwhile to teach young children to recognize and name the letters of the alphabet, though mastery of this skill does not guarantee future reading success. Jana M. Mason (1980) found that letter knowledge can be learned by four-year-olds. She reported that this ability facilitates early reading, and parents can teach it to children before kindergarten.

Language Development

Obviously children's language ability affects their future reading success. Children adept at using oral language have an advantage over peers with immature language skills when they learn to read.

Language abilities can be divided into four areas that develop in this order: *listening, speaking, reading*, and *writing.* Listening, of course, develops very early in life, and children begin to speak at about age one. Most children do not learn reading and writing until they go to school.

Listening and reading are **receptive language abilities.** Similarly, speaking and writing are **productive language skills.** Using a receptive language skill, the child receives a message through her ears or eyes and uses the brain to translate the sounds or symbols into meaning. Using productive language abilities, the child does just the opposite; he creates the idea and then produces it in either speech or writing.

Certainly children who do not understand the meanings of English words cannot successfully read these words. Likewise, children cannot be expected to write words they cannot read. However, most researchers have found that five- and six-year-olds have rather extensive vocabularies. According to William K. Durr and John J. Pikulski (1981) and Violet B. Robinson, Dorothy S. Strickland and Bernice Cullinan (1977), early studies of five- and six-year-olds estimated that their speaking vocabularies averaged between 2,000 and 3,000 words. Later studies found that five-year-olds understand an average of between 5,000 and 6,000 words. Some studies found that first graders understood more than 20,000 words. Thus, most native English speakers enter school knowing the meaning of enough words to begin reading instruction.

The child's knowledge of sentence structure or syntax is also important to language development. Children lacking ability in this area often have trouble learning to read even if they have large vocabularies.

Although there seems to be a strong relationship between language development and future reading success, language skills are not easily measured. At present, definitive tests for predicting reading achievement based on various language abilities do not exist.

Other Readiness Factors

In addition to these readiness factors, many other readiness factors may contribute to young children's future reading performance: interest in reading; gender; visual-motor or visual-perceptual skills; general health; and social and emotional maturity.

Interest in Reading. A child's interest in reading may significantly affect her success, and being exposed to books in the home, preschool, or both appears to increase that interest. Several investigators have found that parents taking time to read aloud to their young children has many beneficial effects. George H. Walker, Jr. and Iris E. Kuerbitz (1979) reported that preschoolers who were read to had higher reading achievement at the end of first grade than their counterparts. Sandra McCormick (1977) reviewed several research studies that showed reading aloud to children improved reading performance (especially for children from lower socio-economic backgrounds), increased interest in and desire to read, and enhanced young children's language development.

Gender. In North America, considerably more boys than girls have difficulty learning to read and ultimately become disabled readers. However, evidence suggests that culture may play a more important role than gender. Downing and Lundsteen (1980) report that research from other countries, such as Germany, India, and Nigeria, reveals that boys there are superior readers. Downing and Lundsteen indicate that attitudes within a culture may affect children's reading performance. In the United States many adults view reading as feminine. Also, young children may be influenced by the gender of their teachers, who are more often women than men in American elementary schools. Some experts be-

lieve that physiological differences between young girls and boys predispose the girls to be better readers. Other theories suggest that beginning reading materials are more motivating for girls than boys or that behavioral differences account for the higher reading achievement of girls. Of course these differences occur among large groups of boys and girls; within any given classroom, many boys may be superior readers and some girls may have trouble reading.

Visual-Motor or Visual-Perceptual Skills. Researchers have often investigated the role visual-perceptual or visual-motor skills play in the learning-to-read process. They have devised ways to measure perceptual abilities and have developed several visual-perception or visual-motor training programs. But such programs often become fads.

Visual-perception programs may emphasize development of form perception, spatial relationships, or the ability to recall visual stimuli. Usually designed to improve students' ability to copy or reproduce visual stimuli, some programs focus on geometric shapes or letters, while others involve gross motor activities or physical coordination tasks.

These approaches all lack substantiation, through research, of their value, perhaps because identifying the particular components that contribute to reading ability is so difficult.

Although some studies show correlations between certain visual-perceptual or visual-motor abilities and early reading success, little evidence supports the effectiveness of training in this area. After reviewing a number of studies, Helen M. Robinson (1972) concluded:

The foregoing studies of the relationship of training in visual perception to reading achievement lead to no clear-cut conclusions. In general, this training results in improvement on tests of visual perception but seldom is resultant reading improvement, if any, substantial or lasting. Even the few early gains reported seem to disappear by second or third grade. (p. 141)

In another review, Stephen E. Klesius (1972) found that only eleven of thirty-eight studies were acceptable on methodological grounds. After close examination of these eleven studies, Klesius concluded:

Of the five studies that included measures of perceptual-motor ability, only two find significantly greater improvement in perceptual-motor ability for the experimental group when compared to the control group and none of these studies finds any concomitant increase in reading achievement. These findings are contrary to claims made for such programs. (p. 157)

Other researchers, including Frank R. Vellutino (1977), Ronald MacKeith (1977), and Jean Harber (1979), have also concluded that instruction based on perceptual approaches has little value in teaching young children to read.

General Health.   Children's general health may affect their success in learning to read, particularly if health problems result in frequent absences during the crucial first two years of school. Children with persistent allergies or frequent colds may temporarily lose some of their hearing, which affects their ability to profit from phonics instruction. Certainly if children come to school tired or hungry, their ability to learn is hampered.

Social and Emotional Maturity.   Although no specific tests or indexes can predict future reading success based on social and emotional maturity, experienced teachers of young children can easily identify those who are not mature enough to respond to early reading instruction.

To learn to read in school, young children must be able to sit still and pay attention during instruction. They also must be able to remain on-task and work independently some of the time. In addition, youngsters have to work cooperatively, handle some frustration, and follow verbal directions. Children without these abilities may benefit from instruction on these specific behaviors before direct reading instruction. In some cases, when teachers and parents are convinced a child needs more time to mature, the child may be held back from entrance to kindergarten or placed in a transition class between kindergarten and first grade. This difficult decision ultimately relies on the experience and good judgment of the classroom teacher and the parents.

Summary of Readiness Factors

Clearly, determining when a child is "ready" to learn to read is a complex task. Existing research suggests that letter knowledge and meta-linguistic abilities are measurable and strongly correlated with future reading success. The latter has emerged only recently and is not widely used as a measure of readiness at this time. Probably further refinement of metalinguistic tests will occur and their use will become more common.

Three other readiness factors seem strongly related to future reading success but are not easily measured: language development, interest in reading, and social and emotional maturity.

Four readiness factors are somewhat related to reading achievement but are either unreliable as predictors or the subject of inconclusive research. These factors are intelligence, visual skills, auditory skills, and general health. Children seriously deficient in any of these areas seem at a disadvantage in learning to read; however, strength or ability in these areas does not necessarily place children at an advantage. These factors are necessary, but not sufficient, conditions for learning to read.

Finally, three readiness factors seem to have little or no predictive value for future reading success: age, gender, and visual-motor or visual-perceptual skills. Research evidence has not established a specific age at which reading should be taught; although more boys than girls experience failure in reading, gender, in itself, is not predictive; and evidence suggests that little is gained from teaching visual-motor or visual-perceptual skills.

Undoubtedly, many abilities and conditions interact to allow a child to profit from reading instruction. Reading readiness is an individual matter. Some children learn to read without what some consider essential prerequisites, while others fail to learn to read even though they possess all the critical readiness skills.

Thus, teachers should be cautious about attempts to *measure* readiness for reading in a quantitative or formulaic way. In actual practice, decisions about what to teach and when to teach it are best made by teachers relying on a combination of performance measures, experience with young children, judgment, and intuition.

ASSESSING READINESS FOR READING

Teachers may use several approaches to evaluate students' readiness for reading: (1) vision and hearing screening; (2) standardized readiness testing; (3) other assessment tests; and (4) checklists and teacher observation.

Vision and Hearing Screening

Since the eyes play such an important role in learning and since vision problems are common, appropriate vision screening should be provided for all children before they begin reading instruction. Unfortunately, many schools still use the **Snellen test** for this purpose. This approach, invented in 1862, consists of a chart of seven rows of letters, decreasing in size from top to bottom. Each child stands 20 feet from the chart and reads as far down the chart as possible. Although this test may provide a fairly accurate measure of far-point visual acuity, it does not evaluate a child's acuity at the typical reading distance. The Snellen test also does not measure other potential visual difficulties, such as astigmatism, binocular ability, and visual fixation.

Two instruments commonly used to provide much more thorough screening of vision are *The Keystone Visual Survey Telebinocular Instrument* (Keystone View Division, Mast Development Company) and *The Master Orthorator Visual Efficiency Test* (Bausch & Lomb Optical Company). If, as a result of the screening or observation, you suspect a child has a vision problem, then refer the child to a professional vision specialist for a complete examination.

Hearing problems occur less often, so routine screening for all children may not be necessary. However, when children exhibit symptoms of hearing difficulty or fail to learn to read successfully, audiometric testing should be done. With proper instruments and a trained specialist, such testing is a simple procedure.

Teachers should (1) remember that some children may fail to learn to read because of correctible vision or hearing difficulties; (2) know the symptoms that mean a referral is in order; and (3) not diagnose such problems, but refer children to qualified specialists for evaluation.

Standardized Readiness Testing

Standardized reading readiness tests have been used for many years to predict future reading success and to identify children's strengths and weaknesses among selected readiness skills. Usually paper and pencil tests, these batteries are administered to kindergarteners or first graders.

Reading readiness batteries may include tests for the following skills or abilities: vocabulary development, listening, letter recognition, numbers, visual-motor abilities, rhyming words, phoneme correspondence, learning rate, auditory discrimination, auditory blending, word recognition, matching of words or symbols (visual discrimination), visual memory, using context clues, and following directions.

No reading readiness battery tests all these areas, and most batteries have only letter knowledge and visual discrimination in common. Even in these two areas the testing approaches vary considerably. Furthermore, many abilities that may be crucial to reading success—such as metalinguistic abilities, attending skills, and experiential background—are *not* evaluated by standardized readiness tests. As Robert T. Rude (1973) has pointed out: "There is a lack of consensus among test authors as to which skills should be assessed as well as the techniques employed to assess them" (p. 575).

Although research has shown that total test scores of readiness batteries predict future reading achievement for *groups* of children, these scores do not predict for *individual* students (Rosalyn A. Rubin, Bruce Balow, Jeanne Dorle, and Martha Rosen, 1978; John Pikulski, 1978; Paul Satz and Jack Fletcher, 1979). Tests seem to predict better for students who score high than for those who perform poorly. Individual subtest scores are usually not very reliable, which limits their diagnostic value. Indeed, authors of reading readiness tests usually emphasize the *predictive* value of the tests, however limited, rather than *diagnostic* benefits.

Nicholas Silvaroli and Warren Wheelock (1966) suggest that group standardized readiness tests are especially inappropriate for children from lower socio-economic groups. These children have particular difficulty following directions and would be better evaluated with individual tests. Any teacher who administers a group paper and pencil test to five- or six-year-olds quickly notices that many children are not sufficiently motivated or appropriately responsive to the testing situation. At the very least, the teacher must proctor the test carefully.

Reading experts have also criticized standardized reading readiness tests for the following reasons:

1. National norms may be inappropriate to the particular children being evaluated;
2. The population on which the test was standardized may not adequately reflect the various socio-economic and ethnic groups in our society;
3. The tests do not indicate what type of instruction would be most appropriate for individual children; and
4. Research has not clearly indicated that the skills typically evaluated on reading readiness tests are, in fact, essential for future reading success.

Thus, there is little value in investing either money or time in standardized readiness batteries. As teachers become aware of the tests' problems, their use declines in American schools. However, these batteries may have *some* value if their limitations are kept in mind. If used as only one source of information to *complement* other types of evaluation, then the tests' data may help in planning the reading readiness program.

These standardized reading readiness tests are commonly used:

- *Clymer-Barrett Prereading Battery*, Personnel Press.
- *Gates-MacGinitie Reading Tests: Readiness Skills*, Teacher's College Press.
- *Harrison-Stroud Reading Readiness Profiles*, Houghton Mifflin.
- *Lee-Clark Reading Readiness Test*, California Test Bureau.
- *Metropolitan Readiness Tests*, Psychological Corporation.
- *Murphy-Durrell Reading Readiness Analysis*, Psychological Corporation.

Other Assessment Tests

Criterion-Referenced Tests. *Criterion-referenced reading readiness* tests may be used as an alternative to standardized batteries. These tests evaluate students' specific abilities in relation to set criteria for mastery, rather than in comparison to a standardized population. Criterion-referenced tests may be readministered frequently, are given to students individually, and generally have greater diagnostic value than a standardized, group-administered test. Cathy Collins (1979) found that one such criterion-referenced test, the *PRS Prereading Skills Test*, was comparable or superior to two standardized readiness batteries in predictive power and diagnostic value.

Many basal reader programs provide criterion-referenced readiness tests, which may have the additional advantage of assessing the specific skills taught in the basal program.

Metalinguistic Interview. The metalinguistic interview, developed by Evans, Taylor, and Blum (1979), can be prepared by a teacher and may yield valuable information about children's readiness for reading. According to the authors, teachers should evaluate children's ability to do the following individual tasks:

1. demonstrate knowledge that the term alphabet and/or ABCs refers to letters;

1.	b	o	b	d	b
2.	R	P	P	R	R
3.	NM	NM	WN	MN	MN
4.	COP	PCO	COP	CPO	POC
5.	q	q	p	q	p
6.	n	u	m	n	n
7.	was	was	saw	saw	was
8.	house	horse	hous	house	huose
9.	were	very	ever	were	every
10.	pot	pet	pot	put	pat

Figure 4–1   An informal test for visual discrimination

2. both identify orally and locate on a page of print a single letter, a word, and a sentence (six different tasks);
3. demonstrate where to begin reading a book, where to begin reading a page, and where to continue reading after the page is completed. (For these three tasks, the child should have a book with a full-page picture as a distractor.)

Give one point for each task completed successfully and compare the children's total scores as a relative indicator of readiness ability. This approach has diagnostic value, since the teacher can easily identify specific metalinguistic abilities needed by each child. For example, if a child does not know the difference between a letter and a word, that skill can be taught directly.

Testing for Visual Discrimination.   Teachers may evaluate other readiness skills through informal testing procedures similar to those used on commercial tests. For example, a teacher can evaluate a child's visual discrimination skills by using a test sheet such as that shown in Figure 4–1.

The directions for this test are as follows: Give the prepared test sheet to the student. If necessary place a marker under each row as you proceed. Say, "I want to see how well you can use your eyes. Put a circle around the letters or words that look exactly like the first one in each line. Look very closely. There may be more than one right answer for each one." Do the first one or two with the child to make sure he understands the directions. You may go over the results with the student to see whether errors resulted from inattention, inability to follow directions, or lack of visual discrimination ability.

Remember, this type of testing is fraught with potential problems. Did the student understand the meanings of key words in the directions, such as *circle, letters, words, exactly like*, and *right answer*? Was the student sufficiently motivated and able to attend to the task? Did the student do well as a result of good guesses? In interpreting the results and comparing performance with that of peers, consider such questions.

The test uses only letters and words, since research shows that these forms are more appropriate for testing and teaching than shapes or other configurations, and it requires the student to make increasingly finer discriminations. You should use a test sheet with letters approximately the size of print the children see in their beginning reading materials. Also, this test should be administered only to those students who appear to have difficulty with this task.

Testing for Auditory Discrimination. To assess a child's auditory discrimination ability, do not give the child a prepared test sheet. Instead, ask the student to respond to pairs of words that you read out loud. The test in Figure 4–2 follows a common format for testing auditory discrimination. Record the child's responses and compare the results with those of other students.

Directions: To be given orally. Seat the child so that she cannot see your lips move. Tell the child: "This is a test to see how well you can use your ears. I will say two words to you. If they are the same, say 'same.' If they are different, say 'different.' Listen very carefully. Let's try some. Look - Look. Are they the same or different? (Pause) Good. How about Tree - Flee? (Pause) Good. Now, here are some more." Make sure the child understands the directions. Allow about ONE second between pairs. Repeat the items the child misses at the end of the test. Only starred items should be called "same" by the child. If starred items are missed, the test may be invalid.

Test:

1. Hat - Fat	11. Lack - Back
2. Pet - Put	12. Though- Show
3. Lag - Laugh	*13. Like - Like
*4. Can- Can	14. Robe - Rove
5. Bad - Bat	15. Should - Could
6. Look - Took	16. Sad - Said
7. Seem - Gleam	17. Tag - Tack
*8. Open - Open	18. Hat - Hot
9. Sit - Set	*19. Chief- Chief
10. Hum - Mum	20. Pass - Path

Figure 4–2 An informal test for auditory discrimination

Directions: Say: "I am going to say two words. If they rhyme, say 'yes'; if they do not rhyme, say 'no.' Listen very carefully. Let's try some: Hat - Mat. If they rhyme, say 'yes'; if they don't, say 'no.' (Pause) Good. How about: Red - Green? (Pause) Good. Now, here are some more."

Test:

1. Sing - Ring
2. Tree - House
3. Sun - Fun
4. Bright - Flight

5. Fast - Nap
6. Page - Life
7. Stop - Hop
8. Ball - Bat

Figure 4–3   An informal test for rhyming ability

Remember, testing may be unreliable, so check that children's errors result from auditory discrimination weaknesses and not other problems. The four starred items, the only like pairs, provide one check of validity. If the child misses any of these, he may have been inattentive or misunderstand the directions, since it is highly unlikely that the child can hear the same sounds as "different." On the other hand, a student may be unable to distinguish sounds that are in fact different (all of the other items on the test), and thus, the student who fails these items may lack adequate auditory discrimination.

Items 1, 6, 7, 10, 11, 12, and 15 test for discrimination of initial sounds, which are both the easiest and most important for most students. Items 2, 9, 16, and 18 test medial vowel sound discrimination. Items 3, 5, 14, 17, and 20 test discrimination of ending sounds, the most difficult and the least crucial prerequisites for reading success.

Testing for Rhyming Ability.   Some teachers assess children's ability to recognize rhyming words by using a format similar to that presented in the test for auditory discrimination. See Figure 4–3.

With this test, you want to see whether the child understands the concept of rhyme. Items 1, 3, 4, and 7 rhyme while items 2, 5, 6, and 8 do not. Item 5 calls for the finest discrimination of the four nonrhyming items.

Testing for Letter Knowledge.   To assess a student's ability to associate letter symbols with letter names, four tests should be given. Present these tests in decreasing order of difficulty, so that once a student demonstrates mastery, additional testing is not required.

The first test evaluates the student's ability to recognize and pronounce letter names when they are scrambled. Test only lowercase letters at this point to save time. If the student knows these, he can also recognize and pronounce the uppercase letters. Figure 4–4 shows this test sheet.

This test intentionally presents a sampling of the most confusing letters, for example, *b*, *p*, *d*, and *q*, to insure that it requires maximum discrimination. It is probably not necessary to test all 26 lowercase letters in this way.

If the student misses even one of the items, administer the next easier test, shown in Figure 4–5.

The remaining lowercase letters are presented in this test. The student identifies the appropriate letters when you pronounce them. This *recognition* task is easier than the *pronunciation* task required on the previous test. If the student passes this test, additional testing is not necessary. However, if the student fails even one item, administer the letter matching test shown in Figure 4–6.

If the student cannot match the appropriate lowercase letter with the equivalent uppercase

Directions: Have the student pronounce each of the letters in order without assistance. Note specific errors made.

b	p	d	q	g
n	u	r	m	
a	h	c	e	

Figure 4–4   An informal test for letter knowledge—most difficult task

letter, you may evaluate the student's visual discrimination ability (see Figure 4–1). If the student cannot complete the visual discrimination task successfully, then teaching such skills and/or a thorough vision examination would be useful before you teach letter knowledge.

Assessing Language Skills.   Although children's language abilities undoubtedly affect their early reading performance, these abilities are difficult to test. Often teacher observation and diagnostic instruction provide the most helpful clues for planning instruction. Jayne DeLawter and Maurice Eash (1966) examined samples of young children's speech and found these common basic errors: (1) failure to focus; (2) poor organization of ideas; (3) failure to clarify questions; (4) lack of supporting ideas; (5) inadequate descriptions; (6) lack of subordination; and (7) stereotyped vocabulary.

Two standardized tests, *The Test of Language Development* (TOLD) (Newcomer and Hammill, 1977) and *The Test of Early Language Development* (TELD) (Hresko, Reid and Hammill, 1981), have been developed to assess children's expressive and receptive language abilities in phonology, semantics, and syntax. These tests provide comparative indexes of children's language abilities but do not provide specific information for prescriptive instruction. The TOLD is designed for most children between the ages of 4 years, 0 months and 8 years, 11 months, while the TELD is intended for children with more severe language difficulties or less proficiency in English between the ages of 3 years, 0 months and 7 years, 11 months.

Many teachers, however, choose to evaluate language abilities as part of a reading readiness checklist.

Checklists and Teacher Observation

Several checklists for evaluating reading readiness have been devised. Figure 4–7 illustrates a brief and easy-to-complete checklist. Observe children over time and evaluate their abilities in

Directions: Have the student point to the letters as you pronounce them. Be sure to pronounce the letters in scrambled order. Note specific errors made.

f	l	t	k	s
i	o	j	z	
y	x	v	w	

Figure 4–5   An informal test for letter knowledge—less difficult task

Directions:	Have the student match the lowercase letter with the uppercase equivalent in the left column.			
1. B	p	b	c	t
2. N	n	m	s	v
3. F	l	p	g	f
4. T	f	t	l	d
5. J	i	n	j	g
6. Y	z	l	j	y
7. D	d	b	p	t
8. P	g	q	p	b
9. G	j	g	p	q
10. R	m	r	n	v
11. H	n	m	r	h
12. A	b	c	a	d
13. E	e	f	c	g

Figure 4–6   An informal test of letter matching of upper- and lowercase letters

	Satisfactory	Unsatisfactory
Interest in Reading		
1. Listens attentively to stories read		
2. Is interested in picture books		
3. Seeks out books to take home		
Oral Language		
1. Has command of a large number of words		
2. Can communicate effectively		
3. Speaks distinctly		
Auditory Discrimination		
1. Can hear rhyming words		
2. Distinguishes differences in sounds represented by letters		
Visual Discrimination		
1. Can see differences in unlike letters		
2. Can see differences in unlike word patterns		
Listening		
1. Recalls stories heard		
2. Can follow simple directions		
3. Can recall a sequence of events		
Left-to-right Orientation		
1. Scans a series of pictures from left to right		
2. Recognizes the left-to-right sequences of letters within words		
Letter Knowledge		
1. Can identify letters named		
2. Can name letters shown		
3. Can relate upper- to lowercase letters		
4. Begins to associate sounds with letters		
Social and Emotional Factors		
1. Can work in groups		
2. Displays self-control		
3. Works independently		
4. Attends to task		

Figure 4–7   An informal checklist for the evaluation of reading readiness

Note. From *The Teaching of Reading*, 6th ed., by Martha Dallmann, et al. Copyright © 1982 by CBS College Publishing. Reprinted by permission of Holt, Rinehart and Winston, CBS College Publishing.

eight important readiness areas; then use this information to determine instructional placements. Many teachers rely primarily on information such as that reported in the checklist to plan instruction for young children.

TEACHING READINESS FOR READING

This part of the chapter presents an overview of kindergarten reading programs and suggests specific procedures for teaching reading readiness skills.

DEVELOPMENT OF PREREADING SKILLS	
Direct Teaching	Incidental Teaching
Objectives projected into experiences.	Purposes arise out of experiences.
Emphasis on intellectual development.	Emphasis on psychological and social climate.
Analysis of knowledge and skills necessary.	Assessment of potential of children and environment.
Sequence of specific learning experiences.	Integrated learning experiences based on needs and interests.
Formal scheduling with definite time allocation.	Informal scheduling through large blocks of time.
Specific skills activities.	Skills embedded in interdisciplinary studies.
Objective evaluation.	Subjective evaluation.

Figure 4–8   Development of prereading skills

Note. From "Prereading Programs: Direct Versus Incidental Teaching" by E.M. King, *Reading Teacher*, 1978, *31*, 505. Copyright 1978 by *Reading Teacher*. Reprinted by permission.

An Overview of the Reading Readiness Program

Clearly many children can learn to read in kindergarten and virtually all children can profit from some form of readiness instruction, but no *one* way of constructing a kindergarten program exists. Ethel M. King (1978) suggests that educators are divided into two camps. One group believes in a focus on young children's cognitive development, with a highly structured and systematic program of teaching that emphasizes the learning of specific skills. The other group focuses on developing the whole child, emphasizes social and emotional development, and integrates incidental teaching of readiness skills into other developmental activities. King labels these two approaches *direct teaching* and *incidental teaching*, as described in Figure 4–8.

Obviously, the kind of kindergarten program a teacher might offer would vary considerably according to the approach used. King also summarized the results of ten studies comparing these approaches and concluded that the categorization of direct versus incidental teaching was, in reality, a false dichotomy. King recommended that teachers blend the two approaches:

Learning to read is too crucial to leave to chance through an incidental approach, and research supports this conclusion, especially for children of lower ability and those from disadvantaged homes. On the other hand, direct teaching will be a misguided effort if it becomes so formal and prescriptive that bored or frustrated children lack the ability to see relationships and make applications. Teaching may be direct without rote learning. However, it is essential to provide an accurate knowledge base for the child to use in informal, playlike activities. (p. 509)

Teachers can use both direct and incidental teaching if they structure and manage an appropriate learning environment, which is not an easy task. Kindergarteners come to school full of energy and excitement but often cannot do for themselves many things that older children manage without difficulty. Also, the teacher must deal with a wide range of interests and abilities.

Teachers, then, should use an eclectic, language-based approach to the development of reading skills in an environment that provides time for both structured, direct teaching and flexible, incidental learning. This approach requires a wealth of materials, such as manipulatives, puppets, reading materials of all kinds, game activities, art materials, and charts. Teachers must provide enough time for language development and pupil interaction through such activities as show & tell, dramatics, dictated stories and other language experience activities, singing, play and movement activities, story reading, and other shared book experiences. Also, students need frequent contact with the written word by seeing labeled objects, writing their own names and other special words, following along while being read to, learning to recognize common signs, color and number words, observing various charts in the room, and learning to read favorite rhymes, picture books, and child-authored stories. Certainly, kindergarten children should learn to love books and what they represent. Young children should be read to daily and allowed to talk about, act out, and otherwise become excited by stories. They should be allowed to "read" books, even if early efforts do not involve actual reading but rather a retelling of a favorite story or an imaginative "reading" as pages are turned. Some teachers may provide a special chair or rug and a read-to-me doll or stuffed animal to encourage such efforts. The room should contain a library filled with books of all kinds for browsing, and children should be taught how to care for books— that books are special and should not be colored in, torn, or destroyed.

Within this context, structured learning activities and direct teaching of important reading readiness skills can occur. Within reason, the teacher should teach specific skills to children in small groups with similar abilities.

Success is essential. Unhealthy competition, persistent failure, and inappropriate pushing have no place; children should view school as a fun and pleasant place to be. As much as possible, reading ability should develop in a natural and satisfying way.

The following suggestions for helping young children develop the skills and abilities needed for successful reading must be viewed in the broader context highlighted above. No formula for an excellent reading readiness program exists, and it would be a mistake to assume that a publisher can package a complete program for all children. Effective teaching of reading readi-

ness skills requires experience, resourcefulness, and effort.

Because an increasing number of children are enrolled in highly structured readiness and beginning reading programs before first grade, a committee with representatives from a number of professional organizations, such as the Association for Childhood Education International, the National Association for the Education of Young Children, and the International Reading Association prepared "A Joint Statement of Concerns about Present Practices in Pre-First Grade Reading Instruction and Recommendations for Improvement" (Strickland and others, 1977). The wise recommendations of this committee appear in Figure 4–9. Readiness instruction should occur within these guidelines.

Techniques and procedures for improving readiness skills in visual discrimination, auditory skills, left-to-right progression, letter knowledge, language development, experiential background, interest in reading, and beginning sight vocabulary follow.

Visual Discrimination

Because all children do not need visual discrimination exercises, use the informal test presented in Figure 4–1 to determine which children can use some instruction.

When teaching visual discrimination, have children look carefully at letters and words and note their distinctive features. You might begin by having children make gross discriminations then work toward increasingly finer discriminations. Because research consistently shows no benefit from using shapes or symbols other than letters or words, you should concentrate on tasks such as the following:

1. First, have children identify matching pairs of *individual letters* by circling the pairs that are alike:

    c p   b l
    c r   and   b b
    c c   b d

2. Next, have children circle all *individual* let-

RECOMMENDATIONS

1. Provide reading experiences as an integrated part of the broader communication process that includes listening, speaking, and writing. A language experience approach is an example of such integration.

2. Provide for a broad range of activities both in scope and in content. Include direct experiences that offer opportunities to communicate in different settings with different persons.

3. Foster children's affective and cognitive development by providing materials, experiences, and opportunities to communicate what they know and how they feel.

4. Continually appraise how various aspects of each child's total development affect his/her reading development.

5. Use evaluative procedures that are developmentally appropriate for the children being assessed and that reflect the goals and objectives of the instructional program.

6. Insure feelings of success for all children in order to help them see themselves as persons who can enjoy exploring language and learning to read.

7. Plan flexibly in order to accommodate a variety of learning styles and ways of thinking.

8. Respect the language the child brings to school, and use it as a base for language activities.

9. Plan activities that will cause children to become active participants in the learning process rather than passive recipients of knowledge.

10. Provide opportunities for children to experiment with language and simply to have fun with it.

11. Require that pre-service and in-service teachers of young children be prepared in the teaching of reading in a way that emphasizes reading as an integral part of the language arts as well as the total curriculum.

12. Encourage developmentally appropriate language learning opportunities in the home.

Figure 4–9   Reading and pre-first grade

Note. From "Reading and Pre-first Grade: A Joint Statement of Concerns about Present Practices in Pre-first Grade Reading Instruction and Recommendations for Improvement" by D. Strickland, et al., *Reading Teacher*, 1977, *30*, 780–81. Copyright 1977 by *Reading Teacher*. Reprinted by permission.

ters that are the same as the first letter given:

c	p	c	r	c
b	d	l	p	b

Both upper- and lowercase letters may be used. These examples illustrate a relatively easy and a more difficult letter-discrimination task. Your practice exercises will include many more examples. Remember the students need not *name* letters at this point. They need only match like letters.

3. Next, have children identify matching *series of letters* by circling the series that are exactly alike:

BR	NR		COP	COP
BR	BR	and	COP	CPO
BR	DR		COP	POC

4. Next, have children circle all *series of letters* that are the same as the first series of letters given:

BR	NR	BR	BR	DR
COP	POC	COP	CPO	COP

5. Now, do the first matching exercise with *words*:

tree	tree		was	were
tree	house	and	was	saw
tree	bird		was	was

6. Finally, have children circle all the *words* that are the same as the first word given:

tree	bird	house	tree	tree
was	was	saw	were	was

Steps 5 and 6 may include words that differ in the following ways:

a. beginning letter; e.g., *dot - hot*
b. ending letter; e.g., *bit - big*
c. medial letter; e.g., *pot - pet*
d. other confusing patterns; e.g., *were - ever, house - horse, around - about.*

Many students have difficulty distinguishing graphically similar words, such as *was* and *saw; what, when,* and *went;* and *where, were, there, every, here, three,* and *their.* Practice with visual discrimination at the readiness stage may help students later when they need to recognize and pronounce common words that appear similar.

The six steps listed above provide a sequential development of visual discrimination abilities using two easy-to-prepare formats. Other formats may be used, such as drawing lines to connect similar pairs, matching pairs on flash cards, and others. In addition, the following activities can be used to reinforce visual discrimination skills:

1. Have children circle letters or words that are alike on a page of print.
2. Have children circle or underline words that are alike on dictated language experience story charts.
3. Have students match words written on flash cards to identical words lined up on the chalk tray or elsewhere in the room.
4. Have children match their names from name tags to the names on a posted chart.
5. Have students complete matching exercises in which dotted letters or words are printed. Students first trace over dotted letters or words, then match them.
6. Have students find a particular or favorite word in several magazines. The words may be cut out and pasted on a page.

Your goal is to help students understand that configuration, not size or color, matters most in identifying letters. In addition, children learn to see the sequences in which letters usually appear. These skills provide the foundation for later word pronunciation when combined with letter recognition and letter-sound correspondence (phonics).

Auditory Skills

Teaching procedures for two types of auditory skills, (1) auditory discrimination and (2) auditory segmentation and blending, follow.

Auditory Discrimination. This skill, along with visual discrimination, auditory segmentation, and blending, is a prerequisite for the application of phonics skills. To use letter-sound correspondences (phonics) to decode, students must be able to distinguish the unique configurations of the letters and the sounds they represent, then blend these sounds together to pronounce the word.

Many children have sufficient auditory discrimination when they enter school and thus do not require instruction in it. You may determine which children need instruction by administering an informal test such as the one in Figure 4–2.

Once again, exercises should proceed from gross discriminations to finer ones, beginning with initial sounds, proceeding to medial sounds, and then finally to ending sounds. Usually the teacher asks students to listen to pairs of words and indicate whether they are the same or different.

One of the best approaches for practicing auditory discrimination with a small group of children is to use the every-pupil-response technique (EPRT) described in Chapter 3. For example, you may seat students in front of you and instruct them to open their eyes if the two words sound the same and close their eyes if the two words are different, thus minimizing students' mimicking. Your instructions to the children could be, "I'm going to say two words. If they are exactly alike, I want you to open your eyes wide like this. (Demonstrate.) If the two words sound different, I want you to close your eyes tight like this. (Demonstrate.) Are you ready?''

Then pronounce various word pairs and observe whether the children understand the directions and can make the discriminations. Examples of word pairs for beginning sounds are *hat - mat, dig - dig, bear - bear*, and *car - far*. Pairs for medial sounds might be *hot - hat, dog - dog*, and *pin - pan*, and examples of final sounds are *big -bit, bad - bad*, and *hum - hut*.

An alternative to open eyes/close eyes is thumbs-up or thumbs-down. Also, teachers can have children mark their responses on paper in some way.

In addition, you may give students practice on word lists. For example, read a few words that begin with the same sound, *dog, doll, dairy, dish*, then ask students to indicate which of the following words *begin* with the same sound: *dig, boy, delicious, door, tomorrow*, etc. This approach gradually helps students learn the meanings of *beginning, middle*, and *end* as well. Children can also practice auditory discrimination by naming other words that begin with the same sound.

One problem may occur if you pronounce words in front of the children; they may discriminate sounds by reading your lips instead of listening carefully. You can avoid this problem by prerecording word pairs on an audio tape recorder, then playing the tape. Or you can hold a card in front of your mouth or use a puppet to distract the children's attention when the words are pronounced.

Sometimes teachers present pictures or objects and have the children pronounce the words they represent and then discriminate between them. However, children often give different names for the picture or object shown. Also, children should focus their attention on the auditory skill, and pictures or objects may distract them.

Be careful, too, about the difficulty of the tasks. No benefit comes from having children discriminate words of more than one syllable. Indeed, applying phonics helps only with one-

syllable units. For larger units, students rely on other decoding methods such as sight recognition, structural analysis, and context clues (see Chapter 6). Therefore, three levels of discrimination—beginning, medial, and final sounds of one-syllable words—are all that is necessary.

Many children even have difficulty discriminating final sounds of one-syllable words. If, after some effort, some children do not improve in this area, do not be overly concerned. The importance of auditory discrimination skill is not clearly established, and some students learn to read quite well in spite of weaknesses in that area.

The procedures noted above essentially test and reinforce auditory discrimination and may not benefit children seriously deficient in the skill unless the teacher assists them individually. In such cases, the teacher should go back to gross discriminations such as *tree - house* and establish a point of success before moving gradually to finer discriminations.

If a child cannot succeed at any point, then one of two possibilities probably accounts for the problem. The child may have a serious hearing impairment, in which case he should be referred to a specialist. Or, the child may lack the ability to follow directions or respond to instruction, in which case teaching efforts should be redirected to other areas and work on auditory discrimination be delayed.

Rhyming ability relates to auditory discrimination and serves as a foundation for later learning of *word elements* or *word families* (discussed in Chapters 2 and 6). This ability can be assessed as in Figure 4–3, and can be taught using procedures similar to those employed in teaching auditory discrimination. In addition, you may read familiar rhymes to children, have them make up rhymes, present the first part of a couplet and have the children supply a rhyming word, provide a word and have the children offer rhyming words, and other similar activities.

Auditory Segmentation and Blending. Increasing evidence suggests that segmentation and blending ability correlate with later reading success. The teacher can use several relatively simple procedures to teach these skills to young children.

Segmentation of sentences into words and words into syllables is easier than segmentation of words into phonemes. To help children practice the easier segmentation tasks, you may:

1. Read a short sentence and ask the children how many words are in it.
2. Read the sentence again, pausing after each word, if they do not respond correctly. Ask them to count the words as you pronounce them. (Obviously, children must be able to count to profit from this activity.)
3. Continue with longer sentences and shorter pauses as the children master the skill.
4. Pronounce a common three- or four-syllable word and have the children indicate the number of syllables.
5. Pronounce the word again slowly and emphasize the syllable divisions, if they do not respond correctly. Instruct them to count the syllables. Frequently, teachers also have the students clap as each syllable is pronounced to emphasize the division.
6. Provide additional practice with multi-syllable words as the children progress.

These same procedures may be followed for segmenting one-syllable words into two or three parts, e.g., *ca - t* or *c - a - t*. However, the procedure becomes more complicated at this point because: (1) the divisions are less discrete and obvious to the children, and (2) the place of division may be dictated in part by the instructional program followed. In synthetic approaches to phonics, children decode words phoneme by phoneme; for example, *cat* would be decoded *c - a - t*. But in analytic programs, less emphasis may be placed on pronunciation of individual phonemes. Thus, segmentation procedures followed may vary.

Lewkowicz (1980) suggests three different techniques for teaching segmentation of one-syllable words. In the first, the teacher empha-

sizes or prolongs the sound of the initial consonant when pronouncing the word, e.g. *b at*, and thus separates the sound of the initial phoneme /b/ from the sound of the phonogram /at/. However, many consonants cannot be sounded in isolation without adding the schwa sound so that *bat* sounds like *buh - at*. This disadvantage could lead to later blending problems for the child.

Second, the teacher can use *iteration*, repeating the first sound two or three times when the word is pronounced, e.g. *b-b-bat*. This method emphasizes the beginning sound and separates it from the phonogram's sound without distorting the beginning sound as in the first method.

In the third method, the teacher pronounces word pairs, e.g. *at, bat*, which does not distort the beginning sound at all.

Blending skills are taught in much the same way as segmentation skills, but the children learn to form whole words from parts rather than vice versa. With multi-syllable words, the teacher may pronounce the word part by part and have the children mentally blend the parts to form and then pronounce the whole word; the teacher says *bas - ket - ball*, students pronounce *basketball*. For additional practice, the students may pronounce the whole word, segment it into parts, pronounce the parts, then (using blending again) pronounce the whole word once more. Another technique for teaching blending, suggested by Lewkowicz, has the teacher give a child a "secret" picture. The child looks at the picture, determines the word it represents, and then pronounces the word in segments (e.g. *tel - e - phone*). The other children try to guess the "secret" picture by blending the parts and arriving at the whole word (*telephone*).

Left-to-Right Progression

Left-to-right progression, sometimes called *left-to-right orientation* or *directionality*, refers to the child's ability to recognize that English words read from left to right on a page and that letters are written from left to right in words. Many entering kindergarteners know this fact—probably as a result of prereading experiences at home or in preschool—and need no special instruction. Other children, unfortunately, do not realize that the squiggly marks on the page represent words. Children also need to learn to distinguish left from right in order to follow many of the directions they receive in school.

Some easy and effective suggestions for teaching left-to-right progression follow:

1. When reading stories to children, occasionally turn the book so that children can see it; by pointing, show them how the words of the story progress from left to right across the page and from top to bottom. You can also demonstrate how the return sweep from the end of one line to the beginning of the next takes place.
2. Use the same procedure with language-experience story charts or charts that accompany low-level basal readers. In this case, run your hand under the words as they are read. Those children who especially need it should then demonstrate the left-to-right progression by moving *their* hands across the chart while the story is reread.
3. Use similar techniques with sentences or stories written on the chalkboard.
4. Arrange pictures from left to right on a flannel board to illustrate a story being told.
5. Children can arrange cut-up cartoons from left to right as they appear in the newspaper.
6. Color the first letter on the left side of a worksheet with "green for go" and the last letter on the right side with "red for stop" as a visual device to remind children of directionality.
7. One teacher uses a visual mnemonic device: In her room the flag is in the front left corner and the clock is in the front right corner. The teacher frequently reminds the children to "read from the flag to the clock."

Letter Knowledge

The term *letter knowledge* may refer to different skills as noted earlier. From easiest to hard-

est the four levels of letter knowledge are as follows:

1. Matching like letters (visual discrimination task, see Figure 4–1);
2. Matching uppercase letters with their lowercase equivalents (low-level recognition task, see Figure 4–6);
3. Identifying letters when the teacher pronounces them (high-level recognition task, see Figure 4–5); and
4. Identifying and pronouncing letters when the teacher points to them in scrambled order (pronunciation task, see Figure 4–4).

Generally, students proceed through the steps in that order, but they can master the third task before the second.

Whether or not to teach letter recognition has been debated. Letter knowledge is highly correlated with future reading success, but correlations do not prove causes, and one can learn to read without being able to name letters. Probably the main reason to teach letter-naming skills, then, is that teachers use letters constantly while teaching. A student who cannot recognize and name letters may get confused when the teacher refers to them during phonics instruction or other times.

The diagnostic steps outlined earlier in the chapter will help you determine which children need instruction in which phases of letter knowledge. Some techniques for teaching letter knowledge follow:

1. Be sure that visual discrimination ability is mastered.
2. Give children practice matching upper- and lowercase letters to their equivalents. The teacher may hold up a card with the upper- or lowercase letter written on it and instruct the children to hold up the card on which the equivalent is written. The students can practice saying the names of the letters as they are shown and matched.
3. Give children practice as above, only have them write the matching letter on paper, small chalkboards, or magic slates.

4. List various letters on the chalkboard or a chart and have children point to the appropriate letter as the teacher calls its name. This can be done with worksheets as well in small groups.

5. List various letters on the chalkboard or a chart and have children name each letter as the teacher points to it.

In addition, a teacher may use several other activities to give students practice with letter knowledge. These include the following:

1. Encourage children to watch *Sesame Street* on television at home with their parents or older brothers and sisters.

2. Teach the alphabet song and have students point to the letters as they sing.

3. Use various commercial games and manipulative letters for practice.

4. Help students recognize and name the letters in their names, the teacher's name, and other important words.

5. Read the various alphabet books with students.

6. Teach upper- and lowercase letters together. Print them on the chalkboard or a chart. Have students find other words in the room in which these letters appear. Refer frequently to the new letters that are taught each day.

7. Use activities from basal reader materials or other readiness materials that practice letter knowledge. Be careful, however, not to overuse workbook pages.

Language Development

Language ability undoubtedly plays a critical role in the development of reading skills. Fortunately, the kindergarten classroom provides an ideal setting for growth in various language skills. As Margaret Early (1972) has stated:

Everything in a good kindergarten room is directed toward these ends: the familiar corners for playing house and store; the collections of living and growing things—plants, flowers, fish, turtles, gerbils; the bins of strange and common objects that excite children's senses and stimulate their imaginations; the art corner where ideas can be expressed in paint and clay and other media; the workbenches where children can literally hammer out ideas; the outdoor play areas where children can stretch their imaginations as well as their muscles. Dancing, miming, dressing up, making believe, listening to stories read by the

Learning to work independently is an important part of reading readiness.

teacher or recorded by others, looking at books, walking tours of school and neighborhood, visits to airports, firehouses, children's museums—all these feed the imagination and loosen tongues. . . . (p. 82)

The development of children's language abilities encompasses many areas, including listening, speaking, and vocabulary enlargement. Language development activities often strengthen children's skills in more than one area. Jayne DeLawter and Maurice Eash (1966) offer three excellent general suggestions for language improvement:

1. Whenever possible, teach in a small-group setting. Groups provide greater interaction for students and better observation for the teacher.
2. Use audio-visual equipment that allows children to see and hear their own speech.
3. Use the language experience approach extensively. (See Chapter 2.)

The following list provides more specific and practical suggestions for developing children's language abilities:

1. Provide time for sharing, perhaps 15 to 20 minutes at the beginning of the day. This time should be a happy, positive experience for children, during which they learn to develop both their listening and speaking skills. Make sure that as many children as possible get to share and that a few do not monopolize the time.
2. Provide some time for free play, so that children can interact informally.
3. Read stories to children frequently and encourage discussion. Occasionally have the children end a story, repeat lines together, or supply missing words.
4. Give children an opportunity to retell or dramatize favorite stories.
5. Provide opportunities for discussion of planned trips, events, or special activities.
6. Use listening centers and prerecorded or teacher-made audio tapes. Also use various commercial records and tapes for listening and following directions activities.
7. Use pictures to develop language skills.

Children may relate a story from a picture book, describe a picture that they are holding, or tell about a picture that they have painted or drawn.

8. Develop some learning centers or stations around the room in areas such as science and art. Encourage children to explore, manipulate, and discuss the items on display.
9. Encourage students to describe various objects in the room. Have classmates try to guess what is being described.
10. Give students opportunities to learn, recite, or sing favorite riddles, rhymes, or songs.
11. Provide creative dramatics and puppetry activities.
12. Let children play the teacher occasionally. Not only valuable for the children, this experience is also revealing for the teacher.
13. Find some time each day to interact with individual children. Encourage them to talk about their interests or concerns while you listen actively.
14. Give students instructions in a series, such as "stand up, walk to the board, and write your name." Then, have the children repeat the instructions in order, then follow them.
15. Encourage students to pay attention by frequently stopping and asking them to repeat what was just said.
16. Have children be very quiet and listen to hear the sounds in the room. Take "listening walks" and ask students to remember the sounds they hear outdoors.
17. Take time to explain the meanings of new words that appear in your speech, children's speech, or books. Teach children the meanings of new words every day. Encourage them to use these words when they speak.
18. Bring interesting objects into the room and teach the new words associated with the objects.
19. Have students act out the meanings of new words when possible.

20. Make language a fun, interesting, and exciting aspect of your instruction. Communicate to children your own excitement about words and ideas.

Experiential Background

Children with varied experiences have an advantage in learning to read and understand concepts presented in books. Many children have had many experiences provided by their parents before going to school, but others are not so fortunate.

As a teacher of young children, you can build many exciting and valuable experiences into the school day. Many of the suggestions for language development will also expand children's experiential background. In addition, you might do the following:

1. Take students on field trips. As simple as school building tours and walking trips in the neighborhood or as elaborate as bus trips away from school, such trips are enjoyable for children, teach them how to behave in different settings, and provide them with the ingredients for many language experience stories and activities.
2. Take care of classroom pets. When possible, make children responsible for the care and feeding of animals in school.
3. Bring in guest speakers to talk about their work, interests, or hobbies. In addition to the children's own parents, other people from the community may be available. Also, various members of the school staff, including custodians, cafeteria workers, and parent aides, might enjoy sharing their experiences with children.
4. Provide classroom demonstrations and experiments in science. Devise simple activities that children can perform themselves.
5. Develop centers for scaled down or imitation experiences, such as stores, building areas, or kitchens. These may be simple or elaborate as space or materials allow.

Interest in Reading

To ignite children's interest in reading and books is one of the most important goals of readiness instruction. In addition to language experience activities, reading to children, and the sharing experiences previously suggested, the following suggestions may help you promote your students' interest in reading:

1. Attractively display a great variety and quantity of children's books.
2. Allow children to browse and explore books with their friends.
3. Bring in storytellers from elsewhere in the school or district or invite children's librarians or parents to read books to your students.
4. Take your children to school and public libraries to visit and check out books.
5. Have students from upper grades read books or their creative writing to your class while your students visit upper-grade classes to read their language experience charts out loud.
6. Make your students' dictated stories into booklets that may be duplicated and shared among classmates.
7. Encourage children to rate their favorite picture books, then list titles on a "best sellers" chart.

Teachers can also make free reading a part of the reading program (see Chapter 11). With the procedure known as Sustained Silent Reading (SSR), all people in a classroom or school read quietly and without interruption for a given period of time. This procedure can work in kindergartens, too; the children "read" by looking at picture books. Just like their older peers, five- and six-year-olds stay on-task and enjoy their books and the solitude of free reading. Children are never too young to read for pleasure.

Beginning Sight Vocabulary

All these reading readiness activities should acquaint children with written language and help them develop the prerequisite skills necessary for translating printed symbols into meaningful sounds. Children need adequate ability in visual discrimination, auditory skills, left-to-right progression, and letter knowledge to "crack the code." In addition, a good background in language development, varied experiences, and an interest in reading aid the learning-to-read process. At some point, however, children must learn to recognize whole words and acquire strategies— phonic analysis, structural analysis, and contextual analysis—for decoding new words. Many teachers provide some phonics instruction as part of the readiness program.

Certain types of whole word learning or sight vocabulary are crucial to beginning reading and are typically taught in kindergarten. This *beginning sight vocabulary* should not be confused with *basic sight vocabulary* (words of high frequency that appear on a prepared list; see Chapter 6).

Beginning sight vocabulary includes words such as children's own names; *mother, father* (or *mom, dad*, etc.); the teacher's name; color words; number words; days of the week and months of the year; position words, such as *over, under, up, down, before, after*; common classroom objects or areas, such as *table, chair, reading corner, library, book*; and any other words important or interesting to young children.

The *key vocabulary* approach to early word learning, described in Chapter 2, may be reread for specific techniques in teaching beginning sight vocabulary. Teachers may also present sight vocabulary by labeling classroom objects or areas, preparing attractive bulletin board displays, and practicing new words with flashcard activities or simple game formats. Students also recognize many new words a week through various language-experience charts and activities.

Once children acquire beginning sight vocabularies—the sight vocabulary for each child will be somewhat different—they will be eager to read simple stories or rhymes. They can also profit from phonics instruction because they can generalize from a list of known words.

At this point many teachers introduce pre-primers. These beginning basal readers usually introduce only a very few words and use them repeatedly to aid students' recognition. At the same time, basal lessons teach other reading readiness skills. Many children are successful with this approach and gradually build ample sight vocabularies and effective decoding strategies. However, not all basal series have stimulating pre-primers. Some present stilted and dull stories and characters.

Alternative approaches, however, are available. Some teachers rely almost exclusively on the language-experience approach and supplement it with children's trade books. Other teachers use *pattern books* extensively; and, of course, many teachers combine basal pre-primers, language experience, pattern books, and other methods and materials.

Pattern books use repetitive language structures, rhyme, sequence, predictable plots, and familiar themes to stimulate children's interest and help them predict next words or lines. Bill Martin writes the best-known pattern books, published by Holt, Rinehart and Winston. Connie Bridge, Peter Winograd, and Darliene Haley (1983) call these pattern books *structured language books* and list more than fifty titles from various authors.

Bridge, Winograd, and Haley also compared the effectiveness of pattern books and basal pre-primers in teaching beginning sight words to slower first-grade readers. They found that the children who used the pattern books learned significantly more words. They also discovered that children taught with the pattern books used context clues more often when they came to unfamiliar words and had more positive attitudes about reading aloud.

Sharon Zinke (1983) developed a series of pattern book materials to accompany pre-primers in a popular basal series. These materials were made into paper fold-up booklets and rhyme cards and field-tested with young children. Zinke found that students made impressive gains in their word learning and that both parents and teachers thought the supplementary materials made an excellent addition to the reading program.

Reading readiness is a complex and challenging subject for the teacher of young children. Teaching readiness skills requires a lot of energy, preparation, and knowledge. However, the satisfaction derived from watching young readers emerge convinces teachers their efforts are worthwhile.

SUMMARY

Many researchers have explored the subject of readiness for reading in recent years. Experts have sought to determine which of the many factors affecting children's early learning actually have an impact on reading ability. Although researchers now know more about readiness factors, many issues remain unresolved. Intelligence, visual abilities, auditory abilities, metalinguistic skills, letter knowledge, language development, interest in reading, general health, and social and emotional maturity seem to interact to affect children's propensity for reading. How various factors affect individual children is less certain, so efforts in teaching readiness skills should be geared to each child's needs.

Thus, teachers use a variety of assessment techniques to identify youngsters' strengths and weaknesses in readiness areas. Children should receive appropriate vision and hearing screening to insure that their eyes and ears are functioning well and to correct defects when necessary. Some schools or districts use standardized reading readiness tests for assessment. Although these batteries have many shortcomings, they may be of some value if used along with other, more suitable diagnostic procedures. Teachers may also rely on criterion-referenced tests or teacher-made informal tests to evaluate children's abilities in readiness areas. In addition, teachers should use the metalinguistic interview, checklists based on their own observation, and other assessment procedures.

Readiness instruction should occur in a stimulating, positive, and supportive environment. Teachers may combine structured, direct teaching and flexible, incidental teaching to develop children's prereading skills. The language experience approach, in combination with a wide range of teaching procedures and techniques, works best in teaching reading readiness.

REVIEW QUESTIONS

1. How is a child's age when beginning reading instruction related to future reading success? Is there an optimal age for beginning reading instruction? Why or why not? Under what circumstances should children be given an early start in reading?

2. For which children are intelligence test scores most predictive of future reading achievement?

3. What is visual discrimination? How is it related to reading ability? Why is the Snellen Test adequate or inadequate as a visual screening procedure?

4. Explain how auditory discrimination ability can be highly correlated with future reading ability yet not be causally related.

5. Discuss the two types of metalinguistic abilities. How does each affect reading readiness?

6. How does letter knowledge relate to reading ability? What are the four levels of letter knowledge?

7. Why is it difficult to prepare tests of language ability that yield results leading to prescriptive instructional procedures?

8. Discuss the extent to which the following readiness factors are or are not related to future reading achievement: interest in reading, gender, visual-motor or visual-perceptual abilities, general health, and social and emotional maturity.

9. If you have a kindergarten student who you suspect has a vision problem, what tests should you use to diagnose the specific vision difficulty?
10. What are the strengths and weaknesses of standardized reading readiness tests?
11. What are the advantages and disadvantages of commercially prepared criterion-referenced tests versus teacher-made informal tests for reading readiness skills?
12. Which readiness skills can be assessed through criterion-referenced or teacher-made tests?
13. Which readiness abilities might best be assessed using checklists?
14. Describe an ideal classroom environment for teaching reading readiness.
15. What are the advantages and disadvantages of a structured, direct teaching approach to reading readiness? Of a flexible, incidental teaching approach? Can both approaches be used in the same classroom?
16. List some specific procedures for teaching the following reading readiness skills: (a) visual discrimination; (b) auditory discrimination; (c) auditory segmentation of sentences into words and words into syllables; (d) oral phonemic segmentation of words into phonemes; (e) blending; (f) left-to-right progression; and (g) letter knowledge.
17. How are every-pupil-response techniques used to teach auditory discrimination?
18. What techniques can help children develop in the following areas? (a) language ability, (b) experiential background, (c) interest in reading.
19. How do pattern books help young pupils build their beginning sight vocabularies?
20. Describe the language experience approach and discuss how it helps children get ready to read.

REFERENCES

Allan, K. K. The development of young children's metalinguistic understanding of the word. *Journal of Educational Research*, November/December, 1982, *76*, 89–93.

Barrett, T. C. Visual discrimination tasks as predictors of first grade reading achievement. *Reading Teacher*, January, 1965, *18*, 276–82.

Barrett, T. C. The relationship between measures of prereading visual discrimination and first grade reading achievement: A review of the literature. *Reading Research Quarterly*, Fall, 1965, *1*, 51–76.

Bond, G. L., & Dykstra, R. The cooperative research program in first-grade reading instruction. *Reading Research Quarterly*, Summer, 1967, *2*, 5–142.

Brezeinski, J. E. Reading in the kindergarten. In W. Cutts (Ed.), *Teaching Young Children to Read*. Washington, D.C.: U.S. Government Printing Office, 1964.

Bridge, C. A., Winograd, P. N., & Haley, D. Using predictable materials vs. pre-primers to teach beginning sight words. *Reading Teacher*, May, 1983, *36*, 884–91.

A closer look at reading and vision. St. Louis, Mo.: American Optometric Association, 1979.

Collins, C. Criterion-referenced prereading skills test to predict first grade reading readiness and achievement. *Reading Improvement*, Fall, 1979, *16*, 182–89.

DeLawter, J. A., & Eash, M. J. Focus on oral communication. *Elementary English*, December, 1966, *43*, 880–82, 891, 901.

Downing, J. *Reading and reasoning.* New York: Springer-Verlag, 1979.

Downing, J., & Lundsteen, S. Understanding new perspectives of early childhood: What does research tell us about children? In L. O. Ollila (Ed.), *Handbook for administrators and teachers: Reading in the kindergarten.* Newark, Del.: International Reading Association, 1980.

Downing, J., & Oliver, P. The child's conception of a word. *Reading Research Quarterly,* 1973–74, *9,* 568–82.

Durkin, D. *Children who read early.* New York: Teacher's College Press, 1966.

Durkin, D. A six-year study of children who learned to read in school at the age of four. *Reading Research Quarterly,* 1974–75, *10,* 9–61.

Durkin, D. Facts about pre-first grade reading. In L. O. Ollila (Ed.), *The kindergarten child and reading.* Newark, Del.: International Reading Association, 1977.

Durr, W. K., & Pikulski, J. J. *Reading research and the Houghton Mifflin reading program.* Boston: Houghton Mifflin, 1981.

Dykstra, R. Auditory discrimination abilities and beginning reading achievement. *Reading Research Quarterly,* Spring, 1966, *1,* 5–34.

Early, M. Components of a language arts program in the primary grades. In R. C. Aukerman (Ed.), *Some persistent questions on beginning reading.* Newark, Del.: International Reading Association, 1972.

Ehri, L. C. Word consciousness in readers and prereaders. *Journal of Educational Psychology,* 1975, *67,* 204–12.

Ekwall, E. E., & Shanker, J. L. *Diagnosis and remediation of the disabled reader* (2nd ed.). Boston: Allyn and Bacon, 1983.

Evans, M., Taylor, N., & Blum, I. Children's written language awareness and its relation to reading acquisition. *Journal of Reading Behavior,* Spring, 1979, *11,* 7–19.

Geissal, M. A., & Knafle, J. A linguistic view of auditory discrimination tests and exercises. *Reading Teacher,* November, 1977, *31,* 134–40.

Groff, P. Reading ability and auditory discrimination: Are they related? *Reading Teacher,* May, 1975, *28,* 742–47.

Harber, J. R. Are perceptual skills necessary for success in reading? Which ones? *Reading Horizons,* Fall, 1979, *20,* 7–15.

Harris, A. J. Discussion: Linguistic awareness and cognitive clarity in learning to read. In M. L. Kamil and A. J. Moe (Eds.), *Reading research: Studies and applications.* Twenty-eighth Yearbook of the National Reading Conference, 1979.

Harris, A. J., & Sipay, E. K. *How to teach reading.* New York: Longman, 1979.

Hresko, W. P., Reid, D. K., & Hammill, D. D. *The Test of Early Language Development.* Austin, Texas: Pro-Ed, 1981.

King, E. M. Prereading programs: Direct versus incidental teaching. *Reading Teacher,* February, 1978, *31,* 504–510.

Klesius, S. E. Perceptual-motor development and reading—A closer look. In R. C. Aukerman (Ed.), *Some persistent questions on beginning reading.* Newark, Del.: International Reading Association, 1972.

Koenke, K. A comparison of three auditory discrimination-perception tests. *Academic Therapy,* March, 1978, *13,* 463–68.

Lesiak, J. Reading in kindergarten: What the research doesn't tell us. *Reading Teacher,* November, 1978, *32,* 135–38.

Lewkowicz, N. K. Phonemic awareness training: What to teach and how to teach it. *Journal of Educational Psychology,* 1980, *72,* 686–700.

Lowell, R. E. Reading readiness factors as predictors of success in first-grade reading. *Journal of Learning Disabilities*, December, 1971, *4*, 24–28.

Lyon, R. Auditory-perceptual training: The state of the art. *Journal of Learning Disabilities*, November, 1977, *10*, 564–72.

MacGinitie, W. H. When should we begin to teach reading? *Language Arts*, November/December, 1976, *53*, 878–82.

MacKeith, R. Do disorders of perception occur? *Developmental Medicine and Child Neurology*, 1977, *19*, 821.

McCormick, S. Should you read aloud *to* your children? *Language Arts*, February, 1977, *54*, 139–43, 163.

Mason, J. M. When do children begin to read: An exploration of four-year-old children's letter and word reading competencies. *Reading Research Quarterly*, 1980, *15*, 203–224.

Morphett, M., & Washburne, C. When should children begin to read? *Elementary School Journal*, March, 1931, *31*, 496–503.

Neuman, S. B. Effect of teaching auditory perceptual skills on reading achievement in first grade. *Reading Teacher*, January, 1981, *34*, 422–26.

Newcomer, P. L., & Hammill, D. D. *The Test of Language Development*. Austin, Texas: Pro-Ed, 1977.

Ollila. L. O. Pros and cons of teaching reading to four-and five-year-olds. In R. C. Aukerman (Ed.), *Some persistent questions on beginning reading*. Newark, Del.: International Reading Association, 1972.

Ollila, L. O. Foundations: What have we learned about kindergarten reading programs? In L. O. Ollila (Ed.), *Handbook for administrators and teachers: Reading in the kindergarten*. Newark, Del.: International Reading Association, 1980.

Paradis, E. E. The appropriateness of visual discrimination exercises in reading readiness materials. *Journal of Educational Research*, February, 1974, *67*, 276–78.

Paradis, E., & Peterson, J. Readiness training implications from research. *Reading Teacher*, February, 1975, *28*, 445–48.

Pikulski, J. Readiness for reading: A practical approach. *Language Arts*, February, 1978, *55*, 192–97.

Richek, M. A. Readiness skills that predict initial word learning using 2 different methods of instruction. *Reading Research Quarterly*, 1977–78, *13*, 200–222.

Roberts, T. Skills of analysis and synthesis in the early stages of reading. *British Journal of Educational Psychology*, 1975, *45*, 3–9.

Robinson, H. M. Perceptual training—does it result in reading improvement? In R. C. Aukerman (Ed.), *Some persistent questions on beginning reading*. Newark, Del.: International Reading Association, 1972.

Robinson, V. B., Strickland, D. S., & Cullinan, B. The child: Ready or not? In L. O. Ollila (Ed.), *The kindergarten child and reading*. Newark, Del.: International Reading Association, 1977.

Rosner, J. Language arts and arithmetic achievement and specifically related perceptual skills. *American Educational Research Journal*, Winter, 1973, *10*, 59–68.

Rubin, R. A., Balow, B., Dorle, J., & Rosen, M. Preschool prediction of low achievement in basic school skills. *Journal of Learning Disabilities*, December, 1978, *11*, 664–66.

Rude, R. T. Readiness tests: Implications for early childhood education. *Reading Teacher*, March, 1973, *26*, 572–80.

Sampson, M. R., & Briggs, L. D. What does research say about beginning reading? *Reading Horizons*, Winter, 1981, *21*, 114–18.

Santa, C. M. Visual discrimination and word recognition. *Reading Improvement*, Winter, 1975, *12*, 245–50.

Satz, P., & Fletcher, J. M. Early screening tests: Some uses and abuses. *Journal of Learning Disabilities*, January, 1979, *12*, 56–60.

Silvaroli, N. J., & Wheelock, W. H. An investigation of auditory discrimination training for beginning readers. *Reading Teacher*, December, 1966, *20*, 247–51.

Strag, G. A., & Richmond, B. O. Auditory discrimination techniques for young children. *Elementary School Journal*, May, 1973, *73*, 447–54.

Teale, W. H. Positive environments for learning to read: What studies of early readers tell us. *Language Arts*, November/December, 1978, *55*, 922–32.

Teale, W. H. *Early reading: An annotated bibliography*. Newark, Del.: International Reading Association, 1980.

Torrey, J. W. Reading that comes naturally. In G. Wallen and G. E. MacKinnon (Eds.), *Reading research: Advance in theory and practice* (Vol. 1). New York: Academic Press, 1979.

Vellutino, F. R. Has the perceptual deficit hypothesis led us astray? *Journal of Learning Disabilities*, 1977, *10*, 375–85.

Walker, G. H., Jr., & Kuerbitz, I. E. Reading to preschoolers as an aid to successful beginning reading. *Reading Improvement*, Summer, 1979, *16*, 149–54.

Wallach, L., Wallach, M. A., Dozier, M. G., & Kaplan, N. E. Poor children learning to read do not have trouble with auditory discrimination but do have trouble with phoneme recognition. *Journal of Educational Psychology*, 1977, *69*, 36–39.

Zinke, S. *Supplementary reading materials for beginning readers*. Master's project, California State University, Hayward, 1983.

5

Assessing and Teaching Sight Words and Basic Sight Words

If each word appearing on the front page of the daily newspaper were listed, certain words would appear over and over again. Some of these high utility words, such as *I*, *and*, and *the*, appear so often that they are called *basic sight words*, words that beginning readers should learn to recognize instantly. Reading researchers and teachers have worked to identify these basic sight words so that they can teach students to know them instantly by late second or early third grade.

Knowing these words on sight is essential for reading fluency; when a child knows 200 different basic sight words, she knows approximately two-thirds of all the words she encounters! For example, the words *the*, *to*, and *and* compose approximately 10 percent of the total words a reader encounters in most reading materials. Eldon E. Ekwall and James L. Shanker (1983) have examined research studies to determine the number of different words that compose certain percents of a passage's total word count. Table 5–1 shows this information.

As you can see from Table 5–1, learning the first 200 different words allows a reader to leap from knowing only 8–12% of words encountered to knowing 66–70% of words encountered.

Basic sight words are high utility words recognized instantly by the reader. Only 200–300 words are used frequently enough to be included in most basic sight word lists. For example, *window* is not used nearly as frequently as *the*; therefore, *the* would be on a basic sight word list, but *window* would not be. Thus, fluent readers generally have the same basic sight vocabulary—the 200–300 most frequently used words in the English language.

On the other hand, *sight words* in general are *any* words known instantly by a reader, not just the high utility ones. A student with a large sight vocabulary has good *word recognition skills*—he does not have to use word analysis skills to decode the words in his sight vocabulary. As students progress in school, their sight vocabularies increase, but of course, each student develops a different one. Fluent readers have similar basic sight vocabularies, then, but their overall sight vocabularies may differ strikingly.

BASIC SIGHT WORD LISTS

Several lists of these basic sight words (high utility words) exist for teachers' use. For example, Edward Dolch (1942) compiled the *Dolch Basic*

Table 5–1 The percent of total running words in reading materials that are composed of different words

Number of Different Words	Percent of Total Running Words[1]
3	8–12%
10	20–25
100	60–65
200	66–70
500	75–80
1000	83–85
1500	87–88
2000	89–90
3000	91–92
5000	92.5–93.5

[1]The total running words are all the words that appear in one section.

Note. From *Diagnosis and Remediation of the Disabled Reader* by E.E. Ekwall and J.L. Shanker (Boston: Allyn and Bacon, 1983), 83. Copyright 1983 by Allyn and Bacon, Inc. Adapted by permission.

Sight Word Test, consisting of what he called not *the* words of highest utility but very common *service* words. Dolch's list contains 220 generally high utility words, but no nouns because nouns sometimes change, come into being, or go out of style with time. Figure 5–1 shows Dolch's well-known basic sight word list.

Other basic sight word lists are the *Harris-Jacobson List* (1980) and the *Fry List* (1980). All the words on the *Harris-Jacobson List* are designated as pre-primer, primer, or first reader. These designations are somewhat arbitrary, based on the researchers' determination of when these words usually appear in textbooks for grades 1 through 6. Because textbooks change, the grade level at which these words actually appear may also change. Fry's list contains 300 words that Fry indicates most readers would probably not master until they reached at least a third-grade reading level. Another basic sight word list, the *Ekwall Basic Sight Word List* (1983), appears in Appendix A. Any of these lists would be appropriate for teaching basic sight words.

REVIEW OF THE RESEARCH

Controversy exists about whether to teach sight

THE BASIC SIGHT WORD TEST. PART 1.					THE BASIC SIGHT WORD TEST. PART 2.			

Name_____Date_____   Name_____Date_____

1.	by	at	a	it	1.	sit	me	to	the
2.	in	I	be	big	2.	not	of	we	so
3.	did	good	do	go	3.	red	too	seven	walk
4.	all	are	any	an	4.	six	start	show	stop
5.	had	have	him	drink	5.	put	round	right	pull
6.	its	is	into	if	6.	no	on	or	old
7.	ask	may	as	am	7.	yellow	you	your	yes
8.	many	cut	keep	know	8.	please	pick	play	pretty
9.	does	goes	going	and	9.	take	ten	they	today
10.	has	he	his	far	10.	my	much	must	together
11.	but	jump	just	buy	11.	own	under	off	over
12.	black	kind	blue	find	12.	out	new	now	our
13.	fast	first	ate	eat	13.	open	one	only	once
14.	help	hot	both	hold	14.	try	myself	never	two
15.	brown	grow	bring	green	15.	us	up	upon	use
16.	four	every	found	eight	16.	with	white	was	wash
17.	from	make	for	made	17.	shall	she	sleep	small
18.	around	funny	always	because	18.	who	write	would	why
19.	long	let	little	look	19.	some	very	sing	soon
20.	away	again	after	about	20.	wish	well	work	will
21.	cold	can	could	clean	21.	ran	read	run	ride
22.	full	fall	five	fly	22.	then	tell	their	them
23.	before	best	better	been	23.	see	saw	say	said
24.	live	like	laugh	light	24.	that	there	these	three
25.	her	here	how	hurt	25.	when	which	where	what
26.	down	done	draw	don't	26.	thank	those	this	think
27.	give	get	gave	got	27.	want	went	were	warm
28.	came	carry	call	come					

Figure 5–1   The Dolch Basic Sight Word Test

Note. From *The Basic Sight Word Test, Parts 1 and 2* by Edward Dolch (Easton, Md.: Garrard, 1942). Copyright 1942 by Garrard Publishing Co. Reprinted by permission.

words in context or in isolation. Kathryn Hampton (1979) studied the effectiveness of both methods with fourth- and fifth-grade remedial reading students. At both grade levels, students learned to *pronounce* more words when the words were taught in isolation. Linnea Ehri and Lee Wilce (1980) had the same results when first graders were taught words in isolation. However, they also found students learned more about the *meaning* of words when those words were taught in the context of a sentence. They concluded that both types of teaching should occur for sight word teaching to be most effective.

Experts also disagree about whether words should be taught in isolation or in relation to pictures representing words. For example, S. Jay Samuels (1967) and Carl Braun (1969) showed that words were *not* learned easier when accompanied by a picture. On the other hand, Ethel M. King and Siegmar Muehl (1965) and Richard Arnold (1968) found that words accompanied by a picture tended to be learned more easily. Arnold, however, found there was no significant difference in student learning between the two methods after 24 hours. Studies by Ruth N. Hartley (1970), Alberto Montare, Elaine Elman, and Joanne Cohen (1977), and John Kiraly and Alexandra Furlong (1974) found no significant differences between the picture and the no-picture methods.

In light of these results, you should not teach words in conjunction with a picture. Furthermore, very few words can be accurately depicted with a picture.

Richard Allington (1974–75) found that when color cues were used to focus attention on discriminating between letterlike figures, students usually retained more than when no color was used. He also found that if a contrasting color was added and then taken away, it produced superior results to using no color or letting the color remain. For example, if a student cannot learn a word or constantly substitutes one word for another, such as *when* for *what*, the teacher can try the color method. The teacher writes the *en* of *when* in red and leaves the rest of the letters black. The student then learns that *when* is partly red and *what* is always completely black.

After the student learns to differentiate between the two words, the teacher quits using the red letters.

Joanna Williams, Ellen Blumberg, and David Williams (1970) concluded that the configuration (word shape) of a word may not be as important for word recognition as knowing the first and last letters. However, older readers tend to use configuration more than younger readers do. They also concluded that the first letter of a word was an important clue to learning while the last letter was used, but less.

ASSESSING STUDENTS' KNOWLEDGE OF SIGHT WORDS

Several basic sight word lists are available. Although there are slight differences in the lists, most of them contain the same "core" words. Therefore, any of them will produce similar results. Five methods for assessing students' knowledge of basic sight words are used, all of which have shortcomings and strong points. However, method 4 should be avoided, *except* under the circumstances described under that method, and method 5 should *always* be avoided.

Computer

A small computer, such as the Radio Shack TRS-80 Pocket Computer, can be programmed to flash each basic sight word (in lowercase letters only) on the screen for approximately 1¾ seconds. The teacher has a numbered list of words and marks each word as correct (+) or incorrect (−) as the student responds to that word. If one uses the basic sight word list in Appendix A, assessing one student takes 8.75 minutes. This method eliminates flash cards and noisy mechanical devices that make it difficult for the teacher to hear student responses. Students can say or read the word as it appears in less than 1¾ seconds, but most teachers need this much time to mark each response. This method of assessing basic sight words seems ideal and will probably become more common as computers move into elementary schools.

The TRS–80 Pocket Computer can be used to effectively test students' knowledge of basic sight words.

Flash Cards

The teacher makes or purchases flash cards for all the basic sight words. The student sits opposite the teacher, who flashes each word for approximately one second or less. The teacher puts all words pronounced correctly in one pile and all those pronounced incorrectly in another. The teacher then makes flash cards or a list of words missed for that student to study and learn. However, the student is often distracted by seeing missed words being put in a separate pile from correct ones. Also, putting the flash cards back in order according to grade level takes time.

As an alternative, the teacher can stop whenever the student misses a word and teach it. A flash card can be made for the student in this case so she will have it to review at some later time. This method allows the teacher to keep the flash cards in their original order. It also works well for grouping students according to words they do not know. The teacher can first test all students on only the pre-primer basic sight words. A student not knowing a word has that word printed on a color card assigned to that level, say *green*. The student keeps the

cards in a file box. Then the teacher tests students on words at the primer level. Again, any student who does not know a word has that word printed on a card, colored according to the primer level, for example, *red*. This procedure continues until all the grade's appropriate levels of basic sight words have been tested. When ready to teach these unknown words, the teacher writes several words to be taught on the overhead projector or chalkboard. Students look through their *red* cards and come to the red group for that day. Their flash cards admit them to the group.

Tape Recorder and Flash Cards

The student sits opposite the teacher. The teacher places the microphone near the spot on the table where cards will be placed after the student has responded to the word on that card. At a steady rate of approximately one per second, the teacher flashes a card to the student, the student responds to each word, and the teacher puts the card on the table. The teacher should not separate right and wrong cards but should focus on the pacing. The cards should be presented in the order they appear on the answer sheet. For example, if you use the list in Appendix A, use the order of that list on the answer sheet.

When the teacher has gone through the list, he plays the tape and marks the answer sheet with (+) for correct and (−) for incorrect answers. He may then make flash cards for each word missed or ask the student to make her own.

List

Students simply read the words from a list. The problem is that when a student comes to a word he does not know, he may just pause and use word analysis skills to decode it. But such a response defeats the purpose of a *sight* words test. However, when students probably know all the basic sight words, and you want to confirm their knowledge, this method can be useful. Give the student a stimulus sheet containing all the words and ask the student to read the words as rapidly as possible. If the student pauses for more than approximately one second on a word, simply mark the word as being incorrect on your copy of the stimulus sheet. When the student has completed reading the words, you may point to words missed, or hesitated over, and see if they were actually not known instantly or if the student paused for some other reason. Generally, however, this method of assessing students' knowledge of basic sight words is not recommended.

Pronounced List

The words on the *Dolch Basic Sight Word Test* are presented in rows of four words each, as shown in Figure 5–1. All students receive a stimulus sheet with 27 or 28 rows of words on it. Students are told that one word in each row will be pronounced and that they are to circle or underline that word. When one word from each row has been called, students get new stimulus sheets, and the same procedure is repeated except a different word is called from each row. Students continue to receive new stimulus sheets until all the words on the *Basic Sight Word Test* have been called.

This method tests all students at once, which seems efficient, but probably wastes the students' and the teacher's time. Extensive research shows that hearing one of four words and circling that word is much easier than seeing a word and pronouncing it. Thus, students may get words correct on the *Basic Sight Word Test* that they could not read in a story or in isolation. Eldon E. Ekwall (1973) gave the *Basic Sight Word Test* to 60 students reading below grade level in grades 3, 4, and 5. Standard procedures were followed. Then individual students were given the same basic sight words flashed on a white screen for approximately 1½ seconds. One-half the students were given the group *Basic Sight Word Test* first and the other half were tested individually first. Students missed an average of 27.95 words on the individual test and 6.23 words on the group-administered *Basic Sight Word Test*, indicating that if one really wants to know which basic sight words a student needs to learn, the student must be tested individually. Even though such testing takes more time, when a student reads, she must look at each word and then pronounce it. To accurately assess a student's knowledge of the basic sight words, then, a teacher must test in a situation analagous or similar to actual reading.

Further, this group procedure allows a student who cannot read even one word to get at least one-fourth of the words correct by guessing. Since knowledge of *each* basic sight word is extremely important, one cannot afford to obtain such inaccurate results.

The Quick Check for Basic Sight Word Knowledge

The Quick Check (See Appendix B) enables the teacher to determine quickly whether a particular student needs to be tested on the entire list of basic sight words. *The Quick Check* was developed by giving 100 students in each of grades 2 through 6 the *Ekwall Basic Sight Word List* in a flash presentation. A computer study then determined which word was missed most often, next most often, etc., in descending order. Then, approximately every eighth word from this list, from the easiest to the most difficult, was put on *The Quick Check* list.

To use this list, a stimulus sheet with the words in the same order as in Appendix B should be prepared. The student receives the stimulus sheet and is told to read the words fairly fast. Students who read all the words quickly and accurately do not need to be tested on the whole list of basic sight words. However, if a student misses or hesitates at one or more words, then he should be tested on the longer list.

Assessing Students' Knowledge of Sight Words in General

As students go through school, certain words should have been encountered enough that they are recognized instantly, without using word analysis skills. If students do not read enough outside the reading class, they are often deficient in their knowledge of sight words in general. You may wish to check on your students' knowledge of these words from time to time.

General knowledge of sight words is usually assessed with a graded word list. These may be prepared by the classroom teacher or ordered from publishers. To prepare these lists yourself, look at the word lists given in the teachers' manuals accompanying basal readers. However, one can simply use one of the prepared lists, such as the well-known *San Diego Quick Assessment List* (see Appendix C). Directions for giving the test accompany the list. Results are given in terms of *independent, instructional*, and *frustration* levels, which are discussed thoroughly in Chapter 10.

When being given such a sight word assessment, students should not pause longer than approximately one-half second before reading each word. If the teacher notes a pause, the student probably does not know the word and has to resort to word attack or word analysis skills for proper pronunciation. Using word attack skills is not innately undesirable, but pausing means that those *sight* words are unknown.

Other sources of graded word lists are as follows:

Bader, L. A. *Bader reading and language inventory.* New York: Macmillan, 1983.

Burns, P. C., & Roe, B. D. *Informal reading assessment.* Chicago: Rand McNally, 1980.

Jacobs, D. H., & Searfoss, L. W. *Diagnostic reading inventory.* Dubuque, Iowa: Kendall/Hunt, 1979.

Johns, J. L. *Basic reading inventory.* Dubuque, Iowa: Kendall/Hunt, 1978.

Rinsky, L. A., & de Fossard, E. *The contemporary classroom reading inventory.* Dubuque, Iowa: Gorsuch Scarisbrick, 1980.

Silvaroli, N. J. *Classroom reading inventory* (4th ed.). Dubuque, Iowa: William C. Brown, 1982.

Woods, M. L., & Moe, A. J. *Analytical reading inventory.* Columbus, Ohio: Charles E. Merrill, 1981.

TEACHING BASIC SIGHT WORDS AND SIGHT WORDS IN GENERAL

Most students learn basic sight words and other sight words in the course of learning to read with a basal reader or other approaches. Therefore, actually teaching basic sight words or any general sight words is usually necessary only for those students needing corrective work, i.e., students who have not learned certain basic or general sight words when they were originally presented.

The research is unclear on the average number of exposures to a word a student needs before it becomes a sight word or before a student no longer needs word attack skills to recognize the word, but the number *is* high. Some studies show that students learn most words in as few as twenty exposures while others show that students need an average of seventy or more exposures before a word becomes a sight word. The number is not important as long as the teacher remembers that most words are not learned until the student has many exposures to them. In developing basal reader systems, authors use basic sight words repeatedly so that students have ample opportunity to learn these words on sight.

However, teachers teach some words before they are encountered in the basal reader. For example, if the word is not phonetically regular, like *scissors*, then it helps students to talk about the word's meaning and show it to students before they read it. However, phonetically regular words should not be put on the chalkboard or overhead projector before the student encounters them in actual reading. This will enable the student to constantly use her word attack skills. If the student probably does not know the meaning of a word, then it can be discussed before the reading lesson; however, it should not be shown to the student.

Since the research is contradictory about introducing and/or teaching a word in context versus in isolation, words should be taught in both. The research also indicates that particularly difficult words, or words that one student miscalls or substitutes, can probably be learned more easily if students have a color cue.

Teachers can teach an unfamiliar sight word in various ways; one successful method follows:

1. Write the unknown word on the chalkboard or on the overhead projector, using it in the context of a phrase or sentence. Underline it.

2. After students see the word, ask them to use word attack skills to pronounce it. It is better not to tell the students the word first, because then they do not have the chance to use word attack skills. If students cannot get the word, then pronounce it for them.

3. Discuss the meaning of the new word or discuss how it is used in the sentence. Try to tie the unknown word to something in the children's experience.

4. Write the word in isolation and ask students to talk about what may help them remember it. Clues in the word's configuration, its descenders, ascenders, length, and double letters, can aid the memory. Also ask them to look for phonograms or word families, such as *all, ell, ill, ent*, etc., in words they already know. Do not, however, ask them to look for little words within the new word being taught; several research studies have shown that this practice misleads

students since a little word within a longer word may have a completely different pronunciation than it would have in isolation. (For example, note the *go* in *government*.) On the other hand, word families or phonograms are usually pronounced the same regardless of their position within a word.

5. Have students write the word, and say it as they write. Research shows that we usually remember 90 percent of what we say as we do a thing, but only 70 percent of what we say in talking. We remember 50 percent of what we see *and* hear, but only 10 to 20 percent of what we read or hear with no other reinforcement.

6. Have students compose new sentences using the word as it was used in the original context. Then have them read each other's sentences, emphasizing the word as it is pronounced.

The Neurological Impress Method

The neurological impress method is one of the fastest and most economical ways to teach students sight words. R.G. Heckelman (1966) explains that in using the neurological impress method, the teacher sits beside a student so that both can see the material to be read. This material should be at the student's instructional level. The teacher explains to the student that he should follow the teacher's reading even if he does not know some of the words. The student listens to the teacher and says the words immediately after they have been pronounced by the teacher. The teacher points to just under each word as it is read, which focuses the student's attention on that particular word as the teacher reads it and the student pronounces it. Teacher and the student continue reading for five to ten minutes. Most students cannot focus their attention on such a demanding task for any longer than that.

Heckelman has reported tremendous success using this method. He stated that you can expect a child to gain as much as one year in grade level for each one or two hours of instructional time, i.e., the total of those short periods

The pocket chart is a helpful, inexpensive device for teaching and reinforcing sight vocabulary.

of time. He reported that some children gained seven to eight grade levels after twelve hours of using this method.

Several later researchers tried to duplicate Heckelman's results while using a tape recorder instead of a teacher. Most of these studies, however, have been less than successful. The important ingredient in this technique seems to be the one-on-one instruction. Also, when a student reads a book and follows a tape recording of the same material, the teacher has no guarantee that the student actually looks at each word as she pronounces it. Therefore, the tape recorder cannot substitute for the teacher.

The Language Experience Approach

Most students learning to read with the language experience approach do so effortlessly and painlessly, and in doing so, rapidly develop their sight vocabularies. (See Chapter 2). However,

Ekwall and Shanker (1983) have an eight-step procedure for using it with individual students:

1. As with a group, find some event of interest to the student and ask the student to record the event on paper.

2. As the student dictates the events, you should write them on a piece of paper with the student seated so that the words can be observed as they are written. . . . The writing may be done on 8½" × 11" paper with a pencil or felt-tip pen.

3. After the story has been completed, you may wish to type it on a pica or primary-size typewriter as appropriate to the grade level of the student. (For third grade and above use regular pica type.)

4. Have the student reread the story, with either you or the student (if able to do it properly) pointing to each word as it is read. Depending on the ability of the student at this stage, the story may be reread sentence by sentence in varying order.

5. Let the student illustrate the story or apply stickers, pictures, or other decoration. Finally, the story should be placed in a booklet to be kept and reviewed each time you meet.

6. You may wish to duplicate the typewritten copies of these stories so that students can cut them up and rearrange, at first the sentences, and later the words within each sentence.

7. Bind groups of experience stories into booklets with illustrated covers and encourage all students to exchange and read each other's booklets.

8. Gradually encourage the student to branch out into the reading of trade books. (p. 104)

A key procedure in using the language experience approach is to have the student point to each word as it is read. Then the teacher knows the student actually looks at each word. A student who has just completed a language experience story can usually recite most of the story from memory, and unless forced to point to each word, may not associate each spoken word with each written word. Also, the procedure is not as effective when the student slides his hand under the words because he may point to one or more words behind or in front of the word being read.

Difficult Basic Sight Words

Eldon E. Ekwall (1981) has several suggestions for teaching especially difficult basic sight words to students. Some of these ideas follow:

1. Have the pupil write troublesome words on cards (8½" × 3"). Trace the word using the index and middle finger. Sound parts of the word as it is traced. After the pupil knows the word, it should no longer be sounded. (Some words do not sound as they are spelled. In this case the sounding part should be omitted.) Use cards to form sentences. Also give sentences with the sight words omitted. Have the pupil fill in blanks with the appropriate word from his or her pile of cards.

2. Use the sight words causing difficulty in sentences. Underline the words causing difficulty as in the following examples:
   a. I *thought* it was you.
   b. I could not go even *though* I have time.
   c. He ran right *through* the stop sign.

3. Have the pupil write troublesome words on a card (8½" × 3") and then pantomime the action described by the word: e.g., *pull, sleep, ride, jump.*

4. Use words commonly confused in multiple choice

situations. Have the pupils underline the correct word. See examples which follow.
   a. He wanted to (walk, wash) his clothes.
   b. He didn't know (when, what) to do.
   c. He put it over (there, their).
   d. I (well, will) go with you.

5. For slow learners who have a great deal of difficulty with certain words, try cutting letters from sandpaper or velvet so that the child can "feel" the word as he or she pronounces it. For certain students it is helpful to put a thin layer of salt or fine sand in a shoe box lid and let them write the word in the salt or sand.

6. Place a piece of paper over a piece of screen wire such as the wire used on the screen doors of a house. Before doing this it is a good idea to cover the edges of the screen wire with book binding tape so that the rough edges do not cut anyone. Writing on the paper on the screen wire with a crayon will leave a series of raised dots. Have the student write basic sight words in this manner and then have him trace over the words, saying them as they are traced.

7. Each day pass out a few basic sight words on cards to students. Each student in turn goes to the board and writes his or her word. The class should try to say it aloud. After it is pronounced correctly, have them write it in a notebook. On some days have students select words from their notebooks and write them on the chalkboard. Then ask various members of the class to say these words. (pp. 29–30)

Games

Using games to teach or reinforce sight words is effective as well as motivating. Dolores Pawley Dickerson (1982) did a study to determine whether children learned sight vocabulary words better when taught using active games, passive games, or selected traditional activities. She used 128 girls and 146 boys in thirty first-grade classrooms, and the study lasted six weeks, sometimes not enough time for students to make adequate progress in learning most skills. However, Dickerson found that while all children gained in their knowledge of sight vocabulary, the groups in the active games situation gained significantly more than the groups in the traditional activities did. In conclusion, Dickerson stated,

These results lend support to educators who believe that games are worthwile learning tools. Statis-

The use of board games often helps reinforce basic sight vocabulary.

tically it was shown that games that involved the most movement were more effective than worksheet activities. . . . Teaming children to work together could be a factor in cooperative and competitive learning, causing greater gain through peer interaction. Incorporating games into regular lessons and not as adjunct activities increases the value of the game, since its objective reinforces the lesson. Additionally, the use of carefully constructed teacher-made games to reinforce a specific concept is a worthwhile effort for both teacher and children. (p. 49)

Remember, however, when you use games in the classroom, students must spend as much time as possible actually engaged in reading words. If they spend too much time rolling dice or moving markers, their word learning may diminish.

SUMMARY

In this chapter you have been introduced to the research on, the testing of, and the teaching of basic sight words and sight words in general. Several basic sight word lists and the rationale for their use were presented. Ways of testing students' knowledge of basic sight words are included, along with problems you may encounter with these methods. You have also been given information on the testing of sight words in general. And finally, suggestions have been given for developing students' sight vocabularies.

REVIEW QUESTIONS

1. What is the definition of a basic sight word?
2. What do the authors mean by sight words in general or other sight words?
3. Would two adult fluent readers probably have basic sight vocabularies the same in size and number?
4. Would two adult fluent readers probably have the same sight vocabularies in general?
5. Why are basic sight word lists limited to somewhere between 200 and 300 words?
6. Why is a thorough knowledge of basic sight words necessary for fluent reading?

7. What are some commonly used basic sight word lists?

8. What problem does one encounter when testing a student's knowledge of basic sight words by having that student read words from a list?

9. Why is it undesirable to test students' knowledge of basic sight words in a group setting?

10. Why are some words designated as pre-primer level, primer level, etc.?

11. What is meant by testing in a situation analagous to actual reading?

REFERENCES

Allington, R. L. An evaluation of the use of color cues to focus attention in discrimination and paired-associate learning. *Reading Research Quarterly*, 1974–75, *10*(2), 244–47.

Arnold, R. D. Four measures of teaching word recognition to disabled readers. *Elementary School Journal*, 1968, *68*, 269–74.

Braun, C. Interest-loading and modality effects on textual response acquisition. *Reading Research Quarterly*, Spring, 1969, *4*, 428–44.

Dickerson, D. P. A study of the use of games to reinforce sight vocabulary. *Reading Teacher*, October, 1982, *36*, 46–49.

Dolch, E. W. *Basic sight word test*. Champaign, Ill.: Garrard Press, 1942.

Ehri, L. C., & Wilce, L. S. Do beginners learn to read function words better in sentences or in lists? *Reading Research Quarterly*, 1980, *15*(4), 451–76.

Ekwall, E. E. An analysis of children's test scores when tested with individually administered diagnostic tests and when tested with group administered tests. *Final research report, University Research Institute*, University of Texas at El Paso, 1973.

Ekwall, E. E. *Locating and correcting reading difficulties* (3rd ed.). Columbus, Ohio: Charles E. Merrill, 1981.

Ekwall, E. E., & Shanker, J. L. *Diagnosis and remediation of the disabled reader* (2nd ed.). Boston: Allyn and Bacon, 1983.

Fry, E. The new instant word list. *Reading Teacher*, December, 1980, *34*, 284–89.

Hampton, K. *An investigation of two methods of teaching basic sight vocabulary*. Master's thesis, California State University, Hayward, 1979.

Harris, A. J., & Sipay, E. R. *How to increase reading ability*. New York: Longman, 1980.

Hartley, R. N. Effects of list types and cues on learning of word lists. *Reading Research Quarterly*, Fall, 1970, *6*, 97–121.

King, E. M., & Muehl, S. Different sensory cues as aids in beginning reading. *Reading Teacher*, December, 1965, *19*, 163–68.

Kiraly, J., & Furlong, A. Teaching words to kindergarten children with picture, configuration and initial sound cues in a prompting procedure. *Journal of Educational Research*, March, 1974, *67*, 295–98.

Montare, A., Elman, E., & Cohen, J. Words and pictures: A test of Samuels' findings. *Journal of Reading Behavior*, Fall, 1977, *9*, 269–85.

Samuels, S. J. Attentional process in reading: The effect of pictures on the acquisition of reading response. *Journal of Educational Psychology*, December, 1967, *53*, 337–42.

Williams, J. P., Blumberg, E. L., & Williams, D. V. Cues used in visual words recognition. *Journal of Educational Psychology*, August, 1970, *61*, 310–15.

6

Assessing and Teaching the Decoding Skills

Reading teachers in the elementary schools must understand and be able to assess and teach the decoding or *word analysis skills,* those skills readers use to pronounce a word when it is not recognized instantly. *Decoding,* "breaking the code" of the language, is the process of taking words in print and changing them to spoken words. The decoding or word analysis skills considered in this chapter are: configuration clues, context clues, phonics, structural analysis, efficiency skills, and dictionary skills. Research into each of these skills will give you a base from which to make decisions about the assessment and teaching of word analysis in your classroom.

CONFIGURATION CLUES

Configuration clues are clues in the *shape* of the word that help a reader identify it. The shape of a word includes its length, x-height, ascenders, and descenders. For example, all the letters in the word *one* are at x-height, whereas the word *high* has two ascenders (*h*) and one descender (*g*).

Review of the Research on Configuration Clues

A study by Gabrielle Marchbanks and Harry Levin (1965) showed that word configuration, however, is not an effective word analysis cue. Marchbanks and Levin had kindergarten and first grade children attempt to match a pseudoword such as *vejat* with one of five other pseudowords. The child looked at the word *vejat* and then saw five other words, each of which was the same in only one way. For example, *vopuf* was the same only in shape, *vetep* was the same only by second letter, *vhjuo* was the same only by third letter, *vumag* was the same only by fourth letter, and *visht* was the same only by fifth letter. The child was to choose one word that was the same as *vejat*. The least used cue for the choice was the shape of the word; the next least used cue was the fourth letter.

Patrick Groff (1974) presented the results of the Marchbanks and Levin study along with a number of other studies. He concluded, "The statements made by most modern writers about how children recognize sight words generally are wrong. The shape of a word is the least-used cue to its recognition by beginning readers" (p. 577).

On the other hand, Ralph Norman Haber and Lyn R. Haber (1981) disputed the Marchbanks and Levin study. They used a passage in which words were omitted and replaced with square

and rectangular forms representing the shapes of various letters. For example, note the outline of the omitted words in this sentence:

(p. 338)

In the abstract of their research they stated,

The present paper counters Groff's argument by showing word shape information, when combined with knowledge of the syntactic and semantic structure of the passage being read, more often than not specifies unique words among all of the alternative high frequency words of English. Groff's error was his failure to consider word shape in the context of semantic and syntactic information, which are also available to the reader. (p. 334)

However, the Haber and Haber rebuttal is not justified by their research. When one reads the sample sentence, one probably uses **context clues** to determine what words are missing. (Context clues are clues to the meaning or pronunciation of a word from the words before or after the unknown one.) Then one *supports* these hypotheses by looking at the word shapes. Also, the Haber and Haber study was based only on *adults'* judgment of word shape. Kindergarten and first grade children learning to read would *not* have the background information to tell them that the words *and, went, for, a, in,* and *the* had their particular configurations or shapes.

Richard Allington and Michael Strange (1977) also studied the import of configuration clues. They had both good and poor fourth-grade readers read sentences in which 5 percent of the words were changed to words used improperly. For example, students read, "He leaned too *fan* over the edge of the wall," and "Bill jumped off the bus and *ram* to the river." The researchers reasoned that if children corrected the wrong word then they were relying more on contextual cues than graphic (configuration) ones. On the other hand, if they read the word as written, then they were relying more on graphic cues than contextual information. Allington and Strange found that both good and poor readers corrected the wrong words 56 percent of the time. They found, however, that good readers more often read the wrong word. They thought that the groups rely equally on contextual information but that good readers use graphic information more than poor readers do.

In a replication of the Allington and Strange study, Robert M. Schwartz and Keith E. Stanovich (1981) obtained almost identical results. Summarizing their study, Schwartz and Stanovich stated, "While good readers seemed able to suspend the contribution of contextual information in their target word responses, poor readers were less able to do so" (p. 269).

Maria A. Ceprano (1981a) reviewed the research on the effectiveness of using pictures to help children differentiate between nouns with similar configurations, such as *bell* and *ball*. She found conflicting results; however, for children who confuse certain nouns, using a picture to illustrate each word may sometimes help.

Research studies on the usefulness of configuration clues have produced conflicting results. More unbiased research is needed to determine how useful configuration clues are.

Assessing Students' Knowledge of Configuration Clues

As indicated by the research, configuration clues may be somewhat important to the reader. However, no tests are available for assessing this skill. Students' awareness of configuration can best be evaluated by informal questioning. For example, you might ask questions such as, "How can we tell the difference between *when* and *what*?" and "What do you think we should do to help you remember the difference between *that* and *this*?"

Teaching Configuration Clues

The research on configuration clues seems to indicate that not much needs to be taught to children about this word analysis skill. Although configuration clues are somewhat important to children as well as adults, very little is known about teaching them. What *is* known can be summarized as follows:

1. The overall shape of a word helps students very little in differentiating one word from another.
2. Children do note first and last letters of words in differentiating one word from another.
3. Children with problems differentiating nouns with similar configurations, such as *bell* and *ball*, often profit from picture cues.

CONTEXT CLUES

Context clues are clues to the meaning or pronunciation of an unknown word from the surrounding words and/or sentences. The reader uses the sense of a sentence or passage to figure out the unknown word.

Review of the Research on Context Clues

In stressing the importance of context clues, Paul Burns and Leo Schell (1975) say that using "context clues may be the major skill which distinguishes connected meaningful reading from reading of word lists" (p. 90).

Maria A. Ceprano (1981b) studied 159 kindergarten children from seven classes in a suburban school to determine whether a "word alone" or "context method" is most useful in teaching context clues. Summarizing, she states

For the practitioner, the present study seems to suggest that a method that focuses the learner's attention on the structural characteristics of the words alone accelerates the rate at which words are learned. However, the ability to read words in text does not appear to be guaranteed by such a method of instruction. Care must be taken to see that the learner develops the ability to effectively utilize context as a means of recognizing words in text. A word alone method may prove beneficial for teaching children who have acquired some reading competency and who need to expand their stock of sight words for a particular reading assignment. For the prereader, however, a slower rate of sight word acquisition may be justifiable if additional skills needed for contextual reading are being acquired conjunctively. (p. 388)

Andrew Biemiller (1977–78) also emphasizes the importance of context clues. Indeed, Biemiller points out that poor readers seem to use context clues as effectively as good readers and that simply practicing the act of reading encourages students to use context clues. He states,

The evidence presented in this paper indicating that slow readers use context as effectively as abler readers to facilitate speed provides further support for the hypothesis that practice emphasizing actual reading may be more useful than discussions aimed at enhancing the use of context. (pp. 250–51)

Janet Ross Kendall and Joyce Hood (1979) compared the reading ability of *high comprehension-low word recognition* students to the ability of those with *low comprehension and high word recognition*. The students with high comprehension abilities tended to use context clues better than those with low comprehension and high word recognition abilities.

They found no difference between groups in their ability to use graphic (configuration) clues. Also important, the high comprehension-low word recognition group answered questions no better than the low comprehension-high word recognition students. The high comprehension group had such low word recognition abilities that they read slowly and had to ponder words, which inhibited their ability to comprehend.

This study indicates that most reading programs do not give students enough time to simply read for pleasure. Reading gives the students multiple exposures to many words, which expands readers' sight vocabulary, which in turn raises their ability to comprehend, and thus make better use of context clues.

Using context clues is an important skill. However, by itself, context usually does not give students enough information to accurately attack each word. In a study by H. Alan Robinson (1963), several fourth graders took a test of basic sight words. These words were presented to students in rapid succession. Words missed were then represented by blank spaces in the context of a passage. Later, the same passage was presented to the students, but configuration clues were added. In the context alone situation, stu-

dents determined which word should go in the blank only one-seventh of one percent of the time. And only 14 percent of the responses given were meaningful synonyms. When configuration was added to context, students still got only one-fifth of one percent of the words. Again, only about 14 percent of the words given were meaningful synonyms. Robinson concluded that students need to learn *how* to use context clues.

Several studies show that simply giving students materials with words omitted and blanks substituted does not contribute much to students' learning how to use context clues. On the other hand, when such an exercise is followed by a discussion of what words *should* be in the blanks and *why*, students benefit considerably.

Assessing Students' Knowledge of Context Clues

Burns and Schell list some characteristics of a student unable to use context clues effectively:

1. The student stops at an unknown word.
2. The student relies too much on other skills, such as configuration clues and/or beginning or ending sounds.
3. The student may practice less effective word analysis techniques, such as signals from the teacher or picture clues.

These characteristics may be noted by simply observing the students' oral reading behaviors. To assess students more formally, use the following techniques. Note the progression in difficulty.

Assess students' ability to *listen* for context clues. Students should understand context clues in oral language before trying to use them in written discourse. This can be done by making a tape recording in which certain key words are omitted and replaced by a bell or beep sound. Then play the tape recording and have the student try to figure out what word has been omitted. The student's responses may be written or oral depending on grade level. A script for such a tape might read:

Mother called Jack to (beep) to breakfast. When Jack (beep) down at the table, he asked his mother for some milk to (beep).

Assess students' ability to fill in a word from context when the first letter is given and the rest of the letters are replaced with *x*'s.

Mother called Jack to *cxxx* to breakfast. When Jack *sxx* down at the table, he asked his mother for some milk to *dxxxx*.

Assess students' ability to fill in a word from context when all letters have been replaced with *x*'s.

Mother called Jack to *xxxx* to breakfast. When Jack *xxx* down at the table, he asked his mother for some milk to *xxxxx*.

Assess students' ability to fill in a word from context when only a blank is given.

Mother called Jack to _____ to breakfast. When Jack _____ down at the table, he asked his mother for some milk to _____.

When using this testing system, remember the following points:

1. Always use material at the student's *independent* or easy *instructional* level. Even students who efficiently use context clues will do poorly on material at their difficult *instructional* or *frustration* levels. (See Chapter 10 for matching children and reading materials.)
2. Make all the blanks the same length in the last technique.
3. Make sure students can do the first technique before proceeding to the next, etc.

Teaching Context Clues

To the teacher and experienced reader, context clues are taken for granted. Thus, the teacher must remember that context clues have to be *taught* to beginning readers. Many children understand how to use context clues without being taught, but others benefit a great deal from con-

text clues instruction. Research shows that students who practice filling in blanks do not improve unless the teacher discusses the passages with students afterwards. To successfully teach context clues, the teacher usually prepares an overhead transparency of the same materials the student uses to fill in blanks. The teacher then discusses why responses given by students *are* or *are not* appropriate. To prepare for this type of instruction try a sequence similar to that of assessing students in this skill:

1. Play a tape recording of someone telling a story or reading a passage. Omit certain words and replace them with a sound. When students hear the "beep," they should write down the word they think should be inserted there. (Younger students may respond orally.)

2. Give students passages in which certain words are omitted, the initial consonant remains, and other letters are replaced with *x*'s. See the following example.

Jim went *tx* visit his aunt who lived *wxxx* his uncle on a farm.

3. Give students passages with certain words omitted. Replace words with *x*'s.

Jim went *xx* visit his aunt who lived *xxxx* his uncle on a farm.

4. Give students passages with words omitted and replaced with blanks:

Jim went _____ visit his aunt who lived _____ his uncle on a farm.

Keep the following points in mind:

1. Make sure omitted words can be easily gotten from the context.

2. Make sure that written materials are at students' *independent* or easy *instructional* levels. When students read materials too difficult for them, they cannot use context clues effectively.

3. Do not use written materials until students can easily fill in the blanks in oral situations. Then do not move to a more difficult activity until students master the one they are working on.

4. When using blanks, make sure they are all the same length.

5. Make an overhead transparency of the materials on which students have been working, discuss possible answers, and discuss why they *would* or *would not* be appropriate.

When discussing materials placed on the overhead projector, cover each word left blank on students' papers with a piece of paper and make a hinge out of masking tape. Then when you come to a covered word, discuss what words the students think might fit in the blank and why they *would* or *would not* be appropriate. After such a discussion, lift the cover from the word and show students the word originally in the blank space.

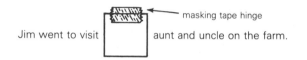

Jim went to visit [ ] aunt and uncle on the farm.

masking tape hinge

As with many other skills, being able to use context clues will improve with practice. Simply providing many opportunities for students to read will help students improve their use of context clues.

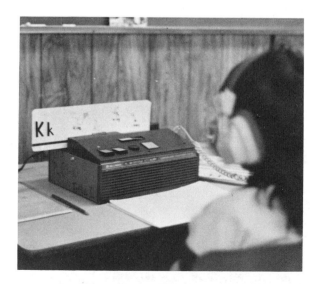

The electronic card reader helps teach phoneme–grapheme relationships.

PHONICS

Phonics is an approach to the teaching of reading and spelling that stresses sound-symbol relationships. Usually used to teach beginning readers, the approach covers several *phonic elements:* initial consonants, consonant digraphs, consonant blends, vowels, vowel combinations, and special letter combinations.

Basic Phonics Information

Reading teachers should have a grasp of the following information so that they can assess and teach phonics.[1]

The vowel sounds are as follows:

Short Sounds		Long Sounds	
a	bat	a	rake
e	bed	e	jeep
i	pig	i	kite
o	lock	o	rope
u	duck	u	mule

W is sometimes used as a vowel, as in the *ow* and *aw* teams. It is usually a vowel on word endings and a consonant at the beginning of words. *Y* is usually a consonant when it appears at the beginning of a word, and a vowel in any other position.

Three consonants usually affect or control the sounds of some, or all, of the vowels when they follow these vowels within a syllable. They are *r*, *w*, and *l*.

r (all vowels)		*w* (*a, e,* and *o*)	*l* (*a*)
car	for	law	all
her	fur	few	
dirt		now	

The consonant sounds are as follows:

b	bear	k	king	s	six
c	cat	l	lake	t	turtle
d	dog	m	money	v	vase
f	face	n	nose	w	wagon
g	goat	p	pear	x	xylophone
h	hen	q	queen	y	yellow
j	jug	r	rat	z	zebra

[1]From *Locating and Correcting Reading Difficulties* (3rd ed.) by E.E. Ekwall (Columbus, Ohio: Charles E. Merrill, Inc., 1981), 136–38. Copyright 1981 by Charles E. Merrill, Inc. Adapted by permission.

The following consonants have two or more sounds:

c	cat	g	goat	s	six	x	xylophone
c	ice	g	germ	s	is	x	exist
						x	box

When *g* is followed by *e, i,* or *y* it *often* takes the soft sound of *j,* as in *gentle* and *germ.* If it is not followed by these letters, it takes the hard sound illustrated in such words as *got* and *game.* When *c* is followed by *e, i,* or *y* it *usually* takes the soft sound heard in *cent.* If it is not followed by these letters, it *usually* takes the hard sound heard in *come. Qu* usually has the sound of *kw;* however, in some words, such as bouquet, it has the sound of *k. S* sometimes takes a slightly different sound in words such as sure.

A **consonant blend** is a combination of two or more consonants that blend together, but the sound for each letter is heard. To say a consonant blend, you retain the sound of the individual letters and change the position of the mouth from the beginning to the end of the sound. The consonant blends are as follows:

Beginning

bl	blue	pr	pretty	tw	twelve
br	brown	sc	score	wr	wrench
cl	clown	sk	skill	sch	school
cr	crown	sl	slow	scr	screen
dr	dress	sm	small	shr	shrink
dw	dwell	sn	snail	spl	splash
fl	flower	sp	spin	spr	spring
fr	from	st	story	squ	squash
gl	glue	sw	swan	str	string
gr	grape	tr	tree	thr	throw
pl	plate				

Ending

ld	wild
mp	lamp
nd	wind
nt	went
rk	work
sk	risk

A **digraph** is a combination of two letters recording a single sound. A **consonant digraph** is a combination of two consonant letters recording a single sound, and a **vowel digraph** combines two vowels in a single sound. To say a digraph, you need not move the mouth's position from the beginning to the end of the sound. (**Consonant cluster** is a term used to mean both consonant digraphs and consonant blends.) The consonant and vowel digraphs are as follows:

Consonant

ch	chute	sh	ship
ch	choral	th	three
ch	church	th	that
gh	cough	wh	which
ph	graph	wh	who

Vowel (Most common phonemes only)

ai	pain	ie	piece	ow	low
ay	hay		(A number of other		
			phonemes are common		
			for *ie.*)		
ea	each	oa	oats		
	or	oo	book		
ea	weather	oo	moon		
ei	weight	ou	tough (*Ou* may be		
	or		either a		
ei	either		digraph or		
			diphthong.)		

A **diphthong** is a combination of two vowels that records a sliding sound. To say a diphthong, you must change the mouth's position from the beginning to the end of that sound. Some diphthongs are as follows:

au	haul[1]	oi	soil
aw	hawk[1]	ou	trout
ew	few	ow	cow
ey	they	oy	boy

Review of the Research on Phonics

Several opponents of teaching phonics have been vocal during the past decade. Josephine Spivack Goldsmith (1981) discusses the research studies done by these opponents and mentions Kenneth Goodman's views on phonics. Goldsmith states,

Goodman (1972) regards training in word perception as a greatly overemphasized, even misguided, aspect of reading instruction. For him, word-centered

[1]Some may hear *au* and *aw* as a digraph.

reading approaches are wrong from several perspectives. First, he views words as artificial constructions of written language which do not exist in the same structured fashion in speech. . . . Individual words . . . are seen as dependent units which derive their meaning from surrounding context. Additionally, Goodman (1972) views the emphasis on word perception as a violation of the skills and style of dealing with language that a child has already developed in learning to speak. As a speaker of language, the child qualifies as an "intuitive grammarian" (Goodman and Goodman, 1977, p. 327). Young speakers have taught themselves to deal with grammatical relations between words and to rely heavily on context to find the meaning of speech. (p. 154)

Goldsmith points out some of the fallacies in Goodman's thinking by quoting the results of other research studies. For example, she mentions a series of studies by A. Biemiller, who found that good readers seem to be better perceivers of words, and particularly of words in isolation. She also mentions his findings that word perception is highly related to comprehension: if a child perceives words accurately, then she probably comprehends better. Goldsmith notes that attention to context is not necessarily the strategy used by good readers, and she stresses that attention to context may not necessarily mean *proper* contextual use. Furthermore, word perception itself involves an active search for meaning, which counters Goodman's claim that when children focus on the accuracy of words, their comprehension is hindered. Goodman also maintains that teachers need not be especially concerned about children's miscalling of words, but Goldsmith says,

Teachers should not be pleased about the syntactic and semantic strengths of poor readers if these reflect strategies which are used because other important skills are missing. It is clearly not acceptable for a reader to have problems with word attack any more than it is acceptable for him/her to be a word caller who does not comprehend. . . . [W]hat distinguishes good from poor readers appears to be not only a more developed array of skills but a more finely tuned synchrony among them. (p. 157)

Finally, Goldsmith points out that

The problem with both the word-centered and

psycholinguistic approaches is not that either has a wrong basis for argument but that both claim too large a share of the field. Essentially, both theories are correct. It is in the insistence on dichotomizing that error exists. Instead of asking which system is more important, researchers must determine which balance between the two approaches is optimal for various combinations of readers and texts. (p. 157)

In a review of the history of phonics instruction, Gwen Fulwiler and Patrick Groff (1980) also note that a long-standing controversy over the effectiveness of phonics instruction exists, and as a result, phonics instruction has waxed and waned over the years. Fulwiler and Groff summarize,

The first such review in this century was that by Chall. Chall concluded from her impressive review of the studies of the effectiveness of phonics that "the research from 1912 to 1965 indicates that a code-emphasis method—i.e., one that views beginning reading as essentially different from mature reading and emphasizes learning of the printed code for the spoken language—produces better results, at least to the point where sufficient evidence seems to be available, to the end of the third grade" (Chall, 1967, p. 307). Dykstra's more recent examination of the research on phonics Chall reviewed, plus that of a like nature carried out since 1965, leads him to the same conclusion. Dykstra judges that this "evidence clearly demonstrates that children who receive early intensive instruction in phonics develop superior word recognition skills in the early stages of reading and tend to maintain their superiority at least through the third grade." It is clear, he concludes, that "early systematic instruction in phonics provides the child with the skills necessary to become an independent reader at an earlier age than is likely if phonics instruction is delayed and less systematic" (Walcutt et al., 1974, p. 397). (p. 50)

Fulwiler and Groff themselves compared two methods of teaching children to read: an intensive phonics approach and a less intensive approach (some sight words taught before children learn any phonics). In the less intensive approach, teachers teach phonics in an incidental manner. Fulwiler and Groff found that students in the intensive phonics program "gained higher levels of achievement in vocabulary, word analysis, comprehension, and in the average of these three skills than did the group of pupils in the less intensive phonics classes" (p. 52). Fulwiler and Groff concluded,

The findings of the present study do not support the contentions of the recent opponents of phonics instruction that phonics teaching is detrimental to the development of children's reading skills, and/or that it should be considered a matter of little or no concern to the reading teacher. To the contrary, the findings of the study reported here reaffirm the findings from past research on this issue. These findings have indicated that intensive phonics brings on greater beginning reading achievement than do reading programs which deemphasize phonics teaching. The present study thus suggests that instruction in intensive phonics is critical to the development of beginning reading skills and therefore is to be recommended. (p. 53)

Fulwiler and Groff also said their findings did not support the contention that teaching word attack skills ultimately hinders the reader's ability to comprehend. Those students receiving intensive phonics instruction also comprehended material better than those who did not.

Several research studies have been undertaken to determine which, if any, phonics rules and/or generalizations should be taught. One such study, by Theodore Clymer (1963), should have led to some reform in what we teach. Clymer examined four "widely used" sets of basal readers to see which phonic generalizations were actually taught in the primary grades. He found five general types of phonic generalizations: "(1) vowels, (2) consonants, (3) endings, (4) syllabication, and (5) miscellaneous relationships" (p. 253). Clymer used several criteria to determine which generalizations were useful. For example, was the generalization stated specifically enough to help the student pronounce a particular word? He also wanted to know which words should be used to decide whether the generalizations were effective. He listed all the words introduced in the four series of basal readers plus the words from *Gates Reading Vocabulary for the Primary Grades*. He then checked the phonetic respelling and the syllabic division of all the words according to *Webster's New Collegiate Dictionary*. By dividing the number of words pronounced,

as the generalization claimed, by the total number of words to which the generalization *could* apply, Clymer computed a utility percentage. Clymer's first criterion for putting a generalization on the list was that it must have at least twenty words to which it might apply. The generalization also had to have at least 75 percent utility. Clymer explained, "If the pupil applied the generalization to twenty words, it should aid him in getting the correct pronunciation in fifteen of twenty words" (p. 255). Clymer's information about phonic generalizations is presented in Table 6–1.

Clymer found that only 18 of the 45 generalizations met the criteria he established: numbers 5, 8, 10, 16, 20, 21, 22, 23, 25, 28, 29, 30, 31, 32, 40, 41, 44, and 45. In his conclusion Clymer stated,

In evaluating this initial venture in testing the utility of phonic generalizations, it seems quite clear that many generalizations which are commonly taught are of limited value. Certainly the study indicated that we should give careful attention to pointing out the many exceptions to most of the generalizations that we teach. Current "extrinsic" phonics programs which present large numbers of generalizations are open to question on the basis of this study. . . . The most disturbing fact to come from the study may be the rather dismal failure of generalization 1 to provide the correct pronunciation even 50 percent of the time. As one teacher remarked when this study was presented to a reading methods class, "Mr. Clymer, for years I've been teaching 'When two vowels go walking, the first one does the talking.' You're ruining the romance in the teaching of reading!" (p. 258)

Look over the 45 generalizations presented by Clymer, which are not necessarily *the* phonic generalizations to be learned, and become familiar with the 18 that met the criteria Clymer set forth.

After Clymer's study, other studies used the same 45 generalizations but different word lists. For example, Mildred Hart Bailey (1967) used words from eight sets of basal readers. She used only those words appearing in two or more of the eight series. She excluded place names, proper names, and foreign words and formed a list of 5,773 words. Bailey thought including gen-

Table 6–1   The utility of phonic generalizations in grades one through six

Generalization	No. of Incidents	No. of Words Conforming	No. of Exceptions	Percent of Utility
1. When there are two vowels side by side, the long sound of the first vowel is heard, and the second vowel is usually silent.	1732	586 (leader)†	1146 (breath)	34
2. When a vowel is in the middle of a one-syllable word, the vowel is short.	1021	730	291	71
Middle letter	430	335 (flank)	95 (her)	78
One of the middle two letters in a word of four letters	478	325 (glen)	153 (long)	68
One vowel within a word of more than four letters	113	70 (depth)	43 (knight)	62
3. If the only vowel letter is at the end of a word, the letter usually stands for a long sound.	38	29 (go)	9 (do)	76
4. When there are two vowels, one of which is final e, the first vowel is long and the e is silent.	578	330 (cradle)	248 (judge)	57
5. The r gives the preceding vowel a sound that is neither long nor short.	1604	1378 (depart)	226 (merit)	86
6. The first vowel is usually long and the second silent in the digraphs ai, ea, oa, and ui.	497	298	199	60
ai	121	87 (acclaim)	34 (plaid)	72
ea	259	143 (bean)	116 (create)	55
oa	66	63 (roam)	3 (broad)	95
ui	51	5 (pursuit)	46 (biscuit)	10
7. In the phonogram ie, the i is silent, and the e has a long sound.	88	27 (grieve)	61 (brier)	31
8. Words having double e usually have the long e sound.	171	148 (exceed)	23 (deer)	87
9. When words end with silent e, the preceding a or i is long.	674	340 (amaze)	334 (give)	50
10. In ay, the y is silent and gives a its long sound.	50	44 (spray)	6 (prayer)	88
11. When the letter i is followed by the letters gh, the i usually stands for its long sound, and the gh is silent.	35	25 (flight)	10 (weight)	71
12. When a follows w in a word, it usually has the sound a as in was.	78	17 (wand)	61 (sway)	22
13. When e is followed by w, the vowel sound is the same as represented by oo.	35	14 (shrewd)	21 (stew)	40

†Words in parentheses are examples, either of words following the rule or of exceptions, depending on the column.

Note. From "The Utility of Phonic Generalizations in the Primary Grades" by T. Clymer, *Reading Teacher, 1963, 16,* 256–58. Copyright 1963 by the International Reading Association. Reprinted with permission of T. Clymer and the International Reading Association.

Table 6–1   (Continued)

Generalization	No. of Incidents	No. of Words Conforming	No. of Exceptions	Percent of Utility
14. The two letters *ow* make the long *o* sound.	111	61 (flow)	50 (scowl)	55
15. *W* is sometimes a vowel and follows the vowel digraph rule.	180	60 (arrow)	120 (drew)	33
16. When *y* is the final letter in a word, it usually has a vowel sound.	518	462 (lady)	56 (key)	89
17. When *y* is used as a vowel in words, it sometimes has the sound of long *i.*	596	63 (ally)	533 (silly)	11
18. The letter *a* has the same sound (ô) when followed by *l, w,* and *u.*	346	119 (raw)	227 (laugh)	34
19. When *a* is followed by *r* and final *e,* we expect to hear the sound heard in *care.*	24	23 (flare)	1 (are)	96
20. When *c* and *h* are next to each other, they make only one sound.	225	225 (charge)	0	100
21. *Ch* is usually pronounced as it is in *kitchen, catch,* and *chair,* not like *sh.*	225	196 (pitch)	29 (chute)	87
22. When *c* is followed by *e* or *i,* the sound of *s* is likely to be heard.	284	260 (glance)	24 (ancient)	92
23. When the letter *c* is followed by *o* or *a,* the sound of *k* is likely to be heard.	428	428 (canal)	0	100
24. The letter *g* often has a sound similar to that of *j* in *jump* when it precedes the letter *i* or *e.*	216	168 (genius)	48 (eager)	78
25. When *ght* is seen in a word, *gh* is silent.	40	40 (tight)	0	100
26. When a word begins *kn,* the *k* is silent.	17	17 (knit)	0	100
27. When a word begins with *wr,* the *w* is silent.	17	17 (wrap)	0	100
28. When two of the same consonants are side by side, only one is heard.	826	809 (dollar)	17 (accept)	98
29. When a word ends in *ck,* it has the same last sound as in *look.*	80	80 (neck)	0	100
30. In most two-syllable words, the first syllable is accented.	2345	1906 (bottom)	439 (attire)	81
31. If *a, in, re, ex, de,* or *be* is the first syllable in a word, it is usually un-accented.	398	336 (reply)	62 (extra)	84
32. In most two-syllable words that end in a consonant followed by *y,* the first syllable is accented and the last is unaccented.	195	190 (pony)	5 (apply)	97
33. One vowel letter in an unaccented syllable has its short sound.	3031	1960 (banish)	1071 (fortune)	65
34. When *y* or *ey* is seen in the last syllable that is not accented, the long sound of *e* is heard.	449	0	449 (ferry)	0

Table 6–1   (Continued)

Generalization	No. of Incidents	No. of Words Conforming	No. of Exceptions	Percent of Utility
35. When *ture* is the final syllable in a word, it is unaccented.	22	21 (future)	1 (mature)	95
36. When *tion* is the final syllable in a word, it is unaccented.	102	102 (notion)	0	100
37. In many two- and three-syllable words, the final *e* lengthens the vowel in the last syllable.	430	198 (costume)	232 (welcome)	46
38. If the first vowel sound in a word is followed by two consonants, the first syllable usually ends with the first of the two consonants.	1689	1311 (dinner)	378 (maple)	78
39. If the first vowel sound in a word is followed by a single consonant, that consonant usually begins the second syllable.	1283	638 (china)	645 (shadow)	50
40. If the last syllable of a word ends in *le,* the consonant preceding the *le* usually begins the last syllable.	211	196 (gable)	15 (crackle)	93
41. When the first vowel element in a word is followed by *th, ch,* or *sh,* these symbols are not broken when the word is divided into syllables and may go with either the first or second syllable.	74	74 (fashion)	0	100
42. In a word of more than one syllable, the letter *v* usually goes with the preceding vowel to form a syllable.	184	119 (river)	65 (navy)	65
43. When a word has only one vowel letter, the vowel sound is likely to be short.	1105	759 (crib)	346 (fall)	69
44. When there is one *e* in a word that ends in a consonant, the *e* usually has a short sound.	149	137 (held)	12 (clerk)	92
45. When the last syllable is the sound *r,* it is unaccented.	761	601 (ever)	160 (prefer)	79

eralizations 1, 7, 12, 13, 15, 17, 18, and 34 in any phonics program was improper because of their low utility. Also, generalizations 13, 16, 30, and 45 had low enough utility to question their use in the classroom. Only generalizations 20, 22, 23, 28, 32, and 40, according to Bailey, were both simple to understand and could be applied to a large number of words with few exceptions. Robert Emans (1967) used words appearing *beyond* the primary level in his study and found

that then generalization number 1 had a utility of only 18 percent!

The problem of sounds represented by various vowel combinations was clarified somewhat by Lou E. Burmeister (1971). Burmeister recorded the vowel-vowel combinations that form a single phoneme for 17,310 words. Table 6–2 shows the frequency and percent of occurrence of each single phoneme for each vowel-pair grapheme. This table, of course, explains why the old

Table 6–2   Frequency and percent of occurrence of each phoneme for each single vowel-pair grapheme

Grapheme		Phonemic Behavior			
Name	Frequency	Pronun- ciation Key	Example	Frequency	Percent
ae	(6)	ē	algae	5	83.3
		ĕ	aesthetic	1	16.7
ai	(309)	ā	abstain	230	74.4
		â	air	49	15.6
		ĭ	mountain	15	4.9
		ə	villain	9	2.9
		ĕ	again	4	1.3
		ã	plaid	1	.3
		ī	aisle	1	.3
ao	(2)	ô	extraordinary	2	100
au	(178)	ô	auction	167	93.8
		ō	chauffeur	5	2.8
		ä	laugh	4	2.2
		ə	epaulet	1	.6
		ā	gauge	1	.6
ay	(137)	ā	gray	132	96.4
		ī	kayak	3	2.2
		ĕ	says	1	.7
		ĭ	yesterday	1	.7
aw	(77)	ô	lawn	77	100
ea	(545)	ē	east	275	50.5
		ĕ	weapon	140	25.7
		ẹ̄	ear	49	9.0
		û	earth	31	5.7
		â	bear	13	2.4
		ä	hearty	18	3.3
		ā	great	14	2.6
		ĭ	guinea	2	.4
		ə	sergeant	3	.5
ee	(290)	ē	sleet	248	85.5
		ẹ̄	peer	36	12.4
		ĭ	been	6	2.1
ei	(86)	ā	reign	34	40.0
		ē	deceit	22	25.6
		ĭ	foreign	11	12.8
		ī	seismic	9	10.5

Table 6–2   (Continued)

Grapheme		Phonemic Behavior			
Name	Frequency	Pronun-ciation Key	Example	Frequency	Percent
ei		â	their	5	5.8
		ə	sovereignty	2	2.3
		ệ	weird	2	2.3
		ĕ	heifer	1	1.2
eo	(15)	ə	pigeon	10	66.7
		ĕ	leopard	3	20.0
		ē	people	2	13.3
eu	(40)	ū	feud	29	72.5
		û	amateur	6	15.0
		o͞o	sleuth	4	10.0
		o͞o	pleurisy	1	2.5
ey	(69)	ĭ	honey	40	58.0
		ā	convey	14	20.3
		ī	geyser	8	11.6
		ē	key	6	8.7
		â	eyrie	1	1.4
ew	(64)	ū	news	39	60.9
		o͞o	flew	22	34.4
		ō	sew	3	4.7
ia		ĭ	carriage	3	60
		ə	parliament	2	40
ie	(156)	ē	thief	56	35.9
		ĭ	lassie	30	19.2
		ī	die	26	16.7
		ə	patient	23	14.7
		ệ	cashier	17	10.9
		e	friend	4	2.6
oa	(138)	ō	road	129	93.5
		ô	broad	9	6.5
oe	(22)	ō	foe	13	59.1
		ē	amoeba	5	22.7
		o͞o	shoe	4	18.2
oi	(102)	oi	moist	100	98.0
		ə	porpoise	2	2.0
oo	(315)	o͞o	lagoon	185	58.7
		o͝o	wood	114	36.2
		ō	floor	9	2.9
		ŭ	blood	7	2.2
ou	(815)	ə	rigorous	336	41.2
		ou	out	285	35.0

Table 6–2 (Continued)

Grapheme		Phonemic Behavior			
Name	Frequency	Pronunciation Key	Example	Frequency	Percent
ou		o͞o	soup	54	6.6
		ō	four	47	5.8
		ŭ	touch	30	3.7
		o͝o	your	25	3.1
		û	journey	22	2.7
		ĕ	glamour	1	.1
oy	(50)	oi	convoy	49	98.0
		ī	coyote	1	2.0
ow	(250)	ō	own	125	50.0
		ou	town	121	48.4
		ŏ	knowledge	4	1.6
ue	(43)	ū	due, cue	27	62.8
		o͞o	clue	16	37.2
ui	(34)	ĭ	build	16	47.1
		o͞o	fruit	10	29.4
		ū	suit	8	23.5
uo	(2)	o͞o	buoyant	2	100
uy	(3)	ī	buy	3	100

generalization, "When two vowels go walking, the first one does the talking," is of such low utility.

Even though certain rules may hold true for certain words of high utility, those rules may not necessarily be the ones to teach elementary students, because students may not be learning those particular words. Burmeister compared the findings of other studies that investigated the value of phonic, structural analysis, and accent generalizations and then decided which of these different rules were most useful to teach. Her recommendations appear in Table 6–3.

Margaret J. Hislop and Ethel M. King (1973) studied how well boys and girls in grades 1 through 3 could apply phonics generalizations to nonsense words before and after receiving instruction on these generalizations. These authors found that "there was a significant difference in performance on the eighteen generalizations when they were being applied after introduction in the basal reader" (p. 410). They also found that phonic generalizations were applied with increasing efficiency as children progressed. Hislop and King stated,

> The evidence indicates that in order to apply phonic generalizations, pupils need specific guidance in arriving at these generalizations. Furthermore, since none of the eighteen generalizations investigated in this study had been mastered by every S [subject], introduction of the phonic generalizations does not appear to be sufficient for mastery. Frequent review of the generalizations and many opportunities to apply them are obviously needed. . . . The explanations offered by the pupils reveal that different methods were used in identifying new words. Very few children stated the phonic generalizations in an acceptable form. Some made reference to relevant cues in the words, but the majority were unable to explain how they had arrived at their pronunciation. Perhaps children are given too few opportunities to discuss the application of phonic principles in words. The procedure of asking for expla-

Table 6–3 Particularly useful grapheme (printed symbol) to phoneme (sound) relationships

Note: A *phoneme* is the smallest unit of sound; a *grapheme* is the symbol we use to represent the sound. The word *cat* has three phonemes and, therefore, three graphemes. The word *main* has three phonemes and, therefore, three graphemes (one grapheme *ai* is spelled with two letters). In this paper grapheme to phoneme relations are described *within* morphemes only (i.e., not between morphemes). Thus syllabication generalizations and grapheme to phoneme relationships dependent upon divisions made because of prefixes, roots, and suffixes are not included.

I. Consonants
   A. Single consonants
      1. Each consonant (except *c, g, s,* and *x*) is highly consistent in representing one sound.
      2. When *c* or *g* is followed by *e, i,* or *y,* it represents its soft sound (city, certain, cycle; gem, agile, gym). When followed by anything else, or nothing, it represents its hard sound (cake, coat, cup, clash, cram, attic; game, goat, gum, glass, grip, flag). Omit *ch* and *gh.*
      3. The letter *s* usually (86 percent of the time) represents its own sound (swim, soft, solo). Its next most frequent sound (/z/–11 percent) is found in words such as resort, raisin, music, desire, treason. Omit *sh.*
      4. The letter *x* represents the sounds found in the following words (/ks/ or /k/ + /s/): ax, box, tax; foxy, taxi, vixen, and (/g/ + /z/): exact, exempt, exist, example.
   B. Double consonants (and triple consonants)
      1. Consonant blends—When two unlike consonants appear side-by-side, usually the sound represented is a blend of the sounds represented by each (*bl*ock, *cl*own, *dr*own, *gr*ow, *sm*ile, *sp*ook, *spl*ash, etc.)
      2. Consonant digraphs—Although spelled with two consonants, consonant digraphs function as single consonants. They are *ch, sh, th, ph, ng,* and *ck. Ch* represents three sounds: /ch/ child, chop – 63 percent, /k/ chorus, christen, orchid – 30 percent, /sh/ chef, chute, mustache – 7 percent; *sh,* as in should, ship, shed; *th* represents two sounds, voiced, as in this, they, rhythm – 74 percent, and voiceless, as in think, thick, youth – 26 percent; *ph* represents an *f* sound, as in elephant, photo; *ng* as in sing, wing, young; *ck* represents a *k* sound, as in chick, package, cuckoo. (*ck* is really two like consonants together, in which *c* represents the *k* sound, and is silent. See 3a).
      3. Silent consonants
         a. Like consonants—When two like consonants are side-by-side, they represent only one sound. (This is not true of *cc* or *gg* when followed by e, i, or y – success, suggest.) E.g., ball, egg, guppy, guerrilla, tattoo.
         b. Unlike consonants—When certain consonants are side-by-side in the same syllable, only one sound is represented. This is true of the following pairs (the only pairs which occur at least once per thousand running words): *initial kn-,* as in kneel, knot; *initial ps-,* as in psalm, pseudo; *initial wr-,* as in wrap, write; *final -dg*(e), as in dodge, bridge; *final -gn,* as in sign, reign; but also *initial gn-,* as in gnat, gnome; *final -lm,* as in calm, palm; *final -mb,* as in bomb, comb; *final -tch,* as in catch, witch.
II. Vowels
   A. Definitions: the five vowels (*a, e, i, o, u*) and two "semi-vowels" (*y* and *w*) are used singly and in pairs and in the final vowel (consonant) *e* position to represent a variety of sounds. The most common sounds are the vowel's own short sound (h*a*t, p*e*t, h*i*t, h*o*t, h*u*t), the long sound (m*ai*n, m*ea*t, s*i*ze, *oa*k, c*u*te), a schwa (*a*bout, cam*e*l, penc*i*l, lem*o*n, circ*u*s, marr*i*age), an *r* modified sound (car, care, her, hear, for), a diphthong (*ou*t, c*ow*, c*oi*n, b*oy*), a *broad a* – or *circumflex o* – *au*to, *aw*ful, b*a*ll; a long and short double *o* (rooster, book).

Note. From "Content of a Phonics Program Based on Particularly Useful Generalizations" by L.E. Burmeister. In *Reading Methods and Teacher Improvement*, edited by N.B. Smith (Newark, Del.: International Reading Association, 1971), 28–33. Copyright 1971 by the International Reading Association. Reprinted with permission of L.E. Burmeister and the International Reading Association.

Table 6–3 (Continued)

B. Single vowel graphemes
   1. Closed syllable (syllable that contains a single vowel and ends with a consonant)—A single vowel in a closed syllable represents its own short sound, its *r* controlled sound when it is followed by an *r*, or a schwa sound.
   2. Open syllable (syllable that contains a single vowel in a final position)—If the single vowel in an open syllable is an *e, o,* or *u,* it usually represents its own long sound; if the vowel is an *a,* it may represent a schwa – 53 percent, a long *a* sound – 32 percent, or a short *a* sound–12 percent; if the vowel is *i,* it may represent a schwa–49 percent, a short *i* sound–37 percent, a long *i* sound–14 percent.
   3. Final *y*—If a word ends with a consonant + *y,* the *y* will represent a long *i* sound if the word is monosyllabic (try, my, thy, cry), but the *y* will represent a short *i* (long *e*) sound if the word is polysyllabic (baby, balcony, century, city).
C. Vowel pairs
   There is no generalization that can be taught to cover a majority of instances of vowel pair grapheme to phoneme relationships. A particular generalization, however, may be taught to cover specific vowel pairs. The vowel pairs listed below need description in a phonics program. They are the only pairs that occur at least 50 times in the 17,310 most common English words selected by Hanna et al.
   1. First vowel long, second vowel silent—If the vowel pair is *ai, ay, ea, ee, oa,* or *ow,* usually the first vowel represents its own long sound, and the second vowel is silent (main, pay, meat, meet, boat, crow). But *ea* often represents a short *e* sound (bread), and *ow* often represents a diphthong (cow).
   2. Diphthongs—The vowel pairs *oi* and *oy* represent a diphthong (coin, boy). The pairs *ou* and *ow* often represent a diphthong (mouse, cow). However, when *ou* is in a suffix, it represents a schwa sound (dangerous, wondrous).
   3. Broad *a* (circumflex *o*)—The pairs *au* and *aw* represent the "broad *a*" sound (auto, awful), just as does *a* when followed by *ll* (ball, fall).
   4. Long and short *oo*—The pair *oo* represents two sounds (rooster, book).
   5. *Ei* and *ie*—The most common sound *ei* represents is *long a* (neighbor, weigh). Otherwise *ei* and *ie* represent the following sounds, in order of frequency: long *e* (ceiling, field), short *i* (foreign, lassie), long *i* (seismic, die).
   6. *Ey* represents a short *i* sound, as in honey, or a long *a,* as in they.
   7. *Ew* represents a long *u* sound, as in news, or an *ōō* sound, as in flew.
D. Final vowel-consonant-*e*
   1. When a word ends with a *single-vowel,* single consonant, and an *e,* the *e* is silent, and the vowel represents its own long sound. The validity level for each vowel is: *a*–78.9 percent, *e*–87 percent, *i*–61.1 percent, *o*–85.6 percent, *u*–78.3 percent.
   2. Exceptions
      a. There are 68 primary level words which are exceptions to this generalization.
      b. Groups of exceptions are (1) *i-e* words in which the *i* represents a short *i* sound: live, give, office, promise; (2) *i-e* words in which the *i* represents a long *e* sound: marine, magazine; (3) *a-e* words in which the *a* represents a short *i* sound, especially -ace, age, ate words: surface, palace; average, courage; senate, delicate.
E. Consonantizing of *i*
   When *io* or *ia* follows *c, t,* or *s,* the consonant plus the *i* combine to represent a /sh/ or /zh/ sound: racial, social; mention, caution; pension, mansion; vision, fusion.
III. Phonic syllabication
(Phonic syllabication generalizations are used only when morphological syllabication generalizations do not apply—i.e., prefix/root/root/suffix.)

Table 6–3   (Continued)

A. Determination of a syllable
   1. There is one, and only one, vowel phoneme (sound) in a syllable.
   2. There is one, and only one, vowel grapheme (symbol) in a syllable. Vowel graphemes are a) single vowels—cap, me, ba-by; b) vowel pairs, or clusters—main, round, beautiful; (c) a final vowel (consonant) e— cake, Pete, home.
B. Generalizations
   1. Situation: two vowel graphemes separated by two consonants (v c c v)
      When two vowel graphemes are separated by two consonants, we divide between the consonants: as-ter, sil-ver, tar-get, but-ler.
      It is suggested that words containing two like consonants between two vowel graphemes not be included in this generalization (except cc and gg when followed by e, i, or y) because only one sound is represented by these two consonants. Instead words containing two like consonants might be included in the v c v generalization [rab(b)-it, car(r)-ot, bal-(l)loon, e-(s)say].
   2. Situation: two vowel graphemes separated by a single consonant (v c v)
      When two vowel graphemes are separated by a single consonant, the consonant may go with the first or the second vowel. In primary level words, it is more likely to go with the first vowel; in more difficult words, it tends to go with the second vowel. At all levels, there is about a 45–55 percent split: liz-ard, lem-on, wag-on, ra-zor, spi-der, ti-ger.
   3. Situation: word ending in a consonant-l-e
      When a word ends in a consonant-l-e, these three letters compose the final syllable (bi-ble, ea-gle, bun-dle, tur-tle, noo-dle).

nations might be revealing and the responses could serve as a basis for diagnostic teaching in subsequent lessons. (pp. 411–12)

Most reading experts recommend teaching the consonant sounds before the vowels. They explain that consonant sounds are usually more consistent than vowel sounds. Martha Steele Williams and June D. Knafle (1977) found this to be true and also reported on the ease or difficulty of learning various letter sounds by kindergarten students. They ranked ten letter sounds from the easiest to the most difficult in the following order: (1) s, (2) k, (3) o, (4) f, (5) a, (6) u and d, (7) e and h, and (8) i. They noted that earlier studies, in contrast, had related order of difficulty to *number* of letters to be learned. Most basal reading programs, as well as supplementary phonics programs, still base their order of presentation of letter sounds on these earlier studies.

Whether to teach vowel sounds in isolation or in phonograms was studied by Susan B.

Neuman (1981), who presented vowels in isolation and vowels in phonograms to two groups of first-grade students. Each group contained approximately 75 students in the lowest quartile of achievement and 75 in the middle quartile. Neuman stated,

The results indicated a differential learning pattern: students in the lowest quartile of achievement scored significantly better than the control using the Vowel in Isolation approach, whereas students at the middle levels of achievement were more successful using the phonogram approach. (p. 264)

Discussing the implications of her study, Neuman stated,

That the primary finding of the vowel knowledge learning was greater among the Phonogram group might lead one to suggest eliminating Vowel in Isolation patterned supplemental instruction altogether. A closer review of the findings indicates, however, that an individualized or grouped program based on elements of both techniques would probably be most effective. (p. 269)

Assessing Students' Knowledge of Phonics

Before assessing any phonics skills, keep in mind that phonics and other word attack skills are only a means to an end—the student's ability to properly attack a word. If a student can already pronounce nearly any word encountered then it is not necessary to teach that student phonic word attack skills. The only people who need to know phonic word attack skills, even though they can already attack words properly, are *teachers!* Teaching word attack skills to children who can pronounce any word they encounter in almost any kind of material not only bores them but wastes their time. They would learn much more simply free reading in material at their independent or easy instructional levels.

Several ways exist to assess students' knowledge of phonic elements or sound-symbol relationships. Eldon E. Ekwall (1981) discusses six of these methods and the problems encountered with each.[2]

METHOD ONE: Using real words to test phoneme-grapheme relationships.

With this method, the teacher might ask the student to pronounce the words *dog, do,* and *done,* to test his knowledge of the /d/ sound. The problem here is that the student probably already knows these words as sight words, and whether he knows the /d/ sound is irrelevant. Many disabled readers have a fairly large sight vocabulary but do not know the initial consonant sound of many words. Or the student, seeing, but unable to pronounce, much more difficult words, such as dispart and despair, may not know the short /i/, the /s/, the /p/, or other sounds and may make no response at all. Thus, the teacher would receive no useful information, finding only that something in the word is unknown.

METHOD TWO: Using nonsense words to test phoneme-grapheme relationships.

In this case, the teacher might ask the student to pronounce a word such as *dupe* to test for knowledge of the /d/ sound. If he can pronounce the word, the student probably knows the /d/ sound. However, if the student makes no response, it might mean one

of several things:

1. He does not know the vowel, consonant, final e rule (vce, as in cake).
2. He may not know the short /u/,/p/, or /d/ sounds.
3. He may not be able to blend the sounds together even if they are known.

METHOD THREE: Testing sounds in isolation.

This method lacks inter-scorer reliability and thus cannot be a valid method of testing students' phonics knowledge. To prove this, simply ask a student to give the sounds represented by the following letters: *f, r, b, w, l, n, m,* and *v,* while you record his responses. Then ask a group of teachers to listen to the tape and mark each response right or wrong. Next, ask each teacher to tell whether the first response was right or wrong, and tally their answers. Do this for each sound given by the student. In most cases, the considerable disagreement among the teachers indicates that this procedure is unreliable and, thus, not valid.

METHOD FOUR: Having students write the first letter or letters of a word pronounced by the teacher.

In using this method, the teacher usually pronounces a word such as *shoe* and asks the students to write the first letter or letters that they hear at the beginning of the word on a piece of paper with numbered lines. See the following example:

1._____

2._____

When the teacher pronounces the stimulus word, as in *shoe* above, the students are to write *sh* in the first blank. Although this method may appear to measure ability to use the *sh* sound in reading, it rarely does so in reality. A study done by Eldon E. Ekwall (1973) showed that students hearing a certain sound miss phoneme-grapheme relationships different from those they would miss on seeing and giving the tester the same sound in a strange word. Obviously, hearing a word and writing the initial consonant is a skill different from seeing and pronouncing the same word as tested in the *El Paso Phonics Survey.* [See Appendix H.] Reading is, of course, a decoding task, and writing an initial consonant sound, when heard, is an encoding task.

METHOD FIVE: Multiple choice.

In using this method, the teacher pronounces a word and the students underline or circle one of four choices, as in the following example:

1. f g d b
2. r p n k

[2]From *Locating and Correcting Reading Difficulties* (3rd ed.) by E.E. Ekwall (Columbus, Ohio: Charles E. Merrill, Inc., 1981), 172–73. Copyright 1981 by Charles E. Merrill, Inc. Reprinted by permission.

Actually, this is also an encoding rather than a decoding task; that is, the students make a written response after hearing an oral stimulus, such as they do in spelling. Furthermore, multiple choice testing usually allows students to get one-fourth of the answers right, regardless of their knowledge.

METHOD SIX: Multiple choice with a stimulus.

This is nearly the same as Method Five, except that the stimulus word is generated by a picture rather than by the teacher. For example, there might be a picture of a fox next to the choices in the first question. The students are told to look at the picture and say the letter that stands for the word's initial sound. This is also an encoding rather than a decoding task and is again multiple choice, allowing a student who knows almost nothing about phonics to get at least one-fourth of the answers right.

The El Paso Phonics Survey, which appears in Appendix H, is an informal testing instrument used to determine whether students know sound-symbol correspondence for the most phonetically regular phonic elements. It will help you avoid most of the problems encountered in the six testing methods just described. Ekwall (1981) describes the use of the *El Paso Phonics Survey* as follows:

In taking the *El Paso Phonics Survey*, the student is shown three easy words: *in, up,* and *am*. The teacher makes sure the student knows each of these words before beginning the test. The student is then shown a stimulus sheet such as the following:

1. p am pam
2. n up nup

The student is told to say the name of the first letter, to pronounce the word in the middle, and finally to say the word formed by adding the initial consonant to the middle word. Although the final word is usually a nonsense word, the teacher is not simply giving the student a nonsense word in isolation. By saying the name of the letter and the small word in the center, the student finds that his only new task is to blend the letter sound with a word that he already knows. The *El Paso Phonics Survey* should not be given unless the student knows each of the three stimulus words, *in, up,* and *am,* before beginning the test. You will also note that vowels, vowel pairs, and special letter combinations are all put together with one of

The student who gets all of the first eight consonant sounds right proves his knowledge of them and shows the teacher whether he knows the vowel sounds that follow. As you can see, the *El Paso Phonics Survey* does not have the disadvantages of the other, previously discussed, six methods of testing phonics knowledge. In taking the *El Paso Phonics Survey*, some students give the nonsense word the wrong ending sound, even though they pronounced the sound correctly earlier. Extensive use of the *El Paso Phonics Survey* shows that this can happen with the student who is not sure of the initial consonant sound and expends so much of his thought in pronouncing it, that he simply does not attend to the pronunciation of the final sound. When this happens, do not count the initial consonant sound as correct, even if pronounced correctly. You will find that if the missed consonant sound is taught thoroughly, the student will not pronounce the ending wrong on the next trial. (p. 174)

The Quick Survey Word List, which also appears in Appendix H, may be used with students who may or may not need a phonics test. Students at approximately the fourth-grade level or higher and generally adequate in their word attack skills should not be tested on sound-symbol correspondence and other phonics skills unless they cannot properly pronounce most words. The *Quick Survey Word List* helps you quickly determine which students have achieved enough knowledge of word attack skills to avoid further phonics testing. It is a list of long nonsense words representing various common phonic generalizations. Students are given a stimulus sheet on which these words appear. If students can read the words on this list without difficulty, then they need not be given the *El Paso Phonics Survey* or any other phonics test and need not be tested on vowel rules and syllable principles. On the other hand, if students have trouble reading the words on *The Quick Survey Word List*, then they should be stopped, because trying to pronounce words such as these, without proper word attack skills, can be extremely frustrating.

Several commercial tests are available for

assessing students' knowledge of phonics skills. These tests are listed in Appendix G. If you use these tests, remember to test in a situation analagous to actual reading *or* analagous to using the skills being assessed.

Teaching Phonics

Teaching phonics is an important part of teaching beginning readers to read. It would be impossible to cover all the individual lessons phonics instruction may entail. However, several approaches and sample lessons appear in this section. Most of them can be modified and applied to any particular phonic element or phonics lesson you wish to teach.

Using Basal Readers.   As with the other word attack skills, sound-symbol correspondence will probably be thoroughly covered in the basal reading program you use. An example of a typical lesson in listening for beginning sounds from a readiness book appears in Figure 6–1.

Figure 6–2 shows a lesson from a pre-primer–2 book. It illustrates how the teacher might teach the beginning consonant cluster (blend) *st* and the *st* and *mp* ending clusters.

Figure 6–3 illustrates a lesson on the digraphs *sh* and *ch* in their ending positions.

The lesson in Figure 6–4 is for students reading at the 3–1 level, and it reviews various vowel sounds. Most basal reading programs not only provide lessons for teaching various reading skills, but also present some follow-up lessons to reinforce skills already taught.

The teacher's manual provides explicit instructions for the teacher. Important advantages of using a basal reader are that the teacher has a structured, sequential program and that such programs are often successful. When the teacher does not use a basal reader or a structured program, students may miss certain important phases of phonic word attack skills, because without some guidance, most teachers cannot deal with the array of skills some students need

to learn to become proficient readers. The comprehensive chart of reading skills (see Figure 1–7) will help you see what reading skills most students should have mastered by the time they reach your classroom.

When teaching phonics skills, you will also want to supplement what is covered in a basal program, because not all students grasp concepts as presented in the basal reader. The basal reader usually teaches skills on the average reader level. Some more adept students need very little work in building word analysis skills, whereas others need more than the basal reader lessons present. If you do not use a basal reading program, you need to monitor the teaching of various word analysis skills much more carefully, perhaps by becoming much more familiar with the comprehensive chart in Chapter 1 (see Figure 1–7). Or, you should follow some logical sequence of teaching the skills needed for word attack. Most publishers of basal readers furnish teachers or administrators with scope and sequence charts with their basal reading programs. Potential or practicing teachers should become familiar with some newer basal reading series, including the student readers, the teachers' manuals, and supplementary materials.

Teaching Phonic Elements.   The following steps for teaching *d* to a group of students may be used to teach any of the consonants, consonant blends, and consonant digraphs. With minor modification, the steps may also be used to teach vowels and vowel combinations. All these steps may not be necessary for many students or for each new phonic element presented. However, they do provide a thorough and sequential procedure for teaching phonic elements.

1—Reestablish Auditory Discrimination

Ask students to listen carefully while you pronounce several words that begin with *d*, for example, *dog, doll, Danny, dairy, dish.* Next, ask the students: "What do you notice about those words?" Presumably, the students will tell you that they all start the same way. If a few stu-

Listening for Beginning Sounds

Help children open their folders and fold them back to page 2.

GREEN ROW   Hold up a copy of the page. Point to *tiger*. Say: Find *tiger* at the beginning of the green row. Put a line under *tiger*. . . . Listen as I name these pictures: *vest, telephone, tent*. Now put a line under each picture in the row whose name begins with the same sound as *tiger*.

BROWN ROW   Point to *pig*. Say: Find *pig* at the beginning of the brown row. Put a line under *pig*. . . . Listen as I name these pictures: *pail, horse, pencil*. Now put a line under each picture in the row whose name begins with the same sound as *pig*.

ORANGE ROW   Point to *nest*. Say: Find *nest* at the beginning of the orange row. Put a line under *nest*. . . . Listen as I name these pictures: *nails, nurse, box*. Now put a line under each picture in the row whose name begins with the same sound as *nest*.

BLUE ROW   Point to *tiger*. Say: Find *tiger* at the beginning of the blue row. Put a line under *tiger*. . . . Listen as I name these pictures: *leaf, table, turtle*. Now put a line under each picture in the row whose name begins with the same sound as *tiger*.

RED ROW   Point to *nest*. Say: Find *nest* at the beginning of the red row. Put a line under *nest*. . . . Listen as I name these pictures: *needle, jeep, newspaper*. Now put a line under each picture in the row whose name begins with the same sound as *nest*.

Figure 6–1   Listening for beginning sounds

Note. From *Getting Ready to Read, Teacher's Guide* (Houghton Mifflin Reading Program) by W.K. Durr et al. (Boston: Houghton Mifflin Co., 1981), 135. Copyright © 1981 by Houghton Mifflin Co. Used by permission.

dents tell you that they all start with *d*, then they may have already mastered some or all of the steps that follow.

To check for auditory discrimination of the *d* sound for individuals within the group, you may add the following every-pupil-response activity. Tell the students to listen for some words that start with the same sound they heard at the beginning of *dog, doll, Danny, dairy*, and *dish*,

and other words that start with a different sound. Say to the students, "If the word I read starts the same way as *dog*, close your eyes real tight. If the word starts with a different sound, open your eyes wide." Have the students repeat the directions so you know they understand. Then read *dentist, boy, Dick, doughnut*, and *tomorrow*. Note if any of the students seem confused or lack adequate auditory discrimination. These stu-

Cluster st (Beginning) (D1·7d)

Print the letters *st* **on the board.** What are these two letters? . . . You know that when the letters *s* and *t* come together like this at the beginning of a word, the sounds they stand for are so close together that they almost seem to be just one sound. You can hear those sounds at the beginning of *store*. Say *store* to yourself and listen for those sounds.

I am going to say two words. One word will begin with the sounds for *st*, and one will not. Be ready to tell which word begins with the sounds that the letters *s* and *t* together stand for. Listen: *stack, sack*. Which word begins with the sounds for *st*? . . . *Stack* begins with the sounds for *st*.

Let's see if you can use the sounds for *st* to figure out a new word. **Print the following sentence on the board, underlining the word that is in boldface type:**

I want to **stay** here.

Have the children read the sentence silently. Then call on individual children to read the sentence aloud and to identify the underlined word.

Clusters st, mp (Ending) (D1·7e)

Print *best* **on the board.** What is this word? . . . What two letters does it end with? . . . **Draw a line under the letters** *st*. You know that when the letters *s* and *t* come together like this at the end of a word, the sounds they stand for are so close together that they almost seem to be one sound. You can hear those sounds at the end of *best*. Say *best* and listen for those sounds.

I am going to say two words. One will end with the sounds for *st*, and one will not. Be ready to tell which word ends with the sounds that the letters *s* and *t* together stand for. Listen: *beast, beat*. Which word ends with the sounds for *st*? . . . *Beast* ends with the sounds for *st*.

Let's see if you can use the sounds for *st* at the end of a word to figure out a new word. **Print the following sentences on the board, underlining the word that is in boldface type:**

I can't find my pencil.
I have **lost** it.

Have the children read the sentences silently. Then call on individual children to read the sentences aloud and to identify the underlined word.

Print the word *jump* **on the board.** What is this word? . . . What two letters does it end with? . . . **Draw a line under the letters** *mp*. You know that when the letters *m* and *p* come together like this at the end of a word, the sounds they stand for are so close together that they almost seem to be one sound. Say *jump* and listen for those sounds.

I will say two words. One word will end with the sounds for *mp*, and one will not. Be ready to tell which word ends with the sounds that the letters *m* and *p* together stand for. Listen: *limp, lip*.

Let's see if you can use the sounds for *mp* to figure out a new word. **Print the following sentences on the board, underlining the word that is in boldface type:**

I can't see.
The **lamp** is not on.

Have the children read the sentences silently. Then call on individual children to read the sentences aloud and to identify the underlined word.

Figure 6–2   Beginning and ending consonant clusters

Note. From *Balloons, Teacher's Guide* (Houghton Mifflin Reading Program) by W.K. Durr et al. (Boston: Houghton Mifflin Co., 1981), 122. Copyright © 1981 by Houghton Mifflin Co. Used by permission.

Digraphs sh, ch (Ending) (D1·7b)

Print the word *fish* **on the board.** What is this word? . . . What two letters does this word end with? . . . **Draw a line under the letters** *sh*. You know that when the letters *s* and *h* come together at the end of a word, they stand for one sound. Listen for the sound for *sh*. **Say:** *fish*. Now you say *fish* and listen for the sound for *sh*.

I will say two words. One word will end with the sound for *sh*, and one will not. Be ready to tell which word ends with the sound for *sh*. Listen: *math, mash*. Which word ends with the sound for *sh*? . . . *Mash* ends with the sound for *sh*.

Print the letters *ch* **on the board.** What are these two letters? . . . You know that when the letters *c* and *h* come together at the end of a word, they stand for one sound. Listen for the sound for *ch*. **Say:** *much*. Now you say *much* and listen for the sound for *ch*.

Now I will say two words. One word will end with the sound for *ch*, and one will not. Be ready to tell which word ends with the sound for *ch*. Listen: *bent, bench*. Which word ends with the sound for *ch*? . . . *Bench* ends with the sound for *ch*.

Let's see if you can use the sounds for *sh* and *ch* to figure out some new words. **Print the following sentences on the board, underlining the words that appear here in boldface type:**

1. Will you get that **dish** for me?
2. Do not **touch** that fish.
3. Can you **reach** that for me?
4. I will **rush** home now.

Have the children read the sentences silently. Then call on individual children to read each sentence aloud and to identify the underlined word.

▬   Practice Book: page 78

Figure 6–3   Ending digraphs

Note. From *Balloons, Teacher's Guide* (Houghton Mifflin Reading Program) by W.K. Durr et al. (Boston: Houghton Mifflin Co., 1981), 112. Copyright © 1981 by Houghton Mifflin Co. Used by permission.

dents may need additional instruction at this level. (See Chapter 4.)

2—Present Letters (Visual Discrimination)

Write the letters *D* and *d* on a chart or the chalkboard; point to the letters and say, "These are both *d*. This one is the uppercase (or capital) *d* and this is the lowercase (or small) *d*." Give each student paper and pencil, magic slates, or small chalkboards and chalk. Have the students describe what *d* looks like to them, print it in upper- and lowercase form, say it, trace it with their fingers, and say it again.

3—Present Key Object or Picture (Optional)

Some teachers or programs present a key object or picture for the children to associate with the new letter-sound. Such an object for *d* might be a doll; a large photograph or poster of a dog would also be appropriate. If a key object or picture is used, print the letter on or near the item selected to help students associate the symbol with the sound it represents.

4—List Appropriate Words (Auditory Cue)

Ask students to name more words that begin with the *d* sound. Print these words on the chart or chalkboard under the symbol. As you list each word, have the students repeat it. Then remind them that "*d* is the *letter* that stands for the *sound* you hear at the beginning of. . . ."

RETEACHING AND ENRICHMENT

RETEACHING BASIC READING SKILLS

Reviewing Vowels and Vowel Sounds (D1•7r)

Say: Who can name the vowels? . . . **(a, e, i, o, and u)** You know that each of these vowels can stand for different sounds. How many vowel sounds do you hear in the word *bus*? . . . How many vowel sounds do you hear in the word *tiger*? . . . Some words, like *bus*, have just one vowel sound. Other words, like *tiger*, have more than one vowel sound. **Print the following words on the board:**

> bank   boat   hide   garden   rooster

Point to *bank*. What is this word? . . . How many vowels do you see in *bank*? . . . How many vowel sounds do you hear when you say *bank*?

Point to *boat*. What is this word? . . . How many vowels do you see in *boat*? . . . How many vowel sounds do you hear when you say *boat*? . . . Even though there are two vowels in the word *boat*, you hear only one vowel sound. The letters *o* and *a* together stand for one vowel sound.

Point to *hide*. What is this word? . . . How many vowels do you see in *hide*? . . . How many vowel sounds do you hear when you say *hide*? . . . The second vowel in *hide* is a final *e*. When you see a word with two vowels and the second vowel is a final *e* separated from the first vowel by just one consonant, there is usually just one vowel sound in that word.

Point to *garden*. What is this word? . . . How many vowels do you see in *garden*? . . . How many vowel sounds do you hear when you say *garden*?

Point to *rooster*. What is this word? . . . How many vowels do you see in *rooster*? . . . How many vowel sounds do you hear when you say *rooster*? . . . There are three vowel letters in *rooster* but you hear only two vowel sounds. The vowels *oo* together stand for one sound. You cannot tell how many vowel sounds a word has by counting the number of vowels. You have to say the word to yourself and listen for the number of vowel sounds.

Now let's see if you can tell how many vowel sounds there are in some other words you know. **Print the following words on the board:**

sweet	basket	cricket	ready
lift	raccoon	street	cane
fluffy	bake	glad	beaver

Point to *sweet*. Who can say this word? . . . How many vowels do you see in *sweet*? . . . How many vowel sounds do you hear when you say *sweet*? . . . **Follow this procedure with the remaining words.**

▬ Assessment: Forms A, B, C
    Reviewing Vowels and Vowel Sounds

Figure 6–4   Reviewing vowels and vowel sounds

Note. From *Spinners, Teacher's Guide* (Houghton Mifflin Reading Program) by W.K. Durr et al. (Boston: Houghton Mifflin Co., 1981), 54. Copyright © 1981 by Houghton Mifflin Co. Used by permission.

5—List from Pictures or Objects (Visual Cue)

Prepare a set of pictures or objects, some that begin with *d*, and others that do not. Present these to the students one at a time and let them decide if the objects start with *d* or not. If they do, add the names to the *d* list. If not, put them on a new list, labeled *not d.* (Either step 4 or 5 provides a good opportunity to point out when upper- or lowercase letters should be used.)

6—Listening in Context

Say to the students, "I'm going to read you a silly story. When I stop, I want you to tell me the next word. The missing word always starts with *d*." Then read a short, silly story, such as the following:

This is about a boy and his pet _____. His dog liked to hide his bones. When he wanted them he would _____ them up. He drank his milk from a _____.

7—Decoding Words in Context

Give students some short, easy sentences to read, such as the following:

1. I have a d_____ that barks.
2. Close the d_____.
3. I like to sing and d_____.

You may need to help students by pronouncing some of the words in the sentences, depending on the size of their sight vocabularies and their knowledge of other phonic elements. Take these factors into consideration when you prepare sentences. However, it is important to teach children from the beginning that they can use the sense of a sentence to figure out unknown words.

8—Blending and Substitution

To apply symbol-sound associations, students must know the sound the letter stands for *and* be able to blend it with other sounds to pronounce a whole word. To teach students to blend, you may begin with a known ending phonogram, such as *-on* or *-in*. (If these are *not* known, teach them first.)

Write the phonogram on the chart or chalkboard and have the students pronounce it. Then place a *d* in front of the phonogram and have the students pronounce the new word. Demonstrate first, if necessary.

As more ending phonograms and beginning sounds are learned, you can have students practice substitution exercises, as illustrated:

don	dan
dig	man
dot	ran
date	fan
dark	tan

It doesn't matter at this point if some of the words are nonsense words. As students become more proficient, you may have them do double initial consonant substitution, as follows: Present pairs such as *dip, tan; man, cat;* and *bell, tend.* Have the students reverse the initial consonants and pronounce the new word, e.g., *dip* and *tan* become *tip* and *dan; man* and *cat* become *can* and *mat; bell* and *tend* become *tell* and *bend.*

9—Fun Activities

Reinforce symbol-sound associations by providing activities such as the following:

1. Pass out magazine pictures. Have students find items that begin with *d*.
2. For visual discrimination practice, ask students to circle words on a newspaper page that begin with *d*.
3. Have each student make a *d* book out of construction paper and list her favorite *d* words.
4. Have a *d* party, serving foods such as dates, doughnuts, chips and dip, and dairy products.

10—Application in Reading

Students *must* have many opportunities to use their new phonic skills in actual reading situations. Prepare easy sentences and simple stories and select trade books and supplementary reading materials that contain many words that begin with *d*.

Other Phonics Lessons. Figures 6–5 through 6–8 show exercises from a workbook lesson designed to teach children the *f* and *j* sounds. Note the sequential development of each lesson. Exercise 1 (Figure 6–5) is designed to help children hear sounds in words (in this case *f*). Children say the name of each object and then decide if the name begins with the *f* sound. If it does, they put a kernel of corn or a button on that square. They then find two rows, columns, or diagonal lines of names beginning with *f*, as indicated by the (2) following the letter at the top of the page. In this case they are to find the following squares: *finger, fork, four, feet,* and *feather* in numbers 24, 8, 3, 16 and 15. They are also to find *fence, fish, fan, football,* and *fox* in numbers 1, 23, 6, 18, and 25.

Exercise 2 (Figure 6–6) is the same type of activity designed to help beginning readers learn to hear the *j* sound in words.

Exercise 3, Section 1 (Figure 6–7, top) now has the reader circle and thus recognize the *f* and *j* in written form in relation to a picture.

Exercise 4, Section 2 (Figure 6–7, bottom) has the student learn to recognize a word beginning with either the letter *j* or *f.* Children now say the name of the picture and then write the word. Students may not be able to *read* the words, but they can recognize the picture, and only one word in each box begins with the correct sound. Thus, students practice hearing and writing words beginning with the sounds being studied.

Exercise 5, Section 3 (Figure 6–8, top) has students say the name of the picture and then *write* the correct letter (*j* or *f*) that stands for the beginning sound they hear. Students now not only hear the sounds being learned but write those sounds when they hear them.

Exercise 6, Section 4 (Figure 6–8, bottom) has students look at each picture and then find the letters in each column that go together to make the correct word for each picture name. They combine the initial *f* or *j* sounds with a phonogram to write a word that stands for the name of the picture. Students adept at this activity can do Exercise 6 without looking back at the other exercises; however, students needing more work on the sounds may look back at the previous exercises for helping in doing this final exercise.

Vowel Rules

Long and short vowel sounds should be taught in conjunction with two common vowel rules:

1. A single vowel in a closed syllable usually has the short vowel sound—*did, not, cat,* etc.
2. In words with vowel-consonant-final *e,* the first vowel is usually long and the *e* silent.

When teaching the vowel sounds, give students words and ask questions, such as:

1. What vowel sound do you hear in each of the following words?

   mat   cat   hat   pat   sat

2. What are some words with the short *a* sound?
3. How many words can you write with the short *a* vowel sound?
4. What vowel sound do you hear in each of the following words?

   came   cape   hate   mate   date

5. What vowel sound do you hear in *cap?* What sound do you hear when an *e* is added to *cap* to make it *cape?*
6. What vowel sound do you hear in *not?* What sound do you hear when an *e* is added to *not* to make it *note?*
7. How many words can you change from the short to the long sound by adding a final *e?*

Two Vowels Go Walking

A rule commonly taught several years ago and still taught some today is that when there are two vowels together, the sound of the first vowel is heard and the second vowel sound is silent. Since Clymer found this rule true only 45 percent of the time, and others have found that in higher level words it is true an even smaller percentage of the time, it should no longer be taught. Burmeister's findings indicate that perhaps it should only be taught for a few vowel pairs: *ai, ay, ea, oa, ee.* Even so, you should point out that *ea* may have either the long *e* sound as in *meat* or the short *e* sound as in

f (2)

Figure 6–5   Teaching *f*

Note. Figures 6–5 through 6–8 from *Diagnostic-Prescriptive Phonics Lessons: Student Puzzle Pages* by E.E. Ekwall (Boston: Allyn and Bacon, Inc., 1981), 31–34. Copyright 1981 by Allyn and Bacon, Inc. Reprinted by permission.

J

Figure 6–6   Teaching *j*

f and **j**

Section 1   Circle the letters that stand for the beginning sound of each picture.

Section 2   Say the name of each picture. Write the word that stands for the name of the picture on the line below the picture.

Figure 6–7   Teaching *f* and *j*

f and j

Section 3 Say the name of each picture. Fill in the letters to make a word that tells what the picture is of.

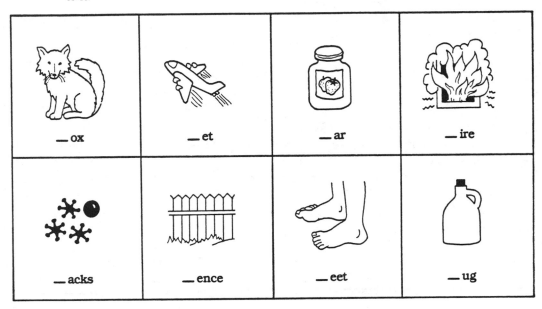

Section 4 Say the name of each picture. Then find letters in each column in the bottom right corner that go together to form a word that stands for each picture. Write the word under the picture.

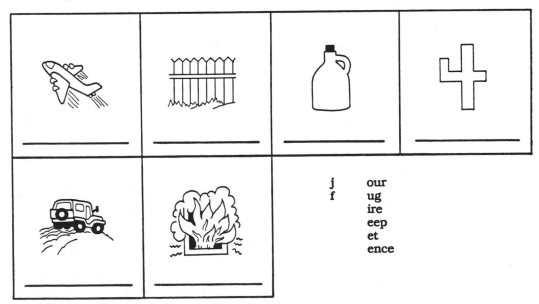

Figure 6–8 Teaching *f* and *j*

head. A memory device for remembering these five vowel pairs is the following sentence: Maids may eat oak trees. Note that Table 6–2 shows that of all the vowel combinations possible, such as *ae, ai, ao, au, ea, ee, ei, eo, eu*, etc., the only ones that follow the "walking" rules are the ones in the sentence, Maids may eat oak trees.

Controlled Vowel

The rule about *r* following a vowel (it usually changes the vowel sound) is quite consistent. You may teach this rule using the discovery method or inductive teaching, which may take slightly longer, but students usually remember the rule much better than if they were simply told the rule and then given examples. The discovery method might be done in the following steps:

1. Ask students to list all the words they can think of that have a vowel followed by an *r*.

2. As students give you words, list them on the chalkboard or on the overhead projector. You might end up with the following list:

star	paper	car	Ernest
zipper	fur	squirrel	far
church	hammer	corn	turtle
far	torn	feather	
bar	bird	shirt	

3. Ask students to group the different sounds using a commonly known word for each sound. This list may then appear as follows:

corn	*car*	*fur*
or	ar	er, ir, and ur

4. Students may then conclude that there are three sounds likely with an *r* controlled vowel, the sounds in the words *corn, car,* and *fur*.

c and g—Two Sounds Each

The rules for *c* and *g* may also be taught inductively. For *c*, use the following steps:

1. Ask students to list all the words they can think of that begin with or have a *c* in them.

2. As students give you the words, list them on the chalkboard or on the overhead projector. You may develop a list like this one:

cent	come	city
card	curl	center
comb	came	
cement	curtain	

3. Ask students to look at the words and decide how many *different* sounds they hear for the *c* in all of them.

4. Group the words according to these two sounds:

s sound (soft)	*k* sound (hard)
cent	came
city	card
cement	curtain
center	curl
	comb
	come

5. Ask students to make up a rule that explains why the words were grouped this way. You may need to give a few hints but do not be overly helpful. Give students plenty of time to think. To get everyone to participate, you can ask each student to write a rule or you can put students in pairs and ask each pair to derive one. Students should eventually derive this rule: When *c* is followed by *e, i,* or *y*, it usually has the soft sound heard in *cent*. If it is followed by any other letter, it usually has the hard sound heard in *came*.

6. When doing this exercise, students may provide a few words that do not fit the rule. You may do a little "educational engineering" and simply tell them that for reasons you will explain later, you will not use those particular words. After the exercise is completed, explain that those words were *exceptions* to the rule.

Follow the same procedure when teaching the hard and soft *g* sounds. As shown by Clymer, the rule for *c* is more consistent than the one for *g*. Thus, the rule (perhaps, more correctly, *generalization*) for *g* should be stated as follows: When *g* is followed by *e, i,* or *y*, it *often* has the soft sound of *j*, as in *gentle* and *germ*. If it is not followed by these letters, it has the hard sound illustrated in such words as *got* and *game.*

STRUCTURAL ANALYSIS

Structural analysis refers to the word analysis skills dealing with the meaningful parts of words. (It is sometimes called *morphology*—because *ology* means *the study of* and *morph* refers to *morphemes,* the meaning bearing units of the language.) It is a word identification technique for breaking a word into its pronunciation units, usually one or more of the following: syllabication, *affixes* (means both suffixes and prefixes), word roots, contractions, compound words, and inflected or derived endings. Vowel rules and syllabication principles can be included in this category because dividing words into syllables often results in meaning units, i.e., root words and affixes.

Review of the Research on Structural Analysis

A question often arises about whether to teach vowel rules and syllable principles. Experts disagree on this point; however, the review of the literature by Patrick Groff (1981) is instructive. Groff concludes:

The number of studies that support the teaching of syllables for word recognition stands in contrast to those that advise against this kind of teaching. It is difficult, in fact, to find empirical data to support the contentions that the successful decoding of words is not related to syllabication skills, that the syllable is too complex a phenomenon to be used by children for word recognition, or that it is impossible for a child to work out the pronunciation of a word through an analysis of the sound of its syllables. (p. 662)

The common problem is that the rules taught for decoding are not the same as those given in the dictionary. Therefore, the dictionary should not be used as the final authority on where a syllable division should occur when using word analysis skills. About this problem Groff stated,

The syllabication taught children for learning to read should not be traditional dictionary syllabication. Despite the fact that dictionary syllabication has often been recommended to teachers, its rules are not based on linguistic research but rather on the arbitrary decisions of typesetters from the early days. Dictionary syllabication rules have little to do with the actual sound patterns of syllables, are often impossible to apply because they are inconsistent, and are not truly usable by children for word recognition. (p. 663)

Russell Stauffer (1969) studied the usefulness or constancy of meaning of various affixes. He concluded that only fifteen prefixes were worth learning (for meaning) because they tended to have consistent meaning in most words encountered by children. One prefix suggested was *in*; it means *input, away from,* or *off.* But knowing the meaning of *in* would not help the student understand a word such as *intense.*

Stauffer based his judgment of the value of suffixes and prefixes on whether their meaning was consistent enough to make them worth learning. However, even with prefixes that consistently mean the same thing, the word roots to which they are attached are so difficult that children in grades 1–6 have trouble understanding the whole word. For example, Stauffer mentioned that the prefix *pro* is consistent in its meaning. However, it is difficult to name five or six words that students will understand because they know the meaning of the attached *pro.* Knowing the meaning of *pro* may help a student decipher such words as *proclaim* or *pronoun,* but the roots in such words as *program* and *provide* have little or no meaning for an elementary student. On the other hand, affixes learned in subject matter areas can be highly useful, such as *bio, aqua, hydro,* etc.

Assessing and Teaching Structural Analysis

Structural analysis is another group of skills that helps the reader decode words. Whereas phonics gives the beginning reader a grasp of individual sounds made up of letters and letter combinations, structural analysis helps the reader with larger word parts: prefixes and suffixes, word roots, syllables, word endings, contractions, and compound words. All these components of structural analysis are important, but only syllable principles (and the resulting vowel rules), prefixes and suffixes, and contractions will be covered here.

Several of the commercial tests available for assessing students' knowledge of certain structural analysis skills are listed in Appendix G. Remember, when using commercial tests, assess in a situation analagous to actual reading or to using the skills being tested.

Assessing Students' Knowledge of Vowel Rules and Syllable Principles.   Eldon E. Ekwall (1981) has suggestions for assessing the most commonly used vowel rules and syllable principles. He stresses that the ultimate goal is that the student can apply the rules, not recite them. Appendix E contains a list of various vowel rules and syllable principles and a list of nonsense words for assessing these rules and principles. It should be kept in mind that students would not normally be tested on most of these rules and principles until they have mastered most sound-symbol relationships. If students do not know the vowel and consonant sounds, then they are not ready to pronounce nonsense words based on vowel rules and syllable principles.

Teaching the Vowel Rules and Syllable Principles.   The purpose of teaching vowel rules is to help the student correctly pronounce the vowel when encountered in an unknown word. Students, as well as teachers, often say there are too many exceptions to the principles to make them worth teaching. Of course, many students cannot recite vowel rules or syllable principles, but that is not the goal of teaching these rules and/or principles. Rather, the goal is to help students pronounce longer words not in their sight vocabularies. If students complain that many words are exceptions to the rules, then explain that these rules are for attacking words. The language was not designed to fit the rules. Then point out that in a three-syllable word there

are at least nine pronouncing possibilities that are reduced to one if all the vowels follow the rules. If the rules hold true for only *two* of the three vowel sounds, then the possibilities are cut from *nine* to *two*. Almost always, at least two of three vowel sounds follow the rules, and the student is left with only two choices. These, when used in the context of a sentence, may help considerably in attacking an unknown word.

Teaching vowel rules and syllabication principles is again a means to an end—being able to break unknown words into syllables so the vowel sound can be determined. If students already have this skill, then there is no need to teach the skill itself. Also keep in mind that some students cannot do the somewhat abstract thinking necessary to achieve competence in these skills. Many students, however, unable to recite the rules, develop a "sixth sense" and know just where to break a word into syllables and thus know what sound to give each vowel. Some students can do this without studying the vowel rules and syllable principles; however, many students also improve with work in this area.

What Rules to Teach

In most basal reading programs, the short and long vowel sounds are taught in relation to two simple vowel rules:

1. A single vowel in a closed syllable (a syllable with a consonant at the end) *usually* has a short sound, as in the word *hat*.
2. In a vowel-consonant-final *e* word, such as *cake*, the first vowel is *often* long and the final vowel silent.

Remember, however, that many of the other vowel rules depend on knowing the position of the vowel in a syllable. After teaching these two rules, then, you should teach students the syllable principles and then the remaining vowel rules.

Using Burmeister's study of the research, you should assess and teach the following syllable principles:

1. When two consonants stand between two

vowels, the word is usually divided between the two consonants. If the two consonants are digraphs or blends, they should be treated as a single sound.

con-text   an-them

(Note: The *th* in *anthem* is treated as a single consonant).

2. When a word ends in a consonant and *le*, the consonant usually begins the last syllable.

ta-ble   ma-ple

3. Compound words are usually divided between word parts and between syllables in these parts.

po-lice-man   dog-house

4. Do not divide between letters that form a blend or digraph. Digraphs and blends should be treated as single consonants. (See number 1.)

5. A principle commonly taught states, when one consonant stands between two vowels, the consonant usually goes with the second syllable.

de-code   lo-cate

Burmeister (1971), however, points out that "In primary level words, [the consonant] is more likely to go with the first vowel; in more difficult words, it tends to go with the second vowel. At all levels, there is about a 45–55 split (liz-ard, lem-on, wag-on, ra-zor, spi-der, ti-ger)." (See Table 6–3, III, B, 2.) Therefore, this principle should not be taught. It would be better to teach children, when one consonant stands between two vowels, the consonant may go with either the first or second syllable.

Then assess and teach the following vowel rules:

1. When a word contains a single vowel letter appearing at the end of it, the vowel letter *usually* has the long vowel sound.

me   she

2. When a word contains a single vowel letter appearing at the end of a syllable, the vowel letter may either be long or short. *Try the long sound first.* (This suggestion means the vowel *can* be either way, but the long sound is more common.)

pre-clude   pro-vide   sha-dow

3. A single vowel in a syllable usually has the short sound if it is not the last letter, or if it is not followed by *r, w,* or *l*. (In other words, a single vowel in a closed syllable usually has a short sound.)

con-duct   can-not

4. Vowels followed by *r* usually have a sound that is neither long nor short.

car   corn   fir   neither   fur

5. A *y* at the beginning of a word has the *y* consonant sound; *y* at the end of a single syllable word, when preceded by a consonant, usually has the long *i* sound; and *y* at the end of a multi-syllable word, when preceded by a consonant, usually has the long *e* sound (some people hear it as short *i*).

yard	yes
fly	my
family	quickly

6. When *ai, ay, ea, oa,* and *ee* are found together the first vowel is usually long and the second vowel is usually silent.

maids may eat oak trees

7. In words ending in vowel-consonant-silent *e*, the *e* is silent and the first vowel may be either long or short. Try the long sound first.

cake   like   have

8. The *ow* sound may be what you hear in either *cow* or *crow*.

9. The *oo* sound may be what you hear in either *moon* or *book*.

10. If *a* is the only vowel in a syllable and is followed by *l* or *w*, then the *a* will usually be neither long nor short.

Method of Teaching

To teach students how to use vowel rules and syllable principles, try a sequence such as the following:

1. Present students with the list of vowel rules and syllable principles outlined previously. Number each rule.

2. Give students several phonetically regular nonsense words to work on.

3. Ask students to draw a vertical line between letters for the syllable division of each word. Ask students to write the *number* of the rule above the vertical line.

4. After words have been divided into syllables ask students to mark the vowel sounds. Have them mark the short vowels with a breve (˘), the long vowels with a macron (¯), the *r,w,* and *l* controlled vowels with these respective letters over the top of the vowel letters, and a combination of a *macron* and a *breve* over vowel letters where the rule states, *try the long sound first.* Then make sure the *macron* is on top of the *breve.* (¯˘)

5. After the vowel sounds have been marked, ask students to write the number of the rule they used to mark each vowel sound. When students complete the sequence, the words should look like these examples:

The teacher who uses this system of teaching vowel rules and syllable principles should remember:

1. Use nonsense words at first to keep students from pronouncing and hearing the points of syllable division in real words they know. This would, of course, defeat the purpose of learning the rules.

2. When students become relatively proficient at dividing and marking nonsense words, then switch to real words they probably do not know and give the same kind of practice.

3. The reason students mark the number over the vertical lines or over the vowels is not to remember the number of the rule but to decide which rules apply. It also shows them how often rules can be applied. Discontinue us-

ing numbers after you are sure students understand and can use each rule or principle.

4. After students have been taught these skills, they may not systematically apply them as they did when they were learning. Do not worry, however, because students develop a "sixth sense" about where to divide words and what sound to give each vowel.

An Alternate Strategy

Some students cannot remember the many vowel rules and syllable principles presented or cannot generalize sufficiently to apply them. An alternative is to teach students to apply the following five steps:

1. Look for prefixes or suffixes.
2. Look for a base or root word that you recognize.
3. Read to the end of the sentence. Think of a word containing those parts (the ones you recognized in steps 1 and 2) that makes sense.
4. Try different sounds, syllables, and accents until you form a word that makes sense.
5. If you still cannot figure the word out, skip it, ask someone, or use the dictionary.

Suppose a student reads the following sentence and cannot decode the word *investigate: The scientist will investigate the problem.* Using the first step, the student identifies and pronounces *in* and *ate* or *gate.* If step 2 does not help, step 3 may, because other words in the sentence often provide enough context clues to help the student decode the unknown word. If the student still does not recognize the word and remains stuck on the *vesti* part, he then tries different sounds, syllables, and accents to see if he can form the word. For many students, this direction helps as much as applying specific vowel rules and syllable principles. If the student still cannot decode the word, then step 5 offers some realistic alternatives. If students must resort to step 5 often, they may not be satisfactorily applying the previous steps or they are reading material too difficult for them.

Ekwall and Shanker (1983) point out that the best way to teach these steps is to model them. Choose several difficult words and put them in sentences. Then demonstrate how you would go through the steps one at a time to figure out the hard word. Use enough examples to show how a student may use a different number of steps each time to get the pronunciation. But always go through them in order. Your goal is to convince students that the first three steps, in order, can help them the most; reassure them that if they practice, they can read big words on their own. (Obviously, students must know some basic phonics and some affixes and have begun to use context clues before they can use this strategy.)

Next, give students some sentences so they can apply the steps; guide them at first, if necessary. List the steps on a chart or blackboard so that students can refer to them often. If they practice, they will begin to memorize the steps and thus be more likely to *use* them. For students who have great difficulty in decoding long words (they take one look and panic), this strategy is concrete, systematic, and helpful.

Finally, students should apply these steps as they read. Persuade them that they must read *a lot* to make this strategy automatic.

To give you an idea of the types of words you might use in teaching this strategy, Ekwall and Shanker (1983) provide the following list of sentences. They are difficult, because most include more than one long word. If they seem too difficult for your students at first, prepare more sentences like number 1 and number 3.

1. The amplifier made the music louder.
2. The archaeologist studied the bones of the dinosaur and the other artifacts found near the caves.
3. Sara is a kind, compassionate person.
4. The twelve contributors contributed five hundred dollars to the charity.
5. That delicatessen has delicious potato salad.
6. After the explosion there was an evacuation of the building.
7. The horizontal lines on the television screen make it impossible to see the picture.
8. The intricate puzzle is very frustrating.
9. The hurricane did substantial damage to our neighborhood.
10. The barometric pressure is falling rapidly. (175–176)

Assessing and Teaching Suffixes and Prefixes. If you use a basal reading program, it will cover the meanings of the few prefixes and suffixes that are worth teaching. Most students, then, will receive considerable instruction in these by the time they leave elementary school. For students able to grasp this knowledge, learning prefixes and suffixes will be an enrichment activity.

Assessing and Teaching Contractions. Assessing students' knowledge of contractions is relatively simple if you use the materials in Appendix F. The teacher needs to know whether or not the student can pronounce each contraction and whether or not the student knows what two words the contraction stands for. In the test for contractions shown in Appendix F, the student has a stimulus sheet, looks at each contraction, pronounces it, and tells what two words the contraction stands for. The levels at which most contractions should have been mastered are shown beside each contraction on the answer sheet.

Teaching contractions hardly differs from teaching any other words. Most basal reader programs emphasize contractions when they are introduced. Perhaps the most important thing to remember in teaching contractions is that students should not only learn the contraction itself but also the two words for which the contraction stands.

EFFICIENCY SKILLS

Sometimes students who have mastered all the word attack skills, according to various tests, still have difficulty reading fluently. These stu-

Multiple exposure to sound–symbol correspondence through various materials is a must in phonics instruction.

dents may have difficulty with speed, accuracy, or both. Some try to read too fast and so stumble on words they can attack and pronounce in isolation. On the other hand, some students are slow to actually use the word attack skills they have, and as a result, read word-by-word and/or phrase improperly. This type of student lacks "efficiency skills." They have picked up faulty reading habits that persist long after they should.

Assessing Students' Efficiency Skills

No formal assessment procedures are available for these students, but close observation of their reading will usually give teachers the information needed for correcting such difficulties. Ekwall and Shanker (1983) suggest a specific procedure for evaluating a student's performance in speed, phrasing, observation of punctuation, and accuracy. They say,

The examiner should have the student read passages orally at two different levels—one at a comfort or independent reading level and a second at the

instruction level. As the student reads, the examiner should complete transcriptions on copies of the passages . . . and evaluate the student's performance in the following areas:
1. Speed—Did the student read too fast, causing unnecessary word-recognition errors, or was the reading speed too slow for acceptable comprehension and adequate rate of learning?
2. Phrasing—Was the phrasing appropriate, or did the student read word by word or with other inappropriate phrasing?
3. Punctuation—Were punctuation cues followed, or did the student ignore or misinterpret punctuation marks?
4. Accuracy—Did the student correctly pronounce the words in the selection, or were words miscalled due to excessive speed or poor phrasing? If omissions, repetitions, insertions, or substitutions occurred, were these a result of poor decoding skills, efficiency problems, or both? (p. 151)

Teaching Efficiency Skills

Some students who have mastered all or enough of the word attack skills to read may still have a problem. This problem may take the form of improper phrasing, word-by-word reading, a reading rate improper for the material, lip movements, lack of observation of punctuation, and finger pointing.

Ekwall and Shanker (1983) suggest these methods for dealing with these problems:

1. Make sure that the decoding skills of basic sight vocabulary, phonics, structural analysis and contextual analysis have been mastered. If not, provide remedial instruction in these areas.
2. Take time to discuss with students the specific nature of their efficiency skill problems and suggest general approaches to solving them. It is often helpful to tape record the student while he or she is reading orally, then play back the recording while the student is listening, so the student can become aware of the specific problem.
3. Do not expect students to read efficiently material that is above the student's meaning-vocabulary level. Generally, use materials that encourage students to read in great quantity.
4. Encourage wide reading from a variety of materials. In addition to the necessary practice this provides, students can be directed to read different types of materials at different speeds and for different purposes, such as pleasure, information, instruction, and so forth. (p. 180)

Echo Reading.   Also recommended for improving students' efficiency skills is a technique called echo reading, which can work on a one-to-one basis or with a tape recorder. The teacher usually reads a thought unit or unit that might be separated from the rest of a passage with a period or comma. After hearing the teacher read, the student tries to duplicate the unit with exactly the same phrasing and intonation. This method helps improve expression and phrasing. If the teacher asks the student to point to words or phrases being read, it can also improve sight vocabulary. However, the purpose of this approach is to develop proper phrasing and expression, and finger pointing can interfere with this process. In the past many professors of reading education have thought that finger pointing in any form was taboo. However, finger pointing can help students learn a sight vocabulary more

quickly and overcome such problems as substitutions, omissions, insertions, etc. (See Chapter 9 for more information.) Most students automatically stop finger pointing when they no longer need it or when they see it interfering with their ability to read more rapidly. If they do not, then it can easily be corrected by simply telling the student to stop doing it.

Precision Reading.   A method called *precision reading* used at the Reading Clinic at California State University, Hayward can also help students overcome difficulties with efficiency. Students get a certain number of sentences to read. They are then told that accuracy of reading (accurate pronunciation and phrasing) will be stressed and that an evaluator will check to see how many of the total number of sentences are read correctly. The student then reads and is evaluated. The teacher determines the number of correct sentences vs. incorrect sentences and computes a percentage of correct sentences. The teacher records these percentages or a graph so that students can see their progress. Students should be given the passages at least one day in advance so that they can practice reading orally.

Repeated Readings.   Still another method of correcting problems with efficiency skills is one called *repeated readings*, as explained by S. Jay Samuels (1979). The student reads a passage of from 50–200 words in length, and the teacher checks for accuracy and speed. This information is then recorded. The student records the passage on audio tape and then practices rereading the material in conjunction with the recorded version. When the student believes she is ready, another test is given and the information is recorded as before so the student can compare the initial reading and the practiced version. The graphing of this information serves as a motivational technique for further improvement.

Other ways to use oral reading for improving students' efficiency skills are:

1. Provide choral reading activities for small groups.

2. Provide plays for students to read.
3. Have students pair off and alternate reading to each other.
4. Have younger students read selections using puppets.
5. Use a reinforcer, such as a clicking sound, each time a sentence is read correctly.

DICTIONARY SKILLS

Assessing Students' Dictionary Skills

Formal tests for most dictionary skills do not exist; therefore, the teacher needs to develop tests for these skills. Unlike many of the reading skills, most of the dictionary skills can be tested using a group survey instrument. Brief examples of items for testing the dictionary skills follow.

Alphabetizing letters. Give students a list of letters and ask them to arrange them in alphabetical order.

Alphabetizing words by first letter. Give students words which all have different letters in the first position and ask them to arrange them in alphabetical order.

Alphabetizing words to second letter. Give students words which have the same first letter but different letters in the second position and ask them to arrange them in alphabetical order.

Alphabetizing words to third letter. Give students words which have the same first and second letters but different letters in the third position and ask them to arrange them in alphabetical order.

Estimating location of word in dictionary. Ask students, individually, to open the dictionary to a letter such as *m, d,* etc.

Deriving word meaning. Ask students to look up the meaning of a word such as *prior* and write the first definition.

Using guide words. Give students a sheet set up as follows:

	Loaf	Location
1. lobby——		
2. lock——		
3. loan——		

Ask students to look at the two guide words (in italics) at the top and decide whether the numbered words would be on the same page as the guide words. Answer with a plus (+) or minus (−).

Interpreting syllables. Ask students to look up a word such as *principal* in the dictionary and write the number of syllables contained in the word. Also show where it would be divided if you were writing a letter and had to divide that word at the end of a line.

Interpreting accent or stress. Ask students to look up a word such as *principal* and determine which syllable would have the most stress on it. Also ask which syllable would have the secondary stress.

Selecting word meaning from context. Give students a sentence such as "The *prior* was praying" and ask them to look up the meaning for the word *prior* as it is used here.

Interpreting pronunciation key. Ask students, individually, how a word with which they are unfamiliar is pronounced as shown in the dictionary.

Using cross reference. Ask students to look up a word that has "SYN. See—" and then explain what it means.

First and second spellings. Ask students to look up the word *prise* and see if it can be spelled another way.

Word origin. Ask students to look up words that have symbols, such as OF., OE, etc. Explain what they mean.

Teaching Dictionary Skills

Some basal reading programs cover dictionary skills thoroughly while others give light treatment. The reason for this variation is that certain textbook publishers provide for the teaching of the dictionary skills in their language arts programs (other than reading). A summary of teaching dictionary skills is not necessary; since you know what these skills are (explained in the previous section) you can test and teach them accordingly. Students who should have learned the dictionary skills, as indicated in Figure 1–7, and have not done so should have corrective help.

SUMMARY

A reader uses decoding, or word analysis skills, to pronounce a word not recognized instantly. This chapter introduces you to the following decoding skills: configuration clues, context clues, phonics, structural analysis, efficiency skills, and dictionary skills.

Readers use the shape of words, the sense of a sentence, knowledge of phonic elements, and word parts to help them "break the code" of an unknown word. As beginners become more proficient in attacking words on their own, they need to improve their efficiency skills so that they become fluent readers. As a result of the decoding skills they develop, they can become more adept at using the dictionary, which in turn helps them decode even more words.

Research on these decoding skills has been presented, and assessing techniques have been covered (for additional information, see Appendices D, E, F, and G). Teaching methods have also been discussed. The sample lessons and exercises and the various approaches can be adapted to the specific decoding lessons you wish to teach in your classroom.

REVIEW QUESTIONS

1. What does research indicate about the usefulness of configuration clues?
2. What does research indicate about the usefulness of context clues when used in isolation?
3. Why is it important to know something about the research on teaching phonic generalizations?
4. What are the phonic elements?
5. Why do we test and teach only certain phonic elements?
6. Explain the methods of assessing phonic elements and list the problems commonly encountered with each method.
7. Why do some vowel rules and/or principles say try the long sound first?
8. Why should the syllable principles be taught before most of the vowel rules?
9. What are the components of structural analysis?
10. What prefixes and suffixes should elementary children know the meaning of?
11. How might you test for students' knowledge of contractions?
12. What methods can you use to teach students how to read more efficiently?
13. What components of dictionary usage should you assess?

REFERENCES

Allington, R., & Strange, M. Effects of grapheme substitutions in connected text upon reading behaviors. *Visible Language*, 1977, *11*, 285–97.

Bailey, M. H. The utility of phonic generalizations in grades one through six. *Reading Teacher*, February, 1967, *20*, 413–18.

Biemiller, A. Relationships between oral reading rates for letters, words, and simple text in the development of reading achievement. *Reading Research Quarterly*, 1977–78, *13*(2), 223–53.

Burmeister, L. E. Content of a phonics program based on particularly useful generalizations. In N. B. Smith (Ed.), *Reading methods and teacher improvements*. Newark, Del.: International Reading Association, 1971.

Burns, P. C., & Schell, L. M. Instructional strategies for teaching usage of context clues. *Reading World*, December, 1975, *15*, 89–96.

Ceprano, M. A. A review of selected research on methods of teaching sight words. *Reading Teacher,* December, 1981a, *35*, 314–22.

Ceprano, M. A. Context versus isolation methods of word instruction: Efficiency assessed by paralleling assessment modes. *Journal of Reading Behavior*, Winter, 1981b, *13*, 381–90.

Chall, J.S. *Learning to read: The great debate*. New York: McGraw-Hill, 1967.

Clymer, T. The utility of phonic generalizations in the primary grades. *Reading Teacher*, January, 1963, *16*, 252–58.

Ekwall, E.E. *An analysis of children's test scores when tested with individually administered diagnostic tests and when tested with group administered tests.* Final Research Report, University Research Institute. El Paso: University of Texas at El Paso, 1973.

Ekwall, E. E. *Locating and correcting reading difficulties* (3rd ed.). Columbus, Ohio: Charles E. Merrill, 1981.

Ekwall, E.E., & Shanker, J. L. *Diagnosis and remediation of the disabled reader* (2nd ed.). Boston: Allyn and Bacon, 1983.

Emans, R. When two vowels go walking and other such things. *Reading Teacher*, December, 1967, *21*, 262–69.

Fulwiler, G., & Groff, P. The effectiveness of intensive phonics. *Reading Horizons*, Fall, 1980, 50–54.

Goldsmith, J. S. Decoding reexamined. *Elementary School Journal*, November, 1981, *82*, 152–59.

Goodman, K. S. Words and morphemes in reading. In K. S. Goodman & J. T. Fleming (Eds.), *Psycholinguistics and the teaching of reading*. Newark, Del.: International Reading Association, 1972.

Goodman, K. S., & Goodman, Y. M. Learning about psycholinguistic processes by analyzing oral reading. *Harvard Educational Review*, 1977, *47*(3), 319–33.

Groff, P. The topsy-turvy world of "sight words." *Reading Teacher*, March, 1974, *27*, 572–78.

Groff, P. Teaching reading by syllables. *Reading Teacher*, March, 1981, *34*, 659–64.

Haber, R. N., & Haber, L. R. The shape of a word can specify its meaning. *Reading Research Quarterly*, 1981, *16*(3), 334–45.

Hilsop, M., & King, E. M. Application of phonic generalizations by beginning readers. *Journal of Educational Research*, May–June, 1973, *66*, 405–12.

Kendall, J. R., & Hood, J. Investigating the relationship between comprehension and word recognition: Oral reading analysis of children with comprehension or word recognition disabilities. *Journal of Reading Behavior*, Spring, 1979, *11*, 41–48.

Marchbanks, G., & Levin, H. Cues by which children recognize words. *Journal of Educational Psychology*, April, 1965, *61*, 57–61.

Neuman, S. B. A comparison of two methods of teaching vowel knowledge. *Reading Improvement*, Fall, 1981, *18*, 264–69.

Robinson, H. A. A study of the techniques of word identification. *Reading Teacher*, January, 1963, *16*, 238–42.

Samuels, S. J. The method of repeated readings. *Reading Teacher*, January, 1979, *32*, 403–406.

Schwartz, R. M., & Stanovich, K. E. Flexibility in the use of graphic and contextual information by good and poor readers. *Journal of Reading Behavior*, Fall, 1981, *13*, 263–69.

Stauffer, R. G. *Teaching reading as a thinking process*. New York: Harper & Row, 1969.

Walcutt, C.C., et al. *Teaching reading*. New York: Macmillan, 1974.

Williams, M. S., & Knafle, J. D. Comparative difficulty of vowel and consonant sounds for beginning readers. *Reading Improvement*, Spring, 1970, *14*, 2–10.

7

Assessing and Teaching the Comprehension Skills, Including Vocabulary

Reading *comprehension* is the meaning gained from what is written on the page. To comprehend is to *understand* what is written. The ability to comprehend is affected by the material being read *and* by the reader. Most reading specialists agree that four factors within the reader affect the reader's comprehension. First, the *knowledge the reader brings to the subject* affects that reader's comprehension. This prior knowledge includes what the reader has experienced, what he has read about the subject, and what special vocabulary he knows about a particular subject. All knowledge humans possess has been learned by tying new information, or comparing new information, to what we already know. People simply cannot learn about a new subject in a vacuum—they must connect it to something they know.

Second, a reader's ability to comprehend depends on her *interest* in the subject, which of course, ties in with prior knowledge. The more interest a reader has in a particular subject, the more likely she is to have already read or talked to someone about it. Such exposure helps the reader know more about the subject and thus comprehend more when reading. Also, when a reader is interested in a subject, she will probably give her undivided attention to it while reading.

Third, a *purpose* for reading contributes to the reader's ability to comprehend. Purpose also ties in with knowledge of and interest in the subject. A reader who knows he must read a certain chapter in his textbook to pass a test has a strong purpose for reading and will comprehend more than a reader who reads the same passage with no purpose in mind. Also, adults often read to gain information about a subject, whether to learn how to do a weekend project or to learn what is happening in the world.

Finally, the *ability of a reader to decode words rapidly* affects comprehension. If a reader must figure out how to pronounce a new word in every line or two, then she becomes so involved with this task that she has little mental energy left for comprehending what is actually written. If a reader is facile at attacking new words, then few of her thought processes are needed for that activity, which means she can concentrate on the subject matter.

COMPREHENSION—THE MATERIAL

Three factors affect the difficulty of material being read. One of these is the *number of hard words*. A word the reader has never encountered be-

fore is more difficult than a word already familiar to the reader.

Also affecting difficulty is the *length of the sentences*. Nearly all reading specialists agree that the longer the sentences, the more difficult the material is. Material written at the pre-primer level is usually written for four-, five-, or at most, six-word sentences, with each sentence being one line long. You have probably encountered sentences in college textbooks as long as 25 to 40 words. Such long sentences often make it difficult to follow the author's train of thought.

Most **readability formulas**, devised to determine a passage's difficulty in terms of grade level, are based on these two factors, number of **hard words** and sentence length. To develop a new readability formula, an author usually uses a specific set of relatively easy words (rather high utility words); any word not on this list becomes a hard word in computing the readability formula. This factor, along with sentence length, then determines the grade level of the passage.

Also recognized as contributing to a passage's difficulty is its **syntax**, the way the author puts words together, or the way words are strung together to form sentences. Second graders, for example, can more easily write materials for other second graders than an adult can, even though the adult may use essentially the same words and the same sentence lengths as the second graders do. Second graders use a syntax that cannot be exactly matched by adults whose reading and writing levels are beyond a second grader's. Even though it is important, syntax has been difficult to use in readability formulas because there is no standard way to measure it.

COMPREHENSION SUBCATEGORIES

For the skill of *division*, a student must be able to *add*, *subtract*, and *multiply*. It is a relatively straightforward task to design a test to see whether a student can add a column of numbers with two digits each or multiply two-digit numbers by two-digit numbers. But it is difficult to pinpoint accurately more than one comprehension subskill. You may think this is strange since you have probably taken, or at least seen, tests supposedly designed to determine whether students could identify the main idea and important details, had the ability to follow directions, etc.

A statistical procedure used to determine the subskills of a broad skill is factor analysis. This procedure determines the percent of some overall skill accounted for by various subskills. However, when factor analysis is applied to the overall skill of comprehension, the only subskill identified with any accuracy is vocabulary. If separate comprehension skills existed, then students' abilities in them could be measured just as students' abilities to add, subtract, multiply and divide can be measured by a diagnostic test in math. In reality, however, a reader adept at getting the main idea, understanding the author's organization, etc. is likely good at all comprehension skills.

Designers of tests for comprehension, however, persist in using nebulous categories. Even though one can question this practice on the basis of statistical procedures, most reading specialists believe that using these categories is still justified. When a teacher concentrates on teaching students to follow directions, for example, they improve in their overall ability to follow directions as well as in their overall ability to comprehend. Perhaps using these categories to ''get a handle'' on teaching comprehension makes them worthwhile.

When a factor analysis is done of comprehension, one subcategory can be identified—vocabulary. Many group standardized reading tests are identified as measuring *vocabulary* and *comprehension.* Technically, this is improper since they are measuring comprehension and its subskill, vocabulary. You should recognize that vocabulary is a subskill of comprehension when assessing and teaching comprehension. This discussion also refers to comprehension *and* vocabulary, even though vocabulary is actually a subskill of comprehension. Since comprehension and vocabulary do exist as separate entities, this terminology can be justified.

REVIEW OF THE RESEARCH

Research on assessing students' comprehension focuses on using standardized reading achievement tests, measuring critical reading, using informal reading inventories, and other ways to measure comprehension. *Standardized reading achievement tests* are given to large samples of the U.S. population—various grade levels, different regions, and different socioeconomic groups. These tests allow teachers to compare their students with a nationwide norm. *Informal reading inventories* are a graded series of increasingly difficult reading passages, usually taken from basal readers, to help teachers see what their students' independent, instructional, and frustration reading levels are. Students reading at their *independent reading levels* need no special preparation in vocabulary or concepts to enjoy and understand what they are reading. The reading level appropriate for a student's textbooks is the *instructional reading level.* At this level, a student has to learn some vocabulary and concepts to understand the material. A *frustration reading level* is the level considered too difficult for an individual student to read and understand.

Research on teaching comprehension focuses on the problems in teaching comprehension, what factors affect comprehension, and the role questioning, chunking, and other teaching methods have in students' learning to comprehend better.

Using Standardized Tests

John E. Readence and David W. Moore (1983) indicate that choosing the best answers to questions (a skill most often called for on standardized tests) may be just one indicator of reading comprehension. Other ways of demonstrating reading comprehension are ''retelling of passages, dramatizing stories, producing miscues, discussing passages, following directions, and supplying words which are thought to be the ones purposely deleted'' (p. 307). They point out that students who do not have a chance to justify their answers do not really have a chance to demonstrate their true ability to comprehend. In their historical perspective on the development of standardized reading tests, Readence and Moore note that these limitations grew out of the early 1900s, when there was a movement toward efficient and scientific management of the schools. They say that the "initial surge in American standardized test production between 1910 and 1918 resulted in at least 84 tests and scales for the elementary grades . . ." (p. 307). In the early days of standardized testing there were many ways to respond to test questions; for example, a student could reproduce a passage word for word or solve written puzzles. However, the influence of Edward L. Thorndike led to "more objective, more accurate, and more convenient measures of . . . a pupil's ability to understand the meaning of words and sentences seen" (p. 310).

Thus, by 1930 answering questions had become the predominant means of assessing comprehension because it was convenient, economical and objective to score. Readence and Moore state,

Perhaps most importantly, questions were adaptable to the multiple choice formats that grew popular in the 1930s, and to computerized scoring in the 1960s— both did much to insure that answering questions would be the primary indicator of reading comprehension at present.

Yet through the years, educators and researchers have pointed out that a reader's ability to comprehend is multifaceted and that relying on a single measure of this complex construct is not warranted. . . . Standardized reading comprehension tests may help us sort students and compare groups according to rough measures of general academic abilities, but those tests provide only limited information about students' specific comprehending abilities. . . .

After all, comprehension is an internal, unobservable phenomenon, and we can only gauge behaviors that reflect it. The more methods we use, the better chance we have of making valid assessments. (p. 312)

Doris C. Crowell, Kathryn Hu-pei Au, and Karen M. Blake (1983) studied the types of questions asked on six different standardized achievement tests. Most tests used more lower level questions, those that only ask the student to recall a passage's details. Most tests also asked some higher level questions, but not necessarily more of them at the higher levels of achievement. If students do grow in their ability to comprehend at higher levels as they progress, then there should be more questions asking for skills such as integration, where the student "combine[s] elements of the story into a coherent structure not necessarily given by the story itself" (p. 316). Crowell, Au, and Blake found, however, that only the California Achievement Test increased the number of higher level questions at higher grade levels.

Measuring Critical Reading and Its Subskills

It is practical to teach and perhaps test students' *critical reading*, their ability to evaluate a passage's meaning and its implications for them. However, it is not practical to measure the subskills of critical reading often listed in the literature. Thomas W. Worden (1981), in his study about developing a model of critical reading and thinking, studied the possibility of developing a test to measure critical reading subskills. In his conclusion Worden stated,

1. A model of critical thinking and critical reading based on professional opinion and the review of the literature in the area can be designed and developed.
2. As a result of this model, certain critical thinking processes and critical reading skills can be identified and defined.
3. The general ability to think and read critically can be reliably measured in students with reading levels ranging from three through six.
4. Individual subskills of critical reading cannot be reliably measured by the *Worden Critical Thinking/ Critical Reading Appraisal.*
5. A model of critical reading with separate subskills may not be appropriate. These subskills, as discussed in the findings, are difficult to measure as separate entities. (p. 282)

Using Informal Reading Inventories

Informal reading inventories may be teacher-made or commercial, in which case they are referred to as commercial informal reading inventories.

An informal reading inventory usually consists of a series of passages (usually two at each grade level) that get progressively more difficult as the student reads. Sometimes teachers make informal reading inventories from their textbooks, in which case, the inventory may not have a designated grade level but simply represent the material in a particular book.

Leo M. Schell and Gerald S. Hanna (1981) asked whether informal reading inventories can reveal strengths and weaknesses in comprehension subskills, and their general conclusion was that they could not. They pointed out that reading experts cannot agree on the classification of questions used in commercial informal inventories. For example, a question listed as *main idea* by the author of an informal reading inventory might be classified as *detail, inference,* or *cause and effect* by someone else. Schell and Hanna stress that questions not being classified carefully enough is one of the main problems with commercial informal inventories. Schell and Hanna also mention that some questions in commercial informal reading inventories are not **passage dependent.** To answer a passage dependent question, the reader has to have read the passage. But in a study by Richard Allington, Laura Chodos, Jane Domaracki, and Sharon Truex (1977), third-grade students could answer 31 percent of the questions on the Diagnostic Reading Scales, by George Spache, without reading the material! A further analysis of individual questions showed that "10 were answered correctly at least 50% of the time with three of these being answered correctly an astonishing 92% of the time" (p. 265). In their conclusion about commercial informal reading inventories, Schell and Hanna said,

The evidence seems overwhelmingly conclusive. Informal inventories do not reveal true strengths and weaknesses in comprehension subskills; therefore, they should not be used for this purpose. It is to be hoped that authors and consumers alike will grow increasingly sensitive to the need for accurate labelling of that which is measured. (p. 267)

Measuring Comprehension by Other Means

Victoria Chou Hare and Douglas C. Smith (1982)

studied whether more could be learned about how students comprehend from their scores on a standardized achievement test (protocol analysis) or from their description of *how* they went about comprehending a passage (retrospection). They believe student retrospection yields more useful information to the teacher. The authors report on some information given by students who use retrospection: "Rereading and imaging remained the most frequently cited strategies for the narrative passage, and rereading and changing speeds remained the most frequently cited strategies for the expository passage" (p. 162). The authors state,

Most of what we learned concerns the students' reported strategies for remembering what they read. We observed students had no trouble whatsoever in reading to remember. And, indeed, students' retrospections about what they thought they did correlated moderately with their reading achievement. (p. 163)

Problems in Teaching Comprehension

Many teachers spend too little time teaching comprehension because they do not know *how* to teach it. For example, Dolores Durkin (1978–79) visited several classrooms and observed almost no comprehension being taught. In an abstract of her research Durkin stated,

Major findings included the fact that almost no comprehension instruction was found. The attention that did go to comprehension instruction focused on assessment, which was carried on through teacher questions. Instruction other than that for comprehension was also rare. It could not be concluded, therefore, that teachers neglect comprehension because they are busy teaching phonics, structural analysis, or word meaning. What they do attend to are written assignments. As a result, time spent on giving, completing, and checking assignments consumed a large part of the observed periods. Sizable amounts of time also went to activities categorized as "Transition" and "Noninstruction." Other findings indicated that none of the observed teachers view social studies as a time to help with reading comprehension. Rather, they see their responsibility as covering content and having children master facts. (p. 481)

Factors Affecting the Teaching of Comprehension

To teach comprehension better, teachers need to know what recent research tells them about how comprehension works.

Interest.   Interest is one of the main factors influencing how much a reader comprehends. Kathleen C. Stevens (1980) studied the effect of interest on the reading comprehension of gifted readers. She stated that superior readers do not always use their maximum reading comprehension power; in her experiment, gifted pupils clearly read passages of lower interest in a substandard way. Only when the students were given challenging and interesting passages did they demonstrate their higher ability levels. This effect was not found for other readers. About her study, Stevens stated,

Individualized programs for gifted students should take the interest factor into account. Classroom teachers might adapt lessons and assignments so that gifted readers can develop their own areas of interest. For example, a reading group of superior students might be allowed to choose individual "research topics," rather than read from a circumscribed "reading program" or basal reader. Reading assignments would be to read several books on the area of interest (book selection may be undertaken in conjunction with the librarian). Thus, one reader might read about spiders, and another might devour five books about rocketry. The group could reconvene for sharing of ideas gained, with the possible side effect of expanding other group members' interests. This "individualized reading" approach to the gifted group would challenge them far more than putting them through textbook paces evolved for the average learner. (pp. 14–15)

Prior Knowledge.   In a study of some known sources of reading difficulty, Taffy E. Raphael (1981) found that three factors influenced seventh graders' comprehension: familiarity with the material being read, text structure, and word frequency. The term text structure refers to syntax or how words are put together. Word frequency means that the more frequent the words, the more familiar they become, and the more familiar words become, the better the reader

comprehends. Familiarity with the material being read refers to background information or previous knowledge of the subject.

Kathleen C. Stevens (1982a) tried to determine whether comprehension can be improved by teaching background information. In this study Stevens mentions that Marilyn Adams and Bertram Bruce (1980) emphasized prior knowledge: without prior knowledge, a complex object such as a textbook is not just difficult to understand, it is meaningless. Stevens also found that teaching students background information significantly increases their comprehension. She stated,

The results of this experiment indicate that teaching background knowledge of a topic to readers can improve their reading comprehension on material concerning that topic.

This experiment also supports the idea that background knowledge can be taught directly. . . . Thus, it is possible to provide students with an ideational scaffold that enables them to better understand information concerning that topic.

An implication for teaching is that some students' apparent "reading problems" may be problems of insufficient background. To improve reading, therefore, one might need to enhance the reader's relevant background information. A teacher of reading might thus be viewed as a teacher of relevant information as well as a teacher of reading skills. (p. 328)

Studies by Judith A. Langer and Mark Nicolich (1981) and David A. Hayes and Robert J. Tierney (1982) also show a clear relationship between prior knowledge and better comprehension. Marie Shantz (1981) pointed out that these factors make material readable:

1. Prior experience
2. Teacher introduction and/or discussion
3. Purpose for reading
4. Format
5. Personal involvement
6. Vocabulary and other linguistic features. (p. 943)

Also, a debate in the reading field exists about whether what the reader brings to the printed page has more to do with helping him understand than what the printed page actually communicates.

This debate is between the *bottom-up* and

photo by Donald Birdd

Building a background of experience facilitates comprehension.

top-down theories. In explaining these theories Michael Strange (1980) says,

Those who adhere to a top-down position believe that the reader brings more information to the page than the page brings to the reader. In other words, when someone is reading s/he has a good deal of prior knowledge about the world and this prior knowledge is used to make good guesses about the nature (relationships, episodes, characters, etc.) of the text. The reader proceeds to confirm or modify the hypotheses as well as to appreciate the nuances that a particular author might bring to the text.

Those experts who adhere to a bottom-up position believe that the page brings more information to the reader than the reader brings to the page. The reader begins reading with little information about the text and the print is sequentially processed until the message is completely understood. The reader continues to gather more information from the page.

These positions are also referred to as concept driven (top-down) and text driven (bottom-up). (p. 392)

Research in the area of prior knowledge is often referred to as schema theory. Strange says,

Schema theory seeks to explain how new information

acquired while reading is meshed with old information already in our heads. It is helpful to think of schema (singular of schemata) as a concept, although a schema is meant to be more inclusive than a concept. (p. 393)

The importance of background information, or *schemata*, in comprehension has also been emphasized by Margaret Stefferson, Chitra Joag-Dev, and Richard C. Anderson (1979). In their research they stated,

When a person reads a story, the *schemata* embodying his background knowledge provide the framework for understanding the setting, the mood, the characters, and the chain of events. It stands to reason that readers who bring to bear different schemata will give various interpretations to a story. (p. 11)

Stefferson, Joag-Dev, and Anderson had subjects from India and the United States read about an Indian and an American wedding. They found that subjects who read about their own culture read the material more rapidly, recalled a greater amount of information, and produced more culturally appropriate elaborations. In their conclusion they stressed their "conviction that differences in background knowledge about the content of text material may be an important source of individual difference in reading comprehension" (p. 28).

Jean Otto (1982) has noted that many basal reader publishers have improved their material because of this new research. She stated, "Basals, while still certainly offering isolated skills worksheets and objectives, now show a new intention to integrate all skills and to include context use and language experiences as word identification strategies" (p. 17).

Cognition and Metacognition. Also contributing to a student's understanding of a passage is the ability to think while reading, or *cognition.* A further intellectual step is learning to think about what one is thinking about, or *metacognition.* Patricia J. Babbs and Alden Moe (1983) say,

Metacognition refers to the ability to monitor one's own cognition; it is thinking about thinking. When applied to the act of reading, this definition suggests

that the reader is able to select skills and strategies appropriate for the demands of the reading task. (p. 423)

Focusing on metacognition as part of reading comprehension may help teachers improve their teaching of reading comprehension more than anything else.

Using Questions in the Teaching of Reading

Isabel L. Beck and Margaret G. McKeown (1981) discuss the role of questions in the improvement of comprehension and note that several taxonomies have been developed for questioning. Most often used is the one by Thomas Barrett (1967), which contains five categories: "1) Literal Comprehension; 2) Reorganization; 3) Inferential Comprehension; 4) Evaluation; and 5) Appreciation" (p. 914).

Beck and McKeown list studies that indicate the most common question types. In discussing these studies Beck and McKeown state,

The common finding of these studies was that more than half of the questions analyzed were of the literal comprehension type, requiring only recall or recognition of story facts. The most often cited recommendation from such studies is that more attention be given to higher levels of comprehension through questions that elicit inferences, evaluation, and appreciation. Taxonomies are then recommended as a guide for establishing appropriate questions. (p. 914)

Questioning does promote comprehension, but it does *just* that. It probably does *not* help the reader learn to comprehend better on his own. Promoting comprehension may be a worthy goal in itself at times, but teachers must ultimately teach readers how to comprehend material without teachers' aid.

Katherine D. Wiesendanger, Ellen D. Birlem, and John Wollenberg (1982) asked whether students' comprehension is improved by questions posed before they read a passage. Of the 22 studies they reviewed, 10 favored prior questions while 12 opposed them. In some studies, the researchers posed the questions, while in others, students posed their own. Summarizing the studies, the authors stated,

It is logical that the objective of the lesson as well as other variables might determine whether or not the teacher should prequestion. For example, the objective might be for the student to skim in order to uncover the general gist of what the author is saying or scan to find out something particularly stated in the material. This would influence a teacher's questioning strategies.

It does seem important to remember that the ultimate goal should be for students to become proficient readers—independent of the teacher's aides. For this reason it seems apparent that we want students eventually to develop their own purposes for reading. Consequently, it would behoove teachers to encourage *student* development of questions, to learn to read the material in order to answer their questions, and to set new purposes for reading. Comprehension is an active process whereby the reader interacts with the material. After taking a number of variables into account, the teacher must use whatever questioning strategy necessary to help the student develop this interaction, so to achieve a degree of independence in reading. (p. 20)

Chunking and Reading Comprehension

The term *chunking* in reading comprehension means reading natural linguistic units, usually phrases. If a student is good at chunking, then that student probably uses proper phrasing while reading. Several researchers have studied students who do and do not chunk properly. The students were given material that had been chunked for them. For example, this story,

> Tim was a boy who lived with his grandmother and grandfather during the summertime. When he was not living with his grandmother and grandfather, he lived at home with his mother and father.

when chunked, might look like this:

> Tim was a boy/who lived/with his grandmother/and grandfather/during the summertime./ When he/was not living/ with his grandmother/and grandfather/he lived with/his mother and father.

One can also chunk material by using spaces instead of slash lines. The *method* of chunking

may be as important as chunking itself, according to some studies.

William G. Brozo, Ronald V. Schmelzer, and Hiller A. Spires (1983) studied the use of chunking. They state, "Several studies have shown that poor readers' comprehension is improved when words are preorganized into meaningful groupings for them. . . . Few, however, have shown that word grouping aids comprehension for competent readers" (p. 442). In their own study, however, students with chunked materials did better than students without chunked materials, whether they were good or poor readers.

Kathleen C. Stevens (1981) also studied the chunking procedure, with 85 boys in the tenth grade of an all-male Catholic high school. In the procedure described by Stevens, students and their teacher discussed a sample chunked paragraph. Stevens stated that the whole procedure took approximately 10 to 15 minutes. Students reading the chunked passages read significantly better than students reading regular passages. She recommends that

> As a first step in teaching "chunking," teachers might present "chunked" reading material to students for discussion. Then, students might point out the phrase units in prose for themselves. The need to "chunk" for every reading task should make the discussion of phrasing and of thought units an ongoing activity. This can be emphasized to students by reading meaningfully and nonmeaningfully "chunked" material. (pp. 128–29)

Other Factors Affecting Reading Comprehension

Reading specialists sometimes believe that certain students, because they lack innate ability, or because of some other reason, simply cannot perform as well as other students. Perhaps this is true to a certain extent, but it appears that the match between the reader's reading level and the material's difficulty strongly influences comprehension. The reader, to comprehend at his peak, must be reading material that is not too difficult.

Grace Malicky and Dennis Schienbein (1981) compared the comprehension processes of average fourth-, average sixth-, and poor sixth-grade readers. They found that if poor readers were allowed to read material commensurate with their instructional levels, then they could make inferences in reading as well as the average readers did. The authors commented,

It would appear, then, that the difficulty level of the material is the crucial variable which must be manipulated if inferencing behavior is to occur. If material is adjusted to the instructional level of poor readers, they are just as capable of making inferences as are good readers. Rather than adjusting instruction by focusing on literal comprehension for poor readers, then, the adjustment should involve level of difficulty of the material. (p. 338)

Using pictures in reading material also plays an important part in comprehension. Dale R. Rice, Robert L. Doan, and Sheila J. Brown (1981) reviewed the literature and conducted their own study on the effect of different kinds of pictures on comprehension. They reported that pictures interfere with comprehension if they are not directly related to the reading material. On the other hand, if pictures are directly related to the text, then the overall comprehension of readers

improves. The pictures do, however, usually slow the reader's speed. The authors ask,

Should pictures be included in a reading text? The answer depends on the objectives the classroom teacher hopes to achieve with the beginning reader. In view of the research, pictures do tend to slow down a reader's speed, but seem to facilitate comprehension. The argument that illustrations help develop positive attitudes toward reading seems to be valid. (p. 312)

ASSESSING COMPREHENSION IN THE CLASSROOM

Teachers have several options for assessing their students' comprehension.

Using Standardized Achievement Tests

Group standardized achievement tests are probably used more than any other kind to assess students' comprehension. They are easy to administer and usually contain enough questions to give the interpreter a fairly good picture of a student's ability to comprehend. Most of these

Locating materials at the child's level is critical in comprehension instruction.

tests are standardized on a large number of students from various sections of the country for as representative a sample as possible. Developers of test norms also try to use students from various socioeconomic levels. Some of the better known tests are listed in Appendix G.

Although group standardized tests have their advantages, they also have disadvantages. These disadvantages may not be so much a part of the test themselves as part of the way they are used. Here are some advantages and disadvantages of group standardized tests.

Advantages.

1. They are easily administered, requiring little of the teacher's time.
2. They give the teacher or administrator a fairly accurate picture of the overall comprehension ability of a class or of all the students at a certain grade level in a district.
3. They allow the teacher or administrator to compare their students' reading ability with students nationwide.
4. They are good for research purposes, enabling someone to study students' improvement from the beginning to the end of a program or a year.

Disadvantages.

Teachers and administrators often misuse them to make major decisions about the welfare of individual students. These are *group* tests, however, and should be used *only* to examine the comprehension of groups. Part of the blame for this misuse can be placed on authors and publishers who often suggest using test scores for individual placement or diagnosis of students. Some studies, as well as many reading specialists, say that using group standardized achievement tests to place students in grades probably puts students at their *frustration* reading levels rather than at their *instructional* levels. Thus, when these tests are used for individual placement, they overplace students. And students reading at their frustration levels, rather than at their instructional levels, cannot deal with the concept load in their reading materials and their comprehension suffers as a result.

Using group standardized achievement tests for determining the reading level of individual students also causes the student reading considerably below grade level to be *grossly overplaced.* Because most group standardized achievement tests use a multiple choice format with four choices for each question, a student who cannot read at all can get one-fourth of the answers correct. Some tests allow students getting one-fourth of the answers correct to be placed near their normal grade level. For example, one college professor has the students in his beginning reading methods class take the intermediate test battery, meant for the fourth, fifth, and sixth grades, of one of the better known group standardized achievement tests. The students pretend that they cannot read even *one* word of English. Therefore, they do not read the questions for the test, but simply mark the answer sheets by chance. After the students mark the answer sheets, they correct them and determine an average reading level according to the group standardized achievement test. The class average is usually about 3.5 or 3.6. In other words, this class of fourth graders is only about 5 to 6 months retarded in their reading levels *even though they have not read the test questions*! In most school districts, this level would not qualify the students for a remedial reading program. Therefore, to suggest that scores on group standardized achievement tests are a good place to start in grouping students for reading instruction is misguided.

Group standardized achievement tests do not accurately measure an individual's reading achievement, but they are especially inaccurate for slow readers. Since nearly all group standardized achievement tests are timed, an especially slow reader, even though reading every word accurately with 100 percent comprehension, is severely penalized in relation to peers. Those peers may be less adept in word recognition or word analysis skills, and even comprehend somewhat less, but they may score higher because they can read faster.

Some group standardized achievement tests still try to measure various comprehension sub-skills. Since nearly every research study shows that testers cannot devise questions to measure various subskills, teachers should discount any subtest results that purport to measure a specific subskill.

Using Informal Reading Inventories

During the past twenty years, both teacher-made and commercial informal reading inventories have gained rather wide acceptance among reading specialists. Many publishers now furnish teachers with informal reading inventories to help them place children in the proper textbook level. A teacher-made informal reading inventory is a series of increasingly difficult passages (usually two passages at each level, one for oral reading and one for silent reading) made from material in basal readers or other material written at a specified grade level. The teacher gives the student several comprehension questions after the completion of each passage.

Commercial informal reading inventories are essentially the same as teacher-made informal reading inventories, except that they have usually been devised by reading experts and are marketed commercially by large publishing companies. Some of the better known commercial inventories are listed in Appendix G. Some advantages and disadvantages of both teacher-made and commercial informal reading inventories follow.

Advantages of Teacher-made Informal Reading Inventories.

1. They are made from students' actual reading materials for students the teacher is actually teaching. This advantage may give a closer match between reading materials and students' reading levels within any one classroom.

2. The questions are often less structured, allowing the teacher to question students in a less formal setting.

Disadvantages of Teacher-made Informal Reading Inventories.

1. Questions on teacher-made informal read-ing inventories may be written with less care than those on commercial inventories. A lot of time is needed to develop a commercial informal reading inventory because questions are tested on students. Some questions, for no obvious reason, are almost impossible for any student to answer. Others are so easy that almost every student, regardless of reading ability, can answer them. Thus, it is much more difficult to write *good* questions for passages than most teachers realize. With all due respect to classroom teachers, it is next to impossible to write *valid* questions for an informal reading inventory without trying each question out on many students and then doing an item analysis on each one.

2. When teachers choose a passage from reading materials, there is no guarantee that the passage actually represents the material as a whole. Many studies on the various reading levels found in most textbooks, especially in the sciences and social studies, show that material written at the seventh grade level, for example, may vary by as much as 4 to 6 grade levels, or even more, from page to page. *Many* materials, including this textbook, vary from 3 to 4 grade levels in reading difficulty from page to page. If the material picked by a teacher does not represent the book as a whole, then the overall purpose of using teacher-made informal reading inventories is defeated.

Advantages of Commercial Informal Reading Inventories.

1. Commercial informal reading inventories are usually put through a rigorous trial period before they are published. Authors usually administer each of the passages to many students and make sure that there are no questions students can answer all the time or others they can never answer.

2. Most authors of commercial informal reading inventories are especially careful to make sure that passages said to be at a certain reading grade level *are* at that grade level. Authors accomplish this validity by using readability formulas.

3. Although as Schell and Hanna point out, questions covering so-called subskills of comprehension are probably not as valid as one might wish, they are probably better than those developed by a classroom teacher. Much more time, effort, and thought goes into a commercial inventory meant to be used over and over again by many teachers.

Disadvantages of Commercial Informal Reading Inventories. Teachers may think that commercial inventories do not help them understand a student's problems with comprehension as well as an inventory derived from the student's actual reading material.

Using Informal Questioning

Informal questioning allows the teacher to immediately question a student on any problem with reading comprehension. It also encourages the teacher to pursue questioning because no fixed set of questions exists. Also, although teachers may not be experts at devising good questions, the opportunity to ask an immediately relevant question sometimes outweighs that problem.

However, it is quite difficult to devise good questions on the spur of the moment, and less than good questions may be almost meaningless. Also, the teacher may not know whether the questions are relevant or not.

Using the Cloze Procedure

The cloze procedure is an effective method for determining how well a student comprehends material. (See Chapter 10 for a more detailed discussion.)

To use the cloze procedure, the teacher uses what the students are reading or will read. The first sentence, or in some cases, the first 25 words of the material is left intact. Beginning around the 25th word, every 5th word is omitted. All omitted words are replaced with blanks of equal length. For third-grade level readers or above, passages should be approximately 250 words in length, plus the initial 25 words and a complete sentence at the end. Teachers give

the passages to students and tell them to read the material and fill in as many blanks as they can.

In correcting cloze passages, the teacher does not penalize the student for spelling but will accept only the exact word omitted as correct. (See Chapter 10 for an explanation of this grading policy.) Then the teacher computes a score indicating the percentage of correct responses and the student's score is judged according to the following criteria:

Independent Reading Level = 57% or better

Instructional Reading Level = 44 through 56%

Frustration Reading Level = 43% or less

Advantages of the Cloze Procedure.

1. The ability to fill in blanks measures comprehension better than other procedures do. Simply regurgitating facts, choosing the right answer out of four, or guessing one in two on a true-false question do not measure comprehension as accurately.

2. There is little guess factor in this procedure. Students can, of course, guess at certain words, but they cannot score up to instructional or independent reading level without actually understanding the material.

3. The student can be given material used in the classroom learning situation.

4. The teacher need not be concerned about the quality of questions.

5. The number of blanks (or what are essentially questions) makes this assessment of comprehension more valid than other measures.

6. The large number of blanks require many types of responses, which probably measure most commonly mentioned comprehension subskills. Yet the procedure does not isolate or separately measure subskills.

7. A teacher can use the cloze procedure to determine whether or not a book or set of reading materials is appropriate for a given class. To make this decision, the teacher looks at many passages throughout the book or reading materials. Then the teacher picks a passage that represents the overall book.

Disadvantages of the Cloze Procedure.

1. Because many teachers do not understand the overall procedure, they balk at using it.

2. The criteria developed for the independent, instructional, and frustration reading levels come from the criteria used for informal reading inventories. However, most reading specialists believe that the criteria for these reading levels are accurate, even though there are few concrete ways of proving their validity.

3. Students often tire easily when using the cloze procedure on long passages. It *is* a strenuous task. Even when students score at the independent level, they can have missed as many as 43 percent of the questions. Young students and adults working at this level become easily discouraged.

ASSESSING KNOWLEDGE OF VOCABULARY

Vocabulary, when it relates to comprehension, does not mean a student's sight vocabulary, or the number of words recognized. Rather, it means the words a student knows the meaning of when listening, speaking, and reading.

Using Group Standardized Achievement Tests

Some of the advantages and disadvantages of using group standardized achievement tests for measuring students' comprehension skills also apply to their use in measuring students' vocabulary skills.

Advantages.   There are five advantages to using group standardized tests for measuring students' vocabulary skills. Four of these advantages are exactly the same as those noted for measuring comprehension. (See p. 217.) The fifth advantage is that some teachers have more faith in the test results of a group.

Disadvantages.

1. Students poor in word attack skills, even though they may have relatively large meaning vocabularies, cannot score up to their potential because they cannot read the questions and/or answers.

2. Many vocabulary tests use words supposedly analogous to the words being tested. But sometimes these supposedly analogous words do not actually mean the same as the word being tested. To some extent, whether a student thinks one word is analogous to another depends more on that student's experiences than on his vocabulary.

3. Group standardized vocabulary tests are timed. A slow reader may be penalized, not because of an inadequate vocabulary, but because of an inability to read quickly.

Using Oral Vocabulary Tests

Teachers should give oral vocabulary tests to students suspected of having problems with word attack skills. For example, if a student cannot read a word being tested or cannot read the synonyms or definitions for that word, then he cannot show his full potential in vocabulary development. Using an oral vocabulary test allows the teacher to determine whether there is a large discrepancy between a student's achievement on an oral vocabulary test and on a written vocabulary test. If the student can perform much better on an oral vocabulary test than on a written one, then one can safely assume that the student has problems with word analysis skills. In this case, the student's problem in vocabulary can be corrected by teaching word attack skills rather than by teaching vocabulary itself.

However, teachers do not administer oral vocabulary tests to most students because it consumes a lot of time. Furthermore, the results have no more, perhaps less, value than those of a written vocabulary test.

TEACHING COMPREHENSION AND VOCABULARY

Barbara Johnson (1982) notes that researchers observing students being taught comprehension found that less than 1 percent of actual classroom time was spent in activities that would improve students' comprehension. Johnson said that first,

... teachers need to acquire some basic concepts about the comprehension process. Second, teachers need to learn instructional strategies that develop children's comprehension. Third, teachers need to implement these strategies so that children's comprehension can be improved. (p. 268)

Johnson's basic assumptions about comprehension are as follows:

1. Comprehension is an active process that requires the reader to think about the author's message. The reader must then accept, reject, or modify the author's ideas.

2. Readers do not really learn anything new in a complete vacuum. Readers, to *understand* what they read, must tie what is on the page to something they already know.

3. Although written words are usually more precise than spoken words, reading is essentially a conversation with the author.

4. Much of what readers learn is "written between the lines." Thus, the more the reader knows about the writer or the subject, the more the reader understands what is read.

Teaching Comprehension

Once teachers understand the comprehension process, they need to develop various strategies for helping students improve their comprehension.

Using Questions.   If students in reading methods courses are asked how they would teach comprehension, they almost always say they would have their students read something and then ask them questions about what they read. But there is a difference between *questioning* and *teaching.* Suppose, for example, that students were taught to do long division by being given several long division problems and *told to do them.* If they could not do them, they would be given more problems the next day, etc. Obviously, they would never master the process. Yet the gap between being given problems and knowing *how* to do long division is the same gap that exists between being asked questions and knowing *how* to comprehend.

If a teacher asks questions about reading students have done, then there should be a purpose for doing so. If the purpose is to *teach* comprehension, then asking questions will probably not accomplish that purpose. If, however, the purpose in asking questions before students read a passage is to help them remember a few specific facts related to those questions, their comprehension of those facts will probably improve. But if your purpose in asking questions before they read is to improve their *overall* comprehension, you will not succeed; their *overall* comprehension will probably not be as good as it would have been if you had asked no questions at all. Students asked specific questions before reading concentrate so much on answering those questions that their overall comprehension suffers.

Teachers also need to be aware that unless they teach students how to ask questions for *themselves*, then they have only served to improve students' knowledge over a small bit of material read on any given day. Teachers should teach students how to look at reading material, how to develop a purpose by skimming that material, and how to ask themselves what parts are important enough to remember.

Using When, Where, Who, What, and Why

Students can be taught how to comprehend more as they read by teaching them to answer the questions when, where, who, what, and why. Gerard Giordano (1981) also suggests a taxonomy for these questions: 1) recapitulative, 2) critical, 3) applied, and 4) judgmental. Giordano illustrates this taxonomy with the story of *The Three Little Pigs*:

recapitulative: Who knocked on the doors of the pigs' houses?
critical: Why didn't all of the pigs build their houses out of bricks?
applied: What would happen if your parents played instead of working?

judgmental: How do you think the pig in the straw house felt after the wolf knocked on his door? (p. 81)

Improving Questioning Techniques

Ronald T. Hyman (1982) suggests improving your questioning techniques by:

1. Using a predictable pattern in questioning. Such a pattern lets all students know they will be called on whether they are reticent or bold.

2. Making it clear that since everyone will be called on, students should not call out answers *unless* called on.

3. Suggesting that a student be named before called on so that everyone knows who should respond. (However, this procedure allows the rest of the class to ignore the question. If a student is not called on until after a question is asked, students get in the habit of listening to *all* questions. Granted, the teacher may have to repeat a few more questions, but students soon realize they may be responsible for *any* question at *any* time.)

4. Breaking your pattern from time to time. For example, you might ask students to react to a *student's* question.

5. Calling on volunteers no more than 10 to 15 percent of the time. A teacher cannot guess the overall percentage of students who know the answers by only asking volunteers to respond.

6. Calling on volunteers mainly during the times students may offer their personal opinions.

7. Asking students questions that are passage dependent. If students realize they can answer most questions from their own experience, they will be less motivated to read beforehand.

8. Using precise questions. For example, if a teacher asks, "Why was Franklin Roosevelt elected President?" one legitimate answer could be, "Because he got the most electoral votes." A better question would be, "What did the passage say were some of the reasons people voted for Franklin Roosevelt?" Hyman also suggests giving clues in your questions, such as "What issues in Roosevelt's platform appealed to labor unions?"

9. Using fewer leading questions, rhetorical questions, and directions phrased as questions. Hyman says, ". . . ask only questions to which you want the students to respond on their own. For example, avoid questions like 'Don't you think Kitty was the one who deserved the medal at the county fair?' and 'Now, why don't we all turn to the end of the story?' " (p. 308).

10. Giving the student ample time to answer. Do not pass the question to another student unless the first student has had *adequate* time to answer it. Several studies have shown that most students have three seconds or less to answer a question, hardly enough time to gather thoughts and respond properly.

Hyman also says we should not ask more than one question at once and then expect a student to remember and respond to them in their proper order.

11. Trying to get all students to answer in some way even if some have less academic potential than others. Teachers should constantly encourage less academic students to answer something even if it means giving them some clues. Encouraged this way regularly, such students will be less likely to say, "I don't know" or to shake their heads.

12. Trying to elicit complete, correct responses from more academically oriented students. Also, teachers should try to get students to formulate their own questions because then they have a stake in the responses, develop a more positive attitude, and become more independent in the way they learn from the text.[1]

QARs

Taffy E. Raphael (1982) suggests that "Children can easily learn three ways to look for answers in a reading passage. While doing so, they learn to look for both explicit and rephrased information and to expect to draw inferences" (p. 186). She calls this strategy the learning of QARs (Questioning-Answering Relationships). Raphael says,

[1]Discussion based on material from "Questioning for Improved Reading" by R.T. Hyman, *Educational Leadership*, 1982, *39*, 307–309. Summarized with permission of the Association for Supervision and Curriculum Development and R.T. Hyman. Copyright © 1982 by ASCD. All rights reserved.

It is important to remember four principles of instruction when teaching QARs: give immediate feedback, progress from shorter to longer texts, build independence by guiding students from group to independent activities, and provide transition from the easier task of recognizing an answer to the most difficult task of creating a response from more than one source of information. (p. 187)

Raphael suggests using three types of questions. The first kind is called *Right There*—"The answer in the story is easy to find. The words used to make the question and the words that make the answer are Right There, in the same sentence" (p. 188).

In the *Think and Search* question, "The answer is in the story, but a little harder to find. You would never find the words in the question and words in the answer in the same sentence, but would have to Think and Search for the answer" p. 188).

The third type of question is called *On My Own.* The answer won't be told by words in the story. Students must find the answer in their heads by thinking, "I have to answer this question On My Own; the story won't be of much help" (p. 188).

Raphael suggests teaching this procedure in four lessons. In lesson 1, the teacher works with students in groups, showing them the terminology with the use of an overhead transparency and a description of the three QARs. Students then learn about the three QARs and how they might find the answers to them. They find out that there are QARs where information for both the question and response are found in a single sentence vs. Think and Search QARs where information must be gotten from integrating at least two sentences.

In lesson 2, the teacher introduces passages of 75 to 150 words and up to five questions for each. Questions should be included from each of the three categories. Discuss the passages and questions and allow for feedback. If students have difficulties, allow them to work in groups to identify the QAR category necessary for answering each question. Finally, the teacher explains why an answer is correct or incorrect on the basis of accuracy and strategy. The teacher should also remember that sometimes more than one type might be appropriate.

In lesson 3, the teacher uses one passage of approximately basal story length. Raphael suggests dividing the story into four parts, each part followed by six questions, two from each category. Then briefly review the first part and let students work independently to complete the last three parts without interruption from the teacher.

In lesson 4, Raphael suggests using material that revolves around typical classroom material, such as a basal reader story or a social studies or science lesson. Give students longer passages to read as a single unit, accompanied by six questions from each QAR category. Students read the unit, respond to each question, identify the QAR, and then provide the answer.

With fourth graders, a weekly review session of the QARs helps students. Raphael concluded

QARs have always been implicit in answering questions. The value of this program lies in its very lack of novelty. An instructor should not be surprised by the QAR concept, but should instead experience a comfortable feeling of recognition. The program merges easily with current instruction. This article should provide readers with an appropriate and systematic means of approaching question answering as a part of the instructional program, making explicit an activity that may otherwise go undiscovered by many readers. (p. 190)

Other Questioning Strategies

Mary M. Kitagawa (1982) tries to get fourth- and fifth-grade students to devise their own questions about stories. She asks previewing questions on the basis of title and picture, such as "What questions do you have just from looking at the title and picture?" or "What are some questions you expect the author to answer?" She also suggests that children be asked occasionally about the main questions the author has answered. She also suggests asking such questions as "What further questions would you ask the author if you could?" or "What would you ask the main character if you were to meet her in person?"

Ruth Cohen (1983) also trained third graders to generate their own questions. The training had two parts: teaching children to discriminate a question from a nonquestion and to discriminate a good question from a poor one. She stated that students taught to generate their own questions comprehended material better than those not taught to do so. She stated, "It appears that self-generating strategies can be taught effectively in the formative years of learning and reading, as early as the primary grades" (p. 774).

Bryce C. Hudgins, James Dorman, and Mary Harris (1979) studied the effects of questions asked before, during, and after material was read on fourth, fifth, and sixth graders. They found that good comprehenders, even at the intermediate grade levels, are like adult readers in that they usually score better when questions are asked after reading instead of before.

George D. Spache and Evelyn B. Spache (1977) also have some suggestions about using questions for the improvement of comprehension:

1. Discussing the material's concepts and perhaps its vocabulary before students read it probably helps them comprehend more than asking them a set of questions beforehand.

2. You may wish to use questions after the material has been read, however.

3. Give slow responders ample time to respond and follow up any inadequate responses with further questions.

4. Make sure students realize there is not always a "specific" answer to questions; some questions require viewpoints or speculations.

Summary of Using Questions

Generally, a teacher's questions about specific facts before students read a passage help students remember those facts but cut down on their overall comprehension. On the other hand, general questions asked after students finish a passage sometimes help them recall more of what they have read.

Students usually recall more facts from a passage when they set a purpose for reading it.

However, the purpose should not be too narrow or students will focus on the few facts related to the purpose.

Teachers should make students understand that not all questions have *an* answer. For some questions, only *speculative* answers exist, and for others, *no* answers exist. In addition, students should learn to ask their own questions as they read and to speculate about what the author is going to say. Cohen (1983) indicated that students can do these tasks effectively as early as the third grade.

Finally, Cathy Roller Wilson (1983) makes a good point about questioning when she writes:

If literal questioning continues in the After phase [the last part of the story], children will get the impression that reading is remembering facts rather than truly understanding. They should realize that the real payoff in reading is to take the information and explore it to see where it fits in with what they already know—where it agrees with what they believe, and where it is different. If teachers continue to ask what color Ginny's sweater was and what type of dog Spot was, instead of allowing wide-ranging discussion, children may not discover this. If instruction has proceeded appropriately before and during reading children will be ready. (p. 389)

The DRTA.   Barbara Johnson (1982) discusses some comprehension activities based on the Directed Reading Thinking Activity as defined by Russell B. Stauffer (1970).

To use the DRTA, teachers give children a story and ask them to develop hypotheses about the story from reading the title or first few lines of text. Children are encouraged to make hypotheses based on the first bit of information they read and on the background information they may have. Teachers allow students ample time to discuss these hypotheses and to change them, according to what they learn from other children.

Children then read the text or story silently to check on the accuracy of their original hypotheses. Teachers ask them to note any sentences or portions of the story that confirm or contradict their original hypotheses.

Then the children discuss what they have read and how it proves or disproves their original hypotheses. The teacher asks questions such as, ''Was your original guess correct?'' or ''Read me the part that proves your original idea was correct.'' You may continue this activity throughout a story by asking students to make hypotheses about what will happen in one part and then to check on the accuracy of their predictions.

Johnson names several reasons for using DRTA. For example, a child is required to think while making inferences and hypotheses. She points out that this process gets the child involved.

Manzo Strategies. Anthony Manzo (1980) describes ''Three Universal Strategies'' for reading in content areas:

One, called the Oral Reading Strategy, is ''text specific,'' i.e., it is designed to be employed with a specific piece of text and to help the student to read it with greater fluency and comprehension. The other two, the C/T/Q and Question-Only strategies are understood better as ''nontextual'' or bracing methods, i.e., intended to help a student to build a richer foundation in the language, thought, and attitude of a discipline, and therefrom to grow in reading and content knowledge. (p. 147)

To use Manzo's Oral Reading Strategy, the teacher should read approximately two textbook pages aloud once a week. While the teacher reads, the students follow along in their textbooks. Manzo suggests that the teacher stop at certain points and ask students to put the material into their own words. The students may have to reread before they understand difficult material. About this method Manzo says,

The confusions revealed, questions raised and informal (incidental) help rendered with vocabulary, author style, basic concepts, and key questions make this a solid content area reading and languaging lesson. (p. 147)

Manzo labels his second method C/T/Q, which reminds the teacher to isolate key Concepts, key Terminology, and key Questions for a unit of study. Manzo suggests that students record C/T/Q points in their notebooks so that the information is available as a reference throughout the unit.

Manzo describes his third method as follows:

Step 1: The teacher announces a topic to the class and explains the rules of the interaction. Students are told that they must learn all that they can about the topic solely by their questions, after which they will be given a test on the topic. The test, they are told, will cover all the information which you, the teacher, consider to be important, whether or not the students extract the information from you with their questions.

Step 2: The class questions and the teacher answers fully but without undue elaboration.

Step 3: The test is given. A class discussion follows in which note is made of the questions raised and those which should have been.

Step 4: Students are directed to read their texts carefully or to listen to a short lecture in order to discover what they failed to learn through their initial questions.

(Optional) Step 5: A follow-up test is given. The combined scores from the first and second tests are a good index of a student's growth in grasp of key ideas and facts. (p. 148)

Other Teaching Strategies. In their article called ''Classroom Practices Can Make Use of What Researchers Learn,'' Diane Lapp, James Flood, and Gary Gleckman (1982) discuss some procedures that consistently bring about better comprehension. One of these is the *Directed Reading Activity*, which is similar to the Directed Reading Thinking Activity previously described. The Directed Reading Activity follows this pattern:

1. The teacher begins the reading assignment by discussing key concepts in the story and relating them to students' experiences.

2. The teacher introduces key vocabulary and holds a discussion related to students' prior knowledge. (The authors point out that researchers in domain knowledge would call this schema development.)

3. The teacher then asks questions that direct students to key content. These questions should give the reader a reason to read the material.

Lapp, Flood, and Gleckman also recommend the ReQuest Procedure, as originally outlined by Anthony Manzo (1969). The teacher asks one or more students to read a sentence or passage from a text. Both the teacher and the students read the material. Then the teacher closes his book and the students ask as many questions as they can to clarify the subject matter. The teacher should answer these questions as clearly and accurately as he can. Then the teacher asks the students questions. Thus, the students gain insight into the questioning process because they are both participants and observers. The procedure should continue until the students can answer questions such as "What do you think is going to happen in the rest of the selection?" (p. 582). This procedure also teaches students to retrieve schemata and concepts.

The Prediction Strategy. Lapp, Flood, and Gleckman also suggest using the prediction strategy devised by Jane Hansen (1981). This strategy is based on the belief that "comprehension improves when readers can integrate the text into prior knowledge." To stimulate this integration, Hansen suggests activities which evoke prior knowledge and encourage its application to textual information. Based on studies with second graders, she recommends that the teacher use the following procedure. (1) Prior to having the children read a story, select a few ideas you find important. (2) Write two questions for each idea, one concentrating on previous experiences which relate to the idea and one requiring the students to make a text-related prediction. (3) Have the students write their answers/predictions. (4) Discuss the students' answers/predictions. (5) Students read the passage. (6) Students answer follow-up questions (using both literal and interpretative questions). (p. 583)

Using Story Frames. Gerald F. Fowler (1982) discusses an interesting method of developing comprehension through the use of story frames, as first described by James Nichols (1980). In a story frame, the teacher begins a sentence about the story's content and then leaves the rest of the sentence blank for the student to fill in. (See Figures 7–1 through 7–5.) Nichols says that, "the intent of the frame is to provide a structure for organizing a student's written responses to a variety of content material" (p. 229). Fowler suggests that story frames be used first with small groups to help students understand how to fit information found in books into a framework.

The children read a story first. The teacher then displays a story frame and discusses possible responses. Remember that the frames are relatively open-ended; no specific words or answers are intended for each space. Thus, children may often use information considerably different from what the teacher might use.

Some examples of story frames to use with students appear in Figures 7–1 through 7–5.

Using Metacognition. Teaching students to think about their own thought processes while reading may be one of the best methods the teacher can use to improve students' reading comprehension. Several studies have verified that if students can be taught to monitor their thoughts while reading, their overall comprehension usually improves. Oran Stewart and Ebo Tei (1983) have suggested many techniques the teacher may use to help students learn to monitor their thinking processes and thus improve their reading comprehension.[2]

Using Who, What, When, Where, and Why

This technique has already been discussed; however, note that asking students to be able to answer these questions when they finish a passage encourages them to monitor their comprehension as they read.

Rereading Parts of Materials

The teacher must teach students that if they find a sentence or paragraph they do not understand, they should go back and reread the material. Many good adult readers do this automatically; however, inexperienced readers cannot be expected to know they *should* reread or to know *when* to reread unless they are taught. You might have students read one paragraph at a time and ask them to ask themselves, "Do I understand what I have just read, or do I need to reread it?" Many adults do this when they

---

[2]Discussion based on material from "Some Implications of Metacognition for Reading Instruction" by O. Stewart and E. Tei, *Journal of Reading*, 1983, *27*, 36–43. Copyright 1983 by *Journal of Reading*. Reprinted by permission.

```
┌─────────────────────────────────────────────────────────────┐
│                                                               │
│           Story Summary with One Character Included           │
│                                                               │
│  Our story is about _____  │
│                                                               │
│  _____. _____is an      │
│                                                               │
│  important character in our story. _____   │
│                                                               │
│  tried to _____.   │
│                                                               │
│  The story ends when _____.   │
│                                                               │
│                                                               │
└─────────────────────────────────────────────────────────────┘
```

Figure 7–1

```
┌─────────────────────────────────────────────────────────────┐
│                                                               │
│                     Important Idea or Plot                    │
│                                                               │
│  In this story the problem starts when _____  │
│                                                               │
│  _____. After that, _____   │
│                                                               │
│  _____. │
│                                                               │
│  Next, _____   │
│                                                               │
│  _____. Then, _____   │
│                                                               │
│  _____. The problem is finally solved when _____    │
│                                                               │
│  _____. The story ends      │
│                                                               │
│  when_____.  │
│                                                               │
└─────────────────────────────────────────────────────────────┘
```

Figure 7–2

Note. Figures 7–1 through 7–5 from "Developing Comprehension Skills in Primary Students Through the Use of Story Frames" by G.L. Fowler, *Reading Teacher*, 1982, *36*, 177. Copyright 1982 by the International Reading Association. Reprinted by permission of G. L. Fowler and the International Reading Association.

Setting

This story takes place _____

_____. I know this because the author

uses the words "_____." Other

clues that show when the story takes place are _____

_____.

Figure 7–3

Character Analysis

_____ is an important character in our story.

_____ is important because _____

_____. Once, he/she _____

_____.

Another time, _____

_____. I think that _____

_____ is _____
          (Character's name)   (Character trait)

because _____.

Figure 7–4

Character Comparison

_____ and _____

are two characters in our story. _____
(Character's name)

is _____
(Trait)

while _____ is _____.
(Other character)   (Other trait)

For instance, _____ tries to _____.

_____ learns a lesson when _____

_____.

Figure 7–5

read directions because they have to perform a task correctly.

Forming a Mental Image

The teacher should encourage students to form mental images of what they read about. To practice, the teacher might ask students to read a descriptive passage and then discuss the mental images perceived by several students. The discussion could also focus on whether or not they did form images and why, or on reasons some students formed different mental images from the others.

Changing Reading Speeds

Students can monitor their comprehension while reading by changing reading speeds. Many students do not get practice in varying their reading rate according to the difficulty of the materials being read. This is one factor that is emphasized a great deal in so-called speed reading courses. Such courses focus not so much on increasing speed as on learning when to

speed up and when to slow down. To teach this concept to students, discuss what materials to skim lightly, such as a newspaper, and what materials to read more carefully, such as directions or a textbook with detailed information.

Predicting What Lies Ahead

Encourage students to guess what the author may discuss next, or what may happen in a story as a result of what they have already read.

Inserting Nonsense Material in the Text

Tell students to read a passage in which you have placed text that does not make sense or does not belong. Then ask students to highlight the material that does not make sense with a highlighter. Or ask them to locate it and discuss it when they have finished reading.

Learning to Anticipate Postreading Questions

This process helps students increase their reading comprehension by helping them discriminate between minor points and major ideas within what they read. You may read a paragraph at a time with the class and then ask students what they think an author or yourself might ask about the paragraph's content.

Retelling a Passage

Tell students that as they read they should remember enough about the passage to tell the rest of the class about it. This technique causes students to work harder at obtaining a mental image and to reread parts they do not understand.

Ranking the Importance of Sentences

Ask students to read a passage and then tell what sentence is most important, next important, etc. This technique also helps students learn the difference between major and minor ideas.

Learning the Vocabulary of Reading

Primary school children may not know the difference between a *sentence*, a *paragraph*, and a *beginning sound*, so teachers should explain such concepts.

Making Students Aware of the Goal of Reading

Authors of basal readers nearly always suggest this technique, also. When students have a particular goal in mind, they usually comprehend more of what is read. The teacher cannot always be present to help students set a goal for reading. Therefore, it is important to teach students to ask themselves what they want to get from a certain story or passage.

Making Students Aware of Headings and Markers

Discuss the reasons for having dark headings in a textbook, as well as illustrations and various other marking devices used by authors.

Using Road Signs or Markers

Teachers can use this technique to make students aware of new words or difficult concepts. You can use YIELD or REDUCE SPEED signs in reading material that contains new words or difficult concepts. After using this technique for several lessons, ask students to determine where *they* would place these signs as they read unfamiliar material. Then discuss the different answers given by students.

Other Comprehension Strategies. This section details ideas on how to teach specific comprehension skills. Although reasearch cannot prove these skills actually exist, these exercises do help students become better at overall comprehension.

Learning to Find Main Idea

Give students paragraphs that contain well-defined main ideas. Ask which sentence represents the main idea and then ask how the other sentences build around or support it. It is often helpful to illustrate paragraphs by using larger rectangles to represent the main idea and smaller rectangles to represent supporting details. For example, give students several sentences that include one main idea and several supporting details. Draw a rectangle for each sentence and ask students to fit the sentences into the rectangles according to their importance, i.e., with the main idea or most important sentence fitting into the largest rectangle. See the following example.

a) Computers save a lot of time and labor for many people.

b) People can easily learn how to use computers.

c) Most businessmen can now afford computers.

d) You should probably own a computer.

Fit the four sentences (by letter only) in the four rectangles at the top of the next page.

This exercise can easily be applied to the sales of articles, for example, by listing all the reasons you should buy a new refrigerator, automobile, etc. The larger rectangle, then, usually contains a statement that summarizes the sales pitch: "For these reasons, Mr. Jones, you should buy a new Ford truck." Other ways to help students get the main idea follow.

1. After reading a passage or chapter from a book ask children to discuss what a proper title for the story's main idea might be. After

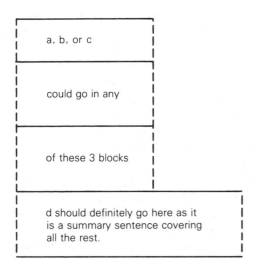

discussing for a while, let children vote and then discuss the vote.

2. Provide short paragraphs or passages and several titles for each one. Discuss the various title alternatives with students, pointing out why some would be better than others.

3. Give children newspaper pages and ask them to use a highlighter to highlight the sentence that contains the main idea in each short article. Use multiple copies of pages, if possible, so that children can discuss why some sentences were and were not picked.

4. Have children write paragraphs that have one sentence carrying the main idea and others that only support the main idea.

5. Cut the titles from several newspaper stories and then mix the stories and titles in an envelope. Have students read the stories and match them to the proper titles.

When teaching the concept of a main idea, remind students that the first and/or last sentence often carries it. Also, remind them that not all paragraphs or passages have a clear-cut main idea sentence.

Learning to Remember Details

Students can be taught to distinguish details from main ideas by using the techniques already outlined for finding the main idea. In addition, a teacher might try the following suggestions.

1. Have students read newspaper clippings and highlight important details. Then discuss the different points students highlighted.

2. Have children listen to a story. Afterwards, have them take a piece of paper (or have several students do the activity on the chalkboard) and list the details as (1) important, (2) helpful, and (3) minor.

3. Have students practice listening to stories with their eyes closed. Tell them not to try to remember a whole series of facts or details but to try to *see* what is going on in the story. This activity usually enhances students' ability to remember details.

4. Give students cards with the words *who, what, why, when,* and *where* written on them in large capital letters. Then have students read newspaper articles and clip them apart, putting each part under the appropriate heading.

5. Give students a passage to read that describes something in minute detail. Have students draw what they have just read about. After students have finished their drawings, have them compare their pictures and discuss things that were forgotten.

Learning to Develop Visual Images

You can help students learn to develop visual images by explaining that this ability can be improved.

1. Begin by having students listen to a short descriptive passage. Then ask them to draw all the details they can from images they pictured when they heard the passage.

2. After doing number 1, tell students that many people can close their eyes, hear a description of a scene, and feel almost as though they are there. Have students put their heads down on their desks and close their eyes while you read a second passage. Again, have students draw all the details they can from the images they saw when they heard the passage. (Be ready to notice a great improvement.) Then explain that people need not close their eyes to get good visual images. The more one practices, the better one gets at remembering images.

3. Discuss common figures of speech and help make students aware of them so that when they hear one, they can visualize it. Some examples of visual figures of speech are:

  a) fat as a hog
  b) big as a bear
  c) fast as a deer
  d) sheets of rain

4. Have children listen to music and either draw or tell about the visual images they see as a result.

Learning to Predict Outcomes

1. As you read a story, stop occasionally, ask children to tell what they think will happen next, and have them justify their answers.

2. Ask children to justify their predictions, if they can, on the basis of what happened earlier in the story.

3. Stop at a certain point in a story and ask students to predict the outcome. Then discuss why certain outcomes almost always take place while others do not. Discuss outcomes in movies or written stories and in truth vs. fiction.

4. Ask students to read headings in a book or chapter and predict what may happen on the basis of these headings.

Learning to Follow Directions

1. Explain that directions are written differently depending on the length of a process and the purpose for which they were written. Help them see that directions for very long procedures should be done step by step, i.e., read some of the directions and then do one step, etc. Other directions can be read all at once and then the procedure completed.

2. Have students write their own directions for getting from one place to another in the room or on the school grounds. After these directions have been written, have other students read the directions and follow them exactly. Discuss why some students cannot get to where they should, either because they have not read the directions properly or because the directions were not written properly.

3. Give students well-written directions, such as for paper folding activities, and ask them to follow the directions. After they complete the projects, discuss why some students had problems following the directions.

4. Write directions for drawing something on a piece of paper. Ask students to follow the directions and draw the picture. Do they all end up with the same drawing?

5. Encourage students to read directions by giving them written rather than oral directions for activities. Do the same for homework assignments. You might put homework assignments on the chalkboard without talking about them, other than to say where the directions are.

Learning to Follow the Author's Organization

1. Most important, the teacher should help students learn how to follow an author's organization by pointing out words that authors often use to show a sequence of events. In the reading field, these words are called full signals. There are also many half signals, which are less obvious to the reader.

Examples of some *full signals* are:

1, 2, 3,   first, second, third,   one, two, three

Examples of some *half signals* are:

  in the beginning, another thing, a last event

Other words used as half signals are:

then, at the outset, to sum up, in addition to, further, on the other hand, finally, besides, in conclusion, in the end, in the beginning, at the same time, more, most, next, soon after, at last, then, later, etc.

Kathleen C. Stevens (1982b) lists many key words that can help students understand difficult sentences:

Connectives which add ideas

also	both . . . and	moreover
and	furthermore	then
besides	likewise	

Connectives which contrast ideas

but	nevertheless	yet
however	still	

Connectives which express choice

either . . . or   nor   or

neither . . . nor   otherwise

Connectives which express result

accordingly   hence

consequently   therefore

Words which express time

whenever   after   until

while   since   when

Words which express cause or reason

since   as

whereas   because

Words which express purpose or result

in order that   that   so that

Words which express condition

unless   provided

if   although (pp. 187–88)

2. Have students read selections and point out words used as half signals or full signals.

3. Examine a social studies or science book and decide how the author has organized the topic. Discuss how authors often organize material and what the most common patterns are.

4. Discuss the terms *former* and *latter* and how they are used. Look for these terms and discuss how they can confuse the reader if one does not pay attention to them.

Learning to Follow a Sequence of Events

1. Cut up comic strips and put them in envelopes. (The teacher can make a copy of the correct sequence.)

2. Do the same with short stories or narrative information found in newspapers. Have students reconstruct the original stories.

3. Give students envelopes with a series of events that can be put in the proper order *without* having to read the story in its original form. Place each event on a separate strip of paper. Putting the events on separate strips of paper allows the students to make changes without having to renumber the whole order of events in case one was inadvertently missed.

Deborah Tresidder Baker (1982) names some activities that can help students learn and/or practice reading a sequence of events.

1. Ask students to think about the events of the day—getting up, dressing, eating, going to school, etc.—and then list them in the order they happen.

2. View a videotaped show and ask students to write down the events they see in it. Then list these events on the chalkboard in the order they happened.

3. Have students follow a particular event in the newspaper (such as a trial) and write daily developments on the chalkboard. (Later you may wish to write these developments on pieces of paper, place them in envelopes, and have students reconstruct the whole story.)

Learning to Read Critically

James W. Cunningham (1980) has stated that "Comprehension is gaining meaning(s) from the page, while critical reading is evaluating the meaning gained and its implications" (p. 165). Teaching critical reading is more difficult to do than other types of reading comprehension. Studies show that most teachers learn to do a better job of teaching reading skills, such as phonics, as they gain experience. However, most teachers' abilities to teach critical reading do *not* improve unless they take a course in critical reading or learn about the tactics used by advertisers, politicians, etc.

Several categories of writing meant to influence the reader exist. In advertising, students should be aware of these:

The Bandwagon. Advertisers try to get people to do something or buy something because *others* are.

Endorsement by an Expert. Advertisers try to influence consumers when they hire movie or sports stars to tell the reasons they use a particular product.

It Is Written in Print. People tend to think that if something is written in the newspaper or in a book, it *has* to be true.

Beautiful People Do It or Wear It. This method is similar to the endorsement by an expert. Clothes are often advertised by showing a young man or woman surrounded by several beautiful people of the opposite sex.

Defamation through Labels. Politicians often use this technique to make their opponents appear in an undesirable light. For example, a politician might label an opponent "rightist," "leftist," "often accused," etc., even though the opponent might not see himself that way.

The Big Lie. This propaganda technique was used by Adolf Hitler: if you tell a lie often enough, people begin to accept it as truth.

Almost Anything, Phrased Right, Sounds Good. One can see this in so many commercials. In effect, it would be better for the product to say nothing.

Example: xxxxxxxxx often brings temporary relief from xxxxxxxxx.

This statement really means that sometimes, maybe often, the product *doesn't work at all*, and when it does, it brings only *temporary* relief!

Example: xxxxxx is often an effective counter-irritant.

This statement actually says that the product is going to have an irritating side effect that may or may not relieve the original problem.

Teaching Vocabulary

Albert J. Harris and Edward R. Sipay (1980) point out that until the 1940s, estimates of most children's vocabularies were inaccurate. Now researchers know that vocabulary probably develops as Edgar Dale (1965) suggests:

If we assume that children finish the first grade with an average vocabulary of 3,000 words, it is likely that they will add about 1,000 a year from then on. The average high school senior will know about 14,000 to 15,000 words, the college senior 18,000 to 20,000. (p. 449)

To help students increase their vocabularies even further, sound instructional methods must be used. Isabel L. Beck and Margaret G. McKeown (1983) reviewed studies of two basal reading programs. They looked at the strategies used to develop vocabulary and concluded:

neither the frequency of encounters with the words presented nor the instructional strategies used were adequate to ensure that words were learned well.

New words introduced for a selection were rarely repeated in subsequent selections, and the strategies for introducing word meanings were superficial, offering little more than a brief definition and one example of the word in context. (p. 622)

Thus, if students are to learn the meaning of a new word, then they must encounter that word many times, preferably in the context of sentences.

The Role of Sustained Silent Reading. There are many ways to improve children's vocabularies, but probably none can do so as easily and effectively as sustained silent reading or the recreational reading that children do on their own. (Chapter 11 explains how to set up and operate a sustained silent reading program.)

Specific Strategies for Teaching Vocabulary. Karen D. Wood and Nora Robinson (1983) discuss a method of teaching vocabulary that they label *VLP* (vocabulary, oral language, and prediction). In the *vocabulary* phase, the teacher examines the reading selection to determine which words are important or difficult. The teacher may highlight these words in the Teacher's Manual. Then the teacher notes what vocabulary skill to teach with the lesson, such as a new word along with the teaching of a long vowel sound. The teacher should then put the new words on cards, noting on the back of each card the page number of the textbook on which that word appears. Then the word can be introduced only on the day that that particular part of the lesson is read. Wood and Robinson then suggest that the teacher place all new word cards on a table in front of students.

The *oral language* part of the lesson should begin with the teacher pointing out or asking questions about each of the words. They recommend questions like the following:

Which word means the same as *students*? What is another name for a herd of cows? . . . Which word means the opposite of old-fashioned? . . . What is another way of spelling weave that means something entirely different? . . . What label can we give to these three words: *spinning, weave, woven*? . . . Group all the words that have something to do with animals.

. . . (For context) People in some parts of our country and in other countries speak a different ———— than we do. . . . Using your dictionaries, find the definition of *supply* that fits in this sentence—"Father bought a *supply* of food for our trip." . . . Which words show action? Which words name something? . . . In which words do you find the same sound as *a* as in *play*? Which words end like examination? (p. 394)

When students begin to realize what the story is about, ask them to *predict* by asking: "Which words probably tell you about the main character?" or "Which words tell where he or she lives?" or "Do any words tell you about the mood of the story?" (p. 394). The authors then suggest that the teacher record the predictions on the chalkboard to be confirmed, rejected, or modified later.

Teachers do not always know each student well enough to know which words may cause difficulty for each. One can assign a committee of students to preview each lesson or chapter several days before the assignment. Then either the teacher or the committee can discuss the new vocabulary words before students read that assignment.

Teachers may also have trouble connecting what students already know with the unknown vocabulary word. Frederik A. Duffelmeyer (1982) suggests that teachers generate synonyms and/or antonyms for new words to help solve this problem. He also suggests that teachers generate two "context rich" sentences for each new vocabulary word, such as "Babe Ruth is *renowned* for his home run record," and "If you became President of the United States, you would be *renowned*."

Other Strategies for Teaching Vocabulary

1. Make students *aware* of new words when they read and teach students not to *skip* them. If you have looked up the meaning of a new word, you probably have noticed that particular word appearing regularly afterwards. This experience shows that readers actually teach themselves to *ignore* words they do not understand. The recurring word had *surely* been there before, but you chose to ignore it!

2. Help students become aware of new words by having contests; who can find the most words that other students do not understand? Limit the contest to a particular book and one day.

3. It is sometimes difficult for students to always look up a new word in the dictionary. Encourage students to keep some 3 × 5 cards in their pockets or purses. When they encounter a new word, look it up, write the meaning of the word on one side of the card, and write down the sentence in which it was found on the other side.

4. Encourage students to be aware of the many contexts words are found in. Have contests to find as many contexts as possible for certain words. Since some words can be used in so many contexts, let the contests run for several days or a week.

5. Encourage parents to discuss things that happen in their homes. Also encourage parents to have their families eat together, as meals are an excellent time to share experiences and build vocabularies.

6. Encourage students to raise their hands whenever someone uses an unfamiliar word. Praise students for asking what a word means and indicate that such students usually have large vocabularies.

7. Encourage children to use the dictionary and the thesaurus as much as possible. Especially encourage using the thesaurus in creative writing.

8. Most children do not learn and retain the meaning of a new word with only one presentation. Therefore, encourage students to think of other words that fit in the same category as the new word. List all those words, plus the new one. Then use each word in a sentence.

SUMMARY

Both the reader and the material being read affect the reader's comprehension of that material. According to the information available about the so-called subcategories of reading comprehension, only the subcategory of *vocabulary* can be identified with any certainty.

There are various ways to assess students' knowledge of comprehension and vocabulary, and each has its strong points and shortcomings.

Research indicates that teachers do not generally do a good job of teaching comprehension. Teachers are generally less competent in teaching reading comprehension than in any other part of the scope and sequence of reading skills. But in defense of teachers, many of them have simply not known *how* to do a better job.

This chapter presents many ways to increase students' ability to comprehend as well as ways of increasing their vocabulary. These suggestions are aimed at teaching you *how* to teach the comprehension aspect of reading skills. These suggestions should give you the needed knowledge and confidence to teach comprehension well.

REVIEW QUESTIONS

1. What affects the reader in comprehending?
2. What affects the difficulty of the material being read?
3. What subcategories of comprehension can be statistically identified?
4. Why label comprehension categories, other than vocabulary, if there is no proof they exist?
5. How specific should assessment devices be for the measurement of so-called comprehension skills?
6. What is meant by cognition? Metacognition?
7. What is meant by schema or schemata?
8. What are some advantages and disadvantages of using standardized reading tests?
9. What are some advantages and disadvantages of informal reading inventories?
10. What is the cloze procedure and what is it used for?
11. What tests are used to assess students' vocabularies?
12. Of what value is questioning in the *teaching* of comprehension?
13. What are QARs? What are Manzo's three questioning techniques?
14. How can you use story frames?

REFERENCES

Adams, M., & Bruce, B. Background knowledge and reading comprehension. *Reading Educational Report No. 13*. Urbana, Ill.: Center for Study of Reading, 1980.

Allington, R. L., Chodos, L., Domaracki, J., & Truex, S. Passage dependency: Four diagnostic oral reading tests. *Reading Teacher*, January, 1977, *30*, 263–68.

Babbs, P. J., & Moe, A. Metacognition: A key for independent learning from text. *Reading Teacher*, January, 1983, *36*, 422–26.

Baker, D. T. What happened when? Activities for teaching sequence skills. *Reading Teacher*, November, 1982, *36*, 216–19.

Barrett, T. C. (Ed.). The evaluation of children's reading achievement. *Perspectives in Reading No. 8*. Newark, Del.: International Reading Association, 1967.

Beck, I. L., & McKeown, M. G. Developing questions that promote comprehension. *Language Arts*, November/December, 1981, *58*, 913–18.

Beck, I. L., & McKeown, M. G. Learning words well—a program to enhance vocabulary and comprehension. *Reading Teacher*, March, 1983, *36*, 622–25.

Brozo, W. G., Schmelzer, R. V., & Spires, H. A. The beneficial effect of chunking on good readers' comprehension of expository prose. *Journal of Reading*, February, 1983, *26*, 442–45.

Cohen, R. Questions as an aid to reading comprehension. *Reading Teacher*, April, 1983, *36*, 770–75.

Crowell, D. C., Au, K. H., & Blake, K. Comprehension questions differences among standardized tests. *Journal of Reading*, January, 1983, *26*, 314–19.

Cunningham, J. W. Reading comprehension is crucial but not critical. *Reading Horizons*, Spring, 1980, *20*, 165–68.

Dale, E. Vocabulary measurement: Techniques and major findings. *Elementary English*, 1965, *42*, 895–901, 948.

Duffelmeyer, F. A. Expanding children's vocabulary. *Reading Horizons*, Fall, 1982, *23*, 64–66.

Durkin, D. What classroom observations reveal about reading comprehension instruction. *Reading Research Quarterly*, 1978–79, *14* (4), 481–533.

Fowler, G. L. Developing comprehension skills in primary students through the use of story frames. *Reading Teacher*, November, 1982, *36*, 176–79.

Giordano, G. Assessing reading disabilities with question sets. *Academic Therapy*, November, 1981, *17*, 179–82.

Hansen, J. An inferential comprehension strategy for use with primary grade children. *Reading Teacher*, March, 1981, *34*, 665–69.

Hare, V. C., & Smith, D. C. Reading to remember: Studies of metacognitive reading skills in elementary school-aged children. *Journal of Educational Research*, January–February, 1982, *75*, 157–64.

Harris, A. J., & Sipay, E. R. *How to increase reading ability.* New York: Longman, 1980.

Hayes, D. A., & Tierney, R. J. Developing readers' knowledge through analogy. *Reading Research Quarterly*, 1980, *17* (2), 258–80.

Hudgins, B. B., Dorman, J., & Harris, M. Some effects of adjunct questions on intermediate grade children with differing reading comprehension abilities. *Journal of Educational Research*, May/June, 1979, *72*, 259–65.

Hyman, R. T. Questioning for improved reading. *Educational Leadership*, January, 1982, *39*, 307–309.

Johnson, B. Helping children construct meaning: Comprehension strategies that work. *Reading Horizons*, Summer, 1982, *22*, 268–74.

Kitagawa, M. M. Improving discussions or how to get students to ask questions. *Reading Teacher*, October, 1982, *36*, 42–45.

Langer, J. A., & Nicolich, M. Prior knowledge and its relationship to comprehension. *Journal of Reading Behavior*, Winter, 1981, *13*, 373–79.

Lapp, D., Flood, J., & Gleckman, G. Classroom practices can make use of what researchers learn. *Reading Teacher*, February, 1982, *35*, 578–85.

Malicky, G., & Schienbein, D. Inferencing behavior of good and poor readers. *Reading Improvement*, Winter, 1981, *18*, 335–38.

Manzo, A. V. The request procedure. *Journal of Reading*, November, 1969, *13*, 123–26.

Manzo, A. V. Three universal strategies in content area reading and language. *Journal of Reading*, November, 1980, *24*, 146–49.

Nichols, J. Using paragraph frames to help remedial high school students with written assignments. *Journal of Reading*, December, 1980, *24*, 228–31.

Otto, J. The new debate in reading. *Reading Teacher*, October, 1982, *36*, 14–18.

Raphael, T. E. The effects of some known sources of reading difficulty on metacomprehension and comprehension. *Journal of Reading Behavior*, Winter, 1981, *13*, 325–34.

Raphael, T. E. Question-answer strategies for children. *Reading Teacher*, November, 1982, *36*, 186–91.

Readence, J. E., & Moore, D. W. Why questions? A historical perspective on standardized reading tests. *Journal of Reading*, January, 1983, *26*, 306–13.

Rice, D. R., Doan, R. L., & Brown, S. J. The effects of pictures on reading comprehension, speed, and interest of second grade students. *Reading Improvement*, Winter, 1981, *18*, 308–12.

Schell, L. M., & Hanna, G. S. Can informal reading inventories reveal strengths and weaknesses in comprehension skills? *Reading Teacher*, December, 1981, *35*, 263–68.

Shantz, M. Briefs: Readability. *Language Arts*, November/December, 1981, *58*, 943–44.

Singer, H. Active comprehension: From answering to asking questions. *Reading Teacher*, May, 1978, *31*, 901–908.

Spache, G. D., & Spache, E. B. *Reading in the elementary school.* Boston: Allyn and Bacon, 1977.

Stauffer, R. G. *The language experience approach to the teaching of reading.* New York: Harper & Row, 1970.

Stefferson, M. S., Joag-Dev, C., & Anderson, R. D. A cross-cultural perspective on reading comprehension. *Reading Research Quarterly*, 1979, *15*, 10–29.

Stevens, K. C. The effect of interest on the reading comprehension of gifted readers. *Reading Horizons*, Fall, 1980, *21*, 12–15.

Stevens, K. C. Chunking material as an aid to reading comprehension. *Journal of Reading*, November, 1981, *25*, 126–29.

Stevens, K. C. Can we improve reading by teaching background information? *Journal of Reading*, January, 1982a, *25*, 326–29.

Stevens, K. C. Helping students understand complicated sentences. *Reading Horizons*, Spring, 1982b, *22*, 184–90.

Stewart, O., & Tei, E. Some implications of metacognition for reading instruction. *Journal of Reading*. October, 1983, *27*, 36–43.

Strange, M. Instructional implications of a conceptual theory of reading comprehension. *Reading Teacher*, January, 1980, *33*, 391–97.

Wiesendanger, K. D., Birlem, E. D., & Wollenberg, J. A summary of studies related to the effects of question placement on reading comprehension. *Reading Horizons*, Fall, 1982, *23*, 15–21.

Wilson, C. R. Teaching reading comprehension by connecting the known to the new. *Reading Teacher*, January, 1983, *36*, 382–90.

Wood, K. D., & Robinson, N. Vocabulary, language, and prediction: A prereading strategy. *Reading Teacher*, January, 1983, *36*, 392–95.

Worden, T. W. Critical reading: Can the skills be measured? *Reading Improvement*, Winter, 1981, *18*, 278–86.

8

Content Area Reading Instruction and the Study Skills

Chapter 8 was written by Ellsworth Berget, Professor of Teacher Education, California State University, Hayward.

PREVIEW OF TOPICS COVERED

☐ How the focus of reading instruction gradually changes from *learning how to read* to *reading to learn*

☐ How to integrate reading instruction into content subjects

☐ The three different approaches to teaching reading in content areas

☐ The effective Instructional Framework for structuring lessons in content areas

☐ How to develop vocabulary in content areas through context clues, structural skills, graphic organizers, and reinforcement

☐ How to use guided reading to help students develop essential reading processes and understand content concepts

☐ How students can use the SQ3R procedure to improve reading comprehension

☐ What other study skills students can learn

Reading skills taught in the developmental reading program should not be considered an end in themselves. Rather, they are a means to an end—that of students becoming independent learners. The old saying, "Give a man a fish and he eats for today; teach a man to fish and he eats for a lifetime," applies to reading instruction. But all too often, reading instruction becomes an end, and the purpose of the instruction is lost.

Teachers may find that intermediate students in particular can complete isolated word analysis drills, but cannot incorporate these skills into their actual reading. When teachers find themselves teaching isolated skills, they need to make sure that students understand *why* they have been taught those skills. Then students should practice the skills in the act of meaningful reading so that they incorporate them into their reading more easily.

However, it is not surprising to find students who have been taught vocabulary, comprehension, and study skills but who cannot read well in *content area subjects*. These subjects are the regular classroom subjects, such as social studies or science. To be an effective teacher of reading, you need to help students develop and apply these skills in content subjects.

READING TO LEARN

The model for reading instruction shown in Figure 8–1 reflects how that instruction changes as students move through the grades. Teachers in the primary grades emphasize *learning how to read*, but this focus gradually decreases. In contrast, teachers place relatively little emphasis on *reading to learn* in the early grades, but this focus increases steadily as children grow older.

Beginning at about the fourth-grade level, the curriculum expands and requires students to do a lot of reading in science, social studies, and other content subjects. Reading to learn begins in earnest. Rather than assume students can use their reading skills, the teacher needs to *insure* they can by teaching them *how* to read their content materials. Unfortunately, many times this instruction does not occur. Instead, the teacher says: "Open your books to Chapter 8. Read it and answer the questions at the end of the chapter. Are there any questions? No? Okay, begin reading."

Also unfortunate, teachers may overemphasize isolated skills and practice drills in the upper grades. Students become accustomed to this approach and initially resist more effective and appropriate techniques. One junior high school reading teacher wanted to use a "Hooked on Books" (Fader and Shaevitz, 1966) approach with his pupils. He had collected a large number and wide variety of high-interest books and other reading material for his students to read. But his students were uncomfortable with this approach at first and argued that "this isn't a reading class." To them, a reading class should have "lots" of worksheets to complete, and they should be graded on how many worksheets they completed and turned in.

The challenge of providing appropriate reading instruction to older pupils is not new. Nila Banton Smith (1965) quotes a statement written by Rebecca S. Pollard in 1889:

> There is quite a general complaint among teachers, principals, and superintendents that pupils in the higher grades are not able to read with ease and expression; they have so little mastery over words that an exercise in reading becomes a laborious effort at word-calling. Pupils read usually very well through the first three readers, according to our present standard of reading in these grades. But the trouble begins in the fourth reader, and by the time the class is in the fifth, the reading recitation is torture to the teacher and a hateful task to the pupil. (pp. 131–32)

Practical, effective techniques for teaching content reading and study skills do exist, however. If you use these methods in your daily instruction, you will help your students to read to learn. This critical ability will, in turn, help them to achieve their full potential as human beings.

Model of Reading Instruction

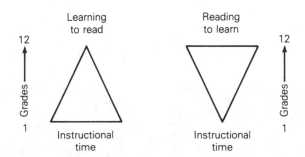

Figure 8–1   A model for reading instruction through the grades

REVIEW OF THE RESEARCH

As early as 1930, J. M. McCallister (1930b) reported on reading difficulties within content subjects. McCallister (1930a) examined the differences between general and specific reading skills and concluded that reading skills differ in mathematics, science, and social studies. He noted that students should be trained in reading activities adapted to the demands of content subjects. Later, McCallister (1932) reported the results of another study of seventh- and eighth-grade pupils in history, math, and science. He listed the skills needed in each subject area and concluded that each subject had its own purposes, forms, and applications and that some skills overlap while others are context-specific.

J. Harlan Shores (1943) investigated the relationship between certain study and reading skills and comprehension of scientific and historical materials. His findings were similar to McCallister's (1932), and he too suggested reading be taught in content subjects.

A. Sterl Artley (1944, 1948) studied the relationships between general reading comprehension and comprehension in specific areas. His results showed a high correlation between general comprehension and social studies comprehension; however, some skills related only to social studies were also found.

E. E. Sochor (1958) investigated the relationship between general reading ability and the ability to comprehend literally and critically in social studies, while E. A. Maney (1958) conducted a parallel investigation in science. They found that when intelligence was constant, literal and critical reading comprehension seemed relatively independent of each other, and critical reading comprehension appeared independent of general reading ability in both social studies and science reading. Experts today usually agree that some reading skills are general in nature while others relate specifically to individual subjects.

John Carney (1977) reviewed the research that related teaching subject area skills in isolation and transferring those skills to the specific subjects to teaching specific skills in subject area classes. He stated that:

The restricted applicability of the principle of transfer across subject matter areas raises serious questions concerning the teaching of reading as a separate entity with the expectation of transfer to content materials. Further, there is no clear evidence from the reported research to suggest that "reading-content" approaches in which reading skills and content are taught within the framework of the subject matter classroom are consistently superior to separate reading instruction, particularly with reference to mastery of content and ability to read materials of the type that are unique to the content areas. (p. 73)

Carney concluded that investigations assessing the effects of the two approaches were inconclusive and suggested further research.

Since 1969, there has been considerable research on the development and evaluation of techniques for improving reading in the content areas. The major source of research in this area has come from the Reading and Language Arts Center at Syracuse University. Harold Herber has edited, with others, a series of reports on research in the content areas (Herber and Sanders, 1969; Herber and Barron, 1973; Herber and Vacca, 1977; and Herber and Riley, 1979).

These four research reports include 24 studies: some dealing directly with content area research, some theoretical position papers, and some reviews of research related to reading in the content areas. The studies include the use of graphic organizers, guided reading, grouping, discussion, preservice instruction, and levels. They also examine different content subjects, including English, social studies, science, and mathematics. The studies have attempted to identify skills needed only in content subjects as well as teaching techniques that can be used effectively in content classes, but the results are equivocal.

More recently, Noble R. Corey found that rewriting science material aided ninth-grade biology students in understanding science concepts and Paul Ankney and Pat McClurg (1981) found that a guided reading procedure was successful with fifth- and sixth-grade students reading social science material but no differences were found in science material. John Tyo (1980) reported that using audio tapes of the social studies material improved poor readers' reading achievement in social studies.

At present, not much research on reading in the content areas is available. One of the first books devoted exclusively to the subject (Herber) was published in 1970. This is, however, a relatively new field that shows promise. There seem to be specific reading skills relating to individual subject areas. And a trend to integrate study skills instruction into the content areas is developing.

Over the years there has been little research on study skills, according to James E. Snoddy (1973), and much of what has been done has focused on the skills management system at the University of Wisconsin (Askov and Kamm, 1982). Experts tend to agree that study skills are particularly important to today's students because of recent technological advances (Dupis and Askov, 1982; Rickman, 1981).

Marilyn Fairbanks and Carolyn Castello (1977) reported that clear findings have not emerged from research on notetaking and underlining. Similarly, James Walker (1982) and Steve Graham (1982) report equivocal research results on SQ3R. Bonnie Armbruster and Thomas Anderson (1981) add the study skills of outlining and writing summaries to the list of those skills whose benefit has not been verified by research.

Armbruster and Anderson believe that any study skills approach *can* help if it helps students process information in an appropriate way. They suggest that students need to know: (1) how to determine the actual task and how to match the study skill to the task; (2) how to identify the properties of texts (including structure) and how to use those properties when studying; (3) about motivation, ability, and background knowledge in studying; and (4) *why, when*, and *how* to use particular study strategies. They concluded that:

Finally, students cannot learn very much about studying by being taught how to study "in general." Studying is not a general process; each content area has its own types of criterion tasks, texts, and preferred study strategies. Content-area teachers are in the best posi-

tion to teach the skills necessary for each particular discipline. Teachers also have a *responsibility* to teach study skills, rather than erroneously assuming that students already know how to study. Teachers need not sacrifice content matter; in fact, teaching students to study will facilitate teaching the content. Our suggestions do not imply a drastic overhaul of the curriculum. These guidelines can be incorporated into the kinds of exercises, assignments, and tests that teachers already employ. (pp. 155–56)

Linda Rickman (1981) surveyed more than 150 administrators, teachers, and counselors in Arizona, and faculty and student teachers at the University of Arizona's College of Education about timing, approaches, and materials used for teaching study skills. She drew the following conclusions: (1) teachers are unprepared to teach study skills, but they are interested in teaching them; (2) teachers feel it is important to teach study skills; the skills should be introduced in elementary school and increasingly complex skills taught through the years; and (3) study skills should be integrated into the content areas; teaching the skills in isolation is artificial and unproductive.

Eunice N. Askov, Karlyn Kamm, and R. Klumb (1977) found that teachers have limited knowledge of study skills and recommended that teachers receive systematic skills instruction before they are expected to teach them. Askov and Kamm (1982) recommended that teachers "carry out skill application as an integral part of teaching every content subject" (p. 5).

Research reported by Ronald E. Wolf (1978) and Barbara Stoodt and Elvira Balboa (1979) showed that students performed better when study skills instruction was integrated in the content subjects. Ed Brazee (1979) also found that study skills were learned more effectively when taught in the content subjects. Also, *teachers* became more aware of study skills when they were presented this way.

Research conducted to date leads to three conclusions: (1) teachers cannot be expected to teach study skills if they do not understand them; (2) instruction in study skills should be integrated into the content areas; and (3) students need to know how to integrate the skills into their own system of study.

TEACHING READING IN THE CONTENT AREAS

At least three different approaches to teaching reading in content areas exist. The first approach involves teaching the skills necessary for content reading in a separate reading class. The teacher identifies the skills needed for success in content subjects and then finds material with which to teach the skills. Often students bring their content textbooks to the reading class and then apply the skills taught to them.

However, this approach focuses on reading skills rather than on reading for information. Also, the skills generate the material to be used. If one is teaching main idea, then one looks for material that has good main ideas. Finally, students often find it difficult to transfer the skills because they may practice the skill only in reading class.

The second approach is used within content classes. The teacher divides the content class into two blocks of time, the first for developing reading skills, the second block for teaching subject matter. Typically, students pick up material from a reading kit when they enter the classroom, take it to their seats, and begin working on the material. After a certain period of time, the students return their reading material, and instruction begins on the content subject matter.

This approach has several disadvantages. First, students learn reading skills in isolation, without direct instruction from the teacher. Second, the teacher has less instructional time for the subject matter, and to transfer reading skills to the subject matter requires still more time. Third, the skills dictate the material used during the transfer time.

The third approach is also used within content classes. However, the teacher teaches reading skills as the students need them to read and understand the content material. With this approach, the materials dictate the skills. For example, when material contains troublesome vocabulary, then it is taught. If the material has a comparison-contrast or cause-effect organizational pattern, then those patterns are taught. In this way, skills become directly relevant to the material read. The teacher does not have to teach reading skills with each content lesson; rather, essential skills can be presented when the students need them to enhance their understanding of a topic. This approach has one disadvantage, at least for inexperienced teachers. Although teachers can plan for some skill lessons, they also have to be flexible, ready to teach any skill at a moment's notice.

Teachers should use this method, however, because it best prepares students to become effective readers and successful learners in the upper grades. It has several advantages: it directly relates reading skills to reading material; it does not drastically reduce the time spent teaching the subject matter; only the reading skills appropriate to the material are taught, and students can quickly transfer skills to the act of reading.

Structure of Lessons

In teaching reading, the elementary teacher in the self-contained classroom has a distinct advantage over the single-subject content teacher. As the students' reading teacher, the elementary teacher knows which skills the students have been taught and which ones they understand. The elementary teacher can therefore use two methods to incorporate reading in the content areas, directly transferring skills taught during the reading period and teaching the reading skills dictated by the content material. Best of all, the elementary teacher can show the students the relationship between the two types of learning.

To teach reading in the content area, the teacher has to understand how and where it fits into the daily lesson plan. In Chapter 3, the Directed Reading Activity (DRA), a format commonly used to teach reading in the elementary school, was described. This approach divides the lesson into four critical components: (1) lesson motivation; (2) vocabulary development; (3) guided reading activities; and (4) extended reading activities.

Presenting study concepts helps students understand content materials.

Instructional Framework. Harold Herber (1978) has modified the DRA to more easily accommodate reading in the content areas. He calls his system for structuring reading instruction in the content classes the *Instructional Framework* (IF). The IF differs from the DRA in emphasis. Herber divides the instructional framework into three areas: (1) preparation; (2) guidance; and (3) independence.

Preparation

Preparation is similar to the first two steps of the DRA. It emphasizes preparing students for reading and understanding the reading selection. Preparation has the following five parts: (1) motivation; (2) background information and review; (3) anticipation and purpose; (4) direction; and (5) language development.

The teacher uses *motivation* to interest students in the material. Thomas Estes and Joseph Vaughn (1978) point out that motivation is one of the most critical elements of learning. When a teacher interests the students in the material, they will usually complete the reading more effectively.

Background information and review provides students with the information necessary for understanding the selection. It may include introducing new information or reviewing information previously learned and applying it to the present subject.

Anticipation and purpose cover two broad areas: "(1) the ideas to be discovered; and (2) the reading processes to be applied" (Herber, 1978, p. 218). After background information and review have been concluded, the student identifies the purposes for reading and anticipates what he will get from it. The teacher focuses on what the student should understand and how to accomplish this understanding. The reading material dictates these processes. You might think of this step as addressing the "why" of reading.

Direction relates to the actual reading and is a critical step. Once purpose is established, teachers should give students directions so that they know exactly how to proceed, what to expect, and how to understand it. Unless students understand the directions, they may read just to "cover the pages."

Language development includes teaching the

assignment's specific vocabulary. Although students may not understand many of the words, *all* potential unknown words cannot be introduced. Otherwise, you might not have time for any other instruction. Therefore, only *key vocabulary* words should be introduced. These words are crucial to students' understanding of the material and its concepts. The words may be easy or difficult to pronounce, but they are the keys to unlocking the material.

Guidance

The guidance portion of the IF is somewhat similar to the guided reading activities part of the DRA, and it has two areas: (1) development of process; and (2) development of concepts.

Development of process means helping students develop reading processes essential to understanding specific content material. This instruction may include guiding students' reading with reading and study guides, preview questions, or SQ3R (to be discussed later in this chapter).

Development of concepts means helping students understand the material's ideas or concepts. For example, one reason to read about United States geography is to understand how parts of the country are similar and different, to recognize what makes the parts unique. Why and how is the climate of Portland, Maine different from the climate of Portland, Oregon? Thus, the student reads to understand concepts relating to climate. Once she understands these concepts, they can be applied to new situations.

Independence

This step in Herber's instructional framework is similar to the extended reading activities of DRA. Independence is the goal of teaching reading in the content areas. It also has two areas, *application of process* and *application of concepts*. These areas are parallel to the ones described under guidance; however, here the teacher helps students to apply reading processes and content concepts independently. If successful, students no longer need guidance in their reading, but can operate independently with new material that presents similar content concepts. Us-

ing the United States geography lesson, the student at this stage should be able to apply climate concepts to material about Columbus, Ohio and Columbus, Georgia, for example.

Vocabulary Development

Vocabulary development is critical to the successful teaching of reading in the content areas. When reading content material, most students encounter many words they do not understand. The teacher cannot possibly introduce all such words. Thus, the teacher needs to select for instruction only those words most important to the students' understanding of the material's concepts. These words are key vocabulary words.

Meaning vocabulary can be divided into three categories: (1) general, (2) technical, and (3) combination. *General vocabulary* refers to words used across content areas, such as *though, abbreviation*, and *thoughtful*. *Technical vocabulary* refers to words relating to a specific subject, such as *osmosis, carburetor, grammar*, and *longitude*. *Combination vocabulary* refers to terms that have both general and technical meanings. The word *property*, for example, means one thing in social studies but has an entirely different meaning in science. The word *graduate* has one meaning in science but a different one in guidance counseling. Students may be familiar with the term in one subject but not in another.

The elementary teacher often knows how to introduce and reinforce general vocabulary, but not technical words or combination words from different subjects. But to help students read in content areas, the teacher *must* focus on technical and combination words.

Teachers often have trouble selecting key words. Rather than being thoughtfully selective, teachers choose every difficult word. However, just because a word is difficult to pronounce does not mean that it is important for developing concepts. On the other hand, many words that are easy to pronounce are critical to the understanding of a selection. The teacher must choose key vocabulary that represents key concepts.

What makes a word important, then? Use two major considerations when selecting key vocabulary: (1) Is the word important for understanding the present concept? and/or (2) Is the word important for understanding future concepts? Some words may be important for the present lesson, but not for future ones. Mathematical terms such as *minuend* and *dividend* may fall into this category.

Other words may be important now and in the future. For example, students may hear *osmosis* for the rest of their lives, and it represents a key scientific concept. Time spent on it at first may insure understanding and save time and frustration later. Merely introducing the word one time does not imprint it on the minds of most students, but tying it in to current discussions and referring to it later may. Any word worth teaching is worth reinforcing. Techniques for teaching technical and combination vocabulary include context clues, structural skills, graphic organizers, and reinforcement activities.

Context Clues.   *Context clues*, clues to meaning and/or pronunciation provided by the context, are probably the best and most commonly used of the vocabulary skills among good readers. Students need to know how to use this skill in both general reading and content reading. The same practices that apply in teaching context clues in the developmental reading class also apply when teaching content area reading. (See Chapter 6 for a more thorough discussion of context clues.)

First, the teacher should review how one finds the meaning of a word through contextual analysis. Then, the teacher might present students with a list of words *in context*, drawn from the reading material. Next, the teacher should assist the students in figuring out the meanings of those words. For example, the teacher might use passages from a social studies text:

1. Today we know that California is not an island. It is part of the western edge of a broad *continent* called North America. A continent is a huge mass of land. Like some islands, continents have oceans around them. They are so much bigger than islands that they have a special name.
2. The soldiers who guarded the missions lived in forts called *presidios*. (Lavender, 1971, pp. 14–15)

The teacher can then show students that context clues may come before or after the unknown word. Students have often learned to identify an unknown word only by rereading the words before it, so teachers should remind them to check after unknown words as well.

Teachers should also take care to find examples easily understood from context. Of course, the meaning of an unknown word cannot always be determined from context alone.

Structural Skills.   Structural skills, or structural analysis skills, can help students develop their vocabulary when reading content material. Structural analysis can be a tool for decoding multi-syllable words. But ***structural skills*** for the purpose of vocabulary development have a different emphasis. Decoding emphasizes recognizing word parts to unlock the *pronunciation* of an unknown word. But in vocabulary the emphasis is on the *meaning* of certain word parts or morphemes. The most helpful morphemes for vocabulary understanding are the affixes (prefixes and suffixes). Content reading instruction gives teachers an ideal opportunity to introduce affixes important to the content subject.

Students studying the life sciences, for example, *must* understand the term *biology*. The teacher can identify the two parts of the word, *bio* and *logy*, and explain that *bio* means *life* and that *logy* means *study of*. Thus, the word *biology* means *the study of life*. If variant forms of the word are included in the reading, they should also be introduced and discussed. For example:

biologist = bio + log + ist
          = life + study of + one who
          = one who studies life
biological = bio + log + ical
           = life + study of + adjective form
           = about the study of life

If other words with similar structures have been studied or will be studied, they may be introduced at this time. For example:

geology = geo + logy
　　　　= earth + study of
　　　　= study of the earth
geologist = geo + log + ist
　　　　= earth + study of + one who
　　　　= one who studies the earth
psychology = psycho + logy
　　　　= mind + study of
　　　　= study of the mind
psychologist = psycho + log + ist
　　　　= mind + study of + one who
　　　　= one who studies the mind

This type of study helps students understand concepts as well as improve their reading. Often students with reading difficulty do not look at the entire word. This activity helps them to see that all parts of the word are important. For example, one student may read: "The biology flew to South America to study rare fish." He is aware of the term *biology*, but he does not bother or know to read the correct ending: *The biologist flew to South America to study rare fish.* Often, too, students use the noun form (*biology*) as an adjective: "the biology forms" instead of "the biological forms."

Structural skills can be reinforced often and easily. For example, the next time any part or form of the word *biology* is found in a reading, it should be pointed out. Do not teach students long lists of affixes. Teach the meaning of affixes only when this information helps students to understand concepts presented in written material.

Graphic Organizers.　　Graphic organizers (Herber, 1978) have been developed over a period of several years (Barron, 1969; 1979; Barron and Earle, 1973). *Graphic organizers* aid students' understanding of material by organizing key vocabulary concepts into a hierarchical classification schema (Lowery, 1974) before or after

reading, and then by defining the relationships between the vocabulary concepts. Barron (1979) has concluded that to use the organizer to its best advantage, the student should actively participate in constructing it, whether "during or following a reading/learning activity" (p. 173).

Two sets of instructions are recommended for developing graphic organizers (Barron and Earle, 1973; Barron, 1979). One set of instructions guides the teacher in developing the organizer without student participation, the second set guides the teacher in developing the organizer with students. Barron and Earle (1973) identify the steps in developing what they call the *structured overview*, or graphic organizer.

1. Analyze the vocabulary of the learning task and list all words that you feel are representative of the major concepts that you want the students to understand.
2. Arrange and/or rearrange the list of key words into a diagram which shows the key relationships among the concepts particular to the learning task.
3. Add to the diagram vocabulary terms which you believe are understood by the students that will clarify relationships between the learning task and the course (or discipline) as a whole.
4. Evaluate the organizer. Have you clearly shown the major relationships? Can the organizer be simplified and still effectively communicate the relationships you consider to be most important?
5. During the introduction of an organizer, display the diagram to the class step by step, having them identify and explain the relationships shown. Briefly explain why you have arranged the terms as you have. Encourage the students to supply as much information as possible.
6. In learning tasks of extended duration (i.e., units of content) relate new information to the structured overview as it seems appropriate. (pp. 84–85)

The first three steps in developing the organizer with students are the same as those listed above. The five additional steps, as presented by Barron (1979), are as follows:

4. Type each of the words included in your graphic organizer on a ditto master.
5. Following the students' reading of the passage or the material to be learned, introduce the idea behind the structured overview to the class with an

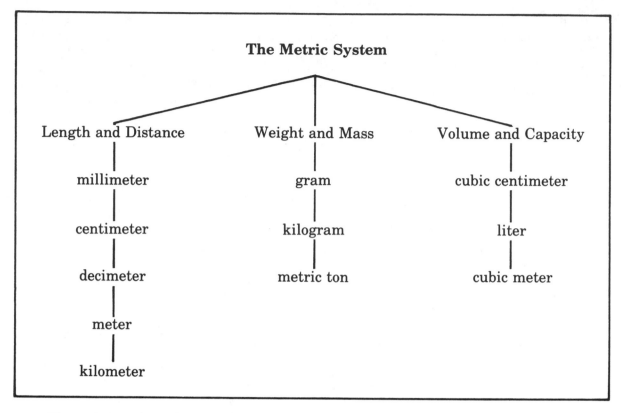

Figure 8–2   A graphic organizer

example at the chalkboard. (This applies when you use the organizer for the first time.)

6. Place the students in groups of two or three and distribute the list of terms and a packet of three by five index cards to each group. [The students write words from the list on the index cards. Then they arrange the cards into a diagram that illustrates the relationships among the learning task's concepts. Then students try to add already known words to the diagram, words that will establish a relationship between the learning task and the course (or discipline) as a whole. It is easier for the students to rearrange the words when cards are used.]

7. As the students work, circulate about the room to provide assistance.

8. Terminate the activity and provide feedback. (pp. 174–75)

Barron (1979) adds a word of caution:

Disagreements will develop since in most pieces of content there is more than one way to correctly view vocabulary relationships. These disagreements and the additional discussion they will produce should be encouraged. (p. 176)

See the example of a graphic organizer in Figure 8–2.

Reinforcement.   Once important vocabulary concepts have been introduced, the teacher should reinforce them. The more students use words, the more they will remember them.

Since many ways to reinforce vocabulary exist, a series of sample vocabulary reinforcement activities is shown in Figures 8–3 through 8–9. These methods can be used before or after reading. However, remember that each activity has a specific purpose: some reinforce recognition, others meaning, and others reinforce both.

Guided Reading

Guided reading fits in well with the instructional framework, because it helps students develop

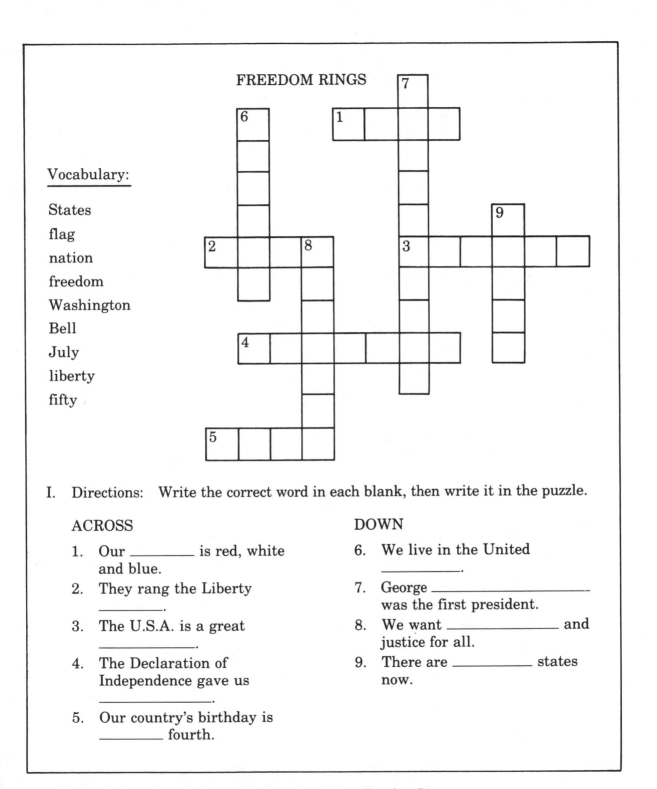

FREEDOM RINGS

Vocabulary:

States
flag
nation
freedom
Washington
Bell
July
liberty
fifty

I.   Directions: Write the correct word in each blank, then write it in the puzzle.

ACROSS

1. Our _____ is red, white and blue.

2. They rang the Liberty _____.

3. The U.S.A. is a great _____.

4. The Declaration of Independence gave us _____.

5. Our country's birthday is _____ fourth.

DOWN

6. We live in the United _____.

7. George _____ was the first president.

8. We want _____ and justice for all.

9. There are _____ states now.

Figure 8–3   A vocabulary reinforcement activity—Freedom Rings

FREEDOM RINGS (continued)

II. Write these words in alphabetical order:

States	nation	July
flag	freedom	liberty
Washington	Bell	fifty

1. _____   6. _____

2. _____   7. _____

3. _____   8. _____

4. _____   9. _____

5. _____

III. Arrange these letters to make the vocabulary words above. Use the cross-word puzzle if you need help.

1. asintWhnog _____ (7 down)

2. alfg _____ (1 across)

3. aitnon _____ (3 across)

4. fyift _____ (9 down)

5. luJy _____ (5 across)

6. dfemoer _____ (4 across)

7. erylitb _____ (8 down)

8. taestS _____ (6 down)

9. lelB _____ (2 across)

Figure 8–3   A vocabulary reinforcement activity—Freedom Rings

WORD PUZZLE

We can not become better
musicians without this:

1. __ __ __ __ __ □ __ __ __ __
2. □ __ __ __ __
3. __ □ __ __ __ __
4. __ __ __ __ □
5. __ __ __ □ __ __ __
6. __ □ __ __ __
7. __ □ __ __ __ __
8. __ __ __ __ □ __ __ __ __

Clues:

1. This touches our mouths when we play an instrument.
2. Clarinets and saxophones need a good one of these.
3. Trumpet players press these to change notes.
4. This is what we all read when we play.
5. You can not play well without good _____.
6. A large instrument. This word also means to play softly.
7. When we tongue a note very hard, it is called an ____ ____.
8. What good musicians are always doing.

Choose from these words:

ligature	accent	music	trumpet
posture	rest	reed	barrel
listening	piano	valves	clarinet
note	trombone	mouthpiece	drums

Figure 8–4   A vocabulary reinforcement activity—Word Puzzle

FIGURE-EIGHT PUZZLE

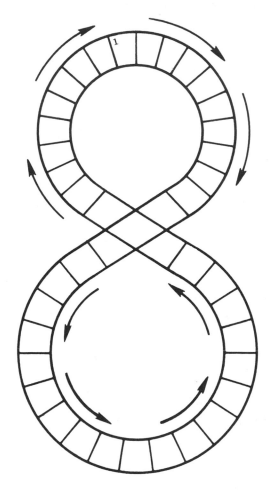

Directions:

Write the first letter of word number one (1) in box number one (1). Then write the rest of the word in the direction shown by the arrow. Do the same for each word. The last letter of each word is the first letter of the next word. The last letter of word number eleven (11) is the first letter of word number one (1).

1. You add two numbers to get their _____.

2. The number 4½ is an example of a _____ fraction.

3. The number 35.788 is an example of a _____ number.

4. You can use a ruler to measure the _____ of a segment.

5. A segment that is 1½ inches long is _____ as long as a segment that is 3 inches long.

6. In the number 619,473, the number in the hundreth's place is _____.

7. A _____ angle has exactly 90 degrees.

8. _____ is a factor of every even number.

9. If a number is not even, then it is _____.

10. To find the circumference of a circle, you multiply the _____ by pi.

11. A segment that goes from the center of a circle to a point on the circle is called a _____.

Figure 8–5 A vocabulary reinforcement activity—Figure Eight Puzzle

THE RANSOM OF RED CHIEF
by O. Henry

MAGIC SQUARE EXERCISE

Directions:

In the left-hand column are vocabulary words found in "The Ransom of Red Chief". In the right-hand column are their definitions. You are to match the definition with the correct word and enter the number to the left of the word into the corresponding box in the magic square below. When this is done correctly, the numbers in each row, column, and diagonal will total 34.

Vocabulary Words

Definitions

___ 1. ransom

A. to keep from sight; to hide

___ 2. kidnap

B. a small farm or farm laborer

___ 3. summit

C. an imposter, a fake; to cheat or trick

___ 4. peasant

D. to give one's consent; to agree

___ 5. fraud

E. a small devil or demon; a mischievous person

___ 6. imp

F. violation of confidence; trickery

___ 7. dastardly

G. a plan of something to be done in a crafty manner.

___ 8. solitary

H. the highest point or part (e.g., of a hill)

___ 9. treachery

I. the habit of talking, writing, or thinking too much about one's self; self-conceit

___10. accede

J. willfully mean

___11. apparition

K. to take someone by force, usually followed by a demand for ransom

___12. egotism

L. one who lives in a particular place as a permanent resident

___13. inhabitant

M. to obtain the release of a person, property, etc., by paying a price demanded

___14. stealthy

N. to move secretly without being noticed

___15. conceal

O. the act of appearing; appearance

___16. scheme

P. single; one; alone

A 15	B 4	C 5	D 10
E 6	F 9	G 16	H 3
I 12	J 7	K 2	L 13
M 1	N 14	O 11	P 8

Figure 8–6   A vocabulary reinforcement activity—Magic Square Exercise

WAR AND PEACE

Directions: The following history terms may be used to describe aspects of war or of peace. Decide which would be terms of war time and which would be terms of peace time. List the terms on the chart. Some terms can go under both categories while others can go under only one.

allegiance	enemy	patriotism
alliance	fascists	persecution
appeasement	fighting	power
armistice	freedom	reform
combat	holocaust	reparations
compromise	internationalism	rights
conflict	invasion	savagery
conscientious objectors	isolationist	seize
convoy	justice	tragic
defeat	liberty	traitors
destructive	military	treaty
disarmament	munitions	warmonger
disastrous	nationalism	weapons

WAR	&	PEACE

Figure 8–7 A vocabulary reinforcement activity—War and Peace

CLASSIFICATION ACTIVITY

U.S. History   Name:_____

Vocabulary Exercise

Directions: Listed below are several words from the unit under consideration.
              They can be grouped under three broad categories. Look for
              relationships among the words and identify the three categories,
              listing them below in the spaces provided. (Rearrange the words
              under the proper category.)

religious freedom	delegate	self-governing
compact	resources	Church of England
democratic	slavery	indentured servant
subsistence farming	democratic	pacifism
representative	Quakers	equality
dissent	representative	tolerance
Puritans	Mother Country	

_____   _____   _____

Figure 8–8   A vocabulary reinforcement activity—Classification Activity

the reading processes and understand content concepts. Remember these two purposes because two assumptions underlie them: (1) students are reading difficult material; and (2) the material is important to understand.

There are usually three steps in the typical content reading assignment: (1) students read the material; (2) they answer questions about it; and (3) these answers are either discussed or turned in to the teacher. However, this method tests rather than teaches or guides. The teacher hopes that asking questions at a particular level (i.e., literal, interpretive, and/or applied) will cause the students to read at that level.

But guided reading sharpens students' reading-thinking processes so that they gain insights into important concepts and improve their reading ability at the same time. The teacher models effective silent reading for the students by preparing reading guides for them. These guides give students clues about what they will read. The teacher prepares statements about the selection's content that students read *before* reading the selection. These statements preview the important information, direct students

CLASSIFICATION OF VERTEBRATES

1.   __ __ ☐ __

2.   ☐ __ __ __ __ __ __

3. __ __ __ __ __ __ __ ☐ __ __

4.   __ __ ☐ __ __

5.   __ __ __ ☐ __ __ __ __

Fill in the blanks with the correct animal name.

1. These animals have gills, scales and fins.
2. These animals provide milk for their young
3. These animals develop first in water, then move onto the land.
4. These animals have feathers and wings.
5. These animals are related to the dinosaurs.

PLACE THE LETTERS FROM THE BOXES ABOVE IN ORDER
ACROSS THE TOP OF THE CHART BELOW

Category					
MAMMAL					
FISH					
BIRD					
REPTILE		E.C.			
AMPHIBIAN		E.C.	E.C.	E.C.	

In each empty box, place the name of an animal for each category. The name must start with the letter in the top box. *1* point for each correct entry. E.C. for extra credit only.

Figure 8–9   A vocabulary reinforcement activity—Classification of Vertebrates

to that information, and show them how to find it.

Some teachers have difficulty accepting the concept of guided reading because they think they "give away" the material. However, if the students have difficulty with the material, they probably do not understand it anyway. So, far from spoiling the material, the teacher helps students gain meaning and develop their reading processes. In fact, the teacher helps students "find the way."

To insure success with the guide, develop meaningful statements. Experience suggests it is better to have a few well-written statements about concepts rather than many trivial ones about details. Details relate to meaningful statements, and they often emerge through discussion without making separate statements for them. Also, group students for discussion so that they can help each other with answers.

Some teachers believe this process leads to students who read only to find specific answers. Indeed, such reading may occur initially; however, if the teacher expects and creates a thorough discussion related to each statement, then students soon learn to read the entire selection carefully.

The purpose of guiding is not to make students depend on guides, but to enable them to develop and answer their own questions as they read. Herber and Nelson (1975) have identified six steps to this independence:

1. The teacher prepares statements for students' reactions. References are added to indicate where students might look in the text to determine if there is information to support the statements (page, column, paragraph if necessary).
2. The teacher prepares statements for students' reactions. No references are given.
3. The teacher prepares questions for students to answer. References are added to indicate where students might look in the text to find information which, when combined, might answer the question.
4. The teacher prepares questions for students to answer. No references are given.
5. Students survey the material, raise their own questions, and answer them.
6. Students produce statements of meaning, concepts, and ideas as they are read. (p. 516)

With this sequence, the teacher begins with dependence and gradually helps students achieve independence. It may be a difficult process, but one well worth the effort.

Two main types of guides exist, the three-level guide and the organizational pattern guide.

Three-level Guides. *Three-level guides* are designed to help students read at the literal, interpretive, and applied levels. No absolute set of instructions must be followed to develop reading guides, but Earle (1969) suggests teachers take three steps before they construct a guide. *First*, examine the material for concepts. What important concepts are students expected to learn? *Second*, examine the material for processes. What important processes are needed to understand the material? Does the student need to read at the literal, interpretive, and/or applied levels? Does the student need to understand relationships, such as comparison/contrast or cause/effect? And so forth. *Third*, determine how much guidance the students need. Obviously, if students can read and understand the material without assistance, no guide is necessary. The reading should determine the type of guidance given; the material should dictate the skills taught. Figure 8–10 shows an example of a three-level guide. The literal-level statements are in level 1 and interpretive-level generalizations in level 2. Level 3 encourages a provocative discussion at the applied level.

Vacca (1981) suggests a five-step sequence for developing three-level guides: (1) begin construction of the guide at the interpretive level; (2) look for information that supports the interpretive-level statements; (3) decide whether to include distractors [false statements]; (4) develop statements for the applied level; and (5) be flexible and develop a format that is appealing by not "crowding too much print on the page" (p. 126). By starting at the interpretive level, the teacher develops inferred main ideas. What is the article about? What is the hidden agenda? What is the author trying to say? The details that the author includes will answer these questions.

After the interpretive-level statements have

THREE-LEVEL READING GUIDE FOR "THE CHAMP"

Level I.   Directions: Read the following statements carefully. Check those
                          statements that are actually stated or paraphrased
                          in the story. Be ready to explain what is inaccurate
                          about the statements that you do not check.

_____ 1.   The Boss, Mr. Smith, had an iron-gray head.

_____ 2.   Herbie Smith was a crippled boy who died.

_____ 3.   Champ excelled in boxing and track.

_____ 4.   Herbie was a kind boy.

Level II.   Directions: The following generalizations may or may not be true,
                          based upon what the author implies. Check those
                          statements that you feel can be supported by the story.
                          Be ready to support your opinions.

_____ 1.   The Boss was an even-tempered man.

_____ 2.   Watson was rehired because he was a hard worker.

_____ 3.   Watson was satisfied at being rehired.

_____ 4.   Smith had felt a lot of pain, but finally had some peace.

Level III. Directions: Below are several famous sayings. In the first column,
                          check those statements that you feel are true. In
                          the second column, check those statements that Mr.
                          Watson would have checked. In the third column,
                          check those statements that Mr. Smith would have
                          checked.

A   B   C
_____ _____ _____   1.   It's not whether you win or lose that counts, but
                         how you play the game.

_____ _____ _____   2.   You've got to think of number one!

_____ _____ _____   3.   All the world needs now is love sweet love.

_____ _____ _____   4.   He ain't heavy, he's my brother.

Figure 8–10   A three-level reading guide

been developed, the teacher constructs the literal-level statements. Literal-level statements are the facts that lead to the inferred main ideas. Some teachers may find it easier to group the literal-level ideas first and let the literal level generate the interpretive level. This process should be followed if the teacher has any difficulty understanding the interpretive level.

There is some debate about the practice of using distractors or false statements (Herber, 1978). Vacca (1981) suggests that each teacher should follow his own instincts; if they work, use them; if they do not work, do not use them.

Developing the third level is often the most difficult step in building a guide. Its purpose is to help students synthesize their own experience and the reading. The teacher should think about what students can do with the new knowledge. Why have they studied it? Also, teachers can use famous quotations or familiar sayings to provoke students' thinking at the third level.

Finally, the teacher should be flexible and try to create an appealing format. Do not use too many statements. The guide then becomes busy work, something to be completed. Students begin to look for answers to specific items, rather than try to connect information or reorganize the material according to their own experience and background.

Organizational Pattern Guides.   Herber (1978) discusses internal and external organizational structure. External organization refers to format and physical features of the reading material, which are part of study skills. Internal organization refers to the patterns authors use to convey their messages. Internal organizational patterns include time order, sequence, compare-contrast, cause-effect, etc. *Organizational pattern guides* help students understand these internal structures. Such knowledge is part of comprehension, because when students are aware of these patterns, they can predict more easily as they read.

The three steps identified previously by Earle also apply to developing organizational pattern guides. Sometimes the process, the content,

and the needs of the students simply dictate the use of pattern guides rather than three-level guides.

In developing an organizational pattern guide, the teacher may elect to use only one or two levels and teach students about the organizational pattern. For example, what is a comparison/contrast relationship? A few introductory activities with concrete objects and pictures that show the concept prove helpful. A graphic organizer may then be used to introduce the reading and illustrate the relationship visually. The students can then understand both the concept of the organizational pattern and the reading itself.

An example of such a graphic organizer is presented in Figure 8–11.

Quite often, when two teachers examine the same story, they focus on different organizational patterns. For example, one teacher may see a comparison/contrast pattern as most important while the second teacher sees a cause/effect pattern as most important. Each teacher should identify the pattern she thinks is most important and then help students understand as much as possible. Internal organizational patterns are usually more explicit in expository material.

Examples of organizational pattern guides that focus on three different organizational patterns are shown in Figures 8–12 to 8–14.

APPLYING STUDY SKILLS

Traditionally, teachers have taught study skills in isolation, if at all. Informal surveys of students in preservice and in-service reading courses suggest that 1 in 15 remembers having been taught study skills while they were in elementary or high school. Curiously, students who remember such instruction often remember a fourth-grade teacher teaching them the skills. The majority of students use study skills, of course, but they learned the skills on their own as college undergraduates. These surveys do not prove that such skills were not taught, but that they were not transferred so that students could apply them. The more capable students develop effective study abilities as

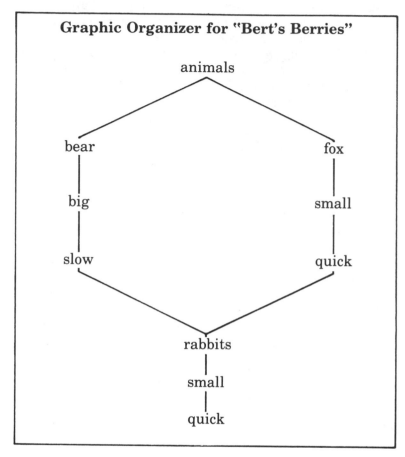

Figure 8–11   A graphic organizer to use before an organizational pattern guide

survival skills—their personal school survival skills— while slower students do not learn these skills and often continue to fail in school.

Students do not need study skills in isolated activities; rather, they need to use them within the context of a reading/learning assignment in a content class. Delva Daines (1982) suggests:

> Students need study skills to contend with the vast array of materials used in different subjects, and the skills are best taught in relation to specific content areas. Focusing on the tasks to be achieved rather than on the skills to be mastered will also enhance the teaching of study skills. (p. 89)

Many skills, when taught within the context of a content class, become meaningful because stu-

dents apply them to get information rather than to simply practice a skill.

To illustrate, a high school reading teacher taught her students to take notes. They became quite accomplished at this study skill in her reading class. One day, while talking to a social studies teacher, the reading teacher asked how Bob was doing in social studies. She discovered that he was failing because he did not take notes in class. When the reading teacher asked Bob why he did not take notes in social studies, he responded that he did not know how to take them. The reading teacher reminded him that they had studied and practiced notetaking in class. Bob replied, "That's reading class, not social studies." He had not transferred the skill

BERT'S BERRIES

I. Listed below are some comparisons from the story. Read the comparisons before you read the story. As you read the story, think about the comparisons. Mark the ones that are included in the story.

_____ A. Bert/fox
_____ B. Bert/rabbits
_____ C. fox/rabbits

II. Listed below are several statements. In the first column, check those statements that are actually stated or paraphrased in the story. In the second column, place the letter of the comparison in Part I that applies. There may be more than one letter for each statement.

(1)   (2)

_____ _____ 1. Bert was a big bear who loved to eat berries.
_____ _____ 2. The fox was small and quick.
_____ _____ 3. The rabbits didn't eat berries when the fox was there.
_____ _____ 4. Bert didn't want to share the berries with anyone.

III. Listed below are several statements that may be true or false depending on what the author implies. In the first column, check those statements which are implied by the author. In the second column, place the letter of the comparison from Part I that applies. There may be more than one letter for each number

(1)   (2)

_____ _____ 1. The rabbits were afraid of the fox.
_____ _____ 2. The rabbits were not afraid of Bert.
_____ _____ 3. The fox was smart.
_____ _____ 4. The fox and Bert became friends.

IV. Listed below are some famous sayings. In the columns at the left, mark those sayings which you think Bert or the fox would check.

Bert   fox

_____ _____ 1. Might makes right.
_____ _____ 2. The bigger they are the harder they fall.

Figure 8–12   An organizational pattern guide for a comparison/contrast pattern

THE MAYFLOWER COMPACT

Read the following statements carefully. The first column includes some reasons (causes) for the Mayflower Compact. The second column includes some of the results (effects) of the Mayflower Compact. In the first column, write the letter of the effect from the second column before those items to which you believe they apply. Some lines may have more than one letter while others may have none.

I. Cause

_____ 1. The "Strangers" on the Mayflower had said they were going to be their own bosses.

_____ 2. The "Saints" did not want anything to happen to divide the small group.

_____ 3. The "Saints" wanted to make some rules that would satisfy everyone.

_____ 4. The people who signed the Mayflower Compact did not want men sent from England to govern them, because in other colonies those men were not always interested in the good of the colony.

_____ 5. There were two very different groups on the Mayflower, one called the "Saints" and one group called "Strangers."

_____ 6. The first winter was very difficult and the Indians were unfriendly at first.

II. Effect

A. A set of rules called the Mayflower Compact was made and signed.

B. Only just and equal laws for the general good of the colony were made.

C. People elected their own governors who knew their problems.

D. It strengthened the idea of self-government in our land.

Figure 8–13   An organizational pattern guide for a cause/effect pattern

HOW TO SOLVE A WORD PROBLEM

Directions: Read each of the sentences listed below. Put them in the order you would do these steps to begin to work a word problem.

_____   Check your answer.

_____   Decide what kind of arithmetic you are going to use.

_____   Read the problem slowly and carefully.

_____   Jot down the facts.

_____   See what the problem is asking you to find.

_____   Do the problem.

Figure 8–14   An organizational pattern guide for a sequence pattern

to his social studies class, even though the reading teacher had used social studies material for the notetaking lectures! This experience seems to be all too common.

This section should help the teacher apply the teaching of study skills to the content areas.

SQ3R

SQ3R was developed during World War II by Francis P. Robinson (1961) to help military personnel understand and remember what they read. SQ3R helps to develop students' ability to interact with material. It should be considered both a process to develop better reading and an end in itself, a study technique.

SQ3R stands for Survey, Question, Read, Recite, and Review. If a student follows these steps, she will thoroughly understand the material.

One teacher guaranteed that any of his students who used the SQ3R would earn an A. The teacher did not "give" the grade, but knew students would "earn" it if they used the technique. It never failed. Many other teachers have discovered the same thing. After a while students shorten the system by eliminating steps they no longer need. The student who uses SQ3R usually becomes a better reader.

Survey.   This step helps the student form a general idea about the material to be read. The teacher tells the student to examine the chapter title, subheadings, italicized words, pictures, graphic aids, summaries, and questions. From this survey, the student should summarize: "This chapter is about . . ."

Because the term *survey* is sometimes confusing to younger students, the synonym *preview* may be used and related to previews of movie or television shows. This comparison seems to help many students understand what a preview is.

When students preview, they check for unknown vocabulary, especially in the title or subheadings. If a word is important enough to use in the title or subheading, it is important enough to learn. For example, a student reading a chapter on the "Antebellum South" and not knowing what *antebellum* meant, had difficulty relating the title to the content of the chapter. Once he learned the definition, a light turned on inside his head. He remarked: "Oh, what the South was like before the Civil War!"

Question. Questioning is a difficult skill to develop as a reader. Yet it is one of the highest critical reading skills because only through questioning can a reader develop a dialogue with the author.

Usually, the teacher directs the student's attention to the chapter title, headings, and subheadings. The student then converts the headings into questions by adding question words. For example:

Chapter 8: Settlers Come at Last

Questions: How did the settlers come?
Why does it say "at last"?
Why did it take them so long to arrive?

Subtitle 1: Father Serra Wanted More Missions

Question: Why did Father Serra want more missions?

Subtitle 2: Soldiers and Settlers Were Needed

Question: Why were soldiers and settlers needed?

Subtitle 3: A New Plan Was Made

Questions: Why was a new plan made? Why was a new plan needed? How were the old plan and the new plan different?

Before the student writes the questions down, she should divide the paper into lengthwise thirds. The questions are written on the first third of the paper on the left side, leaving lots of space on the right side for answers.

Read. The student then reads to discover the answers to the questions. The student should already have a general idea about the chapter's content from the survey, and can now read to answer the specific questions he wrote.

Recite. The student usually writes the answers to the questions down. Some authors suggest that students write answers down as soon as they find them. Other authors suggest that students read to the end of a section before writing answers. Still others encourage students to read to the end of an entire article or chapter before answering questions. The appropriate approach may depend on the particular student's ability. Initially, students may want to write the answer, or at least mark it and then later write it. You may wish to follow this sequence when teaching students this part of the SQ3R procedure:

1. Start by writing the answer down as soon as it is found.
2. Make a check in the margin when the answer(s) is found and write it down at the end of the section before the next question(s).
3. Make a check when the answer is found and only write the answer after the entire selection is completed.

The student's ultimate objective is to arrive at the end of the selection and answer from memory. If the student continually stops to write answers, the flow of the material is broken. Thus, if the student gradually learns to check where the answer is and continues reading, he does not interrupt the reading process.

Review. The student reviews after reading the entire article or chapter by reviewing the questions and answers or by skimming to get an overall summary of the chapter's content.

Although several variations of the SQ3R procedure have been proposed by experts since

Robinson first described the method, all include the same basic ingredients. By whatever name, this approach to study skills should be viewed both as an effective process for becoming a more intelligent reader and as a technique for becoming a better student.

Locating Information

Many teachers assume that students automatically possess the ability to locate information. All too often teachers fail to teach and reinforce this skill because it is such an integral part of the reading process. Locational skills are to a book what the key is to a map. Students can get along without them, but they can acquire information much more easily if they use them. These skills involve using the table of contents, the index, the glossary, graphic aids, and the library.

Table of Contents. Students need to know how to use the table of contents and what information can be found there. They also need to know how to use lists of tables, graphs, and maps. Finally, students should understand that the table of contents outlines the book's structure and organization. The table of contents offers many clues to the book's structure. For example, some books may use the same structure in every chapter even though each one covers a different topic.

Index. For any advanced reading, study, or research, a student has to be able to use an index. The index's most difficult aspect is probably cross-referencing, but with practice, students can use it. The teacher may assist students by discussing how to find additional information through cross-referencing. For example, students studying the 60s civil rights movement might look under only *civil rights.* The teacher can suggest or ask for other appropriate headings, such as *segregation, integration, Dr. Martin Luther King, Jr., racial strife,* etc. Or if students are examining a specific area of civil rights, they could look under *civil disobedience, courts, schools, housing,* or *transportation.*

Glossaries. Once they learn how to use them, glossaries help most students. Designed for individual content textbooks, glossaries present the book's key vocabulary. Often the words found in the glossary are highlighted on the pages where they are introduced.

As each textbook differs so does each glossary. One cannot assume that because students can use a glossary in one text, they can use them in all texts. The teacher should discuss each glossary's peculiarities with students, pointing out how they compare. Then, periodically, the teacher should have the students check vocabulary from assigned readings. These assignments need not be formal, just useful.

Graphic Aids. *Graphic aids,* such as maps, graphs, diagrams, pictures, cartoons, timelines, charts, and tables, are included in texts to clarify or expand textual information. Frequently, readers totally ignore these aids. Students may not use these aids because they want to finish reading as soon as possible, and examining graphic aids takes time. But once they understand how to use the aids, reading and studying them is no longer so bothersome. As students learn to preview properly, they can use these aids more effectively.

The old adage that ''a picture is worth a thousand words'' is often true about graphic aids, for they present information and portray relationships at a more concrete level than does the printed word. Something as complicated as the structure of the federal government can easily be understood through a simple chart, such as that shown in Figure 8–15.

The teacher must explain how to use graphic aids. When introducing a chapter, examine some graphic aids with the students, discuss how to use them, and point out anything unusual or peculiar about them.

Library Skills. Library skills are essential for students to develop independent study techniques. These skills, such as knowledge of the card catalogue and book classification systems, help students locate important information when

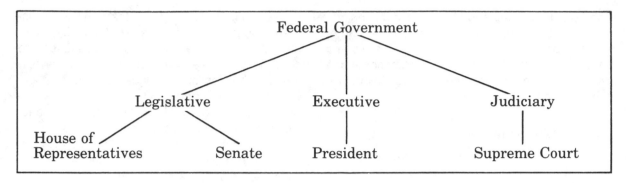

Figure 8–15   A chart showing the structure of the federal government

they want or need it. Sadly, high school students often do not know how to use the library, and they often avoid it rather than reveal they cannot use it. The teacher can easily teach and reinforce these skills when students do research and report writing within elementary school subject areas.

Outlining and Notetaking

Outlining and notetaking require a high level of classification ability. These tasks are best initiated at the concrete level in the early grades. The teacher can use physical objects to teach students to arrange objects in relation to each other. Later, pictures can be organized into group relationships, and finally, words can be classified. The level of sophistication, of course, corresponds to the students' abilities.

Teachers can teach outlining within the framework of the content class and the SQ3R procedure. Figure 8–16 illustrates a sequence for developing this skill. Students receive a nearly completed outline and complete it. As they become more proficient, they get less information and are asked to supply more. This procedure continues until the students receive no information and are expected to outline a certain reading on their own.

Once students understand outlining, it is much easier to teach notetaking. Students use the same basic process, but the teacher presents a lecture from which they take notes. At first, students receive partially filled in outlines

of lecture notes, but then the teacher provides less and less structure until students use no written outline. A side benefit from this activity is that teachers usually become more organized in their presentations!

Flexibility

As students develop in their reading ability, they often become concerned about speed. Although there is considerable disagreement about speed reading, there seems to be little, if any, disagreement about the value of reading flexibility.

Speed reading means reading fast. *Flexible reading* means adjusting reading speed to fit the material. The reading purpose and material dictate the speed. College students often complain about how difficult the textbook is during the semester. But the same students read the same text with speed and excellent comprehension when preparing for the final exam. Then they comment that the textbook was not so difficult after all.

Students need help in reading meaningful units rather than word by word. Reading in phrases and sentences and expanding that to paragraphs and whole unit reading increases both speed and comprehension.

Students also need to develop skimming and scanning. Scanning is faster and means looking for a name, date, place, or other specific information. Skimming takes place when one looks for a main idea or other important information.

OUTLINING

First Step

I. Information given

    A. Information given

        1. Information given

        2. _____

    B. Information given

        1. Information given

        2. _____

        3. Information given

II. Etc.

Final Step

I. _____

    A. _____

        1. _____

        2. _____

    B. _____

        1. _____

        2. _____

        3. _____

II. Etc.

(The student supplies the information that is not given.)

Figure 8–16   A sequence for developing outlining skills

These skills can be practiced regularly in the content class. When students do not remember the exact answer to a question, have them find the answer in the text. Even if they know the correct answer, it is good practice for them to locate it. They may not even realize they are practicing reading skills. When additional information is needed to support an idea, ask the students to skim the material to find it. With this kind of practice, students gradually improve their reading flexibility.

SUMMARY

This chapter covers techniques and procedures for teaching reading and applying study skills in the content areas. The instructional framework is an effective approach for structuring lessons in content areas. Several techniques for teaching and reinforcing general, technical, and combination vocabulary were presented, along with sample exercises or activities. Guided reading activities, centered around three-level guides and organizational pattern guides, were explained and samples illustrated.

The SQ3R procedure, an effective study technique, was reviewed and its five steps discussed. Students need to improve their skills in locating information by using the table of contents, index, glossaries, graphic aids, and the library. Finally, suggestions for teaching outlining and notetaking and helping students increase their reading flexibility were offered.

It is crucial that you find ways to apply the important content reading and study skills proce-dures in your classroom, because your effective-ness in these areas can affect your students' lifetime reading.

REVIEW QUESTIONS

1. What is the difference between *learning to read* and *reading to learn?*
2. Why should reading instruction be incorporated into the content classroom rather than be presented as isolated skills?
3. Why should the reading material dictate the type of reading skills taught?
4. How are the Directed Reading Activity and the Instructional Framework similar? How are they different?
5. Why is vocabulary instruction important in the content areas? Name three methods of teaching vocabulary in the content subjects.
6. What is the purpose of reading guides?
7. What is the purpose of a three-level reading guide?
8. What is the purpose of an organizational pattern guide?
9. What is the purpose of SQ3R?
10. Why should study skills be taught within the content classroom?

REFERENCES

Ankney, P., & McClung, P. Testing Manzo's guided reading procedure. *Reading Teacher*, March, 1981, *34*, 681–85.

Armbruster, B. B., & Anderson, T. H. Research synthesis on study skills. *Educational Leadership*, November, 1981, *37*, 154–56.

Artley, A. S. A study of certain relationships existing between general reading comprehension and reading comprehension in a specific subject matter area. *Journal of Educational Research*, 1944, *37*, 464–73.

Artley, A. S. General and specific factors in reading comprehension. *Experimental Education*, 1948, *16*, 181–86.

Askov, E. N., & Kamm, K. *Study skills in the content areas*. Boston: Allyn & Bacon, 1982.

Askov, E. N., Kamm, K., & Klumb, R. Study skill mastery among elementary school teachers. *Reading Teacher*, 1977, *30*, 484–88.

Baker, R. L. The effects of informational organizers on learning and retention, content knowledge, and term relationships in ninth-grade social studies. In H. L. Herber & R. T. Vacca (Eds.), *Research in reading in the content areas: The third report*. Syracuse, N.Y.: Syracuse University, Reading and Language Arts Center, 1977.

Barron, R. F. The use of vocabulary as an advance organizer. In H. L. Herber & P. L. Sanders (Eds.), *Research in reading in the content areas: First year report*. Syracuse, N.Y.: Syracuse University, Reading and Language Arts Center, 1969.

Barron, R. F. Research for the classroom teacher: Recent developments on the structured overview as an advance organizer. In H. L. Herber & J. D. Riley (Eds.), *Research in reading in the content areas: The fourth report*. Syracuse, N.Y.: Syracuse University, Reading and Language Arts Center, 1979.

Barron, R. F., & Earle, R. A. An approach for vocabulary instruction. In H. L. Herber & R. F. Barron (Eds.), *Research in reading in the content areas: Second year report.* Syracuse, N.Y.: Syracuse University, Reading and Language Arts Center, 1973.

Barron, R. F., & Melnick, R. The effects of discussion upon learning vocabulary meanings and relationships in tenth-grade biology. In H. L. Herber & P. L. Sanders (Eds.), *Research in reading in the content areas: First year report.* Syracuse, N.Y.: Syracuse University, Reading and Language Arts Center, 1969.

Barron, R. F., Melnick, R., Robinson, E., & Moth, W. The effects of expanded directions and interdependent group discussion upon learning of vocabulary relationships in tenth-grade biology. In H. L. Herber & P. L. Sanders (Eds.), *Research in reading in the content areas: First year report.* Syracuse, N.Y.: Syracuse University, Reading and Language Arts Center, 1969.

Berget, E. Two methods of guiding the learning of a short story. In H. L. Herber & R. F. Barron (Eds.), *Research in reading in the content areas: First year report.* Syracuse, N.Y.: Syracuse University, Reading and Language Arts Center, 1973.

Berget, E. The use of organizational pattern guides, structured overviews, and visual summaries in guiding social studies reading. In H. L. Herber & R. T. Vacca (Eds.), *Research in reading in the content areas: The third report.* Syracuse, N.Y.: Syracuse University, Reading and Language Arts Center, 1977.

Brazee, E. Teaching reading in social studies: Skill-centered versus content-centered. *Colorado Journal of Educational Research*, August, 1979, *18*, 23–25.

Brazee, P. E. Reading levels: Are they valid? In H. L. Herber & J. D. Riley (Eds.), *Research in reading in the content areas: The fourth report.* Syracuse, N.Y.: Syracuse University, Reading and Language Arts Center, 1979.

Carney, J. The effects of separate vs. content-integrated reading training on content mastery and reading ability in the social studies. In H. L. Herber & R. T. Vacca (Eds.), *Research in reading in the content areas: The third report.* Syracuse, N.Y.: Syracuse University, Reading and Language Arts Center, 1977.

Corey, A. Do textbook questions stimulate critical thinking? In H. L. Herber & J. D. Riley (Eds.), *Research in reading in the content areas: The fourth report.* Syracuse, N.Y.: Syracuse University, Reading and Language Arts Center, 1979.

Corey, N. R. The use of rewritten science materials in ninth-grade biology. *Journal of Research in Science Teaching*, March, 1977, *14*, 97–103.

Daines, D. *Reading in the content areas: Strategies for teachers.* Glenview, Illinois: Scott, Foresman, 1982.

Dupuis, M. M., & Askov, E. *Content area reading—An individualized approach.* Englewood Cliffs, N.J.: Prentice-Hall, 1982.

Earle, R. A. Use of the structured overview in mathematics classes. In H. L. Herber & P. L. Sanders (Eds.), *Research in reading in the content areas: First year report.* Syracuse, N.Y.: Syracuse University, Reading and Language Arts Center, 1969.

Estes, T. H. The measurement of students' attitudes toward what they study. In H. L. Herber & P. L. Sanders (Eds.), *Research in reading in the content areas: First year report.* Syracuse, N.Y.: Syracuse University, Reading and Language Arts Center, 1969a.

Estes, T. H. Use of prepared guide material and small group discussion in reading ninth-grade social studies assignments: Pilot study report. In H. L. Herber & P. L. Sanders (Eds.), *Research in reading in the content areas: First year report.* Syracuse, N.Y.: Syracuse University, Reading and Language Arts Center, 1969b.

Estes, T. H., Mills, D. C., & Barron, R. F. Three methods of introducing students to a reading learning task in two content subjects. In H. L. Herber & P. L. Sanders (Eds.), *Research in reading in the content areas: First year report.* Syracuse, N.Y.: Syracuse University, Reading and Language Arts Center, 1969.

Estes, T. H., & Vaughan, J. L., Jr. *Reading and learning in the content classroom.* Boston: Allyn & Bacon, 1978.

Fader, D. N., & Shaevitz, M. H. *Hooked on books.* New York: Berkeley, 1966.

Fairbanks, M., & Castello, C. Measuring and evaluating changes in underlining and note-taking skills. In P. D. Pearson (Ed.), *Reading: Theory, research, and practice.* Clemson, S.C.: Twenty-sixth Yearbook of the National Reading Conference, 1977.

Herber, H. L. *Teaching reading in content areas* (2nd ed.). Englewood Cliffs, N.J.: Prentice-Hall, 1978.

Herber, H. L., & Barron, R. F. *Research in reading in the content areas: Second year report.* Syracuse, N.Y.: Syracuse University, Reading and Language Arts Center, 1973.

Herber, H. L., & Nelson, J. Questioning is not the answer. *Journal of Reading*, 1975, *18*, 512–17.

Herber, H. L., & Riley, J. D. *Research in reading in the content areas: The fourth report.* Syracuse, N.Y.: Syracuse University, Reading and Language Arts Center, 1979.

Herber, H. L., & Sanders, P. L. *Research in reading in the content areas: First year report.* Syracuse, N.Y.: Syracuse University, Reading and Language Arts Center, 1969.

Herber, H. L., & Vacca, R. T. *Research in reading in the content areas: The third report.* Syracuse, N.Y.: Syracuse University, Reading and Language Arts Center, 1977.

Karlin, R. *Teaching reading in high school: Improving reading in content areas* (3rd ed.). Indianapolis: Bobbs-Merrill, 1977.

Lavender, D. *The story of California.* Sacramento, Calif.: California State Dept. of Education, 1971.

Lowery, L. *Learning about learning. Classification abilities.* Berkeley: University of California Press, 1974.

Maney, E. A. Literal and critical reading in science. *Journal of Experimental Education*, 1958, *27*, 57–64.

Maxon, G. A. An investigation of the relative effect between questions and declarative statements as guides to reading comprehension for seventh-grade students. In H. L. Herber & J. D. Riley (Eds.), *Research in reading in the content areas: The fourth report.* Syracuse, N.Y.: Syracuse University, Reading and Language Arts Center, 1979.

McCallister, J. M. Guiding pupils' reading activities in the study of content subjects. *Elementary School Journal*, 1930a, *31*, 271–84.

McCallister, J. M. Reading difficulties in studying content subjects. *Elementary School Journal*, 1930b, *31*, 191–201.

McCallister, J. M. Determining the types of reading in studying content subjects. *School Review*, 1932, *40*, 115–23.

Phelps, S. The effects of integrating sentence-combining activities and guided reading procedures on the reading and writing performance of eighth-grade students. In H. L. Herber & J. D. Riley (Eds.), *Research in reading in the content areas: The fourth report.* Syracuse, N.Y.: Syracuse University, Reading and Language Arts Center, 1979.

Pollard, R. S. *Pollard's synthetic method: A complete manual.* Western Publishing House, 1889.

Rickman, L. W. Arizona educators assess the teaching of study skills. *Clearing House*, April, 1981, *54*, 363–65.

Riley, J. D. The effects of reading guides and a directed reading method on word problem comprehension, problem solving ability, and attitude toward mathematics. In H. L. Herber & J. D. Riley (Eds.), *Research in reading in the content areas: The fourth report*. Syracuse, N.Y.: Syracuse University, Reading and Language Arts Center, 1979a.

Riley, J. D. The effects of reading guides upon students' literal, interpretive, and applied level comprehension of word problems. In H. L. Herber & J. D. Riley (Eds.), *Research in reading in the content areas: The fourth report*. Syracuse, N.Y.: Syracuse University, Reading and Language Arts Center, 1979b.

Robinson, F. P. *Effective study*. New York: Harper and Row, 1961.

Robinson, H. A. *Teaching reading and study strategies: The content areas*. Boston: Allyn & Bacon, 1975.

Rubin, D. *Teaching reading and study skills in content areas*. New York: Holt, Rinehart and Winston, 1983.

Sanders, P. L. The effects of instruction in the interpretation of literature on the responses of adolescents to selected short stories. In H. L. Herber & R. T. Vacca (Eds.), *Research in reading in the content areas: The third report*. Syracuse, N.Y.: Syracuse University, Reading and Language Arts Center, 1977.

Shablak, S., & Dixon, C. A. The effects of different types of guide materials on students' written response to short stories. In H. L. Herber & R. T. Vacca (Eds.), *Research in reading in the content areas: The third report*. Syracuse, N.Y.: Syracuse University, Reading and Language Arts Center, 1977.

Shores, J. H. Skills related to the ability to read history and science. *Journal of Educational Research*, 1943, *36*, 584–93.

Smith, C. B. *Teaching reading in secondary school content subjects*. New York: Holt, Rinehart and Winston, 1978.

Smith, N. B. *American reading instruction*. Newark, Del.: International Reading Association, 1965.

Snoddy, J. E. Improving study skills: A review of selected research. In T. Barrett & D. D. Johnson (Eds.), *Views on Elementary Reading Instruction*. Newark, Del.: International Reading Association, 1973, 81–87.

Sochor, E. E. Literal and critical reading in social studies. *Journal of Experimental Education*, 1958, *27*, 49–56.

Stoodt, B., & Balboa, E. Integrating study skills instruction with content in a secondary classroom. *Reading World*, March, 1979, *18*, 247–52.

Thelen, J. N. A scale for rating the individual characteristics of teachers. In H. L. Herber & P. L. Sanders (Eds.), *Research in reading in the content areas: First year report*. Syracuse, N.Y.: Syracuse University, Reading and Language Arts Center, 1969a.

Thelen, J. N. Use of advance organizers and guide material in viewing science motion pictures in ninth grade: Pilot study report. In H. L. Herber & P. L. Sanders (Eds.), *Research in reading in the content areas: First year report*. Syracuse, N.Y.: Syracuse University, Reading and Language Arts Center, 1969b.

Thelen, J. Use of advance organizers and guide material in viewing science motion pictures in ninth grade. In H. L. Herber & R. T. Vacca (Eds.), *Research in reading in the content areas: The third report*. Syracuse, N.Y.: Syracuse University, Reading and Language Arts Center, 1977.

Tyo, J. An alternative for poor readers in social science. *Social Education*, April, 1980, *44*, 309–310.

Vacca, R. T. An investigation of a functional reading strategy in seventh-grade social studies. In H. L. Herber & R. T. Vacca (Eds.), *Research in reading in the content areas: The third report.* Syracuse, N.Y.: Syracuse University, Reading and Language Arts Center, 1977.

Vacca, R. T. *Content area reading.* Boston: Little, Brown, 1981.

Walker, J. Reflections on SQ3R: Retread or retire? In P. L. Anders (Ed.), *Research on reading in secondary schools—A semi-annual report, monograph number 9.* Tucson: Reading Department of the University of Arizona, 1982.

Wolf, R. E. Using subject-matter areas to raise reading achievement scores. *Reading Improvement*, Winter, 1978, *15*, 242–45.

Worthington, J. D. A comparison of three delivery systems for a competency based program to prepare preservice elementary teachers to teach word attack, vocabulary, comprehension, and reading in content areas. In H. L. Herber & J. D. Riley (Eds.), *Research in reading in the content areas: The fourth report.* Syracuse, N.Y.: Syracuse University, Reading and Language Arts Center, 1979.

Bob|and his‖father|like to|work|on old|cars.　His‖father|has five　　(1)

old cars that(belong)to him.　One of them is ~~black~~ ᵇᵃᶜᵏ with a(white)top.　　(2)

Bob is very(young,)so ~~none~~ of the cars(belong)to him.　He‖would　　(3)

like to have his(own)car when he get(s)big.　　(4)

Sometime(s) Bob and his father go to a car ~~show~~ ˢʰᵒᵘ.　At the car ~~show~~ ˢʰᵒᵘ　　(5)

there are many old cars.　　(6)

One time Bob(s) father took his ~~black~~ ᵇᵃᶜᵏ and(white)car to the car

~~show~~ ˢʰᵒᵘ.　One of the men looked at the cars to see which one was best.

He gave Bob(s) father a(prize)because his car was so(pretty.)

9

The Analysis of Oral Reading Errors

Learning to analyze oral reading errors and helping students correct them can probably do more toward making you an effective reading teacher than learning how to give all the commercial reading tests ever devised. To the novice teacher, this approach may seem too elemental. But the experienced teacher has used this approach for years, although perhaps not as consistently as possible.

This chapter describes a code for marking students' oral errors while they read. The new teacher might think that all you have to do is listen to a student read and then analyze that student's reading. However, even experienced teachers know that without a copy of what the student is reading and a system for marking that student's errors, they would do an inadequate job of diagnosing the student's reading problem.

During the past decade reading educators have heard a lot about *miscue analysis*, or the

A critical part of the basal reader program is properly matching child and text. Determining the percentage of oral reading errors helps make this proper fit.

analysis of the *meaning* of students' oral reading errors to help students become better readers. However, miscue analysis, as described from the *psycholinguistic* viewpoint, never became popular. (Psycholinguistics is the study of the language *and* the psychological aspects of the language.) It was too difficult and impractical to use.

This chapter, rather than use the psycholinguistic terminology of miscue analysis, discusses the types of errors commonly made by students when they read orally and how these errors influence a teacher's reading instruction.

ORAL READING AS DIAGNOSIS

Oral reading certainly has its value in the reading program. No beginning reading teacher would seriously attempt to teach a child to read without doing some oral reading. However, most oral reading should be done for diagnostic purposes. Teachers need to know whether a child is calling a particular word correctly, reading word by word, using incorrect phrasing, making repetitions, omitting words, etc. There are other reasons

to use oral reading in the classroom, as mentioned in Chapter 3: to answer a specific question through rereading, to develop fluency and expression, to demonstrate a dialogue, or to do **choral reading.** (Choral reading is two or more students reading aloud at the same time.) However, the main reason is to diagnose. Such diagnosis is most important when the child is first learning to read or when the student is a disabled reader.

In this chapter you will learn a shorthand method of marking students' oral reading errors as well as the characteristics of their reading and be given suggestions on how to correct such errors. Then you will see several cases of students with minor and major reading problems. These passages illustrate how errors serve as a blueprint for instruction in both **developmental** and **corrective** reading. (Developmental reading is for students making normal progress; corrective reading is for students with mild reading disabilities. Both types of instruction are carried out in the regular classroom.) It is not important that you learn *this* shorthand method for marking these errors and characteristics, but it is extremely important that you learn *a* method.

REVIEW OF THE RESEARCH

Miscue analysis stems from Kenneth Goodman's (1969) psycholinguistic model of reading. Yetta Goodman and Carolyn Burke (1972) developed the *Reading Miscue Inventory* to analyze students' oral reading behavior. They call students' errors *miscues* because they assume students' underlying language competence influences their oral reading behavior.

To use the *Reading Miscue Inventory*, the teacher asks the student to read an unfamiliar passage one grade level above the student's usual classroom level. According to Eldon E. Ekwall and James L. Shanker (1983),

The examiner may not aid the student in pronouncing unfamiliar words. After the passage is read, the student is required to retell the story. The examiner asks only general questions to guide the student's retelling. After careful analysis, the examiner is presumably able to determine the reading strategies employed by the student. (p. 403)

Although some teachers find that they understand the reading process better as a result of using this approach, most teachers do not find it particularly practical or helpful. Florence Slegel (1979) clearly shows, for example, that miscue analysis procedures have simply been too burdensome for the average classroom teacher. Slegel states,

Informal discussions with teachers who have studied the method reveal that they are reluctant to use it because: 1) they experience interferences from their habitual use of IRI (Informal Reading Inventory) procedures, 2) they find the procedures too involved for use in the average classroom where schedules are already overcrowded with requirements. It is therefore apparent that many valuable insights into children's reading behaviors can be overlooked for procedural reasons. An adaption of miscue analysis could promote its use. (p. 37)

Karen D'Angelo and Marc Mahlios (1983) studied the insertion and omission miscues of good and poor readers to determine whether the whole analysis process is worth the time usually spent on it. D'Angelo and Mahlios stated,

In classrooms and clinics, qualitative analysis of the types of miscues a reader makes and their effect on comprehension has become an accepted diagnostic procedure. However, considerable amounts of professional time and effort can be involved in the coding and interpreting procedures required. Whether a method involves looking at every type of miscue made or only selected types, the actual analysis is complex and time-consuming. (p. 778)

Criticism of the *Reading Miscue Inventory* has been summarized by George Spache (1981):

Reviewers of the Reading Miscue Inventory point out that the analysis of oral reading errors as suggested by its authors has not been shown to be related to the reading level for instruction. Much of the scoring of miscues is completely subjective, and there are no data regarding the expected frequency of these miscues at any age or grade level. Even the evaluation of the child's recall of the story under guiding or leading questions is completely subjective. The Inventory lacks standardized directions and reading selections, criteria for interpreting diagnostic patterns, norms for interpreting scores, reliability or validity data, and evidence for its prescribed reading strategies. (p. 142)

Karen Wixson (1979) reviewed the research about miscue analysis and summarized its strengths and weaknesses:

Recent promotion of miscue analysis has served the field of reading well. The popularization of miscue analysis has succeeded in bringing about an awareness of reading as a language process, and in sensitizing people to the necessity for a method of evaluation which will accurately reflect this process in operation. However, the exact nature of the relationship between oral reading errors, as analyzed by standard miscue analysis procedures, and the reading process remains unclear. Further, it is unknown whether miscue analysis succeeds in identifying the critical features of readers' oral reading performance which reveal their relative proficiency with the reading process. Accordingly, the current use of miscue analysis procedures as a basis for evaluation and planning in both research and instruction appears at best to be premature. (p. 172)

Elementary reading teachers need not learn all the miscue analysis methods. However, they can learn a lot from simply coding their students' oral reading errors.

TURTLES AT HOME

Turtles are always (at) home.   (1)

If they ^go visit the ~~sea~~ seas, they are at home.   (2)

If they go to the high hill(s) they are at home.   (3)

If ~~they~~ the go far‖away, they have a ~~home~~ house.   (4)

Turtles carry their homes with them.   (5)

Their ~~shell~~ sall is their house.   (6)

Turtles (stay) in their ~~shells~~ salls.   (7)

That‖is‖why‖they are‖always at‖home.   (8)

Figure 9–1   Example of a coded passage

Note. from *Bader Reading and Language Inventory* by L. A. Bader (New York: Macmillan, 1983), 127. Copyright 1983 by Macmillan. Reprinted by permission.

A SHORTHAND METHOD OF MARKING ORAL READING ERRORS

Following is a shorthand method for marking or coding the errors made by children as they read. It is reasonably easy to learn, although it takes considerable practice to become adept at coding students' errors rapidly. To show how the coding looks, a reading passage is shown in Figure 9–1.

Reference will be made to this passage as each oral reading error is explained.

Omissions

Mark omissions by circling the words left out by the reader. In Figure 9–1, the word *at* is omitted in line 1. Omissions may be made either deliberately or nondeliberately.

Insertions

Indicate insertions by using a caret, ^, between words and writing the words added above the caret. For example, the word *go* was inserted between *they* and *visit* in line 2 of Figure 9–1.

Partial Mispronunciations

A partial mispronunciation is a word slightly changed by the reader, such as adding or omitting an *s* at the end of a word or pronouncing a word with a soft *c* when it should be pronounced with a hard *c*. There are two ways of marking partial mispronunciations; use whichever is easiest when the mispronunciation occurs. You can mark a line through the mispronounced word and write the incorrect pronunciation above the word, as illustrated with the word *sea*, which was pronounced *seas* in line 2. Or use a caret and insert an *s* at the end of the word, or circle an omitted letter, as illustrated with the word *hills* in line 3.

Gross Mispronunciations

A gross mispronunciation is a greatly distorted pronunciation of a word, so distorted that the word probably cannot be recognized. Mark gross mispronunciations by drawing a line through the mispronounced word and writing the incorrect pronunciation (phonetic) above it. However, many times students read too rapidly to let you write the entire word as it is mispronounced. Either use a tape recorder and replay the passage later to make sure each error is marked accurately, or draw a line through the mispronounced word and write a *g* over it to indicate a *gross* mispronunciation. However, remember that knowing the word was grossly mispronounced will mean less than knowing the exact mispronunciation. In Figure 9–1 note that the word shell(s) was grossly mispronounced in lines 6 and 7.

Substitutions

A substitution occurs when a reader substitutes one word for another. A substitution differs from a partial mispronunciation in that the word substituted is a *real* word, one that can be used in place of the original. Mark substitutions the same as gross mispronunciations, by drawing a line through the word in the passage and writing the substituted word above it. Line 4 in Figure 9–1 illustrates the marking of a substitution, *house* for *home.*

Repetitions

A repetition occurs when a student repeats a word already read once. It may occur with one word or more. Mark repetitions with a wavy line under the repeated word(s). If the word is repeated *twice* after it is read, use two wavy lines. See line 5 in Figure 9–1. Note that the word *turtles* was repeated twice while the words *carry their* were repeated only once.

Inversions or Reversals

Students make inversions or reversals when they read a whole word backwards, such as *on* for *no* or *saw* for *was.* Since inversions or reversals generally occur rapidly, they are sometimes difficult to distinguish from a substitution. Thus, mark them the same as substitutions, i.e., draw a line through the original word and write the reversal above it. When you have time to go back and examine the passage, you can easily see whether

the error is a reversal or a substitution. Sometimes words are partially reversed, such as *ant* for *nat.* No reversals or inversions are illustrated in Figure 9–1.

Aid

When a student encounters a word she does not know or cannot decode and says nothing, she should be told the word. The teacher gives aid to the student. Marking such words by enclosing them in parentheses. In Figure 9–1, line 7, the student received help with or was told the word *stay.*

Self-Corrected Errors

Students often correct errors themselves, usually because a word does not sound right in context. Use a check mark over words the student self-corrects. See line 4 in Figure 9–1, where the student said *the* for *they* and then corrected it by saying *they.* Self-corrected errors are, of course, a positive behavior.

The following four categories are characteristics of the reader rather than errors. They are usually not scored as errors in informal reading inventories. However, they should be noted so that the teacher can help readers exhibiting these characteristics.

Word-by-Word Reading

A student who reads haltingly, with a short pause between most words, is a word-by-word reader. When coding a student's oral reading, the teacher can note this characteristic by drawing a vertical line before each word the student momentarily halts or stops in front of. However, the teacher need not mark the entire passage this way, since showing it in a line or two indicates the reader's word-by-word reading pattern. A pattern of word-by-word reading is shown in the first part of line 8 in Figure 9–1.

Improper Phrasing

Improper phrasing is similar to word-by-word reading; however, when a student phrases improperly he does not usually halt before *each* word. Rather, he reads haltingly, pausing momentarily in places he would not stop if he were *saying* what was read. The second part of line 8 in Figure 9–1 illustrates a student using improper phrasing.

Lack of Expression

When a student reads without putting proper expression into her voice, as she would normally do when talking, she is reading with a lack of expression. Lack of expression can be noted on a checklist of the reader's characteristics, but would be difficult to code.

Pauses

A student pauses when an abnormally long time occurs before he reads a word. When a student takes an informal reading inventory, the student is usually given aid after a period of approximately 5 seconds. Thus, a pause means a student has waited before saying a word longer than what would be considered normal for word-by-word reading; however, it might also be slightly less than 5 seconds. Mark pauses with two vertical lines before the word at which the student hesitated. See line 4 in Figure 9–1, before the word *away.* Theoretically, a word told by the teacher would always have a pause mark before the parentheses. However, if the student has been given aid, the teacher assumes there has been at least a 5-second pause.

STUDENTS' ORAL READING ERRORS AND HOW TO CORRECT THEM

As you practice listening to students read and marking their errors, you will become more proficient at coding with this method. Then you need to analyze their errors and decide how to help your students correct them.

Omitting Words

Omissions do not occur often; however, they should be noted. There are two categories of omissions—deliberate and nondeliberate. Deliberate omissions may be made because students lack word attack or word recognition skills, i.e., because the reader does not know a word, she omits it. Some students become so adept that their omissions may not be noticed. You can easily determine whether an omission is deliberate or nondeliberate by asking the student to pronounce the omitted word. If the student does not know the word, or takes a while to figure it out, then the word was probably deliberately omitted. Nondeliberate omissions are made because students are careless in noting words and therefore omit them.

Correcting Omissions

The teacher should call the student's attention to the omitted word (either at the time or after the student finishes reading, depending on your philosophy) and ask the student to pronounce it. If the student consistently cannot pronounce or does not know the omitted word, then he has problems with word recognition or word attack skills. If so, determine where to begin your corrective work, as outlined in Chapters 5 and 6. On the other hand, if the student usually knows the omitted word, then you have to help the student correct a bad habit. (In most cases, however, the problem is the student's inability to either recognize or analyze the word.) If the student has a habit of omitting words, determine whether it happens with regularity or not. If it seldom happens, you may ignore the problem. On the other hand, if the student's habit is regular, take the following corrective measures:

1. Call the student's attention to the regular habit. Discuss how omission tends to distort meaning.
2. Tape record a passage the student has read and circle all omitted words. Use this evidence as a basis for discussing the student's need to stop omitting words.
3. Have the student point to each word as it is read. This technique is more effective when the student brings her finger down

The proper coding of students' oral reading errors is an integral part of administering an IRI.

on each word as it is read rather than when she follows along underneath the line. The latter encourages the student to read ahead of or behind the finger, which of course makes the whole procedure fruitless. Some teachers believe it is detrimental for students to point to words as they read, but this fear is unfounded. Most readers who point while reading stop doing so on their own when they find it no longer necessary or helpful.

Inserting Words

Insertions are also made more rarely than other oral reading errors. Students who insert words that make sense within context usually do so

because they think ahead, anticipating what will appear in print. Students often do this when their language ability exceeds their reading ability. One can consider this error carelessness, but it also indicates the student comprehends the material quite well. On the other hand, students who often insert words that do *not* make sense are not comprehending what they read.

Correcting Insertions

If the student inserts words that make sense and does so rarely, it is probably best to ignore the problem. If the student makes *many* insertions that make sense, call the student's attention to this fact. The same procedure as recommended for students' omissions can help.

1. Call the student's attention to the constant insertions. Discuss how insertions often distort the meaning of what is read.
2. Tape record a passage the student has read and indicate where words were inserted. Use the recording as a basis for discussing the student's need to stop inserting words.

If the student's insertions often do *not* make sense yet appear quite rarely, again, it is probably best to ignore them. However, if they appear quite often, then take the same steps used to stop students from omitting words. See steps 1–3 in the previous section.

Partially Mispronouncing Words

A student may partially mispronounce words for several reasons. Such a student often does not know phonics very well. A student with ample knowledge of phonics may mispronounce if the concept load or reading level of the reading material is too difficult. Third, a student may simply be careless or may not carefully observe entire words. A much less frequent cause is that the student has a speech or hearing defect. Finally, the student may have difficulties with word recognition or structural analysis, making such errors as using *ing* instead of *ed* at the end of certain words.

Correcting Partial Mispronunciations

Probably the most common cause of partial mispronunciations is a student's lack of phonics skills. After the student finishes reading and you have a chance to analyze the student's partial mispronunciations, decide what further diagnostic measures to give, as explained in Chapter 6. For example, a student may pronounce words with hard *g*'s or hard *c*'s that *should* be pronounced with soft *g*'s or *c*'s. If so, give the *El Paso Phonics Survey* to insure that your diagnosis is correct, and then teach the student the rules for the hard and soft *g* and *c*. Give ample practice in applying each sound. On the other hand, the student may tend to leave the *s* off

the ends of words or may tend to intermix the endings *ed*, *s*, and *ing*. (Refer to Chapter 6 for how to diagnose all the various phonics problems that students have.) A typical corrective procedure for a student who intermixes *ed*, *s*, and *ing* might be:

Give the student several sentences with several words that should end in *s*, *ed*, and *ing*. Omit the endings and replace them with blanks approximately 3 or 4 spaces long. The student fills in the blanks, using the proper ending depending on how the word is used in context. Usually this error indicates the student has been careless in using the endings or perhaps did not have a teacher who called them to his attention. Doing these sentences calls this problem to the student's attention; after doing several of them, he may become so aware of each ending that he soon corrects his own problem.

A student making partial mispronunciations but with an adequate knowledge of phonics may have reading material at her difficult instructional or frustration level. Students may mispronounce, then, because they are so busy attempting to analyze many new words and to comprehend the material that the concept load becomes too high. If you suspect this problem, give the student something to read at a lower reading level. If the partial mispronunciations decrease sharply, or stop completely, then you know that the student had material that was too difficult for her.

Grossly Mispronouncing Words

Students usually make gross mispronunciations because they lack either word recognition or word analysis skills. In most cases, however, they lack both, i.e., they do not know a word by sight, and when they attempt to use word attack skills, they fail.

Students who continually make gross mispronunciations usually suffer in their ability to comprehend; if they say nonsense words, then they cannot possibly comprehend adequately. Thus, the comprehension problem is only a symptom of the word analysis problem. Comprehension problems often disappear when the teacher gives the student help with word attack skills.

Correcting Gross Mispronunciations

Listen to a student read and code that student's oral reading errors. Is the student having extreme problems with word analysis skills? If so, determine where to begin your analysis of the student's problems in word analysis skills by referring to Chapter 6.

You need not pay attention to comprehension problems, as they are symptomatic of the problem with word analysis skills. When the student overcomes the problem with word analysis skills, difficulties with comprehension will disappear.

Substituting Words

Students usually substitute when they have problems with word recognition; they do not know a word and so substitute another in its place. Students also make substitutions when their oral language ability exceeds their reading ability. When a student substitutes a word, note if it makes sense in context. If most substituted words make sense, then the student comprehends what he reads.

Correcting Substitutions

When a student makes a substitution, note whether it makes sense in the sentence's context. If it does, and happens rarely, then you should probably ignore the problem. On the other hand, if the student continually substitutes words, even though they are right contextually, call the problem to the student's attention. If the student makes substitutions that do not make sense, then the student probably has difficulty with word recognition. Are the substitutions basic sight words? If most of them are, then the student should take a basic sight word test to determine which words are not known. Then teach those words to the student. If you doubt whether or not the student knows the words for which she substitutes, then stop the student after she substitutes and ask her to tell you what the original word is.

Substitutions That Are Correct Within Context.

1. Call the student's attention to the mistake when it is made and ask him to correct it.
2. Ask students to read chorally.
3. Have the student read along with a tape recorded passage.

Substitutions That Mask Word Recognition Problems.

1. If the words the student makes substitutions for are basic sight words, then give the student a basic sight word test and teach the unknown words.
2. If the words the student makes substitutions for are *not* basic sight words, then the student needs help with word analysis skills. You need to diagnose the student's problems and use proper procedures to correct them. Procedures for diagnosis and correction of word analysis skills are in Chapter 6.

Repeating Words

Students repeat words because of poor word recognition skills, poor word analysis skills, bad habits, and/or comprehension problems. Students with poor word recognition and/or poor word analysis skills often back up and reread up to the unknown word, either to give them time to analyze the word or to gain recognition of the word through context clues.

Correcting Repetitions

When a student continually repeats words, the teacher should determine whether the student's error pattern indicates that most repetitions are made just before unknown words. If such is the case, then the student probably has problems with word recognition and/or word analysis skills. But nothing actually needs to be done about the repetitions per se, because they will disappear when the word recognition or word analysis problems are corrected. Problems with word recognition and word analysis have already been discussed. On the other hand, if the student repeats words out of habit or because of comprehension problems, then the teacher needs to determine which of these two problems is the actual cause. If the student reads material at a lower grade level and the repetitions cease, then the problem is one of comprehension. (In that case, the teacher needs to work on the problem as outlined in Chapter 7.) If the student continues to make repetitions at a lower level, then the problem is one of habit. Then the following activities will help:

1. Code the student's repetition errors and base a discussion of the student's need to stop the habit on this information.
2. Have the student read chorally.
3. Have the student read in conjunction with a tape recorder.
4. Have the student bring his finger down on each word as it is read. Remember that sliding the finger under the line is not nearly as effective because the student can move ahead of or behind the finger.
5. Have the student use a 3 × 5 card to cover each line as soon as it has been read.

Inverting or Reversing Letters

Constant inversions or reversals may stem from several causes. The student may have failed to thoroughly learn sight words such as *was* and *saw*, may not use context clues enough, or may have failed to develop left-to-right eye movement patterns. Some experts believe that inversions or reversals are caused by a neurological impairment; however, virtually no research supports this claim. Children often make reversals at an early age, and these errors usually disappear by age 8. An older child reading at first-grade level may make these same errors, but outgrow them as his reading ability improves.

Correcting Inversions or Reversals

The most effective corrective procedures for inversions or reversals are sound decoding instruc-

tion and patience. The decoding approach *must* emphasize context clues. Students who use context clues (think about what they are reading) will probably not read *The boy saw a horse* as *The boy was a horse*.

The following procedures are often recommended for students whose reversals do not disappear over time.

1. Have students type the word(s) being reversed several times. The student can see the word take shape.
2. Use the Nonvisual AKT teaching method: nonvisual, auditory, kinesthetic, and tactile. Have the student close her eyes and give her the letter or word being reversed on a raised or 3-dimensional surface. Then while the student traces the letter or word, as though she were writing it, trace it on her back. You lead the child through the proper movement because she feels the movement of your finger on her back. Have the student pronounce the letter or word as it is traced. For example, if the student reverses *b* and *d*, then while you trace *d* on her back (and she traces it on the 3-dimensional surface), the student says *d*. The theory behind this method of teaching is that the student reverses the letter while it is going from the eye to the brain. This method bypasses the eye.
3. Have the student trace the reversed letter or word in a thin layer of sand or salt in a shoebox lid. The student should say the letter or word as he traces it.
4. Have the student trace the word on a card where it has been written quite large (such as one would use with a large group). Immediately afterwards, have the student write the word with a crayon or pencil. If the student begins incorrectly, stop her and retrace the word until she can copy it correctly.
5. Tell the student you will use a colored letter at the beginning of one of the words being confused. For example, if *was* and *saw* are being confused, then tell the student that for a while everything you give him to read will have the *w* in *was* written in red. When the student no longer confuses the two words, remove the color cue.

Needing Aid

Students need aid either when they do not know a word as a sight word or when they cannot use word analysis skills to pronounce the word.

Reducing the Need for Aid

The student who needs aid does not have the unknown word in her sight vocabulary. Therefore, if a student needs aid, then she must lack word analysis skills. You can usually tell whether students are using context clues with words, and to some extent, whether they comprehend what they are reading. By questioning the student about the unknown word—"How does the word begin?" (phonics) or "What word can be used in place of the one you do not know?" (comprehension) —you can begin to locate the reason the student cannot pronounce the word. Students may often attempt to use word attack skills, also. Ask them to do this aloud, because that will help you decide exactly why they have problems. Using this information, along with the information gained from the chapter on the decoding skills (Chapter 6), you can locate and correct the students' problems with word attack.

Self-Corrected Errors

Students who make self-corrected errors nearly always recognize the error immediately because it does not fit the context of the material. The student may back up, read a few words before the error, and then correct it. Often, the student just corrects the error.

Reducing Self-Corrected Errors

Usually, you need not be concerned about students' self-corrected errors. However, carefully watch which words are corrected and why each correction is made. Ask yourself these questions as a student corrects himself:

1. Did the student apparently think ahead, anticipate what the author had written, guess incorrectly, and then correct the error?

2. Was the original error a substitution of one basic sight word for another? If so, did the words look alike, such as *then* and *they*? Did the student immediately notice this error because the substitution did not fit the context of the sentence? Does this happen often? Does the student tend to confuse several basic, or other, sight words, indicating that he has simply not read these words enough times to make them a part of his sight vocabulary?

Word-by-Word Reading

Students tend to read word by word because they lack word recognition skills, lack comprehension skills, overly depend on phonics, and/or have a bad habit. Before taking corrective action, the teacher needs to determine which of these factors is responsible for the student's problem, because corrective measures for these problems are not the same.

1. To determine if the student's problem is in the area of comprehension, ask the student a series of questions over several passages. If the student comprehends well (75% or better), then the problem is not in that area. Have the student write her own stories. If the student does not use word-by-word reading on the stories she has written, then the problem is probably either in comprehension or word recognition. If the student has considerable trouble with comprehension, then the activities in Chapter 7 should help.

2. Give the student lower level material to read. If the student stops word-by-word reading, then his problem probably is a lack of comprehension or a lack of word recognition skills. Questioning the student about what he has just read should help determine which problem the student has. While the student reads, note whether the words before which the student pauses are ones the student should be familiar with or ones that are naturally questionable (most word-by-word readers do not pause before *every* word). If the student pauses before difficult words, he probably needs work on word recognition skills, but if he pauses before familiar words, then he probably has developed a bad habit. If the stu-

dent continues to read word by word, even at a lower reading level, yet comprehends the material, he is not having difficulty with word recognition.

3. If the student reads word by word even when she comprehends adequately and does not lack word recognition skills, then the student has developed a bad habit and/or tends to rely heavily on phonics.

Correcting Word-by-Word Reading

Comprehension Problems.

1. Give the student reading materials that are easier to understand.
2. Draw slash lines between words to show the student how to phrase properly. Discuss how improper phrasing hinders fluent reading.

Poor Word Recognition Skills.

1. If the student has proper word analysis skills (can eventually say almost every word), then the student simply needs to read more until more words become part of his sight vocabulary. This procedure is the most important and long lasting.
2. Have the student read materials at a lower level of difficulty.
3. Have the student read materials that he has written.
4. Use the Neurological Impress Method. (See Chapter 6.) The teacher points to words and reads orally. The teacher asks the student to read along. As the teacher points to each word, the student looks at it and reads it after the teacher does. Some research studies show that this method increases the size of students' sight vocabularies tremendously in a short time. However, most teachers find this exercise so strenuous that they only do it for 7 or 8 minutes per session. On the other hand, teachers can use this method several times a day and parents can also do it with their children.

A Bad Habit.

1. Have the student read chorally with class members who do read properly.
2. Have the student read with a tape recording of the material. Some teachers find it difficult to read as slowly as students do at the first or second grade level and still maintain proper phrasing. If this is a problem, let students at the same grade level read passages into the tape recorder for the word-by-word reader.
3. Discuss the need for proper phrasing with the student. Use slash lines to separate the passage into proper phrases. Ask the student to try to read all the words between each slash mark as a phrase. Also discuss writing as "talk written down."
4. Have children read and dramatize plays.
5. Practice reading poetry.
6. In a short paragraph, use a different color for each properly used phrase. Ask the student to read each color without pausing.

Phrasing Improperly

Causes of improper phrasing are essentially the same as those for word-by-word reading, i.e., improper word recognition, lack of comprehension, or lack of knowledge about proper phrasing. If students phrase improperly because they lack word recognition skills or comprehension, then the same procedures used for correcting word-by-word reading would be appropriate.

Correcting Improper Phrasing

For students who phrase improperly because they have not learned to do so properly or because they have a bad habit, the following procedures should help:

1. Discuss the need for proper phrasing with the student. Use slash lines to separate the passage into proper phrases. Ask the student to try to read all the words between slash marks as a phrase. Also discuss writing as "talk written down."

2. Use sight phrase cards. The student will get used to reading in phrases as he practices reading the phrases on the cards.
3. Compile lists of prepositional phrases and have students read them as they would say them while talking.
4. Have the student read along with a student who phrases properly or have the student read chorally with several students who phrase properly.
5. Have a good reader make a tape recording of something that is phrased properly. Then the student with phrasing difficulties can practice reading along with the tape recording.
6. Have students read plays, using the same patterns they would use when talking.
7. Practice reading poetry.
8. In a short paragraph, use a different color for each properly used phrase. Ask the student to read each color without pausing.

Lacking Expression in Reading

Students often lack expression in reading because they lack comprehension, are overburdened with the concept load, or have failed to learn to read with proper expression. The teacher can determine whether or not the student lacks comprehension by using informal questioning after the student has read.

Correcting Lack of Expression in Reading

1. Students who lack comprehension should be given instruction as outlined in Chapter 7.
2. Chunking, or reading material in which slashed lines have been inserted between proper phrases, also helps students learn to read material with proper expression.
3. If the teacher suspects the overall concept load is too high for a student, then give the student less difficult reading material. (When the overall concept load is too high, the student tries to use word analysis skills on many new words while also trying to comprehend the material.

These two simultaneous efforts may become too much to deal with, and the student may therefore read with a lack of expression.)
4. The teacher should tape several passages while the student reads and then use these to discuss the need to read material as though one is "talking."

Pausing Before Words

A reader who pauses before words usually does so for one of two reasons. The reader either pauses briefly, as in word-by-word reading, or pauses for a longer time, indicating that the word is not in the reader's sight vocabulary and the reader has to use word analysis skills. If the teacher tells the student the word, then of course the teacher has given aid. In that case, the student not only does not have the word in his sight vocabulary, but also does not have the proper word analysis skills to analyze it.

Reducing Pauses Before Words

A reader who pauses before almost every word for a very short time is a word-by-word reader. (See the section on word-by-word reading.) A reader who pauses for a longer period of time tells the teacher that the word is not in her sight vocabulary, and she had to stop to use word analysis skills on it. A reader who pauses before a lot of words, but gets them, tells the teacher that many words are not in his sight vocabulary. However, the student's ability to say the words, after a momentary pause, indicates that he has good word analysis skills. To eliminate the problem, simply have the student do a lot of free reading so that he comes in contact with enough words, enough times, to make them a part of his sight vocabulary.

It is natural for a reader reading at her independent level to encounter about one word in 100 that she does not know how to pronounce, and thus pause before that word. When a student reads material at his instructional level, then he can expect to not know approximately 5 per-

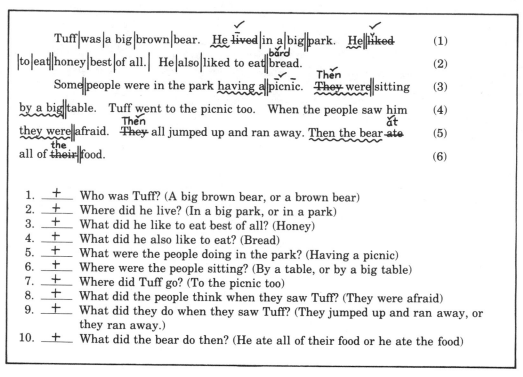

Figure 9–2   Coded passage about Tuff the Bear

Note. From *Ekwall Reading Inventory* by E. E. Ekwall (Boston: Allyn and Bacon, Inc., 1979), 87. Copyright 1979 by Allyn and Bacon, Inc. Reprinted by permission.

cent of the words encountered. It is normal, then, for most students to pause before 5 percent of the words in that material, but to use word analysis skills to get those words. If the student pauses and *misses* more than 4 or 5 percent of the words in a passage, the material is too difficult for the student. That student should be given less difficult reading material.

ANALYZING THE MEANING OF CODED READING PASSAGES

This section contains some passages students have read. Each passage shows how the teacher coded it as it was read. Also included is a list of total errors made by the reader and characteristics of that reader. Each passage is followed by a discussion of the instructional implications of the reader's errors.

0	Omissions
0	Insertions
0	Partial mispronunciations
0	Gross mispronunciations
1	Substitutions
7	Repetitions
0	Inversions or reversals
0	Aid
7	Self-corrected errors
Characteristics of the Reader	
X	Word-by-word reading
X	Improper phrasing
X	Lack of expression
X	Pauses

Figure 9–3   The reader's errors and characteristics

Analysis of Tuff the Bear Coded Passage

1. The first two lines show that this student reads word by word.

2. The word-by-word reading and the many pauses show that the student does not have several of the passage's words in her sight vocabulary.

3. However, it is also evident that she is adept at using her word analysis skills, because she was usually able to say a word after she had paused before it (noted on all lines).

4. Although the student is generally good at using phonic analysis skills, she still has a slight problem with phonics. For example, she mispro-

nounced the word *bread* as *bard* (see line 2). This error indicates that the student probably has a problem with the *br* blend. The student should be given the *El Paso Phonics Survey* to see if she does not know other phonic elements.

5. The student seems to comprehend what she reads quite well, because she corrects the nonsense word *bard* and corrects other words originally mispronounced by using context clues. The number of repetitions also indicates that the student comprehends what she reads and uses context to either correct or help analyze words not in her sight vocabulary.

6. The student has an especially difficult time with the *th* basic sight words, such as *they, then, their, than*, etc. (See lines 3, 5, and 6.) This

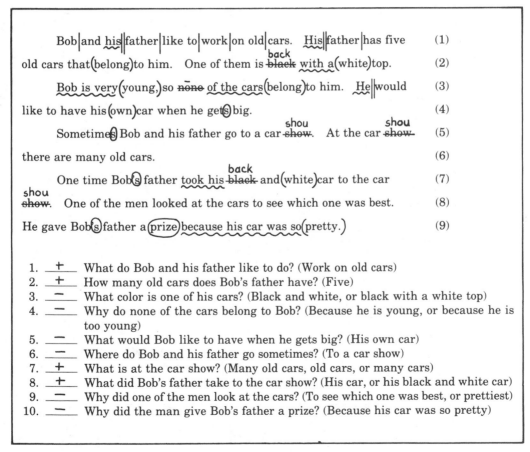

Figure 9–4   Coded passage about Bob and his father

Note. From *Ekwall Reading Inventory* by E. E. Ekwall (Boston: Allyn and Bacon, Inc., 1979), 89. Copyright 1979 by Allyn and Bacon, Inc. Reprinted by permission.

1	Omissions
0	Insertions
10	Partial mispronunciations
0	Gross mispronunciations
0	Substitutions
8	Repetitions
0	Inversions or reversals
7	Aid
0	Self-corrected errors
Characteristics of the Reader	
X	Word-by-word reading
X	Improper phrasing
X	Lack of expression
X	Pauses

Figure 9–5   The reader's errors and characteristics

student should be given a basic sight word test to determine which basic sight words present problems. Those especially difficult for the student should be taught and reinforced.

7. When the student encounters an unknown word and then uses her word attack skills to pronounce it, she knows the word the next time. Although this pattern was not repeated several times, it does indicate that the student learns new words quite easily; if exposed to new words over time, she should soon expand her sight vocabulary.

8. The excellent use of context clues by the student, along with all the correct comprehension answers, indicates that the student has excellent comprehension.

Analysis of Bob and His Father Coded Passage

This student is obviously reading at his frustration level and will likely make wild guesses in some instances. However, an analysis of this student's errors indicates the following:

1. This student is a word-by-word reader as indicated in line 1 (The only line where exact phrasing was marked).

2. This student also does not phrase properly (see line 2).

3. The student seems to have poor word analysis skills, because he needed help with so many words.

4. In a few places the student attempted to use context clues to unlock a word, but was usually unsuccessful. The student may lack the ability to use context clues, but he also is not comprehending adequately. Few students can use context clues successfully when they read at a level so difficult for them.

5. The student does not comprehend well. However, the student made so many errors in his oral reading that he would find it difficult to correctly answer the comprehension questions.

6. This student does not attempt basic sight words such as *black, white, pretty, prize,* and *show.* He should be given a basic sight word test. Words especially difficult for the student should be taught and reinforced.

7. This student might also benefit from some phonics instruction. For example, he has problems with vowel combinations. For example, he does not know that *ow,* found here in the word *show,* often stands for the sound heard in *crow.*

8. The student could possibly profit from some help in learning to phrase or from practice in chunking. However, this problem may only be symptomatic of a very low sight vocabulary. Perhaps when his overall sight vocabulary improves, his word-by-word reading and/or poor phrasing will disappear.

9. The student omits some word endings. This error should be called to his attention, and if he does not stop making it, then some type of corrective measures should be taken. See the section on partial mispronunciations for suggestions.

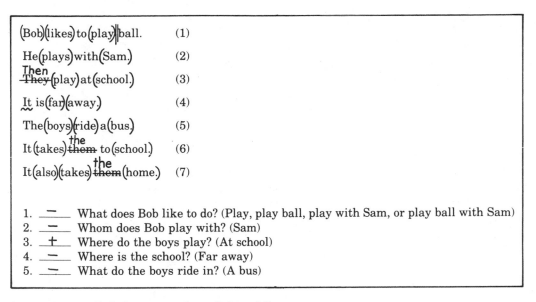

1. ⎯ What does Bob like to do? (Play, play ball, play with Sam, or play ball with Sam)
2. ⎯ Whom does Bob play with? (Sam)
3. + Where do the boys play? (At school)
4. ⎯ Where is the school? (Far away)
5. ⎯ What do the boys ride in? (A bus)

Figure 9–6   Coded passage about Bob and Sam

Note. From *Ekwall Reading Inventory* by E. E. Ekwall (Boston: Allyn and Bacon, Inc., 1979), 86. Copyright 1979 by Allyn and Bacon, Inc. Reprinted by permission.

Analysis of Bob and Sam Coded Passage

1. Probably the most striking characteristic about this reader is that she has *very* few words in her sight vocabulary.

2. This student has almost no word attack skills at all. The only word at which the student paused and then got the word right was *ball* (see line 1).

3. This student seems to know only the *very* most common words she would have encountered a *great* many times, such as *to, a, it,* etc.

4. When the student was told *play* in line 1, she could not get the same word with an *s* at the end of line 2. Furthermore, the student could still not get it in line 3 after having been told twice before.

5. Also, the student was told the word *takes* in line 6 but did not know the same word in line 7.

6. This student is not even sure of one of the three most common words she will encounter —*the* (see line 6). *The* was called correctly in the beginning of line 5, but this student also substituted *the* for *them* on two different occasions. These errors indicate that the student does not know *them* and *they* (and probably

0	Omissions
0	Insertions
0	Partial mispronunciations
0	Gross mispronunciations
3	Substitutions
1	Repetitions
0	Inversions or reversals
17	Aid
0	Self-corrected errors
Characteristics of the Reader	
X	Word-by-word reading
X	Improper phrasing
X	Lack of expression
X	Pauses

Figure 9–7   The reader's errors and characteristics

many *th* basic sight words), and is not sure of *the*, correct only once.

7. This student lacks comprehension as well as the ability to use context clues. Words missed or substituted in context were not corrected, and the student got only one of the five comprehension questions correct.

8. This passage is written at the pre-primer level, the lowest possible level, and the student is still at her frustration level. This student is a nonreader and may need instruction at the readiness level (see Chapter 4).

9. Until this student improves in her word recognition and word analysis skills, she will prob-

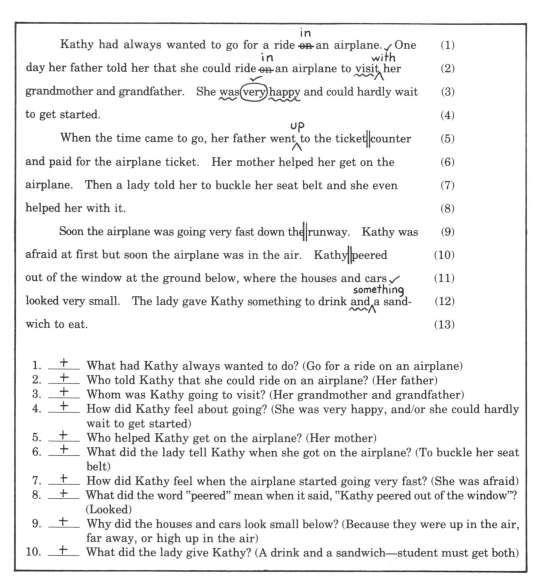

Figure 9–8 Coded passage about Kathy

Note. From *Ekwall Reading Inventory*, by E. E. Ekwall (Boston: Allyn and Bacon, Inc., 1979), 91. Copyright 1979 by Allyn and Bacon, Inc. Reprinted by permission.

ably display all the characteristics of a poor reader, such as word-by-word reading, improper phrasing, lack of expression, and pauses.

Analysis of Kathy Coded Passage

1. Of all the students analyzed thus far, this student is the best reader. His problems are not serious.

2. This student anticipates what words will appear and tends to substitute those words. See lines 1 and 2, where the student substituted *in* for *on*. In both cases, the substituted word made as much sense as the original did and so it was not corrected. Here, the substitution makes no difference in the student's overall comprehension.

3. This student also anticipated the word *with* near the end of line 2. The student noted that he made an insertion and repeated the words *to visit* (line 2) to correct it. However, even if the student had not corrected this error, it would still have made no difference in his overall comprehension.

1	Omissions
3	Insertions
0	Partial mispronunciations
0	Gross mispronunciations
2	Substitutions
4	Repetitions
0	Inversions or reversals
0	Aid
3	Self-corrected errors
Characteristics of the Reader	
	Word-by-word reading
	Improper phrasing
	Lack of expression
X	Pauses

Figure 9–9   The reader's errors and characteristics

4. This student omitted *very* (in line 3), noted the error, and repeated *was* and *happy* to correct the error.

5. A few words do not seem to be in the student's sight vocabulary; however, the student apparently has excellent word attack skills because he got every word before which he paused (see lines 5, 7, 9, and 10).

6. This student also noted that he had incorrectly inserted *something* (probably when he saw *sandwich*) and repeated *and* to correct this insertion (see line 12).

7. You may wish to code this student's oral reading errors and point them out to him, but if nothing were done about these errors, the student would probably not suffer in his reading ability. Some teachers might think that if the student continued to make errors, then they might become worse, having an adverse effect on the student's reading. As a teacher, you would have to decide whether or not to ignore such minor errors.

SUMMARY

In this chapter you have been introduced to the analysis of children's oral reading errors. Most teachers, whether beginning their careers or experienced, can gain more valuable information to help them correct students' reading problems from this method than from most reading diagnostic tests. Both error coding and diagnostic tests have their proper place in the classroom situation, however.

You have been taught a coding system for marking students' oral reading errors. These errors affect the corrective procedures the teacher chooses to take. Finally, passages representative of oral reading errors most often made by students have been analyzed in terms of what corrective work the teacher needs to do in the classroom.

REVIEW QUESTIONS

1. What is meant by each of the following terms: insertion, omission, repetition, reversal or inversion, gross mispronunciation, partial mispronunciation, aid, word-by-word reading, improper phrasing, and pauses?
2. Why is it necessary to code children's oral reading errors rather than simply make a mental note of the errors as they read?
3. Why might a student read word by word?
4. How does a coded passage become a blueprint for instruction?
5. Which errors are usually the most serious?
6. When might a particular error be a cause rather than a symptom of a problem?
7. What is meant by characteristics of the reader?
8. Give some specific procedures to use in helping students overcome certain errors.

REFERENCES

D'Angelo, K., & Mahlios, M. Insertion and omission miscues of good and poor readers. *Reading Teacher*, April, 1983, *36*, 778–82.

Ekwall, E.E., & Shanker, J.L. *Diagnosis and remediation of the disabled reader* (2nd ed.). Boston: Allyn and Bacon, 1983.

Goodman, K.S. Analyses of reading miscues: Applied psycholinguistics. *Reading Research Quarterly*, Fall, 1969, *5*, 9–30.

Goodman, Y.M., & Burke, C.L. *Reading miscue inventory*. New York: Macmillan, 1972.

Slegel, F. Adapted miscue analysis. *Reading World*, October, 1979, *19*, 36–43.

Spache, G.D. Diagnosing and correcting reading disabilities (2nd ed.). Boston: Allyn and Bacon, 1981.

Wixson, K.L. Miscue analysis: A critical review. *Journal of Reading Behavior*, Summer, 1979, *11*, 163–75.

10

Matching Children with Reading Materials

Probably few things you do for your students make as much difference as placing them at the right reading level. When students and materials are well-matched, what students read is not too difficult, yet it presents enough new information and vocabulary to prevent boredom. So many factors are involved in this task that you may doubt your ability to do it well. However, enough information exists to enable a well-informed reading teacher to usually make the proper match between children and the materials they read.

Many reading specialists would say that

the past neglect of this important factor has been a major cause of the failure of many students to become proficient readers. One reading supervisor of a large school district estimates that placing children in materials too difficult for them is the major cause of reading disability for approximately 60 percent of the disabled readers in that school district. Such statistics are, of course, difficult to substantiate since so many factors can covertly contribute to reading disability. However, whether the correct figure is somewhat lower, or perhaps even higher than 60 percent, one cannot deny that matching children with the correct level of reading materials is an all-important task for the reading teacher.

REVIEW OF THE RESEARCH

Reading educators have known for a long time that it is better for students to read materials that allow them to perform at levels that do not frustrate them. Many children become disabled in their ability to read simply because they are asked to constantly perform in reading situations they cannot cope with.

Having children read at the proper level was emphasized by Edward E. Gickling and David Armstrong (1978) in a study of first and second graders. They determined levels of instructional difficulty as they related to on-task behavior, task completion, and comprehension. On-task means engaging in task-oriented behavior, task-completion represents the number of items students complete per assignment, and task-comprehension refers to items students identify and understand on an assignment. In their conclusions Gickling and Armstrong stated,

As the levels of difficulty changed within assignments to conform to frustrational, instructional, and independent conditions, the percentages of task-completions, task-comprehension, and on-task behavior for the two groups of subjects also changed. When assignments were too difficult, the percentages of the three behaviors were relatively low for all. When assignments were at an independent level, comprehension and

task-completions came too easy, leaving large percentages of off-task behavior. However, when assignments were appropriate and subjects were functioning on an instructional level, the percentages of task-completion, task-comprehension, and on-task behavior were consistently high. (p. 565)

In an article discussing the weighting of miscues on informal reading inventories, James V. Hoffman (1980) also stressed student placement at proper levels. He stated,

Many authorities regard this latter task as one of the teacher's foremost responsibilities in reading instruction (Harris, 1961; Botel, Bradley, and Cashuba, 1970). Such emphasis has at its source, first, the awareness that optimum gains in achievement are made by pupils when reading materials are adjusted to their level of ability; and second, the understanding that the selection of inappropriate materials may be in the long run a major contributing cause of reading failure. (p. 136)

Two other leading authorities in the reading field, Albert J. Harris and Edward R. Sipay (1980), make similar statements. In discussing the mismatch between children and their reading materials, Harris and Sipay say, "Such a situation is all too prevalent in the public schools and is probably one of the reasons why normal development of reading skills is not more commonly achieved" (p. 526). Reading experts agree, then, that the proper match between children and their reading materials is crucial for their reading development.

MATCHING CHILDREN'S READING LEVELS WITH MATERIALS

To successfully match children with the proper reading materials, teachers should know about the different ways to accomplish the task. They may use their own judgment, readability formulas, publishers' grade levels, standardized reading achievement tests, informal reading inventories, and/or the cloze procedure. Once familiar with all these methods, teachers may want to use an eclectic approach to matching students and materials.

Using Teacher Judgment

No doubt many teachers are capable of listening to children read and determining whether the materials they are reading are difficult enough to challenge them yet not so difficult as to frustrate them. On the other hand, such decisions are difficult and do not come naturally, even with practice, unless specific guidelines are observed. Most teachers do not know anything about these guidelines because they have simply not been taught, and the knowledge does not automatically come with experience. Without some instruction, a teacher's ability to make a proper match between children and the materials they read does not usually improve.

One reason teachers may not learn how to properly match children and reading materials is that they tend to develop *tunnel vision*; tunnel vision means that when people live and/or work in only one environment, then they have nothing with which to compare it. For example, a teacher working in a high socioeconomic school may seldom have a student who makes an error while reading materials at her grade level. On the other hand, a teacher working in a low socioeconomic school may encounter many students who constantly read at their frustration level. If a teacher seldom hears students reading above frustration level, then a student reading at instructional level may sound like he is reading *above* grade level. Neither teacher realizes how wide the range of reading levels can be, and both teachers could make mistakes in placement because of the levels they are used to.

However, even if the whole spectrum of abilities existed within a school, a teacher without any training in this process would not know what to expect of a child. For example, should a teacher expect a child to read almost 100 percent of the words correctly and comprehend 100 percent of what she reads? Or should a teacher expect a child to read only 80 percent of the words correctly and comprehend 50 percent or less of what he reads?

Albert J. Harris and Edward R. Sipay (1980) emphasize the inaccuracy of teacher judgment in matching children and reading materials. Harris and Sipay state,

Teachers' judgments as to the difficulty of reading materials vary considerably (Jorgensen, 1975). For example, their estimates of the reading level of a first reader selection in Jorgensen's study ranged from first to fifth grade, and for a fourth reader selection from second to eighth grade. (p. 527)

Teachers face similar problems in their classrooms. However, with the proper training, a teacher can learn to accurately match students and the materials they read, perhaps with as much accuracy as any method that now exists.

The Role of Readability Formulas

Readability formulas have been used for some time. Even though they help us determine the grade level at which material is written, they present several problems. The most common readability formulas are based on sentence length and number of hard or unique words. Such words are all those not on a sight word list created by the formula's developer. Also, some hard words are arbitrarily decided upon before the formula is developed. A list of hard words may contain 600 to 3000 words, depending on how the author wishes the formula's rules to operate and on grade levels.

Hard words and sentence length are relatively tangible factors, which may account for the popularity of formulas based on them. However, a third important factor that is more difficult to measure is the syntax of the material. Syntax simply means the way words are put together to make a sentence. Second graders and adults, given the same words and told to write about the same subject, would use different syntax. Because second graders have not developed the complexity in sentence style that characterizes adult writing, their syntax would be easier for other second graders to understand.

In "Syntactic Complexity: A Necessary Ingredient in Predicting Readability," Jean R. Harber (1979) stated,

An analysis of the bases used by numerous readability formulas for readability prediction indicates that two categories of linguistic factors cause the greatest difficulty in reading—syntactic difficulty and vocabulary (or semantic) difficulty. (p. 438)

She reviewed 22 readability formulas and found that 18 included estimates of syntactic complexity. Researchers in reading education obviously know that syntactic complexity is an important factor since so many readability formulas take it into consideration. Yet many reading teachers either do not understand the complex rules involved in using these formulas or refuse to believe that syntax is important. Many do not have the background needed to understand the terminology used in these formulas and do not try to learn it; therefore, they ignore formulas that include syntax and continue to use the popular ones based only on sentence length and hard words.

Harber refers to a study by B. Rosenshine (1969) in which five factors influence the readability of passages. Harber states,

Difficulty was increased by vagueness and ambiguity with the use of indeterminate qualifiers such as *rather* and *quite a bit*, by probability words such as *might* and *possibly*, and by irrelevancy with the use of digressions and unnecessary restatements. Comprehension was aided by frequent use of explaining links such as *because, in order to*, and *if . . . then* (which call attention to a cause, result, or means), frequent use of examples (especially in difficult material), and the use of a rule-example-rule pattern in which a generalization is stated, followed by one or more examples and then is restated. (p. 439)

The beginning teacher, then, can be easily discouraged from trying to sort out the complexities of readability formulas. Harber also examined four series of basal readers to determine if there were a definite sequential pattern in the development of complexity from first through the sixth grade and pointed out that "patterns of increases were irregular with no evidence of systematic planning" (p. 440).

Still other factors make materials readable. For example, Donna Keenan (1982) evaluated how well readability formulas actually measure students' ability to deal with textbooks. The author asked two questions:

1. If a student's reading level is matched to the readability level of a textbook, can he indeed comprehend it?
2. What is the minimal reading level a tenth grader needs to comprehend his textbooks? (p. 124)

Keenan used the *Flesch Reading Ease* and FORCAST formulas to determine the reading level of nine books in English, social studies, and science. She found that all were at or near the tenth-grade level. (An *average* of several different pages from within the book is usually used to determine the overall reading level of a book.) Keenan found that even when a student's reading level is matched to the readability level of a book, a teacher cannot assume the student will comprehend it. She also found that at least 75 percent of the tenth-grade students had to be able to read at the twelfth-grade level to understand their English and science books. And 75 percent of the tenth-grade students had to be able to read at the eleventh-grade level to comprehend their social studies books.

Keenan thought one reason students and materials were mismatched was that the original test used for determining the textbooks' reading levels may not have been valid. (A ***valid*** test or formula measures what it *says* it measures. It is accurate.) She pointed out that *interest* and *style* may be crucial factors, but they are not included in readability formulas. Also, several studies show that motivation for reading the material is extremely important—so important that Keenan stated, "Thus, perhaps the most important variable contributing to readability cannot be processed into a formula" (p. 126). Keenan, as have many others, also noted the variety and frequency of syntactic patterns.

A study done by Susan M. Walker, Charles G. Noland, and Charles M. Greenshields (1979) reinforces Keenan's belief about the importance of interest. They also found, in studying fifth- and sixth-grade students, that *interest* had more to do with some students' ability to read and understand than the criteria set forth in the readability formula used to grade the passage.

An innate problem with some readability formulas is that they are based on materials of

Interesting materials and proper reading level are absolutely critical to a successful reading program.

questionable validity. When developers create a formula, they must first find some material that they *know* or *feel relatively sure* is at a designated grade level. This material then becomes the standard for the grade level placement of all material graded by that formula. However, if the material on which the readability formula stands was inaccurately graded, then the readability formula can never be valid or measure the reading levels of other materials with any accuracy.

For example, Kathleen C. Stevens (1980) points out that a fairly large number of presently used readability formulas are based on the McCall-Crabbs Standard Test Lessons in Reading, which were developed in 1925 and revised in 1950 and 1961. The Lorge Formula, the Flesch Formula, and one of the better known and most used, the Dale-Chall Formula, among others, were based on the McCall-Crabbs Standard Test Lessons in Reading. Stevens states,

While investigating the possible use of the McCall-Crabbs Standard Test Lessons as a research instrument, the author discovered that they are not based on extensive testing and the grade level scores they yield lack reliability and comparability. [A *reliable* test gives the same results each time it is given. It is consistent.] Complete technical information on the lessons is not available from the publisher, because the lessons were never intended to be used as tests. (pp. 413–14)

Stevens states that scores for the lessons were developed to provide motivated instruction, not precise measurement. To emphasize the inaccuracy of the original procedure in terms of grade placement of the original materials, Stevens states,

McCall described the derivation of the scores for the McCall-Crabbs Standard Test Lessons in Reading. "Each test lesson was administered side by side to all grades in the elementary school from Grades III to VI. In some instances the tests were administered only in Grades III, V, and VIII."[1]

Thus, the McCall-Crabbs Standard Test Lessons in Reading were intended only to be practice exercises in reading. The grade level scores were rough

---

[1]Stevens is quoting McCall's personal correspondence to her.

equivalents, provided for students to track their progress. The lessons were never meant to be used for rigorous testing, and were never intended for use as a criterion for readability formulae. . . . Their use "in the rude early days of scientific education" may have been justifiable. That hardly seems the case now. (p. 414)

The problem mentioned by Stevens is surely not limited to the readability formulas based on the McCall-Crabbs Standard Test Lessons. Some formulas are based on other questionable materials, including trade books given reading levels by publishers. If developers base a formula on books simply labeled by a publisher as second grade, third grade, etc., with no concrete basis for these labels, then the readability formula itself can be no better than the publisher's original guesses.

Readability formulas seem quite primitive compared to the accuracy of the sciences. Some formulas, of course, are better than others because of the criteria from which they were developed. Also the whole concept of grade level becomes less apparent in the higher grades. There is a definite difference between the difficulty of first-grade and second-grade material. But there is very little difference between materials written at the eleventh- and twelfth-grade levels. In the higher grades, factors such as syntax, interest, and motivation become much more important than sentence length and percent of hard words.

Near or at the high school level, unless something other than sentence length and number of hard words is considered, a readability formula is fruitless. But in the lower grade levels, a carefully constructed readability formula based only on these two factors still seems plausible. The best and easiest-to-use readability formula is the Harris-Jacobson formula, which is in Albert J. Harris and Edward R. Sipay (1980).

Using Publishers' Designated Grade Levels

Generally, teachers should not use the publisher's designated grade level of materials to match reader and material. However, until teachers become acquainted with the materials and stu-

dents in their classrooms, this approach may be the best. This approach does have several serious problems, though. First, publishers' grade levels may be based on guesses made by someone observing the materials. Since even teachers who constantly work with children vary so much in their estimates of materials' reading difficulty, this procedure is dubious. Is anyone working in a publishing house necessarily any better at judging grade level than a classroom teacher?

However, more and more publishers are using the better readability formulas, such as the Harris-Jacobson or a combination of formulas, for writing and/or grading material. Some companies also specialize in high interest-low vocabulary materials for students reading below grade level. Such books usually have carefully controlled vocabulary and sentence length and often have dependable grade-level designations. Most basal reader series are also written much more carefully than they were in the past and so have more dependable grade levels.

Second, using publishers' designated grade levels does not take into consideration the many students who do not read at grade level. For example, in the second grade, children may read from the first- to third-grade level, while in the sixth grade, the worst reader may read six grade levels behind the best reader. This problem, combined with often inaccurate publisher designations, makes using publishers' grade levels almost meaningless.

Using Standardized Reading Achievement Tests

Can the reading grade levels assigned by standardized reading achievement tests be depended on as accurate, and can they be used for placing students?

Joseph R. Jenkins and Darlene Pany (1978) examined the ability of five different standardized reading achievement tests to measure the content learned in seven commercial reading series at first- and second-grade levels. In doing so, they also discovered some interesting information about the ability of standardized reading tests to place students. They used the following tests:

1. Peabody Individual Achievement Test (PIAT)
2. Metropolitan Achievement Test (MAT)
3. Wide Range Achievement Test (WRAT)
4. Stanford Achievement Test (SAT)
5. Slosson Oral Reading Test (SORT)

In discussing their findings the authors stated,

Achievement test grade equivalent scores are useful, according to some authorities, in placing children within a reading series. However, teachers relying on grade equivalent scores to make a placement decision in a particular curriculum might be led to radically different conclusions depending upon the selection of achievement test and the child's previous reading curriculum. Hypothetically, students who have mastered first grade Ginn vocabulary would obtain SORT grade equivalent of 1.4. The same students, if instead they had read in Economy, could expect a SORT score of 2.2. In one instance children appear unready for second grade material while in the other they appear properly skilled for a second grade placement reading. To further illustrate potential variation in placement decisions as a function of test and curriculum combinations, consider the probable placements for children with an instructional history in SRA, given the PIAT (1.5), the SORT (1.0) or the WRAT (2.1).

What a teacher knows after administering a standardized test is how many words on that particular test a child knows, and how that score compares to other children in the class, and to some children on whom the test was normed. What the teacher does not know is which words a child can read in a *particular* reading series. It is that information which is needed to place a child at an appropriate instruction level in a given curriculum. (p. 354)

Also, all these tests (SORT, PIAT, and WRAT) are word reading tests and do not test students' comprehension; therefore, they give a distorted picture of the student's reading level.

Jenkins and Pany believe that alert teachers have always been able to note students who could skip certain materials and they need not continually test a student to see whether she reads at the proper level. They suggest that no single approach always serves the teacher in

making these decisions and that the results of any test should be tempered with teacher judgment. However, teachers do need to study these problems, or they cannot possibly make the proper judgments.

Using Informal Reading Inventories

Although informal reading inventories were discussed in Chapter 7, here they will be discussed in relationship to placing children in appropriate materials. Two basic kinds of informal reading inventories exist, teacher-made and commercial. Commercial inventories are developed by reading experts, usually contain carefully prepared and tested questions, and usually have passages for a greater number of grade levels. (See Chapter 7 for a detailed discussion of the differences between the two kinds of inventories.)

Information Derived from Informal Reading Inventories. Informal reading inventories provide two main sources of information—the student's reading levels and oral reading error pattern. (See Chapter 9 for a thorough discussion of various errors and their meanings.) An informal reading inventory usually reports a student's reading ability in three levels: *independent, instructional*, and *frustration* levels. Reading authorities disagree somewhat about the criteria for the levels, but the most commonly used criteria were originally developed by Emmett Betts (1946) and set forth in a monograph by Marjorie Johnson and Roy Kress (1965).

Independent or Free Reading Level

At the independent reading level, a student's word recognition should be 99 percent *or better*, and his comprehension should be 90 percent *or better*.

A student reading a library book or something that the teacher does not help him with should be at this level. In other words, anything a student picks up and reads for pleasure, such as a magazine, a story, or a book containing information he wants to know but does not *have* to know, should be at his independent level.

Teachers usually base their decisions about whether a student is reading at independent, instructional, or frustration level on the percentage of comprehension and word recognition errors. However, the teacher may also want to watch for certain behavioral characteristics associated with the independent level. Johnson and Kress listed such characteristics as follows:

Rhythmical, expressive oral reading
Accurate observation of punctuation
Acceptable reading posture
Silent reading more rapid than oral
Response to questions in language equivalent to author's
No evidence of lip movement, finger pointing, head movement, vocalization, subvocalization, or anxiety about performance (p. 6)

If a student reads material and meets or exceeds the independent word recognition and comprehension percentages, then a tendency to finger point, move his head, etc. would not keep him out of the independent level. But students reading materials at their independent level usually do *not* have such tendencies.

Instructional Level

At the instructional level, a student's word recognition should be 95 percent *or better*, and her comprehension should be 75 percent *or better.*

A student should be reading her textbooks, such as a basal reader, a science book or social studies book, at this level. Students should seldom be expected to read material this difficult without *some* preparation by the teacher. Before reading material at their instructional level, students should review the vocabulary and discuss the material's concepts with the teacher. Essentially, then, the teacher discusses the material's vocabulary and concepts and changes it from the student's instructional reading level to her independent reading level before she is expected to read the material on her own. When a student picks up a book or reads a passage from an informal reading inventory without any preparation in vocabulary or concepts, she may be reading at her instructional level. This in itself

is a proper situation. What is not proper is to expect students to *enjoy* reading and comprehending material at these percentages and without help.

To fully understand the concept of the extreme difficulty of material written at the instructional level, first consider an adult's independent level. Most people say that reading material with 1 unknown word in 100, 1 percent, is not unpleasant. (Unknown means the reader does not know how to pronounce a word or does not understand the meaning of it.) On the other hand, material with a new word every 20 seconds seems difficult and unpleasant to read to most people. But the situations are essentially the same. The average adult reads around 285–300 words per minute. If a person reads at 300 words per minute and does not know 1 percent of the words, then he encounters an unknown word every 20 seconds! When put in these terms, reading levels become more concrete than percentages indicate. Remember, too, this example is of an adult reading at the independent reading level. At the instructional reading level and under the same conditions, an adult would encounter an unknown word every 4 seconds! Keep such difficulty in mind when you are trying to place a student in her instructional level.

The related behavioral characteristics for the instructional level are the same as those for the independent reading level.

Frustration Level

At the frustration level, a student's word recognition is 90 percent *or less*, and his comprehension is 50 percent *or less.*

In addition, Johnson and Kress list some related behavioral characteristics for the frustration level. Seeing these characteristics can help a teacher identify students reading at or near this level:

Abnormally loud or soft voice
Arhythmical or word-by-word oral reading
Lack of expression in oral reading
Inaccurate observation of punctuation
Finger pointing (at margin or every word)

Lip movement, head movement, subvocalization
Frequent requests for examiner help
Non-interest in the selection
Yawning or obvious fatigue
Refusal to continue (p. 10)

The teacher should do everything within her power to prevent students from attempting to read material at their frustration reading level. But many students in today's elementary schools are constantly forced to struggle with material so difficult that they become frustrated. This chapter shows you how to avoid such frustrating situations.

Administering Informal Reading Inventories. To administer an informal reading inventory the teacher usually faces the student diagonally across a table. The teacher can watch the student and a copy of what the student is going to read without distracting the student. The goal is to find the student's independent, instructional, and frustration reading levels, but the most important level for the teacher is the student's instructional level. Although the teacher may figure that the student's independent level is one level below the instructional level and the student's frustration level is one grade level above, the student may actually range across three or four grades of instructional levels. The teacher usually begins the inventory at what he thinks will be the student's independent reading level. By having the student read something relatively easy in the beginning, the teacher can establish better rapport with the student.

The teacher usually has the student read the first passage aloud and marks any word recognition errors using the code for oral diagnosis discussed in Chapter 9. After the student completes the oral reading, the teacher takes the material from the student to prevent the student from looking at it again. The teacher then asks several questions, depending on how many the teacher or author decided to use in that particular inventory. An inventory with more questions will probably have higher reliability, while one with fewer questions can be done in less time. After the student reads the oral read-ing passage, she is then asked to read one at the same level silently. When the student indicates she is done with the silent reading, the teacher again takes the material from the student and asks a series of questions over the subject matter. If the first oral and silent reading passages are above the student's independent reading level, then the teacher would use passages at progressively lower levels until the independent reading level is established. The teacher then continues progressively upward with passages until the frustration level is reached. At this point the teacher stops the testing process.

Some authorities disagree about what to call errors on the informal reading inventories. Obviously if some errors are counted and others are not, it takes more errors to reach the instructional level, which means the student may be placed in more difficult material. The following miscues should be counted as errors:

1. Omissions
2. Insertions
3. Substitutions
4. Partial Mispronunciations
5. Gross Mispronunciations
6. Aid (It is customary to wait for five seconds before telling the student the word.)
7. Repetitions

Also you should mark the following reader's characteristics to use in analyzing the student's oral reading pattern, but do *not* count them as errors:

8. Self-corrected words.
9. A disregard for punctuation.
10. A fairly long pause before words (longer than normal but less than 5 seconds, which becomes aid).

Evaluating Data from Informal Reading Inventories. Figure 10–1 portrays the criteria for the independent, instructional, and frustration reading levels.

To figure a student's level, use the following guidelines.

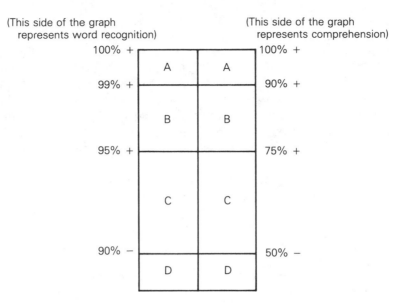

(This side of the graph represents word recognition)

(This side of the graph represents comprehension)

Figure 10–1   Scoring criteria for informal reading inventories

1. If both scores on oral reading or the comprehension score on silent reading fall in the area marked A, then the student is reading at his independent reading level.
2. If both scores on oral reading or the comprehension score on silent reading fall in the area marked B, then the student is reading at her instructional level.
3. If one of the two scores (or both) on oral reading or the silent reading score falls in the area marked D, then the student is reading at his frustration reading level.

Note that the criteria for A and B are listed as percentages with a plus (+), meaning that scores must at least reach these criteria to be at the instructional or independent level. The criteria for the frustration reading levels are marked with a minus (−). The area in C remains unaccounted for in the criteria. Thus, the teacher can judge the seriousness of any reader's errors when deciding which reading level to place the student in. For example, if a student has a word recognition score of 94 percent (in area C, or unaccounted for) but has a perfect comprehension score, then the teacher might give the student the benefit of the doubt and place her at

the instructional level even though the 95 percent word recognition criteria was not quite met. Such a decision can be especially justified if the student makes word recognition errors that are not considered as serious as others, such as repetitions rather than gross mispronunciations. Or suppose a student has a word recognition score of 100 percent but a comprehension score of 70 percent, which does not quite meet the minimum criteria for comprehension at the instructional level. In this case, the teacher might also place the student at the instructional level. On the other hand, if a student's word recognition falls in the lower part of C (for example, 92 percent) and comprehension is also in the middle or lower range of C, then the teacher would probably place the student at his frustration reading level.

Common Problems Encountered with Informal Reading Inventories.   Michael C. McKenna (1983), in a review of issues related to informal reading inventories, points out that Emerald Dechant (1981), a well-known reading authority, estimated that the informal reading inventory is the most frequent means of determining reading levels and diagnosing various reading problems. McKenna also notes that Miles Zintz (1981) has called it "the most accurate test measure that can be provided to evaluate the child's ability to use textbooks for instructional purposes" (p. 99) and that Jerry Johns (1977) has insisted that "we cannot afford not to use informal reading inventories" (p. 136).

McKenna, however, points out many problems that teachers who use informal reading inventories often encounter.

1. If a teacher uses his own inventory, any of the passages chosen may not represent the book as a whole. Many books vary a lot in reading level from page to page. Thus, a student may score in the instructional level on a passage, but have difficulty with the whole book.

2. Interest is a strong factor in how a student does. If a student is interested in a passage, then she will probably comprehend it better than if she read about something she had no interest in. This problem is true of both teacher-made and commercial reading inventories.

3. Choice of questions also affects a student's outcome. In a study by Joe Peterson, Jean Greenlaw, and Robert J. Tierney (1978), three different sets of questions were used for each passage in an informal reading inventory. They found that depending on which set was used, 37 of 57 students in second through fifth grade were identified as being at two different instructional levels.

4. The passage dependency of the questions is also of prime importance. As McKenna points out, "Richard Allington, et al. (1977) found that even the questions used on four highly regarded, individually administered, diagnostic tests of reading were passage independent to a dangerous degree" (p. 673). Also, questions may be passage independent for some students, but not for others. For example, older students may know the answer to questions through experience, whereas a younger student may not. For the younger student, the questions *are* passage dependent.

5. The scoring criteria for passages, stated in percentages for word recognition and comprehension, are still being debated. Furthermore, experts disagree about what miscues should be counted as errors. These factors can greatly influence the outcomes of an informal reading inventory.

6. Scoring criteria often vary with the ability level and IQ of the students. A study by Eldon E. Ekwall, Judy Solis-English, and Enrique Solis, Jr. (1973) found that good readers tend to reach their frustration level with fewer word recognition errors than do students reading at a lower level. They also found that students at lower IQ levels need more errors to reach frustration level than do students with higher IQs.

7. McKenna also notes that students often have dissimilar comprehension scores on their silent and oral readings. Reading orally may place such a burden on the student's mind that he cannot concentrate on what he is reading. Or perhaps a particular student has had more practice reading orally and so can comprehend better orally. Or because each passage has a different set of comprehension questions, comprehension scores may vary accordingly.

8. Although it is common for students to read material in their basal readers silently before reading it aloud, they are usually not asked to do so when taking informal reading inventories. Although this difference may affect a student's score, the original criteria developed for informal reading inventories did not have students read material silently before reading it aloud. Allowing students to read the passages silently first would make the scoring criteria invalid.

9. Teachers often use word lists to determine the starting point for having students read aloud and silently. This practice presents problems, since reading words from a list is different from reading them in context, but it does work better in the lower grades than in the upper ones. McKenna says, "Not surprisingly, Frose (1971) reported that word lists are significantly correlated more often at lower grade levels" (p. 677).

10. Finally, there is the problem of labeling

reading levels at the secondary level. There is much less difference, if any, between grade levels at the secondary level than at the elementary level.

McKenna concludes by saying that in spite of the many problems with informal reading inventories, "All can be mitigated if they are, first of all, recognized as threats to validity and then approached on the best advice available" (p. 677).

McKenna's article contains an excellent review of the research and it offers a lot to the reading teacher. For example, he compiled the following 10 suggestions for constructing and using informal reading inventories:

1. Do not assume that the stories in basal readers all represent the assigned readability level. Check readability with one or more of the better formulas. Once your IRI is complete, stay alert to readability problems as you begin to use it. If you use a commercial inventory, you can have more confidence in stated readability levels, but you should observe these same precautions.
2. Whether constructing your own instrument or selecting a commercial one, make sure the passages in each sequence are from the same general interest area, preferably one of moderate to high interest for both boys and girls of the ages at which the IRI will be given. It is a good idea to ask students individually about their interest in the subjects in the inventory. Make your inquiries prior to a student's exposure to the passages.
3. In writing questions, (1) state each clearly and simply; (2) limit the number of types, perhaps adopting the guidelines provided by Johnson and Kress; and (3) be alert to sets of questions which prove too easy or too hard. In using a commercial test, be wary of tally sheets which show students' responses delineated into a large number of comprehension subskills.
4. Ensure the passage dependency of questions by "field testing" them on some of your brighter students or by using an adult standard of prior knowledge in the subject area. Do not assume that questions in commercial instruments are passage dependent, and do not hesitate to replace some of them with your own.
5. Use the Betts criteria, but do not adhere to them too rigidly. Keep these points in mind: (1) in the lower grades, be lenient with the oral accuracy criteria when comprehension is good; (2) always look for signs of actual frustration in the student's behavior; and (3) when comprehension scores are between 65% and 75%, interpret the performance as instructional unless there is evidence of frustration.
6. Do count repetitions in your error tally. Do not consider the quality (semantic acceptability) of miscues, however. Consider quality in subjectively evaluating overall patterns once the levels have been determined, concentrating on miscues made at and below the instructional level.
7. If there is a difference between oral and silent comprehension scores, use the higher of the two.
8. For miscue analysis, do not allow students to read passages silently before oral reading. When oral accuracy is at frustration level and silent comprehension is at the instructional level, consider the level as instructional.
9. Avoid using word lists except as sight word tests. Look to other information in deciding where to begin in the passages.
10. At the secondary level, beware of commercial inventories that include passages at each of grades 7–12. If constructing your own IRI, combine the upper levels in pairs: 5-6, 7-8, 9-10, 11-12. When evaluating the performance of secondary students, give far more credence to silent comprehension than to oral accuracy scores.[1]

Using the Cloze Procedure

In the cloze procedure, materials a student will be asked to read are retyped with every *nth* (usually 5th) word omitted and replaced with blanks of equal length. Depending on the student's grade level, the passages run 250–275 words long. Students are told to fill in the blanks as best as they can using context to determine what words they write down. The teacher then figures a percentage score. Based on this score, a student is at his independent, instructional, or frustration reading level for that material.

Criteria for the Cloze Procedure.   The criteria for the cloze procedure were originally based

[1]From "Informal Reading Inventories: A Review of the Issues" by M. C. McKenna, *Reading Teacher*, 1983, *36*, 675. Copyright 1983 by the International Reading Association. Reprinted by permission of M.C. McKenna and the International Reading Association.

on the criteria for informal reading inventories. Students using the same materials were given informal reading inventories and the cloze procedure. Half of the students were given the cloze passages first and the other half were given the informal reading inventories first to prevent carryover of knowledge from the materials favoring the method used first. Although there is some disagreement about the criteria for the cloze procedure, the most common criteria used are:

Independent Reading Level: The student must get 57 percent or more of the answers correct.

Instructional Reading Level: The student's answers range between 44 and 56 percent correct.

Frustration reading level: The student gets 43 percent or less of the answers correct.

Other authors use anywhere from 38 to 43 percent for the frustration level.

A study by Anne M. Ferguson (1980), in which she used the cloze procedure to determine what level books children select when they can select their own, showed that more students select books at their independent level. The importance of students being given materials at an appropriate reading level was emphasized by Ferguson, who concluded,

In conclusion, it is reasonable to assume that teachers and librarians can free the child to select trade books on his or her own, for the majority of the sample selected on independent level. The interesting finding in this study is the fact that so few children selected trade books at frustration level. (p. 199)

Other information on the criteria for using the cloze procedure has been provided by Frederick A. Duffelmeyer (1983). Duffelmeyer reviewed some of the original studies on the cloze procedure and several studies done since. He thought that the criterion of 40 percent as the minimum for instructional level may be correct for fourth or fifth graders but he recommended that slightly higher percentages of correct answers be required of students as they reach higher reading levels.

Procedure for Developing a Cloze Passage. First, omit every 5th word and replace it with a line. Some authors suggest omitting every 6th or 7th word, but if you do not use every 5th word, then the original scoring criteria do not apply. Therefore, you should not vary from the "every 5th word" rule. Make sure lines are of equal length.

Then require the student to fill in the exact word from the original text. Studies show that attempting to determine whether certain synonyms should be counted as correct confuses and lowers the reliability and validity of the procedure. Counting *only* the original correct word makes the passages much easier to score and does not harm the student. Teachers are concerned about placing students in material that is too difficult for them to read; they do not need to worry about students reading material that is too easy. If one does *not* count synonyms, then the passages are easier to score, and the student is usually placed in easier materials.

Passages should be about 250 words in length. However, most authorities agree that the first sentence, or the first 25 words, should be left intact so that the student encounters no blanks until after reading the first sentence. Most authorities also agree that the passage should have an entire sentence or at least 25 words left intact at the end. With these intact words, the passages should be around 300 words long. Leaving every 5th word blank in 250 words makes 50 blanks, which makes each correct answer worth 2 percent.

In the original scoring criteria for the cloze, researchers did not count incorrectly spelled words as errors. Thus, do not count misspelled words as errors unless the misspelling is so bad you cannot be sure of the answer.

Placing New Students in Graded Materials.

1. Select approximately 10 passages from a book. Pick them randomly, but from throughout the book, as some basal readers and textbooks are more difficult near the end.

2. Retype the material, omitting every 5th word and replacing it with a blank. As stated before, make sure the blanks are of equal length.
3. Give the tests to the 25–30 students who will use the textbook.
4. Determine the mean score of each passage.
5. Find the *mean* of the *means*. (Find the mean or average score of all the averages.)
6. Select the passage closest to the mean of the means and throw the rest of them away.
7. Duplicate this passage. When a new student comes to your class you can give the student this passage and ask her to read the material and fill in all the blanks she can.
8. If you have several books and need to know which to use with a new student, then you must repeat the above steps for each book. After a passage has been selected from each textbook, clip them together. Give one passage at a time to the new student. Do not ask students to do more than one passage at a sitting. After the student does a passage from each book, correct them and determine which book is at that student's instructional level.

The reliability of this procedure depends on the following factors:

1. If you use longer passages, scores will probably be more accurate, but it takes longer to correct the tests.
2. If more than 10 samples of the textbook are used, the final passage will probably be more representative of the book as a whole.
3. Remember that some materials vary a great deal in difficulty from page to page. If you notice this problem while scoring individual passages, avoid such materials, if possible.
4. The procedure should be followed exactly or the results may not be accurate.

The cloze procedure has been used for a long time and has received both praise and criticism from its users and its researchers. Gary A. Cziko (1983) summarizes the cloze as follows:

Since it appears that the cloze procedure is here for a long stay of widespread use in education as a measure of reading comprehension and general language proficiency, we need to make a serious effort to learn how to make the best of it. (p. 364)

An Eclectic Approach to Matching Children and Reading Materials

It is difficult to make a statement about the absolute merits of any of these methods for matching children with their reading materials. However, based on various research studies and the opinions of various authorities who have studied this subject intensively over the years, an eclectic approach can be recommended.

When you doubt whether a child is reading at his instructional or frustration level, always place the child in easier material. Several research studies show that teachers who consistently get high achievement from their students have their students reading at the proper level, according to their ability and the materials' difficulty. Proper means that the students make few errors when they read the materials.

Informal Reading Inventories. Use informal reading inventories more for miscue analysis than for placement at a certain grade level. And commercial informal reading inventories are probably preferable to teacher-made ones. Because of the innate difficulties in devising good questions and because passages vary so much that any sample may not represent the whole, teacher-made inventories are not as reliable.

When using informal reading inventories, remember you can probe for an answer *if* the student seems confused about the question's wording. However, do not give the student clear choices. Instead, ask "What do you mean by that?" or "Tell me a little more about that."

Grade Levels and Readability Formulas. When using textbooks or trade books that have pub-

photo by Jean Greenwald

A proper match between the child and the level of the text is a *must* in a basal reader program.

lishers' statements about grade levels, check to see if they are estimated grade levels or if the publisher has used one or more of the better-known readability formulas.

Remember that in readability, factors *other* than number of hard words and sentence length become more important in the upper grades. Also, the concept of grade levels becomes vague in the upper grades, especially above the eighth or ninth.

Cloze Procedure.　　Although the cloze procedure has received criticism, it seems one of the most accurate methods of properly matching children with their materials. However, when using the cloze procedure remember the following points:

1. The original percentage scores were based on fourth- and fifth-grade students. You may wish to use slightly more difficult criteria for students in the upper grades, especially at the high school or college level.

2. Doing a cloze passage is a difficult task, even if the material is at the student's independent reading level. Do not expect students to do more than one passage at one sitting.

3. Children below the fourth-grade level probably cannot use the cloze procedure without having a great deal of difficulty.

4. The criteria for the cloze procedure came from comparing it to informal reading inventories. If the criteria for informal reading inventories are not valid, then the criteria for the cloze procedure are probably not valid either.

Other Helpful Techniques.　　Listen to children read when they do not make more than one or two oral reading errors per hundred words and see how it sounds. Keep this in mind when listening to other children read. Stay alert to situations where children may be reading at their frustration levels.

Once you decide to place a student in materials that she will use for some time, do not be satisfied that the original placement is correct. Check on the placement by asking the student to read 100 words and seeing if she makes more errors than she should. If she does, then she may be placed in materials too difficult for her.

Finally, teach students how to select their own library books, or anything to be read for pleasure. Tell them to count 100 words from somewhere in the book and read those words. Tell them that each time they find a word they cannot pronounce, or do not know the meaning of, they should raise one finger. If they have raised more than one, or especially more than two, by the time they read the 100 words, tell them the material is probably too difficult for them.

SUMMARY

In this chapter you have been introduced to the ways traditionally used to match children with the materials they are to read. Matching students and materials properly is one of the most important and most difficult tasks faced by the teacher. Teachers have to consider many factors: readability formulas, publishers' designations, standardized achievement tests, informal reading inventories, the cloze procedure, and finally their own judgment. Thus, you should have a sense of the difficulties involved and a feeling for ways you can accomplish this task in your own classroom.

REVIEW QUESTIONS

1. What does it mean if a certain method of matching children with the proper level of materials is reliable and valid?
2. What does research say about children having to constantly read materials too difficult for them?
3. Discuss how standardized tests may be useful in placing students. Also list their limitations.
4. Discuss grade level in relationship to publishers' recommendations versus readability formulas.
5. On what factors are most well-known readability formulas based? If it were practical, what other factors would you add?
6. What are the strengths and weaknesses of informal reading inventories?
7. Describe how you would use the cloze procedure to match students with reading materials.
8. What are some shortcomings of the cloze procedure?
9. What are some of the elements in an eclectic approach to matching children with the proper level of reading materials?

REFERENCES

Allington, R. L., Chodos, L., Domaracki, J., & Truex, S. Passage dependency: Four diagnostic oral reading tests. *Reading Teacher*, January, 1977, *30*, 369–75.

Betts, E. A. *Foundations of reading instruction.* New York: American Book Co., 1946.

Botel, M., Bradley, J., & Cashuba, M. The validity of informal reading testing. In W. K. Durr (Ed.), *Reading difficulties: Diagnosis, correction, and remediation.* Newark, Del.: International Reading Association, 1970.

Cziko, G. A. Commentary—Another response to Shanahan, Kamil, and Tobin: Further reasons to keep the cloze case open. *Reading Research Quarterly*, Spring, 1983, *18*, 361–65.

Dechant, E. *Diagnosis and remediation of reading disabilities.* Englewood Cliffs, N. J.: Prentice-Hall, 1981.

Duffelmeyer, F. A. The effect of grade level on cloze test scores. *Journal of Reading*, February, 1983, *26*, 436–41.

Ekwall, E. E., Solis-English, J. K., & Solis, E., Jr. Investigating informal reading inventory scoring criteria. *Elementary English*, February, 1973, *50*, 271–74, 323.

Ferguson, A. M. Applying the cloze procedure to children's book selections. *Reading Horizons*, Spring, 1980, *20*, 196–200.

Frose, V. Word recognition tests: Are they useful beyond grade 3? *Reading Teacher*, February, 1971, *24*, 432–38.

Gickling, E. E., & Armstrong, D. L. Levels of instructional difficulty as related to on-task behavior, task completion, and comprehension. *Journal of Learning Disabilities*, November, 1980, *11*, 559–66.

Harber, J. R. Syntactic complexity: A necessary ingredient in predicting readability. *Journal of Learning Disabilities*, August/September, 1979, *12*, 437–43.

Harris, A. J. *How to increase reading ability*. New York: Donald McKay, 1961.

Harris, A. J., & Sipay, E. R. *How to increase reading ability*. New York: Longman, 1980.

Hoffman, J. V. Weighting miscues in informal inventories—A precautionary note. *Reading Horizons*, Winter, 1980, *20*, 135–39.

Jenkins, J., & Pany, D. Curriculum biases in reading achievement tests. *Journal of Reading Behavior*, Winter, 1978, *10*, 345–57.

Johns, J. L. Matching students with books. *Contemporary Education*, Spring, 1977, *48*, 133–36.

Johnson, M. S., & Kress, R. A. *Informal reading inventories*. Newark, Del.: International Reading Association, 1965.

Jorgensen, G. W. An analysis of teacher judgments of reading levels. *American Educational Research Journal*, February, 1975, *12*, 24–42.

Keenan, D. An evaluation of the effectiveness of selected readability formulas applied to secondary texts. *Reading Horizons*, Winter, 1982, *22*, 123–28.

McKenna, M. C. Informal reading inventories: A review of the issues. *Reading Teacher*, March, 1983, *36*, 670–79.

Peterson, J. M., Greenlaw, J., & Tierney, R. Assessing instructional placement with an IRI: The effectiveness of comprehension questions. *Journal of Educational Research*, May/June, 1978, *71*, 247–50.

Rosenshine, B. New correlates of readability and listenability. In J. A. Figurel (Ed.), *Reading and realism*. Newark, Del.: International Reading Association, 1969.

Stevens, K. Readability formulae and McCall-Crabbs Standard Test Lessons in Reading. *Reading Teacher*, January, 1980, *33*, 413–15.

Walker, S. M., Noland, R. G., & Greenshields, C. M. The effect of high and low interest content on instructional levels in informal reading inventories. *Reading Improvement*, Winter, 1979, *16*, 297–300.

Zintz, M. V. *Corrective reading* (4th ed.). Dubuque, Iowa: William C. Brown, 1981.

11

Sustained Silent Reading: A Critical Part of the Reading Program

Because many teachers feel that students in modern elementary and secondary schools do not get enough time to practice the art of reading, they feel the need to develop sustained silent reading programs. *Sustained silent reading* is time set aside, either within a subject matter classroom or a self-contained classroom, for students to read anything they wish. They do not have to account for what they have read, so there is no fear of being tested over the material they choose.

Students, regardless of grade level, no longer spend long winter evenings reading or playing. They spend a lot of time watching television. As a result, they learn *how* to read but often do not become *adept* at reading. They simply lack practice. Teachers also believe that even students who do have extra time do not read because they have not developed a reading habit, do not know how to select books, and/or do not know where to go to select a book. Sustained silent reading is a chance for the student to develop these habits and skills. It also gives the student a chance to broaden his knowledge of the many books available both for pleasure reading and for gaining information.

DIFFERENT NAMES

Sustained silent reading is known by several different names. The term *Uninterrupted Sustained Silent Reading*, USSR, was coined by Lyman Hunt at the University of Vermont, but the acronym drew too much attention and was shortened to *Sustained Silent Reading*, or SSR, by Robert McCracken at Western Washington State College. It has also been called *High Intensity Practice*, or HIP, by Marvin Oliver at Eastern Washington State College and *Some Quiet Uninterrupted Independent Reading Time*, or SQUIRT, by Gary Benedict of the Mukwanago Area Schools, Mukwanago, Wisconsin. It has also been called free reading. Sustained silent reading is the term used most frequently in this chapter.

REVIEW OF THE RESEARCH

Roberta Berglund and Jerry L. Johns (1983) list several important reasons for having sustained silent reading classes. They quote Linda B. Gambrell (1978), who stated that sustained silent reading is "the component in the reading program which gives students the opportunity to transfer and apply isolated skills in a pleasurable, independent reading experience" (p. 328).

Berglund and Johns make a strong case for most students not having or taking the time to read. They cite Barbara H. Long and Edmund H. Henderson (1973), who studied the activities of fifth-grade students over a two-week period. They found that students read for only 3 hours, while they watched television for 30 hours. Also, today's students are often too busy to read because they have to work, because they play sports, or because they take music or some other kind of lessons. Long and Henderson stated that a school program was needed to provide time for reading obviously not being done at home.

In addition, many students perfect their phonics and other word attack skills and can say words, but cannot understand several or many words strung together. Berglund and Johns say that

USSR, by its very nature, releases students from the pressure of reading every word perfectly and remembering every detail. It frees their minds to enjoy reading on their own terms in materials they have selected. (p. 535)

Berglund and Johns also say sustained silent reading programs are a good idea because, as Lyman Hunt points out, oral reading is harmful to low-powered readers. It demands too much perfection before the student knows what the whole reading process is all about.

Finally, Berglund and Johns say a learner has the *right* to read on her own terms, to choose her own books, to decide on her own purposes, and to derive her own meaning from the page.

Kenneth L. Donelson (1969) sees a need for sustained silent reading because "No English teacher, no matter how busy, is so occupied that he can afford to let a year slip away without ample time for free reading in class. Such free reading benefits teacher and student and literature, no matter what the grade or ability level" (p. 545).

Jesse C. Moore, Clarence J. Jones, and Douglas C. Miller (1980) state the need for sustained silent reading:

This attention grew out of the realization that, although much time is spent teaching students how to read, few opportunities are afforded them to practice reading. Adults who know how to read but who do not read "have never gained the reading experience necessary to develop an interest in, or ability to enjoy, reading books or other materials" [LeGrand-Brodsky, p. 948]. (p. 445)

Richard Allington (1975) also points out:

It is not uncommon to find students who can do isolated skill exercises, or who can read isolated word lists, but yet cannot read a book appropriate to skills developed. These learners fill many spaces in some clinics, unidentified because no one presents them with a real word reading task. (p. 212)

Moore, Jones, and Miller also cite Betty S. Heathington (1979), who questioned students in grades five through eight about their reading attitudes and habits. The students perceived themselves as extremely busy, both in and out of school, and felt they had little time left for reading. Even when they did read, they perceived it as difficult and were constantly interrupted. These students also very much wanted to select their *own* materials to read rather than the normally assigned materials.

Richard Allington (1977) has also pointed out some information that has implications for the development of a sustained silent reading program. Allington and his assistants visited a remedial reading classroom and found that during the course of a normal period, no student read over 110 words in context and none read less than 24. Allington stated, "If, in a typical week of reading instruction, students only encounter 150–500 words in context, one has to ask: How they ever gonna get good?" (p. 58).

Robert and Marlene McCracken (1978) have mentioned seven attitudes that students and adults get from sustained silent reading:

1. Reading books is important.
2. Reading is something anyone can do.
3. Reading is communicating with an author.
4. Children are capable of sustained thought.
5. Books are meant to be read in large sections.
6. The teacher believes that the children are comprehending (because he or she doesn't bother to check).
7. The teacher trusts the children to decide when something is well written, when something important has been read (because the teacher expects pupils to share after SSR). (p. 408)

Andrew Biemiller (1977–78) also offers an excellent argument for including a sustained si-

lent reading program in every classroom. After discussing his research results, Biemiller stated,

The second implication of these findings is that more attention might be paid to the small amount of actual reading practice that poor readers receive. There appears to be a potential vicious circle in which initial slow reading may lead to reduced opportunities for practice which in turn reduces opportunities for extracting intraword structure and possibly for increasing general identification speed. Stress on what stories mean, on how participants in stories feel, on pictures, and other activities not directly requiring a child to read words may be doing the young beginning reader a disservice. The evidence represented in this paper indicating that slow readers use context as effectively as abler readers to facilitate speed provides further support for the hypothesis that practice emphasizing actual reading may be more useful than discussions aimed at enhancing the use of context. (pp. 250–51)

Practice in reading is like learning to play tennis or to play the piano. Theodore Mork (1972) has pointed out that in learning such skills, the student expects to have a practice to instruction ratio of approximately 4 to 1. Mork says, "Keep in mind that the practice needed is not just practice in using the backhand or in serving. Much of the practice must be in putting all the skills together for practice in total performance" (p. 440). Mork also mentions the importance of the words *uninterrupted* and *sustained*. He says that teachers often say, "But we do lots of library reading," or "I have children practice reading at home." But Mork says the library period or reading at home is not the same because it is often not *uninterrupted* or *sustained*. Mork also points out that below the third grade, when the student *does* read silently, he is often interrupted by the teacher who asks a question about the passage to check his comprehension.

Byron Callaway's study (1981) illustrates one of the most important reasons for having a sustained silent reading period.[1] Callaway gave a questionnaire to 223 graduate students to determine

---

[1] From "What Turns Children 'On' or 'Off' in Reading" by B. Callaway, *Reading Improvement*, Fall, 1981, *18*, 214–17. Copyright 1981 by *Reading Improvement*. Reprinted by permission.

Time to relax and read is important in today's busy world.

what had encouraged or discouraged them from wanting to read on their own or from wanting to become lifetime readers. The questions were as follows:

1. Has there been anything in your school experience, teacher or otherwise, that "turned you on" in reading? If yes, what happened?
2. Has there been anything in your school experience, teacher or otherwise, that "turned you off" in reading? If yes, what happened?
3. Has there been anything outside of school that "turned you on" in reading? If yes, what was it?
4. Has there been anything outside of school that "turned you off" in reading? If yes, what was it? (p. 214)

Callaway reported various comments about what had turned students on in school, but those closely related to sustained silent reading were:

My first- and fourth-grade teachers read books to the class.

In the sixth grade we ordered paperback books from the school club.

I had an excellent fifth-grade teacher—she put a lot of emphasis on book reports, but wouldn't let us do them in the conventional manner. She thought up all sorts of interesting ways to give a book report.

In fourth grade my teacher allowed us to go to the reading corner after we had finished our work and pick out a book and read.

The librarian really "turned me on" by letting me read just about anything I wanted.

The teachers letting us choose our own material and not giving a "book report." (p. 215)

In addition, nearly all the comments about what turned them on outside of school related to sustained silent reading. For example, Callaway said "Encouragement by parents and making books available were listed more than any other items outside of school or in school" (p. 216). Students mentioned being permitted to select and read books that appealed to them, and not having any books forced on them. Others mentioned discussing and recommending books with their peers. Parents reading to them when they were young was important, and when parents read about subjects they were interested in, students were even more excited about reading. Movies, television, and advertising also encouraged them to read. Callaway included some specific comments about influences outside of school:

My mother read to us at night when we were young. She also kept a number of library books around.

My local library encouraged summer reading programs.

My mother took my brother, sister, and me to the library often when we were young.

A summer reading program that I was enrolled in when I was in junior high school.

My parents read to me or bought me all the books I wanted.

My parents allowing me to choose my own reading material.

My father praising me on how well I was reading.

Reading comic books. (p. 217)

Last, Callaway listed some influences from both outside and inside school that turned children off. For example, one student vehemently rejected his "Enjoying Reading" class! Other comments were:

The librarian would "censor" books. *Uncle Tom's Cabin* could be checked out only by seniors and parents—made one hate librarians.

Each student would stand and read two sentences.

We always did book reports, which made reading less enjoyable. I've done *Hamlet* five times and *Huckleberry Finn* four. Yes, I hate to read out loud, my whole body sweats. SRA labs were a bore.

I think there should be more outside reading for parents teaching them how they can help children. . . . let the parents know their child is not the only one with a learning problem.

My mother always told me I never did enough reading and it seemed like when I did find something I liked she would say, "Why can't you read some *good* books like . . ."

Librarians tried to discourage me from reading mysteries. (pp. 216–17)

Perhaps the most important reason to have a sustained silent reading program is that although reading teachers are building a world of students who know *how* to read, they are not building a world of students who *do* read: according to a survey by the Carnegie Foundation, half the people with bachelor's degrees in the United States never read another book after they graduate from college!

Reading to enhance reading skills is also emphasized in such materials as the August, 1982 *Reading Today*, a membership newsletter from the International Reading Association. In it the editor quoted from a report entitled *Reading Comprehension of American Youth: Do They Understand What They Read?* "At all ages, students who read 'almost every day' performed significantly higher on the reading comprehension exercises than those who reported less frequent spare-time reading" (p. 1).

SUSTAINED SILENT READING IN THE CLASSROOM

Once teachers are convinced they want to have a sustained silent reading program in their school, they need to know some general rules and variations for such a program, how to begin and develop one, why some programs fail, how to get children to read, and what results to expect.

Rules for Operating a Sustained Silent Reading Program

Robert A. McCracken (1971) outlined what he believed should be the *rules* for the sustained silent reading program. McCracken stated that "A simple objective of any school's reading program is to develop each student's ability to read silently without interruption for a relatively long period of time" (p. 521). To achieve these aims, McCracken suggested six rules.

Students Read Silently. The purpose of this was to convince all readers of the importance of silent reading and to encourage other students *not* to interrupt those who were reading silently.

Teacher Also Reads. Nearly every research article on sustained silent reading has stressed this rule as crucial in making the program operate smoothly and efficiently. The teacher should read something he is interested in reading and should *not* use the time to correct papers or do other school work. Students in a sustained silent reading program emulate the teacher.

Students Select a Single Book. McCracken included magazines or newspapers under the term *book*, but he states, "No book changing is permitted" (p. 522). However, many students, especially those new at selecting books, often do not choose ones they wish to read for the entire period. After all, as an adult reader, how many times have you gone to the library, picked out what you thought would be a good book, and then been disappointed? How many times have you chosen three books only to discover you are interested in just one? If the teacher is attempting to develop a student's love of reading, why make that student read or look at a book she is not interested in for an entire period? In other programs, student may select more than a single book for an entire period. McCracken's original rule should not be followed rigidly.

Use a Timer. McCracken and others suggest a timer to mark the end of the sustained silent reading period so that students are not tempted to look at a wall clock and anticipate the end of the period.

Do Not Keep Records.   McCracken says that students should not have to account in any way for reading or understanding a certain amount of material, if they choose not to. In some sustained silent reading programs, students are asked to let the teacher know when they finish a book so the teacher can keep a record of how many books each student reads. Although McCracken is generally right, it is interesting to see just how much reading does go on in a well-run sustained silent reading program. Such record keeping is fine, if the teacher can keep a record of all books read by all children without making it a contest. Students should not know how many books other students have read. Also, although students should not be tested on what they read, many want to share what they have learned from their reading. Therefore, you may ask students to tell you when they have finished a book, and as you write down the name of the book, ask the student to give a 45-second to one-minute synopsis of the book's contents, *if* he wants to. Most students prefer to do this if given a chance. Such a procedure also gives the teacher a chance to see if students are generally

comprehending what they are reading without testing them.

Begin with Whole Classes or Larger Groups. McCracken maintains that when teachers attempt sustained silent reading with smaller groups, such as 10 or less, students feel free to ask questions and to carry on a conversation that involves the entire class. Although such participation is hoped for in most other teaching situations, in sustained silent reading it is better to have larger groups and no interaction.

Variations in the Overall Operation of a Sustained Silent Reading Program

Several types of sustained silent reading programs have been tried throughout the history of reading instruction; regardless of setting, some have been highly successful while others have fallen by the wayside. A program involving the entire school, if the entire school can be motivated to try it, is the best way to operate. On the other hand, not being able to carry on a sustained silent reading program this way should not preclude any teacher, whether in a self-contained or subject matter classroom, from carrying out a successful program.

Within Subject Matter Areas or Self-contained Classrooms.   In this type of sustained silent reading program, the teacher usually allots a certain amount of time to free reading and uses the same general rules set forth earlier. Students are either allowed or asked to bring their own book(s) to read. Or the teacher of a certain subject matter, such as science, may gather as many books, magazines, and pamphlets about science as possible. Students may also bring books they wish to read. As with other types of sustained silent reading programs, the teacher may assign a certain amount of time each day for sustained silent reading or students may use the time they have available after completing assignments for sustained silent reading.

A Schoolwide Free Reading Program.   This type of program, with everyone dedicated to the cause and everyone reading at the same time each day, is the preferred approach. A school with a strong instructional leader as principal usually has higher pupil achievement than a school with a principal without strong leadership abilities. If the sustained silent reading program is used on a schoolwide basis, then the principal probably will be involved to a large degree, and if that is so, then many problems that may plague a teacher will be easier to deal with. For example, the principal can make a specific time available for schoolwide sustained silent reading and can help the classroom teacher secure an ample supply of library books. With the principal involved, teachers need not feel the guilt they may feel when they choose to free read with their students on their own.

Classroom Libraries or Using Books from a Central Library.

Some teachers ask students to bring their own materials to read during the sustained silent reading period. Others try to build a classroom library so that it has a large supply of books. Then students do not have to leave the room to go to the library or remember to bring a book. Others gather a small classroom library to use when a student forgets to bring a book.

However, one factor that separates successful programs from unsuccessful ones is that the successful ones have a classroom library. Any teacher, whether of first grade or of graduate courses, knows several students usually forget to bring their textbooks or library books to class on any given day. Thus, the student is unlikely to spend the full sustained silent reading period in uninterrupted reading. Also, some students do not feel comfortable choosing books from the library, and others may not be able to afford their own books.

In a sustained silent reading program, teachers should not only have classroom libraries but also display books so their covers show. Then students tend to look at books and become fascinated with them during spare moments. When the sustained silent reading period begins, many students already have a particular book in

mind. Remember, students finding books they are interested in is the beginning of a successful sustained silent reading period.

Time Allotments.

Time allotments for a sustained silent reading program depend on the type of program one has. When students free read within a particular subject matter, time allotments often depend on the amount of time left after covering a topic for an entire class or time left after individuals complete an assignment. When all students in the school are involved in sustained silent reading for a specified period of time, time allotments often vary from grade to grade depending on students' levels. However, another factor that separates successful sustained silent reading programs from unsuccessful ones is that the successful programs give students longer periods of time. Regardless of the time allotted for sustained silent reading, remember that McCracken and other researchers suggest that teachers start with a relatively short period of time and gradually increase it until they reach the maximum time period desirable for a particular grade level.

In a discussion about the time that McCracken thought secondary students in subject areas should have, McCracken stated,

Our experience suggests that most classes (90 percent or more) will sustain silent reading for twenty-five minutes or more within one week's time if there are daily sessions. Classes usually need a month of reading under the six rules before the teacher can instigate variations from the six rules. Classes grouped homogeneously as poor readers may require three or four months. (p. 523)

In a similar discussion, but about the lower grades, Gambrell quotes Morton A. Botel (1977), who recommends beginning with a short period of time and gradually extending it to the desired length. Gambrell says Botel suggests starting with only 3 to 5 minutes at the kindergarten/primary level and 10 to 15 minutes in the middle grades. This amount of time is ideal for *beginning* a sustained silent reading program.

Richard Allington (1975), who used sustained silent reading as a classroom teacher, believes that depending on the students' ages, a range of 3 to 10 minutes in the beginning stages is sufficient. However, he adds, "a planned gradual increase in the length of the period will produce middle school children who can easily sustain a 60-minute period. I've observed that it is best to start small and to be lavish with praise" (p. 814).

In the middle grades (usually 4, 5, & 6) students can sustain reading for 50 to 60 minutes. As a rule of thumb, you may use the following guidelines, but only after the program has been in operation long enough to get students up to their maximum times:

Grade 1 (after beginning the second semester)	10 minutes
Grade 2	20 minutes
Grade 3	30 minutes
Grade 4	40 minutes
Grade 5 and up	50 minutes

These times apply to schoolwide sustained silent reading programs or to programs that allot a specified amount of time within each subject matter period to sustained silent reading on that subject. However, students sustain their attention longer when they can choose materials other than subject matter ones.

Beginning a Sustained Silent Reading Program

Barbara Risser (1979), in an article about starting a sustained silent reading program, lists four stages, each of which might take one week. Risser suggests these activities for four weeks:

WEEK ONE—Convince the Faculty
WEEK TWO—Arouse Student Interest
WEEK THREE—Rules of S.S.R.
WEEK FOUR—Get a Book for S.S.R. (p. 439)

Convincing teachers was much easier than Risser anticipated, but having several of the teachers committed to the program is not enough. Nearly 100 percent of the teachers should favor such a program. To get such support, Risser distributed professional journals with articles pointing out the value of sustained silent reading.

She then presented the plan to the faculty in a meeting and outlined various goals.

On the other hand, Marilyn Joy Minton (1980), in describing a less than successful program, believed that the two weeks allotted for teacher orientation was insufficient. She agreed with Risser that if an entire staff is to participate in such a program, then it is essential that everyone be included in the in-service program. She also believed the staff should be completely familiar with the theory underlying sustained silent reading as well as techniques for implementing it in the classroom.

Risser suggests using the second week for arousing student interest with publicity. Risser distributed posters saying "I can't stand it anymore! What's S.S.R.?" and "Do you know what S.S.R. means? No." Risser also made a series of S.S.R. morning announcements, such as "S.S.R. is coming January 4th. Get ready now!" By the end of the week, most students had heard what S.S.R. was, and on Monday of the third week homeroom teachers explained it to everyone and answered students' questions.

During the third week the six rules for S.S.R. were given over the P.A. system in a series of skits and humorous announcements.

Both weeks three and four were geared toward students getting books for S.S.R. Risser tied getting a book in with Christmas.

Even after the program began, a great deal had to be done. For example, the public library system in the county distributed nearly 800 cards to students who had never had one. They also had a book fair where students could buy books. Risser believed the next year, the school could have a paperback book swap. Finally, Risser said there was just one complaint from the faculty after S.S.R. got under way—when the 18 minutes allotted for sustained silent reading was over, no one wanted to stop. Students were also griping because they thought the time was too short.

Paul Ganz and Mary B. Theofield (1974) also suggest that teachers and teacher aides not run duplicating machines or type during the sustained silent reading period. Again, teachers must also read during a sustained silent reading period. Ganz and Theofield also suggest that schools invite parents for S.S.R. days: "It is great public relations. They will experience a high school in . . . absolute quiet and total concentration. But remind them to wear rubbersoled shoes and bring a good book they've been wanting to read" (p. 616).

Finding Time. Time for sustained silent reading can be arranged in several different ways. McCracken suggests having sustained silent reading during social studies one day, during math the next, during science the next, etc. Or have it during first period on Monday, second period on Tuesday, third period on Wednesday, etc. A more workable plan for sustained silent reading on a schoolwide basis, however, is to shorten several subject classes and combine the time from each to create the free reading period. Time should not be taken from music, art, or physical education because students often resent it. And, if time is taken from the normal reading period, students may lose some of the gains made during the sustained silent reading period.

More time, however, can be taken from social studies and science then from other subjects, because students often choose biographies and books about historical and scientific topics on their own. Also, there is no national curriculum in social studies and science; a student in Montana probably studies something different in science from a student in Arizona, even though they are in the same grade. The only common element on achievement tests in these areas is knowledge of vocabulary. In a sustained silent reading program that took much of the time from social studies and science, students actually received higher achievement scores on the vocabulary sections of the *Iowa Test of Basic Skills* than they had when attending social studies and science classes (Ekwall, 1969).

Developing a Classroom Library. Developing a classroom library is crucial to a successful sutained silent reading program. Students cannot be expected to remember to bring a book to class each day, and they certainly cannot be expected to always choose something that sustains their interest for up to 50 minutes. Therefore, the teacher must develop a classroom library.

First, the teacher needs the cooperation of the librarian. Also, in a sustained silent reading program where students read all types of materials, materials should be changed approximately every six weeks. Thus, the teacher must bring *many* books from the school library to the classroom. For a class of 25 to 30 students, you need 80 to 100 new books each time they are exchanged. Obviously, the teacher and the librarian have to work together to find this many books at the reading levels appropriate for your class.

If at all possible, bring books from the main library every six weeks. The librarian may choose the books or the teacher and the librarian can do so. This arrangement should definitely be made with the principal and librarian before starting the program. That way, any hesitation the librarian feels about allowing so many books out of the library for so long a time can be resolved. Librarians can be tactfully reminded that the purpose of a library is to get people to read books. And reading programs done within a library setting do not even begin to encourage the tremendous amount of reading that is accomplished when books are in the classroom.

In addition, there are other sources of materials. For example, Berglund and Johns suggest asking community members to donate paperback books and to hold garage sales to sell paperback books. Gambrell suggests that teachers dismantle old or discarded basal readers and reassemble them into individual story booklets. They can do the same thing with magazine articles. Teachers can hold a book exchange, within a classroom or the school, to secure new and different materials. Gambrell also suggests asking parents to donate old magazines, as well as books. After all, "One child's castaway is another's reading treasure" (p. 329). Allington and Gambrell also remind teachers not to overlook peer-produced materials, such as stories written in a language experience program.

In the beginning of a sustained silent reading program, comic books and magazines can help to whet children's reading appetites, so they are indispensable. Mark K. Monteith (1981) points out,

A large-scale research report done in 1978 for the Book Industry Study Group by Yankelovich, Skelly, and White, Inc. estimated that ninety-four percent of the American public sixteen years of age or older read magazines and newspapers, far more than the number who read books. (pp. 965–66)

Also, at least one book rack should be set aside for paperback books. Allow students to bring any paperback book they own and exchange it for any other paperback book on the exchange rack. (The original cost of the book should be disregarded.) Some students feel proud to own a book, which often means they read a book they otherwise would not.

Developing Successful Sustained Silent Reading Programs

Several procedures are extremely important in developing and maintaining *successful* sustained silent reading programs.

Read!   Nearly every researcher and writer mentions the importance of the teacher reading with students during a free reading program. It may be tempting to correct papers or do other work related to your teaching assignment, but the benefits of reading with students far outweigh the disadvantages of any loss of time.

Have Enough Books.   Having an adequate supply of books within each classroom cannot be overstressed. Many students begin the period with a book they decide they do not like. They should be allowed to quietly browse and to find a more interesting comic book, magazine, or book. As Donelson succinctly says, "Only two rules should be operative; one, that students read, and two that they quit reading any book that bores them, no matter how exciting the book may seem to someone else" (p. 606). Those programs that have less success, ones in which

teachers thought they could not get students to read, are typically the ones that expect students to bring their own reading materials to class.

Display Covers of Books.   Books should be displayed with the covers showing for several reasons. When students are not in the sustained silent reading period, but have a few spare moments, a particular book cover may catch their attention. Then at the beginning of the sustained silent reading period, the students are one step ahead of students with no book in mind. Displaying books with their covers showing also changes the overall image of reading. It makes the classroom different from a library setting, which makes it better for the student who has had unpleasant experiences with libraries or reading. Finally, displaying books with covers, rather than spines, showing makes choosing a book much easier for the student inexperienced in book selection.

Allow Freedom of Choice.   Teachers should not try to cultivate students' cultural tastes. Let them read anything they wish as long as they read. At first, you may wish to have a higher ratio of comic books, newspapers, and magazines than books, but have an ample supply of everything. As students learn to sustain their attention, you may gradually decrease the number of comic books and magazines in relation to the number of books, but do not do so if some students quit reading.

Have Faith in Students.   The more successful programs are characterized by teachers who believe *all* students will read if given a chance. Of course, it takes some students a while to sustain their attention for the allotted time. However, any experienced teacher knows that making a major change cannot be accomplished in one or two days. Students need to get used to what the teacher expects from them, and teachers need to enforce rules with consistency over time to bring about permanent change.

Book racks which display covers rather than spines facilitate childrens' selections of "the right book."

Prevent Fear of Testing. Some teachers and administrators think that any activity students participate in should be reported on or tested. But in successful sustained silent reading programs, there is no required book reporting at all. If students *want* to take a few minutes at the beginning of the period to tell about a particular book they liked, they can do so. Such informal sharing has a positive effect, often making other students want to read that book. Studies in children's literature show that the single most important factor in book selection is peer recommendation.

Encourage Home Reading. Successful sustained silent reading programs also encourage students to check out the books they read during the free reading period and take them home to read or finish. After a student checks a book out of the library, she may discover she is not interested. In a sustained silent reading program, books the students check out are usually ones

they are already interested in. When students are encouraged to take books home, they have been known to read nearly twice as many books as they would have read just during the sustained silent reading period.

A student librarian can be appointed in each classroom. This student's job is to take the card (the student taking the book signs the card) from each book as students leave the room at the end of the day. Little time, then, is taken to check books out to students. When a student returns a book, the student librarian replaces the signed card in the book, and puts it back on the book rack.

Teach Students How to Choose. Finally, successful programs taught children how to find books they could read. Typically, a teacher tells a child to read one page and hold up one finger for each word he does not know. If the child has five fingers up at the end of the page, then the book is too difficult. But there are serious difficulties with this method. First, holding up a certain number of fingers per page has little meaning because the book may have 10 words on a page or it may have 250. The students needs to figure out a *percentage* of words not known per page, not a number of words. Second, if there are approximately 100 words per page, not knowing 5 percent of the words makes any book difficult reading. Such a percentage corresponds to the student's instructional reading level. Students should not be expected to read materials at their instructional reading level unless the teacher can review vocabulary and concepts beforehand. At the *independent* reading level, the student cannot pronounce or understand less than 1 percent of the words encountered. Thus, it is more logical to teach students how to pick books by having them count 100 words and then read them. If they encounter more than one word, and especially more than two, that they do not know, then the material is too difficult for them to read for pleasure.

Why Sustained Silent Reading Programs Fail

Sustained silent reading programs have failed, for the most part, because schools did not follow the procedures discussed in the previous section.

Berglund and Johns (1983) reported on McCracken's discoveries (1978) about why certain programs flounder. McCracken saw the following characteristics in unsuccessful programs:

1. The teacher did not read during the period.
2. Troublesome students did not read.
3. Someone else in the classroom, such as a visitor or aide, did not read.
4. There were too few books or reading materials available.
5. The program began with too long a reading time.

Berglund and Johns also mentioned the failure to formulate ground rules and the failure to keep the program flexible. Rules can sometimes be changed when things do not go as planned.

Mork says some teachers simply do not give the program a long enough time to succeed. He quotes several teachers as follows:

I tried it, but it didn't work.

My children are so immature that they just can't seem to sustain their reading for more than a couple of minutes.

I have a couple of children who will wreck it for the others.

I tried it for a week, but it didn't work. (p. 440)

Mork reminds teachers that children's behavior does not change immediately. It takes time for some children to learn to sustain their attention. He, too, noted that teachers often do not start with a realistic time period.

In Minton's discussion of a program's failure, she mentioned that the Department Chairpersons' Council voted to implement the idea after only a limited proposal by the staff. She thought the two weeks allotted for the decision-making process was inadequate. Minton stated, "If a faculty is to support a new program, it needs to have a stake in that program by being in the decision-making adoption process" (p. 501). Minton also mentioned that sustained silent reading was carried on in physical education classrooms, an atmosphere not conducive to reading.

Getting Children to Read

It is not difficult to get children to read in a sustained silent reading program. Generally students want to emulate their peers, and in a sustained silent reading program, nearly all their peers will be reading. However, here are some ideas about ways to motivate students to want to read.

1. Several movies made from classic stories are available. After such a movie has been shown, students immediately want to read the book. This desire to read the book used for a movie carries over for at least a month to six weeks.

2. From time to time, the teacher can read short selections from books known to be popular with students in the age/grade level he teaches. Read just enough from an interesting part to

whet the students' appetites, and then ask if anyone is interested in reading the book.

3. Advertise books known to be interesting to students in the age/grade level you teach. You can advertise by reading small sections or by putting notices about certain books on the bulletin board or bookrack.

4. Recommendations from peers or adults, more than anything else, cause students to read certain books. Provide opportunities for children to share their opinions about books they have read, in short oral reports (unrequired) or in a book hung from the wall with hook and loop materials. Students may write on a 3 × 5 card and put the card in the book, or they may want to illustrate some interesting scene in the book and include a short explanation.

5. George M. Usova (1979) suggests holding individual reading conferences about books students have read. Usova says,

Quite often the reluctant reader will become a discipline problem in the class in order to be rewarded by attention from the teacher. The attention received in the reading conference becomes a good substitute for the child. In addition, reading conferences (Stewart, 1971) have been shown to increase independent reading, improve reading skill achievement, and enhance favorable attitudes toward reading. (p. 259)

6. For students not used to reading for a sustained period of time or not used to reading through a complete book, provide only small booklets or books with short stories in them at first. Students get a sense of accomplishment from having read an entire book, regardless of size.

7. Creating interest centers can help enhance students' desire to read. These centers may focus on science, social studies, etc. or on any subtopic *within* these areas. For example, in science you can create an interest center on electricity, magnetism, weather reporting, etc. You may also create interest centers around any topic several students are interested in, as long as you have some books on the topic.

8. Book swaps work especially well. If your program does not normally provide for book swapping, then you may have your own from time to time. As mentioned earlier, there is something special about owning your own book.

9. Booklets containing comic strips often motivate students to begin reading. For example, save a number of "Hagar" strips (approximately 20), cut them out, and use rubber cement to fasten them to pages. Then form a whole booklet for students fascinated with "Hagar." Do the same with other comic strips, such as "Peanuts," etc.

Two recommended articles that list ways to motivate children to read are:

Johns, J. L., & Lunt, L. Motivating reading: Professional ideas. *Reading Teacher*, April, 1975, *28*, 617–19.

Roeder, H. H., & Lee, N. Twenty-five teacher-tested ways to encourage voluntary reading. *Reading Teacher*, October, 1973, *27*, 48–50.

The Effectiveness of Sustained Silent Reading Programs

There now exists a lot of research on the effectiveness of sustained silent reading programs. Most programs report a positive attitude on the part of students participating in the program. On the other hand, only a few report increased achievement on standardized achievement tests. A sampling of some research results follows.

Berglund and Johns reported on four studies that showed no measurable results, either positive or negative. However, these were short-term studies, and studies that do not continue for at least eight weeks cannot be expected to show positive results.

Berglund and Johns also reported on a study that showed students' attitudes about assigned reading, going to the school library, reading a book, and the importance of reading in general all improved. However, this same group did not show a statistically significant difference in achievement on standardized test scores over a control group.

Donald Pfau (1966) reported the results of a two-year study of such a program's influence. The experimental group was superior in sight-vocabulary knowledge and in fluency of written language. The experimental group also seemed more interested in reading, showed a greater proficiency in reading skills, and showed better language performance.

Eldon E. Ekwall (1969) found that students in a sustained silent reading program (grades 3 through 8) gained as much in reading vocabulary and comprehension as students the year before had with direct instruction in vocabulary and comprehension; also, many grade levels gained from one-third to two-thirds of a year in *addition* as a result of being in a sustained silent reading program. He also reported that every teacher in the program had a positive attitude about sustained silent reading. In this program, the average number of books read in each classroom was determined. Some examples follow:

1. A second-grade class of 24 pupils read a total of 3290 books during the year, an average of 137 books per pupil.
2. In a third-grade class of 32 pupils, the smallest number of books read was 180, and the greatest number read was 476. The average number of books read per pupil was 369.
3. A fourth-grade class of 21 pupils read 1286 books during the year. One student read only 11, while three others read 132 books each. The average was 61 books per pupil.

McCracken states,

We have reports from hundreds of classrooms with all sorts of pupil populations. We have testimonials from English teachers, machine shop teachers, teachers of the mentally retarded of all ages, teachers of young adults in federal penitentiaries, secondary school reading specialists, and teachers of academic subjects. They report unanimously that SSR works and that it worked almost instantaneously once it was initiated. (p. 583)

Mork says a fifth-grade teacher commented, "For the first time I can remember, pupils in my class are disappointed when they have to stop reading. They want to read and read and read. They are learning to finish whole books, many of them for the first time" (p. 441).

Richard M. Petre (1971) described one such program this way: "Students requested two things: more time for reading and an opportunity to discuss books with others who have read them. Eight hundred high school students read approximately 1000 paperbacks or hardbacks a week—excluding periodicals" (p. 194). And Richard Allington (1975) stated, "As a classroom teacher I found this idea tremendously successful in producing fluent readers" (p. 813).

Moore, Jones, and Miller reported the results of several studies. Most participants in a sustained silent reading program reported an improvement in reading attitude and the number of books read, but only some reported an improvement in reading vocabulary and comprehension. Those programs not extending over a long period (more than a few months) were usually the ones that failed to show an improvement in reading vocabulary and comprehension.

Sustained silent reading programs have been highly successful in improving students' attitudes toward reading. They also have been successful in winning the approval of teachers who have participated in them. On the other hand, in sustained silent reading programs, as with most other experimental programs, little positive change occurs in achievement, as measured by standardized reading achievement tests, unless the program has been in existence for two months or more.

SUMMARY

There are several acronyms for what is often referred to as sustained silent reading, and there are many reasons for having such programs in the public schools. Sustained silent reading programs can be operated several different ways, and the pros and cons of each type have been discussed. Some general rules have been given for operating such a program, and a step-by-step procedure for starting a sustained silent reading program has been presented. Ways to obtain materials and to motivate students are included. The differences between successful and unsuccessful programs have been discussed. Finally, research has been presented to show you what you can expect from students in a well-run sustained silent reading program.

REVIEW QUESTIONS

1. What do the following acronyms stand for: USSR, SSR, SQUIRT?
2. What is the significance of the word *sustained* in USSR or SSR?
3. Discuss the reasons most commonly given for having a sustained silent reading program.
4. What are some general rules for operating a sustained silent reading program?
5. Which of McCracken's rules should be bent somewhat? Why?
6. Discuss various ways to operate a sustained silent reading program.
7. Where can schools find the time for an all-school sustained silent reading period every day? Why can more time be taken from science and social studies classes?
8. What are the characteristics of successful sustained silent reading programs?
9. Based on what you have read in this chapter, is it better to have students bring their own materials to a sustained silent reading program, or is it better to have a classroom library?
10. Where can you obtain materials to begin a classroom library?
11. List the steps, in order, for beginning a sustained silent reading program.
12. What are some common problems encountered in starting a sustained silent reading program?
13. What does the research indicate about the effectiveness of free reading programs?

REFERENCES

Allington, R. L. Attention and application: The oft forgotten steps in teaching reading. *Journal of Learning Disabilities*, 1975, 210–13.

Allington, R. L. If they don't read much, how they ever gonna get good? *Journal of Reading*, October, 1977, *21*, 57–61.

Allington, R. L. Sustained approaches to reading and writing. *Language Arts*, September, 1975, *52*, 813–15.

Berglund, R. L., & Johns. J. L. A primer on uninterrupted sustained silent reading. *Reading Teacher*, February, 1983, *36*, 534–39.

Biemiller, A. Relationships between oral reading rates for letters, words, and simple text in the development of reading achievement. *Reading Research Quarterly*, 1977–78, *13* (2), 223–51.

Botel, M. A. *A comprehensive reading communication arts plan*. Harrisburg: Pennsylvania Department of Education, 1977.

Callaway, B. What turns children "on" or "off" in reading. *Reading Improvement*, Fall, 1981, *18*, 214–17.

Donelson, K. L. Free reading: Another view. *Journal of Reading*, April, 1969, *12*, 545–48, 606–11.

Ekwall, E. E. A free reading-culture program. *Reading Quarterly*, June, 1969, *2*, 7–11.

Gambrell, L. B. Getting started with sustained silent reading and keeping it going. *Reading Teacher*, December, 1978, *32*, 328–31.

Ganz, P., & Theofield, M. B. Suggestions for starting SSR. *Journal of Reading*, May, 1974, *17*, 614–16.

Heathington, B. S. What to do about reading motivation in the middle school. *Journal of Reading*, May, 1979, *22*, 709–13.

LeGrand-Brodsky, K. Hope for reading in America: Practically everyone reads. *Reading Teacher*, May, 1979, *32*, 947–49.

Long, B. H., & Henderson, E. H. Children's use of time: Some personal and social correlates. *Elementary School Journal*, January, 1973, *73*, 193–99.

McCracken, R. A. Initiating sustained silent reading. *Journal of Reading*, May, 1971, *14*, 521–24, 582–83.

McCracken, R. A., & McCracken, M. J. Modeling is the key to sustained silent reading. *Reading Teacher*, January, 1978, *31*, 406–08.

Minton, M. J. The effect of sustained silent reading upon comprehension and attitudes among ninth graders. *Journal of Reading*, March, 1980, *23*, 498–502.

Monteith, M. K. ERIC/RCS report: The magazine habit. *Language Arts*, December, 1981, *58*, 965–66.

Moore, J. C., Jones, C. J., & Miller, D. C. What we know after a decade of sustained silent reading. *Reading Teacher*, January, 1980, *33*, 445–49.

Mork, T. A. Sustained silent reading in the classroom. *Reading Teacher*, February, 1972, *25*, 438–41.

Petre, R. M. Reading breaks make it in Maryland. *Journal of Reading*, December, 1971, *15*, 191–94.

Pfau, D. W. *An investigation of the effects of planned recreational reading programs in first and second grade*. Unpublished doctoral dissertation, State University of New York at Buffalo, 1966.

Reading Today—A Membership Newsletter of the International Reading Association, August, 1982, 1.

Risser, B. Sustained silent reading: Here's how to begin! *Clearing House*, May, 1979, *52*, 438–40.

Stewart, D. *Individual conferences to promote independent reading*. A report on the field test. ERIC, November, 1971, 7–8.

Usova, G. M. Helping the reluctant reader: Principles and practices. *Reading Improvement*, Fall, 1979, *16*, 258–60.

12

Teaching Children with Special Needs

Reading researchers and teachers often focus on the methods and procedures used to teach children how to read. How nice it would be if reading instruction were merely a systematic set of teaching behaviors that, when applied to students, would result in successful learning for all of them. Of course, it does not work that way. Children are *individuals* with unique needs that the teacher must consider. To be a truly successful teacher of reading (or any other subject, for that matter), you must understand children's special needs and be able to alter your instruction to accommodate those needs. Problem readers, gifted learners, and children who speak either a nonstandard dialect of English or a language other than English all have special needs and all are frequently seen in elementary classrooms. Federal legislation defines the schools' responsibilities to handicapped students, another group with special needs. Mainstreaming uses an identification and planning process to include these students in the regular classroom.

EXCEPTIONAL CHILDREN

Paul C. Burns and Betty D. Roe (1980) define the *exceptional child* as

one whose development deviates from that of a normal child to such an extent that maximum benefit cannot be derived from a regular classroom experience without some additional or different curriculum features. The deviation may range from minimal to extreme and may occur in the areas of language, intelligence, hearing, vision, perception, health, and behavior. (p. 423)

Of course, all people are exceptional to some extent, but the term means children who require an adjusted curriculum. The discussion here does not include those children with special needs so great, such as profound or multiple emotional and physical handicaps, that they require a completely separate program.

Virtually every elementary school classroom includes some students with special needs. Teachers must accept this fact and not assume that a specialist should be responsible for educating such children. Because of space limitations, not all special needs can be addressed here.

However, the most common types of exceptional students are covered, and suggestions offered that should benefit all children in your classroom.

REVIEW OF THE RESEARCH

Children with special needs vary in many ways. For example, what research tells us about students who speak a nonstandard dialect may not apply to slow learners. However, most students with special needs share a common problem: their low achievement relative to their peers. Research has been conducted to explore how teacher expectations influence student achievement. Teacher expectations seem highly correlated with pupils' achievement, but research cannot prove a cause-effect relationship.

Thomas L. Good (1981) comprehensively reviewed the research on this correlation. Since educators assume that teachers' behavior influences the self-concepts, motivation, and aspirations of students, then levels of student achievement reflect the teacher's original assumptions or expectations about students' ability. Many investigators have explored this self-fulfilling prophecy. Good found that most studies focused on the following question: Do teachers treat high- and low-achieving students differently? In general, teachers do behave differently toward these two groups. Good reported that teachers' behavior varies specifically by:

1. Seating slow students farther from the teacher or in a group (making it harder to monitor low-achieving students or treat them as individuals).
2. Paying less attention to lows in academic situations (smiling less often and maintaining less eye contact).
3. Calling on lows less often to answer classroom questions or make public demonstrations.
4. Waiting less time for lows to answer questions.
5. Not staying with lows in failure situations (providing clues, asking follow-up questions).
6. Criticizing lows more frequently than highs for incorrect public responses.
7. Praising lows less frequently than highs after successful public responses.

8. Praising lows more frequently than highs for marginal or inadequate public responses.
9. Providing low-achieving students with less accurate and less detailed feedback than highs.
10. Failing to provide lows with feedback about their responses more frequently than highs.
11. Demanding less work and effort from lows than from highs.
12. Interrupting the performance of low achievers more frequently than that of high achievers. (p. 416)

Good pointed out that *all* teachers do not treat students differently. He also suggested that "sameness" toward high- and low-achievers is not necessarily desirable; after all, "teachers can err by treating students too alike or too differently" (p. 416). But teachers should examine the ways they behave toward successful and unsuccessful students and be sure they set appropriately high expectations for all. Children with special needs may require different amounts and types of attention, but teachers should not respond to exceptional children in ways that reinforce continued low achievement.

TEACHING THE PROBLEM READER

Many types of problem readers may appear in the elementary classroom. Attempts to categorize such students are difficult because many problem readers belong in more than one category and some do not fit neatly into *any* category. Nonetheless, teachers need to realize that students fail to read for different reasons. Table 12–1 shows five categories of problem readers.

The Slow Learner

The *slow learner* is a child with below average ability. Many slow learners achieve below their peers in reading and other academic subjects. Thus, teachers should be most concerned about slow learners when they fail to achieve at their *own* potential, not when they fail to read as well as more capable students. The category of slow learners generally does *not* include children with severe mental handicaps. Slow learners usually score in the 70 to 85 or 90 range on an IQ test.

(Scores of 90 to 110 indicate average ability.) Students who score below 70 are often assigned to special classes for the mentally handicapped.

However, you should not put too much faith in students' IQs. Research by Merle B. Karnes and others (1970) found that educational intervention at home by mothers of disadvantaged infants led to significantly superior intelligence test scores for the children involved. In other words, IQ is not a permanently fixed characteristic for most children. Even more important, a particular IQ score reported to you may be inaccurate because of clerical error, improper test administration or scoring, atypical performance by the child, or other reasons. Since teacher expectations have a profound effect on the children they teach, they should not put too much stock in a potentially inaccurate or misleading IQ score. Such data should not be ignored, but IQ is only one of many factors you should use to evaluate your students' academic potential.

Most slow learners can learn to read if they receive appropriate instruction. Unfortunately, these children often suffer emotionally because parents, teachers, or peers expect either too much or too little of them academically. The percentage of slow learners in a particular school or classroom varies according to the definition employed and the school community. But 15 percent is not unusual. Certainly it would be unusual for you to teach a class without any slow learners.

The Reluctant Reader

Dechant defines the *reluctant reader* as a child who *can* read but chooses not to. Dealing with reluctant readers means changing their attitudes toward reading. Often these children receive very little stimulation or incentive to read at home. Sometimes they have tuned out reading because of a school's inappropriate instructional practices. Whatever the cause, the teacher is in an ideal position to motivate reluctant readers.

Most teachers find that their classrooms contain a few students who read every chance they

Table 12–1 Characteristics of various poor readers

Slow Learner	Reluctant Reader	Disadvantaged Reader	Disabled Reader	Underachiever
Ability level is below 90 IQ.	Can read but will not.	Potential often far exceeds performance.	Is usually of average or above average intelligence, although a disabled reader could also be a slow learner.	Ability level is substantially above average.
Generally reads on ability level.	The root of the reading difficulties is the mental attitude of the pupil.	Generally can learn and wants to learn.	Does not read on ability level.	Generally reads at or above grade level.
Generally reads below grade level; in terms of the requisites for success the pupil cannot achieve at his or her chronological grade level.	Solution to the reading problem must begin with a change of attitude.	The major deficiencies are language- and experience-related.	May or may not be reading below grade level.	Reads substantially below ability level.
Instruction needs to be adapted to the pupil's limited ability; the pace of instruction and teacher expectations must be realistic.		Often is deficient in auditory attention. Needs to learn how to learn.	May show blocks to learning, especially emotional or neurological, which keep the pupil from learning to read.	

Note. From *Improving the Teaching of Reading*, 3rd ed., by E.V. Dechant (Englewood Cliffs, N.J.: Prentice-Hall, 1982). 432. Copyright © 1982 by Prentice-Hall, Inc. Reprinted by permission.

Children with learning difficulties may need the special help of a resource specialist teacher.

get, even rereading books over and over if new titles are unavailable. The reluctant reader is just the opposite, showing little interest in reading, even about subjects otherwise exciting to him. Sustained silent reading procedures, if followed faithfully, should decrease the number of reluctant readers in your classroom.

The Disadvantaged Reader

The *disadvantaged reader* is a child who often achieves below her potential because of language- and experience-related deficiencies. For example, many disadvantaged readers speak a nonstandard dialect or a language other than English. Also, children who live in conditions of economic poverty are often considered disadvantaged. However, remember that some children from impoverished backgrounds are academically gifted. A child is not a disadvantaged reader unless environmental conditions contribute in some way to the reading failure. Of course, a disadvantaged reader can also be a slow learner or a reluctant reader; remember, these categories are somewhat arbitrary and may overlap.

The Disabled Reader

Disabled readers read below their ability level. Often the term describes apparently capable children with serious reading difficulties. Reading disability may be caused by a variety of physical, psychological, socioeconomic, and educational factors that seem to combine to deter normal reading development.[1] Reading professionals have a limited ability to precisely identify the causes of an individual's reading disability. This limitation may not be important, though, since the identification of causes does not necessarily lead to a blueprint for solutions.

With appropriate training and experience, you can learn to diagnose and remediate the difficulties exhibited by many disabled readers in a regular classroom. The more severe cases may require special assistance from a reading specialist in small groups or a clinical setting.

Some disabled readers seem to make little progress even when they receive a lot of help.

---

[1] For a more thorough discussion of the causes of reading failure, see Chapter 1 in *Diagnosis and Remediation of the Disabled Reader*, 2nd ed., by E. E. Ekwall and J. L. Shanker (Boston: Allyn and Bacon, 1983).

These students are particularly challenging and frustrating, for often there is no apparent reason why they cannot learn successfully. Such children are often called *learning disabled*. The terms **learning disability** and *specific learning disability* are frequently used, but unfortunately, no commonly accepted definitions exist for them.

In 1968, the National Advisory Committee on Handicapped Children presented a definition of learning disabilities to Congress, which became part of the landmark federal legislation of 1975 that addressed the educational rights of the handicapped. The committee's definition is:

Children with special learning disabilities exhibit a disorder in one or more of the basic psychological processes involved in understanding or in using spoken or written languages. These may be manifested in disorders of listening, thinking, talking, reading, writing, spelling, or arithmetic. They include conditions which have been referred to as perceptual handicaps, brain injury, minimal brain dysfunction, dyslexia, developmental aphasia, and so on. They do not include learning problems which are due primarily to visual, hearing, or motor handicaps, to mental retardation, emotional disturbance, or environmental disadvantages. (P.L. 94–142, 1975, p. 142)

This definition is not very precise or specific; but even as broad as it is, some experts disagree with parts of it. Some believe, for example, that emotional difficulties and environmental factors should be included in a definition of learning disabilities.

Whether educators use the term *learning disabilities* or the equally imprecise term *dyslexia*—which to most people suggest a neurological dysfunction, possibly inherited—the labeling may lead to several serious problems for the teacher:

1. You may be less willing to help seriously disabled readers if you believe they suffer from a disease for which you have no cure;
2. You may believe that traditional, sound instructional procedures are inappropriate for these children, when in fact, they may represent the best hope;
3. You may feel that only a specialist can provide the assistance required;

4. You may have inappropriately low expectations for these children that then become a self-fulfilling prophecy, leading to continued failure;
5. The children themselves—once they know they are labeled as dyslexic or learning disabled—may feel like freaks, resulting in lowered self-concepts, less effort, and continued poor performance; and
6. Rather than facilitating communication among educators and parents, the labels may actually inhibit understanding since the parties may not agree on the definitions of the terms.

Perhaps educators would be better off to acknowledge that a few children fail to learn to read, and we simply don't know why. Then, teachers could concentrate their efforts on teaching children as *individuals.* Their instruction would reflect their assessment of each child's unique strengths and weaknesses, and they would spend less energy in identifying and placing so-called learning disabled students.

Directors of separate reading clinics for more than ten years, Ekwall and Shanker have supervised the instruction of hundreds of severely disabled readers. Many dramatically improved in a short time. Others made gradual, steady progress in reading. A few grew only marginally. But *every* child improved. Many students, whom others had written off as hopelessly dyslexic or unable to learn to read due to "minimal brain dysfunction," learned effectively once their instruction was properly tailored to their needs.

The improvement possible in a clinical situation cannot be duplicated in a public school setting because it is not realistic to expect the classroom teacher or the reading specialist to provide a great deal of individual attention to severely disabled readers. Teachers should realize, however, that the deficiency is usually not so much in the student as in the institution's inability to adapt instruction as needed.

Although no clear definition of learning disability exists, it helps teachers to know some of the symptoms associated with a *severe* reading disability. These symptoms often appear in clusters.[2] Note that normal readers may also exhibit these symptoms to some extent.

1. *Reversals of letters or words.* In the case of letters, the student may reverse *b*'s and *d*'s, *p*'s and *q*'s, or less commonly, *n*'s and *u*'s, thus making *bad* read *dab* or *baby* read *dady*; in the case of words, parts of words may be reversed as in *ant* to *nat*, or entire words may be reversed as in *saw* to *was* or *on* to *no*.

2. *Short or erratic memory for words.* Words that a normal reader would learn in teaching-learning situations may require many more exposures for the disabled reader. Also, a word can be remembered and spoken correctly one time and not recognized the next time. This failure to recognize may occur within a period of minutes.

3. *Oral rereading not improved following silent reading or a first oral reading.*

4. *Inability to hold information in memory until needed.* Memory problems are exhibited in the use of context clues; that is, the student cannot remember what has been read and so cannot derive a new word from context. Problems are also exhibited in use of phonics or structural analysis for word attack. In sounding a word with three phonemes the student may forget the first one or two by the time the third appears.

5. *Difficulty with concentration.* Some students simply cannot attend to a paragraph or story as it is being read or cannot listen for periods beyond half a minute. This problem becomes apparent when dealing with abstract relationships such as sound-symbol correspondence. Students with subtle difficulty in concentrating may not have obvious hyperactivity or other behavior problems.

6. *Inability to see whole relationships or form a gestalt.* This difficulty is illustrated by the phonetic speller who is unable to form a mental image of a word. Also, words are often spelled exactly as they sound, e.g., *liks* for *likes* or *hav* for *have.*

7. *Emotional instability.* Most students become irritated when they fail to experience some success. Students with severe reading disability, however, have a tendency to become extremely irritable on

meeting a task at which they are not immediately successful. Their moods may also change rapidly.

8. *Impulsiveness.* This problem is illustrated by the student who guesses at words rather than working them out using word attack skills. Impulsiveness is best demonstrated when pictures are represented on a page. The student may say *bunny* for *rabbit* when the word *rabbit* is accompanied by an illustration of a rabbit.

9. *Poor eye-motor coordination.* This problem can be measured using tests. It can also be noted by observing the student write or engage in motor activities such as cutting with scissors or coloring. Tests have the advantage of providing scoring criteria or norms from which to judge the student's performance. However, the eye of an experienced teacher may be just as capable in identifying eye-motor coordination problems.

10. *Difficulty with sequencing.* This problem arises in poor spelling but may be more common in reading when the student has difficulty remembering the specific order of words in a sentence, events in a paragraph, days in a week, or months in a year.

11. *Inability to work rapidly.* This problem arises in reading assignments but is equally common in written work. The student is always behind the pace set by others and gets irritable if rushed. There is also a tendency to perseverate, or dwell on a particular point for an extra long time.

12. *Omissions of words and phrases.* It should be emphasized that many students omit an occasional word, but some severely disabled readers consistently omit words, especially unknown words. There is also a tendency to skip whole phrases or lines and to constantly lose place.

13. *Directional confusion.* This may show up, as mentioned before, in lack of ability to distinguish *b* and *d*, and so forth. Confusion can extend, however, to inability to distinguish left and right, front and back, before and after.

14. *Poor auditory discrimination.* This condition may be present even when the student's auditory acuity is excellent. Again, many students have difficulty with auditory discrimination, but the severely disabled reader has trouble learning minute differences in words such as *pen* and *pin* or even *him* and *hen.* Disabled readers are also erratic in their ability to discriminate sounds.

15. *Hyperactivity.* The hyperactive student frequently has a short attention span and is wiggling and

[2]From *Diagnosis and Remediation of the Disabled Reader*, 2nd ed., by. E. E. Ekwall and J.L. Shanker (Boston: Allyn and Bacon, 1983), 317–19. Copyright 1983 by Allyn and Bacon, Inc. Reprinted by permission.

squirming, tapping fingers, etc. These signs are more apparent when the student is under stress, such as when completing an assignment.

16. *Poor syntax, stuttering, and halting speech.* The student who exhibits speech problems seems to need to think ahead when talking; that is, words do not flow smoothly, or when they do the order of the words is illogical.

17. *Achievement in arithmetic considerably higher than in reading and spelling.* Perhaps there is a physiological explanation for this. Some people who have suffered strokes have been left unable to read but still able to solve difficult math problems.

Following the discussion of the underachiever, many suggestions for teaching problem readers in the regular classroom will be presented. Many of these specific procedures benefit severely disabled readers.

The Underachiever

As shown earlier in Table 12–1, the underachiever does not lack ability. Rather, this student tends to perform well below his ability level even if the achievement is on grade level. Quite often the underachiever is a gifted student but a reluctant reader. Usually, as with reluctant readers, the

Children with special needs often require individual attention.

underachiever needs to alter her attitude toward reading and school.

In the section on gifted students, the specific suggestions may be appropriate for working with underachievers.

Suggestions for Working with Problem Readers

Because neither research nor experience has identified a specific set of procedures to use with all problem readers, no such procedures will be prescribed here. Instead, general and specific suggestions that have proved successful with most teachers when used judiciously are presented. Most of these suggestions apply to slow learners or disabled readers. Some also apply to reluctant readers, disadvantaged readers, and underachievers. When considering any suggestion, however, be most concerned about its appropriateness for the student in question, regardless of the problem's label.

General Suggestions.   In working with problem readers, try the following general approaches.

Build a Good Relationship

Take time to build a positive, accepting, encouraging, and trusting relationship with the student. Many problem readers have given up on themselves and may initially put forth more effort to please you than to help themselves. The more the student believes in and trusts you and your ability to help, the more the student tries to produce.

Encourage Follow-through

Have the student follow through on your instruction. Students with reading problems simply do not improve without considerable reading practice. Most of this practice must take place when you are not present. The more responsibility the student takes, the greater the progress. The degree of commitment obviously varies according to the student's age and the nature of the problem.

Involve the Family

Involve the student's parents and family

members in treating the problem. If you do not discuss the student's problem with his parents, you may lose the opportunity to acquire valuable insights about the student. In addition, parents and siblings can often help to reinforce learning or to create a proper study environment. Parents, however, should *not* actually teach reading skills to their children. Such a practice often does more harm than good for everyone concerned.

Provide Success

Provide the student with as much success as possible. For most students, there is simply no substitute for success. In addition to giving the student verbal praise when she succeeds, you can provide visual evidence of the student's improvement with graphs and charts. If possible, tape record the student when she reads on several occasions. Then replay the tape and let the student actually hear her improvement.

Individualize Instruction

Provide instruction that is as individualized as possible. It is not realistic for most teachers to individualize reading instruction for each child. However, for the problem reader, some degree of individualization is essential. Try to adjust instruction and assignments, but also give the problem reader some individual time, if only a few minutes a day. Ability to individualize increases as experience grows.

Choose Proper Materials

It is crucial to match problem readers with appropriate reading materials. Of course, difficulty level must be considered; the student should be reading materials that are neither too easy nor too hard. But interest level and subject matter are also important for problem readers. Highly motivating selections can be especially effective with some reluctant readers, disadvantaged readers, and underachievers. Materials for teaching skills must also be chosen carefully: are the skills presented in a logical, systematic fashion and is the program properly balanced? Most important, do *not* merely assign paper and pencil tasks or busywork to these students.

Specific Suggestions. These more specific suggestions incorporate principles of instruction that have proven effective with most problem readers.

1. Introduce new skills slowly, allowing for small increments of learning.
2. Review materials and skills previously learned as often as needed to make responses automatic.
3. Introduce materials in various ways. Use a multisensory approach to instruction whenever possible.
4. Instruction usually should be highly structured, with clear expectations for the student's performance and carefully planned lessons.
5. Use short periods of instruction, with the learning paced to accommodate the student's ability to acquire new information or skills.
6. Using a variety of audiovisual aids often proves effective.
7. Be sure that directions are clear and limited. For example, divide a three-part assignment into three separate segments and provide directions for each segment separately.
8. Provide reasonable short-range goals. If assignments take too long, the student may not be able to persist.
9. Allow the student time to respond to questions. Research shows that most teachers wait as little as one-half second for responses. If you wait five or even ten seconds, problem readers may respond more often and thoughtfully.
10. Experts sometimes recommend that teachers orally present material to students with reading difficulties. Unfortunately, this approach reinforces the problem rather than solves it. When possible, adjust the material's difficulty, provide additional help with the reading, or allow the student more time to complete the assignment.
11. Do not constantly change the approaches you use. A profusion of unrelated meth-

ods seldom proves effective. Also, a method must sometimes be used over time to achieve the desired effect. On the other hand, be flexible; do not remain permanently wedded to techniques that continue to fail.

12. Encourage the student to use crutches for a while, if needed. Some students need to use a finger, pencil, or marker (such as a ruler or piece of paper) to keep their place when reading. Although students may not actually need these devices, they do provide temporary security. Over time, aids that impede reading performance can be gradually eliminated.

TEACHING THE GIFTED STUDENT

Although it might seem as though gifted students could be readily identified, sometimes such students conceal their giftedness under poor attitudes. Also, it can be more difficult to teach the gifted than one might assume. The curriculum is often geared to the average student, gifted children may have behavioral problems because they are bored, etc. However, many ways exist to help a teacher lessen these problems and challenge gifted children.

Characteristics of Gifted Children

The term *gifted student* often refers to students of superior mental ability. Other terms used include: academically talented, bright, able, and intellectually gifted. In the past, these students were identified by administering intelligence tests. Usually an IQ of 130 or higher determined giftedness. Approximately 3 percent of the population falls into this category. Currently, assessment methods are much broader and are often established at the local level. Many students with superior abilities or creative talents are now included among the gifted, even if they do not score among the highest on an IQ test. Thus, **gifted students** possess some combination of the following attributes: (1) superior intellectual

ability; (2) academic aptitude; (3) creative thinking ability; (4) special ability in the creative arts; and (5) leadership ability. Some experts also include students with exceptional psychomotor ability, outstanding athletes, among the gifted.

When teachers or parents refer to a child as gifted, they usually mean a student with superior intellectual or academic ability. Usually, the special abilities these children have appear at an early age. They often begin speaking before age one and soon develop impressive vocabularies. They often can read before they enter school, having apparently taught themselves or picked up the skills from observing others. If gifted students have not learned to read before kindergarten, they usually progress quickly in kindergarten or first grade, unless discouraged or prevented from reading.

According to Dorothy A. Sisk (1977), a noted authority on giftedness, gifted students often possess the following characteristics:

1. Early use of advanced vocabulary;
2. Keen observation and curiosity;
3. Retention of a variety of information;
4. Periods of intense concentration;
5. Ability to understand complex concepts, perceive relationships, and think abstractly;
6. A broad and changing spectrum of interests; and
7. Strong critical thinking skills and self-criticism.

Problems in Teaching Gifted Students

Giftedness is often a mixed blessing. Many gifted children suffer from social and emotional problems. Because they are different from other children, misunderstanding and unrealistic expectations may result. Adults easily impressed by their talents and sophisticated thinking may forget that the gifted are *children,* not small adults. Gifted students often respond emotionally the way their peers do, rather than as adults expect. Also, many gifted students have social problems. Often without intending to, gifted students show up, threaten, or challenge their peers. In addition, many gifted youngsters are self-critical and perfectionistic in their behavior.

Most teachers find it difficult to accommodate gifted students' needs. Curricula in the schools (as in this book) emphasize instruction for the average or slower child. Thus, many gifted students are neglected or forced to follow the same lock-step curriculum presented to other children, which often leads to boredom, frustration, restlessness, and ultimately, discipline problems.

Sometimes teachers recognize that a child is gifted, but adjust by providing more of the same rather than something different. This misguided response often causes more problems than it solves. For example, many teachers give *extra* workbook assignments to gifted students while placing them in a basal reader that presents no challenge or interest. They may assume that bright students who think quickly also work quickly, but many gifted students actually complete paper and pencil tasks slowly. Thus, the teacher who piles on extra work may unintentionally punish the gifted child.

In this situation, the student may be better off reading independently during basal lessons, assuming that some bright students cannot be grouped. However, it is sometimes a mistake to single out gifted children. Like other children, they may prefer being in a group, even if it is not challenging. Simply *ask* a child what he prefers in such a situation. If the child wants to participate in a reading group, assign him to the highest one and provide more challenging and appropriate assignments for seatwork and independent activities.

As noted earlier, many gifted children learn to read before kindergarten. Invariably highly skilled sight readers, they may or may not know all the phonics rules. Because these rules are guides for children who *need* them, already fluent decoders should be spared countless lessons and worksheets on phonics. Alas, exactly the opposite often occurs.

Using gifted students extensively as tutors can hinder their progress. Although gifted children may enjoy this role and possess the skills to play it effectively, too much time spent helping others may prevent gifted children from pursuing their own learning and may lead to negative social consequences.

The teacher should, therefore, adjust the instructional program to stimulate and challenge the gifted child without harming either the intellectual or emotional needs of that child. Inappropriate practices, such as those described, have turned many gifted students into underachievers or reluctant readers.

Suggestions for Teaching Gifted Students

John Hoback and Phyllis Perry (1980) suggest that teachers of gifted students should themselves possess several special attributes, which include:

1. Skill in identification of giftedness in students;
2. Flexibility and tolerance for the unexpected;
3. Secure and unthreatened personality;
4. Intellectual acumen;
5. Mature judgment and leadership in handling groups; and
6. Imagination and creativity.

Indeed, these attributes are ones that all teachers should strive to possess.

Hoback and Perry also suggest modifying school organization to best serve gifted students. Effective gifted programs allow flexibility in time and subject matter and an opportunity to explore learning beyond classroom walls. In addition, schools need to provide opportunities for gifted pupils to interact with each other and to draw upon a wealth of instructional resources, such as extensive libraries and well-supplied laboratories.

Martha Dallman and others (1982) describe three general plans for meeting gifted students' needs: (1) *enrichment*; (2) *acceleration*; and (3) *special grouping*. *Enrichment* plans include special activities for the gifted within the regular classroom. These activities are usually challenging, more complex, and somewhat open-ended. *Acceleration* refers to earlier admittance to school or double promotion once students have begun school. Naturally, teachers and parents are concerned about the possible adverse effects of acceleration on gifted pupils' self-esteem. However, research shows that in general, this is not a problem. Schools may provide *special classes* for gifted students for either all or part of the day. Most experts think an ideal program for gifted children includes both enrichment in the classroom and special grouping part of the time.

Other possible programs for the gifted include: (1) *advanced placement*—generally for high school students so that they can attend college courses before they graduate from high school (a form of acceleration); (2) *resource rooms* with materials for independent exploration or study (such rooms may be staffed by specialist teachers or volunteers); and (3) *mentor programs* that match gifted pupils with community professionals or other resource people.

Suggestions for helping gifted students develop their reading and language skills follow. Remember, many can also benefit underachieving students and reluctant readers, even if they are not identified as gifted. Teachers can incorporate most of these ideas into a regular classroom enrichment program.

1. Provide enough time and opportunity for students to read widely in school.
2. Arrange for students to have open access to the school library.
3. Be sure your classroom contains as many books, magazines, newspapers, and other reading materials as you can accumulate.
4. Encourage students to read a variety of literary forms, both fiction and nonfiction.
5. Offer a variety of methods or media for students to use when reporting on books read.
6. Encourage students to read all the books or articles written by a favorite author.
7. Teach students how to do library research and other study skills.
8. Suggest interesting research projects for students to pursue on their own or in pairs or small groups.

9. Provide topics or ideas for creative projects, such as art or drama activities.
10. Offer direct instruction on higher-level comprehension skills.
11. Provide frequent, challenging vocabulary-building activities. (Many books are available to help you.)
12. Supply students with brain teasers, puzzles, mysteries, etc.
13. Adjust the basal reader program as needed for gifted students. Do not require busywork on previously mastered skills.
14. Ask gifted students to occasionally tutor other students or to read stories to younger children. Encourage them to plan carefully for their instructional responsibilities.
15. Provide many opportunities for writing, such as:
    (a) keeping a journal or diary;
    (b) writing plays;
    (c) corresponding with a pen pal;
    (d) writing poetry;
    (e) preparing annotated bibliographies of favorite books for fellow students; and
    (f) preparing a newspaper or literary magazine with fellow students.
16. Form small groups of gifted students for special purposes, such as:
    (a) discussing novels or other materials read by all group members;
    (b) planning of special reading-language activities for the class; and
    (c) preparing their own bulletin board.

Although such stimulating enrichment activities can and should be part of any classroom, working with gifted children does require special effort. As Albert J. Harris and Edward R. Sipay (1979) point out,

Mentally superior children are our nation's most precious natural resource. They are usually curious and interested in learning, if the school does not blunt this interest by stressing conformity and repetitive drill. The best policy with such children is to make the finest books available and accessible to them, and to assist them in making as much progress as possible. (p. 491)

TEACHING THE STUDENT WHO SPEAKS A DIFFERENT DIALECT

Spoken languages have many regional and social variations known as *dialects.* Dialects vary from each other in at least three ways: (1) *phonologically*, or in the way pronunciation of the same words varies; (2) *lexically*, or in the way vocabulary varies; and (3) *grammatically*, or in the way sentence construction varies.

Dialects are often related to geographical location, specific groups, or communities. However, speakers of different dialects can usually understand each other because they speak the same language. The variations *within* that language do not prevent communication. Furthermore, many people can speak more than one dialect and can switch dialects under the appropriate circumstances.

Standard English (SE) is the form of English most commonly spoken by well-educated members of the society. For example, newscasters in various parts of the country speak standard English.

The most common form of nonstandard English, and the dialect most often associated with reading problems, is ***black English*** (BE). Actually, speakers of black English have several different regional dialects. Also, not all blacks speak black English, and some whites, particularly those who live in close proximity to blacks, speak black English.

The major differences between SE and BE are phonological and grammatical. A few lexical differences exist, such as *kin* for *family*, but they are minor. Examples of some phonological and grammatical differences between SE and BE follow.

Phonological Feature	SE	BE
Omission of /r/ and /l/ in some words	yard	yod
	store	stow
	help	hep
Change of initial /th/ to /d/	then	den

Grammatical Feature	SE	BE
Linking verb	He is going.	He goin'.
Verb agreement	He has a car.	He have a car.
Plural marker	She has five cents.	She got five cent.

Many other differences between SE and BE exist, but remember, the similarities between BE and SE far outnumber the differences.

Scholars disagree about the quality and usefulness of nonstandard dialects like black English. Two main theories explain how nonstandard dialects differ from standard English, the deficit theory and the difference theory.

In the early to mid-60s the deficit view suggested that nonstandard dialects resulted from inadequate physical and social environments. These dialects were deficient and prevented speakers from fully developing their linguistic abilities.

From the mid-60s on, the difference position became generally accepted. The difference model views nonstandard English (especially black English) as different but equal. Sociolinguists espousing the difference view claim that the deficit position is linguistically unsound and reflects distorted cultural values. These experts demonstrate that black English is a systematic, fully developed linguistic system.

However, some people still have misconceptions about speakers of black English, misconceptions that teachers should guard against having. Robert C. Aukerman and Louise R. Aukerman (1981) list and rebut the following ten false beliefs about speakers of black English:

1. *They make errors as they speak and read English.* As noted above, many so-called errors are actually distinctive, regular features of black English. Teachers must learn to distinguish between reading errors that are a function of dialect and those that are a function of poor decoding.

2. *Black English is inferior.* From a linguistic point of view, black English is neither inferior nor superior. It is merely different. However, certain dialects clearly carry more social status than others.

3. *Children who read standard English with black English translations are guilty of miscues.* Teachers need to evaluate the quality of miscues. Dialect rendering may, in fact, reflect high-level comprehension.

4. *Black children are nonverbal.* There is no evidence to support this statement.

5. *Speakers of black English are lip-lazy.* There is no evidence to support this statement.

6. *Black English is merely simplified standard English.* Though some features of black English dialect simplify standard English forms, BE is more than merely a simplified form of SE.

7. *Speakers of black English have something wrong with their hearing.* There is no evidence to support this statement.

8. *All blacks speak black English.* This is not true.

9. *Black English causes reading failure in massive proportions in inner-city schools.* The evidence suggests this is not the case.

10. *Black English should be replaced with standard English.* As Aukerman and Aukerman point out, efforts to do so have consistently failed. Furthermore, "a child's home and environmental language is never replaced, but a second language should be learned for survival and achievement in 'outside' situations, such as in the schoolroom and in the larger mainstream society" (p. 453).

The Effect of Black English on Reading Ability

A greater percentage of black children than white children fail to learn to read. And most failing black students speak black English. However, this correlation should not be confused with a cause-effect relationship. In the late 60s and early 70s, many sociolinguists did just that. These investigators suggested that the mismatch between the black child's spoken language and beginning materials' written language was a major cause of reading failure among black children. This belief became known as the *dialect interference theory.* However, this theory was not the product of sound research.

Several investigators have discredited the dialect interference theory. When Judith J. Schwartz (1982) reviewed ten studies on the relationship between black English and reading achievement she found several serious methodological flaws. Schwartz stated: "The proposition that dialect has a measurable effect on reading achievement has never been demonstrated, although it is a popular belief" (p. 441). Richard Rystrom (1970) and Bonnie Lass (1980) drew similar conclusions.

Proponents of the dialect interference theory claim that black children perform better on listening tasks when teachers present materials in black English instead of in standard English (Joan Baratz, 1969). However, Rose M. Branisel (1977) found that black kindergarten children comprehended stories written in SE better than they did stories in BE. Margaret A. Cagney (1977) found the same true of black first graders.

Apparently, the key to both listening and reading comprehension is receptive linguistic ability. Black-English-speaking children can usually understand standard English very well, even if they cannot speak or write standard English.

Rystrom (1972) summarized the evidence on the effect of black English on reading ability in an address to the National Council of Teachers of English:

There is virtually no evidence to indicate that dialect is causally related to reading failures. . . . Any regional or social dialect is, so far as has been determined, an equally effective vehicle for learning to read as any other regional or social dialect.

Approaches to Teaching Reading to Black-English Speakers

At least six different approaches have been tried for teaching black-English-speaking children to read. Proponents of each approach believe that their method reduces the rate of illiteracy among black children. However, most of the approaches assume that the second dialect somehow interferes with the acquisition of reading ability.

The first approach uses materials written in black English. Although such dialect-specific materials have not been commercially developed, some experimental materials have been produced. Proponents assume that using dialect-specific readers for initial reading instruction helps children learn to read by avoiding dialect interference. But virtually no research supports this approach. In addition, there are practical difficulties in developing these materials, and research shows that black parents and black teachers often disapprove of these materials.

A second approach is called dialect neutralization, which requires texts that use only neutral language. The text minimizes the discrepancies between the child's oral language and standard English. But most experts agree that this approach is either too artificial or too impractical to be considered seriously.

A third approach has teachers teach black-English-speaking children to speak standard English before teaching them reading. This approach also assumes that dialect-interference exists. Although it seems logical, developing oral language skill in standard English through formal instruction has little evidence to support it. Unsuccessful attempts to use this approach were reported by Rystrom (1970 and 1968), who conducted research with urban blacks in California and rural blacks in Georgia, and Victor Rentel and John Kennedy (1972), who used this approach without success with rural Appalachian white children. Dorothy Strickland (1972) reported on a special literature program developed to aid black-English-speaking kindergarten children that succeeded. But Strickland used the concept of language expansion (broadening one's language stock), not language substitution (the subjugation of one dialect to another). This research suggests that factors other than standard English facility may contribute to reading gains.

A fourth approach uses culturally relevant materials written in standard English. Proponents assume dialect is not the culprit but inappropriate or unmotivating story content is. Contemporary basal readers usually do present stories that appeal to various ethnic groups. In addition, several supplementary series are designed to appeal to certain ethnic groups. To a large extent,

then, teachers now use this approach with most black-English-speaking children.

Fifth, some teachers use the language experience approach for beginning reading. Proponents think it is particularly well-suited for the black-English-speaking student. By drawing on the language and experience of the child, the approach eliminates dialect mismatch and keeps motivation and interest high. Existing evidence, however, does not show that the language experience approach is clearly superior to other beginning reading approaches.

The sixth approach uses existing materials, but allows black-English speakers to read in their own dialect. Dialect rendering suggests it is appropriate for the black-English speaker to read a sentence in black English even if it is written in standard English. For instance, the child might read, "Have they gone there?" as "Is they gone there?" As long as no meaning is lost, experts say dialect rendering is acceptable. Indeed, such rendering is a sophisticated linguistic process: the child reads the material in standard English and then translates it into black English where appropriate.

The key to using dialect rendering is the teacher's knowledge of the dialect and attitude toward the child. If the teacher cannot distinguish between reading miscues resulting from dialect rendering and those from inadequate decoding, then the teacher may unfairly but unknowingly misdiagnose decoding problems. Such misdiagnosis may lead to inappropriate directions to the student, improper placement, and confusion and failure for the child. Thus, teachers of nonstandard-dialect-speaking children *must* become familiar enough with that dialect to distinguish reading miscues that result in meaning loss from those that do not.

Patricia Cunningham (1976–77) examined the correcting behavior of graduate students enrolled in reading courses at four universities in different geographic areas. Cunningham found that the students corrected significantly more black-dialect-specific miscues (78 percent) than non-dialect-specific miscues (27 percent). Cunningham attributed the inappropriate evaluations to ignorance rather than racism and recommended that potential teachers receive more instruction about black dialect. Larry Ditto (1974) found that teachers who received such training perceived fewer dialect-related responses as reading errors than those who did not receive such instruction.

In summary, using dialect-specific materials, dialect neutralization, or instruction in standard English before reading instruction have little to recommend them. Using culturally relevant materials written in standard English and language experience activities for beginning readers are sensible, appropriate approaches to combine with a belief that dialect rendering is acceptable when there is no meaning loss. Teachers should know about the nonstandard dialects spoken by their students and understand the culture from which the dialect comes. Teachers must always be sensitive to their students' self-concepts and recognize the damage that may result when children believe their home language is inferior.

TEACHING THE NON-ENGLISH-SPEAKING STUDENT

As an elementary school teacher, you will probably teach children who are not fluent English speakers. If you teach in certain areas of the country, a majority of your students may be speakers of a native language other than English. Large numbers of people speak Spanish instead of English, particularly in the Southwest and some large cities throughout the United States. Many families speak Chinese, either Mandarin or Cantonese, in San Francisco, Oakland, Los Angeles, and New York. In addition, languages such as Korean, Tagalog, Vietnamese, Samoan, Portuguese, various American Indian languages, and many others are spoken by students in many parts of the United States. John D. McNeil, Lisbeth Donant, and Marvin C. Alkin (1980) point out that public schools in the city of Los Angeles, for example, must serve students who speak 82 different languages. Similar challenges face teachers in other large cities and in many smaller cities and towns. Given the number of immi-

grants entering the United States, the need to teach non-English speakers how to read English will continue. Furthermore, the regular classroom teacher will probably continue to be responsible for providing this instruction, whether he possesses special training or not.

Although *bilingual* often refers to students who speak a language other than English, it should be reserved for students who are fluent in *two* languages, such as Spanish and English. Bilingual students are by no means disadvantaged. Rather, the student who speaks or reads a *second* language but cannot speak or read English has special needs. The non-English speaker faces a different problem from that faced by the nonstandard-dialect speaker. The speaker of a second dialect understands spoken standard English and need only learn how to read it. The non-English speaker, in contrast, usually does not understand spoken English and therefore lacks a primary foundation for reading comprehension.

Whereas dialect interference need not impede reading ability, second *language* interference can make learning to read difficult. For example, many phonological and grammatical variations exist between Spanish and English. Some English vowel and consonant sounds are not pronounced in Spanish, including short *i* and short *a*, as well as the consonant sounds /j/ and /sh/. Spanish omits the plural marker (*two book* instead of *two books*) and uses negatives differently (*He no go away* instead of *He will not go away*). A complete summary of variations in English and Spanish can be found in Doris C. Ching (1976) or Albert J. Harris and Edward R. Sipay (1979). Ching also lists variations between English and Cantonese.

Harris and Sipay point out that native Spanish speakers may have difficulty pronouncing some English words; however, the teacher should not emphasize proper pronunciation during reading. As long as the reader understands what she reads, precise pronunciation is not required. Too great an emphasis on pronunciation may have a negative effect on the child's self-concept.

Approaches to Teaching Reading to Non-English Speakers

Three main approaches, with variations, have been used to teach English reading to non-English-speaking children. Controversy exists about which approach is most appropriate for which children. Unfortunately, educational research has not yet provided data to resolve the controversy. Each approach has its advocates, and the method used in each school may reflect the biases or politics of the decision-makers or practitioners in that area.

Melting Pot.   Frank May (1982) calls it the *melting pot approach.* (Others call it the do-nothing approach.) Teachers make no special effort for the non-English-speaking child. The teacher teaches oral language and reading skills in English and hopes the child picks up English speaking and reading ability through constant exposure. Unfortunately, this approach is frequently used. Many English speakers find this approach used in foreign schools where English is not the native language. Of course, some students succeed in spite of this approach. But either of the following approaches is a better alternative.

ESL.   The second approach is called the *English-as-a-second-language* (ESL) *approach.* Reading instruction is delayed while the non-English-speaking child receives oral language instruction to improve listening and speaking skills in English. Once these abilities are established, reading instruction in English begins. ESL programs often pull children out of the regular classroom for instruction. The time devoted to ESL varies according to the personnel and space available. The instruction itself is usually quite structured and may involve teacher modeling, pupil response, and repetitive drill.

The ESL approach provides direct help to the non-English-speaking student and assists the child in learning English without the frustration of trial and error. Teachers of ESL are generally fluent in the second language, and classroom teachers welcome their ability and expertise. In addition, some teachers find that students who improve their English language skills through ESL instruction succeed better in English reading.

The ESL approach has several possible disadvantages, though. For one thing, not all experts agree that the delay of reading instruction is necessary or advisable. In addition, if students leave the classroom for ESL instruction, then they miss some of what their peers receive. Also, the regular classroom teacher may mistakenly assume that children receiving special ESL instruction do not require any other assistance. Similarly, the ESL help may not match the regular classroom program. Some critics of the ESL approach believe it emphasizes fluent English speech too much and values the child's first language too little.

Vernacular.   The third approach is called the *vernacular* or *native-vernacular* method. Children learn to read in their native language first, while they are exposed to English informally or receive formal instruction in oral English. This *bilingual approach* places initial value on the children's mother tongue, then shifts to English reading as they develop English language skills, usually before the end of third grade.

The vernacular approach has many advantages. Children begin reading early in their native language, which often (as in Spanish) has a more consistent sound-symbol system. Syntax presents no special problems because children are already comfortable with the oral language. Presumably, learning to read English later is easier because the students have already mastered the learning-to-read process. This approach seems to benefit the children's self-concepts, since they learn to read in foreign language materials that highlight the positive characteristics and cultural experiences of the children's ethnic group. Parents can participate more actively in the beginning reading process, and children are less likely to feel stigmatized by their language differences.

One possible disadvantage of the vernacular approach is the need for teachers able to communicate in the second language. Also, teachers do not always have enough materials to teach reading in languages other than English. Although more and better materials are appearing, some schools lack the funds to purchase them. Critics of the vernacular approach argue that many children have difficulty reading when they transfer from the second language to English. They cite a lack of evidence about the benefits to later English reading achievement. Frank May (1982), an advocate of the vernacular approach, acknowledges that:

there is presently insufficient evidence to show that the bilingual approach actually works. . . . Most of the arguments for the bilingual approach at the present time are based on logic, politics, subjective observations, and humanitarian concern. (p. 464)

Many citizens strongly oppose programs that teach children to read in any language other than English. Certainly some parents would prefer that their children be taught to read in English. Language learning *is* a controversial area, and the program employed usually reflects an area's political climate.

Concurrent

McNeil, Donant, and Alkin (1980) describe two variations of the bilingual approach. In the *concurrent method*, students learn language skills in both languages at the same time. Often, children are grouped for oral language development and reading instruction according to their abilities. Children learn to read first in their dominant language. If this is the non-English language, then the children begin English reading as they develop sufficient language readiness. In some concurrent programs, the goal is not only to teach children to read in English but also to *maintain* the children's ability to speak and read in the other language. Other concurrent programs emphasize English reading and downplay the maintenance of the native language.

Immersion

Another variation is the *immersion program*. This program emphasizes learning in a language other than English and is often designed for native-English speakers. In a sense, the immersion program is the opposite of the melting-pot approach. Instruction is in the second language, say Spanish, as much as possible, while English is clearly deemphasized. Students in these programs often emerge as fully bilingual, because they were fluent English speakers when they began.

Various Language Needs of Elementary School Students

Two main problems make deciding which approach to use with second-language students difficult. First, research evidence does not yet show which method is pedagogically most effective. Second, a great variety of language differences are possible among students.

Figure 12–1 illustrates the possibilities. Note that the chart assumes only two different languages. When more than two languages occur in the classroom, the number of possibilities increases accordingly.

Student #1 speaks English only and is a nonreader. This student might be a typical kindergartener or beginning first grader. Unless he is in a bilingual program, your goal is to teach him to read in English.

Student #2 both speaks and reads English. She does not require beginning language instruction unless she is in a bilingual program.

Student #3 speaks only another language. He must learn to speak and read English and perhaps to read the other language as well, depending on the approach. He may be a candidate for ESL instruction, a vernacular approach, or the concurrent method.

Student #4 both speaks and reads another language. She is probably a candidate for an ESL approach, followed by instruction in English reading.

Student #5 speaks two languages but cannot read either, a common situation. In some schools, he would learn to read in English. Many bilingual programs, however, would first determine which language is dominant. Reading instruction would then begin in the dominant language.

Student #6 speaks and reads English, but

	English		Other Language	
	Speaks	Reads	Speaks	Reads
Student #1	x	-	-	-
Student #2	x	x	-	-
Student #3	-	-	x	-
Student #4	-	-	x	x
Student #5	x	-	x	-
Student #6	x	x	x	-
Student #7	x	-	x	x
Student #8	x	x	x	x

Figure 12–1   The variety of possible language differences in the elementary classroom

only speaks the other language. She does not require beginning language instruction unless bilingualism is a goal of the program.

Student #7 speaks and reads another language, but only speaks English. This student needs to be taught to read English.

Student #8 speaks and reads both English and the other language. She obviously does not require beginning language instruction. Unfortunately, this student is quite rare.

As can be seen in Figure 12–1, non-English speakers in your classroom can further complicate your efforts to create and manage reading groups. Organizing for reading instruction is difficult enough before adding this factor. Exemplary bilingual programs do exist where students' reading and language needs are met through small group instruction. However, this feat has been accomplished by spending extra funds for specialists, aides, special materials, and equipment.

Fortunately, most elementary teachers have only a few non-English speakers in their classrooms. These children's special needs can be met by using the following suggestions.

Suggestions for Teaching Language and Reading to Non-English Speakers

Audrey Weitkamp and Joan Donnelly (1982) present many excellent, commonsense suggestions to help you help non-English speakers adjust to your classroom and begin learning English. Some of these suggestions are:

1. Relax and help the student relax. If he has just arrived in the United States, he needs time to adjust.
2. Learn to pronounce the student's name correctly and show the student you are pleased to have her in your class.
3. If possible, seat the child next to a helpful classmate. Encourage other students in the class to help the new student.
4. Set up a conference with the student's parents, using an interpreter if necessary. Use this conference to reassure the parents, learn more about the student, and answer the parents' questions.
5. Give the student a picture dictionary.
6. Write down simple words and phrases as the student learns them.
7. Encourage the student as he begins to speak English, and do not be concerned about imperfect pronunciation.
8. Allow the student some free time to observe other students and classroom activities.
9. Be patient with the student's rate of language acquisition. Many students learn English more rapidly than you realize.
10. Try to understand the student's frustrations and difficulties, and teach your other

students to be kind and understanding as well.

Additional ideas for assisting non-English speakers can be divided among these four areas: (1) Motivation and self-concept; (2) Auditory skills; (3) Language development; and (4) Beginning reading instruction. Many of these ideas come from Doris C. Ching (1976) and Joan T. Feeley (1983).

Motivation and Self-concept.   A strong relationship exists among teachers' expectations, students' self-concepts and motivation, and students' achievement. To demonstrate your confidence in your non-English-speaking students, consider the following:

1. Treat the students with warmth, understanding, and consideration. Express an interest in their language and cultural background.

2. Provide books and other materials that will interest the students.

3. Arrange for other children or adults who speak the students' native language to spend some time with them.

4. Allow the students to begin expressing their interests in safe situations, such as small groups or play experiences. Do not force them to speak in front of the whole class until they are ready.

5. Prepare a study unit on the non-English-speaking students' culture. Encourage classmates to participate fully in these activities. Encourage the non-English-speaking students to bring in stamps, coins, clothing, and food unique to their culture. Show appropriate movies and filmstrips and display books relating to the culture.

6. Encourage adults of the same cultural background to visit and speak to the class about their interests and achievements.

Auditory Skills.   Many experts believe that instruction and activities in auditory skills particularly benefit non-English speaking students. Some possibilities include:

1. Provide activities to make students aware of the sounds around them, such as listening walks, listing pleasant and unpleasant sounds, closing eyes and listening carefully, and guessing mystery sounds created by the teacher.

2. Play games that require students to listen carefully. These include *Simon Says*, in which the directions given (sit down, raise your hand, etc.) are to be followed only if preceded by "Simon says"; *The Telephone Game*, in which a whispered message is passed from student to student and the final message is compared to the original; and *Going to the Grocery Store*, in which the first student says, "I'm going to the grocery store to buy some ____," the next student repeats the line and adds an item, and so on.

3. Provide classroom listening centers for many activities, including listening to commercially prepared tapes while following along in books; listening to teacher-prepared tapes of favorite stories, rhymes, poems, or interesting sounds; or listening to tapes prepared by other children. Listening centers can easily be adapted to "recording studios" if a microphone and blank tapes are provided. Students can then listen to their own speech or reading.

4. Read to children frequently. You may include activities that encourage careful listening, such as stopping occasionally and having students guess what word or event comes next.

5. Provide storytelling and creative dramatic activities.

Language Development.   Obviously, language development possibilities are numerous. Some of this development occurs without teacher involvement, through students' exposure and direct experience. However, much of the important language learning requires careful planning and active participation by the teacher. Some effective language development activities are summarized below:

1. Develop oral language through participation in many enjoyable classroom activities, such as storytelling and creative dramatic activities,

general conversation, guided discussions, telephone conversations, oral reports, announcements, directions or explanations, and choral speaking activities. (See Ching, 1976, pp. 26–32, for more details.)

2. Expand vocabulary and concept development through direct experience, teaching specific vocabulary, naming objects or placing familiar objects in a surprise box, dramatizing words, using various media to illustrate words or concepts, using pictures and picture dictionaries, using new words often and in various contexts, and broadening students' experiences through field trips.

3. Enhance ability to use English syntax effectively by using an audiolingual approach. The teacher models the language element and repeats it several times, then provides cues for the student to respond to; then the student uses the element correctly in a variety of situations. Other activities include using the tape recorder or Language Master, sentence building activities, drills, and student tutors.

Beginning Reading Instruction.   Teachers may introduce beginning reading skills through language experience techniques (see Chapter 2) and pattern books (see Chapter 4). Many teachers encourage the dictation and reading of simple sentences or dialogues, such as: "My name is _____. I like to _____. I am happy when _____." Activities in which students first listen to a simple selection and then read it are often successful. Some teachers also use so-called linguistic reading approaches or the Distar program (see Chapter 2).

MAINSTREAMING AND THE EXCEPTIONAL CHILD

Children with exceptional needs have not always received public school instruction; in fact, handicapped children were excluded from public education until the mid-nineteenth century. Until quite recently, handicapped children were educated, if at all, in segregated residential institu-

tions or treatment centers. Growing dissatisfaction among parents of handicapped children and research showing that segregated education was frequently ineffective led to litigation and ultimately to changes in the federal law.

In 1975, Congress passed *Public Law 94–142,* known as the Education for All Handicapped Children Act. This law, which became effective in 1977, encompassed and expanded earlier federal laws. P.L. 94–142 guaranteed the right to a "free, appropriate public education" designed to meet the needs of all handicapped students between the ages of 3 and 21. The term *handicapped students* includes students who are mentally retarded, hard-of-hearing, deaf, speech-impaired, visually handicapped, seriously emotionally disturbed, orthopedically-impaired, or learning disabled. Although the definition of learning disabled is somewhat vague, many problem readers in elementary classrooms are considered learning disabled.

According to Ernest L. Boyer (1979), former U.S. Commissioner of Education, the law specifies that states and local school districts must:

1. locate handicapped children, giving first priority to the most severely handicapped;
2. assess the learning needs of each child, with the participation of the child's parents;
3. plan an individualized education program (IEP) for each child;
4. place the child in the "least restrictive environment" possible, whether this is a hospital, state institution, special private or public school, or a regular classroom;
5. periodically evaluate the child's progress and make adjustments as needed, again with the parents' participation; and
6. set up impartial hearing, appeal, and other procedures to assure parents of due process.

Referrals for special services may be made by parents or guardians, public school personnel, public or private agencies, community members, or the children themselves. After students are referred and parental consent is obtained, students are assessed. The law provides guidelines for assessment, which include:

1. testing and assessment materials must not be racially, culturally, or sexually discriminatory.
2. testing and assessment materials must be administered in the child's native language by qualified personnel.
3. no single procedure may be used as the sole criterion for the student's educational placement or program.

Several people develop the IEP. This team usually consists of the teacher, one or both parents, the child (when appropriate), a public school employee other than the child's teacher (typically the principal), and other educational specialists.

According to P.L. 94–142, Section 121a.346, the *individualized education program* for each child must include:

1. a statement of the child's present levels of educational performance;
2. a statement of annual goals, including short-term instructional objectives;
3. a statement of the specific special education and related services to be provided to the child, and the extent to which the child can participate in regular educational programs;
4. the projected dates for initiation of services and their anticipated duration; and
5. appropriate objective criteria and evaluation procedures and schedules for determining, on at least an annual basis, whether the short-term instructional objectives are being achieved.

Mainstreaming, the process of integrating handicapped pupils into the regular educational program whenever possible, includes a clause about the *least restrictive environment.* According to Section 121a.550 of the law, each public agency shall insure:

1. that to the maximum extent appropriate, handicapped children . . . are educated

with children who are not handicapped, and
2. that special classes, separate schooling, or other removal of handicapped children from the regular educational environment occurs only when the nature or severity of the handicap is such that education in regular classes with the use of supplementary aids and services cannot be achieved satisfactorily.

The child's parents must approve the IEP and consent to the student's placement. They also, of course, must be informed about the child's progress and about adjustments to the instructional program. If they are dissatisfied, they have the right to pursue an impartial due process hearing.

Although virtually all educators agree with the intent of Public Law 94–142, it has led to some litigation between parents and school districts and a rather cumbersome instructional planning process. For example, schools in Alameda County, California follow 11 steps in the instructional planning process for each handicapped child:

1. Search
2. Referral
3. Parent notice
4. Assessment plan/Parent consent to assess
5. Assessment conducted
6. Individualized Education Program team meeting scheduled
7. Parent notified of eligibility and planning meeting
8. Individualized Education Program developed/Parent consent to IEP
9. Placement
10. Review—annual and third year
11. Third year reevaluations

Your best source of information and guidance about mainstreaming and the exceptional child will probably be your school principal, who can tell you which policies and procedures are being followed in your school.

Many of the suggestions made earlier about

teaching children with special needs are also appropriate for mainstreamed students. Teachers do not need prescribed or special techniques to include handicapped children in their reading classrooms. Rather, they should simply use the same principles of good reading instruction they follow with other students: awareness of individual differences; knowledge of frustration, instructional, and independent reading levels; approaches and materials that match students' needs; individual attention, etc. And as indicated earlier, teachers' attitudes and expectations greatly influence how much their students achieve.

SUMMARY

When teaching reading to children with special needs, teacher expectations are important.

Various types of problem readers appear in elementary classrooms, and general and specific suggestions for teaching these students were discussed.

The characteristics of gifted students, some problems you may encounter when teaching them, some approaches used to educate the gifted, and many suggestions for helping gifted students develop their reading-language skills were presented.

Although the United States has many dialects, this chapter focused on black English and the reading difficulties of black children. Six approaches for teaching reading to black children were presented along with recommendations for you to employ when working with black-English-speaking students in your classroom. These suggestions apply to students with other dialects, also.

Teaching the non-English-speaking child is a challenge; various approaches are used in elementary schools to meet this challenge. Specific suggestions for teaching language and reading to non-English speakers were discussed.

Finally, the highlights of federal legislation designed to insure a free and appropriate public education for all handicapped students were reviewed.

REVIEW QUESTIONS

1. What did Thomas L. Good discover about teacher behaviors and high- and low-achieving students?

2. What characteristics do the following types of problem readers have? (a) slow learners; (b) reluctant readers; (c) disadvantaged readers; (d) disabled readers; and (e) underachieving readers.

3. Give a hypothetical example of a student who might fit more than one category of problem readers.

4. Why can't experts agree on a definition of learning disabilities?

5. What are some dangers in applying labels such as dyslexic or learning disabled to children who have difficulty learning to read? What are some possible advantages?

6. What are some symptoms associated with severe reading disability?

7. List some general and specific suggestions for working with problem readers.

8. What type of problem reader is the gifted child most likely to be?

9. What are some characteristics of gifted students?

10. What are some problems in teaching gifted students?

11. What are some approaches to educating the gifted?

12. List some specific techniques for teaching reading to gifted students.

13. Discuss the deficit and difference views of nonstandard dialects.

14. What is the dialect interference theory? What does research say in support of or opposition to this theory?

15. Describe the six approaches to teaching reading to black-English speakers. What are the possible advantages and disadvantages of each?

16. Describe the following approaches to teaching reading to non-English speakers: (a) melting-pot approach; (b) English-as-a-second-language approach; (3) vernacular approach; (4) concurrent approach; (5) immersion program.

17. How might the selection of the approach used to teach reading to non-English speakers be affected by language needs of individual children? Give examples.

18. What are some techniques you may use to help a non-English speaking child?

19. Describe the critical elements of Public Law 94–142.

20. How might the requirements of Public Law 94–142 affect you as a classroom teacher?

REFERENCES

Aukerman, R. C., & Aukerman, L. R. *How do I teach reading?* New York: John Wiley, 1981.

Baratz, J. C. A bi-dialectal task for determining language proficiency in economically disadvantaged children. *Child Development*, December, 1969, *40*, 889–901.

Boyer, E. L. Public Law 94–142: A promising start? *Educational Leadership*, February, 1979, *36*, 298–301.

Branisel, R. M. A study of black kindergarten children's auditory comprehension of stories presented in standard English versus black English. Master's thesis, California State University, Hayward, 1977.

Burns, P. C., & Roe, B. D. *Teaching reading in today's elementary schools* (2nd ed.). Boston: Houghton Mifflin, 1980.

Cagney, M. A. Children's ability to understand standard English and black dialect. *Reading Teacher*, March, 1977, *30*, 607–10.

Ching, D. C. *Reading and the bilingual child.* Newark, Del.: International Reading Association, 1976.

Cunningham, P. M. Teachers' correction responses to black-dialect miscues which are non-meaning changing. *Reading Research Quarterly*, 1976–1977, *12*, 637–53.

Dallman, M., Rouch, R. L., Char, L. Y. C., & DeBoer, J. J. *The teaching of reading* (6th ed.). New York: Holt, Rinehart and Winston, 1982.

Dechant, E. V. *Improving the teaching of reading* (3rd ed.). Englewood Cliffs, N.J.: Prentice-Hall, 1982.

Ditto, L. D. *The effects of language characteristics in oral reading.* Unpublished doctoral dissertation, Michigan State University, 1974.

Ekwall, E. E., & Shanker, J..L. *Diagnosis and remediation of the disabled reader* (2nd ed.). Boston: Allyn and Bacon, 1983.

Feeley, J. T. Help for the reading teacher: Dealing with the limited English proficient (LEP) child in the elementary classroom. *Reading Teacher*, March, 1983, *36*, 650–55.

Good, T. L. Teacher expectations and student perceptions: A decade of research. *Educational Leadership*, February, 1981, *38*, 415–22.

Harris, A. J., & Sipay, E. R. *How to teach reading.* New York: Longman, 1979.

Hoback, J., & Perry, P. Common sense about educating the gifted and talented. *Educational Leadership*, January, 1980, *37*, 346–50.

Karnes, M. B., Teska, J. A., Hodgins, A. S., & Badger, E. D. Educational intervention at home by mothers of disadvantaged infants. *Child Development*, December, 1970, *41*, 925–35.

Lass, B. Improving reading skills: The relationship between the oral language of black English speakers and their reading achievement. *Urban Education*, January, 1980, *14*, 437–47.

May, F. *Reading as communication.* Columbus, Ohio: Charles E. Merrill, 1982.

McNeil, J. D., Donant, L., & Alkin, M. C. *How to teach reading successfully.* Boston: Little, Brown, 1980.

Rentel, V. M., & Kennedy, J. J. Effects of pattern drill on the phonology, syntax, and reading achievement of rural Appalachian children. *American Educational Research Journal*, 1972, *9*, 87–100.

Rystrom, R. *The effects of standard dialect training on Negro first graders learning to read.* Unpublished doctoral dissertation, University of California, Berkeley, 1968.

Rystrom, R. Dialect training and reading: A further look. *Reading Research Quarterly*, Summer, 1970, *5*, 581–99.

Rystrom, R. Dialect differences and initial reading instruction. Address given at National Council of Teachers of English Conference, November, 1972.

Schwartz, J. I. Dialect interference in the attainment of literacy. *Journal of Reading*, February, 1982, *25*, 440–46.

Sisk, D. A. What if your child is gifted? *American Education*, October, 1977, *13*, 23–26.

Strickland, D. S. A program for linguistically different, black children. *Research in the Teaching of English*, Spring, 1972, *7*, 79–86.

Weitkamp, A., & Donnelly, J. Tips from teachers on helping non-English-speaking children. *Learning*, September, 1982, *11*, 99, 102.

13

Reading Instruction:
Its History and
Its Future

Reading instruction in the United States has gone through several distinct periods, each of which differed in *orientation* (or philosophy) and in the *materials* and *methods* used. Political events, economic situations, religious pressures, individual influential books, and mere chance have all shaped our early, middle, and more modern reading instruction. Figure 13–1 shows the different periods of reading instruction in this country, according to Nila Banton Smith.[1]

In a sense, reading instruction is just now coming into its own, because researchers have begun to determine what important factors result in optimum achievement for students.

[1]*Note.* The discussion of American reading instruction that follows is based on material from *American Reading Instruction* by N. B. Smith (Newark, Del.: International Reading Association, 1965). Copyright 1965 by the International Reading Association. Used with permission of the International Reading Association.

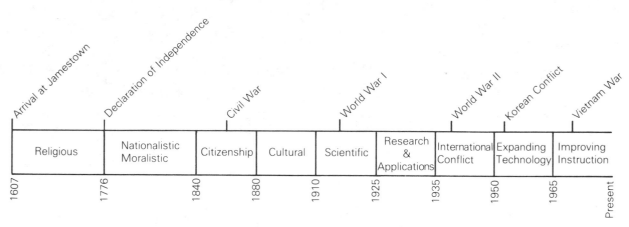

Figure 13–1   Orientations of reading instruction in U.S. history

A HISTORY OF READING INSTRUCTION

At first, American reading instruction was often controlled by circumstances. For example, reading itself was limited by the materials available, and reading instruction depended on competent and influential people to write usable materials. Also, many of our ideas about reading came from foreign countries: a knowledgeable American educator would visit a foreign country, learn a new technique, bring it home, and implement it.

Since then, many different methods of teaching reading have been tried, most without much research into their effectiveness. However, our history of reading instruction is a history of increasing research and knowledge about reading processes, materials, and teaching methods. The more recent and careful research into the effectiveness of various methods has produced better and more cohesive reading programs. Also, researchers and writers (such as A. Sterl Artley [1981], who recounted the results of the *First Grade Reading Studies)* have repeated time and again that not so much the materials' quality as the teacher's ability accounts for quality reading instruction.

Researchers such as Charles Fisher, Richard Marliave, and Nikola N. Filby (1979) as well as David Berliner (1980) show that reading educators can learn still more about concrete ways to improve children's chances of becoming better

readers. A careful analysis of the research by S. Jay Samuels (1981) shows that exemplary reading programs consistently have certain characteristics. Such information is invaluable, because now other schools can work to duplicate those characteristics in their own programs.

1607–1776: Religious Beginnings

Reading instruction for children was dominated by religious materials and values. Memorization of the alphabet and passages from the Bible was important, along with oral reading.

Orientation.   Beginning reading in the United States was all oriented toward religion. Learning to read was necessary so that readers could interpret the Bible for themselves. If people knew what the Bible had to say about Satan and his evil ways, Satan could not lead people astray. Nila Banton Smith quotes Martin Luther about reading. He recommends:

"Above all things, let the Scriptures be the chief and most frequently used reading book, both primary and high schools and the very young should be kept in the gospels. Is it not proper and right that every human being, by the time he has reached his tenth year, should be familiar with the holy gospels, in which the very core and marrow of his life is bound? (5:321) (p. 11)

During this period, if religion was not directly emphasized, strong moral values were.

The Hornbook and the Bible were among the earliest reading materials in America.

Materials

The Hornbook

One of the earliest books used for reading instruction in the United States was the hornbook, a small, paddle-shaped object made of wood, iron, pewter, silver, ivory, or even gingerbread! It was about 3″ × 4″ and contained the alphabet and some selections from the Bible, including the Lord's Prayer. It was covered with skin or paper upon which letters or words could be written. The transparent scale of a cow's horn covered the book and paper, keeping them clean. Hornbooks were evidently published in England as there is no record of any of them being made in the United States. The hornbook had two purposes: catechizing in church and giving children their first reading instruction. An early motivator, according to Smith, was to let a child eat a gingerbread hornbook.

The ABC

A manual of church services, the ABC was called a primer. It served as a school book as well as a church book, and it was one of the first books sold at a moderate price. However, it was not used as widely as the hornbook and the Bible.

The Psalter

The Psalter contained a variety of reading and spelling lessons and instructions for reading verse. It also contained some accounts from the Old Testament, books of the prophets, and the Apocryphal books and some material from the New Testament.

The Bible

The Bible was used as a reader and for memorizing. It was considered literature, necessary reading, as well as being a way to learn to read.

The Protestant Tutor

The Protestant Tutor was the first textbook printed in the United States. It contained the Roman small letters, the syllabarium (lists of syllables and words), the Lord's Prayer, the Creed, the Ten Commandments, John Rogers' biography and verses, words of two to seven syllables, the proper names (from Scripture), a catechism, and other religous selections.

The New England Primer

The first reading textbook designed for use in the American Colonies was probably printed in England, making its debut in a London stationer's store in 1683. *The New England Primer* became the standard reading textbook throughout the colonial period, and its use extended far into the eighteenth century. The *Primer* included several crudely drawn pictures, many depicting a dreadful scene, such as a man being burned at the stake with his wife and family watching.

The first page and a half of *The New England Primer* had the alphabet, the vowels and consonants, double letters, italics, and capitals. Then came the syllabarium, beginning with columns of **phonograms** or word families, syllables beginning with vowels, and progressing in the next four pages to words of five or six syllables! Then came the alphabet verses, which were "sentences of religious or moral import, arranged in the form of couplets, each couplet containing some outstanding word to illustrate a letter of the alphabet" (p. 24). These verses were followed by Alphabet Lessons for Youth, sentences from the Bible arranged in alphabetical order according to the first letter of each sentence. The primer also usually contained the Lord's Prayer, the Creed, verses that John Rogers bequeathed to his children, and other miscellaneous verses.

Spellers

Although *The New England Primer* was probably the most famous and most used book for teaching reading, many editions of spellers were published during the 1700s. One speller, *England's Perfect School Master*, was first printed in the United States. The spellers taught spelling, as well as reading, religion, and morals. They contained one- to six-syllable words, to be spelled in whole words *and* in syllables, and they gave rules for spelling, punctuation, and grammar. They too contained a lot of religious material, including the Lord's Prayer and various Bible verses.

Methods.   Children had to learn the ABCs by rote, one letter at a time. They learned them both forward and backward, and if the teacher named a letter, they were supposed to be able to point to it. After the child mastered the alphabet, he was introduced to the syllabarium. The syllabarium was a series of syllables such as *ba, be, bi, bo, bu*, etc.

After working with the hornbook, the ABC, and the syllabarium, the child learned short words and began to read orally. Oral reading was an important part of the reading curriculum; articulation and elocution were emphasized. Students memorized certain verses and passages from the Bible. Because materials were so scarce, the Bible often served as the only reading material and literature; many early colonists, however, could not afford even that.

The usual method of teaching reading was the **alphabetic method**, which followed these steps:

1. Learn the alphabet forward and backward and learn to identify any letter wherever it appeared.
2. Work with the syllabarium, lists of syllables.
3. Learn to read some words and memorize some sentences.
4. Memorize important passages of the Bible.
5. Do oral reading.

1777–1840: Nationalistic-Moralistic Period

The United States began to stress reading to promote patriotism, materials became less exclusively religious, and good oral reading continued to be emphasized.

Orientation.   According to Smith, reading instruction between 1777 and 1840 was working to purify the American language. Second, it fostered loyalty to the traditions of the new nation—its occupations, institutions, and resources. It also continued to develop the morals and high ideals considered necessary for the citizenry of a new nation. Reading instruction, then, had a nationalistic and moralistic slant. These two concerns came together in the colonist's belief that being good led to the good life for individuals and for the country. This nationalistic orientation can be seen in some of the period's popular titles:

The American Spelling Book, An American Selection of Lessons in Reading and Speaking, The Columbian Orator, The American Preceptor, American Popular

Reader, Class Book of American Literature, A History of the American Revolution, National Preceptor, and the *American Manual.* (p. 37)

Materials. Reading materials used between 1777 and 1840 emphasized some new things. For example, they contained exercises designed to overcome the dialects and diversity that appeared with the influx of people from different lands. Authors designed patriotic materials to awaken children to the talent of people in their country. Other materials acquainted children with the history of Europe as it affected America. Some materials helped children appreciate their new environment. Also, oratorical selections helped develop *elocutionary* ability, the art of effective public speaking, so important for life in a democracy.

In most cases, writers who wrote readers, such as Noah Webster, Caleb Bingham, and Lyman Cobb, also wrote spellers, and their books became extremely popular. To illustrate how popular, Smith says Noah Webster and his family supposedly lived, during the 20 years he was writing his dictionary, on the profits from his speller, *The American Spelling Book.* It became so popular, it eventually outsold the popular *New England Primer.*

Methods. Smith says that J. Leavitt best summarizes the methods of the Nationalistic-Moralistic Period in a set of rules from his 1829 text, *Easy Lessons in Reading:*

1. Be careful to *call* your words right.
2. Learn to *pronounce* them properly.
3. Speak with a *clear* and *distinct* voice.
4. Do not read too *fast.* Read *slowly* and *carefully* so as not to make any *mistakes.*
5. Be very particular to observe all the *stops.*
6. Learn to use the proper *Emphasis* and Inflection of voice. Ask your teacher to show you what these mean and how to do it.
7. Try to understand every word as you go along. *Study* your reading lessons very carefully before you read.
8. Try to read as if you were telling a story to your mother or talking with some of your playmates. *Reading is talking from a book.*

9. Take pains to read poetry, not to sing it.
10. The emphatic words are printed in *Italic letters.* (pp. 72–73)

1841–1880: Citizenship Period

During this period, reading instruction focused on making students intelligent citizens, books designed for each grade appeared, and basal readers began to emphasize repetition more in the primary grades and content and comprehension in the upper grades.

Orientation. During the period, from 1840 to 1880, reading teachers educated students to be intelligent voters in a democracy. American reading instruction was greatly influenced by Pestalozzean principles and methods. Pestalozzea, a famous Prussian educator, believed in teaching reading by relating words to actual objects. He also thought beginning readers should concentrate on concrete words—nouns, adjectives, and verbs—and not worry about articles, prepositions, and conjunctions. Horace Mann visited Prussia at this time and came back espousing the use of the five senses in reading. Horace Mann, according to Smith, did more than anyone else to shape the educational principles of the time. For example, Mann called for using letter sounds rather than letter names in learning to read.

Materials. Around 1840, a book for each grade and the concept of grade levels appeared. More emphasis was placed on history, science, nature study, geography, and general information, much less emphasis was placed on religion, and somewhat less emphasis was placed on citizenship. At the beginning of the period, there was still a lot of material on morals, but such materials gradually disappeared in the next forty years.

McGuffey's complete set of readers was published between 1836 and 1844, and they were the first readers to include one book for each grade. They were immediately popular and continued to be for 40 years. Smith says the "last editions intended for general school use were printed by the American Book Company in

1896 and 1907'' (p. 105); however, Henry Ford had a private edition printed in 1925!

Methods.   After 1840 more emphasis was placed on working from simple words to the more complex, and fewer words were introduced in primers. As a result, these was much more built-in repetition of words. Before 1940, many words were not repeated except by chance, a method that made learning to read very difficult.

Josiah Bumstead's work led to a new method: during the first few weeks, children learned words. Then they learned letters and letter sounds, going back to the alphabetic-phonetic method. Much more emphasis was placed on learning letter sounds than on learning letters per se.

Reading instruction also shifted to an emphasis on meaning in the upper grades. Teachers asked questions about the material's content as well as the words' meanings. Such lessons must have been built into the readers since no teachers' manuals were available.

During the latter part of this time period, teachers moved from the alphabetic-phonetic method to a word, sentence, and story method. However, even more elaborate phonetic methods, including changes in alphabet markings, continued to be developed.

1881–1910: Cultural Period

Beginning in about 1880, reading was thought of as a cultural asset, professional books about teaching reading appeared, and both whole word and more complex alphabetic-phonetic methods were used.

Orientation.   Between 1880 and 1910, educators stressed getting good literature into the hands of children. Efforts were made to get students to appreciate what was considered good literature. Smith quotes a selection from the course of study at the Rochester Public Schools (1901) that summarizes this period:

The objects of reading lessons are two: First, to give the pupil the power to secure from the written or

printed pages an intelligent and appreciative knowledge of the thoughts of the authors as recorded and expressed in literature. Second, to give the pupil the power to impart to others the knowledge thus obtained in a clear, sympathetic, pleasing manner. The teacher should always bear it in mind that the content of the reading lesson is of more value than its form, and that an appreciation of good literature is worth more than the mechanical ability to read. Careful attention should be paid in all grades to correct enunciation, and pronunciation, to proper use of the vocal organs and of the organs employed in breathing and the carriage of the body; and vocalization of both vowels and consonants should be employed when needed. (p. 121)

Another statement showing the emphasis of the period appeared in a course of study from Flint, Michigan (1902–03): ''The purpose of the courses in reading is threefold: first, to teach children to read; second, to cause children to like to read; third, to enable them to know and prefer good literature'' (p. 121).

Materials.   Several professional books appeared on how to teach reading, but most were incomplete. For example, a book by Sarah Louise Arnold, *Reading: How to Teach It* (1899), was mainly devoted to teaching an appreciation of literature. What H. Alan Robinson (1977) considers the first scientific contribution to reading instruction, Edmund Burke Huey's *The Psychology and Pedagogy of Reading*, was published in 1908. It was reprinted in 1968 for its historical value, but more important, for its still pertinent discussion of ideas about and problems in teaching reading.

Courses of study were developed that distinguished between various grade levels. It became common practice to put additional sets of basal readers in each classroom and prescribe how much of each was to be covered during a certain period of time.

In the upper grades, students read classic literature in separate books.

Methods.   A great shift in reading instruction occurred when elaborate alphabetic-phonetic methods were developed. Elocutionary rules disappeared and moralistic selections began to lose their foothold. Basal readers changed to having content almost wholly from literature. Smith says, for example, that Mother Goose rhymes and folk tales were used for the first time.

The books themselves also changed: cloth bindings replaced cardboard covers, the print got larger and clearer, and colored pictures began to be used.

Several reading texts introduced the whole word method, and phonics was used after a core of sight words had been learned. Also, at the end of this period, several new scientific alphabets appeared, but they were short-lived.

1911–1925: Scientific Period

During this time, reading educators conducted 436 reading studies! Teachers' manuals and standardized tests were developed, individualized instruction became important, and teachers emphasized silent reading and speed.

Orientation. The *study* of reading became important, and researchers investigated various materials and methods. Group as well as individualized standardized reading tests began to influence the reading curriculum. Because these tests called for silent reading, the reading curriculum became more oriented in that direction. And because many soldiers during World War I could not read well enough to function properly in a military setting, more silent reading was added to the curriculum. Also, research began to show that silent reading practice produced more fluent readers and readers who comprehended better.

Materials. Huey's *The Psychology and Pedagogy of Teaching Reading* remained a popular text, and new editions came out in 1912 and 1915. Robinson (1977) reports that many cities produced courses of study as part of an English or overall **curriculum guide.** These written plans describe a school's curriculum. Although they vary in scope and detail, they usually discuss philosophy, specific objectives, and ways to arrive at those objectives. Also, many new read-

ers appeared and teachers' manuals proliferated, new and revised, to accompany these readers. Much of the material focused on silent reading, and more of it was not strictly literary. He also states that there was an abundance of materials such as flash cards and seatwork activities designed to improve comprehension.

Methods. Silent reading and speed were emphasized. The language experience approach began to be used for teaching reading. Also, the sentence or story method was used more frequently, and individualized instruction was stressed.

1926–1935: Research and Application Period

Planned sequences of skills and student-generated activities both became important, pre-primers were introduced, and reading readiness was formally recognized.

Orientation. Reading experts identified and plotted a sequence of reading skills to be learned. In addition, experts believed children could often meet their own reading needs by solving their own problems and generating their own activities. Robinson (1977) reports that research in reading improved and that much of it focused on reading disabilities. Another group of research studies focused on reading readiness. Although there was still interest in silent reading, the intense focus on it began to wane.

Materials. Robinson reports that many of the professional books published at this time were on reading. They included such subjects as remedial reading, audience reading, vocabulary development, and factual and recreational reading. He also says teachers' manuals became less dogmatic, giving the teacher many suggested or optional activities. Supplemental materials, some of which came in sets, also became abundant. The language experience approach continued to be used, and pre-primers were introduced.

Sixteen sets of basal readers existed at this

time, which gave the teacher a wide variety to choose from. Table 13–1 analyzes the content of some typical primers of this period and Table 13–2 analyzes the content of some typical fourth-grade readers.

Methods.   The *Fernald technique,* having the student use her touch, hearing, seeing, and muscles to learn words, was used more often. The concept of reading readiness was formally recognized and materials for teaching it were published. Teaching reading in the content areas became more popular, but regular reading classes were still held. Phonics was still taught to some extent in nearly all classrooms.

1936–1950: International Conflict Period

Reading instruction focused on developing social understanding and helping students deal with the complexities of American life, both readiness materials and adult reading materials were developed, and grouping was used to individualize instruction.

Orientation.   Systematic reading instruction and reading in contemporary life were the focuses of reading instruction in this period. Reading was seen as a way to help people develop social understanding and deal with life's complexities. To make sure adults could read, many developmental reading programs were begun in high schools, colleges, and for adults in general. Much of this reading instruction was integrated with the teaching of other subjects.

Robinson points out that several reading clinics opened, focusing attention on the disabled reader. This development probably grew out of the many research studies done in this area during the preceding period.

Materials.   A lot of material was published in reading readiness, including more pre-primers per series. The number of vocabulary words per book was cut and words were repeated more often. Also, skill charts began to appear along with basal reading series. The number of teachers' manuals increased.

Many materials were designed for teaching upper level reading skills in high schools and beyond. This material focused on teaching reading in the content areas. Several important professional books were published, such as Albert J. Harris' *How to Increase Reading Ability* and Emmett A. Betts' *Foundations of Reading Instruction*, and they did more than anything else to shape the course of reading during the next few decades.

Methods.   Grouping was often used to provide for individual needs. Word recognition techniques were isolated and taught, perhaps more systematically than they had ever been before. Also, educators moved toward teaching reading as a *part* of overall communication or language arts—reading, writing, speaking, and listening. There was renewed interest in systematic instruction, and the diagnosis of reading problems became common.

1951–1965: Technological Period

Technological knowledge expanded and influenced the teaching of reading, more materials for teaching higher level skills appeared, and programmed texts were often used.

Orientation.   Some textbooks showed a *linguistic orientation,* teaching words by grouping them in word families. An example would be: "Mat the fat cat sat on the hat."

Interest continued to grow in the higher level reading skills. Reading programs were expanded in high schools and junior colleges as well as in four-year colleges. Services for disabled readers expanded greatly, as seen by the large number of reading clinics that opened.

Materials.   The United States government entered education more by providing money for the purchase of reading machines and other materials. The use of linguistically oriented materials grew and *programmed materials* without hardware also became popular.

Programmed textbooks break a skill into very

Table 13–1   The content of primers

Primers	Realistic Narratives	Old Tales	Modern Fanciful Tales	Informational Selections	Poetry	Fables	Silent Reading Exercises
Children's Own Readers (1929)	113						9
Child-Story Readers (1927)	44	15					6
Work-Play Books (1930)	112						8
Child's Own Way Series (1926)	120						
New Wide Awake Readers (1929)	103		16				2
Story and Study Readers (1928)	81		6		3		21
Smedley and Olsen Series (1926)	66	9	12		10		21
Newson Readers (1927)	69	22	11		2		14
True Story Series (1928)	135				9		8
New Path to Reading (1929)	172						
Total { Number of pages	1015	46	45		24		89
{ Percent of pages	83.26	3.77	3.69		1.97		7.30

Note. From *American Reading Instruction* by N.B. Smith (Newark, Del.: International Reading Association, 1965), 218. Copyright 1965 by the International Reading Association. Reprinted with permission of the International Reading Association.

Table 13–2   The content of fourth-grade readers

Fourth Readers	Realistic Narratives	Informational Selections[1]	History Stories	Civics Stories	Silent Reading and Study Exercises	Old Folk Tales	Modern Fanciful Tales	Myths	Fables	Poetry
Story and Study Readers	74	71	18	6	60		77	2		25
Child-Story Readers	47	88	37	46	92	25				12
Children's Own Readers	52	63	48	38	13		11	25		15
Pathway to Reading	61	48	23	2	27	46	59			19
Newson Readers	72	46	39		16		108		3	40
Study Readers	54	92	31	3	81	15	23	8		8
Total { Number of Pages	360	408	196	95	289	86	278	35	3	119
{ Percent of pages	19.26	21.83	10.49	5.08	15.46	4.60	14.87	1.87	.16	6.37

[1]This includes geography, nature, industry, and science.

Note. From *American Reading Instruction* by N.B. Smith (Newark, Del.: International Reading Association, 1965), 220. Copyright 1965 by the International Reading Association. Reprinted with permission of the International Reading Association.

"Up front"—1943.

small parts. The learner responds to these parts, step-by-step, and gets immediate feedback on the accuracy of the responses. Several systems of teaching reading became well-known; however, the program that probably gained the most fame was Sir James Pitman's Initial Teaching Alphabet, which had 44 symbols to represent the 44 sounds Sir James Pitman maintained were part of spoken English. (See Figure 2–8.)

Multiple textbooks at each grade level were more widely used so that students reading above and below grade level had materials. More materials also became available for teaching higher level reading skills in developmental and corrective reading courses in high schools, junior colleges, and four-year colleges.

Methods.   In general, eclectic methods were

used, mixtures of those methods that had been successful in previous years. For the first time, scholars could use information gained from past research. Also, individualized reading emerged on what Robinson calls "a sound conceptual basis" (p. 55).

1966–Present: Questions and Answers

Reading educators worked to prepare their students for an age bombarded with information. The standard middle class white family of earlier basal readers began to be joined by people of other races, and female characters were no longer always housewives. Research into different methods and materials continued, as researchers tried to answer some of the persistent questions asked by people in the reading profession.

Is the Testing and Teaching of Perceptual and Perceptual-Motor Skills Worthwhile?

The question about perceptual and perceptual-motor training has been around much too long. The very people involved in the development of such programs often do not read the research on the effectiveness of their own programs. Otherwise, they would surely take them off the market.

A popular test of children's visual perception and eye-motor coordination problems has been the *Developmental Test of Visual Perception*; the *Frostig-Horne Training Program* has been popular for correcting these problems. Other materials in the field are the Getman, Getman-Kane, and Kephart programs.

One can still find such materials in the modern classroom, even though the question about using them should have been laid to rest with the publication of "Visual-motor Processes: Can We Train Them?" by Donald Hammill, Libby Goodman, and J. Lee Wiederholt (1974). In this article the authors examined the usefulness of the Frostig-Horne, the Kephart, Getman, and the Getman-Kane materials in developing eye-motor and visual-motor coordination to help children learn to read. After a thorough survey of the literature about the effectiveness of these programs, they wrote:

To conclude, the results of attempts to implement the Frostig-Horne materials and Kephart-Getman techniques in the schools have for the most part been unrewarding. The readiness skills of children were improved in only a few instances. The effect of training on intelligence and academic achievement was not clearly demonstrated. Particularly disappointing were the findings which pertained to the effects of such training on perceptual-motor performance itself. For if the training is not successful in this area, can the positive benefits of such instruction reported by a few authors be anything other than spurious?

We have little doubt that any interested person who reads the efficacy literature will conclude that the value of perceptual training, especially those programs often used in schools, has not been clearly established. If he concludes that such training lacks solid support, he may begin to question the purchase of attractively packaged materials which some companies offer teachers along with unsubstantiated claims concerning their merits, the practice of providing perceptual-motor training to all school children in the name of readiness training, and the assumption that a lack of perceptual-motor adequacy causes a considerable amount of academic failure. (p. 476)

In fairness to the publishers and users of materials for the development of visual perceptual skills, the instruments used for measuring these skills usually did not measure them in relationship to reading. If measuring instruments more closely related to reading are developed, considerable research will be needed to prove that training of visual perceptual skills improves children's reading more than direct instruction in reading does.

But at this time, claims made by the makers of such programs have been refuted by Hammill, Goodman, and Wiederholt. When a school uses such programs, it does not help the students, and in fact, it harms them because the programs take time away from other activities that might really help.

Does Any Set of Teaching Materials Consistently Bring About Higher Achievement?

During the 1964–65 school year the United States Office of Education, in the U.S. Department of Health, Education, and Welfare, funded 27 studies to determine if one reading method was better than any other for teaching first graders to read. These studies, popularly known as *The First Grade Reading Studies,* involved approximately 30,000 children and about 1000 teachers.

In the first large attempt to determine if any one method was superior to any others, a wide variety of approaches were studied, such as basal series, linguistic programs, the language experience approach, new alphabets, individualized reading, phonics emphasis approaches, etc. A. Sterl Artley (1981) best summarizes the results of these studies:

After all has been said and done there is still strong evidence to show that it is not the method, the materials, the approach, or the room arrangement which make the major difference in pupil adjustment and achievement. Though the approach or materials may affect student reading achievement, in the final analysis it is the teacher who has the greatest effect.

This not surprising fact was brought out in the *First Grade Reading Studies* (Bond and Dykstra, 1967), which attempted to determine if there were differences in reading achievement that could be accounted for by different methods and materials. On the basis of this comprehensive experimental study the authors concluded that it was what teachers did in their relation with children that made the major difference in reading achievement. This fact was dramatized by the discovery that frequently there were greater differences in pupil achievement between teachers using the same method than between teachers using different methods. (pp. 149–50)

The findings of the First Grade Reading Studies and the statement by A. Sterl Artley ring true. No doubt some teachers work better in materials that force them to be structured and vice versa, but after all factors are taken into account, it is finally the teacher, not the materials, who makes the difference between students' high or low reading achievement.

Do Students Read as Well as They Used To?   Roger Farr (1977), who has researched this question extensively, stated:

The status of reading achievement in the United States cannot simply be labeled "good" or "bad" or "improved" or "declining." Such achievement is a complex and constantly changing picture, but we can make some definite statements about its present status:
1. If, in observing changes in children's reading achievement, we consider a period of at least 30 years—from 1946 to 1976—there is no question that on the average students read better today than in the past.
2. If we consider a relatively short period—say 1970 to 1976—then it appears that students in the lower grades read better than their 1970 counterparts. However, at the upper grade levels, students in 1976 are not reading any better on the average than those in 1970. They may, in fact, be reading less well.
3. In general, students at the lower grade levels are scoring very high on basic skills tests in reading. There is some indication that this is the result of the heavy emphasis on specific reading skills encouraged by federally funded reading projects.
4. Almost all students in the United States do achieve

a minimal level of reading literacy. However, at higher levels of reading literacy—such as inferential reading—the performance of high school students is declining. (p. 522)

In a speech Farr (1980) gave at the Silver Anniversary of the International Reading Association, he referred to Harold Hodgkinson's "What's Right With Education." In the past 30 years, reading teachers have done for over 75 percent of their students in both elementary and secondary schools what they did for only about 25 percent of them in 1950. Today, there are some students in school that would not have been in 1950 because they were not as academically inclined. However, even with that added burden, Farr says, "More importantly, any age comparisons of the reading abilities of children today with those of former years, say 20 or 30 or more years ago, indicates that today's youth read better" (p. 905).

Paul Copperman (1979), however, points out that the picture may not be quite so rosy. He agrees there has been a steady achievement increase in the primary grades. However, above the third- or fourth-grade level, reading achievement has decreased somewhat from a peak reached around 1963 or 1964. Copperman's figures, in fact, show that in grade eight and above, the drop was serious from 1970 to 1978. In discussing Farr's studies, Copperman stated,

Roger Farr's 1974 study of changes in reading achievement in this century does an excellent job of analyzing changes prior to the early 1960s, but a very poor job after that point. Farr fails to look at any renorming studies or at SAT or ACT data. . . . Farr was IRA president last year and apparently feels that his interests and perhaps those of the IRA will be served if he can supply the public school establishment with statistical evidence that the public schools are doing a good job. (p. 739)

Mary Wray Dubbs (1979) compared the reading achievement of eighth-grade students in 1978 with eighth-grade students in 1917. They took the same test and were compared on reading comprehension and reading vocabulary subtests. She also studied the same students' achievement at the sixth-grade level. Dubbs said,

Within the limits of the present study, it appears that today's students fare quite well indeed when compared with yesterday's students. Eighth graders in 1978 showed slightly lower achievement than 1919 eighth graders on a vocabulary test, but the difference was not statistically significant. Furthermore, on inferential literal comprehension of a paragraph, 1978 sixth graders scored at a significantly higher level than sixth graders in 1917. (p. 933)

John T. Guthrie (1980) reports that in 1970, a sample of the United States population read a paragraph and then answered questions about it. He noted the following results:

1. The item was answered correctly by 96.8 percent of the adults tested.
2. The item was answered correctly by 98.7 percent of the 17-year-olds tested.
3. The item was answered correctly by 83.7 percent of the 9-year-olds tested. (p. 750)

In a later article, John Micklos, Jr. (1982) stated,

Overall, the most recent evidence paints an encouraging picture, especially regarding achievement in the primary grades. The data show that reading achievement in grades 1–3 is consistently rising, while the basic skills of students at all levels remain stable. The figures also indicate, however, that older students may not be developing the higher level reading skills that are so necessary to function effectively in today's complex world. (p. 760)

An article in the *El Paso Times* (1982) reported that students' scores on the Scholastic Aptitude Test were higher that year for the first time in 19 years. George Hanford, president of the College Board, was quoted as saying,

This year's rise, however slight, combined with last year's holding steady, is a welcome sign for educators, parents and students that serious efforts by the nation's schools and their students to improve the quality of education are taking effect. (p. 8A)

Thus, research shows that the profession is doing a better job of teaching reading at the primary grade level than at any time in the past. However, from 1970 to 1978, there was a drop in students' achievement from approximately the fifth-grade level and above. This drop was especially pronounced at the eighth-grade level and

above. Much of the problem at the secondary level, where achievement has not been so marked, stems from students not *practicing* the skills learned earlier. No matter how much students are coached, they will not develop good reading skills unless they practice. But many junior high and secondary students have days so full of other activities that they have little time left for reading for pleasure. That is why a sustained silent reading period is so crucial to a school's reading program (see Chapter 11).

Also, remember that reading achievement trends are complex. They involve more than teachers and their methods; such trends also involve societal factors, educational philosophy in general, parent and student attitudes, and a host of other known and unknown factors.

THE FUTURE: BECOMING BETTER TEACHERS

Because research shows how crucial the teacher is to reading instruction, reading teachers feel great responsibility. They want to improve, to help their students achieve more, but they do not always know how to do so. Recent research about academic learning time and exemplary reading programs give them a handle on what they need to do to become better teachers.

Academic Learning Time

An important concept in the research of recent years is *academic learning time*. Charles Fisher, Richard Marliave, and Nikola N. Filby (1979) explain this concept as the amount of time a student spends engaged in an academic task that she performs with high success.[2] Thus, the basic components of academic learning time are *allocated time*, *student engagement*, and *student*

[2]*Note.* The following discussion comes from "Improving Teaching by Increasing 'Academic Learning Time'" by C. Fisher, R. Marliave, and N. N. Filby, *Educational Leadership*, October, 1979, *37*, 52–54. Quoted portions are reprinted with permission of the Association for Supervision and Curriculum Development and C. Fisher, R. Marliave, and N. N. Filby. Copyright © 1979 by the Association for Supervision and Curriculum Development. All rights reserved.

success rate. In explaining these terms the authors say,

engaged time is that portion of allocated time during which the student is paying attention.

The amount of student learning is influenced not only by the amount of engaged time, but also by the "match" between the task and the particular student. If the task is so difficult that the student produces few correct responses, then not much learning will result. On the other hand, if the student produces many correct responses, he/she is more likely to be learning.

Academic Learning Time occurs when all three of these conditions apply simultaneously; that is, when time is allocated to a task, the student is engaged in the task, and the student has a high rate of success. (pp. 52–53)

As part of a beginning teacher evaluation, Fisher, Marliave, Filby, and others measured the academic learning time accumulated in reading and mathematics instruction by students in grades two and five. This time was then compared with their achievement. Six students from each of 25 second-grade classes and 21 fifth-grade classes were given achievement batteries in October, December, and May. During this time, students were intensely observed to obtain allocated time, engagement rates, and success rates for each individual. The researchers found that in fifth-grade reading and reading related activities, the average amount of allocated time varied from about 60 minutes a day to as much as 140 minutes a day. The average engagement time was about 50 percent—the students actively worked only 50 percent of the time allocated. But in some classes, engagement time ran as high as 90 percent. Students also varied considerably in their success rates. The average student spent only about 50 percent of the time working on tasks that he succeeded in. Students who spent more time than average in successful activities had higher achievement scores in the spring and better retention of learning over the summer. They also had more positive attitudes towards school.

Fisher, Marliave, and Filby summarized:

Allocated time, engagement rate, and success

rate—the three ingredients of Academic Learning Time—are all associated with student achievement. Students who accumulate more Academic Learning Time generally have higher scores on achievement tests. This means that Academic Learning Time can be interpreted as an immediate, ongoing measure of student learning. (p. 53)

David Berliner (1980) discussed his and other studies in which allocated time varied in reading classes, with ratios of most allocated time to least allocated time being as high as 2:1 or even 3:1.[3] Berliner states,

In reading we have evidence that the average child in one class receives 357 minutes per school year in comprehension activities such as paraphrasing, synthesizing, or drawing inferences from stories. Yet in another class, the average child receives 3,081 minutes of such activities over the school year. These are differences of a magnitude of 10:1. If you could bet on which class would perform better on comprehension tests, you would do well to follow common sense notions. Teachers who provide their classes with greater amounts of allocated time in a subject matter area than their colleagues will have classes that usually achieve higher in that subject matter area. (p. 303)

In discussing engaged time Berliner states that

in a pilot study under way now, we are amazed to find after six days of observation in one classroom that we have a student who appears to be engaged under 10 percent of the time while another student in that class appears to be engaged over 90 percent of the time. That is, ratios of 9:1 in the percent of the engaged time are showing up in this one class! (p. 303)

About success rates, Berliner says that

in general, a high success rate during learning is a positive predictor of school achievement. A rather unsurprising corollary bit of knowledge also has been gained. It is found that materials and activities that yield a low success rate for students (i.e., where there are high error rates) are consistently and negatively correlated with achievement. (p. 304)

---

[3]*Note.* Quoted portions from "Using Research on Teaching for the Improvement of Classroom Practice" by D. C. Berliner, *Theory Into Practice,* Autumn, 1980, *19,* 303–304, 307. Copyright 1980 by *Theory Into Practice.* Reprinted by permission.

In his discussion of the implications for staff development, Berliner states,

The conclusions reached from these studies and the attempt to define direct instruction leads to a simple one-sentence statement that best summarizes what we now know: If the tests they use are matched to the curriculum they teach, then elementary school teachers who find ways to put students into contact with the academic curriculum, and keep them in contact with that curriculum, while maintaining a convivial classroom atmosphere, are successful in promoting reading and mathematics achievement. Staff development efforts that try to work on these issues will be likely to succeed in improving the academic achievement of young children. (p. 307)

Exemplary Reading Programs

S. Jay Samuels (1981) studied the characteristics of seven exemplary reading programs and found 15 factors common to almost all of them. These characteristics are summarized in Table 13–3. These 15 common variables were:

Strong Leadership. Administrators were aware of existing problems and expressed strong support for efforts to raise achievement.

High Expectations. People believed that teachers can make the difference. Administrators, teachers, and parents help maintain high expectations for both teacher and students. As Samuels says, "Failure was unacceptable" (p. 257).

Teacher Aides. Aides participated in direct instruction. They did not run off mimeo or ditto sheets and, in general, did not do menial tasks. They were directly involved in the teaching of children, thus making a much smaller pupil-teacher ratio.

Reading Specialists. There was a reading specialist present. The reading specialist worked directly with teachers and teacher's aides to help them upgrade their skills in teaching reading. Samuels calls this the multiplier effect: ten teachers learn, then work with 300 pupils. The reading specialist who works with only 10 children gains little compared to the specialist who works with 10 teachers.

Teacher Training. Teachers were trained in the program methods the school was using.

Teacher Role. The teacher's role was to present, diagnose, and remediate. The teachers taught the material in the program. They then diagnosed their students to see if they had achieved certain program objectives. If some students had not learned the material, they were given remedial work.

Specific Reading Objectives. The teachers had specific objectives; they knew exactly what they wanted to accomplish and set about to do so.

Skills Centered Curriculum. Teachers focused on certain skills to facilitate word recognition, etc. As Samuels says, "This should not be taken to mean that comprehension was unimportant, but that an early focus was given to those skills which facilitate word recognition" (p. 258).

Instruction and Materials Relevant to Goals. Specific objectives were stated, and instruction was focused to accomplish these objectives. Materials were appropriate for the purpose.

Structured Environment. Classroom environment aided the teacher in accomplishing the objectives.

Positive Classroom Climate. Teachers believed that students could learn regardless of their socioeconomic level and that they themselves were all capable of teaching. Token rewards were given when students needed extra motivation. Students were in an academic environment, but they also felt good about themselves.

Efficient Use of Time. Daily routines were carefully structured so that teachers and students could use time efficiently.

Table 13–3   Common variables of exemplary reading programs

Components	Weber (1971)	Hawkridge, Tallmadge, and Larsen (1968)	Wargo et al. (1972)	CRAFT (1966)	NY State Office of Ed. (1974)	Direct Instruction (1977)	Wilder (1977)
Strong administrative leadership	+	+	+		+	+	+
High expectations and belief that the teacher can make the difference	+		+	+	+	+	
Teacher aids used in direct instruction	+	+	+			+	
Reading specialist	+		+			+	+
Teacher training	+	+	+		+	+	+
Teacher role—present, diagnose, remediate	+	+	+			+	
Specific reading objectives	+	+	+	+		+	+
Skills centered curriculum	+		+	+		+	+
Instruction and materials relevant to goals	+	+	+			+	+
Structural environment	+		+		+	+	
Positive classroom climate	+		+		+		
Efficient use of time	+	+	+	+		+	+
High intensity of treatment	+	+	+	+		+	+
Frequent evaluation of student progress	+	+	+		+	+	
Supervision of teachers			+			+	

A + means that component was identified in the report.

Note. From "Characteristics of Exemplary Reading Programs" by S.J. Samuels in *Comprehension and Teaching: Research Reviews*, J.T. Guthrie, ed. (Newark, Del.: International Reading Association, 1981), 265. Copyright 1981 by International Reading Association. Reprinted with permission of S.J. Samuels, J.T. Guthrie, and the International Reading Association.

High Intensity of Treatment.   Students had to pay attention and the teacher went from one activity to another without wasting time.

Frequent Evaluation.   Students were evaluated frequently, so that those not making proper progress could be given remedial work on specific tasks or skills.

Supervision of Teachers.   Teachers were first trained in the program's methods and materials and then carefully monitored to make sure teachers were using those methods and materials.

The concept of academic learning time gives reading teachers a way to evaluate their own contribution to the work done by students in the classroom. Observing academic learning time partially answers why some teachers more efficiently stimulate pupil achievement than others do. Samuels' identification of what makes a reading program successful also gives teachers a tangible grasp of ways to improve their reading programs. Teachers and administrators now know what to change and can begin the hard work of implementing those changes in their own school systems.

SUMMARY

Reading instruction's orientation, materials, and methods have changed greatly during the United States' history: from religious to literary to social values, from the hornbook to basal readers, from rote learning to individualized approaches, from trial and error to research. What has remained constant during all these changes, however, is the teacher's influence in making students better readers; the teacher always has more to do with students' success than materials do.

Such responsibility has led to research into what happens in classrooms and schools that produce superior readers. The impact of the research on academic learning time and exemplary reading programs will influence reading instruction in the United States for years to come.

REVIEW QUESTIONS

1. Why do teaching materials change?
2. How might students' overall achievement compare grade-by-grade, in colonial times to now?
3. Why have people in the United States felt the need to learn to read?
4. Is there any superior method of teaching first-grade students how to read?
5. Compare, using as many points as possible, the way reading is taught in today's elementary schools to the way it was taught in the earliest years of the United States' history.
6. Discuss why reading teachers spent so much time in the past in training visual or visual-motor processes.
7. What is academic learning time, and why is it important?
8. What are the characteristics of schools that achieve superior results?

REFERENCES

Arnold, S. L. *Reading: How to teach it*. Newark: Silver Burdett, 1899.

Artley, A. S. Individual differences and reading instruction. *Elementary School Journal*, November, 1981, *82*, 143–51.

Berliner, D. C. Using research on teaching for the improvement of classroom practice. *Theory Into Practice*, Autumn, 1980, *19*, 302–308.

Betts, E. A. *Foundations of reading instruction*. New York: American Book Co., 1946.

Bond, G. L., & Dykstra, R. The cooperative research program in first-grade reading instruction. *Reading Research Quarterly*, Summer, 1967, *2*, 5–142.

Copperman, P. The achievement decline of the 1970s. *Phi Delta Kappan*, June, 1979, *60*, 736–39.

Dubbs, M. W. How good were readers in the good old days? Replication of two studies. *Reading Teacher*, May, 1979, *32*, 933–39.

Farr, R. Is Johnny's/Mary's reading getting worse? *Educational Leadership*, April, 1977, *34*, 521–23, 525–27.

Farr, R. International Reading Association's silver anniversary, 1980, 25 years of accomplishment in reading. *Reading Teacher*, May, 1980, *33*, 904–906.

Fisher, C. Marliave, R., & Filby, N. N. Improving teaching by increasing "academic learning time." *Educational Leadership*, October, 1979, *37*, 52–54.

Guthrie, J. T. Three facts of reading achievement. *Reading Teacher*, March, 1980, *33*, 81–83.

Hammill, D., Goodman, L., & Wiederholt, J. L. Visual-motor processes: Can we train them? *Reading Teacher*, February, 1974, *27*, 469–78.

Harris, A. J. *How to increase reading ability*. New York: Donald McKay, 1961.

Hodgkinson, H. What's right with education. *Phi Delta Kappan*, November, 1979, *61*, 159–62.

Huey, E. B. *The psychology and pedagogy of reading*. Cambridge, Mass.: MIT press, 1908.

Leavitt, J. *Easy lessons in reading*. Keene, N. H.: J. & J. W. Printiss, 1829.

Micklos, J., Jr. A look at reading achievement in the United States: The latest data. *Journal of Reading*, May, 1982, *25*, 760–62.

Robinson, H. A. Reading instruction and research in historical perspective. In H. A. Robinson (Ed.), *Reading and writing instruction in the United States: Historical trends*. Urbana, Ill.: ERIC Clearinghouse on Reading and Communication Skills, and Newark, Del.: International Reading Association, 1977.

Samuels, S. J. Characteristics of exemplary reading programs. In J. T. Guthrie (Ed.), *Comprehension and teaching: Research reviews*. Newark, Del.: International Reading Association, 1981.

Scores rise for college entrance exam. *El Paso Times*, September 22, 1982, p. 8A.

Smith, N. B. *American reading instruction*. Newark, Del.: International Reading Association, 1965.

Appendices

BASIC SIGHT WORDS

Should be known by			*Words*			
1.9	a	him	then	time	find	red
	did	look	who	after	is	that
	have	run	can	came	other	way
	know	we	good	he	something	blue
	one	be	in	now	very	give
	to	for	not	she	around	may
	and	his	this	tree	fly	ride
	do	make	will	all	jump	them
	her	said	come	could	over	went
	like	what	has	help	stop	by
	play	big	it	old	want	green
	too	get	of	so	as	me
	are	house	three	up	from	sat
	down	my	you	am	let	there
	here	the	your	day	ran	when
	little	where	about	how	take	saw
	put	but	call	on	was	they
	two	go	had	some	back	would
	away	I	mother	us	funny	yes
	eat	no	see	an	man	
2.5	again	well	stand	please	morning	happy
	dog	been	yellow	think	under	walk
	boy	any	were	tell	party	much
	if	far	before	better	black	fun
	brown	ask	white	than	pretty	must
	into	fast	five	four	long	girl
	buy	at	why	thank	pull	name
	just	laugh	light	or	Mr.	got
	cold	ate	with	their	rabbit	never
	new	night	soon	out	more	high
	color	ball	work	these	read	shall
	sleep	walk				

Note. From *Locating and Correcting Reading Difficulties* by E.E. Ekwall (Columbus, Ohio: Charles E. Merrill, 1981), 170–71. Copyright 1981 by Charles E. Merrill Publishing Co. Reprinted by permission.

Should be known by	*Words*					
2.9	always	another	because	best	both	box
	bring	carry	clean	cut	does	each
	end	every	fall	first	found	friend
	gave	full	left	own	start	year
	last	our	six	wish	kind	open
	sit	while	keep	only	show	which
	hurt	once	should	warm	hot	men
	near	school	until	home	say	those
	hold	many	round	thing	hand	made
	right	ten	grow	live	pick	sure
3.5	dear	drink	present	seem	sing	such
	today	use	write	done	people	seven
	small	try	wash			
3.9	draw	eight	upon	leave	its	goes

B Quick Check for Basic Sight Word Knowledge

QUICK CHECK FOR BASIC SIGHT WORD KNOWLEDGE

Answer Sheet

Name: _____ Date: _____

School: _____ Tester: _____

Directions: As the student reads the words from the stimulus sheet, mark those read correctly with a plus (+) and those read incorrectly with a minus (−) or write in the word substituted. If the student says he does not know an answer then mark it with a (?).

(IF A STUDENT MISSES ANY WORDS ON THIS TEST THEN HE SHOULD BE GIVEN THE FULL LIST OF BASIC SIGHT WORDS).

1. I _____

2. the _____

3. you _____

4. down _____

5. here _____

6. he _____

7. fly _____

8. help _____

9. this _____

10. happy _____

11. tree _____

12. his _____

13. hot _____

14. end _____

15. ride _____

16. saw _____

17. light _____

18. sat _____

19. pretty _____

20. again _____

21. thank _____

22. only _____

23. well _____

24. first _____

25. thing _____

26. any _____

27. also _____

28. while _____

29. should _____

30. upon _____

31. sure _____

32. always _____

33. than _____

34. present _____

35. such _____

36. hurt _____

Note. From *Locating and Correcting Reading Difficulties* by E.E. Ekwall (Columbus, Ohio: Charles E. Merrill, 1981), 206–07. Copyright 1981 by Charles E. Merrill Publsihing Co. Reprinted by permission.

QUICK TEST FOR BASIC SIGHT WORD KNOWLEDGE

1. I	13. hot	25. thing
2. the	14. end	26. any
3. you	15. ride	27. also
4. down	16. saw	28. while
5. here	17. light	29. should
6. he	18. sat	30. upon
7. fly	19. pretty	31. sure
8. help	20. again	32. always
9. this	21. thank	33. than
10. happy	22. only	34. present
11. tree	23. well	35. such
12. his	24. first	36. hurt

C San Diego Quick Assessment

The San Diego Quick Assessment is a quick way to gauge a student's reading ability. It is a graded word list, formed by drawing words randomly from basal reader glossaries, and from the Thorndike list. Words initially were assigned levels according to these sources, with some shifting on the basis of students' responses.

The graded word list has two uses: 1) to determine a reading level; 2) to detect errors in word analysis. One can use the test information to group students for corrective practice or to select appropriate reading materials for those students.

The list is remarkably accurate when used for these purposes. During the last two years we have had students in our undergraduate reading classes give this test to children in our campus laboratory school. Following testing, we asked them to recommend appropriate reading levels for these children. In all but four cases out of more than one hundred, their recommendations coincided with those of the classroom teachers who had been working with these children for a large portion of the year.

The list, like other instruments, is not appropriate for all students. Among high school and adult groups, we find it most effective for those who have poor decoding skills. Junior high students need not be so disabled for this to be an effective instrument.

Administration

1. Type out each list of ten words on an index card.
2. Begin with a card that is at least two years below the student's grade level assignments.
3. Ask the student to read the words aloud to you. If he misreads any of the list, drop to easier lists until he makes no errors. This indicates the base level.
4. Write down all incorrect responses, or use diacritical marks on your copy of the test. For example, *lonely* might be read and recorded as *lovely*. *Apparatus* might be recorded as *a per' a tus*.
5. Encourage the student to read words he does not know so that you can identify the techniques he uses for word identification.

Note. From "The Graded Word List: Quick Gauge of Reading Ability" by M. LaPray and R. Ross, *Journal of Reading,* January, 1969, 305–07. Copyright 1969 by the International Reading Association. Reprinted with permission of M. LaPray, R. Ross, and the International Reading Association.

6. Have the student read from increasingly difficult lists until he misses at least three words.

PP	Primer	1
see	you	road
play	come	live
me	not	thank
at	with	when
run	jump	bigger
go	help	how
and	is	always
lock	work	night
can	are	spring
here	this	today

2	3	4
our	city	decided
please	middle	served
myself	moment	amazed
town	frightened	silent
early	exclaimed	wrecked
send	several	improved
wide	lonely	certainly
believe	drew	entered
quietly	since	realized
carefully	straight	interrupted

5	6	7
scanty	bridge	amber
certainly	commercial	dominion
develop	abolish	sundry
considered	trucker	capillary
discussed	apparatus	impetuous
behaved	elementary	blight
splendid	comment	wrest
acquainted	necessity	enumerate
escaped	gallery	daunted
grim	relativity	condescend

8	9	10
capacious	conscientious	zany
limitation	isolation	jerkin
pretext	molecule	nausea
intrigue	ritual	gratuitous
delusion	momentous	linear
immaculate	vulnerable	inept
ascent	kinship	legality
acrid	conservatism	aspen
binocular	jaunty	amnesty
embankment	inventive	barometer

11
galore
rotunda
capitalism
prevaricate
risible
exonerate
superannuate
luxuriate
piebald
crunch

Analysis

1. The list in which a student misses no more than one of the ten words is the level at which he can read independently. Two errors indicate his instructional level. Three or more errors identify the level at which reading material will be too difficult for him.

2. An analysis of a student's errors is useful. Among those which occur with greatest frequency are the following:

Error	*Example*
reversal	*ton* for *not*
consonant	*now* for *how*
consonant clusters	*state* for *straight*
short vowel	*cane* for *can*
long vowel	*wid* for *wide*
prefix	*inproved* for *improved*
suffix	*improve* for *improved*
miscellaneous	(accent, omission of syllables, etc.)

3. As with other reading tasks, teacher observation of student behavior is essential. Such things as posture, facial expression, and voice quality may signal restlessness, lack of assurance, or frustration while reading.

D Publishers of Reading Materials

A.B. Dick Co.
5700 Touhy Avenue
Chicago, IL 60648

The A.N. Palmer Co.
1720 West Irving Park Road
Schaumbug, IL 60193

ARO Publishing, Inc.
P.O. Box 193
Provo, UT 84601

A-V Concepts Corp.
30 Montauk Boulevard
Oakdale, NY 11769

Abingdon Press
201 8th Avenue South
Nashville, TN 37202

Abrahams Magazine Service
56 East 13th Street
New York, NY 10003

Academic Press
111 Fifth Avenue
New York, NY 10003

Academic Therapy Publications
20 Commercial Blvd.
Novatio, CA 94947

Acropolis Books Ltd.
2400 17th Street N.W.
Washington, DC 20009

Addison-Wesley Publishing Co.
Jacob Way
Reading, MA 01867

Addison-Wesley Testing Service
2725 Sand Hill Rd.
Menlo Park, CA 94025

Albert Whitman & Co.
5747 West Howard Street
Niles, IL 60648

Allied Educational Press
P.O. Box 337
Niles, MI 49120

Allyn and Bacon, Inc.
7 Wells Ave.
Newton, MA 02159

American Council on Education
One Dupont Circle
Washington, DC 20036

American Guidance Service
Publishers' Building
Circle Pines, MN 55014

American Library Association
50 East Huron Street
Chicago, IL 60611

American Printing House For The Blind
P.O. Box 6085
Louisville, KY 40206

Ann Arbor Publishers, Inc.
P.O. Box 7249
Naples, FL 33940

Arista Corporation
2440 Estand Way
Concord, CA 94524

Association for Childhood Education International
3615 Wisconsin Avenue N.W.
Washington, DC 20016

Audio-Visual Research
1317 Eighth Street S.E.
Waseca, MN 56093

Avon Books
959 8th Ave.
New York, NY 10019

Baker and Taylor Co.
1515 Broadway
New York, NY 10036

Bantam Books Inc.
School and College Marketing Division
666 Fifth Avenue
New York, NY 10019

Barnell Loft, LTD
958 Church Street
Baldwin, NY 11510

Barnes and Noble Sale Annex
126 Fifth Ave.
New York, NY 10011

Basic Skills Program
Office of Basic Skills Improvement
Room 1167, Donohoe Building
400 Maryland Avenue, S.W.
Washington, DC 20202

Bell and Howell
Audio-Visual Products Division
7100 N. McCormick Rd.
Chicago, IL 60645

Benefic Press
1250 Sixth Avenue
San Diego, CA 92101

Bobbs-Merrill Educational Publishing
4300 West 62nd Street
P.O. Box 7080
Indianapolis, IN 46206

Borg-Warner Educational Systems
600 West University Drive
Arlington Heights, IL 60004

Bowmar Noble Publishers, Inc.
4563 Colorado Blvd.
Los Angeles, CA 90039

Burgless Publishing Co.
7108 Ohms Lane
Minneapolis, MN 55435

C B H Publishing Inc.
P.O. Box 236
Glencol, IL 60022

C.C. Publications, Inc.
P.O. Box 23699
Tigaro, OR 97223

C. Lucas Dalton
5720 Caruth Haven
Suite 130
Dallas, TX 75206

CTB/McGraw-Hill
Del Monte Research Park
Monterey, CA 93940

Carlson-Dellosa Publishing
1946 S. Arlington Road
Akron, OH 44306

Center for Applied Research in Education, Inc.
P.O. Box 130
West Nyack, NY 10995

Centurion Industries, Inc.
167 Constitution Dr.
Menlo Park, CA 94025

Charles E. Merrill Publishing Co.
1300 Alum Creek Drive
Columbus, Ohio 43216

Chicago Tribune
435 North Michigan Avenue
Chicago, IL 60611

The Children's Book Council
67 Irving Place
New York, NY 10003

Children's Press
1224 West Van Buren Street
Chicago, IL 60607

Clarence L. Barnhart, Inc.
P.O. Box 250, 1 Stone Place
Bronxville, NY 10708

Clarion Books
52 Vanderbilt Ave.
New York, NY 10017

Communacad
Box 541
Wilton, CT 06897

Consulting Psychologists Press, Inc.
577 College Ave.
Palo Alto, CA 94306

Contempoary Books Inc.
180 North Michigan Avenue
Chicago, IL 60601

Continental Press Inc.
Elizabeth Town, PA 17022

Coronado Publishers, Inc.
1250 Sixth Avenue
San Diego, CA 92101

Coronet
65 East South Water Street
Chicago, IL 60601

Council For Exceptional Children
1920 Association Drive
Reston, VA 22091

Creative Curriculum, Inc.
15681 Commerce Lane
Huntington Beach, CA 92649

Creative Publications
P.O. Box 10328
Palo Alto, CA 94303

Crestwood House
P.O. Box 3427
Mankato, MN 58001

Crown Publisher, Inc.
1 Park Avenue
New York, NY 10016

Curriculum Innovations, Inc.
3500 Western Avenue
Highland Park, IL 60035

Curriculum Review
517 S. Jefferson Street
Chicago, IL 60607

D.C. Heath and Co.
125 Spring Street
Lexington, MA 02173

DES Educational Publications
25 South Fifth Avenue
P.O. Box 1291
Highland Park, NJ 08904

Dale Seymour Publications
P.O. Box 10888
Palo Alto, CA 94303

Delacorte Press
c/o Montville Warehousing Co., Inc.
Changegridge Road
Pine Brook, NJ 07058

Dell Publishing Co.
Education Dept.
245 East 47th St.
New York, NY 10017

Department of Defense
Office of Dependent Schools
2461 Eisenhower Avenue
Alexandria, VA 22331

Dormac, Inc.
P.O. Box 1699
Beaverton, OR 97075

Doubleday and Co., Inc.
501 Franklin Avenue
Garden City, NY 11530

Dreier Educational Systems
25 South Fifth Avenue
P.O. Box 1291
Highland Park, NJ 08904

EBSCO Curriculum Materials
P.O. Box 11521
Birmingham, AL 35202

EDITS
P.O. Box 7234
San Diego, CA 92107

EDL Division
Arista Corporation
2440 Estand Way
P.O. Box 6146
Concord, CA 94524

EDL/McGraw-Hill
1221 Avenue of the Americas
New York, NY 10020

EDUCAT Publishers Inc.
P.O. Box 2158
Berkeley, CA 94702

E.H. White and Co.
Suite 710
1025 Vermont Avenue, N.W.
Washington, DC 20005

E.M. Hale and Company
Harvey House Publishers
128 West River Street
Chippewa Falls, WI 54729

E and R Development Co.
Vandalia Road
Jacksonville, FL 62650

ERIC Clearinghouse on Reading and Communication
   Skills
National Council of Teachers of English
1111 Kenyon Road
Urbana, IL 61801

ESP, Inc.
1201 E. Johnson Ave.
P.O. Drawer 5037
Jonesboro, AR 72401

ETA (Educational Teaching Aids)
159 West Kinzie Street
Chicago, IL 60610

Econoclad Books
2101 N. Topeka Blvd.
P.O. Box 1777
Topeka, KS 66601

The Economy Company
P.O. Box 25308
1901 North Walnut Street
Oklahoma City, OK 73125

Educational Activities
P.O. Box 392
Freeport, NY 11520

Educational Development Corp.
8141 East 44th
P.O. Box 45663
Tulsa, OK 74145

Educational Progress
Division of Educational Development Corp.
P.O. Box 45663
Tulsa, OK 74145

Educational Service, Inc.
P.O. Box 219
Stevensville, MI 49127

Educational Teaching Aids Division
555 West Adams Street
Chicago, IL 60606

Educational Testing Service
P.O. Box 999
Princeton, NJ 08540

Educators Publishing Service
75 Moulton Street
Cambridge, MA 02138

Educulture
1 Dubuque Plaza, Suite 150
Dubuque, IA 52001

Elsevier-Dutton Publishing Co., Inc.
2 Park Avenue
New York, NY 10016

Encyclopedia Britannica Educational Corp.
425 North Michigan Avenue
Chicago, IL 60601

Essay Press, Inc.
P.O. Box 2323
La Jolla, CA 92037

Farrar, Straus, & Giroux, Inc.
19 Union Square West
New York, NY 10003

Fawcett Books Group
Educational Marketing Dept.
1515 Broadway
New York, NY 10036

Follett Publishing Co.
Dept D.M.
1010 West Washington Blvd.
Chicago, IL 60607

Frank E. Richards Publishing Co., Inc.
P.O. Box 66
Phoenix, NY 13135

Franklin Watts, Inc.
730 Fifth Ave.
New York, NY 10019

Frank Schaffer Publications
1028 Via Mirabel, Dept. 34
Palos Verdes Estates, CA 90274

G. and C. Merriam Company
Publishers of Merriam-Webster Reference Books
47 Federal Street
Springfield, MA 01101

G.P. Putnam's Sons
Coward McCann & Geoghegan, Inc.
200 Madison Avenue
New York, NY 10016

Gamco Industries, Inc.
Box 1911
Big Spring, TX 79720

Garrard Publishing Co.
1607 North Market Street
Champaign, IL 61820

Ginn & Co.
191 Spring St.
Lexington, MA 02173

Globe Book Co.
50 West 23rd Street
New York, NY 10010

Good Apple, Inc.
Box 299
Carthage, IL 62321

Greenhaven Press, Inc.
577 Shoreview Park Road
St. Paul, MN 55112

Grosset & Dunlap, Inc.
Education Division
51 Madison Avenue
New York, NY 10010

Groves Press, Inc.
196 West Houston Street
New York, NY 10014

H.W. Wilson Co.
950 University Avenue
Bronx, NY 10452

Hammond Inc.
515 Valley Street
Maplewood, NJ 07040

Hampden Publicatons, Inc.
P.O. Box 4873
Baltimore, MD 21211

Harcourt Brace Jovanovich, Inc.
757 Third Ave.
New York, NY 10017

Harper & Row. Inc.
10 East 53rd Street
New York, NY 10022

Harper & Row, Inc.
c/o Order Dept.
Keystone Industrial Park
Scranton, PA 18512

Hawthorn Books, Inc.
260 Madison Avenue
New York, NY 10016

Hayden Book Company, Inc.
50 Essex Street
Rochelle Park, NJ 07662

Heinemann Educational Books, Inc.
4 Front Street
Exerter, NH 03833

Hertzberg-New Method Inc.
Vandalia Road
Jacksonville, IL 62650

Highlights For Children
2300 West Fifth Avenue
P.O. Box 269
Columbus, OH 43216

The Highsmith Co., Inc.
P.O. Box 800 A, Highway 106 East
Fort Atkinson, WI 53538

Holiday House, Inc.
18 East 53rd St.
New York, NY 10022

Holt, Rinehart and Winston
CBS Inc.
383 Madison Avenue
New York, NY 10017

Houghton Mifflin
1 Beacon Street
Boston, MA 02107

Hutchinson Books, Inc.
Chestnut Street
Lewiston, ME 04240

I/CT-Instructional/Communications Technology, Inc.
10 Stepar Place
Huntington Station, NY 11746

ITA, A Non-Profit Educational Foundation
Hofstra University
Hempstead, NY 11550

Ideal School Supply Co.
11000 South Lavergne Avenue
Oak Lawn, IL 60453

Imperial International Learning Corporation
P.O. Box 548
Kankakee, IL 60901

Incentive Publications
2400 Crestmoor Rd.
Nashville, TN 37215

Incentives for Learning, Inc.
600 West Van Buren Street
Chicago, IL 60607

Innovative Sciences, Inc.
300 Broad Street
Stanford, CT 06901

Instructional Fair
P.O. Box 1650
Grand Rapids, MI 49501

Instructor
Dansville, NY 14437

Instructor Publications
7 Bank Street
Dansville, NY 14437

International Reading Association
800 Barksdale Road
Newark, DE 19711

J. Weston Walch, Publisher
321 Valley Street
Portland, ME 04104

Jamestown Publishers
P.O. Box 6743
Providence, RI 02940

Janus Book Publishers
2501 Industrial Pkwy. West
Hayward, CA 94545

Julian Messner
1230 Avenue of the Americas
New York, NY 10020

Kenworthy Educational Service, Inc.
Box 60, 138 Allen Street
Buffalo, NY 14205

Keystone View
Division of Mast Development Co.
2212 East 12th Street
Davenport, IA 52803

Kimbo Educational
P.O. Box 477
Long Branch, NJ 07740

King Features
235 East 45th Street
New York, NY 10017

The Kingsbury Center
2138 Bancroft Place, N.W.
Washington, DC 20008

The Klamath Printery
628 Oak Street
Klamath Falls, OR 97601

Knowledge Industry Publications, Inc.
701 Westchester Ave.
White Plains, NY 10604

Kraus-Thomson Organization, Ltd.
Rt. 100
Millwood, NY 10546

Laidlaw Brothers
Thatcher & Madison
Riverforest, IL 60305

Language Research Associates, Inc.
P.O. Drawer 2085
Palm Springs, CA 92262

Lansford Publishing, Co.
1088 Lincoln Avenue
P.O. Box 8711
San Jose, CA 95155

Learning Arts
P.O. Box 179
Wichita, KS 67201

Learning Associates, Inc.
P.O. Box 561167
Miami, FL 33156

The Learning Line
P.O. Box 1200
Palo Alto, CA 94302

Learning Periodicals Group
19 Davis Drive
Belmont, CA 94002

Learning Resources Corporation
8517 Production Avenue
San Diego, CA 92121

Learning Systems Corp.
60 Connolly Parkway
Hamde, CT 06514

Learning Tree Publishing, Inc.
7108 South Alton Way
Englewood, CO 80112

Learning Well
200 South Service Road
Roslyn Heights, NY 11577

Lerner
241 First Avenue North
Minneapolis, MN 55401

Leswing Press
P.O. Box 3577
San Rafael, CA 94901

Library of Congress, National Library Service for the
  Blind and Physically Handicapped
1291 Taylor Street N.W.
Washington, DC 20542

Listening Library, Inc.
1 Park Avenue
P.O. Box L
Old Greenwich, CT 06870

Little, Brown and Company
College Division
34 Beacon Street
Boston, MA 02106

Litton Educational Publishing, Inc.
7625 Empire Drive
Florence, KY 41042

Longman Inc.
19 West 44th Street
New York, NY 10036

The Macmillan Company
Front and Brown Streets
Riverside, NJ 08370

Macmillan Education
Houndmills, Basingstoke, Hampshire
England
RG212XS

Macmillan Publishing Co., Inc.
866 3rd Ave.
New York, NY 10022

Mafex Associates, Inc.
90 Cherry St.
P.O. Box 519
Johnstown, PA 15907

Mast Development Co.
2212 East 12th Street
Davenport, IA 52803

Mastery Education Corp.
85 Main Street
Watertown, MA 02172

McCormick-Mathers Publishing Company
A Division of Litton Education Publishing, Inc.
7625 Empire Drive
Florence, KY 41042

McDonald Publishing Co.
925 Demun Avenue
St. Louis, MO 63105

McDougal, Littell & Co.
P.O. Box 1667-C
Evanston, IL 60204

McGraw-Hill Book Co.
1221 Ave. of the Americas
New York, NY 10020

McGraw-Hill Ryerson LTD.
330 Progress Avenue
Scarborough, Ontario
Canada M1P 2Z5

Media Basics
Larchmont Plaza
Larchmont, NY 10538

Media Material, Inc.
Department MDR
2936 Remington Avenue
Baltimore, MD 21211

Media-Pak/82
P.O. Box 541
Wilton, CT 06897

Melody House Publishing Co.
819 N.W. 92nd Street
Oklahoma City, OK 73114

Midwest Publications
P.O. Box 448
Pacific Grove, CA 93950

Milton Bradley Co.
Springfield, Mass. 01101

The Morgan Co.
4510 N. Ravenswood Avenue
Chicago, IL 60640

NCS/Educational Systems Division
4401 West 76th Street
Minneapolis, MN 55435

National Associations For the Deaf
814 Thayer Avenue
Silver Springs, MD 20910

National Council of Teachers of English
1111 Kenyon Road
Urbana, IL 61801

National Public Radio
2025 M Street, N.W.
Washington, DC 20036

National Textbook Company
8259 Viles Center Road
Skokie, IL 60077

The New American Library, Inc.
1633 Broadway
New York, NY 10019

Newsweek
The Newsweek Building
Livingston, NJ 07039

Nystrom
3333 Elston Avenue
Chicago, IL 60618

Oceana Educational Communications
75 Main Street
Dobbs Ferry, NY 10522

Optimal Corporation
Open Court Publishing Company
La Salle, IL 61301

PIRT
c/o Tact
P.O. Box 1052
Daylestown, PA 18901

Pendulum Press, Inc.
The Academic Building
Saw Mill Road
West Haven, CT 06516

Penguin Books
299 Murry Hill Parkway
East Rutherford, NJ 07073

Phonovisual Products, Inc.
12216 Parklawn Drive
P.O. Box 2007
Rockville, MD 20852

Pitman Learning, Inc.
6 Davis Drive
Belmont, CA 94002

Plays, Inc.
8 Arlington Street
Boston, MA 02116

Pleasantville Media
Suite E-61
P.O. Box 415
Pleasantville, NY 10570

Pocket Books
1230 Avenue of the Americas
New York, NY 10020

Prentice-Hall
Educational Book Division
Englewood Cliffs, NJ 07632

Pro-Ed
5341 Industrial Oaks Blvd.
Austin, TX 78735

Programs for Achievement in Reading, Inc.
Abbott Park Place
Providence, RI 02903

Pruett Publishing Company
3235 Prairie Avenue
Boulder, CO 80301

The Psychological Corp.
757 Third Avenue or
304 E. 45th Street
New York, NY 10017

Psychological Test Specialists
P.O. Box 9229
Missoula, MT 59807

Publishers Test Service
2500 Garden Road
Monterey, CA 93940

R.R. Bowker Co.
1180 Avenue of the Americas
New York, NY 10036

Radio Shack
Publicity Dept.
300 One Tandy Center
Fort Worth, TX 76102

Raintree Children's Books
205 West Highland Ave.
Milwaukee, WI 53203

Rand McNally and Co.
P.O. Box 7600
Chicago, IL 60680

Random House, Inc.
201 E. 50 St.
New York, NY 10022

The Reading Laboratory
P.O. Box 681
South Norwalk, CT 06854

Readers Digest Services, Inc.
Educational Division
Pleasantville, NY 10570

Reflections & Images
6607 Northridge Drive
San Jose, CA 95120

Regents Publishing Co., Inc.
2 Park Avenue
New York, NY 10016

Resources
Instructional Communication Technology, Inc.
Huntington Station, NY 11746

Resources for the Gifted
P.O. Box 15050
Phoenix, AZ 85060

Richard C. Owen Publishers
P.O. Box 14007
Chicago, IL 60614

Riverside Publishing Co.
P.O. Box 1970
Iowa City, IA 52244

Rourke Publishing Group
P.O. Box 711
Windermere, FL 32786

SVE Teacher's Choice
2750 North Wayne Avenue
Chicago, IL 60614

Santillana Publishing Co.
575 Lexington Avenue
New York, NY 10022

Scarecrow Press, Inc.
52 Liberty Street
P.O. Box 656
Metuchen, NJ 08840

Scholastic Book Service
904 Sylvan Avenue
Englewood Cliffs, NJ 07632

Science Research Association, Inc.
155 North Wacker Drive
Chicago, IL 60606

Science Research Associates, Inc.
College Division
1540 Page Mill Road
P.O. Box 10021
Palo Alto, CA 94303

Scott, Foresman and Company
1900 E. Lake Ave.
Glenview, IL 60025

Silver Burdett Co.
8301 Ambassador Row
Dallas, TX 75247

Simon & Schuster
1230 Avenue of the Americas
New York, NY 10020

Sirs
P.O. Box 2507
Boca Raton, FL 33442

Skillcorp Publishers, Inc.
P.O. Box 712
Columbus, OH 43216

Slosson Educational Publications
P.O. Box 280
East Aurora, NY 14052

Smithsonian Institution
475 L'Enfant Plaza
Suite 4800
Washington, DC 20560

Society for Visual Education
Dept. LX
1345 Diversey Parkway
Chicago, IL 60614

South Western Publishing Co.
5101 Madison Road
Cincinnati, OH 45227

Special Learning Corporation
42 Boston Post Rd.
P.O. Box 306
Guilford, CT 06437

Steck-Vaughn Co.
P.O. Box 2028
807 Brazos St.
Austin, TX 78767

Stemmer House
2627 Caves Road
Owings Mills, MD 21117

Step, Inc.
P.O. Box 887
Mukilteo, WA 98275

Stoelting Co.
1350 S. Kostner Avenue
Chicago, IL 60623

Strine Publishing Co.
P.O. Box 149
York, PA 17405

Sunburst Communications
Room U 23 or VR-6
39 Washington Avenue
Pleasantville, NY 10570

Sundance
Newton Road
Littleton, MA 01460

TSC, A Houghton Mifflin Co.
Dept. 70
P.O. Box 683
Hanover, NH 03755

Teachers & Writers Collaborative
84 Fifth Avenue
New York, NY 10011

Teaching Resources Corporation
50 Pond Park Road
Higham, MA 02043

Thinking Skills
P.O. Box 448
Pacific Grove, CA 93950

Thurman Publishing Co.
1428 Harvard Avenue
Seattle, WA 98122

Trend Enterprises, Inc.
P.O. Box 43073
St. Paul, MN 55164

Troll Associates
320 Rt. 17
Mahwah, NJ 07430

United Learning
6636 West Howard Street
Niles, IL 60648

United States Government Printing Office
Washington, DC 20402

University of Chicago Press
5801 South Ellis Avenue
Chicago, IL 60637
or
Journals Dept.
11030 South Langley Avenue
Chicago, IL 60672

University of Illinois Press
54 E. Gregory Dr.
Champaign, IL 61820

University of Michigan Press
P.O. Box 1104
Ann Arbor, MI 48106

University of Nebraska Press
318 Nebraska Hall
901 North 17th Street
Lincoln, NE 68588

Viking Penguin, Inc.
625 Madison Avenue
New York, NY 10022

Visual Materials, Inc.
4170 Grove Avenue
Gurnee, IL 60031

W.W. Norton & Company, Inc.
500 Fifth Avenue
New York, NY 10036

Webster Division of McGraw-Hill Book Company
1221 Avenue of the Americas
New York, NY 10020

Weekly Reader
Long Hill Road
Middletown, CT 06457

Weekly Reader/Secondary Unit Books
1250 Fairwood Avenue
P.O. Box 16618
Columbus, OH 43216

Western Psychological Services
12031 Wilshire Blvd.
Los Angeles, CA 90025

Weston Woods Studios
Weston, CT 06883

William C. Brown Company
2460 Kerper Boulevard
Dubuque, IA 52001

William H. Sadlier, Inc.
11 Park Place
New York, NY 10007

William Morrow & Company
105 Madison Avenue
New York, NY 10016

The World Almanac, Education Division
1278 West Ninth Street
Cleveland, OH 44113

World Book-Childcraft International, Inc.
Merchandise Mart Plaza
Chicago, IL 60654

Xerox Education Publications
1250 Fairwood Avenue
Columbus, OH 43216

Youngheart Records
P.O. Box 27784
Los Angeles, CA 90027

Zaner-Bloser
2500 West Fifth Avenue
P.O. Box 16764
Columbus, OH 43216

Zweig Associates
1711 McGraw Avenue
Irvine, CA 92714

E Vowel Rules and Syllable Principles

When testing for knowledge of vowel rules and syllable principles,* remember that the ultimate goal is to enable the student to *use,* not just to *recite,* the rule or principle that applies to each word. Phonics research in the past ten to fifteen years has not always been used to the best advantage; too many outdated rules appear in textbooks and teacher's manuals. The material on the following pages is designed to test the student's knowledge of phonics rules in terms of using, rather than reciting them.

As you test the student on the vowel rules, you may wish to simply ask him to go on to the next nonsense word on the stimulus sheet, rather than continue saying, "Would you please pronounce the nonsense word by number two?" etc.

Vowel Rules

1. In *words* containing a single vowel letter that appears at the end of the word, the vowel letter usually has the long vowel sound. Say to the student, "Would you please pronounce the nonsense words by number one?" (*ra, de, po*)
2. In words containing a single vowel letter that appears at the end of the syllable, the vowel letter may have either the long or short vowel sound. Try the long sound first. Say to the student, "Would you please pronounce the nonsense words by number two?" (*mola, gamo*)
3. A single vowel in a syllable usually has the short sound if it is not the last letter, or if it is not followed by *r, w,* or *l*. Say to the student, "Would you please pronounce the nonsense words by number three?" (*loc, pid, lap*)
4. Vowels followed by *r* usually have a sound that is neither long nor short. Say to the student, "Would you please pronounce the nonsense words by number four?" (*der, bir, cur, par, por*)
5. A *y* at the beginning of a word has the *y* consonant sound; *y* at the end of a single syllable word, when preceded by a consonant, usually has the long *i* sound, and *y* at the end of a multi-syllable word, when preceded by a consonant, usually has the long *e* sound. (Some people hear it as short *i*.) Say to the student, "Would you please pronounce the nonsense words by number five?" (*bly, cly, noppy, dalry, yamp, yorp*)
6. In words ending with vowel-consonant-silent *e*, the *e* is silent and the first vowel may be either long or short. Try the long sound first. Say to the student, "Would you please pronounce the nonsense words by number six?" (*nike, lode, pake*)
7. When *ai, ay, ea, ee,* and *oa* are found together the first vowel is usually long and the second vowel is usually silent. Say to the student, "Would you please pronounce the nonsense words by number seven?" (*tay, neap, toap, tain, tee*)

* The terms *rule* and *principle* have been used interchangeably.

Note. From *Locating and Correcting Reading Difficulties* by E.E. Ekwall (Columbus, Ohio: Charles E. Merrill, 1981), 200–202. Copyright 1981 by Charles E. Merrill Publishing Co. Reprinted by permission.

8. The *ow* sound may be the same you hear in *cow* or *crow*. Say to the student, "Would you please pronounce the nonsense words by number eight?" (*mow, fow*) If the student gives the same response both times say, "Yes, that is right, but can you tell me another way to pronounce the last nonsense word?"

9. The *oo* sound may be the same as you hear in *moon* or *book*. Say to the student, "Would you please pronounce the nonsense words by number nine?" (*moop, toon*) If the student gives the same response both times say, "Yes, that is right, but can you tell me another way to pronounce the last nonsense word?"

10. If *a* is the only vowel in a syllable and is followed by *l* or *w*, then the *a* will usually be neither long nor short. Say to the student, "Would you please pronounce the nonsense words by number ten?" (*hal, baw, kal, kaw*)

VOWEL RULES

1. ra   de   po
2. mola   gamo
3. loc   pid   lap
4. der   bir   cur   par   por
5. bly   cly   noppy   dalry   yamp   yorp
6. nike   lode   pake
7. tay   neap   toap   tain   tee
8. mow   fow
9. moop   toon
10. hal   baw   kal   kaw

Syllable Principles

1. When two consonants stand between two vowels, the word is usually divided between the two consonants. If the two consonants are digraphs or diphthongs they should be treated as a single consonant. Say to the student, "Would you please tell me where you should divide the words by number one?" (*alpil, oppor, botnap, curron*)

2. When a word ends in a consonant and *le*, the consonant usually begins the last syllable. Say to the student, "Would you please tell me where you would divide the words by number two?" (*nable, frable*)

3. Compound words are usually divided between word parts and between syllables in these parts. Say to the student, "Would you please tell me where you would divide the words by number three?" (*cowperson, dogleg*)

4. Do not divide between letters that form a blend or digraph. Digraphs and blends should be treated as single consonants. Say to the student, "Would you please tell me where you would divide the words by number four?" (*bachop, bashil*)

5. When one consonant stands between two vowels, the consonant usually goes with the second syllable unless the vowel on the right is a final *e*, in which case there is no syllable division. Say to the student, "Would you please tell me where you would divide the words by number five?" (*monan, fadop*)

SYLLABLE PRINCIPLES

1. alpil   oppor   botnap   curron
2. nable   frable
3. cowperson   dogleg
4. bachop   bashil
5. monan   fadop

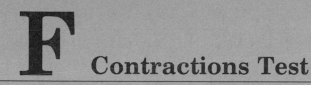

F Contractions Test

TEST FOR KNOWLEDGE OF CONTRACTIONS

KNOWLEDGE OF CONTRACTIONS ANSWER SHEET

NAME _____ DATE _____

SCHOOL _____ TESTER _____

Directions: Say, "Here is a list of contractions. I want you to begin with number one and say the contraction and then tell me what two words it stands for." Following each contraction are two lines. If the student is able to pronounce the contraction correctly, put a plus (+) in the first blank. If he can then tell you what two words it stands for, put a plus (+) in the second blank. Mark wrong answers with a minus (−). The grade-level designation following each blank stands for the point at which the contraction should be known.

1. let's	____	____	2.9	25. wouldn't	____	____	3.5
2. didn't	____	____	2.9	26. she'll	____	____	3.5
3. it's	____	____	2.9	27. here's	____	____	3.5
4. won't	____	____	2.9	28. ain't	____	____	3.9
5. that's	____	____	2.9	29. couldn't	____	____	3.9
6. can't	____	____	2.9	30. they're	____	____	3.9
7. wasn't	____	____	2.9	31. they'd	____	____	3.9
8. isn't	____	____	2.9	32. you'll	____	____	4.5
9. hadn't	____	____	2.9	33. she'd	____	____	4.5
10. don't	____	____	3.5	34. weren't	____	____	4.5
11. I'll	____	____	3.5	35. I'd	____	____	4.5
12. we'll	____	____	3.5	36. you've	____	____	4.5
13. I've	____	____	3.5	37. you'd	____	____	4.5
14. he'll	____	____	3.5	38. we'd	____	____	4.5
15. hasn't	____	____	3.5	39. anybody'd	____	____	4.5
16. haven't	____	____	3.5	40. there'll	____	____	4.5
17. aren't	____	____	3.5	41. we've	____	____	4.5
18. I'm	____	____	3.5	42. who'll	____	____	4.5
19. he's	____	____	3.5	43. he'd	____	____	4.5
20. we're	____	____	3.5	44. who'd	____	____	4.5
21. you're	____	____	3.5	45. doesn't	____	____	4.5
22. what's	____	____	3.5	46. where's	____	____	4.5
23. there's	____	____	3.5	47. they've	____	____	4.5
24. she's	____	____	3.5	48. they'll	____	____	4.5

Note. From *Teacher's Handbook on Diagnosis and Remediation in Reading* by E.E. Ekwall (Boston: Allyn and Bacon, 1977), 82–83. Copyright 1977 by Allyn and Bacon, Inc. Reprinted by permission.

KNOWLEDGE OF CONTRACTIONS TESTING SHEET

1. let's
2. didn't
3. it's
4. won't
5. that's
6. can't
7. wasn't
8. isn't
9. hadn't
10. don't
11. I'll
12. we'll
13. I've
14. he'll
15. hasn't
16. haven't
17. aren't
18. I'm
19. he's
20. we're
21. you're
22. what's
23. there's
24. she's
25. wouldn't
26. she'll
27. here's
28. ain't
29. couldn't
30. they're
31. they'd
32. you'll
33. she'd
34. weren't
35. I'd
36. you've
37. you'd
38. we'd
39. anybody'd
40. there'll
41. we've
42. who'll
43. he'd
44. who'd
45. doesn't
46. where's
47. they've
48. they'll

G Reading Tests Available

COMMERCIAL INFORMAL READING INVENTORIES
GROUP STANDARDIZED READING ACHIEVEMENT TESTS
TESTS OF WORD ANALYSIS SKILLS

ADDRESSES OF TEST PUBLISHERS

COMMERCIAL INFORMAL READING INVENTORIES

Test	Skills or Areas Measured						Other Information				
Name and date	Vocabulary	Comprehension	Word attack	Speed	Listening	Other	Time for administration	Number of forms	Grade level	Group (G) or individual (I)	Publisher
Analytical Reading Inventory (1981)	X	X				Graded word lists	Varies	3	2–9	I	Charles E. Merrill
Bader Reading & Language Inventory (1983)		X	X			Spelling Graded word lists	Varies	3	pp–12	I	Macmillan
Basic Reading Inventory (1978)	X	X				Graded word lists	Varies	3	pp–8	I	Kendall/Hunt
Classroom Reading Inventory (1982)	X	X				Graded word list Spelling	12 min.	4	pp–adult	I	William C. Brown
Contemporary Classroom Inventory (1980)	X	X				Group cloze tests & Graded word list	Varies	3	2–9	I	Gorsuch Scarisbrick
Diagnostic Reading Inventory (1979)	X	X			X	Graded word list & Phrase list	Varies	1	3–8	I	Kendall/Hunt
Ekwall Reading Inventory (1979 & 85)	X	X	X			May be used for listening	Varies 21–30 minutes	2	pp–9	I	Allyn & Bacon
Informal Reading Assessment (1980)	X			X	X	Graded word list	Varies	X	pp–12	I	Rand McNally
Sucher-Allred Reading Placement Inventory (1981)	X	X					20 min.	1	p–9	I	Economy

GROUP STANDARDIZED READING ACHIEVEMENT

Test (Name and date)	Vocabulary	Comprehension	Word attack	Speed	Listening	Other	Time for administration	Number of forms	Grade level	Group (G) or individual (I)	Publisher
Assessment of Reading Growth (1981)											Jamestown Publishers
Level 9	X	X					50 min.	1	2–4	G	
Level 13	X	X					50 min.	1	6–8	G	
Level 17	X	X					42 min.	1	10–12	G	
California Achievement Tests (1977)	X						45–60 min.	2	K–12	G	CTB/McGraw-Hill
Comprehensive Tests of Basic Skills (Espanol-Reading)	X	X					45–60 min.	1	K–8	G	CTB/McGraw-Hill
Comprehensive Tests of Basic Skills S&T (Reading) (1973)	X						45–60 minutes	2	K–12	G	CTB/McGraw-Hill
Comprehensive Tests of Basic Skills U&V (Reading) (1981)	X	X					45–70 minutes	2	K–12	G	CTB/McGraw-Hill
Gates-MacGinitie Reading Tests (1978)	X	X					65 min.	2		G	Riverside Publishing Co.
Basic R	X	X							1.0–1.9	G	
A	X	X							1.5–1.9	G	
B	X	X							2.0	G	
C	X	X							3.0	G	
D	X	X							4–6	G	
E	X	X							7–9	G	
F	X	X							10–12	G	
Iowa Tests of Basic Skills (1982)											
Early Primary	X	X		X	X	Also subtests for language, math, work-study skills	2 hrs. to	1	K–1.9	G	Riverside Publishing Co.
Primary	X	X		X	X		2 hrs.	1	1.7–3.5	G	Riverside Publishing Co. & Houghton Mifflin Co.
Multilevel	X	X					40 min. to 4 hrs.	1	3–8	G	Houghton Mifflin Co.
							40 min.				
Iowa Tests of Educational Development (1978)	X	X				Language arts and math	2¼ hrs.	2	9–12	G	Science Research Associates

GROUP STANDARDIZED READING ACHIEVEMENT

Test Name and date	Vocabulary	Comprehension	Word attack	Speed	Listening	Other	Time for administration	Number of forms	Grade level	Group (G) or individual (I)	Publisher
Metropolitan Achievement Tests (1978)	X						30–50 min. depending on level	2	K–12.9	G	Psychological Corp.
Nelson-Denny Reading Test (1981)	X	X		X			35 min.	2	9–12 College & Adult	G	Riverside Publishing
Nelson Reading Skills Test (1977)	X					Word meaning	33 min.	2	3–9	G	Houghton Mifflin Co.
School and College Ability Tests (1979)	X	X					20 min.	2	3.5–12.9	G	Addison-Wesley
Sequential Tests of Educational Progress											
Primary Levels A–D (1974)	X	X			X		Various	2	pp–3.5	G	Addison-Wesley
Intermediate & Advanced (1979)	X	X			X		40 min.	2	3.5–12.9	G	
SRA Achievement Series (1978)											
Primary Levels A–D	X	X			X	Auditory discrimination	2½–3 hrs.	2	K–3	G	Science Research Associates
Upper Levels E–H	X	X					3 hrs.	2	4–12	G	
Stanford Achievement Series (1982–1983)											
Stanford Early School Achievement	X				X	Sounds & letters, Word Reading	Various	2	K–1.9	G	Psychological Corp.
Stanford Achievement Test	X	X			X	Spelling	Various	2	1.5–9.9	G	
Stanford Test of Academic Skills	X	X				Spelling	Various	2	8–13	G	
Tests of Achievement and Proficiency (1982)	X					Study skills	4 hrs.	1	9–12	G	Riverside Publishing
Test of Reading Comprehension (1978)	X	X					Varies	1	2–12	G	Pro-Ed

WORD ANALYSIS SKILLS

Test (Name and date)	Vocabulary	Comprehension	Word attack	Speed	Listening	Other	Time for administration	Number of forms	Grade level	Group (G) or individual (I)	Publisher
Botel Reading Inventory (1978) Spelling Placement Test Word Recognition Test Word Opposites Test Decoding Test	X	X	X			Used to find student's highest instructional level	Varies	1 2 2 1	All	G I G I	Follett
Diagnostic Reading Scales	X	X	X		X	Graded word lists, Reading passages	Varies	1	1–8 and above	I	CTB/McGraw-Hill
Durrell Analysis of Reading Difficulty	X	X	X	X	X	Spelling. Auditory discrimination	Untimed Approx. 40 min.	1	1–6	I	
Sipay Word Analysis Tests (1974)			X			Tests of various areas of word analysis	Varies	1	All	I	Stoelting Co.
Woodcock Reading Mastery Test (1974)	X	X				Letter identification	20–30 min.	2	K–12	I	American Guidance Service

ADDRESSES OF TEST PUBLISHERS

Addison-Wesley Testing Services
2725 Sand Hill Road
Menlo Park, CA 94025

Allyn and Bacon, Inc.
7 Wells Ave.
Newton, MA 02159

American Guidance Service
Publishers' Building
Circle Pines, MN 55014

CTB/McGraw-Hill
Del Monte Research Park
Monterey, CA 93940

Charles E. Merrill Publishing Co.
1300 Alum Creek Drive/Box 508
Columbus, OH 43216

The Economy Company
P.O. Box 25308
1901 North Walnut Street
Oklahoma City, OK 73125

Follett Publishing Co.
4506 Northwest Highway
Crystal Lake, IL 60014

Gorsuch Scarisbrick Publishers
576 Central
Dubuque, IA 52001

Houghton Mifflin Company
One Beacon Street
Boston, MA 02108

Jamestown Publishers
P.O. Box 6743
Providence, RI 02940

Kendall/Hunt Publishing Company
2460 Kerper Boulevard
Dubuque, IA 52001

Macmillan Publishing Co. Inc.
866 Third Avenue
New York, NY 10022

Pro-Ed
5341 Industrial Oaks Blvd.
Austin, TX 78735

Psychological Corporation
757 Third Avenue
New York, NY 10017

Rand-McNally & Company
Box 7600
Chicago, IL 60680

Riverside Publishing Co.
8420 Bryn Mawr Avenue
Chicago, IL 60631

Science Research Associates, Inc.
155 North Wacker Drive
Chicago, IL 60606

Stoelting Co.
1350 S. Kostner Ave.
Chicago, IL 60623

William C. Brown Company Publishers
2460 Kerper Boulevard
Dubuque, IA 52001

H The El Paso Phonics Survey

In taking the *El Paso Phonics Survey*, the student is shown three easy words: *in, up,* and *am*. The teacher makes sure the student knows each of these words before beginning the test. The student is then shown a stimulus sheet such as the following:

1. p am pam
2. n up nup

The student is told to say the *name* of the first letter, to pronounce the word in the middle, and finally to say the word formed by adding the initial consonant to the middle word. Although the final word is usually a nonsense word, the teacher is not simply giving the student a nonsense word in isolation. By saying the name of the letter and the small word in the center, the student finds that his only new task is to blend the letter sound with a word he already knows. However, the *El Paso Phonics Survey* should not be given unless the student knows each of the three stimulus words—*in, up*, and *am*—before beginning the test. You will also note that vowels, vowel pairs, and special letter combinations are all put together with one of the first eight initial consonants tested on the survey. The student who gets all of the first eight consonant sounds right proves her knowledge of them and shows the teacher whether she knows the vowel sounds that follow. In taking the *El Paso Phonics Survey*, some students give the nonsense word the wrong ending sound, even though they pronounce the sound correctly earlier. Extensive use of the *El Paso Phonics Survey* shows that this can happen with the student who is not sure of the initial consonant sound and expends so much of his thought in pronouncing it, that he simply does not attend to the pronunciation of the final sound. When this happens, do not count the initial consonant sound as correct, even if pronounced correctly. You will find that if the missed consonant sound is taught thoroughly, the student will not pronounce the ending wrong on the next trial.

The Quick Survey Word List

The *Quick Survey Word List* on page 410 is used to eliminate phonics testing for those students who have already mastered the phonics skills necessary for accurate pronunciation. When testing a student who you suspect has no difficulty with phonics skills, you may wish to simply show her the long words on the *Quick Survey Word List* and ask her to pronounce them. If the student can readily pronounce these words, she would not need to take the *El Paso Phonics Survey* or a test for such skills as knowledge of vowel rules or syllable principles. She has already shown mastery of these skills by pronouncing each word accurately. Also remember that if the student can use these skills, she need not be able to recite the rules that apply in each case. If the student hesitates and cannot pronounce the first couple of words, the use of the list should be discontinued, lest you lose rapport with the student. Upon examining the words on the *Quick Survey Word List*, you will note that many of the important phonics rules must be known in order to make the proper response. The proper pronunciation of each word on the list appears on p. 410.

Note. From *Locating and Correcting Reading Difficulties* by E.E. Ekwall (Columbus, Ohio: Charles E. Merrill, 1981), 174–82. Copyright 1981 by Charles E. Merrill Publishing Co. Reprinted by permission.

QUICK SURVEY WORD LIST

wratbeling	twayfrall
dawsnite	spreanplit
pramminciling	goanbate
whetsplitter	streegran
gincule	glammertickly
cringale	grantellean
slatrungle	aipcid

PRONUNCIATION OF QUICK SURVEY WORDS

răt′-běl-ĭng	twā′-fräl
däs′-nīt	sprēn′-plĭt
prăm′-mĭn-cĭl-ĭng	gōn′-bāt
hwĕt′-splĭt-tər	strē′-grăn
jĭn′-kyool	glăm′-mər-tĭck-ly
crĭn′-gāl	grăn′-tĕl-lēn
slăt′-rŭn-gəl	āp′-sĭd

PRONUNCIATION KEY

l — litt<u>le</u>	ə — tamp<u>e</u>r
ə — <u>a</u>bout	hw — <u>wh</u>at
ä — f<u>a</u>ther	kyoo — <u>cu</u>te

El Paso Phonics Survey:
General Directions

1. Before beginning the test, make sure the student has instant recognition of the test words that appear in the box at the top of the first page of the survey. These words should be known instantly by the student. If they are not, reschedule the test at a later date, after the words have been taught and the student has learned them.

2. Give the student the *El Paso Phonics Survey* stimulus sheet pages.

3. Point to the letter in the first column and have the student say the name of that letter (not the sound it represents). Then point to the word in the middle column and have the student pronounce it. Then point to the nonsense word in the third column and have the student pronounce it.

4. If the student can give the name of the letter, the word in the middle column, and the nonsense word in the third column, mark the answer sheet with a plus (+). If he cannot pronounce the nonsense word after giving the name of the letter and the word in the middle column, mark the answer sheet with a minus (–), or you may wish to write the word phonetically as the student pronounced it.

5. If the student can tell you the name of the letter and the small word in the middle column but cannot pronounce the nonsense word, you may wish to have him give the letter sound in isolation. If he can give the sound in isolation, either the student is unable to "blend" or does not know the letter well enough to give its sound and blend it at the same time.

6. Whenever a superior letter appears on the answer sheet, you may wish to refer to the Special Directions sheet.

7. To the right of each answer blank on the answer sheet, you will note a grade level designation under the heading "PEK." This number represents the point at which most basal reading series would have already taught that sound. Therefore, at that point, you should expect it to be known. The designation 1.9 means the ninth month of the first year, and so forth.

8. When a student comes to two- or three-letter consonant digraphs or blends, as with *qu* in number 22, she is to say *q-u* as with the single letters. *Remember:* the student never gives letter sounds in isolation when engaged in actual reading.

9. When a student comes to the vowels (number 59), she is to say "short *a*," and so forth, and then the nonsense word in column two. If the student does not know that the breve (˘) over the vowels means short *a, e,* and so forth, then explain this. Do the same with the long vowels where the macron (ˉ) appears.

10. All vowels and vowel combinations are put with only one or two of the first eight consonants. If any of these first eight consonants are not known, they should be taught before you attempt to test for vowel knowledge.

11. You will note that words appear to the right of some of the blanks on the answer sheet. These words illustrate the correct consonant or vowel sound that should be heard when the student responds.

12. Only phonic elements have been included that have a high enough utility to make them worthwhile learning. For example, the vowel pair *ui* appears very seldom, and when it does it may stand for the short *i* sound as in *build,* the long *oo* sound as in *fruit,* or the short *u* sound as in *luck.* Therefore, there is really no reason to teach it as a sound. However, some letters, such as *oe,* may stand for several sounds but most often stand for one particular sound. In the case of *oe,* the long *o* sound should be used. In cases such as this, the most common sound is illustrated by a word to the right of the blank on the answer sheet. If the student gives another

correct sound for the letter(s) then say, "Yes, but what is another way that we could say this nonsense word?" The student must then say it as illustrated in the small word to the right of the blank on the answer sheet. Otherwise, count the answer as wrong.

13. Stop the test after five consecutive misses, or if the student appears frustrated from missing a number of items even though he has not missed five consecutive items.

EL PASO PHONICS SURVEY:
SPECIAL DIRECTIONS

[a]3. If the student uses another s sound as in *sugar (sh)* in saying the nonsense word *sup*, ask, "What is another s sound?" The student must use the s as in *sack*.

[b]15. If the student uses the soft c sound as in *cigar* in saying the nonsense word *cam*, ask, "What is another c sound?" The student must use the hard c sound as in *coat*.

[c]16. If the student uses the soft g sound as in *gentle* in saying the nonsense word *gup*, ask, "What is another g sound?" The student must use the hard g sound as in *gate*.

[d]17. Ask, "What is the y sound when it comes at the beginning of a word?

[e]23. The student must use the *ks* sound of x, and the nonsense word *mox* must rhyme with *box*.

[f]33. If the student uses the *th* sound heard in *that*, ask, "What is another *th* sound?" The student must use the *th* sound heard in *thing*.

[g]34. If the student uses the *hoo* sound of *wh* in saying the nonsense word *whup*, ask, "What is another *wh* sound?" The student must use the *wh* sound as in *when*.

[h]69. The student may give either the *oo* sound heard in *moon* or the *oo* sound heard in *book*. Be sure to note which one is used.

[i]70. If the same *oo* sound is given this time as was given for item 69, say "Yes, that's right, but what is another way we could pronounce this nonsense word?" Whichever sound was *not* used in item 69 must be used here; otherwise, it is incorrect.

[j]71. The student may give either the *ea* sound heard in *head* or the *ea* sound heard in *meat*. Be sure to note which one is used.

[k]72. If the same *ea* sound is given this time as was given for item 71, say, "Yes, that's right, but what is another way we could pronounce this nonsense word?" Whichever sound was *not* used in item 71 must be used here; otherwise, it is incorrect.

[l]78. The student may give either the *ow* sound heard in *cow* or the *ow* sound heard in *crow*. Be sure to note which one is used.

[m]79. If the same *ow* sound is given this time as was given for item 78, say, "Yes, that's right, but what is another way we could pronounce this nonsense word?" Whichever sound was *not* used in item 78 must be used here; otherwise, it is incorrect.

Note: Numbers of items refer to answer blanks on *El Paso Phonics Survey Answer Sheet* (which follows immediately).

EL PASO PHONICS SURVEY:
ANSWER SHEET

Name _____ Sex _____ Date _____

School _____ Examiner _____

Mark Answers as Follows

Pass   +

Fail   − (or write word as pronounced)

PEK   *Point at which phonic element is expected to be known*

	Answers PEK		*Answers PEK*

Initial Consonant Sounds

1. p	pam	_____ 1.9
2. n	nup	_____ 1.9
[a]3. s	sup	_____ 1.9
4. t	tup	_____ 1.9
5. r	rin	_____ 1.9
6. m	min	_____ 1.9
7. b	bup	_____ 1.9
8. d	dup	_____ 1.9
9. w	wam	_____ 1.9
10. h	hup	_____ 1.9
11. f	fin	_____ 1.9
12. j	jin	_____ 1.9

13. k	kam	_____ 1.9
14. l	lin	_____ 1.9
[b]15. c	cam	_____ 1.9
[c]16. g	gup	_____ 1.9
[d]17. y	yin	_____ 1.9
18. v	vam	_____ 1.9
19. z	zin	_____ 1.9
20. c	cin	_____ 2.5(sin)
21. g	gin	_____ 2.9(jin)
22. qu	quam	_____ 1.9

Ending Consonant X

[e]23. x	mox	_____ 1.9

Note: Superior letter refers to a note listed in *El Paso Phonics Survey: Special Directions.*

Initial Consonant Clusters

24. pl   plup   _____ 1.9

25. fr   frin   _____ 1.9

26. fl   flam   _____ 1.9

27. st   stup   _____ 1.9

28. bl   blin   _____ 1.9

29. tr   trin   _____ 1.9

30. gr   grup   _____ 1.9

31. br   brin   _____ 1.9

32. sh   shup   _____ 1.9

ʳ33. th   thup   _____ 1.9 (thing)

ᵍ34. wh   whup   _____ 1.9 (when)

35. ch   cham   _____ 2.5 (church)

36. dr   drup   _____ 2.5

37. pr   pram   _____ 2.5

38. sl   slup   _____ 2.5

39. cl   clin   _____ 2.5

40. gl   glam   _____ 2.5

41. sm   smin   _____ 2.5

42. sk   skam   _____ 2.5

43. cr   crin   _____ 2.5

44. tw   twam   _____ 2.5

45. sn   snup   _____ 2.5

46. sch   scham   _____ 2.5

47. sp   spam   _____ 2.9

48. sc   scup   _____ 2.9

49. str   stram   _____ 2.9

50. thr   thrup   _____ 2.9

51. shr   shrup   _____ 2.9

52. squ   squam   _____ 2.9

53. sw   swup   _____ 3.5

54. spr   spram   _____ 3.5

55. spl   splin   _____ 3.5

56. wr   wrin   _____ 4.5

57. dw   dwin   _____ 4.5

58. scr   scrup   _____ 4.5

Vowels, Vowel Teams, and
Special Letter Combinations

59. ă   pam   _____ 1.9

60. ĭ   rit   _____ 1.9

61. ĕ   nep   _____ 1.9

62. ŏ   sot   _____ 1.9

63. ŭ   tum   _____ 1.9

64. ī   tipe   _____ 2.5

			Answers PEK				Answers PEK
65.	ē	rete	_____ 2.5	[l]78.	ow	owd	_____ 2.5 (cow or crow)
66.	ā	sape	_____ 2.5	[m]79.	ow	fow	_____ 2.5 (cow or crow)
67.	ū	pune	_____ 2.5	80.	or	orm	_____ 2.5 (corn)
68.	ō	sote	_____ 2.5	81.	ir	irt	_____ 2.5 (hurt)
[h]69.	oo	oot	_____ 2.5 (moon or book)	82.	ur	urd	_____ 2.5 (hurt)
[i]70.	oo	oot	_____ 2.5 (moon or book)	83.	aw	awp	_____ 2.9 (paw)
[j]71.	ea	eap	_____ 2.5 (head or meat)	84.	oi	doi	_____ 2.9 (boy)
[k]72.	ea	eam	_____ 2.5 (head or meat)	85.	ou	tou	_____ 2.9 (cow)
73.	ai	ait	_____ 2.5 (ape)	86.	ar	arb	_____ 2.9 (harp)
74.	ay	tay	_____ 2.5 (hay)	87.	oy	moy	_____ 2.9 (boy)
75.	oe	poe	_____ 2.5 (hoe)	88.	er	ert	_____ 2.9 (her)
76.	oa	oan	_____ 2.5 (soap)	89.	ew	bew	_____ 2.9 (few)
77.	ee	eem	_____ 2.5 (heed)	90.	au	dau	_____ 2.9 (paw)

EL PASO PHONICS SURVEY

Test Words | in   up   am |

1. p	am	pam	16. g	up	gup
2. n	up	nup	17. y	in	yin
3. s	up	sup	18. v	am	vam
4. t	up	tup	19. z	in	zin
5. r	in	rin	20. c	in	cin
6. m	in	min	21. g	in	gin
7. b	up	bup	22. qu	am	quam
8. d	up	dup	23. m	ox	mox
9. w	am	wam	24. pl	up	plup
10. h	up	hup	25. fr	in	frin
11. f	in	fin	26. fl	am	flam
12. j	in	jin	27. st	up	stup
13. k	am	kam	28. bl	in	blin
14. l	in	lin	29. tr	in	trin
15. c	am	cam	30. gr	up	grup

31.	br	in	brin	50.	thr	up	thrup
32.	sh	up	shup	51.	shr	up	shrup
33.	th	up	thup	52.	squ	am	squam
34.	wh	up	whup	53.	sw	up	swup
35.	ch	am	cham	54.	spr	am	spram
36.	dr	up	drup	55.	spl	in	splin
37.	pr	am	pram	56.	wr	in	wrin
38.	sl	up	slup	57.	dw	in	dwin
39.	cl	in	clin	58.	scr	up	scrup
40.	gl	am	glam	59.	ă	pam	
41.	sm	in	smin	60.	ĭ	rit	
42.	sk	am	skam	61.	ĕ	nep	
43.	cr	in	crin	62.	ŏ	sot	
44.	tw	am	twam	63.	ŭ	tum	
45.	sn	up	snup	64.	ī	tipe	
46.	sch	am	scham	65.	ē	rete	
47.	sp	am	spam	66.	ā	sape	
48.	sc	up	scup	67.	ū	pune	
49.	str	am	stram	68.	ō	sote	

69.	oo	oot	80.	or	orm
70.	oo	oot	81.	ir	irt
71.	ea	eap	82.	ur	urd
72.	ea	eam	83.	aw	awp
73.	ai	ait	84.	oi	doi
74.	ay	tay	85.	ou	tou
75.	oe	poe	86.	ar	arb
76.	oa	oan	87.	oy	moy
77.	ee	eem	88.	er	ert
78.	ow	owd	89.	ew	bew
79.	ow	fow	90.	au	dau

I Glossary

Ability groups Assigning students of similar reading ability to small groups for reading instruction.

Affixes Both suffixes and prefixes.

Allocated time The amount of instructional time scheduled for a particular subject.

Alphabetic method A method of teaching reading and spelling used from ancient times until the early part of the 19th century. The student first identified letters by their names; next spelled out syllables; then words; next read sentences; and finally read short stories.

Analytic phonics Students learn that letters stand for sounds rather than letters make sounds. **Phonic elements** are introduced as part of whole words rather than as isolated letter sounds. For example, *b* is the letter that stands for the sound at the beginning of *ball, bat, base,* and *banana.* See **synthetic phonics** for a different approach.

Ascender The part of a lowercase letter that goes above its *x*-height.

Auditory acuity The ability to hear sounds at various pitches (or frequencies) and at different volume levels.

Auditory analysis See **oral phonemic segmentation.**

Auditory discrimination The ability to hear likenesses and differences among spoken sounds.

Auditory segmentation or segmentation The ability to recognize that oral language, when translated into print, can be divided into discrete units: sentences, words, and **phonemes** (individual sounds).

Auditory synthesis see **blending.**

Basal reader approach The teacher relies on a series of graded books, with accompanying teachers' manuals, workbooks, and testing materials, to teach students to read. **Basal readers** are designed to be compehensive, developmental, continuous-progress programs that provide for the sequential and systematic learning of all reading skills.

Basal reader A textbook used for the teaching of reading.

Basic instructional plan A plan for organizing daily reading instruction that allows for small group directed teaching, seatwork, and independent activities.

Basic sight word A word of relatively high utility that appears on a researcher's list. Students should know these words instantly by late in grade two or early in grade three. The word *relatively* is used because the words are not always of the *highest* utility; for example, some basic sight word lists contain no nouns.

Beginning sight vocabulary The first words children learn to recognize, including their own names; names of other important people; color, number, and position words; days and months; and names of common classroom objects and areas.

Behavioral objective A statement about the nature and degree of measurable performance expected for a specified instructional outcome under certain conditions: "When the learner has finished this unit, she can look at a list of five previously unknown words and pronounce each correctly."

Bilingualism The ability to speak two languages fluently.

Black English A variety or dialect of English spoken by most blacks in the United States; an example of a nonstandard English dialect.

Blending The ability to hear a series of isolated speech sounds, then recognize and pronounce them as a whole word. This is an **auditory segmentation** ability.

Choral reading Two or more students reading aloud at the same time.

Code-emphasis programs An approach to reading instruction. Initial emphasis is placed on decoding skills, especially **phonics. Phonics-based basal readers** are examples of code-emphasis programs.

Cognitive clarity A term used by John Downing. Downing believes most children approach the task of reading in a state of cognitive confusion. Once they understand how the written system matches oral language, they achieve cognitive clarity.

Combination vocabulary Multiple-meaning vocabulary. Some meanings of the words are general and others are technical.

Comprehension Meaning gained from what is written on a page (when read) or heard (when spoken).

Configuration clues Identifying a word by its shape: its length and x-height (The word *one* has only one x-height vs. *high* which has two **ascenders** (*h*) and one **descender** (*g*).

Consonant blend Two or more consonant letters that blend together, but the sound that each letter stands for is heard. (To say a consonant blend, the mouth's position must change from the beginning to the end of the sound.) Examples are *bl* in *blend* and *cr* in *crow*.)

Consonant cluster A term meaning both **consonant digraphs** and **consonant blends.**

Consonant digraph A combination of two consonants recording a single sound. (To say a consonant digraph, the mouth's position need not change from the beginning to the end of the sound.) Examples are *ch* in *church* and *ck* in *kick*.)

Content area subjects Regular classroom subjects with an information base, such as science or history.

Context clues Clues to the meaning and/or pronunciation of an unknown word derived from the words preceding or following that word. For example, one can easily figure out that the missing word in the next sentence is *dog*: The _____ was barking all night and kept me awake.

Controlled vocabulary The careful introduction and limitation of new words for the beginning reader, with sufficient repetition to allow the child to learn these words easily.

Corrective reading Reading instruction in the regular classroom for students experiencing mild reading disabilities. Such instruction aims to prevent the development of more serious disabilities.

Criterion referenced test Evaluates students' specific abilities in relation to a set of criteria for mastery rather than in relation to a standardized population.

Critical reading Evaluating the meaning and implications of what is read on the basis of the reader's experience.

Curriculum guide A written plan describing the curriculum of a school or school system. Curriculum guides vary in scope and detail, but usually give the philosophy, specific objectives, and ways of carrying out a program of studies.

Decoding The process of taking words in print and changing them to spoken words.

Departmentalization An organizational plan in which teachers teach specific subject areas and students move from class to class.

Descender The part of a lowercase letter that falls below its x-height.

Developmental reading Reading instruction in the regular classroom for those students making normal progress.

Dialect Regional or social variations of spoken languages; dialects vary phonologically, lexically, and grammatically.

Dialect Interference Theory The assumption that a mismatch between the spoken language of the black child and the written language of beginning reading materials causes reading failure among black children. This theory has not been supported by research.

Digraph A combination of two letters recording a single sound. There are **vowel digraphs** and **consonant digraphs.**

Diphthong A combination of two vowels recording a sliding sound. To say a diphthong, the mouth's position must change from the beginning to the ending of that sound.) Examples are *ow* in *cow* and *oi* in *oil.*

Direct instruction A teaching approach that is academically focused, sequential, and structured. The teacher presents information to the students and monitors the pacing and learning of the material.

Directed reading lesson or Directed Reading Activity Instruction that usually takes place during the directed teaching segment of the basic instructional plan. The directed reading lesson has four parts: (1) lesson motivation; (2) vocabulary development; (3) **guided reading** activities; and (4) extended reading activities.

Directed Reading-Thinking Activity (DRTA) An alternative to the **directed reading lesson.** Students assume greater responsibility for determining the purposes for reading and the teacher assumes a more facilitative role.

Directionality See **left-to-right progression.**

Eclectic or Meaning-based basal readers (or **balanced** or **sight word basal readers**) Basal readers that emphasize language development and other readiness skills and then introduce a core vocabulary of words to be learned as sight words. Usually an **analytic phonics** approach is used with controlled vocabulary in the early books. Other decoding skills are taught along with phonics. The most common type of basal reader.

Efficiency skills Beyond the ability to decode words, the ability to use punctuation and other cues to read smoothly and easily, without hesitation.

El Paso Phonics Survey An informal instrument used to determine whether students know sound-symbol or phoneme-grapheme correspondence for the most phonetically regular **phonic elements.**

Elocutionary The style of reading or speaking in public.

Engaged time or On-task time The amount of time a student is actually involved or engaged in the learning task.

Every-pupil-response-techniques (EPRT) Teaching techniques to use with small groups. All students can respond together while the teacher evaluates individual student's mastery of concepts.

Exceptional child A student who differs from normal children in the areas of language, intelligence, hearing, vision, perception, health, or behavior to such an extent that adjusted or modified instruction is required for effective learning.

Fernald technique A technique for learning words that involves looking (visual), saying (auditory), and tracing (kinesthetic). Usually used with students who have severe reading disabilities.

First Grade Reading Studies A series of studies, sponsored by the Federal Government in the early 1960s. Various methods of teaching reading were compared to determine whether any one method was better than the others.

Flexible reading Adjusting reading speed to fit the requirement of understanding the text. Purpose for reading and type of material to be read dictates speed.

Free reading See **sustained silent reading.**

Frustration reading level A reading level much too difficult for the reader.

General vocabulary Words used across content areas.

Gifted student A student who possesses some combination of the following attributes: (1) superior intellectual ability; (2) academic aptitude; (3) creative thinking ability; (4) special ability in the creative arts; (5) leadership ability; and (6) exceptional psychomotor ability.

Grapheme The written representation of a **phoneme.** There is always a one-to-one correspondence between graphemes and phonemes. However, there is not always a one-to-one correspondence between phonemes and letters. For example, long *i* may be spelled *ie, eye, igh, aye,* etc., but all these graphemes stand for the long *i* sound.

Graphic aids Maps, graphs, diagrams, pictures, cartoons, timelines, charts, and tables included in texts to clarify or expand textual information.

Graphic organizer or Structured overview A technique designed to organize and present key vocabulary concepts in a hierarchical classification schema before and/or after the reading of a text.

Guided reading A system to help students understand concepts and develop reading processes in important but difficult reading material.

Handicapped student According to federal law, students who are mentally retarded, hard-of-hearing, deaf, speech-impaired, visually handicapped, seriously emotionally disturbed, orthopedically-impaired, or learning disabled.

Hard words When devising a **readability formula,** the author usually begins with a list of rather easy or high utility words. Any word not on that list is considered a hard or unique word.

Heterogeneous grouping Random assignment of students to grades or classes without regard to intelligence or special abilities.

Hip High intensity practice, essentially the same as **Sustained silent reading.**

Holistic approach A teaching-learning approach that emphasizes wholes of subject matter. A completely holistic approach to teaching reading would include few or no subskills of reading.

Homogeneous grouping The assignment of students to grades or classes based on intelligence or special abilities.

Independent reading level The reading level considered appropriate when a student is reading for pleasure. No special preparation should be needed for the student to understand and enjoy material at this level.

Individualized educational program (IEP) A written plan, composed by a committee of parents, teachers, and other educational experts after a careful assessment, to help the handicapped child learn successfully. The IEP must include short and long range goals and objectives, a statement of special services to be provided, and the extent to which the child will participate in the regular instructional program.

Individualized reading An approach to reading instruction originated in the 1950s that emphasizes self-selection rather than the basal reader. Instruction of reading skills is usually done on a one-to-one basis or in very small groups. The teacher uses individual conferences often. This approach emphasizes a personalized, motivating approach to reading instruction.

Inflection   A change in word form. Examples of inflectional endings are *s, ed,* and *ing.*

Informal reading inventory   A graded series of increasingly difficult passages, usually taken from basal readers, used to make an informal diagnosis of one or more levels of reading performance, such as **independent, instructional,** and **frustration.** There are usually two passages at each level, one for oral reading and the other for silent reading.

Initial Teaching Alphabet   A method of teaching reading invented by Sir James Pitman. Our regular Roman Alphabet augmented with enough extra letters to give a one-to-one correspondence between the sounds of English and those letters. Sir James Pitman maintains there are 44 sounds in the English language.

Instructional framework (IF)   A system designed to structure reading instruction in the content classes. It has three steps: (1) preparation, (2) guidance, and (3) independence.

Instructional reading level   The reading level considered appropriate for a student's textbooks, such as a basal reader, science, or social studies book.

Joplan Plan   Intergrade grouping of reading instruction for fourth, fifth, and sixth graders to reduce teachers' number of preparations and to limit the range of abilities in each reading class.

Key vocabulary   Those words critical to a reader's understanding of a text's concepts. They may be easy or difficult to pronounce, but are key vocabulary because they unlock the mystery of a concept.

Key vocabulary approach   Words that have special or intense meaning to a child are elicited by the teacher and used as a vehicle for beginning reading instruction.

Language experience approach   An approach to learning to read. The student's or group's own words are written down and used as materials for instruction in reading, writing, spelling, speaking, and listening. Thus, this approach relies on children's oral language background to develop their reading skills. This approach is considered more personalized and motivating, though less systematic or sequential than other approaches.

Learning disability   A frequently used term that lacks precise definition; usually refers to children with disorders of the psychological processes required for using or interpreting language. Learning disabled children

generally do *not* have problems associated primarily with visual, hearing, or motor handicaps, mental retardation, or emotional difficulties.

Least restrictive environment   According to federal law, settings where handicapped children are to be educated; when possible, handicapped children should be in classrooms with children who are not handicapped.

Left-to-right progression or Directionality   The ability to recognize that English words read from left-to-right on a page and that letters are also written from left-to-right.

Letter knowledge   The ability to discriminate, recognize, and name the letters of the alphabet.

Letter-sound correspondence   The relationship between a letter and the sound it stands for.

Linguistically oriented   Linguistically oriented materials teach several words in the same word family, such as "Mat the fat cat sat on the hat." To some extent the story line or interest is sacrificed to use phonetically regular words.

Linguistic approaches   Reading programs that emphasize the regularity of letter-sound associations through consistent spelling patterns.

Mainstreaming   The process of integrating handicapped pupils into the regular educational program when possible.

Main-line reading program   The principal reading program being used to teach reading as contrasted with supplementary materials also being used.

Management system approaches   Reading instruction provided through individualized, carefully monitored, and skill-focused programs. May be used separately from, alongside of, or in addition to, basal reader programs.

Meaning-emphasis programs   Reading instruction that initially emphasizes reading for comprehension. Some experts think eclectic readers are examples of meaning-emphasis programs.

Metalinguistic interview   A set of questions designed to assess children's knowledge of metalinguistic concepts.

Metalinguistic skills   The ability to consciously manipulate language. Metalinguistic skills are of two types: (1) awareness of specific terms and concepts related to reading; and (2) the ability to identify and isolate units of language.

Miscue   An error made while reading orally.

Miscue analysis   Studying the types of errors made

by students while they read orally. The teacher analyzes the errors to help the student become a more proficient reader.

Modified alphabet approaches Reading materials written with an artificial orthography that more closely matches English spelling and sounds. The **Initial Teaching Alphabet** is an example of a modified alphabet approach.

Morpheme A meaning-bearing unit of the language. For example, the letters *d, o,* and *g* themselves have no meaning. However, when put together, they refer to an animal. There are two kinds of morphemes, *bound* and *unbound*. An unbound morpheme can stand alone and have meaning, such as the word *dog.* A bound morpheme cannot stand alone and have meaning, such as the letter *s*. Only when *s* is put with *dog* does it take on meaning by changing *dog* from its singular to its plural form.

Morphology The study of morphemes, the meaning-bearing units of the language. Morphology is often used synonomously with the term **Structural analysis.**

Nongraded schools The grouping of students in a nongraded unit, usually to replace grades 1, 2, and 3.

On-task time See **engaged time.**

Open schools An architectural arrangement in which classrooms with few or no interior walls surround an open-space area. Or a highly child-centered and individualized philosophy of teaching; students have considerable freedom to direct their own learning while teachers assume a facilitative role.

Oral phonemic segmentation or Auditory analysis The ability to isolate and articulate each of a word's sounds in the proper order. It is an **auditory segmentation** ability, the opposite of **blending.**

Organizational pattern guide A reading guide designed to help the reader understand the internal organizational structure of the text (time, comparison/contrast, cause/effect, etc.).

Passage dependent question A passage dependent question cannot be answered by chance; the student has to have read the passage to know the answer. If a question can be answered whether or not the student read the passage, then it is a passage independent question.

Pattern books or Structured language books Books that employ repetitive language structures, rhyme, sequence, or predictable plots and familiar themes to stimulate children's interest and help them predict the next words or lines.

Phoneme The smallest unit of speech sound in the language.

Phonic elements Phonic elements are initial consonants, consonant digraphs, consonant blends, vowels, vowel combinations, or special letter combinations to be learned in the study of **phonics.**

Phonic or Phonetic method Teaching reading by emphasizing the sounds represented by letters and letter combinations.

Phonics An approach to teaching reading and spelling that stresses sound-symbol relationships. Usually used in beginning reading.

Phonics-based basal readers Basal readers that strongly emphasize **phonics** for beginning reading instruction.

Phonogram or Word family A series of letters that begin with a vowel and are often found together, e.g., *all, ell, old, ime,* etc.

Process-product research Research about teaching that evaluates the relationship between the processes of teaching (such as teacher behaviors) and the products of teaching (usually the students' achievement gain as measured by *standardized tests*).

Productive language abilities Speaking and writing; a child creates an idea, then communicates or produces the idea in either speech or writing.

Programmed materials approaches Students learn to read with materials that enable them to work independently and at their own pace. Students receive continual feedback on their performance, learning occurs in small increments, and skills are presented in a sequential and systematic way.

Programmed textbooks or Programmed instruction A skill or subject matter is broken up into very small parts. The learner responds to each part, step-by-step, and gets an immediate check on the accuracy of each response.

Psycholinguistics A study of the language (linguistics) along with the psychological aspects of that language.

Public Law 94-142 Legislation passed by Congress in 1975 to provide for the education of all handicapped children.

Readability formula A method of determining the difficulty or the grade level of reading materials. A book labeled 3.8 would mean that it is appropriate for a third grader in the eighth month of school (providing the student reads at grade level). Readability formulas are often based on sentence length and the percent of **hard words** in a passage. Some formulas also take other factors into consideration such as **syntax.** However, difficulty of syntax is much more difficult to measure than percent of hard words or sentence length.

Reading readiness Both the child's state of preparedness for reading and the type of instruction a child receives prior to the formal teaching of reading.

Receptive language abilities Listening and reading; a child receives a message through the ears or eyes and uses the brain to translate the sounds or symbols into meaning.

Reliability A term used to show that a test gives the same results each time it is given; it is consistent.

Remedial reading Reading instruction outside the regular reading classroom for students with serious reading disabilities.

Self-contained classroom The traditional organizational arrangement in American elementary schools. One teacher teaches all subjects to a group of approximately thirty students.

Semantics Usually refers to meaning.

Sight vocabulary All the words known instantly by a reader. The size of sight vocabularies varies, depending on amount of education, how much is read, and how many exposures to a word are necessary for learning it, etc. Once a word is in a sight vocabulary, the reader does not have to use **word attack skills** on it.

Skills oriented approach An approach to the teaching of reading. Based on the belief that most students must learn certain skills to learn how to read. Most teachers who believe in this approach know that some students learn these skills on their own without any formal training; however, these teachers also recognize that some students cannot break the code of reading without learning certain skills first.

Snellen Test An inappropriate vision screening procedure commonly used in schools. Due to this test's limitations, many vision defects that may affect reading are not detected.

SQ3R A study technique designed to develop study skills: S = Survey, Q = Question, R = Read, R = Recite, and R = Review.

SSR An acronym for **Sustained silent reading.**

Staggered reading An organizational plan that reduces class size for reading instruction by dividing students into two groups. One group begins school an hour early for reading, while the other stays an hour later in the afternoon.

Standard English That form or dialect of English most commonly spoken by well-educated members of the society.

Standardized readiness tests Group administered, paper and pencil reading readiness batteries; commercially developed and standardized with norms established for the purpose of predicting the future reading success of young children.

Standardized reading achievement test Tests given to large samples of the population of the United States, usually to various grade levels from different locations and different socioeconomic levels. (These students, who originally take the test, are usually referred to as a norm group.) Using a normed test allows the teacher to compare a student or group of students with a large sample of the country.

Structural analysis A word identification technique for breaking a word into its pronunciation units. These units are: **affixes,** word roots, contractions, compound words, **inflected** or derived endings, and sometimes syllabication.

Structural skills Skills used for unlocking the pronunciation and meaning of words through an understanding of their structure (prefixes, suffixes, etc.).

Structured language books See **pattern books.**

Sustained silent reading Practicing the act of reading. The classroom teacher or the whole school sets aside time for simply reading.

Syntax The structure of grammatical sentences in a language; the way we string words together in writing.

Synthetic phonics method An approach to teaching **phonics.** Students are taught the individual sounds that each letter stands for and then how to blend these letter sounds to decode words. See **analytic phonics** for a different approach.

Team teaching An organizational arrangement in which teachers work together to teach some or all subjects and rely on each teacher's particular strengths in the subject areas.

USSR An acronym for uninterrupted sustained silent reading, another term sometimes used for the concept of **sustained silent reading.**

Validity A term to show whether a test really measures what it says it measures. If it does, then the test is valid; the test is truthful, accurate.

Visual acuity The ability of the eyes to accurately resolve detail.

Visual discrimination The ability to see likenesses and differences among visual stimuli, particularly among letters and words.

Visual-motor or Visual-perceptual skills These terms are not clearly defined; sometimes a third term, visual-motor perception is used. Terms may refer to fine motor skills, visual-motor coordination, figure-ground perception, spatial relationships, gross motor or physical coordination abilities, or visual memory.

Vocabulary Knowing the meaning of words in a student's listening, speaking, and reading vocabulary. However, it sometimes simply means the number of words a reader recognizes; or a reader's sight vocabulary.

Vowel digraph A combination of two vowel sounds recording a single sound. Examples are *oa* in *coat* and *oo* in *book*.

Word analysis or Word attack skills The skills a reader must use to pronounce a word when it is not recognized instantly. The skills making up the word analysis skills are usually considered to be **configuration clues, context clues, phonics, structural analysis, efficiency skills,** and **dictionary skills.**

Word discrimination Noting differences in words, especially in their visual outlines or overall shapes.

Word recognition skills The ability of a reader to recognize words without the aid of **word analysis.**

Index